P9-EER-180

Saints & Revolutionaries

Essays on Early American History

156652

Saints & Revolutionaries

Essays on Early American History

Edited by

DAVID D. HALL

JOHN M. MURRIN

THAD W. TATE

974.02

S157

W · W · NORTON & COMPANY

New York · London

Alverno College
Library Media Center
Milwaukee, Wisconsin

Copyright © 1984 by W. W. Norton & Company, Inc.
All rights reserved.
Published simultaneously in Canada by
George J. McLeod Limited, Toronto.
Printed in the United States of America.

The text of this book is composed in VIP Baskerville,
with display type set in Typositor Caslon 471.
Composition by Vail-Ballou Press, Inc.
Manufacturing by The Murray Printing Company
Book design by Laurel Wagner
First Edition

Library of Congress Cataloging in Publication Data
Main entry under title:
Saints and revolutionaries.
Includes index.
1. New England—History—Colonial period, ca. 1600–1775
—Addresses, essays, lectures. 2. United States—
Civilization—To 1783—Addresses, essays, lectures.
3. Morgan, Edmund Sears. I. Hall, David D.
II. Murrin, John M. III. Tate, Thad W.
F7.S24   1984   974'.02   82-22439

ISBN 0-393-01751-6

W. W. Norton & Company, Inc.
500 Fifth Avenue, New York, N.Y. 10110
W. W. Norton & Company Ltd.
37 Great Russell Street, London WC1B 3NU

1 2 3 4 5 6 7 8 9 0

To

EDMUND S. MORGAN

and
to the memory of

HELEN M. MORGAN

Contents

THREE
Culture, Society, & the Revolution

Preface

The essays in *Saints and Revolutionaries* deal with the century and three quarters that lies between the founding of the American colonies and the Revolutionary era. These essays take up three broad aspects of this period: religion and mentality; law and politics; and culture, society, and the Revolution. Some of them provide new depths of factual precision. Others start with well-known materials and review them from a different angle. What all these essays have in common is a willingness to reconsider certain story lines or categories that we often take for granted.

Another kind of common ground is this: the authors have been students of Edmund S. Morgan. *Saints and Revolutionaries* is dedicated to him, with gratitude and affection, by all of his Ph.D. degree students. Whether growing out of work in progress or prepared especially for this volume, these essays seek to honor him as a teacher and a historian.

In these two roles, Edmund Morgan has never slackened in his curiosity about the past. To review his more than forty years of creativity is to recognize that two events have deeply touched him, the revolution wrought by Perry Miller and the reaction against the Progressive historians. Morgan would enhance and help consolidate each one of these great transformations.

Coming out of Harvard in the days when Perry Miller was overturning our most basic assumptions about the Puritans, Morgan found it natural to write his dissertation on some aspect of Puritanism. *The Puritan Family* (1944) was another blow against false stereotypes, though its main purpose was to explore how the covenant theology—the central theme in Miller's grand revisionism—affected the structure of the family. In later work, as Morgan continued to pursue the history of New England Puritanism, the emphasis would shift away from Miller's categories. In Miller's first book *Orthodoxy in Massachusetts,* he read the history of modern denominationalism back into the Puritan movement in the early seventeenth century. He assumed that Puritanism had fragmented into several groups, each

ix

with its distinct interpretation of church order. This premise enabled Miller to resolve a famous puzzle in the history of New England, that is, the origins of congregationalism; they lay, he argued, in the emergence of "non-separating congregationalism" in England just before the great migration.

As Morgan was preparing a course of lectures on the Puritans and their demand for purity, he made a surprising discovery that overturned this argument. A feature of congregationalism, or so it was assumed, had been the doctrine of the gathered church: a membership restricted to the godly. Morgan found that Puritans of all persuasions had been in favor of a gathered church. "Presbyterian" and "congregational" were consequently terms without much relevance. "The fact is," he would declare in *Visible Saints: The History of a Puritan Idea* (1963), "that before the disputes of the 1640s, virtually all Puritans agreed on certain basic principles of church organization, and on the basic nature of the church." A traditional theme, not one unique to a few individuals, had taken hold and flourished in New England.

In a short biography of John Winthrop, the first governor of Massachusetts Bay, Morgan returned again to the classic sources and emerged with a new answer to another problem in New England history, the enfranchising of a group of colonists in 1630–31. The list of names in the Massachusetts records is headed by a statement of tantalizing simplicity: "The Names of such as desire to be made Freemen." What did this statement mean? Important writers on the seventeenth century had understood the word *desire* to mean that the people had grown restive with the magistrates' authority. According to one historian, the people "demanded the franchise"; according to another, they "confronted" the magistrates "with an ominous petition for citizenship." But as Morgan would argue persuasively in *The Puritan Dilemma* (1958), the verb may mean that these men were responding to an open invitation. Indeed, said Morgan, John Winthrop opened up the franchise because he viewed society as organized around a covenant that entitled all the godly to participate in government.[1]

In the background of *The Puritan Dilemma* looms a question we associate with the Progressive historians. Did the structure of politics in early America embody a clash between the haves and the have-nots? Behind every political movement, the Progressives detected

---

1. The relevant sections from the Massachusetts Bay Colony records are reprinted, together with the interpretations of several historians—the two cited here are by Samuel Eliot Morison and Perry Miller, respectively—in Edmund S. Morgan, ed., *The Founding of Massachusetts: Historians and the Sources* (Indianapolis, 1964).

the presence of economic issues that divided people. Political ideas were to be taken seriously, not on their own terms, but as counters in some more fundamental game. A key example was the colonists' behavior in the years before the Revolution. Progressives read events to mean that the issue was taxation, not the principle of representation.

When Morgan turned to consider the Revolutionary crisis, he rejected this line of argument. Above all, he insisted, colonial patriots developed a set of consistent principles and stuck with them from 1764 to 1774. Without this intense commitment, there would have been no Revolution. Only after 1774, when the options narrowed and the consequences of resistance became much grimmer, did Americans begin to shift. Turning to natural rights as the last line of defense against a Parliament that would not listen to less alarming constraints, the colonists rejected crown and empire to venture on a daring experiment in self-rule. But still they remembered why they had resisted Britain's claims. By making taxation with representation a viable reality, the Constitution resolved the central problem of the age in a way that neither Britain nor the Articles of Confederation had found. This consistency is the central argument of *The Stamp Act Crisis* (1953) and *The Birth of the Republic* (1956), in which Morgan drew together and consolidated all of the emerging scholarship opposed to Charles Beard. Morgan has never doubted the continuity of the Constitution with the nation's Revolutionary heritage, nor its manifest superiority to the Articles as a framework for federal government.

Considered as art, *The Stamp Act Crisis* is an unusual achievement. In it Edmund and Helen Morgan strive for objectivity through dramatic subjectivity, identifying as they do with the dilemmas of each major figure in the story. The most sympathetic portraits in the book depict the agonies of stamp masters and other royal servants, good men trapped on the wrong side of a great constitutional and political divide. Only by telling a dramatic story, by respecting the narrative mode as the ultimate form of history, do the Morgans uncover the fullest meaning of the imperial crisis and its revolutionary implications.

Morgan has often seen links between the Puritan experience and the Revolution. A mark of his integrity as a historian emerged when he failed to discover quite the connection he had expected. At one time he planned a large study of the Protestant work ethic in America. It affected all of the colonies, he believed, not just New England or Quaker Pennsylvania. To this end, he published a prize-winning essay in 1967, "The Puritan Ethic and the American Revolution," an

essay that, said one historian of the South, made Thomas Jefferson
too much of a Puritan. Morgan was already reaching a similar conclusion from the opposite chronological direction. In his paper "The
Labor Problem at Jamestown," he found not a trace of the work ethic
in the early years of England's first permanent colony in North
America.[2] To Morgan this disappointment became a challenge. The
outcome was *American Slavery, American Freedom: The Ordeal of Colonial Virginia* (1975), perhaps a more profound and desperate story
of social conflict than anything the Progressives had ever written about
colonial America. Planters often kept busy, no doubt, but their success rested overwhelmingly on their ability to coerce others into
working for them. In *American Slavery, American Freedom* the story is
one of unrelenting brutality and exploitation, whether involving
Indians and whites, whites and Africans, or only the whites themselves. Perhaps it is going too far to suggest that the book was Morgan's response to the war in Vietnam, a war replete with senseless
massacres and exploitation. What this grim, ironic story surely rep-
resents is a curiosity infused with moral passion.

There was a time when Morgan seemed to represent "consensus"
history.[3] His conservatism is real, but its essence is not in the myth
of a conflict-free society. He outgrew this myth (if he ever shared it),
as he outgrew Miller. Change and growth are constants in the forty
or so years that lie behind him. Another constant is his temperament. Morgan expects of every historian the same honesty that
informs his own research into the past. Inflated rhetoric can make
him deeply angry, as can a special, introverted logic. The bicentennial celebration of the Revolution left him bemused by the cliché of
"the people" and their role in bringing on the crisis. This skepticism
puts us once again in touch with his conservatism. There is no doubt
that he admires John Winthrop and the Constitution, seeing in each
of them a middle way between extremes. What he also admired in
Winthrop was the governor's tolerance of strong-minded foes like
Roger Williams. Morgan argues that Americans agreed with one
another. But this "consensus" remains open-ended, as useful to the
left as to the right. An instinctive tolerance, a passion for intellectual
honesty, an understanding of the past that insists on openness—are
these the qualities of a conservative or of a radical? Perhaps the best
way to answer this question is to quote the final paragraph from one
of Morgan's own essays on the Revolution:

2. Edmund S. Morgan, "The Puritan Ethic and the American Revolution," *William
and Mary Quarterly*, 3d ser., 24 (1967): 3–43; "The Labor Problem at Jamestown," *American Historical Review* 76 (1971): 595–611.
    3. Marian J. Morton, *The Terrors of Ideological Politics: Liberal Historians in a Conserva-
tive Mood* (Cleveland, 1972), chap. 5.

If, then, the American Revolution produced a consensus among the victorious Americans, it was not a static consensus but one with the genius to
serve changing times and needs. It was a consensus that invited conflicts
and still invites them, a consensus peculiarly adapted to a growing people,
a people on the move both geographically and socially. It could not have
contained, but it did not produce, the kind of conflict that gave Charles I
his Cromwell. It made instead for a society where a Hamilton had his Jefferson, a Hoover his Roosevelt, and a Nixon—might profit by their example. If this be conservatism, it is radicals who have made the most of it.[4]

The other constant is Morgan's love of clear, expressive prose. He
learned from and admired the writing style of his former Harvard
teacher Samuel Eliot Morison. But here again the role of temperament is large. Someone skillful with his hands, someone with a keen
sense for the intricacies of nature (especially the wonders and delights
of birds), is a man who wants things to be tangible and accurate. In
his efforts to avoid the false note in prose, Morgan has always sought
to be specific, to make each sentence be as firmly real as possible.
Our statements about the past must be as true and honest as any act
of birdwatching. Ideally they must have the same ring of the crafts-
man. The voice of the historian in twentieth-century America remains
ambiguous, responsive as it is both to the apparatus of professional-
ism and to the deep, instinctive hunger of us all to understand the
past. For Morgan, the way of satisfying both demands lies in a prose
that makes the past concrete and real.

Helen M. Morgan, to whom this book is also dedicated, was a historian in her own right. She befriended many of her husband's students, sharing with them, in her quiet way, the strength of purpose,
the joy of living, and the instinct for craftsmanship that made her so
completely his collaborator. We remember her with affection.

Anyone who works with Morgan soon learns the lesson of unend-
ing curiosity. The essays in *Saints and Revolutionaries* bear out this
lesson by their diversity. Some begin where he leaves off, elaborating
on themes and issues that he has dealt with. Others, and especially
the essays on law and politics, reflect his encouragement of work
quite different from his own. Collectively, these essays should make
it clear that no Morgan "school" exists, no point of view sustained by
generations of disciples. His confidence in intellectual history and
his longstanding interest in the Puritans have had their consequences. But the richest tribute anyone can pay to him is to take that
second glance, to think anew about the past, to set out on a voyage
of discovery.

4. Edmund S. Morgan, "Conflict and Consensus in the American Revolution," in *Essays
on the American Revolution*, ed. Stephen G. Kurtz and James H. Hutson (Chapel Hill,
1973), 309.

The essays in Part 1, "Religion and Mentality," start with familiar documents and issues. Stephen Foster reappraises the development of New England congregationalism, arguing that changing circumstances in 1630s England sequentially affected events and attitudes in Massachusetts. Christine L. Heyrman, in describing the reaction to religious deviants in Essex County, Massachusetts, finds that witchcraft accusations often involved the Quakers and their kin. David D. Hall uses the diary of Samuel Sewall as the basis for a study of mentality, the less formal attitudes and responses that infuse New England Puritanism.

The essays in Part 2, "Law and Politics," all focus on New England, but as a whole they shift attention away from Massachusetts toward the other colonies in the region. Gail Sussman Marcus investigates criminal justice in New Haven Colony, which Perry Miller once described as "the essence of Puritanism, distilled and undefiled." G. B. Warden looks again at Rhode Island's law code of 1647, which seems, perhaps deceptively, to be more English than Puritan. John M. Murrin traces the history of trial by jury through all of the New England colonies in the seventeenth century and finds an astonishing range of extremes, again represented by New Haven and Rhode Island. Turning to politics, Joy and Robert Gilsdorf use eighteenth-century Connecticut to scrutinize the concept of deference in a way that no one else has yet attempted.

If the four essays in Part 3, "Culture, Society, and the Revolution," seem to mirror Morgan's own deep interest in the subject, they nonetheless offer abundant support for the proposition that there is no Morgan "school." Two of the essays, Robert Middlekauff's "Why Men Fought in the American Revolution" and Jonathan Clark's "The Revolution at Home: Community and Politics in Poughkeepsie, New York, 1765–1790," emphasize the unifying influence of the American Revolution. But neither author is much concerned with ideas of political consensus or social harmony. Instead, each—one by examining the soldiers who served in the Continental army and the other by analyzing a bitterly divided New York town—views the Revolutionary experience as having nurtured a strong sense of community that transcended the personal hardships or sharp political differences of the struggle. The remaining essays, James H. Hutson's "The Origins of 'The Paranoid Style in American Politics'" and T. H. Breen's "The Culture of Agriculture: Tobacco and Society in Pre-Revolutionary Virginia," trace revolutionary changes that occurred in political ideology and in the dominant culture of the Virginia colony.

Six of the essays in *Saints and Revolutionaries*—those by Foster, Hall,

Murrin, Clark, Middlekauff, and Hutson—were presented at a conference in New Haven on 19 and 20 October 1979. The others were written especially for this volume. The editors are grateful to several of the commentators at the conference for their suggestions. The principal expenses of the conference were generously borne by W. W. Norton and Company; additional support came from Harcourt Brace Jovanovich, Inc., and from Yale University. On behalf of all the conferees, the editors wish to thank the university and the two publishers. This volume has been made possible by James Mairs, senior editor and vice-president of W. W. Norton.

Jonathan Clark, professor of history at Vassar College, died unexpectedly in February 1983. Clark's essay stands not only as a tribute to his mentor but also as a token of his own great promise and abilities.

Permission to reprint "The Mental World of Samuel Sewall" from the *Proceedings of the Massachusetts Historical Society* 92 (1981): 21–44, has been granted by the Massachusetts Historical Society. Permission to reprint "Why Men Fought in the American Revolution" from the *Huntington Library Quarterly* 43 (1980): 135–48, has been granted by the *Quarterly*.

ONE

---

*Religion
&
Mentality*

English Puritanism and the Progress of New England Institutions, 1630-1660[*]

STEPHEN FOSTER

Few of us have the combination of straightforwardness and imagination needed to call a book simply *The Puritan Dilemma,* announcing a central theme quite explicitly without forfeiting the author's obligation to intrigue his readers. Mostly, we just take the easy way out by luring the unwary in with a cryptic title and wait until the humdrum subtitle to give the game away (if then). A piece written in honor of Edmund S. Morgan, however, should have the decency to admit to its argument fairly early on, and the reader is accordingly forewarned that the operative word in this title is *progress,* used in the older sense of "journey" or "movement."

Thanks to Edmund Morgan's own work and to the scholarship he has inspired, we have a real sense of the progress of American Puritanism and, especially, a sense of the adaptive and protean qualities of New England culture, of the ways in which the world of Ezra Stiles has become different from, yet still heir to, the world of John Winthrop. The challenge accepted in this essay is to build a little on these insights by bringing into the story of gradual change in New England another and more abrupt series of changes—the extraordinary disruptions in the religious life of the English Puritans that turned the loosely integrated movement in the 1620s into a bitterly fragmented group of warring denominations by the time of Cromwell's death, in 1658. In the same period the New England Way took on much of its

 *This piece was written while the author enjoyed a sabbatical leave from Northern Illinois University and a fellowship for independent study from the National Endowment for the Humanities. He wishes to acknowledge his gratitude to both institutions and to thank the Newberry Library for the many courtesies extended to him. Revision of this essay has profited from the criticisms and suggestions offered by David Hall, Robert Pope, and William Breitenbach.

definition, and it seems reasonable to suggest that the shape of American Puritanism was in some way affected by the simultaneous upheavals in the parent movement. Englishmen continued to move to America at a steady rate throughout the whole decade of the 1630s, and while immigration had all but ceased by 1642, New Englanders remained acutely aware of affairs at home through correspondence, remigration, and their participation in the brutal pamphlet wars over "Independency," as well as through such unwelcome imports as English military forces in 1654 and Quaker missionaries in 1656 and afterward. A claim for English influence in America in these thirty years, from 1630 to 1660, may seem unexceptionable and therefore too obvious to be interesting. Yet an understanding of the changing transatlantic relationship can help to pin down the enduring and essential qualities of American Puritanism for the whole of the period in which it remained the dominant force of New England culture.

In many respects the religion that stood on tiptoe in England in 1630, ready to depart for points west, was a very different thing from the faith of the embittered survivors of the Laudian regime who brought in the Root and Branch Petition only ten years later. Arguably, the fate of English Puritanism was already sealed in the year of the Winthrop fleet, but it retained a degree of flexibility, a sense of a common cause, and, even in 1630, a number of friends at court and in the episcopal establishment. When the subcommittee on religion in the parliament of 1629 brought in its resolutions, the grievances were familiar and, with one exception, not very far-reaching. There were the usual complaints about the multiplication of papists at home and about the menace abroad of a coalition of Catholic powers "aiming at the subversion of all Protestant churches in christendom," as well as another instance of the regular demand for "a godly, able minister in every parish church of this kingdom." The subcommittee struck a relatively new and highly ominous note only when it dwelt upon the toleration and covert official encouragement of ceremonialism and Arminianism.[1] In 1629 a Laudian ascendancy may have been fearfully anticipated, but it was yet to come—and with it the whole attempt to restore the Church of England to its pre-Reformation wealth and grandeur. The Laudians would introduce a drastic change by repudiating the traditional Calvinist consensus and attacking the previously respectable Puritan causes of Sabbatarianism and the provision of a preaching ministry, they would openly and rigidly enforce ritualism, and, above all, they would launch a wide-ranging assault on the incumbent Puritan ministry, filling a variety of New England and Dutch pulpits with refu-

1. S. R. Gardiner, ed., *The Constitutional Documents of the Puritan Revolution, 1625–1660*, 3d ed. rev. (Oxford, 1906), 77–82.

gee clergy and, incidentally, shattering the unity of clerical Puritanism. The New England settler of 1637 or 1638 had renounced an England very different from the country left behind by the immigrant of 1631 or 1632, and the direction of New England institutions accordingly registered the change. In America a modus vivendi was worked out between old Puritan and new; in England the decade of the 1640s would demonstrate that the case was quite otherwise.[2]

The immigrants who sailed for America with the Winthrop fleet or who came over in the next few years had, to be sure, perfectly good reasons for getting out of England, many of them perfectly good Puritan reasons. The events of the 1620s, and especially the last five years, were like a crescendo of thunderclaps, the ever louder warnings of an ever angrier God. In rapid succession come the loss of the Palatinate, the victories of Tilly over Protestant forces, the English failures at Cadiz and the Isle of Rhé, the fall of the Protestant citadel of La Rochelle, and, at home, the disorderly Parliaments of 1626 and 1628–29, culminating in the incredible final session of the Commons in 1629, with its abortive resolutions against Arminianism and arbitrary taxation. The list is long and almost rhythmical in its alternation of hope and despair. The dominant sense is not of depression or of bitterness but of crisis, fueled both by the repeated political and military failures and by abrupt fluctuations in the harvests and sudden depression in the cloth-working regions, as well as by the outbreak of popular disorders in East Anglia and the West Country. John Winthrop in 1629 was ready to predict a social war in England and, looking abroad, to declare that "all other Churches of Europe are brought to desolation, and it cannot be, but the like Judgment is comminge upon us: and who knows, but that God hathe provided this place [New England], to be a refuge for manye, whom he meanes to save out of the general distruction?" Charles Chauncey had much the same thing to say to his congregation at Ware, in Hertfordshire, a few months later, in January of 1630, when he caused "a great distraction and feare amongst the people" by linking the planned New England migration with rumors of a French invasion and the warning that "the preaching of the Gospel would be suppressed."[3] A year later the burden of Thomas Hooker's farewell sermon, *The Danger of Destruction,* was similarly apocalyptic:

2. There now exists a considerable body of scholarship on the relationship between the English and American Puritans, but most of it, unfortunately, remains unpublished. A useful bibliography of this material may be found in Francis J. Bremer, "In Defense of Regicide: John Cotton on the Execution of Charles I," *William and Mary Quarterly,* 3d ser., 37 (1980): 104 n. 5.

3. Allyn B. Forbes et al., eds., *Winthrop Papers, 1498–1649* (Boston, 1929–47), II, 114, 124; "Articles objected by his Majesties Comissioners for causes Ecclesiatical against Charles Chauncey . . . ," *Proceedings of the Massachusetts Historical Society,* 1st ser., 13 (1873–75), 340.

God begins to ship away his Noahs, which prophesied and foretold that destruction was near; and God makes account that New England shall be a refuge for his Noahs and his Lots, a rock and a shelter for his righteous ones to run unto; and those that were vexed to see the ungodly lives of the people in this wicked land, shall there be safe.[4]

The diagnosis is undeniably grim. England has broken her "external covenant" with a God who had held her especially dear and who will consequently punish her especially severely. "The poor native Turks and Infidels," says Hooker, "shall have a more cool summer-parlor in hell than England shall have; for we stand upon high rates."[5] The faithful remnant will accordingly pray for her recovery and His mercy—from a distance. England is guilty, however, precisely because she has failed to realize an extraordinary potential. Her magistrates have not suppressed vice, her court indulges papists and tolerates immorality, her church has stalled in its advance on superstition and atheism. (If anything, the ritualism of John Cosin, the theology of Richard Montagu, and the high-handed administration of William Laud at London were marked signs of a backward drift.) But the sin, though black, remains a case of laxity and weakness, of a few wicked men among those in high places abetted by many timeservers and lukewarm "politicians." Few would have suggested in 1630 that Antichrist was running the machine; that verdict would require Laud at Canterbury, Richard Neile at York, Matthew Wren at Norwich. The practices of these prelates, William Prynne would complain in 1637, making a significant conjunction, "have caused thousands of godly Christians (the best Preservatives against Plague and Judgements) to file out to forraigne Countries and Plantations, Hundreds to separate from our Church as now quite Romish and Antichristian; And made thousands ready for to separate."[6]

Just recently we have become aware of the important ways in which English regional differences left their mark in the founding of the colonies. Yet when it comes to the shaping of the most characteristically Puritan of New England institutions, there is a still more significant variable—time. The religion transferred to Salem, Charlestown, Boston, Roxbury, and other towns in the early 1630s was not quite the same thing as the more militant, more explicitly sectarian faith that was imported with Laud's exiles a few years later. The latter were bitter, disillusioned individuals who had seen a painstakingly pieced-together set of compromises within the Church of England repudiated at one blow, and it would be a serious mistake to accept

4. George Williams et al., eds., *Thomas Hooker: Writings in England and Holland,* Harvard Theological Studies, 28 (Cambridge, Mass., 1975), 246.
5. Ibid., 252.   6. *A Quench-Coale* ([Amsterdam], 1637), 36–37.

their very distinctive brand of Puritanism as somehow normative. Even at the moment of the colonies' inception, New England had a "past" of sorts in the long and eventful history of the English Puritan movement until that time. The Puritanism of 1630 may seem a little short on unqualified affirmations, but it was in no sense inchoate or incomplete. Rather, it should be understood as the matured position of the radical end of the English Puritan spectrum, the tempered, resilient product of seventy years of English history and not merely as the church of the Cambridge Platform in embryo. Though their situation was already showing some erosion by 1630, the first commitment of the more radical Puritan ministry and their prominent lay allies and patrons was still to the established church: they continued to consider it the primary means of bringing both civility and Christianity to the English people, most of whom, in their view, lacked more than formal touches of either. In their current form the resources of the Church of England were glaringly inadequate for the great task, according to the radicals, who demanded a quantum improvement in the number and ability of the preachers, indicted episcopal discipline as disorderly and sterile, and objected to the required ceremonies as inconvenient or (in some cases) unlawful. Still, for men who were nonetheless proud to be a part of it, the Church of England had accomplished much and possessed the capacity to do much more. Their record of success in begetting the Godly, John Cotton claimed in 1630, proved in itself that the English parishes were true congregations endowed with a true ministry, "for god is not wont to blesse the bedd of an adulteresse with greater increase then the bed of the married wives."[7]

Radical ministers legitimated their ambivalent official establishment by a process of subtraction, discovering enough right at bottom in their individual congregations to excuse any unlawful "addition" imposed from above. (The term was singularly understated as a description of the judicial and administrative hierarchy.) Such a stance was in part casuistry—a neat formula for accepting inherited arrangements more tolerable than not—but also in part a genuine description of the situation of many Puritan clergy. The more successful the minister and the longer a parish enjoyed a string of such ministers, the greater the body of "saints of God," or "the children of God," or (as it was most frequently put) "the Godly." Their presence was used to "justifie the congregations in which they are called," but when the ministerial apologist went further and suggested that

7. David D. Hall, ed., "John Cotton's Letter to Samuel Skelton," *William and Mary Quarterly,* 3d ser., 22 (1965): 482. Cf. Thomas Hooker, *The Christians Two Chiefe Lessons* . . . (London, 1640), 203–4.

the Godly were already in some sense a separated people, he was doing more than engaging in a theoretical exercise. He was making a virtue of a king-size problem.

The Godly evidently thought that as saints they deserved something more than the privilege of hearing the word truly preached and sharing the sacrament rightly administered cheek by jowl with the carnal majority. They took to their own forms of collective activity—psalm singing, conferences for scriptural exegeses and the resolution of personal doubts, private fasts for public misfortunes.[8] These select private exercises were so popular and so deeply ingrained in the religious life of the Puritan laity that they continued uninterrupted in New England, protected by law in both the Bay Colony and Connecticut.[9] In England, Laudian-sponsored attempts in the 1630s to crack down on the time-honored tradition of "conventicling" merely drove the Godly underground, increasing both their sense of autonomy from clerical control and their already well-developed conceit of themselves as the saving remnant in a wicked and persecuting world. Oliver Heywood's reminiscence of his youth in Lancashire during "the heat and heght of the Bishops tyranny over godly ministers," for example, carries a certain suggestion of the primitive church gathered furtively in the depths of the Roman catacombs:

> I can remember something of the warm spirit of prayer in those days . . . that when at my father's house they had a private fast when I was a child, they set me a singing, about doores, that when the [a]paratour . . . came he might not hear them pray.[10]

8. For instances and discussion, see Patrick Collinson, "Towards a Broader Understanding of the Early Dissenting Tradition," in *The Dissenting Tradition: Essays for Leland H. Carlson,* ed. C. Robert Cole and Michael E. Moody (Athens, Ohio, 1975), 3–38; R. C. Richardson, *Puritanism in North-West England: A Regional Study of the Diocese of Chester* (Manchester, 1972), chap. 3; Stephen Foster, *Notes from the Caroline Underground: Alexander Leighton, the Puritan Triumvirate and the Laudian Reaction to Nonconformity,* Studies in British History and Culture, 6 (Hamden, Conn., 1978), 3–10, 17–19; Ronald A. Marchant, *The Puritans and the Church Courts in the Diocese of York, 1560 to 1642* (London, 1960) 37–38, 41, 47–48, 58, 81, 187–88; W. J. Sheils, *The Puritans in the Diocese of Peterborough, 1558–1610,* Publications of the Northamptonshire Record Society, 30 (Northampton, 1979), chap. 9.

9. *Good News from New-England* (London, 1648), in *Collections of the Massachusetts Historical Society,* 4th ser., 1 (1852): 213; *The Book of the General Lawes and Libertyes Concerning the Inhabitants of the Massachusetts* (Cambridge, Mass., 1648), 19; J. H. Trumbull and C. J. Hoadly, eds., *The Public Records of the Colony of Connecticut* (Hartford, 1850–90), I, 311–12.

10. J. Horsfall Turner, ed., *The Rev. Oliver Heywood, B.A., 1630–1702* (Brighouse, 1881–85), I, 98. For other instances, see Nehemiah Wallington, *Historical Notices of Events . . . in the Reign of Charles I,* ed. R. Webb (London, 1864), I, 132–33; Kenneth W. Shipps, "Lay Patronage of East Anglian Puritan Clerics in Pre-Revolutionary England" (Ph.D. diss., Yale University, 1971), 241–42 (Great Yarmouth), 297–98 (Norwich); Marchant, *Puritans and the Church Courts,* 115.

The Puritan clergy were inclined to regard these lay initiatives with a marked degree of ambivalence. Welcome, palpable proof could be found in the vigor and frequency of the exercises for the claim that deep down below many a parochial surface lay a true church of voluntarily gathered saints. But if the sectarian impulse behind the conventicling urge ever reached its full expression, it could end in one form or another of Separatism: a rejection of any kind of comprehensive mission for church and ministry in favor of the withdrawal of the Godly into their own exclusive societies. As one relatively moderate Separatist writer put it in the early 1620s, "it is a sequestration, and not a reformation that will heale us, helpe us, and give us a right church estate to joyne unto."[11] Though the Separatists did not make all that many outright converts prior to 1630, judging by the regularity with which the ministry warned their constituents to stay away from the subject, as well as by the subsequent resistance on the point in New England, the Godly in England often bridled at the idea of mixed communion, even if they did not bolt their parish assemblies entirely. The demand for exclusivity in the sacrament picked up substantial clerical backing over time, but it seems to have begun with the laity and to have remained their special property. While Thomas Shepard did not see the evil of mixed communion until well into the 1630s, in 1626 or so Thomas Hooker was already lecturing his congregation that exclusion of the unworthy was the job of "those that have public authority in their hands" and that it was no sin for godly persons to share the sacrament with the wicked multitude when control of the matter rested with their superiors. "We confess the fault; let it lie where it is; we cannot reform it. We can only mourn for it, and that God will accept." Fourteen years later, writing from the vantage point of New England, Richard Mather would flatly reject this same proposition that "the people of God may without sinne, live in the want of such Ordinances as superiours provide not for them," but here he was, like most of the Puritan ministry, a follower and not a leader of the popular demand.[12]

The clergy found the Godly heady and uneasy, but necessary, allies. Their presence justified the clergy's very claim to legitimacy, and their support was certainly vital when the rest of the body of parish-

11.Robert Coachman [i.e., Cushman], *The Cry of a Stone* . . . (London, 1642), 16–17. For the dating of this tract, see Stephen Foster, "The Faith of a Separatist Layman: the Authorship, Context, and Significance of *The Cry of a Stone*," *William and Mary Quarterly*, 3d ser., 34 (1977): 375–83.

12. Michael McGiffert, ed., *God's Plot . . . Being the Autobiography and Journal of Thomas Shepard* (Amherst, Mass., 1972), 55; *The Carnal Hypocrite*, in Williams et al., eds., *Thomas Hooker*, 111; [Richard Mather] *Church-Government and Church Covenant Discussed* (London, 1643), 35 (1st pag.).

ioners was liable to contain so many condemners of the truth. Besides, unless the Godly were allowed to release their energies through some variety of exclusivist exercises, they might move into the Separatist camp. Thomas Hooker also warned the saints of Chelmsford that they were obliged to avoid *private* contact with the vulgar or even with those of the Godly who persisted in some sort of serious error—a kind of social excommunication in lieu of the sacramental one.[13] And Hooker also sponsored a regular meeting that took on the aspects of a private church, complete with discipline and excommunications but, paradoxically, without the sacraments.[14] John Cotton's technique was similar: while continuing to give communion to the whole parish, he also separated out a covenanted inner ring for supplementary administration of the sacrament in their own restricted ceremony.[15]

If the Puritan Dilemma is that of maintaining both social commitment and personal integrity, then the collective religious life of the Puritans on the eve of the Great Migration is really its ecclesiastical face. For all Puritans the church was still the custodian and evangelical arm of the official Calvinist culture; if there was ever to be an advance upon the dark, it would be the agent. For the more radical Puritans, however, the church was also already, before the Great Migration, defined in a basically congregational way as the voluntary and deliberate gathering of the faithful, a formulation that expressed something very close to the fact of the matter in some English parishes, where lay pressure and ministerial indulgence had combined to create regular private exercises.[16] And English Puritanism also displayed a clericalist propensity in the frequent clubbing together of the clergy, generally through exercises accompanying the widespread combination lectureships. Like conventicling, ministerial

13. Williams et al., eds., *Thomas Hooker*, 117.

14. F. J. Powicke, ed., "Some Unpublished Correspondence of the Rev. Richard Baxter and the Rev. John Eliot . . . ," *Bulletin of the John Rylands Library* 15 (1931): 159–60.

15. Hall, ed., "John Cotton's Letter to Samuel Skelton," 484; Cotton, *The Way of Congregationall Churches Cleared* (London, 1648), 20.

16. This is not the place for a full-length consideration of the continuing controversy over the extent to which New England ecclesiology embodied an already well-developed English theory of "nonseparating congregationalism." However, for the sake of clarity in my own argument, let me put in a guarded endorsement of Perry Miller, *Orthodoxy in Massachusetts, 1630–1650: A Genetic Study* (Cambridge, Mass., 1933). Regardless of the degree of formality it enjoyed in the early 1630s, there was already a congregational conception of the church, in outline at least, advocated by most of the leading figures of the New England Way *before* they crossed the Atlantic. See, for example, the evidence presented in Miller, pp. 107–19; for further information on John Cotton, see his definition of a church in 1630, in Hall, ed., "John Cotton's Letter to Samuel Skelton," 483. Richard Mather copied out and preserved Cotton's letter less than nine months after the latter wrote it and is himself to be found writing a fluent defense of congregationalism within a year of his own migration. Ibid., 478–79, 485; below, n. 53.

meetings were so useful and so well entrenched an institution that they were transferred to America almost immediately in the form of the frequent "consociation" of the ministers of the Puritan colonies. The practice reaffirmed the distinct, corporate status of the ministry as an order of society separate from the laity and united to one another through their shared vocation, but it occasioned only minor criticism even from the most hardened opponents of clerical power.[17]

Puritanism in New England was always defined by these same three elements: a standing ministerial order, a religious establishment charged with an evangelical and civilizing mission, and a set of particular churches composed of visible saints. Within this trivalent culture, however, the balance among the competing forces shifted sharply in response to the deteriorating situation in England—toward a markedly sectarian concept of church and state in the later 1630s, followed by a slowing of all movement in the 1640s as a result of English criticism, and climaxed by the attainment of a nervous, irritable equilibrium in the 1650s. The resumption of the task of 1630, forging an American establishment capable of feeding the faithful while bringing enlightenment and salvation to the unconverted, would have to wait until the Restoration settlement excluded the English Puritans from any further part in their state church, leaving their New England brethren as the sole custodians of the original vision. Unproductive as this period of advance and retreat in America may seem in retrospect, through its fluctuations New England Puritanism did manage to survive intact; the English half of the movement disintegrated into its component parts.

English Puritanism suffered in large part from being, as of 1630, too well integrated into its society. Lay patrons among the gentry and nobility and Puritan factions in the municipal oligarchies had managed over seven decades to hollow out islands of zeal within the established church, and much of the hierarchy of that church itself had become more indulgent during the period of rapprochement under the moderate Archbishop George Abbot at Canterbury and a succession of Calvinist archbishops at York. Discreet clergymen who had retained the loyalty of their flocks while making some concessions to episcopal authority suddenly found that the technique of compromise put them in an untenable position when they were dealing with a William Laud or a Matthew Wren. "Know I am not more zealous of Ceremonies this day, then when you first called me to

17. Patrick Collinson, "Lectures by Combination: Structures and Characteristics of Church Life in Seventeenth-Century England," *Bulletin of the Institute of Historical Research* 48 (1975): 182–213; Robert F. Scholz, "Clerical Consociation in Massachusetts Bay: Reassessing the New England Way and Its Origins," *William and Mary Quarterly,* 3d ser., 29 (1972): 391–414.

Groton," William Leigh wrote to his former patron John Winthrop in 1636. "I then wore the Surpliss, lesse frequentlie for your sake; now more frequentlie for my Ministeries sake." Winthrop was not much impressed; and neither, as it turned out, was Wren: he suspended Leigh anyway for refusing to read the Declaration of Sports.[18] More pliable ministers simply caved in whole and adopted a dash or two of Laudianism, exchanging the ascetic pleasure of running with the hares for the more fleshly delights of hunting with the hounds. The penalty for this clerical complaisance was lay disgust and the growth of various forms of Separatism. Muriel Sedley Gurdon, the stalwart Puritan wife of a no less stalwart Puritan member of the Suffolk gentry, lamented in 1636 "that in so short a time so many of Gods faithfull ministers should be silenced: and that which is wars [worse]; many that seemed to be zealous doe yield obedience to the inventions of men: it will be a hard matter to chous the good and lav [leave] the evill." By 1640 the authors of the Root and Branch Petition were prepared to open their list of prelatical sins with a blast at the ministry in general for their toadying to the bishops. Before they got around to denouncing the episcopacy for silencing the uncompromising clergymen, they scored "the faint-heartedness of ministers to preach the truth of God, lest they should displease the prelates" and the "encouragement of ministers to despise the temporal magistracy, the nobles and gentry of the land; they abuse the subjects, and live contentiously with their neighbours, knowing that they, being the bishops creatures, shall be supported." A short time later, in January of 1641, the Norfolk royalist Thomas Knyvett, witnessing without comprehending the whirlwind harvest first sown by Matthew Wren's episcopate, reported to his wife that "heers like to be such a Purgation of Black-Coates, as, if the Parliament intertanes all the complantes of the Brethren, I knowe not wher they will finde newe ones to put in. Con[ven]ticles every night in Norwich, as publikely knowne as the sermons in the day, and they say much more frequented." The Norwich "brethren," Knyvett concluded, had respect for only two preachers in the entire city—"the rest all Praters." It had not in the end proven as hard to choose the good and leave the evil as Muriel Gurdon had feared.[19]

For conscientious moderates, lay and clerical, the Laudian ascen-

---

18. *Winthrop Papers,* III, 311, 353, 380, 391.
19. Muriel Sedley Gurdon to Margaret Winthop, 4 April 1636, *Winthrop Papers,* III, 243; Gardiner, ed., *Constitutional Documents of the Puritan Revolution,* 138; Thomas Knyvett to Katherine Knyvett, 17 January 1641, Bertram Schofield, ed., *The Knyvett Letters, 1620–1644,* Publications of the Norfolk Record Society, vol. 20 (London, 1949), 98–99. See J. F. Maclear, "Popular Anticlericalism in the Puritan Revolution," *Journal of the History of Ideas* 17 (1956): 443–70.

dancy was especially bitter. They had trusted in the offices of good bishops to overcome the malice of high-flying prelates and to advance the common cause, and they now found their allies either powerless or turncoats. Some of these disillusioned individuals for one reason or another managed to resist the high-church innovations, at least in part, without budging from their allegiance to traditional goals. A parish was still a parish, no matter how misgoverned; the keys to its membership and discipline still belonged in the hands of the church governors, not in those of the laity, however godly.[20] More will be said of these proto-Presbyterians shortly, but from the standpoint of colonial history a more interesting type in the general falling out of the late 1630s is that of the Newcastle coal merchant and mercer John Blakiston. Blakiston was a feisty individual and a Puritan of no uncertain convictions, who wrote of the New England migrants in 1635: "What worthy Jewells are cabinett in those Ship[s] now agoeinge I hear by New England men that God blesses the place exceedingly both with Spritualls and temporalls. It is in all the best mens opinion a place likeliest for the people of God to escape into whome he gives liberty to remove."[21] He had, however, been born into the self-perpetuating and nearly hereditary episcopal oligarchy in County Durham (his father was a prebendary of Durham cathedral and his sister married John Cosin), and he respected the learned and unimpeachably Calvinist bishop of Durham, Thomas Morton. But by 1638, as "superstition" grew "upp like the hemlock" in the churches of Newcastle and the high-church vicar whom he charged with Arminianism schemed to appeal over Morton's head to Laud, Blakiston knew the new lesson the Lord was teaching him in his adversity:

> for myne owne part I purpose to follow the light I have which the Lord hath bestowed to discerne their wicked plotte and cursed aymes, and never put my necke under this miserable bondage [the ceremonies], I lament that I have stooped and yielded in former more tollerable services so much as I have done, I finde the Lord is asquareinge of my heart and furnishinge of my spirit to doe him some service in an active or passive way.[22]

As it turned out, the way was active. As MP for Newcastle in the Long Parliament, Blakiston was a war-party man, an early republi-

20. See, for example, John Ball, *A Friendly Triall of the Grounds Tending to Separation* (London, 1640). A first-rate account of the growth of the polarization of Puritan opinion can be found in Peter Clark, *English Provincial Society from the Reformation to the Revolution: Religion, Politics, and Society in Kent, 1500–1640* (Hassocks, Sussex, 1977), 361–71.

21. Blakiston to William Morton, 22 May 1635, SP16/540, pt. 4, f. 355, Public Record Office. Blakiston also lent money to a number of Newcastle inhabitants who sailed for New England, and, judging from the dates of these loans, he was probably bankrolling their passage and settlement. See *New England Historical and Genealogical Register* 38 (1884): 79.

22. Blakiston to Morton, 2 March 1637/38, SP16/540, f. 29.

can, and, in 1649, a signatory to the death warrant of Charles I.[23] The changes that came over the English Puritans, the "squaring" of their hearts, had consequences in America as well, in the form of a new concern for rigorous definition and for an appropriately altered polity, both civil and ecclesiastical. The reign of the saints in America was not the product of any specifically Puritan millennialism that simply came to full flower in the unrestricted environment of the New World; rather, everything depended on where a migrant stood in relation to the English church he had left behind, and that, in turn, depended on the state it was in when he left it.

Perhaps the most dramatic contrast between the original broadly based Puritanism of the early migration and its more militant successor can be found in Connecticut, where by an odd set of circumstances the leadership in the river towns ended up largely free from the influence of the later migrants and the dominant group in the New Haven Colony was unalloyed with any moderate elements from the first settlements. Though claiming a settlement date of 1636, two of the three river towns that originally composed Connecticut had begun much earlier as gathered congregations—Hartford at Newtown (later Cambridge), in the Bay in 1633, Windsor earlier still, at Dorchester in 1630 (or at the New Hospital in Plymouth, England, a few months before that, depending on definitions). Both John Warham of the Windsor church and Thomas Hooker of Hartford had left England early in the decade of the 1630s, and the former had defended mixed communion during his early days in the Bay, while the latter rejected the more rigorous tests for church membership introduced in some Massachusetts churches between 1634 and 1636. In Connecticut, as is well known, their churches adopted relatively generous tests of visible sainthood, and both men were advocates of a liberal standard for baptism. The colony itself, unlike the Bay and New Haven, never required church membership as a condition for voting and holding office.[24] By contrast the last of the Puritan colonies to be founded, New Haven, was also the strictest. The gathering of the first church under John Davenport's leadership took well over a year because of the scrutiny with which the would-be pillars looked into the work of saving grace in each other's souls, and this rigor was

23. *Dictionary of National Biography*, s.v. "Blakiston, John"; Mervyn James, *Family, Lineage, and Civil Society: A Study of Society, Politics, and Mentality in the Durham Region, 1500–1640* (Oxford, 1974), 116–17, 136, 167–76; Roger Howell, Jr., *Newcastle upon Tyne and the Puritan Revolution: A Study of the Civil War in North England* (Oxford, 1967), 126–29 and passim.

24. Edmund S. Morgan, *Visible Saints: The History of a Puritan Idea* (1963; pbk. ed., Ithaca, 1965), 106–8; Frank Shuffelton, *Thomas Hooker, 1586–1647* (Princeton, 1977), 168–70, 289–91; Robert Pope, *The Half-Way Covenant: Church Membership in Puritan New England* (Princeton, 1969), 22, 31.

not relaxed in subsequent admissions. Only a saint so carefully certified, however, could participate in political affairs, and for good measure the New Haven Colony enjoyed the distinction of being the only Puritan polity in America to adopt whole into its laws John Cotton's biblically derived "Moses his judicials." Before the union with Connecticut in 1664, there was no wavering from these standards, not even to the limited degree granted by the Bay Colony's franchise laws, and under Davenport's leadership the churches of the colony vigorously resisted the Half-Way Covenant of 1662.[25]

Ironically, the New Haven Colony's guiding light had originally been the most moderate of the English ministers who eventually became major figures in New England. Richard Mather never used the ceremonies, Thomas Shepard vacillated regarding their use, and John Cotton abstained but equivocated. John Davenport was an unabashed conformist as late as 1631, and in 1632 he went out of his way to denounce as schismatic the Independent church in London that had originally been gathered by the early congregationalist Henry Jacob.[26] Davenport spelled out his early philosophy in the mid-1620s when he called on all parties to undertake a common battle, through the enhancement of the preaching ministry, "against those who oppose us in Fundamentalls." In the church of Archbishop Abbot the ceremonies could be dismissed as superficial ornaments on a basically sound structure. The real danger came instead from the Catholic menace, incipient Arminianism of the Montagu stripe, and the old enemies of vice and irreligion. "Who can, without sorrowe, and fear observe how Atheisme, Libertinisme, papisme, and Arminianisme, both at home, and abroad have stolne in, and taken possession of the house, whilest we are at strife about the hangings and paintings of it?"[27]

Davenport was a perfect instance of Jacobean Puritanism at its most respectable, content to pour its energies into preaching campaigns and Sabbatarianism until the Laudians repudiated both and incorporated ceremonialism and Arminianism into the very fabric

25. Isabel M. Calder, *The New Haven Colony* (New Haven, 1934), chaps. 4–5; Pope, *Half-Way Covenant*, 264–65; Morgan, *Visible Saints*, 108–9. See also the accounts of the New Haven Colony towns of Milford and Guilford in Gerald F. Moran, "Religious Renewal, Puritan Tribalism, and the Family in Seventeenth-Century Milford, Connecticut," *William and Mary Quarterly*, 3d ser., 36 (1979): 238–40; Paul Lucas, *Valley of Discord: Church and Society along the Connecticut River, 1630–1725* (Hanover, N.H., 1976), 32–34.

26. Increase Mather, *The Life and Death of . . . Mr. Richard Mather* (Cambridge, Mass., 1670), reprinted in *Collections of the Dorchester Antiquarian and Historical Society* 3 (1850): 49–51, 56; McGiffert, ed., *God's Plot*, 48; Champlin Burrage, *The Early English Dissenters in the Light of Recent Research (1550–1641)* (Cambridge, 1912), II, 260–64, 298; Isabel M. Calder, ed., *Letters of John Davenport, Puritan Divine* (New Haven, 1937), 13–16, 19, 33–38.

27. Calder, ed., *Letters of John Davenport*, 23–24.

of the episcopacy. Men in that position had a longer way to fall than did the Richard Mathers and Thomas Hookers, and they landed harder and meaner. The same kind of disillusionment that made a radical of John Blakiston in England turned John Davenport into the unbending patriarch of the New Haven Colony.

In the Bay Colony the process of sectarianization was more subtle because the new immigrants regularly interacted with the old over the course of the whole decade of the 1630s. Yet there was a discernible drift—or rush—toward purity, toward a definition of the church that gave first thought to the calling of the saints and deduced the terms of the Puritan mission from their needs and privileges. As the enthusiasm for the pure church rose in New England, the failings of the English churches seemed progressively more serious. New Englanders continued to find saving graces in at least some English parishes, but old and new Puritans increasingly adopted a de facto Separatism in their concept of the whole parochial system. By the time Ezekiel Rogers and his Yorkshire company arrived in the Bay, in 1638, they encountered no opposition when they declared that they "had of a good time, withdrawn themselves from the church communion of England, and that for many corruptions which were among them. . . . Hereupon they bewailed before the Lord their sinful partaking so long in these corruptions, and entered a covenant together to walk together in all the ordinances, etc."[28] The Yorkshire group may have been one step ahead of the previous settlers of the Bay Colony, but in 1638 it was one step only. Less than two years later John Cotton was discovering the Church of England in the thirteenth chapter of Revelation, in the beast risen from the sea, and informing his hearers that if they were unwise enough to return to the mother country, "you will finde the body of the church rent from you, or you will be rent from the body, if you shall walk roundly and sincerely in the ways of God."[29]

This shift was not absolutely predictable in the first years of the Bay Colony. In 1631 the General Court, such as it was, had restricted the franchise to church members, though almost certainly in order to keep the few really wicked from the reins of power rather than to place them exclusively in the hands of the few really deserving. At the time only a handful of churches had actually been founded and no very restrictive tests for admission had been laid down, nor had communion with the Church of England been formally rejected. The

28. John Winthrop, *The History of New England from 1630 to 1649*, ed. James Savage (Boston, 1853), I, 335 (hereafter cited as Winthrop, *History*).

29. John Cotton, *An Exposition upon the Thirteenth Chapter of the Revelation* (London, 1655), 19–20. (The unpaginated preface indicates that these sermons were preached between January and April of 1640.)

Boston church, in particular, began its existence on a very cautious note, affirming in so many words that its new pastor, John Wilson, enjoyed his ministerial status by virtue of his episcopal ordination in England and not of his election to a pulpit in America: "We used imposition of hands, but with this protestation by all, that it was only a sign of election and confirmation, not of any intent that Mr. Wilson should renounce his ministry he received in England."[30]

These earlier churches began by late 1634 or early 1635 to suffer the consequences of their informal beginnings. The growing disillusionment with moderation imported from England year in and year out could be seen in schisms or near schisms as well as in the measures necessary to prevent further trouble. Local conflicts and personal animosities determined the particular form of these disputes, but whether at Salem or at Lynn or, a few years later, at Scituate (in Plymouth Colony) the terms of the divisions were more or less the same. Some portion of the membership, as the champions of purity, called into question the casual manner in which the church had been founded and run, "withal making question, whether they were a church or not."[31]

"Only" is a dangerous word to employ in discussing academic historiography, but I am going to venture it: to the best of my knowledge only *The Puritan Dilemma* had drawn attention to the overall rise in Separatist sentiment in Massachusetts that accompanied the heavy immigration of the mid-1630s.[32] Most of the more famous ecclesiastical institutions of the Bay Colony derive in one way or another from efforts to damp this potentially explosive element in the population—efforts that were on the whole successful, in marked contrast to the disintegration of Puritan unity in England in the same period. The most direct and immediate response was the covenant renewal, a device initiated to prevent divisions in the 1630s and not an invention of the revivalist 1670s. The new covenants were expanded, tightly defined documents that supplied any elements in congregational polity that might have been lacking, without necessarily acknowledging that the earlier church foundations were void *ab initio*. The Boston church, as well, on the occasion of the "distractions" at Lynn and Salem, took the further precaution in 1636 of indulging the Separatist penchant for purification rituals by including a portion of the renewal ceremony in which the members

30. Winthrop, *History*, I, 38–39.
31. Ibid., 187 (referring to Lynn); Richard P. Gildrie, *Salem, Massachusetts, 1626–1683: A Covenant Community* (Charlottesville, 1975), 31–38; Samuel Deane, *History of Scituate, Massachusetts, from Its First Settlement to 1831* (Boston, 1831), 60–88.
32. Edmund S. Morgan, *The Puritan Dilemma: The Story of John Winthrop* (Boston, 1958), 73–76.

"acknowledged such failings as had fallen out, etc."[33]

The same kind of expiatory ritual, not strictly Separatist but very close to it, would be used at the gathering of the church of Concord in 1637 to absolve the New England ministry of ever having upheld an unlawful calling by accepting episcopal ordination. The intellectual formula was, in fact, very similar to the covenant renewal. The earlier practice was not totally denied: the ordained ministry had been true ministers in England despite their sinful ordinations because they had received a call, explicit or implicit, from the people to whom they ministered. But the crime of coupling this legitimate call with a usurped, episcopal one was acknowledged and repented of, and the privilege of the saints, their unique and precious right to constitute a church, was emphatically affirmed when the clergy denied that they were ministers at all except at the call of a gathered, covenanted, and certifiably gracious society. (The conclusion was the opposite of the claim made at John Wilson's ordination in 1630, again in just so many words.) This arrangement did not explicitly repudiate past commitments, yet it satisfied any purist less extreme than a follower of Roger Williams—the question of the ministerial call, indeed, was moved on this occasion "by one sent from the church of Salem."[34] To purists who *were* as extreme as Williams, a more summary answer could be given: exile to Rhode Island. But most of the time the Separatists were not repressed; they were assimilated.

Even the levelheaded John Winthrop showed the effects of the new rigorism, in his changing perceptions of the schism at Lynn in 1635 and 1636. At the time, he had been primarily interested in getting the business settled, with an acknowledgment of the importance of church ordinances rightly ordered, certainly, but above all as quietly and bloodlessly as possible. He accepted with relief an early and familiar compromise (later repudiated) that found Lynn a true church on the basis of "consent and practice."[35] (That is, however incomplete the outward gathering of the church, the members had now been doing the right things long enough to provide their polity with a retrospective baptism by desire.) Two years later, in 1638, after the Lynn church had been regathered under careful outside supervision and "with much ado," he compared the new arrangement with similar disorders at Weymouth and attributed Lynn's subsequent success to its repentance for its original laxity:

33. Winthrop, *History*, I, 216; Gildrie, *Salem*, 51–55; Alonzo Lewis and James R. Newhall, *History of Lynn, Essex County, Massachusetts* (Boston, 1865), 165–67. At Scituate, however, the liberal admissions party used a covenant renewal in 1642 to assert its separate and prior existence as a church, in answer to the claims of the purist faction: Deane, *History of Scituate*, 60–61.

34. Winthrop, *History*, I, 259–60.   35. Ibid., 187.

> . . . they did not begin according to the rule of the gospel, which when Lynn had found and humbled themselves for it, and began again upon a new foundation, they went on with a blessing.[36]

Evidently, the atmosphere in the Bay Colony must have been very rarefied if it could make the likes of Winthrop a little pixilated. He was still the same political animal trying to find a middle ground that accommodated all except the extremes in the colony, but as the boundaries of his field of operations shifted leftward, so did the middle point.

Responding to these repeated contentions, actual and potential, the General Court issued its well-known order of 3 March 1636 requiring the majority of the colony's magistrates and ministers to be present at the gathering of any new churches.[37] While the law has a repressive air to it, its original purpose was mainly prudential: "the sad breaches which other churches have had" demonstrated that if these mixed councils of civil and ecclesiastical officers were not present at the start of any new church, they would sooner or later be called in anyway to deal with the claim of some aggrieved faction that errors in the foundation invalidated the whole edifice.[38] Nevertheless, indirectly the mid-1630s crisis did force a greater degree of uniformity on the churches of the Bay, for the significance of these statutory councils lies in their function as devices for determining and adjusting common goals. As at Concord in 1637, in each instance the ministry in full regalia told the new church—and each other— what the New England Way was all about and where it was headed.

The earliest authorized council, held during the first attempt to gather the Dorchester church, in April of 1636, had the most profound consequences for the religious life of the Bay Colony and New Haven. On this occasion the resident clergy taught their newly learned lessons in exactness to a newcomer, Richard Mather, when they rejected his would-be pillars on the grounds that their conversions were spurious and for the most part merely "legal" (resting on faith in their own abilities rather than on a sense of their total dependence on free and unmerited saving grace). Thomas Shepard, who had organized the first public demonstration of the members' saving faith at the gathering of his own Cambridge church, two months earlier, took the lead in halting the Dorchester proceedings under the new

36. Ibid., 243–44, 346.
37. Nathaniel B. Shurtleff, ed., *Records of the Governor and Company of the Massachusetts Bay in New England* (Boston, 1853–54), I, 168 (hereafter cited as *Mass. Recs.*).
38. The origins and purpose of the law appear clearly ibid., 142, in *Winthrop Papers*, III, 231, and its preamble. See also John A. Albro, *The Life of Thomas Shepard* (Boston, 1847), 216.

statute because, as he told Mather, "we come not here to find [i.e. discover] gracious hearts, but to see them too. 'Tis not faith, but a visible faith, that must make a visible church, and be the foundation of visible communion."

The Dorchester episode always seems a little puzzling, partly because Richard Mather, who devoted most of his intellectual life to questions of polity, should have been the last man in New England to gather a church carelessly, partly because the development cannot be readily explained as a qualified accommodation with the growing Separatist spirit. (The classic Separatists of Amsterdam and Leyden did not require conversion narratives as part of the procedure for admission to church fellowship.) The affinity of the requirement promulgated at Dorchester is probably with the Antinomian controversy in the church of Boston, which erupted later in the same year and which also centered on discerning the difference between a legal and a truly gracious conversion. At Dorchester no less than at Boston, we are dealing with a reaction to the Laudian attack on the long-standing predestinarian consensus of the mother church and to the feebleness with which most English contemporaries resisted these new (or newly revealed) episcopal corruptions. "Though the light be hindered with us with the Foggs and Mists of Pelagian and other heresyes," an English Puritan declared, "there [in New England] it breakes forth and shines." The New England clergy might have been responding "Amen" when they faulted poor Richard Mather's pillars because "they expected to believe by some power of their own and not only and wholly from christ." In the face of the dwindling minority ready to do their duty by opposing the episcopacy, and because of the increasing exaltation of the few who had actually migrated for truth's sake, it became necessary, for reasons of principle and prudence alike, to demonstrate as publicly as possible the *visible* sanctity of the genuine remnant as they arrived and built their churches in America. Even as Anne Hutchinson was just beginning to object in Boston to the overly charitable standards used in awarding sainthood in New England, she was already being answered at Dorchester. "By this means, I believe and hope that the communion of saints will be set at a higher price," Shepard told Mather—significantly, at the very moment when he was about to assume the lead in blunting the Antinomian threat in the colony.[39]

39. Albro, *Shepard,* 215–16; Winthrop, *History,* I, 218–19; Morgan, *Visible Saints,* 100–102; Richard Walker preaching at Saint Leonard's Eastcheap in 1640, SP16 / 164, fol. 83r.-v. I have offered some suggestions on the English context of American Antinomianism in "New England and the Challenge of Heresy, 1630–1660: The Puritan Crisis in Trans-Atlantic Perspective," *William and Mary Quarterly,* 3d ser., 38 (1981): 624–60.

Undeniably, the test for saving grace had its theoretical roots in the elaborate manuals for self-examination that had always made up much of the literary corpus of church Puritans.[40] Yet the institutionalization of the test, the insistence that a church cannot be right without some version of it, must be understood as a manifestation of the spirit of embittered extremism characterizing the refugee politics of those Puritans desperate enough and angry enough to choose exile after Laud came to power at Canterbury. The driving force was the collapse of the comfortable world of the old nonconformity and the sense of freedom that came, not from the expanses of America, but simply from the release from the necessity of compromise. The expatriate church that gathered at Arnhem, in the Netherlands, under the ministry of Thomas Goodwin and Philip Nye instituted the same test at about the same time without the benefit of any American influence, and its ministers and congregation alike would become prominent members of the Independent cause in England on their return home in the 1640s. Indeed, the Arnhem group had almost ended up in New England in the first place: before they had settled in the Netherlands as their place of exile, Nye had already been serving (in 1635 and 1636) as the agent for a proposed home at Saybrook for these "gentlemen," as the Puritan ultras were prudently termed. In their different ways, the congregations at Arnhem, Dorchester, and Boston were responding to a single impulse.[41]

In this context there was nothing anomalous in Richard Mather's becoming the first New England minister to have his church found wanting in vital matter. Throughout his career Mather was the foil of John Davenport, and the two men were appropriately ranged on opposite sides of the Half-Way Covenant at the very end of their lives. In the wilds of the diocese of Chester, Puritan clergymen like Mather had enjoyed a unique degree of freedom until Neile's first visitation of the northern province. He had never used any of the ceremonies whatever, nor had he ever been forced to face the issues of mixed communion or of the legitimacy of a national church orga-

40. Morgan, *Visible Saints*, 67–73.

41. For the test, see John C. Miller, ed., *The Works of Thomas Goodwin, D.D.* (Edinburgh, 1861–65), XI, 536. There is evidence of a similar practice in use at Rotterdam as of 1637: see the confession of Sidrach Simpson in W. H. D. Longstaffe, ed., *Memoirs of the Life of Mr. Ambrose Barnes, Publications of the Surtees Society* 50 (1866): 131. "The gentlemen" were Sir William Constable, Sir Matthew Boynton, Sir Richard Saltonstall, and Henry Lawrence. All are in the *DNB* except Boynton. For full details, see *Winthrop Papers*, III, 211, 212, 226–27; Arthur Percival Newton, *The Colonising Activities of the English Puritans* (New Haven, 1914), chap. 7; J. T. Cliffe, *The Yorkshire Gentry from the Reformation to the Civil War* (London, 1969), 306–8; Burrage, *Early English Dissenters*, II, 291. The actual covenanting of the Arnhem group took place at Misbourne, Buckinghamshire, in the winter of 1636 or the spring of 1637. See Thomas Edwards, *Antapologia: or, A Full Answer to the Apologeticall Narration . . .* (London, 1644), 22–23, 35.

nized on parochial lines. Until he was abruptly deprived of his English calling, in 1634, he had ministered to the "chapelry" of Toxeth Park, a voluntary, gathered body so intensely Puritan that its little tract of Lancashire was called "the Holy Land."[42] The situation was not unusual in the sprawling, undersupervised diocese. Just across the Mersey from Mather's Toxeth Park lay Samuel Eaton's parish of West Kirby, which, according to its minister, "consisted of the choycest Christians of many Parishes, who met constantly together upon the Lords day, and enjoyed the Word, and seales of the covenant, and maintained a Pastor to dispense the same unto them, and never or very rarely repaired to such Parishes where their habitations were."[43] For both Mather and Eaton during their English ministries, their saints were already visible without any special scrutiny, and their removal to America did not require them to repudiate any previous concessions to ritual, hierarchy, or parochial communion. Mather, in fact, recorded his reasons for leaving: when he came here, he was simply looking for work and for a refuge that merited God's protection. (Like Winthrop in 1630, he fled the wrath of God, not the face of Antichrist.) But doing what came naturally at Dorchester, he promptly ran afoul of those of his colleagues who had been reborn in the 1630s and who were making up for the time he himself had never lost by a thoroughgoing reversal of their earlier caution. Eaton similarly collided with John Davenport over another central issue of the new sectarianism—the church member franchise—and returned to Cheshire, where, back in his own milieu, his still unchanged commitments now made him a disruptive radical.[44] Mather, who was better at acclimating himself to differing environments, stayed on in New England and managed to get an acceptably exclusive church

42. See above, n. 26, and Richardson, *Puritanism in North-West England*, 16–17, 17–22, 97–99. See also Marchant, *Puritans and the Church Courts*, chap. 4.

43. Samuel Eaton and Timothy Taylor, *A Defence of Sundry Positions, and Scriptures, Alleged to Justifie the Congregationall-Way* (London, 1645), 2. For Eaton, see the *DNB* and A. G. Matthews, *Calamy Revised* (Oxford, 1934), s.v. "Eaton, Samuel."

44. Increase Mather, *Richard Mather*, 57–68; Cotton Mather, *Magnalia Christi Americana*, ed. Thomas Robbins (Hartford, 1853), 585–86; J. S. Morrill, *Cheshire, 1630–1660: County Government and Society during the English Revolution* (Oxford, 1974), 35–37, 53, 164–65. Cotton Mather's description of the opposition between Eaton and Davenport is questioned in an important reinterpretation of the founding of the New Haven Colony: Bruce Steiner, "Dissension at Quinnipiac: the Authorship and Setting of *A Discourse about Civil Government in a New Plantation whose Design is Religion*," *New England Quarterly* 54 (1981): 14–32. This is not the place to review the whole of Steiner's argument, but I should note that I consider his unsupported rejection of Cotton Mather's testimony on Eaton unconvincing. Moreover, Cotton's father, Increase Mather (whose authority in other matters Steiner does credit), was the main source of information on the New England men in Anthony à Wood's *Athenae Oxonienses*, one of whom was Samuel Eaton. See Matthews, *Calamy Revised*, s.v. "Mather, Increase"; and Anthony à Wood to Increase Mather, 12 June 1690, *Collections of the Massachusetts Historical Society*, 2d ser., 7 (1818): 187–88.

formed a little later in 1636, but he remained one of the earliest and, without deviating into any form of Presbyterianism, certainly the most consistent advocate of a broader definition of church membership.[45] It is a left-handed compliment to the New England Way that the man with the most generous concept of the church's agenda should be its single most ingenuous congregationalist.

If the concatenation of New England innovations is added up, the composite picture by 1638 undercuts most of the force in the clergy's repeated claim that they revered particular English parishes as basically true churches. No new migrant was allowed to join a New England church on the basis of his former good standing in an English parish, while New Englanders returning home were enjoined from participating in mixed communion, and, after the Dorchester council, the effective standards for locating the residue of gracious souls in the mixture were raised considerably. A true English reformation, according to John Cotton (more right than he knew), was all but impossible because it would require the would-be reformers "to shut out the greatest part of a kingdom from the Lords Table."[46] In the meanwhile the hierarchy was held to be "wholly Antichristian" (Ezekiel Rogers's words), and to take ordination at its hands was a sin even when joined with a lawful popular call. Further given the covenant renewals required to reform the earlier Massachusetts churches, even when the English parishes were able to get out from under the control of the bishops, as they did after 1640, they "could not be right without a renewed covenant at least, and the refusers excluded."[47] It was all very well for New Englanders to attempt to find "implicit" truth in some English congregations (left unspecified) for the benefit of their old friends in the Puritan clergy now under increasing fire from the Separatists and the militant wing of the laity— the same kind of laity that migrated to New England to insist on purity there. "Implicit" legitimacy was not worth much under the circumstances. "That much favor will be granted us by the strictest of the separacion," a correspondent of Governor Winthrop's shot back in 1637 and suggested for good measure that the cause of the moderate Puritans was not being helped by letters from New England calling the members of the English churches (in no implicit terms)

45. Pope, *Half-Way Covenant,* 17–23, 33–35, 134–135.
46. *Exposition upon the Thirteenth Chapter of the Revelation,* 259. Cf. Richard Mather, *Church Government and Church Covenant Discussed,* 30–36. See E. Brooks Holifield, *The Covenant Sealed: The Development of Puritan Sacramental Theology in Old and New England, 1570–1720* (New Haven, 1974), 163–64; Foster, "Faith of a Separatist Layman," 398–99.
47. Williston Walker, ed., *The Creeds and Platforms of Congregationalism* (pbk. ed., Boston, 1960), 138 (hereafter cited as Walker, *Creeds*).

"dogs and swine, especially those of the profaner sort among us, nor questioning our ministry and calling to it."[48]

From about 1636 on the New England clergy began to receive detailed complaints from their sometime colleagues in England. When they responded with tact and circumlocution, they were met with rejoinders that were a notch less brotherly than the original criticisms. The further replies were less generous and more argumentative in their turn, and before long the whole correspondence ended up as part of the ferocious polemical exchanges that erupted into print in the ever proliferating pamphlet warfare of the Interregnum.[49] The whole business converted no one (or almost no one—John Owen and one or two others claimed to have come over to the Independents after reading John Cotton's apologies for congregationalism). Yet in an important way English criticism did begin the gradual cooling down of the New England colonists' love affair with purity. In the 1640s the ministers, caught short by the rising volume of English Puritan attacks, took stock of themselves and halted their continuing indulgence of lay initiatives. Consequently, they found themselves in an off-again, on-again round of skirmishing with the laity that produced few casualties and no victors. But this round of drawn engagements did effectively stop further movement in a sectarian direction.

New England writers in the Presbyterian-Independent controversies never seemed to understand precisely what it was their opponents were attacking—or, more likely, they chose not to understand. Charged with embracing Separatism, they responded by examining "rigid" Separatist writings of the Jacobean period and then congratulated themselves on finding that New England congregationalism differed in major ways from the polity of Henry Ainsworth and John Robinson. The English critics, however, were worried less about competition from Amsterdam and Leyden than about a much more pervasive revolt of the laity. For moderates the burden of the Laudian years had been the multiplication of impromptu, lay-dominated exercises and the concomitant growth in impatience with clerical leadership—developments abetted by a few ministerial hotheads who had taken to announcing that "it is the peoples duety to labore to manetayne the gospell" in the face of the new episcopal onslaught.[50] At the same time and for the same reason, the moderates were similarly threatened by the increasing aggressiveness of very loosely

48. *Winthrop Papers,* III, 398–99.
49. Winthrop, *History,* I, 331; Walker, *Creeds,* 134–41. See also below, nn. 52, 53, 54.
50. A visiting preacher filling the pulpit (left empty by Wren's visitors) of Saint Mary's Tower, Ipswich, on 23 April 1636, quoted in Shipps, "Lay Patronage of East Anglian Puritan Clerics," 261.

organized clusters of Separatists in such places as the Kentish Weald and the city and suburbs of London and by the activities of such groups as the Bristol conventiclers, who withdrew from parochial communion "when the clergy began to be high" in order to start the private meetings that evolved into the Broadmead Baptist church in the next decade.[51] For all these groups the New England example was all too apposite in its condemnation of mixed communion, set prayer, and episcopal ordination and in its endorsement of gathered churches. Reports from the New England colonies, thirteen Puritan ministers claimed in 1637,

> have so taken with divers in many parts of this kingdome that they have left our Assemblies because of a stinted Liturgie, and excommunicated themselves from the Lords Supper, because [of] such as are not debarred from it. And being turned aside themselves, they labour to ensnare others, to the griefe of the godly, the scandall of Religion, the wounding of their own soles . . . and great advantage to them, that are wily to espy, and ready to make use of all advantages to prejudice the truth.[52]

Whatever their natural inclinations, the New England clergy by example and, when they were put to it, by explicit statements were aligning themselves with the most sectarian of the new critics of the English church. They left their former brethren with no shred of comfort, even on the most delicate and dangerous of all the issues involving the perquisites of the English clergy and their gentry protectors. New Englanders rejected lay patronage out of hand, and, while they pursued an ambiguous course on compulsory maintenance of the clergy, they objected to the whole idea of tithes.[53] More awkward still, their official spokesmen, as early as 1636 or even earlier, explicitly endorsed gathering true (that is, fully congregational)

51. Roger Hayden, ed., *The Records of a Church of Christ in Bristol, 1640–1687*, Publications of the Bristol Record Society, vol. 27 (Bristol, 1974), 83–91; Murray Tolmie, *The Triumph of the Saints: The Separate Churches of London, 1616–1649* (New York, 1977); Clark, *English Provincial Society*, 369–73; Geoffrey F. Nuttall, *Visible Saints: The Congregational Way, 1640–1660* (Oxford, 1957), 48–49; Ball, *Friendly Triall*, preface, sig. Bv; Andrew Foster, "Richard Neile" (D.Phil. thesis, Oxford University, 1978), 254 ("Brownists" around Macclesfield, Chester, and Manchester, Lancashire, in 1633), 264 (covert lay activity in Yorkshire).

52. Simeon Ashe and William Rathband, eds., *A Letter of Many Ministers in Old England . . . Written Anno. Dom. 1637* (London, 1643), Sig. Azv. The original MS (which has the full list of signatories) is in Prince Collection, Cotton Papers, pt. 2, no. 9, Boston Public Library.

53. Cf. The Cambridge Platform in Walker, *Creeds*, 215, 221; B. Richard Burg., ed., "A Letter of Richard Mather to a Cleric in Old England," *William and Mary Quarterly*, 3d ser., 29 (1972): 94; Clark, *English Provincial Society*, 368–69; William A. Shaw, *A History of the English Church during the Civil Wars and under the Commonwealth, 1640–1660* (London, 1900), II, 175–286; Richard Mather, *Church-Government and Church Covenant Discussed*, 77 (last pag.); Margaret James, "The Political Importance of the Tithes Controversy in the English Revolution, 1640–60," *History*, n.s., 26 (1941–42), 1–18.

churches separated from the parish assemblies and in flat defiance of the authorities, civil and ecclesiastical.[54]

In the 1630s there was not much that middle-of-the-road English Puritans could do about the Separatist threat besides issue irrelevant calls for forbearance and repeat the same familiar apology for true, but imperfect, churches that now was beginning to wear thin. Liberated at last by the fall of Laud in 1640, they rushed to the Presbyterian cause as the last hope for retaining a national church with a comprehensive mission, only to find that the disappearance of the episcopal courts and the High Commission left their Separatist and neo-Separatist opponents stronger than ever. What was worse, the respectability lent to congregationalism by the rather distant example of New England was now enormously increased by the Holland exiles, returned to become the Dissenting Brethren in the Westminster Assembly, and by a sprinkling of ex–New Englanders and prestigious English converts (including Henry Burton and John Goodwin). Yet, maddeningly, there was nothing concrete to attack. Thomas Gataker in 1640 found himself grumbling about "a great noise in England" for the last three or four years in favor of "a New Light and a New Way," which, unlike bona fide Separatism, was never spelled out "yet further than by private letters and clancular manuscripts" originating from abroad.[55] The "dark lanthornes," however, still did not shine brightly after the calling of the Long Parliament and the Westminster Assembly: with the exception of a few of the Separatists and the ever intrepid Burton, the English Independents mostly held their hand, refusing to come up with a full statement of church polity or even, in the case of the Dissenting Brethren, to admit before 1644 that they so much as constituted a distinct party.

At this juncture, between 1642 and 1645, the correspondence begun with New England suddenly and conveniently appeared in

54. John Cotton, *The Doctrine of the Church to Which Are Committed the Keyes of the Kingdome of Heaven,* 2d ed. rev. (London, 1643), 13; Burg., ed., "A Letter of Richard Mather," 89; Richard Mather, *Church-Government and Church Covenant Discussed,* 34–36. The dating of the Cotton piece is uncertain. He began work on it on 25 January 1635, and I suspect it to be the letter of his mentioned by a correspondent of Governor Winthrop as in circulation in England ca. May 1637, but there is no definite evidence that the earlier, manuscript versions carried the inflammatory assertion that "the gathering of saints or churches according to the Order of Christ and the guidance and walking of both according to his Will, is no just offence to the civil Magistrate." See Larzer Ziff, *The Career of John Cotton: Puritanism and the American Experience* (Princeton, 1962), 264; Winthrop Papers, III, 399.

55. Preface to William Bradshaw, *The Unreasonableness of the Separation,* 2d ed. rev. ([The Netherlands], 1640), unpaginated. The authors of the manuscripts in question were clearly members of New England churches and of the Rotterdam and Arnhem congregations: they were described as having originally gone abroad but now "come home again by weeping crosse" or "still abiding in forraine parts" for fear of their English reception.

print. In his *Antapologia* of 1644 the notorious Thomas Edwards (of *Gangraena* fame) claimed that during the formal truce between the Dissenting Brethren and the Presbyterian majority in 1642 and 1643 the Independents simply got around the peace terms by bringing out account after account of New England polity.[56] Actually, both sides played the same trick: the defense of the parochial system in the 1630s against New England innovations also appeared in print in the 1640s, grafted onto the new Presbyterian campaign against Independency. Nothing loth to respond, the New England clergy promptly took up the next round in the dispute anyway, and for the rest of the decade they were active and eager literary contributors to the anti-Presbyterian camp, even though that group included English allies who would very quickly have wound up in Rhode Island if they had ever set foot in Massachusetts or Connecticut.

As an issue, however, Presbyterianism changed the nature of the debate in New England no less than in old. The English criticism of the late 1630s could be written off as misinformed (as it was on some points), and charges of apostasy were answered with the double reply of new light and new liberty. In America, free from episcopal interference, the New England clergy had grown in grace and realized to their sorrow that in some instances they had engaged in unlawful acts in England; further, many things not strictly unlawful in the English church were thoroughly inconvenient, and it was surely the New Englander's moral duty to reform what was amiss, now that they no longer had to tolerate these undesirable impositions from above as the price of continuing their ministry. The presumption was that if the English ever had the like freedom they would immediately do as the New Englanders did in the case of inconvenient practices (they would, for example, reorganize their churches with explicit covenants) and that they might very well come to accept the New England view of the lawful, as well, after the new light broke out on their side of the Atlantic. Instead, after 1640 the New Englanders found themselves replying for the first time to full-blown doctrinal Presbyterianism, not the semi-Erastian compromise that eventually emerged from the Long Parliament and that could easily be faulted for its obvious imperfections, but a wholly theoretical system of indisputably Reformed pedigree. Issues of congregational polity that had been handled piecemeal before, and in their own terms, now had to be faced systematically and defined against a plausible alternative system. Presbyterianism, therefore, became the burning question of the 1640s. Anti-Presbyterian conventions of the

56. *Antapologia,* 220, 240–43.

whole body of the New England clergy were held at Cambridge in 1643 and 1645, while the full-scale synod that held its sessions there from 1646 to 1648 was confessedly looking over its shoulder at England at regular intervals during the course of hammering out a platform of discipline. (Virtually all of its ten-page preface is an apology for gathered congregations and a rejoinder to Presbyterian charges of schism.)[57]

Most of the defense of congregationalism was a theoretical exercise. A genuine Presbyterian sentiment in New England could be found only in a few towns, and when the Massachusetts Remonstrants of 1646 sought broader support for an alteration in civil and ecclesiastical polity, they had little success.[58] But the very fact of having to go on the defensive affected the American clergy's conception of themselves and the churches to which they ministered. They became aware, to begin with, of the relatively extreme position that they had gradually adopted in the 1630s. As early as 1642 Thomas Hooker affirmed the ministry's isolation when he declined an invitation to the Westminster Assembly on the ground that he did not intend "to go 3,000 miles to agree with three men" (actually five).[59] As a result it became necessary to build paper bridges to the Presbyterians while denying any very direct debt to the Separatists.

The New Englanders and the Independents hit on the joint strategy of labeling their congregationalism a "middle way" between Brownism and the Presbyterians, an assertion historically untrue— Presbyterianism was not a live issue for the exiles in the 1630s—but polemically useful. To the extent, however, that the New England clergy bent their efforts to distinguishing their polity from its alleged Separatist parent, they did become more reluctant to endorse anything that looked like an advance beyond the situation achieved by the end of the 1630s. In particular, they reemphasized the sacerdotal and distinct qualities of their office through the Cambridge Platform's gingerly endorsement of ordination by the laying on of hands of the eldership rather than the laity. And when they came to a detailed definition of that amorphous and traditional formula of church government as an unspecified blend of clerical aristocracy and lay democracy, the clergy usually spelled out the particulars for the benefit of their own side. The Cambridge Platform of 1648 in small but significant ways takes back something of what the laity had gained in the last eighteen years, and in the course of defining terms,

57. Winthrop, *History,* II, 165, 304–5; *Mass. Recs.,* II, 154 (the call for the synod in 1646); Walker, *Creeds,* 195–262. See also below, n. 62.

58. Robert Emmet Wall, Jr., *Massachusetts Bay: The Crucial Decade, 1640–1650* (New Haven, 1972), 202–3.

59. Winthrop, *History,* II, 92. See also David D. Hall, *The Faithful Shepherd: A History of the New England Ministry in the Seventeenth Century* (Chapel Hill, 1972), 117–19.

it formulates them in a manner that precludes further lay encroachments. In this one area, the status and power of the clergy, the sectarian drift was actually reversed in the course of demonstrating how
far the New England Way was from Separatist "popularity."[60]

For the most part the "democracy" did not put up much of a sustained opposition to the clerical resurgence. Nasty controversies over
ministerial power broke out in a few churches, most notably at Hartford in the 1650s, but the brunt of the laity's concern was elsewhere.[61] They were English refugees, not Scottish, and seventeenth-
century saints, not democrats: the aspect of Presbyterianism they
feared most was impurity, not inequality, a revival in a new form of
a comprehensive national church. That specter was fought at every
turn, whenever any possible change could be construed as defining
a church as any body other than a single gathered and covenanted
society of saints. The demands for more liberal baptismal membership that originated with the clergy from 1645 on always ran directly
into lay resistance, while anything that hinted at interchurch organization was sure to provoke criticism from one segment or another
of the laity. At Woburn in 1642 the members of the congregation
insisted on ordaining their minister themselves, fearing that the laying on of hands by ministers of other churches "might be an occasion
of introducing a dependency of churches, etc. and so a presbytery."
The Cambridge Synod drew opposition on similar grounds in 1646
from "some of Boston, who came lately from England, where such a
vast liberty was allowed, and sought for by all that went under the
name of Independents." Among the deputies the fear of Presbyterian inroads was so strong that the General Court twice had to adopt
equivocal formulas to deal with the synod, first in calling for its
assembly in 1646 (a recommendation only, though not one that
implied any incompetence to require a synod), then in accepting the
final results in 1651 ("approbation" only was awarded, and that on
the murky grounds "that for the substance thereof it is that wee have
practised and doe believe").[62]

Ordinarily, we think of the 1640s as a decade of achievement and
the attainment of "maturity," and in a sense they were years of definition, but what was achieved by 1650 was really a stasis. The dramatic movement of the 1630s was stopped but not really reversed.
The Cambridge Platform, the summa of the decade, indeed of the
first thirty years of Puritanism in America, simply spelled out the
stalemate article by article. Both its language and its politics demonstrate mainly that the ministry had become anxious over the distance

60. Ibid., 102–16.   61. Ibid., 207–18.

62. Winthrop, *History*, III, 169–70, 329. See also ibid., II, 338–39; *Mass. Recs.*, II,
155–56; III, 240; IV, 57–58; Walker, *Creeds*, 167–74, 186–88.

they had traveled from so many of the men in England with whom they had once shared a common cause, while the laity had no intention of tolerating the least step in the direction of the schemes of polity and discipline now advocated by all but a relative handful of these same Englishmen. On the whole, each side in New England respected the other and was willing to allow the Platform, with its weights and counterweights, to serve as the basis for discussion in future conflicts, but further substantial change in the New England Way was ruled out for the time. The area of greatest urgency, the redefinition of eligibility for baptism, was too controversial, however, even for discussion: the Platform simply skips the issue.[63] The ordeal of English Puritanism in the 1630s had spurred rapid and significant redefinition in New England; in the 1640s the fissures in the English movement gave the impetus for a series of alarums and excursions that canceled each other out and left the New England Way back at dead center by the time the Massachusetts General Court nerved itself, in 1651, to approve the Cambridge Platform primarily on the grounds that it did not change anything.

The next ten years brought more of the same. Presbyterianism largely faded away as an issue in the 1650s, to revive in the Connecticut River Valley in the 1660s, but only in a distinctly local form in response to distinctly local problems.[64] The improvisatory, neo-Erastian religious establishment of the Commonwealth and Protectorate periods came closer to resembling the New England Way than did any prior or subsequent English arrangement, but that was little consolation in America for other, more sinister developments in the mother country. Under the prevailing conditions of de facto toleration, the sectarian fragmentation of the radical wing of the Puritan movement, which began as early as the 1620s, reached its luxuriant full growth in Seekers, Ranters, Muggletonians, Fifth Monarchists, every variety of Baptist, and, most enduringly, in the Quakers. The Puritan colonies had given only sporadic attention to their own Baptists, and to the Gortonists, in the early 1640s, but beginning in 1649 they registered their recognition that the "Opinionists" had come into their own in England by the remarkable alacrity with which they elaborated their own heresy statutes to take cognizance of species of error undreamed of in the simpler days just passed, when heresy and casual blasphemy were difficult to distinguish and principled heterodoxy rarely got beyond denying infant baptism.[65]

63. Pope, *Half-Way Covenant*, 17–19.   64. Ibid., chaps. 3–4.
65. For example, cf. *Mass. Recs.*, 176–79, a loosely drawn omnibus statute of 1646 listing a few heterodox opinions but mostly taken up with scoffing and irreligion, with the tightly written act of 1652 (ibid., IV, 78), or with the anti-Quaker act of 1656, which singles that particular group out by name (ibid., 227–78).

The respective general courts were facing a real threat: heresy was a much more palpable danger than the mainly external menace of Presbyterianism. In 1650 the Bay Colony lost one of its oldest and most distinguished magistrates, William Pynchon, for writing a confessedly Socinian book, and in 1654 Henry Dunster, the president of Harvard, defected to the Baptists.[66] Both men were at least recondite in their errors, but the Puritan colonies got a closer look at the crude face of popular religion in 1654 and 1655, courtesy of the Commonwealth's armed forces: the area was the staging ground for a projected invasion of the New Netherlands during the first Anglo-Dutch War, and it was almost continuously a rear area for the entire duration of the "Western Design" against Hispaniola and Jamaica.[67] One can only imagine, for example, the horror with which the General Court of the Bay Colony must have treated the case of Benjamin Saucer, a soldier in the fleet sent to take New Netherlands, who was indicted during a stopover in Boston after he uttered the "most prophane and unheard of blasphemy, saying that Jehovah was the devill, that he knew no God but his sword." One can also imagine the frustration of a colony in external covenant with the Lord when Saucer resolved the complex procedural tangle his case precipitated by breaking jail and taking sanctuary in his warship.[68]

A more formidable challenge to orthodoxy appeared for the first time in 1656 with the start of regular invasions by Quaker missionaries. At first Mary Fisher and Ann Austin and their successors must have seemed merely the next step up in blasphemy from Benjamin Saucer, but they were actually something new in New England experience. The Quakers offered an uncompromisingly thorough critique of every facet of orthodox Puritan religious life, and, unlike most of the Baptists, they took the offensive without waiting for the authorities to come to them. They were as aggressive as the Gortonists and far more comprehensible, and, unlike Samuel Gorton and his company, they repeatedly came back for more, no matter how severe the previous punishment.[69] Judging from their English record,

66. For Pynchon, see *Mass. Recs.*, IV, 29–30, 48–49, 72; Herbert J. McLachlan, *Socinianism in Seventeenth Century England* (Oxford, 1951), 234–39. For Dunster, see Samuel Eliot Morison, *Builders of the Bay Colony*, rev. ed. (Boston, 1964), 183–216.

67. See Calder, *New Haven Colony*, 198–202, 212–14; S. A. G. Taylor, *The Western Design: An Account of Cromwell's Expedition to the Caribbean* (London, 1969), 56, 126–27, 131, 206; *Calendar of State Papers, Colonial Series, 1574–1660*, 431, 432, 434–438; Bernard Bailyn, *The New England Merchants in the Seventeenth Century* (Cambridge, Mass., 1955), 93–94.

68. *Mass. Recs.*, IV, 213; John F. Noble and John F. Cronin, eds., *Records of the Court of Assistants of the Massachusetts Bay, 1630–1692* (Boston, 1901–28), III, 34–38.

69. John Gorham Palfrey, *History of New England during the Stuart Dynasty* (Boston, 1882–85), II, 461–85; Hugh Barbour, *The Quakers in Puritan England* (New Haven, 1964), 216–18.

the Quakers were equally remarkable for their ability to appeal to committed saints, who found in the Society of Friends the next logical step in the pilgrimage begun with the Independents or the Baptists, and for the attraction of their universalism to previously unconverted souls who had found themselves excluded from the narrow way to salvation laid down in orthodox predestinarianism. While the Quakers ultimately made only limited headway in the Puritan colonies, their rapid growth in Interregnum England demonstrated clearly enough their capacity to combine religious enthusiasm and political radicalism with a tightly disciplined and highly effective organization.[70] Their failure to do better in New England had less to do with the notorious exercises of wholesome severity, which quickly petered out, than with the overall strength of the establishment that the American Puritans were in the process of erecting. The Quakers made their converts mainly on the periphery of orthodoxy, where the mechanisms for inculcating the Puritan message were absent or impaired: in Rhode Island, in Kittery in Maine, on Long Island, far out on the Cape in Plymouth Colony, and in pockets of endlessly festering, ever combustible Salem.[71] It was a rare thing for the members of the Puritan leadership to underestimate themselves, but in the case of the Quaker persecutions, they were disastrously in error in believing they could not withstand this "cursed set of haereticks lately risen up in the world" without the help of the gallows and the whipping post.

Because of its central location as the entrepôt for English immigrants and English ideas, the colony most exposed to the English contagion was Massachusetts, where the frantic attempts of the authorities to construct a theological cordon sanitaire around the inhabitants began at times to approach the obsessive. As early as 1652 the magistrates were complaining of the spread of "erroneous books

70. Barbour, *Quakers in Puritan England*, chap. 3; Clark, *English Provincial Society*, 394; Gildrie, *Salem, Massachusetts*, 130–37; Richard T. Vann, *The Social Development of English Quakerism, 1655–1755* (Cambridge, Mass., 1964), 21–31; Margaret Spufford, *Contrasting Communities: English Villagers in the Sixteenth and Seventeenth Centuries* (Cambridge, 1974), 281–86; Alan Cole, "The Quakers and the English Revolution," in Trevor Aston, ed., *Crisis in Europe, 1560–1660* (1965; pbk. ed., Garden City, N.Y., 1967), 358–76; Christopher Hill, *The World Turned Upside Down: Radical Ideas during the English Revolution* (London, 1972), chap. 10; Barry Reay, "Quaker Opposition to Tithes, 1652–1660," *Past and Present*, no. 86 (1980): 98–120.

71. In addition to the study of Salem by Gildrie cited above, n. 70, see Sydney V. James, *Colonial Rhode Island: A History* (New York, 1975), 38–47; Jonathan Moseley Chu, "Madmen and Friends: Quakers and the Puritan Adjustment to Religious Heterodoxy in Massachusetts Bay during the Seventeenth Century" (Ph.D. diss., University of Washington, 1978), chaps. 5–6; George D. Langdon, Jr., *Plymouth Colony: A History of New Plymouth, 1620–1691* (New Haven, 1966), chap. 6; Arthur J. Worrall, *Quakers in the Colonial Northeast* (Hanover, N.H., 1980), 20–21, 29–31, 67–73.

brought over into these parts," and they were very prompt indeed in calling in and burning a Muggletonian tract almost as soon as it reached the colony in 1654. In the same year the General Court demonstrated a change in attitude toward reading and education generally when, in contrast to its earlier declaration "of the necessity and singular use of good literature in managing the things of greatest concernment in the commonwealth," it now held that "it greatly concerns the welfare of this country that the youth thereof be educated, not only in good literature, but sound doctrine." The overseers of Harvard and the selectmen of the towns were accordingly charged to be especially careful about the lives and opinions of the individuals responsible for the instruction of the young. Even the very first theological work to be printed in America, a 1652 collection of sermons by Richard Mather, is a melancholy sort of a first, embodying with painful clarity the dominant preoccupation of the decade that produced it: weighed down at one end by three overblown prefaces and at the other by an absurdly inappropriate index, the thin body of the little tract is nothing more than yet another refutation of Antinomian heresies, designed by its worried author as "some few helpes for a christian preservation in the truth from the prevailing power of error" at a time when unsound opinions "and some of them very pernicious are scattered abroad."[72]

During the course of the 1640s, the Bay Colony had been singularly unsuccessful in rousing its ordinarily lethargic neighbors to respond to threats to orthodoxy, but under the changed conditions of the next decade, it did manage at last to export its anxieties.[73] In 1649 and 1650 Plymouth Colony finally acceded to a request from its northern neighbor and squelched a newly formed Baptist church at Rehoboth, and in the next few years the colony whose deputies had approved universal toleration in 1645 proceeded to put its first comprehensive set of repressive laws on its statue books.[74] When the Bay Colony first put forward its suggestion for common anti-Quaker legislation through the medium of the commissioners of the United

72. See John Endicott et al., to Sir Henry Vane, 20 October 1652, *Collections of the Massachusetts Historical Society*, 3d ser., 1 (1825): 36; *Mass. Recs.*, II, 167; IV, 183, 199. (See also the fast day for "the abounding of errors" in England ordered on 14 May 1656, ibid., IV, 276.) Richard Mather, *The Summe of Certain Sermons upon Genesis 15.6* (Cambridge, Mass., 1652), "The Authors Preface to the Reader," sig. A3r. (Mather's is the earliest *extant* collection of sermons printed in New England, but I have called it simply the earliest of any sort because its alleged predecessors are almost certainly ghosts.)

73. The earlier, abortive attempts to light a fire under the other colonies may be traced in Nathaniel B. Shurtleff and David Pulsifer, eds., *Records of the Colony of New Plymouth in New England* (Boston, 1855–61), IX, 20, 28, 81.

74. Ibid., II, 147, 156, 162; Langdon, *Pilgrim Colony*, 65–68. Cf. *Winthrop Papers*, V, 55–56.

Colonies in 1656, Plymouth, New Haven, and even moderate Connecticut responded promptly, and until Massachusetts carried off the dubious palm by hanging four Quakers between 1658 and 1661, it was something of a toss-up as to where in New England missionary Friends were treated worst and subjected to the most outrageous legal restrictions.[75]

Outrageous is the right word by contemporary standards, despite all subsequent attempts to excuse the mistreatment of the Quakers on the grounds that midseventeenth-century Puritans were too fanatical to know any better. (This line of argument is, curiously, strongest among historians sympathetic to the Quakers and always seems to lead to the related inference that the New England colonies were on the march to secularism when they lost the will to exterminate or mutilate their religious dissidents.) In point of fact, the more severe forms of repression were immediately unpopular and were quickly modified, first in Connecticut, then in New Haven, and finally in the Bay, where the "cartail act" of 1661, for all its ferocious provisions, was actually a way of breaking off the lethal contest with the Quakers. Inevitably in the Quaker-Puritan story the pathos of the victims comes off as the most dramatic and appealing aspect of an otherwise awful business, but the waivering, irresolute draconianism of the persecutors is, historically, the more interesting phenomenon. The latter group knew better—the immediate revulsion at the executions proves as much, as does the opposition aroused by the harshest legislation and the rapidity with which it was repealed. Yet in the nervous atmosphere of the 1650s, with one eye and sometimes both eyes cocked on the disintegrating Puritan movement at home, the New England leadership for a few fatal years felt that they had to keep their Quaker adversaries from calling their bluff. The Quakers, and only they, had the satisfaction of following their consciences to the last extremity. The recoil that followed the executions did help markedly in the organization of the first sustained efforts at toleration in the Bay, though it was the less objectionable, ultimately more dangerous Baptists who were to be the main beneficiaries in the 1660s.[76]

Because of the English situation there was little opportunity for further adjustments in the New England Way after 1649 or for any-

75. Shurtleff and Pulsifer, eds., *Plymouth Records*, X, 155–56; Langdon, *Pilgrim Colony*, 71–75; Calder, *New Haven Colony*, 95–98; Trumbull and Hoadly, eds., *Public Records of the Colony of Connecticut*, 283–84, 303, 308.

76. The divisions within the Bay Colony and in New England generally are well brought out in Palfrey, *History of New England*, II, 472–73, 475–76, 478–83; E. Brooks Holifield, "On Toleration in Massachusetts," *Church History* 38 (1969): 188–200. The moderating of the anti-Quaker statutes may be found in Trumbull and Hoadly, eds., *Public Records of Connecticut*, I, 324 (1658); Charles J. Hoadly, ed., *Records of the Colony and Plantation of New Haven* (Hartford, 1857–1858), II, 363 (1660); *Mass. Recs.*, IV, pat. ii, 2–4 (1661).

thing very much other than caution. In the 1650s even otherwise inoffensive steps were viewed with suspicion. Twice, in 1652 and 1653, the newly founded North Church in Boston tried to ordain Gabriel Powell to its ministry despite his lack of formal education, and twice the General Court intervened against him, not out of any doubts of his orthodoxy or his ability to preach, but only "considering the humour of the times in England, inclined to discourage learning."[77] A little later in 1653 the court's nervous, reactive conservatism led to an attempt to restrict lay preaching, a well-established Puritan practice, through a strict licensing system. The court quite candidly announced that it feared that "persons of bolder spirits and erroneous Principles may take advantage to vent their errours, to the infection of their hearers and the disturbance of the peace of the country." The act, however, ran so thoroughly against the grain of the country that the court repealed it, reluctantly, during the very next session, only to return to the attack in 1658, "in this houre of temptation, wherein the enemy designeth to sowe corrupt seed," with a new statute that followed a solemn and awful preface with a rather meager restriction.[78] Action on the most pressing problem facing the churches was similarly desultory throughout the decade. In a number of New England towns, ministers proposed some version or other of what was to become the Half-Way Covenant, their churches discussed the proposals and in some instances approved them, and then nothing happened anyway unless, as always, the parents of the child to be baptised were already in full communion.[79] If the decade merits a lone adjective, it must surely be "indecisive."

The brief hegemony of the English Independents proved a double burden to the American Puritans. Both the formidable bureaucracy created in the republican period and the vacancies in the clergy that resulted from the thoroughness with which the Committee for Plundered Ministers did its work lured back to England much of the younger talent in the colonies, who could otherwise have been the group most likely to reopen the old debates. Those of the rising generation who did remain in America had to play second fiddle to surviving members of the founding generation, some of whom took an unseemly length of time to rest from their labors.[80] Massachu-

77. *Mass. Recs.*, IV, 113–14, 177.

78. Ibid., IV, 122, 151, 328. See also the protest of Woburn in 1653, *Collections of the Massachusetts Historical Society*, 3d ser., 1 (1825): 138–45, and the opposition to a similar (and equally unprecedented) exercise of prior restraint to block the calling of a minister, at Malden in 1651, in *Mass. Recs.*, IV, 42–43.

79. Pope, *Half-Way Covenant*, 19–39.

80. Hall, *Faithful Shepherd*, 185–86. See also Harry Stout, "The Morphology of Remigration: New England University Men and Their Return to England, 1640–1660," *Journal of American Studies* 10 (1976): 151–72; William L. Sachse, "The Migration of New Englanders to England, 1640–1660," *American Historical Review* 53 (1948): 251–78.

setts, for example, did not elect a deputy governor who was not a member of the original magistrates of the 1630s until 1665, and it was another eight years before the same could be said of the colony's governor. Both men turned out to be veterans of the Cromwellian period who put that experience to good use as advocates of toleration, but both had endured a very long wait for their call to office.

The impasse in New England's religious life would probably have been broken sooner or later anyway, but when the Puritan colonies finally resumed their progress with a noisy, divisive creativeness in the 1660s, they were immeasurably the freer for the fall from power of the English movement at the beginning of the decade. England, of course, could not be ignored after 1660: the threat of intervention was as real as ever and growing, while contacts with English Nonconformity were still of major political and intellectual significance to New Englanders. But the English Puritans no longer faced the challenge of reconciling sainthood with dominion because they were no longer a part of the national religious establishment; they had no further obligations except to the faithful souls who singled themselves out for social and legal penalties by continuing to follow their deprived clergy. As Richard Baxter wrote to John Eliot in 1668, even the Presbyterians were inadvertent congregationalists under the new order:

> The restraint of other meetings occasioneth the private assemblies in England to be now ordered just like the congregational way, or rather as the old Separatists, in many places. But if they were as much at liberty as formerly they were as ready to fall together by the eares.[81]

The traditional Puritan mission had come under terrible strain in England in the 1630s, and in the Interregnum it had all but collapsed except in name. With St. Bartholomew's Day, 1662, even that name was abandoned, and Puritanism passed over into Dissent— except in America. American Puritans had never abandoned the original vision of a faith that was at once the engine of culture and the special treasure of gathered knots of saints, and the New England ministry, for all its twistings and turnings, remained intact as the mediatory body between the two ideals. In the 1630s, however, the saints had loomed ever larger in American calculations on the optimistic assumption that they would constitute most of the population "and have liberty," in John Cotton's words, "to cast themselves into that Mould or Form of a Commonwealth which shall appear to be best for them."[82] After 1660 both the saints and, increasingly, the

81. Powicke, ed., "Correspondence of Baxter and Eliot," 446.
82. From the subtitle of John Davenport, *A Discourse about Civil Government in a New Plantation Whose Design Is Religion* (Cambridge, Mass., 1663). For the authorship of this tract, see Steiner, "Dissension at Quinnipiac."

liberty came in more rationed doses, forcing a recovery of the initial balance that had defined the Puritan commitment for most of his history until the Great Migration. The New England churches would now have to find means to reextend their reach and, no less significant, as their ministry began to lose its direct magisterial protection, the clergy would have to rediscover the multiple ways to envelop the people of New England in a pervasive, irresistible set of values. Clergymen would convert and nourish still, but in the future they would also educate and interpret, so that a New Englander could hardly escape their influence from the time he learned to read on their primers to the day he was buried and they preached his funeral sermon. Important as the extension of church membership was after 1660, it was no more essential to the enduring Puritan mission than the simultaneous growth in schooling and the increase in the productions of the local printing presses. With the Restoration of Charles II, the Puritan movement, in its American refuge, entered at last into its austere golden age.

Specters of Subversion, Societies of Friends: Dissent and the Devil in Provincial Essex County, Massachusetts*

CHRISTINE LEIGH HEYRMAN

Colonial Quakers seldom missed an opportunity to castigate the Puritans for the persecution that the Friends had suffered at the hands of Massachusetts Bay's magistrates and clergymen. Throughout the seventeenth and eighteenth centuries, spokesmen for the Society of Friends recounted the stories of fines, whippings, imprisonments, and the notorious executions of four Quaker missionaries on the Boston Common. This litany of suffering left a lasting impression upon scholars of the late nineteenth and early twentieth centuries who departed from the earlier, filiopietistic histories of George Bancroft and John Gorham Palfrey that had hailed the Puritans as champions of religious freedom. Instead, Brooks and Charles Francis Adams, James Truslow Adams, and Vernon Parrington depicted Puritan leaders as a particularly prejudiced and narrow-minded lot and attributed their persecution of the Quakers to "the bigotry and greed of power of a despotic priesthood." Only in the 1950s was the emphasis upon Puritan intolerance leavened by the perspective of historians like Perry Miller who pointed out that New England Congregationalists were no more or no less disposed toward religious prejudice and persecution than were most of their European contemporaries.

In addition to underscoring the unexceptional character of early

* I would like to thank William Presson and Deborah Goodwin of the Cape Ann Historical Society and Lorraine Bishop of the Town Clerk's Office in Gloucester City Hall for all of their assistance. I have also benefited from the criticism and suggestions of Jonathan Dewald, John Patrick Diggins, David Hall, William Hamilton, Edmund and Helen Morgan, and John Murrin.

Puritan antipathy to dissent, these more recent studies of intersectarian relations have also argued for the relatively rapid penetration of Bay society by more tolerant attitudes toward the Quakers. Both colony laws and ministers' sermons point to a clear progression from persecution of the heterodox to an acceptance of religious pluralism on the part of Massachusetts's civil and ecclesiastical establishment. Following a period of severe repression between 1656 and 1665, colony leaders granted a grudging toleration to a somewhat less militant Quaker movement until the outbreak of King Philip's War, in 1675. Sectarian hostilities rekindled during this conflict with the Indians which the Friends regarded as divine retribution for New England's past persecutions and which the Puritans interpreted as punishment for permitting the presence of heretics in their new Israel. The colony government reacted by passing stringent anti-Quaker legislation while the Friends retaliated with displays of defiance and protests to the king. But relations between the Quakers and the Bay's civil and spiritual leaders improved with the cessation of warfare, and after 1691 the freedom of worship accorded all dissenters under the new Massachusetts charter promoted a progressive easing of discriminatory legislation. At the same time, the concern of the Congregationalist clergy over efforts to extend the influence of the Anglican church in New England enhanced their interest in a rapprochement with other dissenting sects like the Quakers and softened their strictures against the Friends in sermons of the later colonial era.[1]

But did relations between Puritans and Quakers living in Massachusetts towns reflect the relaxation of religious discrimination suggested by clerical commentaries and province laws? Did the orthodox laity during the late seventeenth and eighteenth centuries adopt the more tolerant attitudes toward dissenters promoted by many civil and clerical leaders? Although most historians have assumed that the majority of ordinary, orthodox Bay inhabitants followed or even forced their leaders in the direction of greater religious liberalism, a

1. For some examples of the historiography emphasizing Puritan bigotry, see Brooks Adams, *The Emancipation of Massachusetts* (Boston, 1887), 128–78, James Truslow Adams, *The Founding of New England* (Boston, 1921), 262–77, and Vernon L. Parrington, *Main Currents in American Thought* (New York, 1927), 26–106. Later revisions of this stereotype include Perry Miller, "Puritan State and Puritan Society," in *Errand into the Wilderness* (1956; reprint, New York, 1964), 144–45, and Daniel Boorstin, *The Americans: The Colonial Experience* (New York, 1958), 38–39. For an illuminating discussion of liberty of conscience in seventeenth-century New England, see Edmund S. Morgan, *Roger Williams: The Church and the State* (New York, 1967), esp. 115–42. The most recent study of Quakerism in colonial New England is Arthur Worrall, *Quakers in the Colonial Northeast* (Hanover, N.H., 1980). Earlier accounts include Rufus Jones, *The Quakers in the American Colonies* (London, 1911), and Frederick Tolles, *Quakers and the Atlantic Culture* (New York, 1960).

closer look at the experience of dissenters at the local level indicates that the case for an attenuation of sectarian prejudice in provincial Massachusetts could be overstated. In Gloucester, for example, orthodox Puritan laymen steadfastly resisted accommodation to their town's Quaker minority. Here relations between the Congregationalists and the Friends deteriorated steadily during the late seventeenth century, and the formal, legal toleration that the mother country forced upon the Bay after 1691 actually augmented the antagonism that the local Puritan laity felt toward dissenters. By the middle of the eighteenth century, in response to sectarian prejudice, most of the town's dissenters had either moved on or entered the orthodox fold. The Congregational church retained its monopoly of religious life to the virtual exclusion of all competing sects as dissenting influence actually waned in town with the passing of time. Gloucester's experience with the Quakers was not exceptional. Over the same period, other Essex County towns like Newbury and Salem where the Friends had formerly shown some strength saw a similar reduction in Quaker ranks. The sustained animosity toward the Quakers in Gloucester, Salem, and Newbury is of particular significance because all three towns were seaports, more cosmopolitan places that supposedly accommodated religious diversity with greater ease. But the strongholds of Quakerism in provincial Massachusetts were not the largest commercial centers: they were instead the smaller fishing and farming villages like Lynn and Amesbury to the north and Dartmouth and Tiverton to the south.

The lag between the growth of legal toleration and the actual acceptance of religious diversity in many towns raises questions about the specific ways in which dissenting status affected social relationships within a community and about the sources that sustained sectarian prejudice among ordinary New Englanders well into the eighteenth century. For throughout the later colonial period in Gloucester as well as in other Essex County ports, religious differences aroused impassioned conflicts among people for whom sectarian distinctions were integral to social identity. Well into the eighteenth century, the division between orthodoxy and dissent was a basic element shaping social life.

Outside of the vicinity of Lynn and Salem, the largest single concentration of Quakers in seventeenth-century Essex County was probably in the town of Gloucester, on Cape Ann, a developing center of the fishing industry and trade. After 1660 traveling missionaries for the Society of Friends aggressively evangelized in the communities north of Salem that had been settled by emigrants from the West of England, but Gloucester's Quakers probably contracted their heterodox sympathies in southern Bay settlements where they had formerly resided or where family members still lived. A history of difficulties with Essex magistrates drove Nathaniel Hadlock to Cape Ann after his indictment for declaring that "he profitted more by going to the Quakers' meeting" than he did by hearing the Salem minister John Higginson. Gloucester's Elizabeth Kendall Somes and several of her children, including a stepdaughter, Mary Hammond, joined the Quakers after adopting the beliefs of their kin, the Kendalls of Cambridge and Essex County's most outspoken dissenter, Thomas Maule of Salem. The Someses' influence also brought their neighbors in Gloucester, the Pearces, under conviction.[2]

While settlements to the north and south often dealt harshly with their Quaker dissenters, moderation marked Gloucester's initial response to the development of religious diversity. Orthodox inhabitants had little reason to feel threatened by local Friends: their numbers were small, a schism over the practice of male celibacy had deeply divided the Essex sect, and the civil government of the Bay remained officially committed to the defense of the established Congregational churches. Another circumstance that encouraged coexistence was the Quakers' willingness to occupy an obscure, circumscribed position on the outskirts of local society. Quite literally, Friends resided on the fringes of late-seventeenth-century settlement, at Goose and Lobster coves and along the Ipswich line. Forming a community apart, they never exercised any significant influence upon local affairs or held important political offices. During the 1670s and 1680s, the town routinely reported their absences from public worship to the courts, but orthodox inhabitants resorted to reason rather than to stringent repression in order to combat heresy. In 1678, when John Pearce, Jr., invited the Reverend John Emerson to a Quaker meeting at the home of the senior Pearce, the pastor "Labored to convince him of the evil of it and the breach of the Law of this Commonwealth but he was very impudent and bold and sayd they were neither afrayd of the Laws nor Magestrates nor any man I answered I thought he sayd very true for I believed they neighter feared God nor reveranced man." Emerson was dismayed that Pearce left "stiff and obstinate," but neither the minister nor any of his parishioners interfered with the young Quaker as he went from "house to house to invite

2. On the strength of Quakerism in the West of England and the West Country origins of many Essex County Quakers, see David Grayson Allen, *In English Ways: The Movement of Societies and the Transferal of English Local Law and Custom to Massachusetts Bay in the Seventeenth Century* (Chapel Hill, 1981), 11. On Hadlock, see *Records and Files of the Quarterly Courts of Essex County, Massachusetts*, ed. George Francis Dow (Salem, Mass, 1911–21), IV, 74–75; V, 356; VII, 367 (hereafter cited as *Essex Ct. Recs.*).

mens children and servants the most part of that night."[3] The tithingman Thomas Day tried the same approach with the Quaker Mary Hammond that Emerson had attempted with her neighbor Pearce:

> I asked her the resen why she did hinder her dafter Mary from Coming to meting to which she said that when shee Came hom I tould her that she might goe to meting if shee wold but she should not have my consent to which I replyed you then wer as good say that shee should not goe: why Thomas said she you have Childeren would you be willing to let them goe to hell if you could help it to which I said noe I wold doe what I cold to hinder them and then said I why is goeing to meting the way to hell yea said she to goe to here your parson or prest or what you will Call him is the way to hell then said I it is not the way to hell to goe to John Pearces to her him and some time he ses nothing noe said she.[4]

Gloucester's Quakers remained under conviction, but with local Congregationalist leaders disposed only to debate, more militant sectarians who courted suffering had to leave town in order to attain these satisfactions: Elizabeth Somes's eldest son, John, moved to Boston, where the magistrates obliged him with a whipping for publicly proclaiming that King Philip's War was divine punishment for New England's past persecutions. But among some Friends who stayed in town, the Congregationalist community's relatively tolerant attitude encouraged accommodation. John's brother Joseph Somes joined other young townsmen in the fight against King Philip and gave his life to the cause.[5]

But beneath the apparent willingness of townspeople to suffer the dissenters in their midst ran an undercurrent of apprehension, an anxiety reflected in a peculiar spate of criminal prosecutions that coincided with the initial appearance of Quakerism in town. Prior to the 1670s, crimes involving sexual misconduct were uncommon in Gloucester: aside from the charge of lewdness leveled against the fisherman John Jackson, only one newlywed couple had been pre-

---

3. The location of the residences of Quakers in Gloucester can be ascertained from John J. Babson's "Map of Gloucester, Cape Ann," which appears on the frontispiece of his *History of the Town of Gloucester, Cape Ann, including the Town of Rockport* (Gloucester, 1860). On Pearce, see *Essex Ct. Recs.*, VII, 150, 243, 367. Jonathan Chu has also detected a restrained response to local Quakers among the orthodox Puritans of Kittery and Salem during the middle of the seventeenth century. Chu, "The Social and Political Contexts of Heterodoxy: Quakerism in Seventeenth Century Kittery," *New England Quarterly* 54 (1981): 365–84; idem, "The Social Context of Religious Heterodoxy: The Challenge of Seventeenth Century Quakerism to Orthodoxy in Massachusetts" (forthcoming, *Essex Institute Historical Collections*).

4. *Essex Ct. Recs.*, VII, 367.

5. *Records of the Court of Assistants of the Massachusetts Bay Colony, 1630–1692* (Boston, 1901–28), I, 12; Babson, *History*, 162.

sented for fornication. But in 1673, John Pearce, Sr., and his new wife appeared in court to answer allegations of premarital impropriety, and the servant maid Christian Marshman accused John Stannard of having fathered her bastard child. During the next year, Timothy Somes and his bride were also prosecuted for fornication, and in 1682 it was the turn of the newlyweds William and Naomi Sargent. This sudden outbreak of indictments for sexual misconduct before marriage was not the result of intergenerational tensions or the decline of parental discipline: the defendants John and Jane Pearce were a middle-aged couple with grown children. But the Pearce connection makes all of the other prosecutions comprehensible, for by his marriage to the former widow Jane Stannard, John Pearce became the stepfather of John Stannard and subsequently the father-in-law of Timothy Somes and of William Sargent, whose wives were Jane's daughters. The household of John Pearce, Sr., was the site of the Quakers' meetings in Gloucester.[6]

There is no evidence to suggest that Jane Stannard Pearce or any of her children contracted Quaker convictions from the Pearces, but Gloucester's orthodox inhabitants were watching closely and suspecting the worst about anyone in town connected with the small coterie of Quaker families clustered around Lobster and Goose coves. The Congregationalist community encouraged local scandal over sexual misconduct as a way of discrediting the dissident sect and deployed criminal prosecutions as a way of disciplining people like the Stannards who consented to alliances with Quakers. The logic behind their selecting the charge of fornication specifically derived from the longstanding association of all forms of religious antinomianism with sexual libertinism. Fornication was also an apt metaphor for conveying the Congregationalist perception of intersectarian unions as essentially illicit. Whether Jane Stannard Pearce and her children were actually guilty of breaching the boundaries of sexual propriety is uncertain, but it is unquestionable that they had stepped outside the pale of sectarian exclusivity. The Quakerism of John Pearce made less than legitimate, in the eyes of local Congregationalists, not only his union with Jane Stannard but also the marriages between his stepchildren and the sons and daughters of orthodox families. The Puritans were consistent in their belief that religious affinities ran in families. Just as the assumption underlying the "Half-Way Covenant" was that one generation of "visible saints" would transmit their virtuosity to another, so informing the suspicion of the Pearce-Stannard marriages was the conviction that the contagion

6. *Essex Ct. Recs.*, V, 231, 250, 358, 359; VII, 368. Aside from Quakers prosecuted for fornication, only one other local couple was presented between 1673 and 1682.

of heresy spread in the same way.[7] Like the Quaker Mary Hammond, John Pearce would try to stop the members of his family from going to hell.

As the prosecutions of the Stannards and their partners suggest, Congregationalist suspicions fastened not only on the Quakers themselves but also on those people whose social ties to the Friends raised questions about their own religious loyalties. The Congregationalist Clement Coldom became a source of local concern in the 1660s because of his son-in-law Francis Norwood. Norwood had come to New England after the restoration of the Stuart monarchy made England an inhospitable environment for someone with his radical religious and political convictions. Francis first kept a tavern in Lynn, a center of early Baptist and Quaker enthusiasm, but after a few years he settled in Gloucester, at Goose Cove, amid the Pearces and Hammonds, and married Coldom's daughter in 1663.[8] In 1666, the local militia company, "upon some difference . . . or dislike of some among them," stripped Coldom of his rank as ensign. Stung by this humiliation, Coldom atoned for his daughter's defection by personally policing the border between the orthodox and dissenting communities. It was Coldom who tore John Pearce's door from its hinges to expose the illicit intimacies attending his neighbor's wooing of the widow Stannard; Coldom also testified in court against John Stannard, alleging that "he saw John Stainwood and Christian Marshman together outdoors . . . and he was kissing her." Undeterred by the testimony of local midwives that Christian had never been pregnant, Coldom appeared in court the following year as a witness against Timothy Somes and his wife.[9] But if Coldom managed to acquit himself of guilt by association through his vigilance in exposing the evildoing of dissenters, he was unable to arrest the spread of heresy within his own family: Francis Norwood, Jr., fulfilled his grandfath-

7. Edmund S. Morgan, *The Puritan Family: Religion and Domestic Relations in Seventeenth Century New England* (1944; reprint, New York, 1966), 173–86.

8. Babson, *History*, 118. The name of Francis Norwood, Jr., appears in the Salem Monthly Meeting Records, but I could find no direct evidence confirming his father's Quakerism. However, everything about Francis Senior's career points to this conclusion: his emigration after the Restoration because of his religious and political convictions; his choices of residence in Lynn and in Gloucester's Quaker enclave; his reputation as a wizard; his failure to join the First Church; and his purchase of land from John Pearce, Jr., when the latter left town in 1682. The lack of Quaker records for much of the seventeenth century makes criminal prosecutions the best source for identifying members of the Society of Friends. In Gloucester, however, older members of the Quaker community tended to be more circumspect about confronting the Congregational establishment than were younger people. This makes it more difficult to identify the mature, adult members of the local Quaker community.

9. *Essex Ct. Recs.*, III, 338; V, 231, 250, 358–59. On Coldom's role in the witchcraft trials in 1692, see Paul Boyer and Stephen Nissenbaum, eds., *The Salem Witchcraft Papers* (New York, 1977), II, 457 (hereafter cited as *Witchcraft Papers*).

er's worst fears by inheriting the Quaker convictions of his father and namesake.

Gloucester's orthodox opposition to Quaker dissenters living in their midst was muted for most of the seventeenth century, expressed mainly in indirect modes bespeaking an underlying uneasiness. But in the closing years of that century, intersectarian tensions in town steadily increased in intensity. While the sources of this greater animosity toward the Friends are complex, its manifestations are unmistakable, for they figured in a familiar and intensively studied episode in early American history—the witchcraft hysteria that swept through several Essex County towns during the year 1692.

Although the witchcraft outbreak started in Salem Village in the winter of 1692, discrete outcroppings of mass panic occurred in at least two other towns, Gloucester and neighboring Andover. In Andover, where the hysteria over witchcraft began in the summer of 1692, the first flurry of allegations resulted in a roundup of all the usual suspects: Martha Carrier, the acid-tongued wife of a Welshman whom everyone in town had for years regarded as a witch; Mary Parker, a crazed, impoverished widow who had lost a son in King Philip's War; Samuel Wardwell, the village fortune-teller, who read palms and "mayd sport" of his misdeed. But following these eccentrics and outcasts to prison were nearly forty other Andoverians who were all solid and respectable members of the community. This group of suspected witches included the wife of Deacon John Frye, the wife of the militia captain John Osgood, two of the Reverend Francis Dane's daughters, his daughter-in-law, and several of his grandchildren, and the wife of Dudley Bradstreet, the town's representative to the General Court. These defendants provided the judges of the Court of Oyer and Terminer with full confessions of conversations with feline "familiars," trips by broomstick to Salem Village for coven gatherings, and rebaptisms by Satan himself (who preferred full immersion to sprinkling) in the Shewsheen River.[10] Almost immediately after the Andover outbreak, the hysteria spread to Gloucester, triggered there by a number of inhabitants who claimed they had sighted Frenchmen and Indians in the remote reaches of Cape Ann. The failure to find these invaders led locals like the Reverend John Emerson to the conclusion that "Gloucester was not alarumed . . . by real French and Indians, but that the devil and his agents were the cause of all the molestation which . . . befell the town." The search for the source of these disturbing apparitions eventuated in the arrest of an assortment of village scolds, misfits, and poor

10. Sarah Loring Bailey, *Historical Sketches of Andover* (Boston, 1880), 194–237.

widows during September of 1692.[11]

As Emerson's observation suggests, the susceptibility to hysteria that instigated these two outbreaks of witchcraft in northern Essex County was fostered in part by popular fears of vulnerability to attack by the French and Indians. Most locals could remember the Indian raid on Andover in 1676 that had killed several inhabitants; now the onset of King William's War exposed both towns to the same perils again. This climate of dread and apprehension, coupled with the contagion emanating from Salem Village, caused panic in Gloucester and Andover to coalesce into accusations of witchcraft, an alchemy that Cotton Mather captured in his *Wonders of the Invisible World,* written a few months after the outbreak of the delusion in northern Essex County. Deftly conflating fears over earthly armies with those of Satanic legions, Mather conjectured that "there is a sort of Arbitrary, even Military Government among the Devils. . . . Think on, Vast Regiments, of cruel and bloody, French Dragoons, with an Intendant over them, overrunning a pillaged Neighborhood."[12]

That anxieties over military attack contributed to the climate producing the witchcraft panic in northern Essex County is also suggested by the character of the delusion in Andover. Accusations reached into the top of the local social structure with surprising speed; furthermore, many townspeople admitted freely to covenanting with Satan or charged members of their own families with doing so. Those who at first denied diabolical dealings were easily persuaded of their mistake by close friends and relatives. Many Andoverians

---

11. Gloucester's "invasion" by French and Indians is described in Babson, *History,* 212; David T. Konig, *Law and Society in Puritan Massachusetts: Essex County, 1629–1692* (Chapel Hill, 1979), 167. Emerson's account of the town's spectral enemies is in Cotton Mather, *Magnalia Christi Americana* (Hartford, 1855), 621–23. The most detailed narrative of the involvement of Gloucester inhabitants in the witchcraft trials of 1692 is Marshall W. S. Swan, "The Bedevilment of Cape Ann," *Essex Institute Historical Collections* 117 (1981): 153–77. Eleven women connected with Gloucester were arrested for witchcraft in that year. The first two suspected witches, Abigail Somes and Anne Doliber, had formerly resided in town but were living in Salem at the time of their arrests and were accused by Salem Village's "afflicted girls." Somes was an invalid, and Doliber, the daughter of Salem's Rev. John Higginson, was a poor, deranged woman who, after being deserted by her husband, a Gloucester mariner, returned to Salem and depended upon her family for support. *Witchcraft Papers,* III, 733–37; Babson, *History,* 81. Among the six Gloucester women arrested in September, probably in connection with the "spectral invasion," Elizabeth Dicer was the wife of a Boston seaman who had drifted into Gloucester; the widow Margaret Prince, whose daughter Mary and in-law Phebe Day were also accused, was notorious among her neighbors for her history of loud, violent domestic quarrels; the widow Joan Penney was too poor to be rated in 1693; and another widow, Rachel Vinson, belonged to a family implicated in an earlier witchcraft case. *Witchcraft Papers,* II, 651–53, 641–42; John J. Babson, *Notes and Additions to the History of Gloucester,* 2d ed. (Salem, 1891), 72; *Essex Ct. Recs.,* I, 301; IV, 440; VI, 116.

12. Cotton Mather, *Wonders of the Invisible World* (Boston, 1693), 232. The Indian attack on Andover is described in Bailey, *Historical Sketches of Andover,* 173.

probably confessed to save themselves, but the town's unique pattern of recriminations against relatives and community leaders and of frequent self-incriminations also constituted a kind of collective purgation. Seventeenth-century New Englanders commonly construed catastrophes like epidemics or wars as "afflictions" sent by God to punish an entire community, either for collective backsliding or for failure to chasten individual sinners in their midst.[13] So in response to the renewal of warfare, Andoverians sought to preserve themselves from another scourging by the rod of divine wrath by a frenzied searching out of secret sin within individual souls, family circles, and high places, followed by mass admissions of wrongdoing.

Meanwhile Gloucester's townspeople also sought to stave off suffering at the hands of external enemies by rooting out internal subversives and hidden sin within their community. But the hysteria here assumed a configuration different from Andover's course because the source of divine displeasure with Gloucester was more apparent to its inhabitants. While uncertainty over how they had transgressed sent Andoverians into widening spirals of suspicion, the panic among Gloucester's people did not spawn mass confession but came to focus upon a single case of sorcery that points to a distinctive source of communal anxiety—namely, the possession of Mary Stevens.

Even before her alleged bewitchment in the fall of 1692, Mary Stevens had probably become an object of local concern because of her courtship by Francis Norwood, Jr., the Quaker grandson of Clement Coldom. The marriage of Mary to Francis would not have been the first merging of orthodox and dissenting families in Gloucester, but it was a union of tremendous social significance. For Mary was not a servant maid or the daughter of an ordinary local farmer up in Goose Cove, but the child of Deacon James Stevens of the First Church, one of Gloucester's most prominent citizens; and Francis was not the stepson of an obscure Quaker farmer, but an avowed Friend from a fairly affluent family. Francis's suit of Mary Stevens thus marked the first movement of the Friends in Gloucester out of their position on the periphery of local society and the neighborhood of the remote northern Cape and into the mainstream. Their betrothal persuaded Lt. William Stevens, Mary's older brother and a major local merchant, that only demonic influences could have prevailed upon his sister to accept the attentions of a Quaker. As alarmed by the discovery of dissenting affinities among his own kin as Clement Coldom had been earlier, William Stevens acted to defend his

13. Edmund S. Morgan, *The Puritan Dilemma: The Story of John Winthrop* (Boston, 1958), esp. 69–83.

family's integrity and to dissuade his sister from a disastrous alliance by declaring that she was bewitched. Stevens also sent for four of Salem Village's "afflicted girls," the instigators of the witchcraft trials held earlier in 1692, who claimed to have the power to discern who troubled the victims of malefic magic.[14] But when William Stevens sought assistance from Salem Village, he and his neighbors already suspected who had bewitched his sister—her prospective father-in-law, Francis Norwood, Sr., whom everyone in Gloucester had long believed to be a wizard. In 1679, when the Newbury household of William Morse became the haunt of evil spirits that made strange noises and sent objects flying about the room and down the chimney, Morse's suspicions fastened upon his young servant Abel Powell, whose first apprenticeship had been served under Gloucester's sorcerer. "He was brought up under [Francis] Norwood," the Reverend John Emerson told the county court, "and it was judged by the people there [in Gloucester] that Norwood studied the black art."[15]

John Emerson and his parishioners deemed their neighbor Norwood a wizard because seventeenth-century Puritans linked religious heresy not only with sexual license but also with witchcraft. While all of the contending religious groups of this period commonly claimed that their competitors were in league with the devil, the Friends especially were subject to charges of being possessed or of practicing witchcraft because of their emphasis on continuous revelation and the light within and because of the bodily convulsions manifested by believers at Quaker meetings.[16] New England Puritan leaders quickly appropriated the allegations of witchcraft made against the English founder of Quakerism, George Fox, in their attacks upon his followers who crossed the Atlantic. In 1656, Massachusetts magistrates ordered midwives to search for "witches marks" on the bodies of Ann Austin and Mary Fisher, two of the first Quaker missionaries to arrive in the Bay Colony, and in the early 1660s Gov. John Endicott alleged that three other Quaker women imprisoned at Boston were witches.[17] Alarmed by the Friends' conversions in his own congregation, Salem's minister, John Higginson, characterized the "Quakers Light" as "the Devil's Sacrifice" and "a stinking Vapor from Hell," while the pastor of Barnstable charged that local Friends had

14. Babson, *History*, 211–12; Thomas F. Waters, *Ipswich in the Massachusetts Bay Colony* (Ipswich, Mass., 1905), I, 298; Mather, *Wonders of the Invisible World*, 232.

15. *Essex Ct. Recs.*, VII, 355–60. Although Abel Powell was the focus of Morse's suspicions, the testimony of their neighbors resulted in the conviction of Morse's wife for witchcraft in 1679. However, she was later reprieved by the Court of Assistants in 1681. *Records of the Court of Assistants*, I, 159, 190.

16. Keith Thomas, *Religion and the Decline of Magic* (New York, 1971), 477, 487.

17. George Bishop, *New England Judged by the Spirit of the Lord* (London, 1703), pt. 1, p. 12; pt. 2, pp. 21, 404–5.

bewitched his daughter to death as retribution for the distraint of their goods.[18] Ordinary New Englanders shared the suspicions of their civil and clerical leaders. At Portsmouth, where Mary Thompkins disrupted the discourse of Thomas Millet, Gloucester's former elder, "some of his unruly Hearers" threw her down a flight of stairs, "which might reasonably have broke her Neck, and which they themselves confessed, had she not been a witch (as they said of her . . .)." Shortly thereafter at Newbury, Mary was disputing with the Reverend Thomas Parker: John Pike heard her stomach growl and concluded that "She has a Devil in her."[19] The widespread belief that the Quakers, and particularly female heretics, practiced witchcraft continued even after the most vigorous attempts to suppress the sect had ended in the mid-1660s. In 1669, Nathaniel Morton ascribed the miscarriages of both Anne Hutchinson and the Quaker Mary Dyer to their pacts with Satan.[20] During the 1680s, the connection between Quakerism and diabolism received renewed emphasis in the writings of Increase Mather, the pastor of Boston's Second Church and a leading member of the second generation of New England clergymen. Like his Puritan predecessors and contemporaries, Increase believed that the Quakers were subject both to demonic possession and to the practice of malefic magic. In *Illustrious Providences,* he linked the Friends to a group of Ranters on Long Island suspected of bewitching their neighbors and recounted the havoc that poltergeists created in the home of a Portsmouth Quaker.[21]

But the most forceful assertion of the traditional association between Quakerism and diabolism appeared in the years between 1689 and 1691 as a response to the open evangelism of George Keith in New England. A onetime Quaker schoolmaster turned itinerant preacher, Keith arrived in Boston in June of 1688 and promptly posted "in the most public place" a paper calling upon the Puritans to repent of their "degeneracy" and challenging four local ministers, Cotton Mather, John Allin, Joshua Moodey, and Samuel Willard, to an open debate. Keith failed to draw Boston's clergymen into a confrontation, but on his return to Philadelphia a few months later, he published an attack upon the doctrine, polity, and ministry of New England's Congregational churches and a refutation of Increase

18. Ibid., pt. 2, pp. 394, 492–93.   19. Ibid., pt. 2, p. 223; pt. 2, pp. 394, 400.
20. Nathaniel Morton, *New-Englands Memoriall* (Cambridge, Mass., 1669), 106–10.
21. Increase Mather, *An Essay for the Recording of Illustrious Providences* (Boston, 1684), 160, 188, 341–46. Increase also described the haunting of the Morse house in 1679, although he did not make any connection between this case and the Quakers. Possibly it was Francis Norwood, Sr., to whom Increase was alluding when he reported, on p. 156, that some in Newbury "were apt to think that a seaman suspected . . . to be a Conjurer, set the Devil on work thus to Disquiet Morse's family."

Mather's earlier imputations against the Quakers.[22] This outspoken tract prodded Boston's ministers into a heated pamphlet exchange with their persistent critic. In 1689, Cotton Mather defended the view of his father, Increase, that "Diabolical Possession was the thing which did dispose and encline men unto Quakerism" by bringing out a long account of the bewitchment of the four children of John Goodwin, one of whom had resided for a time in Cotton's household. The latter, an adolescent girl at the time of her "affliction," was able to read "a Quaker or Popish book" but not the Bible or any other edifying orthodox literature; her brother's bewitchment assumed the form of "torment" at being taken to the Congregational meetinghouse that subsided only when his father spoke of going to other assemblies, "particularly the Quakers." According to Cotton, what finally reclaimed the Goodwin children from "the strange liberty which the Devils gave unto them to enjoy the Writings and Meetings of the Quakers" were the prayers of those same Boston clergymen so maligned by George Keith.[23] Throughout the next year, 1690, Mather and his colleagues kept up their attacks, producing two passionate denunciations of the Friends that reiterated the affinity between Quakerism and demonic forces. Keith retaliated in kind later that year by alleging that the efforts of Boston's ministers to relieve the young Goodwins' suffering were nothing less than "a conjuring of the Devil." This charge aroused a last retort from Cotton Mather in 1691: after accusing Keith of blasphemy, he reminded his readers of the resemblance between "quaking" and diabolical possession and of an early Quaker woman who had appeared naked in Puritan assemblies "like a Devil."[24]

With this kind of anti-Quaker polemic as prologue—and particularly the repeated linkage of the Friends with the Devil's legions that poured from Boston's presses and pulpits in the years immediately prior to 1692—it is not surprising that William Stevens perceived his sister's acceptance of a Quaker suitor as evidence of demonic posses-

22. George Keith, *The Presbyterian and Independent Visible Churches in New England* (Philadelphia, 1689), esp. 198–228; *The Diary of Samuel Sewall*, ed. M. Halsey Smith (New York, 1973), I, 172.

23. Cotton Mather, *Memorable Providences, Relating to Witchcrafts and Possessions* (Boston, 1689), 1–47; appendix, 1, 6–7.

24. John Allin, Joshua Moodey, and Samuel Willard, *The Principles of the Protestant Religion Maintained and the Churches of New England Defended* (Boston, 1690), preface; Cotton Mather, *The Serviceable Man* (Boston, 1690), 34–36; George Keith, *A Refutation of Three Opposers of the Truth* (Philadelphia, 1690), 71; idem, *The Pretended Antidote Proved Poyson* (Philadelphia, 1690); Cotton Mather, *Little Flocks Guarded against Grievous Wolves* (Boston, 1691). Keith had the last word in this exchange; he issued two tracts rebutting Mather in 1692. But by now Keith was becoming embroiled in another theological controversy, this time with his own brethren in Pennsylvania. Their differences resulted in the Keithian schism and his formation of the Christian Quakers.

sion. What is more unexpected is that the seduction of the deacon's daughter by the spells of a Quaker wizard did not set the stage for a wholesale purging of dissenters from Gloucester through a campaign cloaked in accusations of witchcraft. Strangely enough, after the "afflicted girls" of Salem Village told William Stevens of seeing three people "sitting on his sister until she died," they charged not the Norwoods but three local women, all relatives of accused witches. Stranger still, although everyone in Gloucester suspected that the sorcery of Francis Norwood was the source of Mary Stevens's possession, William and his neighbors accepted the guilt of the "witches" named by the girls.[25]

What endows the story of Mary Stevens with some importance for understanding the history of heterodoxy in Massachusetts is that this case was not singular. In fact, the same fears of heresy's infecting orthodox families through intermarriage or other ties to dissenters that stirred William Stevens underlay many of the other witchcraft prosecutions in Essex County during 1692. The center of the hysteria that had peaked earlier in that year was Salem, the town with the largest concentration of Quakers in the county. As in Gloucester, the connection in Salem between actual prosecutions for witchcraft and religious heterodoxy was indirect: few Quakers, and none of Essex County's most prominent Friends, were accused of the crime. The situation in Salem differed from the Stevens possession in Gloucester in only one way: here it was the "witches" rather than the bewitched who had ties of blood, marriage, affection, or friendship to the Quakers. But many of the Salem trials, like the Stevens case, reflect the same anxieties over the merging of the orthodox and dissenting communities.

A substantial number of the witches accused by Salem Village's "afflicted girls" came from families or households that included Quaker members. A case in point is the apparently puzzling prosecution of Rebecca Nurse. The pattern of indictments in Salem conformed to that of Andover and Gloucester insofar as those initially accused were all social outcasts in some sense—poor or shrewish women prone to violent or unseemly behavior, and usually reputed to have practiced malefic magic against their neighbors.[26] The sole

25. The three women implicated in Mary Stevens's affliction all had family ties to other suspected witches: Abigail Row was Margaret Prince's granddaughter; Rebecca Dyke was Anne Doliber's sister-in-law, and Esther Elwell was the daughter of Grace Dutch, who had been charged with witchcraft earlier in the seventeenth century. *Witchcraft Papers*, I, 305–6; Babson, *History*, 81; *Essex Ct. Recs.*, I, 301.

26. The four women indicted before Rebecca Nurse in 1692—Sara Good, Sara Osborne, Martha Corey, and Tituba, a Negro slave—all conform to this description. See Paul Boyer and Stephen Nissenbaum, *Salem Possessed: The Social Origins of Witchcraft* (Cambridge, Mass., 1974), 203–4, 193–94, 146–47; Konig, *Law and Society*, 184, 146–47.

exception was Rebecca Nurse, a paragon of matronly piety, a pillar
of respectability, a church member, and the wife of a substantial Salem
Village farmer, Francis. There was only one reason that her neighbors had for disliking Rebecca Nurse: namely, that in 1677 the young
Samuel Southwick, the orphaned son of a local Quaker farmer, John
Southwick, chose the Nurses as his guardians and that they took the
boy into their home.[27] Rebecca and Francis were not Quakers, but
their ward was.

Among those accused of witchcraft later in the trial proceedings
were a large number of people who shared with Rebecca Nurse the
same kind of indirect Quaker affinities, connections of kinship, and
friendship with religious dissidents. There was the Proctor family,
for example, of which five members—John, his wife, Elizabeth, and
three of their children—were charged with witchcraft. What made
the Proctors suspect in the eyes of their neighbors was less that John
ran a tavern on the Ipswich Road than that his wife's family, the
Bassets of Lynn, included a large number of Quakers. Joining the
Proctors in prison were two members of the Basset family, along
with four members of Lynn's Hawkes, Farrar, and Hart families, all
of whom had Quaker connections.[28] The same was true of the
Andover residents Samuel Wardwell, his wife, and two daughters,
all relatives of the Quaker Lydia Wardwell, who in 1663 had appeared
naked in the Newbury meetinghouse to protest persecution by the
Puritans.[29] Another accused witch, Job Tookey of Beverly, had for
years denied the gossip that his father, an English clergyman, was
"an anabaptistical quaking rogue that for his maintenance went up
and down England to delude souls for the Devil."[30] And in at least
one instance, an accusation of witchcraft figured as a way for one of
the "afflicted girls" of Salem Village to disassociate herself from the
Quaker community. Ann Putnam, Jr., described to the Court of Oyer
and Terminer "an old gray head man" whom "people used to call

27. *Essex Ct. Recs.*, VI, 294.
28. On the Proctor family, see *Witchcraft Papers*, II, 655–95; Charles Upham, *Salem
Witchcraft* (Boston, 1867), II, 307. The accused witches Elizabeth Proctor and Mary DeRich
were the daughters of the Lynn Quaker William Basset, Sr.; the accused witch Mary
Basset was his daughter-in-law and the wife of William Basset, Jr., another Lynn Quaker.
Mary Basset's maiden name was Hood, which connected her to another Lynn Quaker
family. Thomas Farrar, Sr., charged with being a wizard, was the father of the Lynn
Quaker Thomas Farrar, Jr. The accused witches Sarah and Margaret Hawkes also had
Quaker connections, but I have been unable to trace their precise family relationship to
Quakers in the Hawkes family. This reconstruction of Quaker connections is based upon
names culled from the Records of the Salem Monthly Meeting, microfilm reel 1, Rhode
Island Historical Society, Providence, R.I., and from Alonzo Lewis and J. R. Newhall,
History of Lynn, Including Lynnfield, Saugus, Swampscott and Nahant (Boston, 1865), I, 295,
298, 305.
29. Bailey, *Historical Sketches of Andover*, 212; *Essex Ct. Recs.*, III, 64.
30. *Essex Ct. Recs.*, VIII, 330–38.

father pharaoh" who tormented her by insisting that he was her grandfather. The old man whom Ann Putnam, Jr., publicly denied as a blood relative was Thomas Farrar, Sr., the father of a leading Lynn Quaker.[31] Shortly after the trials, one of Salem's leading Friends, Thomas Maule, hinted that some linkage existed between dissenting affinities and the witchcraft prosecutions, comparing the trials to the Quakers' sufferings and expressing relief that none of his "relations" had been charged.[32]

Along with the bonds of blood and marriage, geographic propinquity to the Quaker community characterized many of the accused witches of Salem Village. Since most of these accused witches lived in Salem Village's more prosperous eastern part, situated adjacent to Salem Town, and since the majority of the accusers came from the more remote and economically stagnant western side, it has been suggested that western farmers both envied and resented the east's exposure to the affluent, cosmopolitan town. But more prominent in the thinking of the western Villagers than the greater proximity of their eastern neighbors to commercial Salem Town may have been the even shorter physical distance separating the residences of the accused from Salem's Quaker enclave.[33] This close geographic connection appears to have encouraged some eastern Villagers to take on some of the characteristics of their Quaker neighbors, forms of behavior that blurred sectarian boundaries in the same way that close social ties to dissenters did. The justices examining the suspected wizard George Jacobs, Sr., for example, asked, "Are you not the man that made disturbance at a Lecture at Salem?" "No great disturbance," Jacobs replied.[34] John Proctor's appeal to Boston ministers to take the trials out of Salem echoed the language of earlier Quaker denunciations of Puritan persecutions as "very like the Popish cruelties. . . . They have already undone us in our Estates, and that will not serve their turns, without our Innocent Bloods." Anticipating Thomas Maule's charges, Proctor contended that the supporters of the trials were "inraged and incensed against us by the Delusion of the Devil."[35] A testimony on behalf of John and Elizabeth Proctor signed by several of their Quaker neighbors probably helped to seal

31. Lewis and Newhall, *History of Lynn*, I, 295.
32. Thomas Maule, *Truth Held Forth and Maintained* (New York, 1695), 206–7.
33. This geographic propinquity appears when one compares the names of Salem's Quakers against a map of Salem Village in 1692 prepared by Charles Upham. For a comprehensive list of Salem Quakers, see Chu, "Social Context of Religious Heterodoxy." The "Map of Salem Village, 1692," with an accompanying key is in Upham, *Salem Witchcraft*, I, following p. xvii.
34. *Witchcraft Papers*, II, 476.
35. "Petition of John Proctor to the Ministers of Boston," 23 July 1692, in *Witchcraft Papers*, II, 476.

their fate. Sarah Good's end was in sight when from the scaffold she threatened Salem's assistant minister Nicholas Noyes, "if you take away my life, God will give you blood to drink." In these words Noyes found his vindication, because Marmaduke Stevenson and William Robinson had thirty years earlier addressed the same sanguinary prophecy to Boston magistrates just before the two Quakers had been hanged.[36]

Even among the accused who had no familial or geographic affinities with the Friends, the sort of behavior most likely to invite suspicion, to attract unfavorable notice, or to incur the censure of the presiding magistrates was distinctly Quaker-like. During the examination of the Boston mariner John Alden, "all were ordered to go down into the street where a ring was made; and the same accuser cried out, there stands Aldin, a bold fellow, with his hat on before the judges. . . ."[37] Alice Parker of Salem Town first incriminated herself by foretelling the fates of men at sea, her claim to prophetic powers evoking an association with Quakerism.[38] And the general characteristics displayed by or ascribed to many of the accused—the caviling questioning of authority, the refusal to confess error in spiritual loyalties, and, among women, publicly dominant, assertive behavior in dealing with men—were all traits familiar to Essex County residents and magistrates in the context of their experience with Quakerism.

In a few cases tried in 1692 and even earlier, the relationship between Quakerism as well as other forms of religious heterodoxy and witchcraft accusations was direct and unmistakable. Phillip English and his wife, who fled Salem Town to New York after being indicted in 1692, were both vocal supporters of the Church of England; George Burroughs, the former minister of Salem Village who was executed as a wizard, held Baptist convictions; Abigail Somes, the invalid daughter of the Gloucester Quaker Elizabeth Somes, lived in the household of Samuel Gaskill, one of Salem Village's leading Friends, until her imprisonment for witchcraft. Even before the Salem hysteria, deviance from orthodoxy could invite indictment for malefic magic: Goody Glover, the old woman charged with bewitching the Goodwin children in 1689, was an Irish Catholic.[39] But more

36. Cited in Boyer and Nissenbaum, *Salem Possessed*, 7–8; compare with the "Letter of Marmaduke Stevenson and William Robinson from the Boston Jail," August 1659, in Bishop, *New England Judged*, pt. 1, p. 237.

37. Mather, *Wonders of the Invisible World*, 211.   38. *Witchcraft Papers*, II, 623.

39. On Phillip English, a Jerseyman who was an outsider ethnically as well as religiously, see Henry W. Belknap, "Phillip English, Commerce Builder," *Proceedings of the American Antiquarian Society*, n.s., 41 (1931): 17–24, and Konig, *Law and Society*, 184. Mary Warren, a servant in the Proctor household, was the first to accuse Abigail Somes,

typically the accused witches were not themselves members of dissenting sects, and their connections with heterodoxy consisted in more tangential ties to dissenters among blood relatives, in-laws, household members, or neighbors and friends. Even in the case of Abigail Somes, accusations passed over Samuel Gaskill, for decades a central figure in the Salem Meeting, and focused instead on his ward, the child of an orthodox father and a heretical mother. Her background and that of many other accused witches suggest that the focus of anxiety was less on dissenters themselves than on those individuals who because of their relations or residences fell under suspicion of harboring if not heterodox sympathies then at least sympathy for the heterodox. The very ambiguity of their affinities and the division of their religious loyalties by the ties of family and friendship made such figures even more threatening to the maintenance of orthodoxy than known dissenters.[40]

The widespread anxiety over religious allegiances that was reflected in the witchcraft hysteria had been building for almost a decade before it erupted into panic at Salem and Gloucester in 1692. At its source were changes forced upon Massachusetts Bay by the mother country that challenged the hegemony of Congregationalist orthodoxy. For more than fifty years, the government established by the charter of 1629 had supported the public worship of God in the Congregational way and had protected the colony's churches from dissent. But in the 1680s, imperial policy "destroyed the accustomed order of things by which the Puritans had maintained supremacy and supposedly advanced God's kingdom."[41] The ambition of the Stuart kings to centralize the administration of their empire throughout North America resulted in the confiscation of the old

who admitted during her examination that she was the sister of John Somes, the Quaker cooper earlier punished by Boston authorities. No verdict survives in the Somes case, but Abigail was not executed, possibly because she alleged to the court that she was herself afflicted by "many persons [that I have seen] at my mother's camp at Gloucester." *Witchcraft Papers*, III, 733–37. I am grateful to John Murrin for bringing to my attention that George Burroughs had refused to have his younger children baptized, something that came up during his examination by the justices. See Upham, *Salem Witchcraft*, II, 157–63. On Goody Glover, see Mather, *Memorable Providences*, 7, 9. The correspondence between ties to dissenters and suspicions of witchcraft may have figured in earlier prosecutions as well. For example, John Godfrey, a herdsman indicted for witchcraft several times during the 1650s and 1660s, was originally a servant of John Spencer, a follower of Anne Hutchinson. In a detailed study of Godfrey, John Demos describes the alleged wizard's tendency to "startle," "confuse," and "deliberately provoke" his neighbors, assertive traits often associated with the Quakers and other Antinomian dissidents. ("John Godfrey and His Neighbors: Witchcraft and the Social Web of Massachusetts," *William and Mary Quarterly*, 3d ser., 33 (1976): 244–45.)

40. David Konig makes a similar argument respecting the significance of accusations against women married to non-English men. *Law and Society*, 184.

41. David S. Lovejoy, *The Glorious Revolution in America* (New York, 1972), 180.

Massachusetts charter in 1684 and in the consolidation of all of the New England colonies into a single entity, the Dominion. By abolishing the colony's elected assembly, restricting town meetings, and according all powers of taxation and legislation to a royally appointed governor and his council, the Dominion radically altered the government that Massachusetts Puritans had established under their former charter. The abrasive Sir Edmund Andros, a military officer and the governor of New York, who was named to head the Dominion in 1686, pursued a course still more alarming to Bay colonists. Andros not only threatened their livelihoods by calling land titles into question and by strictly enforcing the Navigation Acts, but he also implemented policies aimed at undermining the close relationship that had existed between the state and the Congregational churches. He remodeled the procedure for jury selection to reduce the influence of church members and insisted upon swearing on the Bible in the courts, a practice repugnant to the Puritans. He ousted church members from important positions in the militia and replaced them with Anglican officers. And finally, Andros imposed liberty of conscience on Massachusetts Bay.

The extension of toleration to all dissenters in the Dominion afforded the Friends complete freedom of worship and gave the Quaker missionary George Keith license to preach freely in the streets of Boston. At the same time, the Bay's small Anglican minority, formerly forced to attend Puritan worship services and compelled to contribute to the support of Congregationalist ministers, now enjoyed the particular favor of the new Episcopal governor. To the Puritan majority's dismay, after the Bishop of London assigned the Reverend Robert Ratcliffe to Boston as the Bay's first resident Episcopal priest, Andros seized part of a public burial ground as the site for an Anglican church, King's Chapel. And while it was being constructed, he commandeered the Congregationalists' Old South meetinghouse for Episcopal services. These developments, combined with Andros's revocation of tax support for the salaries of orthodox clergymen, led many Congregationalists to fear that the Dominion's policy would pass from protecting liberty of conscience to persecuting the Puritans and attempting to establish Episcopalianism as the state religion.[42]

The successful rebellion of Massachusetts inhabitants against Andros in April of 1689—an event that followed in the wake of the Glorious Revolution in England—did little to restore order to the troubled colony. While Bay colonials waited for the new king, William III, to determine their future, Massachusetts endured three years of chaos under a temporary government unable to deal with the disarray in the colony's judicial system and military defenses, a serious trade recession, and the continuing threat of French and Indians on the frontier. But the aftermath of the rebellion did reveal the depth of anxieties occasioned by the Dominion's challenges to Puritan preeminence. Uncertainty over the fate of the colony and internal difficulties notwithstanding, the interim government immediately began making inroads upon Andros's imposed toleration by reinstating tax support for ministerial maintenance and by turning a deaf ear to the dissidents' complaints of mistreatment. At the same time, the orthodox clergy campaigned to reclaim any souls that they had lost to competing sects during the period when liberty of conscience had prevailed. Boston Anglicans, whose new chapel had been vandalized and threatened with total destruction during the upheaval, came under virulent attack for their alleged complicity in a "Catholic conspiracy" to deliver all of England's colonies to the pope.[43] But the Anglicans, badly discredited by their close ties to the hated Dominion regime, were not the chief concern of the Congregationalist leaders. It was, instead, the Quakers that Cotton Mather singled out in his election sermon of 1690 as the Bay Colony's "Most Malicious as well as most Pernicious Enemies" who "by Writing, Railing, and the Arts peculiar to themselves . . . are Labouring to Unchurch all the Lord's People here."[44] In June of 1689, just two months after the overthrow of Andros, Mather and other members of the Boston clergy initiated their counteroffensive against George Keith, "to furnish the Churches in this Land with an Antidote against the contagion of Quakerism." Besides calling up the old associations of Quakerism with witchcraft, the flurry of treatises and sermons published by Mather and his colleagues between 1689 and 1691 advised Massachusetts laymen on how to confute Quaker proselytizers, providing specific responses to all controverted theological points. Although Mather and his brethren believed that "our Churches have yet had very little Impression from any [Quaker] Seducers hitherto," the frequency with which they administered these "Antidotes" belies their expressed confidence in the immunity of their congregations to the infection of heresy.[45]

Almost a decade of confusion in all spheres of the colony's life and of concern over the maintenance of social order and authority came to an end in the fall of 1691 when William III finally gave Massachu-

43. Ibid., 238–45, 281–88, 324–25, 350–53.
44. Mather, *Serviceable Man*, 34–35.
45. Allin et al., *Principles of the Protestant Religion Maintained*, preface.

setts Bay a new charter that provided for rule by a royally appointed governor and an elected assembly. But other items included in the new charter only aggravated the apprehensions aroused by the Dominion's attack on the Congregationalist establishment. The new constitution precluded the possibility of religious discrimination in voting rights in that it substituted a property qualification for church membership as the basis of the franchise; it also guaranteed liberty of conscience to all Christians except Catholics. While the king allowed the Bay government to continue the policy of supporting the Congregationalist clergy by taxes on all inhabitants, orthodox and dissenters alike, the charter imposed once and for all a real liberalization of religious life on Massachusetts.[46]

The progress of legal toleration was an unwelcome and unsettling development for most Massachusetts colonials, who still regarded themselves as a people in covenant with God to uphold orthodoxy. But the developments of the intercharter period had placed the Bay's civil and clerical leaders in a delicate position, presenting them with political exigencies that dictated their lending lip service at least to liberty of conscience. Andros's aggressive pro-Anglican policies had demonstrated that toleration might be a principle worth upholding for the protection of Puritan orthodoxy itself. During the years between 1689 and 1691, when the Bay colony's agents were negotiating for a new charter with the king and his ministers, several Massachusetts spokesmen had proclaimed their adherence to religious liberty, hoping by this strategy to limit royal interference in ecclesiastical affairs. And after 1691 the Bay's leadership continued to support publicly the official policy of toleration as the price for preserving the other privileges restored to the colony under the new charter.[47]

The situation that had evolved in Massachusetts between 1684 and 1691 thus made it impolitic and impossible to renew civil repression aimed directly at religious dissenters. But over the same period, intersectarian tensions were stretched to the breaking point: hysteria over rumored papist conspiracies, attacks upon King's Chapel and its adherents, and especially the impassioned invective against the Quakers expressed the extreme excitability over religious differences that gripped the orthodox laity. They had long held that to profane holy commonwealth by granting religious equality to dissenters was to invite divine retribution in the form of Indian wars, epidemics, or natural disasters. And by 1691 the prospect that a gen-

46. Lovejoy, *Glorious Revolution in America*, 347–48; Timothy Breen, *The Character of the Good Ruler* (New Haven, 1970), 183–84.

47. Worrall, *Quakers*, 49–50; see also Increase Mather, *A Vindication of New England* (Boston, 1690), passim; Cotton Mather, *Serviceable Man*, 35.

uinely pluralistic religious culture would supplant orthodox purity and distinctiveness seemed a real and ominous possibility. Not only had the new charter compromised the Bay's original spiritual mission by outlawing the civil suppression of heresy and by according political rights to propertied dissenters, but the accommodation to heterodoxy had also started to manifest itself at the local level. The amalgamation of orthodoxy and dissent exemplified in the courtship of Mary Stevens and in the merging of Congregationalist and Quaker families in the neighborhood networks of Lynn and Salem augured the emergence of a new order that profoundly threatened the majority of pious Puritans.

This background of popular resistance to religious liberalization provides one context for understanding the Essex County witchcraft panic of 1692. Although political exigencies ruled out the persecution of known dissenters by the state, they did not prevent an alarmed laity from trying to reclaim "marginal" members of orthodox society, those whose religious loyalties, had been rendered ambiguous by either social ties or geographic propinquity to the dissenting community. If the civil government could no longer stamp out heresy at its source, other measures might at least contain its contagion by arresting the spread of dissenting influence through families and neighborhoods. The closing of ranks among the Congregationalists in Essex County was expressed in allegations of diabolical possession and accusations of witchcraft made against people linked to the Quakers. William Stevens could not attack the Norwoods themselves, but he could try to intimidate his sister into rejecting a Quaker suitor by insisting that she was possessed by the devil. Neither could Salem Villagers strike directly at the Friends in their midst, but they could demand that their neighbors with Quaker ties confess to being in league with Satan's legions and publicly repudiate the connection.

Irreducible to any single source of social strain, the witchcraft hysteria of 1692 reflected a wide array of antagonisms and uncertainties. Many accusations within Salem Village grew out of longstanding factional rivalries. Other allegations figured as a collective retaliation against village scolds or women long suspected of using malefic magic against their neighbors. Still others spilled over from disputes between near neighbors over land and livestock or from tensions generated by the renewed anxieties over military attack, as the Andover outbreak illustrates. Many of these simmering local antagonisms boiled over in charges of witchcraft because of disruptions in the judicial system during the intercharter period: the creation of the powerful court of Oyer and Terminer in 1692, commissioned to adjudicate only witchcraft cases, encouraged Essex County residents to couch

all of their complaints in supernatural terms.[48] But yet another source
of the witchcraft delusion was popular fear over the spread of religious dissent. Although sectarian tensions cannot account for all of
the prosecutions, they figured in enough cases to indicate that religious differences played a significant role in shaping the witchcraft
outbreak and that the episode constituted in part a counteroffensive
against the Quaker heresy under the conditions imposed by the new
Massachusetts charter.

As several historians have pointed out, the entire intercharter
period displayed the vulnerability of many of the "boundaries"
established by the old colonial order in Massachusetts Bay.[49] Political
upheaval created uncertainties over land titles, the powers and jurisdictions of the judicial system, and the authority of a succession of
colony governments. Military crisis simultaneously raised fears over
preserving the security of Massachusetts's physical borders from
attack by the French and the Indians. The witchcraft delusion came
as a response to the stress and insecurity created by these confusions
of social, legal, and territorial boundaries. But the hysteria also registered the strain resulting from the blurring of boundaries in the
realm of religious life, the diffusion of sectarian divisions portended
by the policy of official toleration. Cotton Mather's account of the
witchcraft hysteria expressed aptly both the collective anxieties
induced by the anticipated obliteration of older distinctions under
the new charter and the strategy of New England's counterattack:
"such is the Descent of the Devil at this day upon ourselves, that I
may Truly tell you, the Walls of the Whole World are broken down!
The usual walls of Defense about Mankind have such a Gap made in
them that the very Devils are broke in upon us. . . ." Mather placed
witchcraft within the succession of other afflictions that had befallen
New England, the "sorcery" of hostile Indians, the loss of the old
charter, the onset of King William's War, and "Seducing Spirits," the
Quakers and other heterodox sects. He advised unity among the
faithful: "Let us not be a Troubled House, altho' we are so much
haunted by Devils." To insure that no one missed his meaning,
Mather included an account of "a sort of daemon" who "stirred up
Strife" among the inhabitants of a ninth-century German village. "He
uttered Prophecies, he detected Villanies, he branded People with

48. Among the recent historians of the witchcraft hysteria, Paul Boyer and Stephen
Nissenbaum emphasize the village antagonism while Kai Erikson and David Konig place
the delusion within a wider context of cultural disorientation and institutional disrup-
tion occasioned by the intercharter period. Erikson, *Wayward Puritans: A Study in the
Sociology of Deviance* (New York, 1966), 137–59; Konig, *Law and Society*, 158–68.

49. See Kai Erikson and David Konig on this point, and also Lovejoy, *Glorious Revolution in America*, 353, 373–74.

all kinds of Infamies. . . . Let us be aware lest such Daemons do, Come hither also!"[50] "Daemons" of this description had a great deal in common with Quakers, who were also given to prophecies and to strictures against the orthodox majority. Lt. William Stevens did not want his sister to marry one.

But neither the Court of Oyer and Terminer nor the admonitions of Cotton Mather could remedy the difficulties in the "Troubled House" of William Stevens: those accused of having afflicted Mary Stevens were set free as the hysteria subsided in 1693, the same year in which she wed Francis Norwood, Jr. The prosecutions also failed to drive the devils out of the "Troubled House" of New England: the trials at Salem backfired badly as a device for shoring up orthodox loyalties, and revulsion at the complicity of local clergymen like Samuel Parris and Nicholas Noyes in the discredited prosecutions produced a wave of Quaker conversions in the area around Lynn and Salem.[51] In Gloucester, inhabitants also felt compunction for their participation in the panic, and for a brief period the suspicion of dissenters also receded. In 1694, enough voters were willing to overlook the Quakerism of John Pearce to elect his son-in-law Timothy Somes to a term on the board of selectmen. When Samuel Bownas, a traveling English Quaker missionary, stopped in town in 1706, some curious Congregationalists deserted the Sabbath services at the First Church to attend his two meetings, "It being a New Thing." Even the Reverend John White came to the second of Bownas's meetings and attempted to confute the Quaker's erroneous beliefs about water baptism, perfection, and election. Over the same period, some additional Quaker families arrived in town— shipwrights, mariners, and blacksmiths attracted by Gloucester's growing maritime economy and its more hospitable treatment of dissenters.[52]

But this lull in intersectarian hostilities did not outlast even the first decade of the eighteenth century, and the anxieties that the Quakers had aroused within the Congregationalist camp did not die out with the witchcraft delusion. Despite his "quiet and civil" reception at Cape Ann, Bownas admitted to having encountered "great

50. Mather, *Wonders of the Invisible World*, 42, 48, 60–61. Mather endorsed legal toleration, but he remained a stringent critic of Quakerism until the last years of his life. See esp. Robert Middlekauff, *The Mathers: Three Generations of Puritan Intellectuals, 1596–1728* (New York, 1971), 316–17.

51. Worrall, *Quakers*, 49–50.

52. Babson, *History*, 585; Samuel Bownas, *An Account of the Life of Samuel Bownas* (Philadelphia, 1759), 127–29. During the first decade of the eighteenth century, the Quaker shipwrights Thomas and Nathaniel Sanders, the Scituate blacksmith Jonathan Springer, and the Lynn mariner Joseph Goodrich settled in Gloucester.

opposition" in Gloucester.[53] By 1706, antipathy to dissenters was rising again in town: the orthodox resumed closing ranks, and reprisals against local Friends took a more direct and effective form. Throughout the opening decades of the eighteenth century, the Congregationalist majority in Gloucester made increasingly plain its unwillingness to incorporate dissenters within the community by actions calculated to discourage Friends from staying on in town. The career of Gloucester's most prominent Quaker in this period reveals both the strength and the efficacy of local exclusivism.

The blacksmith Jonathan Springer came to Gloucester from Scituate in 1704 and set himself up as a general retail merchant, selling provisions for fishing voyages, running a packet trade to Boston, and peddling locally produced commodities along the Atlantic coast. Springer's commercial investments and connections were impressive compared with the scale of other local operations at the time: he held partial interest in four small sloops and a valuable stock in trade with two Quaker partners, John Maule of Salem and Walter Newberry of Boston, and he dealt directly with major fish exporters in the capital.[54] But despite the advantages of financial backing by nonlocal coreligionists, opposition from within town thwarted Springer's schemes for seizing the opportunity offered by Gloucester's infant fishery. His suit for debt against John Vittum in 1712 reveals the extent to which religious intolerance limited business success. Springer had hired Vittum, a mariner, to pilot a sloop to Boston, where a cargo of bullets, tar, and bread was waiting. Vittum loaded part of the goods sitting on the Boston wharf but sailed off before the Negro porter who was transporting the commodities from a warehouse to the dock had completed the lading. Questioned later about why he had left half of Springer's merchandise behind, Vittum replied that he "did not care what became of the rest of the goods but the bullets . . . but the Quaker dog shall never have one of them again for a negro is noe evidence in court and it is as good going a privateering as taking anything from him [Springer] as from a french man for I doe account him noe better."[55] Nor was Vittum's attitude an isolated instance of antipathy toward Springer specifically and the Friends in general: a year later, when Springer went to court again, this time suing Adam Cogswell, a member of a prominent landed family in

53. Bownas, *Account*, 127.
54. Essex County Probate File no. 26043, Registry of Probate, Essex County Courthouse, Salem, Mass. (hereafter cited as EPF). For a full discussion of the ways that religious fellowship benefited the businesses of Philadelphia Quakers, see Frederick Tolles, *Meetinghouse and Countinghouse: The Quaker Merchants of Colonial Philadelphia, 1682–1763* (1948; reprint, New York, 1963), 68, 89–90.
55. Springer v. Vittum, 1712, Files of the Court of Common Pleas for Essex County, Superior Courthouse, Salem, Mass. (hereafter cited as FCCP).

Ipswich, the defendant related the history of Springer's hard dealings with him, including a demand for payment in "a Railing, Reviling Letter after the Manner of the Quakers."[56]

These cases represent only a small portion of the many legal difficulties that blighted Springer's business career in Gloucester. Until his early death, in 1714, he appeared constantly before the court, both as a plaintiff charging malfeasance on the part of his pilots and as a defendant in suits brought by farmers who alleged that he had embezzled the profits of produce on consignment. Even after Springer died, litigation involving his affairs continued to crop up on court dockets as Maule and Newberry attempted to recover debts due his estate.[57] Springer's Quakerism did not dissuade all orthodox local residents from doing business with him, and he did not always have to resort to the courts in order to collect his obligations. But considering his capital, his influential connections in other ports, the growing local demand for his stock of provisions, and the limited availability of all these resources in Gloucester around 1710, Springer's inability to attract a larger clientele is surprising. Only a handful of inhabitants had book debts or bonds due to his estate in 1714, and for credit he remained almost totally reliant on outsiders, especially on the more affluent Friends of Lynn, Salem, and Boston. His venture into the Gloucester fishery was a failure, and he died insolvent.[58]

Springer's origins outside of town and the periodic military crises of the first decade of the eighteenth century may have hampered his chances for success, but among his orthodox contemporaries were other recent immigrants engaged in similar enterprises who managed to make money in Gloucester. The real source of Springer's troubles in establishing a local trade was his status as a dissenter: the resentment and mistrust resulting from his religious nonconformity both limited the willingness of inhabitants to deal with him and gave those orthodox farmers and mariners who did deal with him a pretext for exploiting him economically.[59] Intolerance trapped Springer

56. Springer v. Cogswell, 1713, FCCP.
57. Springer v. Elwell, 1714; Putnam v. Springer, 1712; Estate of Springer v. Tarr, 1719, v. Babson, 1719, v. Bennet, 1719, v. Elwell, 1719, FCCP. Estate of Springer v. Sanders, November 1717 and 20 May 1718, Minutebooks of the Superior Court of Judicature, Office of the Clerk of the Supreme Judicial Court for Suffolk County, Suffolk County Courthouse, Boston, Mass. (hereafter cited as MSCJ).
58. EPF no. 26043; "Petition for the Sale of Real Property," 8 November 1715, MSCJ.
59. Max Weber, "Religious Rejections of the World and Their Directions" and "The Protestant Sects and the Spirit of Capitalism," in *Essays from Max Weber*, ed. H. H. Gerth and C. Wright Mills (New York, 1946), 302–22, 329. On the Quaker reputation for slyness and dishonesty in business dealings and its currency throughout the Anglo-American world during the seventeenth and eighteenth centuries, see Tolles, *Meetinghouse and Countinghouse*, 47–48, 60–61.

in a vicious circle: the orthodox perception of Quakers as unscru-
pulous, litigious sharpsters discouraged the fair treatment of dissenters in business dealings, and Springer's recourse to the courts to
collect his debts simply reinforced the prevailing stereotype.

The in-group economic morality that operated in Gloucester both
within defined geographic limits and within a narrow cultural com-
pass impaired not only Jonathan Springer's business career but those
of other Gloucester Quakers as well. The difference that religious
orthodoxy made in determining commercial success is especially evident in the disparate careers of the Sanders brothers, who came to
Gloucester from Plymouth at about the same time when Jonathan
Springer did and who set up a shipyard in the southern harbor. Both
Thomas and Nathaniel Sanders initially held Quaker sympathies and
invested in vessels with Springer. But Thomas abandoned the
Friends: he became a pillar of the First Church, claimed the title of
"captain" for having commanded a government sloop during the
Indian wars of the 1720s, and amassed one of the largest estates in
town by the middle of the eighteenth century. Nathaniel retained his
Quaker connection and drifted out of town sometime in the 1730s
without sharing his brother's success.[60] The same sanctions against
according Quakers commercial opportunity prevented the effective
economic ostracism of dissenters that bankrupted Jonathan Springer,
but neither John Maule nor any of his fellow Friends succeeded
Thomas Maule into the ranks of Salem's major traders.[61] Most Essex
County Quakers with commercial aspirations moved to more con-
genial communities, to the north in Maine and New Hampshire and
to the south in Rhode Island and Pennsylvania.

While Quakers became, because of their involvement in trade, the
most visible and vulnerable targets for popular religious animosity,
intense suspicion also continued to surround individuals of more
obscure status whose ties to the Friends were only through the affiliation of family members. An example is the career of James Dyke,

60. Babson, *History*, 241. At the time of his death, Thomas Sanders's estate was worth
£632 sterling. EPF no. 24778. For a certificate of ownership of a vessel with Springer,
see *Massachusetts Archives*, vol. 7, dated November 1707, the Statehouse, Boston, Mass.
See also the Minutebooks of the General Sessions of the Peace for Essex County, 17 July
1728, Office of the County Clerk, Superior Courthouse, Salem, Mass. (hereafter cited
as MGSP).

61. On the Salem province tax list of 1700, four Quakers ranked in the top decile of
taxpayers, including Thomas Maule and two members of the Buffum family who also
had commercial interests. But in the province tax list of 1748, only two Quakers, both
farmers, ranked in the top decile and no Quakers appeared among the town's major
merchants. See Tax and Valuation Lists for Massachusetts Towns, comp. Ruth Crandall,
Harvard University Microfilm Edition, reel 8. As Frederick Tolles points out, in *Meetinghouse and Countinghouse*, p. 36, the use of economic weapons for religious persecution
of the Quakers dates from the time of the sect's origin in seventeenth-century England.

who appeared more frequently in court than any other Gloucester inhabitant between the 1720s and 1740s. Dyke's first offense, in 1720, was bringing into town a child judged likely to become a public burden; four years later he allegedly introduced another "chargeable" child to Gloucester, a bastard that he fathered but refused to support. During the same decade, Dyke also brought suit against the town proprietors, protesting that they had deprived him of his rightful share in the division of the commons. Throughout the 1730s and 1740s, Dyke's legal difficulties continued: in 1735, he was imprisoned for assaulting his neighbor Nathaniel Rust, and he compounded his offense by breaking jail with a fellow prisoner convicted of rape; a few years later, the town took him to court for enclosing part of a common highway. James Dyke did not conform to the pattern set by Gloucester's other petty criminals: a long-established resident of Second Parish, a steady farmer, a full church member, he seems an unlikely habitual offender. But something did set Dyke apart from his fellow townsmen: his two sisters were Quakers.[62] As Thomas Sanders's successes suggest, it was possible for some former religious dissenters or for those with heterodox family connections to ingratiate themselves with local society. But James Dyke was not a military hero like Sanders, and for him acceptance never came.

What explains the persistence of popular anti-Quaker animus in provincial Essex County? Why were local Friends widely regarded with suspicion, mistrusted as businessmen, disdained as marital partners, and discouraged from settling in town? In part the continuing prejudice against the Quakers reflects the preservation of the past in the long memory of local society: one orthodox generation's recounting to another the peculiarities of Quakerism's prophetic period in the middle of the seventeenth century, repeating to it the traditional association of heresy with witchcraft, reminding it that religious distinctiveness should not be lost to the encroachments of diversity sustained sectarian friction into the eighteenth century. But the cast of mind capable of equating Quakers with Frenchmen and dogs and intent upon eliminating dissenters from local life seems less like the residue of an inherited antagonism than the product of a present provocation. What made the antipathy seem still more anomalous is that it occurred in the period in the early eighteenth century when Quaker doctrine and practice was coming increasingly to resemble Congregationalism and when the Friends themselves were underplaying their sectarian peculiarities.[63]

62. Babson, *History,* 81; MGSP, 28 June 1720 and 1 January 1726; MSCJ, 28 October 1735 and October 1724; Records of the Salem Monthly Meeting, 1728, 1731.
    63. Worrall, *Quakers,* 43–80.

Doctrinal differences continued to divide Puritans from Friends in provincial New England, but popular interest in these theological discrepancies peaked in intensity early in the eighteenth century and subsided thereafter. A few days before his arrival in Gloucester, Samuel Bownas had faced a less "quiet and civil" audience of Congregationalists at Newbury, where he finally stilled the crowd by "urging as the Reason for it that I had the Word of God in my Hand, such a great Regard they paid to my Bible." As Bownas cited Scripture to corroborate the truth of Quaker doctrine, "there were many Bibles then appeared," and his auditors tested against revelation the truth of the missionary's message.[64] But the gathering that occasioned the most intense interest in Essex County was the apostate George Keith's debate with the English "Public Friend" John Richardson at Lynn in 1702. Keith, whose local notoriety dated from his former incarnation as a Quaker evangelist, had now defected to the Episcopal church and had become a missionary for the Society for the Propagation of the Gospel. With all the zeal of a convert, he "had boasted much of what he would prove against the Friends," and so "in great Expectation to hear the Quakers run down . . . a great many People gathered together of Several Professions and Qualities . . . coming from every Quarter to see and hear How matters would go."[65] Yet after the first decade of the eighteenth century, theological discrepancies began to pale in importance as a point of division between the Friends and the orthodox. Missionaries like Bownas and even ardent Foxian laymen like Thomas Maule attempted to minimize their sect's doctrinal divergences from orthodoxy, and their efforts told in the comment of one Congregationalist clergyman who confided to Bownas in the 1730s that the Friends' theology had become "more refined" than their earlier doctrine.[66]

During the same period when Quaker doctrine was becoming more acceptable, the sect's ecclesiastical practices were conforming more to the Congregationalist model. Supplanting the self-appointed or popularly acclaimed spiritual leaders of the seventeenth century were ministers chosen by the Friends' business meetings after a formal examination. Sitting on raised "facing benches," Quaker ministers and elders presided over worship services that had by the early eighteenth century become more restrained gatherings than their enthusiastic antecedents had been.[67] Even as their own polity assumed a less lay centered character, Quakers kept up their objections to Con-

---

64. Bownas, *Account,* 123.
65. John Richardson, *An Account of the Life of John Richardson* (Philadelphia, 1759), 95, 106.
66. Bownas, *Account,* 177.   67. Worrall, *Quakers,* 91.

gregationalism's "hireling" clergy, to whose support the Friends were compelled to contribute until 1728.[68] Yet this Quaker critique of the establishment actually enhanced the sect's appeal to some orthodox laymen who believed that maintenance by taxation compromised the clergy's stance as "otherworldly prophets." The appearance of Samuel Bownas in Gloucester emboldened one member of John White's church to declare that "Religion could never prosper, so long as it was made a Trade to get Bread by."[69]

The discipline of members and the arbitration of personal and economic differences was another area in which Quakers created a set of institutions similar in character to those of the orthodox community. The Congregational system for regulating the behavior of members involved the pastor, the saints, and, in some congregations, the lay ruling elders, who heard testimony concerning the transgressions of backsliders or the quarrels between individuals and then punished the guilty or adjudicated the controversy. Private conferences outside of the church with the parties involved were often a preliminary to public proceedings. The Quakers undertook a similar oversight of their members' behavior: the "Discipline" set forth in 1708 codified rules for conduct essentially similar to orthodox standards, and the Salem Meeting put into effect in the same year a system of two-man committees that regularly visited all families of Friends in the area—an institution similar to the visitations conducted by Congregationalist pastors and elders.[70] A related means of regulating the behavior of members was the travel certificate, the Quaker counterpart to the pastoral letter of dismission used to acquaint the Congregational churches of other communities with the piety and good character of migrating members. Quaker certificates improved upon the orthodox system by including both members who moved permanently and those who traveled on business or as missionaries. James Goodrich, for example, "being bound to sea," received a letter from the Salem Meeting attesting to his good conduct and to his status as a single man; John Maule acquired a similar recommendation before moving to Philadelphia. Certificates served religious, social, and economic functions for traveling sectarians, establishing their integrity with distant meetings as well as with prospective marital partners and business associates. At the same time, such letters of introduction helped to confine the contacts of members on the move to Quaker circles by insuring their welcome. Meetings did not grant such recommendations as a matter of course and

---

68. Ibid., 122–23.   69. Bownas, *Account,* 129.
70. Records of the Salem Monthly Meeting, 1708; Worrall, *Quakers,* 70.

often withheld certification from members as a means of discipline; in 1717, the Salem Friends strengthened their restrictions on mobility even more by voting against admitting "any stranger" without a certificate to their monthly meeting.[71]

One Quaker practice, however, continued to incite intense controversy during the eighteenth century: preaching by women. While Congregationalists were willing to listen to dissenting views on questions of doctrine and polity, to visit the meetings of traveling male missionaries, and even to attend Quaker marriages, attempts by female friends to pray aloud or to testify publicly disrupted any gathering with a large orthodox attendance. Samuel Bownas recounted his meeting at Newbury in 1706 where the Quaker Lydia Norton "having a very strong Manly Voice extended it very loud but to no purpose, for the People were as loud as she, calling for a Dram and sporting themselves in their Folly." John Richardson attended a meeting a few years earlier in Boston where "when one of the . . . worthy Women was declaring Excellently . . . as the Manner of Inhabitants of Boston had been for many Years to Encourage, or at least suffer a rude Mob to bawl and make a Noise, they did so now." The basis for orthodox objections was Saint Paul's proscription of female preaching: "We hold it unlawful," a Newbury justice of the peace informed Bownas, "therefore we think it not proper to give them a hearing."[72] But in addition, the assertiveness of female preachers and the greater equality accorded to all women within the Quaker community was tinged in the orthodox imagination with a suggestion of sexual libertinism. George Keith created a considerable stir in Lynn with his charge that the Quakers "used many Ceremonies, as taking one another by the Hand, and Men saluting one another, and Women doing so to one another, and he said that Women did salute Men; yea, they had done it to him." Keith afterward retracted this "foul Reflection" to the relief of local Quaker women "especially before their zealous Neighbors the Presbyterians who . . . fell hard upon our Women Friends about their Saluting Men . . . as was generally understood in the Plural. . . . [and] probably might have twitted them."[73] This merging of fears over women's publicly assuming priestly roles with anxieties over the exhibition of aggressive female sexuality surfaced again in New England during the Great Awakening, in the debate over female New Light exhort-

---

71. Records of the Salem Monthly Meeting, 1689, 1707, 1717.

72. Bownas, *Account*, 121; Richardson, *Account*, 71. Thomas Maule defended the role of women in "prophecy," but he explicitly denied them any place in church government, for in participating in these matters, "she comes to Usurp Government over the Man." *Truth Held Forth and Maintained*, 124.

73. Richardson, *Account*, 98, 103–4.

ers and in the criticism of the open emotionalism of many women converts.[74]

But aside from the Friends' sustained support of "Women's Preaching," there was little in Quaker practice during the early eighteenth century that affronted orthodox sensibilities. The Friends themselves had forsworn ritualized displays of defiance: no more did naked Quaker women march down the aisles of meetinghouses, nor did Quaker prophets stridently publicize in the streets the errors of the Congregationalist establishment. With its prophetic period past, the sect settled down to strengthening its institutional structure, developing a hierarchy of monthly, quarterly, and yearly meetings, promulgating a "discipline," and evolving measures for its implementation. This concern with enhancing internal organization became particularly pronounced in the Salem Meeting as local Friends attempted to capitalize on the conversions that occurred in the wake of the witchcraft trials. No less than the Congregationalist clergy in Massachusetts, but much more successfully, the Friends' ecclesiastical leaders sought to consolidate their control over membership, to maintain uniformity in doctrine and practice, and to establish clear lines of authority.[75]

This institutional reorganization was precisely what sustained the suspicions of eighteenth-century Congregationalists about the Friends. Unlike Baptist evangelicals in the eighteenth-century South, the Quakers in Essex County did not constitute a "counterculture"; they did not represent a striking alternative to orthodox values, ideals, and models of behavior, but they called on their members to adhere to essentially the same standards for personal conduct that every Congregationalist clergyman in the province urged on his parishioners.[76] But while eighteenth-century Quakerism no longer constituted a "counterculture," the Friends had by the eighteenth century become a "countercommunity," a network of institutions for ordering the lives of their members separate from, but closely parallel to, those within individual New England towns. What lay behind the animus against the Quakers in places like provincial Gloucester was less an objection to the Friends' private religious convictions and their conduct than uncertainties about their public loyalties.

74. For an example, see Ebenezer Turrell, *Mr. Turrell's Directions* (Boston, 1742).

75. Worrall, *Quakers*, 67–80. Among Congregationalists, the proposals of 1705, the Saybrook Platform, and the formation of ministerial associations were intended to effect the same kinds of centralizing reforms. See G. William T. Youngs, *God's Messengers: The Religious Leadership of Colonial New England, 1700–1750* (Baltimore, 1976), 64–76.

76. Rhys Isaac, "Evangelical Revolt: The Nature of the Baptists' Challenge to the Traditional Order in Virginia, 1765 to 1775," *William and Mary Quarterly*, 3d ser., 31 (1975): 345–68.

Quaker discipline encouraged sectarian solidarity and separateness and the strengthening of social bonds within the fellowship by proscribing activities that enhanced the orthodox majority's contact with and control over individual Friends. While the Congregationalists employed informal pressures to prevent mixed marriages but stopped short of using church discipline to discourage such alliances, the Quakers used stronger institutional sanctions: in 1706, for example, the Salem Meeting sent Samuel Collins to speak with Edward Webb about "his Marrying outside the Unity of the Friends." The Society also frowned upon members' marrying "contrary to the Good Order of Truth," in a service conducted by a clergyman or a civil magistrate. Quaker marriage customs prescribed that a couple first declare their intentions, then give proof of being single, and finally gain the consent of the entire meeting. The wedding ceremony itself took place without the presence of clergy. After Nathaniel Wood violated these procedures, in 1706, the Salem Meeting insisted that he write "a public paper of self-condemnation," the usual penalty for "outgoing."[77] Quakers perceived an equally potent threat to the integrity of their fellowship in an array of offenses surrounding the participation of their members in the sociability of neighborhood taverns. Throughout the opening decades of the eighteenth century, the Salem Meeting frequently chastised members for "disorderly behavior" in such places, for keeping "bad company," and for retailing liquor illegally, the last offense being the subject of an explicit stricture in 1730.[78] Congregationalists also discouraged excessive drinking, but their discipline of members for this offense was more occasional, and the churches left the punishment of illegal retailers entirely to the courts. The source of the more intense concern among the Quakers over conviviality and the illicit sale of spirits was twofold: first, the regular contact of individual Friends with their orthodox neighbors at local inns or private stills increased the likelihood of their integration into the wider network of the neighborhood community; at the same time, Friends involved in the illegal sale of alcohol provided secular magistrates with a legitimate pretext for exercising their authority over dissenters.

This concern with keeping secular authority at bay is also evident in the Salem Meeting's opposition to members' suing each other in the Court of Common Pleas. In 1689, after the Lynn mariner Jacob Allen and the Salem merchant Thomas Maule had quarreled over a vessel, the Friends deputed two arbitrators to treat with Allen about

77. Records of the Salem Monthly Meeting, 11 and 14 November 1706. See also Kenneth Carroll, *Quakerism on the Eastern Shore* (Baltimore, 1970), 71–78.
78. Records of the Salem Monthly Meeting, 11 February 1713, 14 February 1722, and 12 March 1730.

settling the dispute privately, "so that the difference may be disposed of without going to law"; at the same time, James Goodrich also complained that Allen had slandered him "to the world's people," probably a reference to another civil suit.[79] Congregationalist clergymen deplored the litigiousness of their parishioners from the pulpit and attempted to resolve disputes arising over bad debts and business deals privately, but the churches did not penalize members for recourse to the courts. It was otherwise with the Quakers: when Allen proved obdurate and resisted private arbitration of his differences with Maule and Goodrich, the Friends denied him a certificate of travel. To his coreligionists, Allen's decision to redress his grievances against fellow Friends outside of the Salem Meeting, in the civil courts controlled by Congregationalists, constituted a betrayal.

The Friends attempted to curtail their members' contact with and dependence upon the Congregationalist community not only by imposing strong sanctions against intermarriage, tavern haunting, and recourse to the courts but also by providing certain benefits. Essex County Quakers maintained a private fund for relieving their own poor and sick, and in 1716 the Salem Meeting proposed that "friends have Schooles Amongst themselves and not Suffer our Children to be brought up in the Corrupt Customes and Fashions of Our Enemys."[80] In order to further the religious education of adults, members circulated among themselves the writings of George Fox and other books supplied by the London Meeting. Quakers even had a cemetery in Salem separate from the burial places of the Congregationalists.[81] Informally, Friends favored each other in their economic activities, as Jonathan Springer's reliance on his fellow Quakers in Boston and Salem indicates. So close was the connection between sectarian membership and daily subsistence for some men that the sundering of ties to the Quaker community meant a loss of livelihood. Ostracized by the fellowship for failure to attend meetings regularly, Richard Oakes of Marblehead protested that "the Friends had denied him for Nothing, and that they have Ruined him and his family."[82] The Salem Meeting's ability to supply members' needs for relief, education, employment, and credit served to reduce the influence of both civil government and orthodox society over the lives of dissenters.

In some ways, the growth of the Quaker countercommunity gave

79. Records of the Salem Monthly Meeting, 18 July 1689; cf. Tolles, *Meetinghouse and Countinghouse,* 58–59, 73–74, 75–76.
80. Records of the Salem Monthly Meeting, 1712, 11 August 1716, 13 May 1731, and 11 September 1744.
81. Records of the Salem Monthly Meeting, 1713, 1720. The Quaker cemetery was situated on land in Salem donated by Thomas Maule.
82. Records of the Salem Monthly Meeting, 15 January 1717.

the Congregationalists just what they wanted: as little as possible to do with religious dissidents. But on another level, the development of Quakerism from an antiauthoritarian aberration into an effective, authoritative, institutional church was what made the Friends so threatening: they had created an alternative not only to the Congregational church but also to the local community itself. Although Essex County Quakers established specific institutions that replicated the functions served by those of the orthodox churches and civil society, the Friends' social organization had one singular characteristic: it was translocal. The Salem Meeting stands out on the social landscape as one of the few voluntary organizations that cut across the borders of individual towns and involved the inhabitants of several distinct geographic areas. Its membership included not only families from Salem but also residents of Boston, Lynn, Marblehead, and Gloucester as well as visitors from more distant places. Until the founding of Saint Michael's Episcopal Church at Marblehead in 1714, the only other religious fellowship in the county that commanded such strong translocal loyalties was the suspected witch coven that was also centered at Salem. In addition, through their quarterly and yearly meetings and their far-flung business contacts and networks of intermarriage, the Essex County Quakers maintained close and regular connection with their coreligionists elsewhere in New England and in New Jersey, Long Island, and Pennsylvania. When the Boston Quakers had become numerous enough to establish their own meeting, the Friends in Essex County contributed to a fund for building their new place of worship; when Salem Quakers suffered from epidemics, they received relief funds from the Philadelphia Meeting.[83] Because the Friends identified themselves as members of a religious fellowship that transcended geographic boundaries rather than as inhabitants of a particular town, their first loyalty was to fellow sectarians irrespective of where they resided.

By contrast, among the orthodox the purely localistic identification based on residence in a particular town was considerably more intense, and intercourse among Congregationalists from different geographic communities was far less frequent, particularly in northern Essex County with its strong tradition of congregational autonomy. Unlike the Salem Meeting, whose membership came from several surrounding communities, orthodox congregations comprised families who all lived in the same town, and membership within the church enhanced the sense of belonging to that town. Occasions that brought together the representatives of different churches from

83. Records of the Salem Monthly Meeting, 1709; Tolles, *Meetinghouse and Countinghouse*, 69–70, 89.

separate towns—ordinations, meetings of ministerial associations, and ecclesiastical councils—aroused suspicion among a large segment of the laity and the clergy who feared that such gatherings infringed on the independence of individual congregations and encroached on the integrity of local life.[84] The same exclusivistic ethos characterized the rituals of civil society at the local level, many of which aimed at defining the community and preserving it from contamination by external influences: the annual "perambulations" of town borders delineated the physical boundaries that separated Gloucester from adjacent communities; town selectmen "warned out" families not admitted as inhabitants. Effecting any public improvement that entailed cooperation between two towns required infinite patience on the part of county officials, who had to cope with the inevitable clash of particularistic concerns: the simple process of building a bridge between Ipswich and Gloucester took years because of haggling between the two towns.

The inhabitants of colonial New England's communities prized their autonomy, and nowhere was this local identity more intensely and uniformly felt than in northern Essex County, where the native son John Wise made independence from centralized control as much an object of folk adoration as he made ancestors.[85] Only the Friends withheld homage from this icon. The Quaker fellowship was not just indifferent to geographic boundaries; its essential ethos was antilocalistic. The Salem Meeting not only limited and discouraged its members' engagement in the town community but also fostered actively their antagonism to local society itself by the ritualized accounting and recounting of "sufferings." Obligations like the minister's rate, the meetinghouse fund, and militia training that the orthodox accounted as identifying badges of membership within the community the Quakers styled as "sufferings," contributions distrained from dissenters. The Salem Meeting's leading laymen made regular "inspections" of these losses and entered "what friends suffered, when and at whose hands" in a ledger that it "may not be forgotten but that it may stand upon record for generations yet unborn, to see how faithful friends took Joyfully the Spoyling of their goods for the answer of a good Conscience towards God. . . ."[86]

84. Youngs, *God's Messengers,* 92–98.
85. See esp. John Wise, *The Churches Quarrel Espoused* (1710), 2d ed. (Boston, 1715) and *Vindication of the Government of New England Churches* (Boston, 1717).
86. The records of the Salem Monthly Meeting contain several "Accompts of Sufferings" interspersed throughout the minutes. In 1712 the Salem Meeting ordered published the "sufferings" of two Quakers forced to serve in the Port Royal expedition, and in 1716 the meeting reminded members to keep a precise record of their financial losses in goods distrained to pay the minister's rate.

It was this antilocalistic animus of provincial Quakerism that constituted the link between social experience and religious prejudice among the orthodox into the eighteenth century. The Friends' real heresy lay less in their challenge to religious loyalties than in their subversion of proper social loyalties by eroding the claim of individual towns to the allegiance of inhabitants. As the Friends enhanced their denominational cohesion in the early eighteenth century, they developed an increasingly ambiguous relationship to the localities where they resided: Quakers were in the community but not of it. Membership in a translocal religious organization claiming their primary allegiance made the Friends' civic status suspect, a situation similar to that of American Catholics until quite recently. Or to draw a parallel closer in time: just as ambiguous sectarian loyalties made people vulnerable to accusations of witchcraft in 1692, so ambiguous social and political loyalties sustained discrimination against dissenters during the eighteenth century. As objections to Quaker doctrine and practice diminished after 1690, this new source of friction maintained an old antagonism.

In 1726, Samuel Bownas returned to northern New England and passed through Essex County. The state of his sect at Newbury was dismal: the growing port held "only a very few Friends . . . not above nine or ten in all." An equally dispiriting reception awaited him in the vicinity of Lynn and Salem. Here the Friends retained some numerical strength, but the promising growth in the earlier part of the eighteenth century had not continued: their ranks consisted chiefly of the descendants of believers, while the absence of any significant traders and their proneness to "constant Cavil or Dispute" attenuated their influence.[87] Bownas did not even bother to stop at Cape Ann. There the evolution of informal mechanisms for restricting membership in the community to the orthodox had effectively suppressed all sectarian competition. Perhaps by 1730 Gloucester's orthodox majority had come to regard the Friends as "a benign if heretical sect."[88] If so, the inhabitants had little occasion to express this enlightened outlook, for the town had spent the last forty years excluding Quaker families from their community.

87. Bownas, *Account,* 175, 178.
88. Worrall, *Quakers,* 43. Besides those of the sisters of James Dyke, no names of Gloucester inhabitants appear in the records of the Salem Monthly Meeting after 1730; probate records also identify no inhabitants as Quakers. Four people were fined for absence from public worship in Gloucester after 1730, and two of these may have had Quaker sympathies, since they were members of the Hadlock family.

The Mental World of
Samuel Sewall

DAVID D. HALL

Samuel Sewall (1652–1730) was a Bostonian and proud of it. A sometime suitor, father, and husband, he suffered more than his due share of difficulties in each of these roles. From time to time he fell ill; when in good health, he spent an inordinate amount of time by the bedsides of others who were sick or dying. He attended a great many funerals. He dreamed once that a French fleet was descending on Boston. And each spring he rejoiced to hear the "chippering" of the swallows in the thin sunshine of April.[1]

These diverse items are known to us through the diary that Sewall kept throughout his adult life. The importance of this diary to historians of colonial politics has long been recognized. Sewall stood near the center of Massachusetts politics, and he left behind a richly detailed account of issues and alliances within the circle of the governing elite. The importance of the diary to historians of the family became clear in 1944, with the publication of Edmund S. Morgan's *The Puritan Family*. No other source is so revealing of how kinship was understood among the colonists or of the relationship between courtship and marriage.[2] Still more recently, and in keeping with the shift among historians to a point of view upon religion and culture that may loosely be termed anthropological, the importance of the diary for our understanding of broader, more elusive beliefs and attitudes in provincial New England has begun to be acknowledged.[3] What follows is an interpretation of the diary from this point of view,

---

1. *The Diary of Samuel Sewall, 1674–1729*, newly edited from the manuscript at the Massachusetts Historical Society by M. Halsey Thomas, 2 vols. (New York, 1973), 2:829, 685. I have also used the *Letter-Book of Samuel Sewall*, 2 vols., *Collections of the Massachusetts Historical Society*, 6th ser., 1–2 (1886–88), to which references in the text appear as LB 1 or LB 2.

2. Edmund S. Morgan, *The Puritan Family* (New York, 1966 ed.), 150–60.

3. David Stannard, *The Puritan Way of Death* (New York, 1977), 68–70, 113–16.

75

a reconstruction of Sewall's mental world as it is revealed in his responses to many kinds of phenomena, from the sounds he heard at night to the scriptural texts of Sunday's sermon.

Scriptural texts and sounds are but two of the patterns of information that run through the diary. It is these patterns that provide the clues to Sewall's deeper and persisting attitudes. He kept track of rainbows and bolts of lightning, of illnesses and deaths, of bearers at a funeral. He noted down the times at which hundreds of events occurred and the names of those who brought him any kind of news. Such patterns (and there are many more) tell us something about his sensibility. Further clues lie in certain words that recur in the diary, words like "startled" and "sudden." Sewall's mental world is especially evident in the interweaving of the patterns in the diary. They flow into one another just as Sewall in his thinking moved back and forth between all sorts of moods and information.

Altogether, the notations in the diary lead us into a mental world that would otherwise be largely hidden from us. This world is very different from ours. Sewall was a Puritan, of course, and we are not, but the distance between his sensibility and ours grows out of several other circumstances. Simple changes make a difference. We are accustomed to brightly lit space, and our sense of sight is correspondingly acute. Sewall lived in relative darkness and depended more on his sense of sound than on his sense of sight. Lacking most of what we know as science and medicine, he viewed earthquakes, comets, and disease as outward, physical equivalents of moral and spiritual forces. It is almost a cliché for historians to observe that people living in preindustrial society understood time in a way that differs from ours, and this is true of Sewall. His Puritanism is something the diary says much about, but in this context most statements by historians become irrelevant. Sewall's religion is less a matter of textbook doctrines than of deeply felt responses to the great crises and *rites de passage* of human life. Religion added to the anxieties that loom so large in Sewall's mental world. It was also a means of reassurance, providing him with ritual modes of surmounting conflict and crisis. As we enter Sewall's mind through his diary, we should expect some of our assumptions about him and his times to be confirmed and others to be challenged.

I

Sewall's Boston was a dark place at night. In the confusion that darkness brought, someone standing outside Sewall's door swung a club at a small boy, thinking he was a dog (1:29). People coped with the dark by going to bed early and arising at daybreak. The town became quiet once the streets were empty, so quiet that the beat of a drum in Charlestown could be heard across the water in Boston (1:266). Any sudden sound awakened all who slept. "At night a great Uproar and Lewd rout in the Main Street [as a drunken man wandered about]. Many were startled, thinking there had been fire, and went to their windows out of Bed between 9. and 10. to see what was the matter" (1:144). Time and again, thunderstorms roused Sewall from his bed (1:400). At night, thunder was hard to distinguish from "great guns" (1:330), like those that were fired on Castle Island late one evening after news had arrived of a son's being born to James II. The guns, bells, and drums that celebrated the birth of Prince James caused "Alarm" for "fear of fire . . . the thing was so sudden, People knew not the occasion" (1:175).

At any hour of the night or the day, the cry of "fire" sent Sewall and his fellow townspeople to their windows or into the streets. No minister could hope to hold his audience if the alarm—someone shouting or a bell ringing furiously—reached the ears of the congregation. "Uproar in N[orth] M[eeting] House by Cry of Fire" (1:301). "When Mr. Willard was in his first Prayer, there was a Cry of Fire, which made the People rush out" (1:262). Panic was rooted in the very real danger that people faced in a town of closely packed wooden houses and without any effective means of putting fires out.

The dangers of this urban environment were many. A robber crept into Sewall's house one night and made off with a load of silver (1:568). Waves of disease swept over the town, taking lives by the score. Sewall himself came close to dying from a case of smallpox, in 1678 (i:xxxiii). Thereafter the "fear" he had of the disease was akin to his fear of fire. When the news of a fresh case reached him, it caused a "great startling, lest it should spread as in 1678" (1:126). With the safety of his children in mind, he noted the location of reported cases, since distance was some indication of peril or safety (1:100). None of his children were to die from smallpox. None became so hungry as to riot for food, as some townspeople did in the winters of 1710 and 1712 (2:638, 715). No sons were impressed to become victims of badly managed expeditions against the French (2:844). More fortunate in some ways, the Sewalls were not spared in others. Samuel would bury eight of his own children (LB 1:236) and attend the funerals of many kin and close friends. Asleep at night, he "dreamed that all my Children were dead except Sarah" (1:328) and that his wife, Hannah, had died (1:219).

The street life of provincial Boston occasioned other nightmares. Every so often carts rumbled by carrying Indians or pirates to the

Common to be executed (1:21, 22). Great spectacles these, with thousands attending and printers hurrying to publish narratives of the event. Beforehand, people would jam the meetinghouse to view the condemned as they listened to their final sermon (1:97). Going to the Common once when pirates he had helped to apprehend were being executed, Sewall was astonished at the size of the crowd; the "River was cover'd with People" packed aboard at least 100 boats. The sounds were just as remarkable: "When the Scaffold was let sink, there was such a Screech of the Women that my wife heard it sitting in our Entry next the Orchard" a mile away (1:509). Some months later came the emotional response. "Last night I had a very sad Dream that held me a great while. As I remember, I was con-demn'd and to be executed" (1:518).

Sewall's dream life came closer to reality in his recurring night-mare that the French were attacking Boston (1:544; 2:829). The fre-quent wars between France and Britain never actually led to such a battle. But even in times of peace Sewall and his fellow townsmen were kept on edge by "Rumors and Fears" (1:76) of Indian conspir-acies. Sewall's uneasiness about the future was rooted in a broader fear of change. As he walked about the town or listened to the sounds outside his home, the rhythms of unwelcome change became appar-ent to him in the noise of a dueling ceremony (1:137) or intrusions on the Sabbath (1:502). Meanwhile, the world of politics in which he moved was losing its coherence. Leaders, he believed, should act as one: "Agreement makes Kingdoms flourish" (LB 1:278). The quar-reling he overheard among the ministers (1:270) or encountered in meetings of the council (1:363) was disturbing evidence of the dif-ference between the ideal and the actual. Politics was now a matter of factions—for or against the governor, the Mathers, the old charter, the new. The old guard, the "true New England" men (1:385) who cherished the ways of the holy commonwealth, reassemble at certain ordinations and funerals (1:180). At others, the alliances that come and go in Massachusetts politics become momentarily evident in the designation of participants. People watch to see where any new-comer to the scene will attend church services (1:169). No longer do the elite close ranks on ceremonial occasions. The governor skips the lecture service (2:900), while the pew reserved for "Gentlewomen" is almost empty (2:881).

Preferring unity to conflict, Sewall usually retreated when dis-agreement turned into anger. Any kind of violence upset him. When his father-in-law complained of something he had done, Sewall felt so ashamed—and disturbed—that he changed into Latin when he set down the episode (1:35). Yet there was no way he could avoid the anger that people high and low felt about their situation. He was present in Old South when "in Sermon time there came in a female Quaker, in a Canvas Frock, her hair disshevelled and loose like a Periwigg, her face as black as ink. . . . It occasioned the greatest and most amazing uproar that I ever saw" (1:44). Anonymous threats to burn down certain houses (1:34) and the fires actually set by discontented servants and slaves (1:37, 531) menaced life and property. He read or heard of printed "Libels" circulating about the town or pinned up on someone's fence (1:21, 97, 81). And on one awful occasion, he learned that the Reverend Increase Mather, furious at being forced out of the Harvard presidency, was prophesying that "some great Judgment will fall on Capt. Sewall, or his family" (1:455).

Sewall worried over Mather's words because he felt that prophecies of judgment were all too likely to come true. The changes overtaking Boston were changes sure to anger the God who had singled out and protected the founders of New England. Inheriting their vision of a holy commonwealth, Sewall also shared with them the fear that any breach of faith with God was certain to be punished. On his own he did what he could to uphold the customs and restrictions of the old days. He broke up street games and encouraged shopkeepers to stay open on Christmas Day (2:795). In court he urged passage of a law against incest, believing it would strengthen the covenant between God and the colonists (1:333–34). Back home he followed anxiously the signs of the times. Good news was any victory over the French in North America or Europe (1:306), or the death of Louis XIV. But all too often the news was bad. Expeditions against the French have ended in disaster (1:574). Rumor is replaced by fact: the king still lives (1:492). The governor was insisting that persons place their hands upon the Bible when they take an oath in court (1:117). The Huguenots were being persecuted (1:102). Such "evil tidings" seemed to portend a yet greater "Darkness," the vaster gloom that was the "Night" of God's disfavor (LB 2:31–32). Given what was happening in New England, would the darkness of the final days foretold in Revelation ever be succeeded by the sunrise? Who could be certain of the future?

Coming home at night, Sewall left the darkness behind him as he entered his house. Here he was on safe ground; here peace and quiet reigned: *"Laus Deo"* (1:470). The same feeling of transition from danger to safety came over him as he reentered Boston from a trip elsewhere: "by this means I had the pleasure to view the Wall of our City, and pass in, and out at the Gate. . . . The LORD keep the City!" (2:860). Outside the walls that enclosed his home and city, safety could be found in close friendships, the kinds he formed with Harvard classmates and some kin. "Glad to hear that you intend to visit us again," he wrote a cousin, "because real friends are the principal comfort and relief against the evils of our own Life" (LB 1:86). Security could be found in Third Church, where reassurance flowed from being part of a tight community and from hearing Samuel Willard preach that "God would not forget the Faith of those who came first to New England, but would remember their Posterity with kindness" (1:127). And feelings of security came occasionally from dreams, as when he imagined "that our Saviour in the dayes of his Flesh when upon earth, came to Boston and abode here" (1:91). Surely in the end light would triumph over dark!

II

Craving security himself, Sewall also sought it for his family. As he went about this task, he could not separate the welfare of his wife and children from that of New England. Family, church, town and country, all shared in a collective destiny. He linked them together at a private fast: "Pray'd for Sister Dorothy, my family, New England, that God would fit me for his good pleasure in doing and suffering" (1:277). At another fast, he begged for blessings upon his children and their kin, the governor and the General Court, missionaries to the Indians and Old South, Connecticut and New York, "all the European Plantations in America," the queen and "all Europe" (1:589). The close at hand and the distant were both deserving of his care. Yet the family still came first in order of concern. There were steps he took to protect them, to build strong walls around their house, that he did not take for others.

A new addition to his house is under way. Before construction begins, Sewall consults with a minister as to whether the times are propitious (1:287). While the floor is being laid, he drives a pin into the frame (1:317), an act he will repeat for the houses of friends and kin and for occasional ships and meetinghouses (1:11, 300; 2:639). Soon after he and the family move into their new rooms, they hold a private fast asking God to bless the place where they now live (1:337). Some years later, Sewall sets up wooden carvings on gateposts in front of the house, two "cherubims heads" that symbolize the presence of protecting forces (1:400; see Exodus 25:18–22).

The children born to him and Hannah are carried to the meetinghouse during their first week of life to be baptized. In later life Sewall liked to remember the occasions when he had held a newborn child in his arms as it was baptized "upon the Sabbath Day in the Solemn Assembly of God's saints" (1:313, n. 14). Naming the children is no casual task, for the right choice may add protection (1:175, 324). For his children he also seeks the benefits of "Blessings" from old men, on one occasion transporting the whole family to the bedside of a man whose word (or touch?) he deems of special worth (1:282) and on another, presenting "all my stock" to the Reverend Nehemiah Walter of Roxbury, "desired his Blessing of them; which he did" (1:407).

Back within their home, father, mother, and children gather each morning and evening for a service of family devotion. Year in and year out the Sewalls pray, sing psalms, and read Scripture together. The prayers are explicit in their reference to family problems: the efforts of a married daughter to conceive (1:496), a son's quest for a suitable apprenticeship (1:327). Scripture reading proceeds "in Course" (1:115) as they go through Old and New Testaments in a sequence that resumes once the entire Bible has been read. Everyone in the family takes his turn at reading, Sewall's son Joseph commencing when he is ten years old (1:384) and his sisters at a later age (1:404).

The psalms they all sing together have a particular significance. Sewall lists by number in the diary the psalms he sang not only in household devotions but also in private meetings, in Old South, and in the "closet" of his own bedchamber. All this attention to record keeping rested on scriptural texts that described the saints in heaven as full of song. When Sewall burst out in song himself, he felt as though he caught a glimpse of heaven and its joys. The singing of psalms carried him closer to God. "I give you this Psalm-Book," he told a relative, "in order to your perpetuating this Song; and I would have you pray that it may be as an Introduction to our Singing with the Choir above" (2:731). Noting the death of a Harvard classmate, he recalled that they had "sung many a Tune in Consort; hope shall sing Hallelujah together in Heaven" (2:878). Together with his family, he shared the same feelings of joy as they sang the stanzas of their favorite psalms.

The shared experience of reading Scripture was rich in benefits. It was, of course, Sewall's means of ensuring that his children learned the truth essential to salvation. Scripture was life-giving and life-sustaining: "Thy life to mend/this book attend" ran a verse in *The New England Primer.* The routine of learning Scripture was also an act of religious devotion. Every evening the Sewalls could in this manner renew their sense of oneness with God's will. And for Sewall himself, reading Scripture was another way by which he compensated for the evils of the world. It was a comfort and a shield; it helped him place things in perspective. On the evening after the thief who had robbed him had been caught, Sewall turned to a famous Puritan commentary on Job 5:2 and read how "The humble submission to the *stroke* of God, turns into a *Kiss*—which I thank God, I have in this Instance experienced" (1:568). Leaving a long meeting of the council, "weary and uneasy," Sewall came home and found it "a singular Refreshment to me to read 2 Cor. 6. especially from the 14th to the end" (2:632).

Reading, indeed, often became a "cordial" (1:454), heartwarming and heart-renewing refreshment, like *The Mourners Cordiall,* written by his pastor, Samuel Willard. Sewall gave away copies of this book (1:287) in order to extend its benefit. All his life he enjoyed giving books away—books of his own composing or commissioning, like Cotton Mather's *American Tears upon the Ruines of the Greek Churches* (1:560), great sets of scriptural commentary by Matthew Poole (2:741), Psalters bound in "Turkey-Leather" (2:731), or New England classics like John Cotton's *Gods Promise to His Plantation* (1:120), which he gave to soldiers in his militia company as the old charter government was coming to an end. Sewall's eagerness to make such gifts was not the eagerness of an author or patron seeking recognition. He saw the gift relationship as a means of helping others gain comfort and a better understanding of God's will. In effect he gave away books as a form of blessing. Seeking the assurance of blessings for himself and his children, he was generous in exchange. The books and broadsides that circulated between him and his friends sustained a complex web of mutual caring and protection (1:554).

III

Sewall came to know the Bible practically by heart. After all those hours of reading Scripture, he could very nearly think in terms of biblical texts. When a woman died from choking on a piece of meat, Sewall's mind ran to 1 Corinthians 10:31: "Whether therefore ye eat, or drink, or whatsoever ye do, do all to the glory of God." Visiting with a woman who was ill, they talked of the fatal accident, and she too cited this verse (1:287). The coincidence was significant to Sewall. He was ever alert to special harmonies between events and scriptural texts. A stormy scene in council was preceded by his reading accidentally "Mr. Strong's Notes on Revelation 12 . . . : The last words were, prepare for it" (1:363). Could this really have occurred by accident? One way of finding out was by keeping track of texts. Hence the hundreds of entries in the diary, for the act of recording references to Scripture was essential if he was to perceive and profit from coincidences that someday might be clear.

The hundreds of references to time are complementary, in that keeping track of the rhythms of the universe was another way of comprehending the will of God. Sewall actually lived amid several modes of time. As a merchant, he had to cope with slow and uncertain communication with his business partners overseas. Months would go by before he knew whether a ship was lost or safe in port (LB 1:86). But while the rhythm of work was irregular and slow-paced, the rhythm of historical time was fixed in a certain pattern. The bits and pieces of news from abroad that reached Sewall fell into order as evidence that the sequence described in Revelation was rapidly unfolding. Historical time—the reign of a particular monarch, the phases of a war, the events in Massachusetts politics—was really prophetic time, and Sewall poured his energies into deciphering the relationship between the two. Time for him was also a complex structure of coincidences. For this very reason, it was essential to know when an event had occurred, for the correlations he detected could be specially revealing of God's will. Time was finally "GOD's time" (2:660) in the sense that the ultimate rhythm of life was arbitrarily determined by God. As Sewall lay in bed listening to the clock tick away the minutes, its sound was cause for reflection on the profound contingency of life. To know this, to know time, was to feel that at any moment life could end.

Sewall could follow the passing of literal time in several ways. For him as for everyone who lived in preindustrial society, the rising and setting of the sun were key reference points in the cycle of the hours. When meetings of the council or the Superior Court ran late, it was "Candle-Light" when they ended, not this or that hour of the evening (2:773; 1:360). Traveling once to Springfield without his watch, Sewall was entirely dependent on light and dark as his temporal frame of reference: "a little after sunset," "by duskish," "when night came" (2:829–30). But in Boston he usually knew the time in hours, either by consulting his watch or (if he was at home) the clock he owned (1:177; 2:675) or by listening to the town bells.[4] His notations of the time in hours are invariably in the form of a "between," as in "between 3 and 4. p.m." (1:383), which suggests that his watch, like an hourglass, told time only by the hour. To tell the time in minutes, he had to be at home near his clock (2:707).

Spared the modern urgency to be punctual, Sewall worried nonetheless about the right and wrong ways of observing time. The days of the week were God's creation; the seven days of Genesis carried over into human history. Arguing unsuccessfully for legislation to

4. A [7th] *Report of the Record Commissioners of the City of Boston, Containing the Boston Records from 1660 to 1701* (Boston, 1881), 97.

replace "Tuesday, Thursday, and Satterday" with "Third, fifth and seventh," Sewall reminded his fellow councilors that "the Week only, of all parcells of time, was of Divine Institution, erected by God as a monumental pillar for a memorial of the Creation perfected in so many distinct days" (1:351). That being understood, it followed, according to Sewall, that the calendar should be cleansed of corruptions like the pagan names for days of the week. In the diary itself he kept up the practice of using numbers in place of names long after the almanacs published in New England had reverted to unpurified English practice.[5] And though the government would not reform the calendar, he used his powers as a magistrate to impede the celebration of Christmas and April Fools' Day. Hearing that some Boston schoolchildren were playing tricks on 1 April, Sewall exploded in a letter to their schoolmasters: "What an abuse is it of precious Time; what a Profanation! What an Affront to the Divine Bestower of it!" (LB 1:365). Sewall's sense of what was sacred had been rubbed the wrong way; for him the units of the calendar were a measure or mark of God's presence here on earth.

Meanwhile Sewall was filling the diary with notations of time that would help him understand the temporal relationships among events. To find that the "very day" a child had died he himself "accidentally lit upon, and nail'd up the verses" commemorating one of his own children was cause for reflection (1:429). As the diary lengthened into a record of activities, it enabled him to search out connections between past and present. Turning back the pages, Sewall discovered in 1691 that a fast he had kept "to pray that God would not take away but uphold me by his free Spirit" occurred "the very day of the week and year as much as could be that I set out for New York, which made me hope that twas a token for good that God would pardon that Sin and Sins since committed" (1:277). The coincidences that occurred in public events were many, some of them distressing, like the deaths of prominent persons "one after another" (1:16), and others reassuring, like the "News of the 18. Indians kill'd, and one Taken last Tuesday; which heard of just after the Appointment" of a day of prayer for the military expedition against Port Royal (1:562). All such relationships bespoke what the moral condition of the people in New England was and whether God was angry with them. The sequence of things, indeed the very flow of time,

5. The earliest of the New England almanacs to survive, those of Samuel Danforth from the mid-1640s, employ the compromise form of "the 1st month called March," etc. Josiah Flynt eliminated the names of the months from his puristic *An Almanack, or, Astronomical Calculations . . . For the Ensuing Year 1666* (Cambridge, Mass., 1666), but in the following year the compromise reappeared, and by 1673 the almanac makers were abandoning numbers altogether.

fluctuated in accordance with individual and collective faithfulness.

The deeper, more far-reaching rhythm that Sewall sought to capture was the rhythm foretold in Revelation. An eager reader of each "news letter" reaching Boston from abroad, he tried to discern in European history any evidence that the prophecies were being realized. "Out of the State of Europe for April, I read the project of the Marquis de Langalerie, formerly a great General, Of planting a Colony of Protestants in the Morea, supposing that he is the person God will improve for pulling down the Throne of Antichrist, is so designed in the Revelation" (2:826). News of the Company of Scotland and its scheme to colonize the Isthmus of Panama excited him to write the ministers of the Darien expedition about the meaning of their venture. "So soon as I was informd of it, and of their Expedition to Darien, I said within my self Surely the Company of Scotland is the Sixth Angel; And within this week, I am confirmed in my Opinion, having seen the Golden Girdle wherewith the Officers and privat Souldiers are girded" (LB 1:228). Closer to home, there were other coincidences in which he could rejoice. Discussing the prophecies with a houseguest, he was told "of a converted Turk, and of strange Visions at Meccha, in the year 1620, to be seen in Clark's Examples. It being the same year with Plimouth it affected me" (1:393). Here the emotion sprang from his ability to link the prophecies with the founding of America.[6] To be sure, there were coincidences that troubled him, as when Joseph Dudley received 666 votes in an election (1:61). His endless puzzling over witnesses and seals could sometimes aggravate his fear of what might lie ahead (LB 2:53–54). But on the whole, prophetic time was reassuring evidence of the promise of America and the coming victory of the saints.

Sewall nonetheless sensed that time was never to be understood as permanent or regular. Though prophecy unfolded, though the clock ticked away the hours by an unvarying beat, though the seven days of Genesis were stamped immutably upon the calendar, the will of God stood over and above any structures, even structures He created. All existence was contingent, all forms of time suspended, on His will. The unexpected crash of a glass to the floor (1:378) was like the crash of God's anger breaking in upon the flow of time: "How suddenly and with surprise can God destroy!" (1:418). The diary entries pile up as Sewall records the happening of the unexpected— the roaring of a cow in the street (1:288), the cry of fire or the "amaz-

---

6. Sewall's major effort to link prophecies of the kingdom to the history of America is *Phænomena quædam Apocalyptica . . . Or, Some Few Lines towards a Description of the New Heaven* (Boston, 1697). His millennialism is described in James W. Davidson, *The Logic of Millennial Thought* (New Haven, 1977), 22–23, 65–70.

ing News" (1:564) of someone's sickness, news of war or of a change in governors, and, most frightening of all, the deaths that happen without warning. Sewall was fascinated by such cases:

> all the town is filled with the discourse of Major Richards's Death, which was very extraordinarily suddain; was abroad on the Sabbath, din'd very well on Monday (1:318). Capt. John Wincoll mounting his Horse to ride . . . to the Point, falls off his Horse; in falling cries, Lord have mercy upon me, and dies immediately (1:322).
> We have had many very sudden deaths of late; but none more amazingly sudden, than that of the Learned President of Harvard . . . who when he was calld to pray in the Hall . . . was found dead in his bed! (LB 2:166).
> Our Neighbor . . . died extreme suddenly about noon. . . . People in the Street much Startled at this good Man's sudden Death (1:87).

Other entries reveal that Sewall had a special interest in those situations where, a "day Sennight," he himself had encountered someone in perfect health who now lay in the grave (1:326, 437).

The words that recur in entries of this kind are "sudden," "surprising," "unexpected," "startled," and "amazing." When Sewall adds the words "doleful" or "awfull," as he sometimes does (1:58; 2:796), the language is suggestive of his inner feelings. For himself a time had been appointed (1:81), yet he knew it not, and he therefore lived in fear that he would fall before he was prepared. "If we are not prepared, if Death surprise us, we are Everlastingly Undone" (2:753).

IV

Sewall's sense of hearing was like his sense of time, a faculty attuned to meanings that the slightest sound could carry. The beat of a drum and the rumble of guns, the "Hew and Cry" of the sheriff and the voice of the cryer of fish (1:10, 97, 78), these made up a system of signals that were commonplace events in a culture that depended upon such sounds for communication. Yet when an eccentric old woman wandered into Sewall's house one day and "much scare[d]" his children, the cries they made were "amazing" (1:369) to him, something unexpected and therefore frightening. The natural world provided many such experiences. However pleasant the "chippering" of the swallows every spring, the thunderstorms that awakened him at night were something else. Dozens of entries indicate his interest and concern. He was not unique in this regard: "Much Lightening . . . toward the Castle, which many observ'd and talk'd of" (1:280). And he shared with others his reaction to an earthquake. "I congratulat with you [he wrote a friend] our having survived the late terrible Earthquake. . . . Yet the crashing Noise was very amazing to me. . . . The young people were quickly frighted out of the Shaking clattering Kitchen, and fled with weeping Cryes into our Chamber, where they made a fire, and abode there till morning" (LB 2:229). The hysteria is evident, as is Sewall's artless attempt to reproduce in words the jumble of sounds he heard that morning. But there was more to report and ponder on. The rumbling continued, and someone living in Portsmouth had "heard a fine musical sound, like the sound of a Trumpet at a distance. He could not distinguish any Tune that he knew; but perceiv'd a considerable Variety of Notes" (LB 2:232).

In some part of Sewall's mind lay a reasoned understanding of thunder and lightning, and even of earthquakes.[7] But in his immediate behavior, and again in the diary, a deeper level of thought and feeling lies exposed. Abrupt and unexpected sounds were signals of a different order, deriving their meaning from prophecies of judgment. Describing Christ's return to earth in *The Day of Doom*, Michael Wigglesworth made much of its accompanying sounds—the crash of thunder, the blare of trumpets, the shrieks of the distressed. Any encounter with thunder, trumpets, or shrill cries in everyday life stirred associations in Sewall's mind with their meaning in the Book of Revelation. And more generally, abrupt sounds were the sensate medium of God's anger. Hence Sewall's automatic response to the cries of his children when the old woman frightened them: "The Lord save me and his people from astonishing, suddain, desolating Judgments" (1:369).

Like scriptural texts and time, moreover, sound derived its meaning from the structure of coincidences. It was rare for Sewall not to feel that thunder was related to some other evidence of God's presence. His mind ranged widely in seeking out these associations. The "day of the Coronation of K. Charles the 2d," dimly remembered from his childhood in England, was also a day of remarkable sounds: "the Thunder and Lightening of it" (l:xxx). At home one evening, Sewall listened to Cotton Mather "mentioning that more Ministers Houses than others proportionably had been smitten with Lightening; inquiring what the meaning of God should be in it." All at once a storm of hailstones smashed the windows of the room. Amid several efforts at interpretation, Sewall reminded Mather that "Monmouth made his discent into England about the time of the Hail in '85, Summer, that much cracked our South-west windows" (1:330, 331). Here the pattern of sound has become fused with the Protes-

7. Samuel Eliot Morison, "The Harvard School of Astronomy in the Seventeenth Century," *New England Quarterly* 7 (1934): 3–24.

tant cause, and, more broadly, with prophecy. Indeed the person who listened closely to the sounds of the universe could hear the Spirit speak, as in the music that echoed through the woods (LB 2:232), or perhaps in the mysterious "Noise of a Drumme in the air, Vollies of Shot, Report of Cannons" described in letters from Connecticut (1:49), or in the words emerging from a child too young to know their meaning. "About Monday night last as Joseph was going into the Cradle, He said, News from Heaven, the French were come, and mention'd Canada" (1:281).[8] To a father who dreamed of the French fleet descending on Boston, and who imagined that Louis XIV was an agent of the Antichrist, these words had to seem of supernatural origin.

It was from the heavens, after all, that the Holy Spirit would descend in the final days, bringing peace to some and judgment to others. Sewall knew of one moment in recent times when the Spirit had descended, a miraculous occasion at a college in Edinburgh when "the Lord came down with the Shout of a King among them" creating in that instant a "Heaven on Earth" (1:352). He would not experience any such revival in his own lifetime. But in his eagerness to hasten the Second Coming, he arranged for sound effects that anticipated those of Revelation. On New Year's Day of 1701, Sewall's townsfolk awoke in the morning to the sound of trumpets saluting the new year, the new century, and by implication the kingdom that lay just ahead (1:440). Such was the hope of the man who hired the trumpeters.

V

Day in and day out, Sewall was constantly aware of portents. The range of signals was immense. Only once did he chance upon the "rare and awful Sight" of Siamese twins (2:729, 730). Comets and eclipses were items more frequently observed, though his commentary on them dwindled over time to a bare notation (1:426). Early on, during King Philip's War, he responded strongly to an eclipse: "Morning proper fair, the wether exceedingly benign, but (to me) metaphoric, dismal, dark and portentous, some prodigie appearing in every corner of the skies" (1:12). As in this example, most of what he saw or heard became associated in his mind with anxiety and fear—fear for the welfare of his family and New England, anxiety about his own relationship to God, fear of being caught unprepared.

8. Edward Taylor records a story told by Urian Oakes, the president of Harvard, about an infant who spoke from his cradle. William P. Upham, "Remarks," *Proceedings of the Massachusetts Historical Society*, 2d ser., 13 (1899–1900): 128.

But whenever a rainbow appeared in the heavens, he felt better. A rainbow in 1687 attracted wide attention—"People were gazing at it from one end of the Town to tother"—no doubt because it seemed to mean that the troubles of that period would soon end (1:131).[9] Thirty-five years later, Sewall was greatly relieved when a marvelous rainbow appeared while he and his council colleagues were distressed about events: "A Rainbow is seen just before night, which comforts us against our Distresses as to the affairs of the Expedition" (1:568). In his letter book he expanded on his feelings:

> At Boston upon the Lord's Day . . . about 6. p.m. a Noble *Rainbow* was seen in the Cloud, after great Thundering, and Darkness, and Rain: One foot thereof stood upon Dorchester Neck, the Eastern end of it; and the other foot stood upon the Town. . . . For the entire Compleatness of it, throughout the whole Arch, and for its duration, the like has been rarely seen. . . . I hope this a sure Token that CHRIST Remembers his Covenant for his beloved *Jews* under their Captivity and Dispersion; and that He will make haste to prepare for them a City that has foundations, whose Builder and Maker is GOD (LB 2:248).

Here as elsewhere his mind flowed easily from rainbows to prophecy, and from prophecy to assurance.

The hopes and fears that mingle in his entries about portents are notably entangled whenever the subject is death. Death was always present in his mind, whether manifested in his dream life or a topic of explicit reflection (1:183–84). Often it was someone's illness that prompted him to think of death, for sickness and death were equivalent in being outward signs of spiritual impurity. "Sin," as Sewall said to Increase Mather, "is the Sting of death" (LB 1:391). Cotton Mather made the point succinctly in a sermon he "preach'd of God's Punishing Sin with Sickness" (2:736). Expressed in slightly different terms, the relationship between the spiritual and the physical involved "afflictions" that God "measure[d] out" to persons who could benefit from them. It was God who "appointed . . . pain," though the reasons for His doing so, Sewall explained to his aunt, were usually hidden from those who suffered (LB 1:80). Sickness and death, then, were aspects of the process by which God distinguished true believers from false, the humble from the proud. It is no wonder that one of Sewall's servants could not sleep at night because she "was afraid she should dye" (2:731) or that Sewall's son Samuel, reminded by his father of another young child's death, should "burst out into a bitter Cry" because "he was afraid he should die" (1:249).

9. Cotton Mather expands on the meaning of rainbows in *Thoughts for the Day of Rain. In Two Essay's. I. The Gospel of the Rainbow. . . . II. The Saviour with His Rainbow* (Boston, 1712). The relevant scriptural texts are Genesis 9:13 and Revelation 4:3.

But as real as these fears were, death was also an experience charged with hope and joy. Sitting by the bedsides of the dying, Sewall witnessed patience and a feeling of oneness with Christ far more often than terror or undue concern. To be sure, the pain was difficult to bear when no physical remedies were at hand to ease it (2:866). Many prayed for death to come quickly and spare them more distress; the sooner it came, the sooner they would be with Christ. Sewall's friend John Bayley had to wait many months. Visiting him in January 1706, Sewall found Bayley "in a very pious humble frame in submitting to the afflicting hand of God" (1:539). In that October, Bayley "said he had been a long time in a storm at the Harbours Mouth, hop'd he should not be swallow'd on Quicksands, or split on Rocks. God had not yet forsaken him. . . . Said, Here I Wait!" (1:553). In the next month, his words to Sewall were "I long to be at home; why tarry thy chariot wheels?" (1:555). Death came at last in January 1707. If few had to wait this long, others shared with Bayley the joyous expectation of entering paradise. A Quincy relative of Sewall's, feeling the end approach, spoke "pretty freely to me. Saith he must run with open arms to a dying Saviour" (1:384). And a woman who at first complained that dying was hard ended by saying, "How long Lord, how long? Come Lord Jesus!," and when asked what she had said, answered, "How good is God" (1:343). The God who appointed pain was the same God who pardoned the repentant and granted them eternal life. "Our HULDAH's gone to Gods *Jerusalem*," Sewall affirmed in his epitaph for Judith Hull; this faithful wife and mother had "Triumph'd over . . . DEATH. Perfect in *Thoughts, Words, Deeds,* She soars on high" (1:335). To her, as to many others, the trumpet blast that ushered in the day of judgment was also herald of the gospel, the joyful news of God's promise to the faithful.

These contradictions of hope and fear were resolved, or at least the tension between them was lessened, in ritual practice. Confronting sickness and death, Sewall turned to prayer as the means of aiding others through their crises. The remedy for sin was clear: to seek pardon and relief from the "Great Physician" (LB 2:12). Prayer was the means by which Sewall turned doubt into hope, fear into assurance, sickness into health, death into life.[10]

Hannah awakens him in the night and says she is going into labor. Sewall rises, prays, then sends for the midwife. Once it is daybreak,

---

10. Puritan devotional practice is described in rich detail in Charles Hambrick-Stowe, "The Practice of Piety: Puritan Devotional Disciplines in Seventeenth Century New England" (Ph.D. diss., Boston University, 1980). David Stannard has distorted our understanding of Puritanism by citing in *The Puritan Way of Death* only those parts of the *Diary* which describe someone's fears of dying.

he walks to the house of Samuel Willard "and desire[s] him to call God." When he returns, "The Women call me into chamber and I pray there." He sends for Cotton and Increase Mather to pray, and, when problems persist, to yet another minister (1:459). Major Walley has a badly infected foot. A group of ministers and councilors gather at his bed to pray. "Major Walley was easy all the time of the exercise, had not one Twinging pain" (2:674). One of Sewall's daughters has given birth. Suddenly she worsens. It is late at night. Servants try "to call up Mr. Wadsworth; but could not make the family hear." Sewall thinks of another minister, "who came and pray'd very well with her" (2:645). No doctor is summoned.

With death the ritual is even more rigorously pursued and its meaning made more explicit. "My little Judith languishes and moans, ready to die. . . . About 2 *mane*, I rise, read some Psalms and pray with my dear Daughter. Between 7. and 8. . . . I call Mr. Willard, and he prays. Told Mr. Walter of her condition at [a funeral the day before], desiring him to give her a Lift towards heaven" (1:266). The poignant moments are many, but for Sewall the grief was lessened by his practice of devotion. Toward his daughter Elizabeth, dying as an adult, he stretched out every possible "Lift towards heaven." There was prayer in a private meeting, there were prayers at her bedside by some five different ministers, there were prayers requested of the minister who preached the Thursday lecture and of the minister of Old South. Sewall and his wife were continually at her side in prayer (2:823–24).

Sewall was scarcely less generous with his prayers when friends and even ordinary people asked him for assistance. Many a day and night he spent with someone who found solace in his prayers. Often he arranged for a minister to pray on a person's behalf during the regular church service. The "notes" that were the means of making these requests become themselves symbolic tokens. "I asked [a sick man] whether I should put up a Note for him. He seem'd very desirous of it; and said he counted it the best Medicine" (2:863).[11] There was always a dissenting voice, that of the man who on his deathbed asked a group of ministers gathered around *not* to pray. On the spot they spoke "pretty roundly" to him, and the dying man relented. But Sewall was aghast: "His former carriage was very startling and amazing to us" (1:267).

---

11. A note that Sewall put up for himself after he recovered from illness, and another by his son Joseph, are quoted or paraphrased in the *Diary*, 2:699, 695. The notes put up in Northampton during Jonathan Edwards's ministry are described in Stephen J. Stein, " 'For their Spiritual Good': The Northampton, Massachusetts, Prayer Bids of the 1730s and 1740s," *William and Mary Quarterly*, 3d ser., 37 (1980): 261–85.

Amazing, indeed, to someone who prayed as often and as passionately as Sewall (2:617). Prayer had discernible effects. Like reading, it was an act of devotion that consoled. "I got up pretty early, being forc'd to it by a laxness. Had sweet communion with God in Prayer, and in reading the last two Sermons I heard in London, about Assurance etc." (1:425). For the sick and dying it was another form of "cordial," easing pain and removing doubt. Believing wholly in prayer, Sewall saw it as an instrument of grace; and when in the course of aiding an old woman he asked Samuel Willard "to give her one Lift more heaven-ward" (1:343), he meant those marvelous words exactly. The soul rose to heaven on the wings of prayer.

VI

Second only to prayer in importance as a ritual was the fast day. Sewall took part in at least seventy-five fasts during the years covered by the diary, and his care in describing many of these services is revealing of his strong hopes for them as means of reconciliation. Fasts were occasioned by a variety of events—drought and military defeats, the sickness or death of someone prominent, politics at home and abroad (1:166). He and his family observed a number of private fasts, as did the religious "meeting" he attended. Old South, the General Court, the council, each of these larger communities practiced the ritual with Sewall in attendance. No governor could declare a fast without having Sewall scrutinize the fast-day bill to see whether it was adequate (1:361, 475).

Ever anxious to increase his family's share of blessings, Sewall arranged for private fasts at key occasions and transitions. The change to new quarters in his house was a step completed by a fast that included three ministers and several members of the council. "I appointed this day to . . . bless us in our new house. The Lord pardon and doe for us beyond our hopes, contrary to our Deserts" (1:337). Some twenty-odd years later, shortly after Hannah Sewall died, a large group gathered at the house for a "Family Sacrifice" that Sewall spent a week arranging. The scriptural text central to the exercise was Psalm 79:8: "O remember not against us former iniquities: Let thy tender mercies speedily prevent us; For we are brought very low" (2:878–80).

Sewall's Puritanism cannot be understood save in terms of rituals like the fast day, and these in turn cannot be understood save in terms of his clear feeling that he had sinned. Of the feelings and responses that make up his religious sensibility, this one is most crucial. Time and again he recognizes that human nature is corrupt.

Time and again he acknowledges that God holds him to account for his sins (2:655) and will cast him off unless he repents. Repentance is what he seeks to express; pardon is what he begs in all his prayers. He knows that wrongdoing will increase his jeopardy. He knows it is dangerous to feel secure. When "afflictions" strike, as so often happens, they must be understood as signals that he is wandering from the faith. Adversity is good (1:512), Sewall insists, because it sharpens his determination to trust and obey (2:617). Afflictions can be "sanctified" and turned into blessings, as when a fire in his house is discovered and extinguished. "The good Lord sanctify this Threatening; and his Parental Pity in improving our selves for the Discovery of the fire, and Quenching it. The Lord teach me what I know not; and wherein I have done amiss help me to doe so no more!" (2:622). Vows to obey, to do one's duty more earnestly and fully, arise out of such crises. His brother Stephen, lying ill, "Is very desirous to live, and makes vows to serve God better, if his life be spared" (1:299). Sewall himself pledges to "Walk in New Obedience" even while wondering whether he can ever do enough (2:861, 622). Obedience means a life of self-denial (1:449). God is just, and all depends upon His will: "help me to live upon Him alone" (1:417).

The anxiety is evident. Sewall's piety was rooted in his fear of being punished because he had not done enough. He had this feeling about the human relationships in his life; the dreams he had of his wife and children being dead flowed from a sense of guilt about his role as husband and father (1:65, 328). But the focus of his prayers for pardon was upon another, more important relationship. It was God as judge who made Sewall feel so anxious about each rite of passage in his life. Was he unworthy to become a member of the church (1:39)? Did his children die because he stumbled in his faith? Would death find him unprepared? These uncertainties extended beyond his family to include the church, New England, and the cause of true religion. Would the church lapse from purity if he accepted any change in the basis of membership (1:76)? Would he betray the mission of New England if he placed his hand upon the Bible as he took an oath (1:165–66)? So many things seemed uncertain, so much was precarious!

Yet still he persevered. After all, this world was transient. Ahead lay Canaan, "infinitely the best Country, wherein are all Friends and no Enemies; all Conveniences and no Inconveniences, for perpetuity" (LB 2:88). And God was merciful. He answered many prayers and fasts with favoring providences: the rains came (2:857), the sick were restored to health, defeat turned into victory. Whatever the literal consequences, fasting and prayer functioned to transmute

anxiety into assurance. They were Sewall's means of resolving contradictions, acts that he performed "incessantly" (1:xxxiii) to give
himself security.

VII

Incessant is indeed the word for much of his behavior. The diary is
put together out of thousands of entries that arrange themselves into
a handful of patterns. The patterning was purposeful, a means of
establishing the coincidences that so fascinated Sewall. The diary
helped order his world. It enabled him to link the small-scale to the
large, the microcosm of the Sewall family and events in Boston to
the macrocosm of God's plan for redemption. Turning back to older
entries, he could see how things came together, how times and scriptural texts and thunderstorms were all conjoined. Often, of course,
he could not tell the meaning of his data. But it was reassuring to
believe that all would someday become clear.

To any modern reader of the diary, the mental world of Samuel
Sewall must seem very distant. We no longer think of sudden deaths
and rainbows as portentous. Nor can we participate in so magical an
understanding of the universe—magical in the sense that connections and coincidences exceed cause-and-effect relationships as we
conceive them, and also in the sense that Sewall believed he could
manipulate the spiritual forces that flowed about him. Certainly the
diary leads us into a world that is not our own. Sewall views truth as
fixed and unchanging (LB 2:48). His sense of time is fundamentally
ahistorical, for the same basic scheme is repeated in all that happens.
Time is really time*less* as Sewall, like the makers of New England
gravestones, looks ahead to eternity.[12]

Perhaps he lived in greater fear than we do. So, at least, some
historians have argued in regard to the people who lived in early
modern Europe.[13] Yet in the light it throws upon his piety, the diary
suggests the remarkable capacity of Sewall's religious culture to meet
the basic human need for security and consolation.[14] His piety sustained and enlivened a range of ritual practices, and the diary allows
no doubt that he drew real comfort from them. The cycle of repentance and renewal, whether formalized in the structure of the fast
day or experienced in personal meditations, was the deepest rhythm
of Sewall's psychic life. And as the diary reveals in astonishing detail,

12. Ian Watt, *The Rise of the Novel* (Berkeley, 1971), 21–23.

13. Robert Mandrou, *Introduction to Modern France, 1500–1640: An Essay in Historical
Psychology* (New York, 1976), 241, 236–37.

14. For an argument to the contrary, see Keith V. Thomas, *Religion and the Decline of
Magic* (London, 1971), 51–70.

he was not limited to Christian belief in responding to the crises of existence. When Sewall gave away the coin he referred to as an "Angel," as he did on innumerable occasions, he was invoking the rite of the king's touch, the magical power to heal that supposedly went with kingship.[15] Whether or not he was conscious of the connection, he regarded the coin as having special powers to bless (2:862–63). When he drove a pin into a new building, he performed a ritual act rooted ultimately in pagan folklore.[16] The cherubim that guarded his front gate, the care he took with personal names, his sense of urgency about baptism, all suggest that Sewall's world view was infused with beliefs that owed little to Puritanism per se. To take Sewall whole, to see that all the patterns coalesce, is an act that stands in the way of any simplifying labels for his kind of thinking.[17]

Sewall was present for the dedication of the new Town House in 1713. Interpreting the moment in a brief speech, he saw in the process of destruction and rebuilding an emblem of repentance and renewal. So too the light that flooded the "Court-Chamber," streaming in through a "large, transparent, costly Glass," should "serve to oblige the Attorneys always to set Things in a True Light." "Light and Truth," these together were God's doing. Just as light would ultimately prevail over darkness, so the God who "is a Consuming Fire" was also the God who would bless and protect: "And since he has declar'd that He takes delight in them that hope in his Mercy, we firmly believe that He will be a Dwelling place to us throughout all Generations." Here spoke the Sewall for whom all existence was contingent, but for whom there was also permanence. Here spoke the Bostonian, proud of the better building that rose in place of the one that had burned. And here spoke the man who believed he could infuse this house, as he had his own, with blessings: "If we thus improve this House, they that built it, shall inhabit it; the days of this people shall be as the days of a tree, and they shall long enjoy the work of their hands" (2:713–14).

15. *Oxford English Dictionary,* s.v. "angel."

16. Henry W. Haynes, "Driving a Pin or Nail," *Proceedings of the Masachusetts Historical Society,* 2d ser., 4 (1887–89): 101–2, 219–21.

17. Historians of the early modern period have been struggling to describe a collective mentality that encompasses Christian and pre-Christian belief, oral culture and the culture of print. Similarly, historians have been wrestling with the relationship between "elite" and "popular" belief. For some interpreters, the key distinction lies between "traditional" and "modern," or "rational." No one of these categories is clearly applicable to Sewall. He had yet to withdraw from the street life that was an important element of "popular" culture in Boston; his interest in executions is a case in point. The special nature of literacy for persons like Sewall is described in David D. Hall, "The World of Print and Collective Mentality in Seventeenth-Century New England" in *New Directions in American Intellectual History,* ed. John Higham and Paul Conkin (Baltimore, 1979), 166–80.

TWO

Law
&
Politics

"Due Execution of the Generall Rules of Righteousnesse": Criminal Procedure in New Haven Town and Colony, 1638–1658[1]

GAIL SUSSMAN MARCUS

To the Puritan founders of New England, the punishment of crime was a religious imperative. They saw themselves as a "New Israel," joined with God, like the Israel of old, in a national covenant. If they used "all due means to prevent sin" in their communities, God would reward them with prosperity and peace. If they allowed sin to flourish, He would loose His wrath upon them. Since the Puritan God's anger took the form of indiscriminate disasters, from storms and droughts to shipwreck and disease, fulfilling the national covenant was a matter not of inclination but of survival.[2]

Puritan communities could protect themselves from God's "revenging justice" by punishing those sins, or crimes, which came to public attention.[3] Through punishment, Puritan governments "bore witness" before a jealous God to the community's effort to

1. This essay is derived from a chapter of my forthcoming dissertation, " 'All Due Means to Prevent Sin': The Criminal Justice System as a Means of Social Control in Colonial New Haven, 1638–1665."

I would like to thank Joan Annett, Tom Green, David Hall, John Langbein, John Murrin, and Thad Tate for their comments and suggestions on this article, and the American Association of University Women for much-needed financial assistance. My gratitude to Barbara Black, Martin Marcus, and, most especially, Edmund S. Morgan for their indispensable advice and encouragement, is unbounded.

2. *Ancient Town Records*, vol. 1, *New Haven Town Records, 1649–1662*, ed. Franklin B. Dexter (New Haven, 1917), 393–94 (hereafter cited as ATR I). On the social, or national, covenant, see Perry Miller, *The New England Mind: The Seventeenth Century* (Boston, 1961), 463–91.

3. See John Davenport and William Hooke, *A Catechisme Concerning the Chief Heads of Christian Religion, Published at the Desire and for the Use of the Church of Christ at New Haven* (London, 1659), 44–45, which describes the categories of sins.

combat sin. The sentencing magistrates were God's instruments, attracting the lightning of His wrath away from the group and conducting it, in the form of criminal punishment, to the particular evildoers who incurred it. But the punishment would satisfy God's requirements only if the criminal justice system that administered it was itself a righteous one. The problem was to embody abstract Puritan ideals in a practical legal apparatus, and the settlers' solutions are revealing. The records of colonial New England's courts indicate the success of Puritan leaders in imposing their ideas of social order on their communities. They demonstrate, too, what priorities emerged when Puritan ideology confronted reality, and how those priorities affected the early development of colonial law.

Of all the New England records, the most illuminating are those for the town and colony of New Haven, from its founding in 1638 until its absorption into Connecticut in 1665. The court records of Plymouth, Connecticut, and Massachusetts are either incomplete or preserve accounts of only those criminal cases serious enough to reach the higher provincial or county courts.[4] New Haven's records are nearly complete for the colonywide courts of superior jurisdiction; and those of the lowest level of jurisdiction, the town court, are preserved in their entirety. The scope of these records is as important as their depth. They contain details of court proceedings found almost nowhere else in New England archives.[5] New Haven provides an unmatched record of the routine administration of Puritan criminal justice and of its impact on the people who passed through the system. Particularly during the administration of Gov. Theophilus Eaton, from 1639 to 1658, the colony possessed the kind of continuous, purposeful, and centralized direction that makes it an ideal laboratory for study.

"New Haven," Perry Miller concluded, "was the essence of Puritanism, distilled and undefiled; the Bible Commonwealth and noth-

4. Eli Faber, "Puritan Criminals: The Economic, Social and Intellectual Background to Crime in Seventeenth Century Massachusetts," *Perspectives in American History* 11 (1977–78): 97. See also David H. Flaherty, "A Select Guide to the Manuscript Court Records of Colonial New England, *American Journal of Legal History* 11 (1967): 107–26, and John M. Murrin, "Magistrates, Sinners, and a Precarious Liberty: Trial by Jury in Seventeenth-Century New England," printed in this volume, pp. 152–206.

5. Records of the Court of Magistrates, which heard "weighty and capitall" criminal cases from all the towns in the New Haven Colony, and of the Colony General Court, which on rare occasions heard a capital case, are missing after April 1644 until May 1653. All of New Haven's court records have been published, with the exception of some testimony in a few cases that the editors deemed too salacious for publication. See *Records of the Colony and Plantation of New Haven, 1638–1649*, ed. Charles J. Hoadly (Hartford, 1857) (hereafter cited as CR I), and *Records of the Colony or Jurisdiction of New Haven, 1653 to the Union (1663)*, ed. Charles J. Hoadley (Hartford, 1858) (hereafter cited as CR II). The manuscripts are in the Connecticut State Library, Hartford.

ing else."[6] Certainly its leaders, the Reverend John Davenport and Chief Magistrate Theophilus Eaton, would have rejoiced in Miller's judgment. Their ambition to practice a purer Puritanism led them and their followers away from the political tumult of Massachusetts in 1638 and toward the isolation of Quinnipiac Sound.[7] Yet their disagreements with other Puritans were minor. Both men were influential members of early New England's religious establishment.[8] Despite their peculiar reforming zeal, the structure and pattern of criminal justice administration in New Haven resembled in most particulars that in Massachusetts and Connecticut. New Haven's eccentricities, such as they were, highlight Puritan doctrine by illustrating the extreme to which some of its practitioners would go in imposing their religious beliefs on secular institutions. As a result, criminal procedure in New Haven provides insights into Puritan justice that apply, generally, to the rest of New England.

Like other Puritans in New England, New Haven's leaders based their criminal justice system on Scripture. Foremost among their ideals and fundamental to the others was the obligation of the New Haven judiciary to "further the execution of justice according to the righteous rules of God's word."[9] To ensure that the legal system would conform to God's standards and not to profane ones devised by godless men, the town's founders entrusted its administration to magistrates selected according to the criteria for fit rulers that God gave to Moses. Town magistrates were expected to be wise, pious, courageous, understanding, and God-fearing.[10] In electing such men to office, the church members instructed them to judge righteously and to "do justice to all without partiality."[11]

Exactly how the magistrates dispensed justice was largely up to

6. Perry Miller, "Review of *The New Haven Colony* by Isabel M. Calder," *New England Quarterly* 8 (1935): 584. Miller wrote, on p. 583, "The Colony of New Haven is the ideal laboratory in which to study the germ of Puritanism."

7. Although dissertations and articles on the New Haven Colony have appeared recently, the most recent book focusing on it, Isabel M. Calder's *The New Haven Colony*, appeared in 1934 (New Haven).

8. See Calder, *New Haven Colony*, 8–21, 28–30, 32–49.

9. CR I, 37, and Colony Laws of 1656, CR II, 569. See also *The Laws and Liberties of Massachusetts: Reprinted from the Copy of the 1648 Edition in the Henry E. Huntington Library*, ed. Max Farrand (Cambridge, Mass., 1929), preamble, and *The Public Records of the Colony of Connecticut*, ed. J. Hammond Trumbull (Hartford, 1850), I, 39, 509.

10. John Davenport, *A Discourse about Civil Government in a New Plantation Whose Design Is Religion* (Cambridge, Mass., 1663), 16–17. See also Exodus 18:21, Deuteronomy 1:13, and CR I, 11–17, 21. On the authorship of *A Discourse*, see below, n. 12.

11. CR II, 616, Magistrates' Oath, also Deuteronomy 16:18, 19, 20. Because this article on criminal procedure concerns primarily the years 1639 through 1657, I have avoided using the Colony Laws of 1656 (CR II, 596–616) as the sole authority for any of my assertions. These laws do contain some coherent statements of policies and practices followed in criminal cases by the courts from 1639 through 1657, however, and I have cited these.

them. The New England colonists never produced a manual for criminal procedure, and its absence suggests that most of the procedural details so prominent in English courts were unimportant to them. The founders of New Haven preferred to concentrate on the greater purposes of the criminal process. According to *A Discourse about Civil Government in a New Plantation Whose Design Is Religion*, a tract written as a guide for New Haven's founders, magistrates were to execute the laws "according to God's appointment." They were bound only to "consult with Men of God in all hard cases, and in matters of Relition [*sic*]."[12] Like another Puritan leader, John Winthrop of Massachusetts, New Haven's founders believed that since God selected magistrates according to their adjudicative abilities, they deserved the freedom to apply the skill He gave them.[13] As long as New Haven remained the central town of an independent colony, its magistrates, and the deputies elected to assist them, controlled all aspects of the criminal process, from investigation through prosecution, trial, and sentencing. During those years they attached few legal rudders to their judicial ship, relying instead on the moral rectitude of individuals to keep it on a heading toward righteousness.

Despite the imprecision of court procedures, most criminal cases conformed to a general pattern. Like any task that becomes routine, the judges' handling of accused criminals took on an identifiable form that applied to all crimes, from minor offenses to capital ones, and in all courts, town and colony alike. Under the administration of New Haven's first magistrates, from 1639 until Eaton's death, in 1658, criminal procedure in New Haven followed two stages: preliminary examination and trial.

The criminal process in New Haven began after one of the magistrates learned of an offense and sent the marshal or his deputy to bring in the suspect for examination.[14] Examinations took place pri-

12. Davenport, *Discourse*, 15. There is some dispute about the authorship of the *Discourse*, which is attributed on its title page to John Cotton. Cotton Mather, in his *Magnalia Christi Americana*, gives credit for it to Davenport. Isabel M. Calder thought Cotton wrote it, and Bruce Steiner in a recent article argues that Davenport did. I agree with Steiner. But the correct authorship of the *Discourse* is not crucial here. There is no disagreement that the purpose of the tract was to direct New Haven's founders, who generally did follow its recommendations. See Isabel M. Calder, "The Authorship of *A Discourse About Civil Government in a New Plantation Whose Design Is Religion*," *American Historical Review* 37 (1932): 267–69, and Bruce E. Steiner, "Dissension at Quinnipiac: The Authorship and Setting of *A Discourse About Civil Government in a New Plantation Whose Design Is Religion*," *New England Quarterly* 54 (1981): 14–32.

13. John Winthrop, *The History of New England from 1630 to 1649*, ed. James Savage (Boston, 1853), II, 280–82 (hereafter cited as Winthrop, *Journal*). Some Massachusetts colonists feared that too much judicial freedom could be as fatal to justice as too little of it, but if anyone in New Haven agreed with them, his opposition went unrecorded.

14. By 1650 or so, if not earlier, the magistrates probably issued a simple "warrant," requiring the accused's attendance, to the marshal for delivery. See ATR I, 30, 57, and CR II, 615, for the form of the summons.

vately, usually at the home of the chief magistrate, in the presence of one or more of the other magistrates and possibly some deputies as well. The purpose of an examination was "to find out the trueth."[15] The presiding magistrate asked the suspect what he had to say to the charges made against him, and often brought him face to face with his accusers. Examinations were inquisitorial proceedings: the judge, rather than the parties, determined the course of events. The accused could contest the complainants' allegations, but primarily he answered the magistrates' questions.[16]

If an examinant convinced the examining magistrates of his innocence, or if they could not gather sufficient proof of his guilt, they dismissed him, or dropped a charge, if it was one among several.[17] If he confessed, or if the magistrates felt they could prove the charges, they usually referred the case for trial. Unlike magistrates in Massachusetts and Connecticut, those in New Haven had no power to dispose of criminal cases independently. Criminal cases went to trial (and therefore, to our good fortune, into the record) no matter how minor they were. Furthermore, major criminal cases proceeded to trial in the same manner as minor ones. Elsewhere in New England, alleged capital offenders received special treatment. Grand juries convened and formally indicted them before trial.[18] New Haven rejected this device.[19] Whether a case went to trial or not depended only on the informal decision of one or more magistrates.

When the magistrates decided to hold a public trial of a case, they ordered the examinant to appear at the next court session. Those accused of capital offenses and a few repeat offenders stayed in jail

15. ATR I, 491.

16. Examinations are recorded at CR I, 22–24, 26, 62–69, 170–71, 221–24, 243–50, 253, 327–28, 454–55; ATR I, 3, 9, 30–31, 497–98; CR II, 31–36.

17. Dropping charges: ATR I, 253. The court told this suspect, charged with and convicted of lying and swearing, "that further things are intimated against him, wch the court forbeares to mention till they may have further proofe." Though this criminal was probably not examined before trial, it seems reasonable to assume that the magistrates refrained from bringing unprovable charges against examined suspects as well. (See also my later discussion of cases ending in nonconvictions.)

Dismissals: CR I, 301. Since examinations were recorded only if they resulted in trial, this case is one of few that give evidence of cases dismissed after examination. By protesting his innocence, the examinant Samuel Hotchkiss cleared himself with the authorities, but he could not clear his conscience. Eventually he confessed his crime voluntarily and mentioned the aborted examination at his trial. See also ATR I, 55–56.

18. See George Lee Haskins, *Law and Authority in Early Massachusetts: A Study in Tradition and Design* (New York, 1960), 32, 175–76, and *Public Records of Connecticut*, I, 57, 91, 545, 546, and Julius Goebel, Jr., "King's Law and Local Custom in Seventeenth Century New England," in *Essays in the History of Early American Law*, ed. David H. Flaherty, (Chapel Hill, 1969), 112 (Plymouth).

19. In the Colony Laws of 1656, there is a section headed "Indictments." This is an example of a lay use of a legal term by New Haven's legislature, which uses *indicted* to mean "legally charged with" a crime. This usage has no particular procedural connotation, and indeed the section itself has to do with the government's right to seize the lands and goods of anyone accused of a capital crime who escapes justice. CR II, 595.

before trial, and a few other suspects had to post bail. But almost all New Haven suspects (probably close to 190 out of 201) received only a verbal "warning" to appear in court. Pending trial they returned to their normal activities.[20] New Haven's criminal justice system rested on widespread confidence in the magistrates. Apparently the magistrates placed similar confidence in the townspeople, even in alleged criminals, relying on the suspect's sense of responsibility or, in the great number of cases involving an unmarried suspect, on the integrity of the head of his family, to bring the accused into court as ordered.

The system worked. If the records of court attendance are complete, only four suspects did not appear for trial at the town court after they had been warned to attend.[21] When three of the four showed up at the court meeting a month later, the judges added contempt of authority to the original charges against them. Thomas Robinson, a household head, was the only New Havener between 1639 and January 1658 to leave town after formal criminal proceedings against him had begun. Four more suspects tried to escape but were caught and returned in time to keep their original court dates. The cautious treatment given these four after their examinations—two were servants who had been remanded to their masters' custody, and two had been imprisoned—indicates that the magistrates were able to separate the good risks from the bad.[22] Presumably, if a substantial number of offenders not mentioned in the records were escaping prosecution, the magistrates would have ordered bail or imprisonment more frequently than they did.

Like suspects, witnesses to criminal offenses faithfully appeared to give their testimony at trials. Although only illness, infirmity, or dis-

20. Only 6 of 201 suspects tried were certainly imprisoned before trial. Four of these were accused of capital offenses (CR I, 68–73, 295; ATR I, 174, 249–52; and CR II, 57, 169–71), and two were notorious repeat offenders (CR I, 89, and cr II, 188). It is likely that a few more than 6 New Haven suspects were imprisoned before trial, although the records do not mention where they stayed. For examples, see CR II, 137–39, and MSS Records of the Colony of New Haven, Connecticut State Library, Hartford, pp. 89–91 (hereafter referred to as CR II MSS), and ATR I, 33, 327. When the magistrates questioned the strength of a suspect's attachment to the community, they allowed a surety to post bail for him, or, if he was a servant, remanded him to his master's custody. ATR I, 3, 81, 327; CR I, 109, 404, 420. The scarcity of references to bail or the like in otherwise detailed records of criminal cases suggests that the New Haven court resorted to such measures infrequently. For examples of verbal "warnings," see CR I, 233, and ATR I, 256.

21. If asked, the magistrates would permit a criminal suspect to be absent from the court he had been ordered to attend, providing he had an acceptable reason for his request. But these excused absences are not usually noted in the records. See ATR I, 125–26. For the four suspects who did not appear for court as ordered and had no excuse, see CR I, 233–39, 454, and ATR I, 125–26.

22. Thomas Robinson, CR I, 233. James Clements, leader of a local crime ring, also escaped prosecution, but he apparently left town before his operations had been discovered. ATR I, 3–11. For attempted escapes by New Haveners, see ATR I, 3, CR I, 89, and CR II, 188.

tance excused a witness from testifying in person,[23] and although the magistrates seem not to have bound witnesses over for appearance in court, court records disclose no criminal case delayed because a witness failed to attend. The complacency with which magistrates ordered the court attendance of witnesses and defendants and the response their orders received attest both to the ease of attending local courts and to a widespread acceptance by New Haveners of the legitimacy of their government.

Once ordered to attend a court session, examinants and their accusers had little time to wait. The magistrates tried almost all New Haven offenders in the town "Particular" or "Plantation" Court. In practice, cases came to trial in less than the month that elapsed between town court meetings. Those few suspects whose offenses were so serious that the magistrates referred them to the Colony Court of Magistrates (which included the magistrates of the other New Haven Colony towns as well as New Haven's) might in theory wait for up to six months before trial at one of the court's semiannual meetings. But here, too, practice favored speedy trials. The magistrates called the higher court into special session to try serious criminal cases that arose more than a month or so before a scheduled sitting.[24]

Some criminal cases in New Haven came to trial without having been screened at a preliminary examination. A victim might bring his own complaint against a suspect without first consulting the magistrates. He could pay the town secretary to issue a warrant requiring the accused's appearance in court, bring in his own witnesses, and prosecute the case himself.[25] From this distance, we cannot deter-

23. In cases of a witness's justified absence, the court accepted written testimony taken on oath out of court before a magistrate. See Colony Laws CR II, 614–15; for examples in practice, see CR II, 26–27, and ATR I, 126. Even when written testimony was read at trial, unless the witnesses were disabled, they appeared in court to affirm it. See ATR I, 169–70, and CR II, 137. This was English practice too: see John H. Langbein, *Prosecuting Crime in the Renaissance* (Cambridge, Mass., 1974), 26–29.

24. For example, CR II, 187–89, 224–26. Also to prevent delay, Colony Laws granted a town court attended by two visiting magistrates jurisdiction equal to that of the Court of Magistrates, CR II, 571, in practice, CR I 467. See also ATR I, 31. The only recorded instances of delays of over a month between accusation and a court appearance occurred in the cases of Thomas Hogg and of John Frost, CR I, 295, and CR II, 169–71. In Hogg's case the delay was part of his "strict examination." (See my discussion of strict examinations, below, pp. 118–19.) The magistrates thought Frost might deserve execution for having deliberately set fire to his master's house, so they waited to try him in the Colony General Court, which, as the legislature, could declare his offense capital.

25. For example, CR I, 175, 380, 418–19, and ATR I, 151–52. The accepted modern distinction between civil and criminal cases does not hold for New Haven. A victim who prosecuted a criminal case might receive damages for his efforts, or he might not, depending on the offense charged. Similarly, even if the magistrates prosecuted, they might award damages to the victim, again depending on the offense charged. In my dissertation I go into this question more fully, in order to explain how I decided which cases were criminal and which ones were not.

mine why some victims followed this procedure while others turned instead to the magistrates. Sometimes the magistrates seem to have omitted a preliminary examination in cases they conducted themselves, although they did question before trial the witnesses who testified in such cases. For instance, it seems likely that the magistrates had not examined Rebecca Meekes before bringing her to trial for "intertaining mens servants in the night season when ther Governers were in bed" and for receiving stolen property, because at her trial "she was bid to speake if she had anything to say to cleere herselfe." Had Rebecca previously discussed her case with the magistrates, they would either have dismissed the case already or have called on her in court to confess her crime.[26]

A person who committed or unwittingly confessed to a crime while he was in court on other business also faced trial without prior examination. The disappointed litigant in a civil case who grumbled in the courtroom about the magistrates' judgmental abilities promptly found himself sentenced for contempt of authority.[27] The court's habit of discarding procedure in favor of immediate dispensation of justice must have unnerved unsuspecting litigants like John Meggs. Meggs sued for debt, but the proof he offered in his own behalf convinced the court that he had deceived his customers and "incouraged" his opponent to "doe evil." Besides granting damages to the people Meggs cheated, the court levied a heavy fine on him for his unrighteous behavior.[28]

William Blayden also unwittingly incurred the court's wrath. Having neglected to bring his arms to church on Sunday, as required by town order, he should have expected to pay a small fine. But Blayden justified his absence from worship. On Sunday morning his clothes were still damp from Saturday's rain, he explained, and he had no wish to risk illness by putting them on. Instead he stayed in bed. The court rejected this excuse, fined him the usual amount for the violation, and then gave a surprised Blayden the chance to "hold forth sight of his sine in profanely neglecting to come" to church. Blayden remained as blind to his sin as he had been to the magistrates' predictable reaction to his explanation. Such incomprehension made him a criminal. For "dispising" God's laws "through sloathfulness," the magistrates sentenced Blayden without further ado to be publicly whipped.[29]

26. See the discussion of unexamined cases, below, pp. 127–28. ATR I, 12. For examples of other cases that appear to have been unexamined before trial, see CR I, 470–71, and ATR I, 172, 178–79.
27. CR I, 42, 123, 261; ATR I, 30.   28. CR I, 345–53, also 174–75.
29. CR I, 322, 324.

When the criminal demonstrated his guilt in the courtroom, as Blayden and Meggs did, criminal procedure collapsed into a statement of the charge, which was also a judgment, and sentencing. Otherwise, the trial procedure for both examined and unexamined defendants paralleled that of an examination. The presiding magistrate read the charge, occasionally along with a written record of the examination, and called for the defendant's answer. When a victim was the prosecutor, he initiated the trial by reciting his complaint.[30] If the accused confessed, the court proceeded to sentence. If he did not, the magistrates called on the witnesses to testify before again asking the defendant to speak.

This orderly procedure could now and then break down, as in the case brought by Susan Clark's father against Ellis Mew. Susan, whose parents lived in New Haven but who herself lived with John Jones and his wife as their servant, accused Mew, who also stayed with the Joneses, of lewd behavior toward her. In the town court, her father complained that one day when Susan was alone Mew threw her on a bed, kissed her, and, "pull[ing] down his breeches," attempted to violate her. Had he succeeded, he would have stood trial for his life. The charge as stated was grave enough. Susan confirmed it, but Mew denied the attempted rape, saying he "discovered not her nakedness nor his owne." Apparently no one asked him specifically about the rest of the allegations. Then the trial became something of a free-for-all among the spectators. In response to questioning by the townspeople, John Jones and others who knew Mew asserted that he had always been truthful. The judges ruled that "this proves nothing" in the case, citing as precedent a biblical story of an honest man turned liar under pressure. Then Jones's wife reported that "she had taken the girle in some untruthes." Again the magistrates rejected the evidence, arguing that a young girl would be unlikely "to be so imprudent as to charge such carriage upon a young man when it was not so." Instead of curtailing discussion, this second judicial pronouncement caused further debate from the floor about Susan's disposition; her mother and her mistress offered opposing observations. Finally the judges called a halt. For lack of better evidence, they again asked Mew to "declare the truth." Once more he denied having tried to violate Susan, insisting that she had told him to leave her alone when he had kissed her—that was as far as he had gone. The judges convicted Mew only of the acts he confessed.[31]

Other than denying the charge, or part of it, as Mew did, a

30. In one case, the nonmagisterial prosecutors were two upstanding citizens appointed by the town to prosecute an offender in the Colony Court. CR I, 222.
31. ATR I, 182–83.

defendant who intended to defend himself in New Haven's courts had two options. He could present his own witnesses to contradict the testimony against him, or he could attempt to disqualify the prosecution witnesses themselves. His accusers could rebut his allegations against them, though it appears that they did not respond to him directly, just as the defendant could not directly cross-examine witnesses. Accused and accusers spoke to the presiding magistrate, who controlled court proceedings by holding the reins of conversation.[32]

Whether the accused defended himself or confessed, the magistrates, and, in the town court, the deputies, consulted about the judgment and the sentence. There was no jury in any New Haven trial. The deputies and magistrates apparently heard the opinions of the presiding magistrate (who was usually also the colony governor) before passing sentence by majority vote. Once the magistrates announced the court's decision to the waiting defendant, the trial was over.[33] There were no appeals in criminal cases, although New Haven courts did accept requests for mitigation of the imposed sentence.[34]

Once begun, criminal cases in New Haven reached speedy conclusions. The magistrates postponed for a month or more the trials of only 28 out of 201 New Haveners tried, including the trials of the three suspects who failed to appear on the date for which they had been called. The court delayed ten of these from one monthly Particular Court to the next, in two cases at the request of the defendant, but usually in order to allow the prosecution time to gather additional evidence against the accused. They referred fifteen "weighty" or "capitall" cases from the town court to the Colony Court of Magistrates, which were thus delayed usually for one month, and perhaps for as many as five months, before their final resolution.[35]

32. For examples of defense efforts, see CR I, 39, 46, 221–25, CR II, 152, and CR II MSS, 92–93.

33. CR I, 307, CR I, 113, and Colony Laws CR II, 570–71. If the votes of the judges were equal, the "casting vote" went in the Colony Court of Magistrates to the governor or, in his absence, to the deputy governor; in the town Plantation Court, those two officials had the same right, and if neither was present, then the presiding magistrate cast the decisive vote.

34. Although the fundamentals of town government promulgated in 1643 seem to allow appeals (CR I, 113), by 1655, when the Colony Laws were compiled, New Haven's leaders had decided to limit appeals to noncriminal cases (CR II, 572, "Appeales"). There are no examples in the New Haven court records of appeals directly from any court's decision in a criminal case. Since the magistrates would not entertain suggestions that they had proceeded unrighteously—suggestions to that effect earned the complainant a fine—the change in the wording of the law made no practical difference. See CR I, 362, 402; ATR I, 81.

35. CR I, 114. After 1653, when the complete set of Colony Court records makes specific calculation possible, no trial in a case referred to the Court of Magistrates was

Only four New Haven residents tried on criminal charges in New Haven between 1639 and 1658 appeared in cases that the court did not resolve or whose resolution the court reporter neglected to record.[36]

The structure of New Haven's criminal justice system, like that of Massachusetts and Connecticut, was English. The position of magistrates in New England paralleled that of seventeenth-century English justices of the peace, who administered both local government and local justice. New Haven's criminal procedure duplicated in many ways that followed by the JPs in trying those minor offenses over which they had jurisdiction singly or in pairs. When JPs learned of a crime, they ordered the suspect to appear before them, examined him and his accusers, and decided the sentence, although there was probably no delay between examination and judgment in these summary proceedings. In more serious criminal cases, English JPs possessed investigatory and committal powers that resembled the examination, imprisonment, and bail practices of New Haven's magistrates. One or two JPs could not try serious offenses themselves. After preparing the case for trial, they, like magistrates, passed it on to a higher court, either to Quarter Sessions or to Assizes. Procedure at that level differed substantially not only from that of New Haven but from that of Massachusetts and Connecticut as well.[37]

The resemblance between the judicial powers of Puritan magistrates and English justices of the peace is not surprising. Especially where scriptural guidance was scanty, as in the case of criminal procedure, godly men could adopt those English customs and institutions which were consistent with God's law. But while the floor plan of New Haven's criminal justice system may have been English, the furnishings were designed according to scriptural specifications, and they had a distinctly Puritan style.

The most distinctive feature of New Haven's judicial edifice was

---

delayed for more than a month. The absence of higher court records prior to that means that the closest determination of the delays of trials is between one and five months, depending on when the Court of Magistrates was due to sit next. The Court of Magistrates sent one case to the New Haven town court for resolution. CR II, 224–26, and ATR I, 317–18. The two cases delayed at the defendants' request: CR I, 39, 46, 385.

36. CR I, 153, 163, 385, and ATR I, 3–14 (Captive's case). These do not include cases referred to the Court of Magistrates for sessions whose records are no longer extant. The court referred two cases "to further consideration" (ATR I, 16–17, 268), but in both we later learn that this meant the court "passed by" the offense without a fine.

37. See Haskins, *Law and Authority in Early Massachusetts,* 77; Langbein, *Prosecuting Crime in the Renaissance,* 75–116. Another study by Langbein, though, suggests that even at Assizes the criminal trials resembled New Haven's: in speed, absence of defense counsel, expectation that the accused answer the charges (in addition to entering a formal plea), and judicial questioning of witnesses. John H. Langbein, "The Criminal Trial before the Lawyers," *University of Chicago Law Review* 45 (1978): 277–84.

the absence of juries. Those town founders who unanimously agreed that "the Scripturs doe holde forth a perfect rule for the direction and government of men in all dueties"[38] always measured their actions against their own scriptural yardstick. When Scripture was silent, they often borrowed solutions devised by Massachusetts Puritans (without ever acknowledging a nonscriptural source, as Massachusetts did, for example, when it modeled magistrates on JPs).[39] In the case of juries, however, New Haven rejected the example not only of Massachusetts but of the rest of New England as well. While the other Puritan colonies adopted the English practice of convening grand and petit juries in capital cases, after 1643 the New Haven Colony magistrates, acting *en banc*, decided weighty and capital cases on their own.[40] The records nowhere explain this anomaly, but the reasons were probably both religious and practical. The Bible entrusts judicial matters exclusively to God-chosen judges; lay juries do not appear in Scripture. Then too, the pool of potential jurors in New Haven, landowning male church members who attained the franchise as freemen, was small.[41]

In abandoning juries, New Haven did not empower magistrates to make all judicial decisions alone. Each town in the New Haven Colony elected two to four deputies annually (four in New Haven Town), who assisted the magistrates in the town court and, after 1643, passed sentence with them by majority vote. Presumably the deputies or

38. CR I, 12; see also CR I, 21.

39. CR I, 571. For example, New Haven adopted Massachusetts's laws on theft and on exemptions from military training. CR II, 575 and 605, and *Laws and Liberties of Massachusetts*, 4–5 and 41–42. See also George L. Haskins and Samuel E. Ewing, "The Spread of Massachusetts Law in the Seventeenth Century," in *Essays in the History of Early American Law*, ed. Flaherty, 189–91. On the similarity between magistrates and JPs, see Haskins, *Law and Authority*, 32.

40. CR I, 113–14, CR II, 571. Prior to 1643, New Haven tried its own capital and weighty criminal cases in the town General Court—the town meeting, where all freemen could vote. After New Haven became a colony, the magistrates did, at least once, bring a capital case to trial in the Colony General Court, made up of magistrates and two deputies elected from each town (CR II, 169–71). This case, involving arson by a fourteen-year-old boy, apparently went to the General Court because arson was not a capital offense by law and because the magistrates thought this criminal deserved execution. Though the court spared his life because of his youth, it did pass a law making malicious arson capital. On New England juries, see Murrin, "Magistrates, Sinners, and a Precarious Liberty."

41. By the end of New Haven's first year of government, it had seventeen enfranchised settlers, or freemen. Thereafter the town admitted to freemanship an average of fewer than 10 residents per year, up to an estimated total of 77 by 1646 and 98 by 1658. Because of deaths and departures from New Haven, there were probably never more than 75 freemen in the town at any one time, including the three magistrates. (The list of freemen at CR I, 9, is a partial one. See also CR I, 147, 156, 171, 230, 277, 381, 387, 404, 405, 456, 463; ATR I, 32, 72, 204, 277, 313, 316. Internal evidence—for example, a deputy who was nowhere listed as a freeman, though only freemen could hold that position—suggests that the records of admission to freemanship are incomplete.)

"ordinary judges"[42] developed some judicial expertise—enough, at least, to fulfill scriptural requirements for judges in lesser cases. Paradoxically, while New Haven's freemen allowed their magistrates greater power over the lives and deaths of criminals than did their counterparts in any other New England colony, they imposed more restraint on magistrates in routine criminal matters. Those minor offenses which Massachusetts and Connecticut magistrates could punish acting singly or in pairs, New Haven magistrates could try only at town court sessions and punish only with the concurrence of the deputies. But if the presence of lay deputies enhanced the power of freemen, it had little discernible effect on the outcome of New Haven's criminal cases. The same freemen who voted to give magistrates unfettered discretion in major criminal cases seem, as deputies, to have been equally content with magisterial policies and to have willingly passed cases on to the higher, entirely magisterial court.[43]

The common bond of Puritanism may explain why, except in the matter of juries, criminal procedures in New Haven matched those of its neighbors. Among the "generall rules of righteousnesse" that Scripture laid out for men and magistrates was a specific rule of evidence. To find an alleged criminal guilty, God required that two witnesses testify to the crime.[44] In applying this evidentiary standard, first at examination and later at trial, New Haven's judges accepted an interpretation promulgated by the church elders of New England, John Davenport among them, in 1641. The ruling arose from a question put to the elders by the magistrates of Massachusetts. Intending to abide by the two-witness rule in criminal cases, they were troubled when they recognized that the rule, if taken literally, would make conviction impossible in certain cases where factual guilt was incontrovertible. No witnesses to the crime were needed, for instance, when an unmarried woman became pregnant. To deal with such anomalies, the elders decided that where "the fact itself speaks" or the offender confessed, another "witness" was unnecessary. The two-witness rule existed, they reasoned, to eliminate doubt.

---

42. CR I, 22–23, 113–14, 130, 191; in practice: CR I, 252, 334. Before 1643 the New Haven deputies were to "assist the courts by way of advice, but not to have any power by way of sentence." CR I, 78. This initial division of power suggests the possibility that town court deputies came into being as a substitute of sorts for a jury, perhaps to satisfy some settlers who were not entirely content to give up juries.

43. CR I, 221, 257, 422; ATR I, 252, 324. When the need arose, a New Haven town court could also constitute itself as a court with jurisdiction equivalent to that of the Court of Magistrates by adding to the bench two magistrates from outside towns. CR I, 571. Here, too, there seems to have been no disagreement between deputies and magistrates. CR I, 467–76.

44. Deuteronomy 17:16; 19:15. See also CR II, 572.

Therefore they decreed that "one clear witness with concurrent and concluding circumstances" would satisfy the rule.[45]

New Haven's magistrates accepted as "clear witness" verbal testimony by people who had seen either the crime itself or physical evidence of it, or who had heard the accused make an admission of guilt.[46] The judges occasionally also took as "clear witness" hearsay evidence reported by a person in a position of authority over the original source of the information; a husband might speak for his wife, or a master for his servant. But when the subordinate was the principal accuser, he appeared at trial in person.[47]

If a defendant disputed the testimony of a "clear witness," the witness could confirm it by repeating it under oath, although the accused might first try to disqualify his accuser from taking an oath at all. To the Puritan leaders of New Haven, swearing an oath was an "Extraordinary act of Religion." They considered carefully before allowing anyone to take one, and they punished casual swearers for profanation.[48] The magistrates explained the rationale behind this policy to the one suspect in the court records who volunteered to swear to his own innocence. They refused his offer, made in the face of concrete evidence of his guilt, and warned him against

> his bold and sinfull way of protestations and offering to take oath, as if by confident contradictions he would drive men from the truth they knew. . . . minding [him] of that [biblical] rule, 'let your communication be yea, yea, nay, nay oathes even in certain truthes are not lawfull till they be necessary and duely called for.' Profane men indead in other places who little attend truth, thinke they must swere that they may be believed; and in [this] case it would be noe other than a high breach of the third commandment [against taking the Lord's name in vain].[49]

Because of the danger of individual damnation for violating God's law and because of the peril to the community if the magistrates provoked God's wrath by encouraging such an evil, they would ask a witness to take an oath only if the defendant "duely called for" it.

Defendants in New Haven's courts seldom demanded that their accusers take oaths.[50] What happened in the still rarer instances when a suspect tried to disable the witness from testifying under oath is

45. Winthrop, *Journal*, II, 56–57.
46. For examples of each, see CR I, 170, and ATR I, 55–56, 124.
47. CR I, 176, 387.
48. As in CR II MSS, 92–93, ATR I, 151–53, CR I, 242–52. See ATR I, 88–89, prosecution for swearing.
49. CR I, 223–24. See also CR II MSS, 92–93. For the religious significance of the oath, see Davenport and Hooke, *Catechisme,* 51.
50. Witnesses took oaths in only ten cases (CR I, 46, 66–69, 233–39, 242–52, 253–56, 297; ATR I, 88–89, 165–68, CR II, 137–39, CR II MSS, 92–93), and the accused requested

illustrated by the case of Mrs. Lucy Brewster. After denying the sixteen charges leveled against her, which ranged from spreading disaffection with church doctrines to selling liquor without a license, Mrs. Brewster insisted she had been wronged and misinterpreted. She "laded the witnesses with reproach that she might disable their testimony. [A]ll of them were lyars," and two "were hypocrits and she would prove them soe, what they spake was to currey favour that [one of them] might get into the church again." The witnesses contested these claims and presented people who attested to their good character. Mrs. Brewster then produced other witnesses, who claimed that her principal accuser, a servant named Elizabeth Smith, "was of a crooked disposition and apt to speake untruthes." Elizabeth's master added that "when himselfe or his wife had called her to account for miscarridges she would seeme to be affected and promise amendement but they could never see much amendement in her." To this "the Governor replyed, that the court would duely proceed against any of the witnesses according to allegation and proofe in due season." (It did. At the same session, the court convicted Smith of fornication and another of Mrs. Brewster's accusers of defaming a magistrate.)

Yet a criminal record did not necessarily disqualify a witness. The magistrates and deputies judged Elizabeth and the rest of the witnesses against Mrs. Brewster competent to testify under oath. Perhaps Elizabeth did indeed convince the court of her reliability. The mistress who impugned her character was herself implicated by Elizabeth's testimony, and Elizabeth had repented her crime and married her lover by the time of the trial.[51] On the other hand, the judges' ruling probably owed as much to an inclination to resolve issues in favor of conviction as to any other considerations. It was difficult, if not impossible, since there are no instances in the records where it occurred, to get the magistrates to disqualify a witness.[52] Once Mrs. Brewster's accusers repeated their allegations under oath, her defense

that his accuser take an oath in one other case (ATR I, 151–53) but backed down before the man was sworn. The English common law of the period required that prosecution witnesses give their testimony under oath (Langbein, *Prosecuting Crime in the Renaissance,* 25). Therefore a New Haven defendant who was discouraged from demanding sworn testimony by the sanctity with which he and / or the court viewed oaths sacrificed a right that he would have retained in England. A defendant who called for sworn testimony, though, did enjoy some protection. While the only people who could take oaths were those the court would believe anyway, whatever testimony they could not swear to was discredited. Since New Haven's residents took the oath seriously, they did not automatically swear to everything they were otherwise willing to state in court. See below, p. 114.

51. Mrs. Brewster's case, CR I, 242–52.

52. See, for example, the court's insistence that a woman's accusation against a man for sexual assault would be no less credible because she had been a thief. CR I, 235, 239.

collapsed. She dared not question the truth of testimony sworn by God's holy name.

The importance of the oath as a precipitator of truth in New Haven cases is illustrated by the presiding magistrates' evidentiary ruling in a 1652 assault case. Thomas Beech alleged that Edward Camp had beaten him, but Beech's witnesses could testify only to a quarrel between the two men, for they had not seen the attack itself. Governor Eaton cited the example of a case of rape described in Deuteronomy. In both the scriptural and the New Haven cases, there were no witnesses. But since the complainant had a visible injury and the accused could not clear himself, Eaton ruled that the willingness of the accuser to take an oath was determinative.[53]

As this judgment reveals, New Haven's magistrates assumed that most witnesses were unwilling to jeopardize their souls by swearing falsely. Magistrates and townspeople shared the same scruples about swearing by God's name. Beech's offer to swear to his story not only disposed the judges to believe him; it also affected Camp. The thought that he would cause an unnecessary oath so troubled Camp that he confessed rather than force Beech to swear. In other cases, witnesses who were called to repeat their testimony under oath modified their statements in spite of the embarrassment it entailed. Although the court never asked anyone to swear to anything except what he "was clear in," it might blame a witness for making ill-considered assertions in the first place.[54]

The persistence and eventual decline of this reverential attitude toward oaths among magistrates and citizens would be a useful gauge of piety in Puritan New England. As religious fervor decreased (or its emphasis changed), the oath probably lost some of its terror, and therefore some of its value as an arbiter in court disputes. If we could discover when New Haveners became like those "profane men in other places" who swore "that they might be believed," we would also learn when they ceased to be Puritans of the sort John Davenport or John Winthrop would have recognized.

Whether or not a witness testified under oath, his evidence provided only one "clear witness" to the accused's guilt. Unless the suspect confessed, sufficient proof of guilt in all New Haven criminal cases consisted of two or more "clear witnesses," or of one plus "concurrent and concluding circumstances." Possession of stolen property, for instance, was a fact sufficiently incriminating to count as one clear witness but was not in itself incontrovertible proof of guilt. It served to convict the accused only when augmented by proof of

53. ATR I, 151–52.   54. CR I, 243, 253.

other suspicious circumstances, ranging from testimony that a suspect had had specific opportunity to commit the crime to inconsistencies in the excuses he made to the magistrates.[55]

Most of the circumstantial evidence evaluated by New Haven's judges seems reasonable to a modern reader. But some of their suspicions rested on assumptions about causation that have changed since the seventeenth century. Like other Christians, New Haveners believed that God directed every event on earth, no matter how trivial, but they acted more consistently on this conviction. God's intervention in some circumstances, for example, provided evidence of an otherwise unknowable crime. Whenever a sow gave birth to a deformed piglet, they perceived this event as a signal that someone had committed bestiality with the monster's mother, although in one case they could find no peculiarity in the monster sufficient to point to a particular person.[56] Another "monstrous" birth led the magistrates to examine the appropriately named Thomas Hogg on suspicion of bestiality. The logic that gave rise to the accusation also prompted an "experiment" to test it. When Hogg denied the charge, two magistrates—the governor and the deputy governor of the colony—took him down to the pigsty, where they had him scratch the mother of the monster and another sow. The magistrates' suspicions were confirmed when Hogg's alleged partner in crime reacted with "lust" to his touch and the other sow remained unmoved.[57]

God was not the only supernatural agent capable of influencing earthly events in New Haven. The devil might also be abroad, and the townspeople occasionally found evidence of the witchcraft that his agents might be practicing. The magistrates suspected Elizabeth Godman of being a witch and examined her after hearing neighbors' reports of disquieting occurrences. One witness, after gossiping about the suspect, began to fear that Godman, if she was a witch, would take revenge on her by harming her cows. On that same day the woman's fears were realized. One of her cows fell sick. She besought God to deliver the beast if it did indeed suffer under an evil spell. When the cow recovered, this good townswoman, rejoicing at the efficacy of her faith, concluded that the source of her cow's illness

---

55. See ATR I, 285, a theft case that did result in conviction, and ATR I, 252–53, one that did not. The Colony Laws included a provision that the nonappearance for trial of a person charged with a capital crime would count as one clear witness against him, but there is no case in the extant court records in which a capital offender escaped trial.

56. CR I, 62–63, 295; ATR I, 158–59.

57. CR I, 296. Note that the magistrates were so intent on proving Hogg's probable guilt that they required no "control" for their experiment. Only Hogg scratched the sows.

had been the accused witch. Godman denied the charge.[58]

"Circumstantial" evidence based on a belief in the intervention of supernatural forces caused the magistrates to imprison both Hogg and Godman for further questioning. But the New Haven courts never convicted anyone on such evidence alone. Tales of enchantment or even a litter of monstrous piglets amounted to only "concurrent and concluding circumstances." Without one clear witness to confirm them, all the circumstantial evidence that the magistrates could garner would not bring the New Haven judges to a verdict of guilty.[59] Unlike the judges at the Salem witch trials, they resisted their emotions, and never convicted any criminal on supernatural evidence, which by their own standards was insufficient. The judges of New Haven insisted on one proof that a mere human could verify—though it could be a confession—before they would convict. Both Hogg and Godman went free.[60]

Practical experience with the two-witness rule led the government to supplement the ruling of the elders in 1641. The magistrates feared that a problem might arise, for example, in a case of slander. A slanderer careful to repeat the same lies to one person at a time might insulate himself from criminal prosecution. If each incident was considered alone, no two witnesses could testify to either one. As in the case of the unwed mother, adherence to the two-witness rule could thus lead to the absurdity that a crime known to the entire town was unpunishable. After much debate about the solution to this dilemma, the town's church members, with Davenport's support, concluded that "the wisdom of God in the Scriptures" contained "perfect rules [which] duly attended will prevent all such dangerous consequences." Due attendance to the two-witness rule must therefore mean that even though two people witnessed an offense on different occasions, together their testimony would suffice to convict the accused.[61]

One church member disputed this decision. Ezekiel Cheever argued that the new ruling negated the purpose of the original: to prevent anyone from being punished on the word of a single witness. Now, he insisted, any malicious person could bring unjust accusations against his enemy "in hope another such witness may come

58. ATR I, 250–51.

59. ATR I, 252–53, CR I, 454–55, 470–71, noncapital offenses.

60. Hogg was acquitted of the charge of bestiality only; at his trial in the town court on that charge, he was convicted of a number of lesser offenses unrelated to it. CR I, 295–96; witchcraft case, CR II, 29–36, 181, ATR I, 249. See also CR II, 223–34, where two witnesses could prove only attempted bestiality, not the capital offense itself.

61. "The Trial of Ezekiel Cheever," *Collections of the Connecticut Historical Society* 1 (1860): 22–51, quotation on 28. See also Laws, CR II, 572.

in." The accuser could testify without fear of contradiction, almost as if the two-witness rule did not exist. The visible saints of New Haven disagreed. In their opinion Cheever was overly concerned that accusers would abuse their godly duty to report crime, and not worried enough about the possible guilt of a suspect who, after all, had managed to get himself accused.[62] Deciding this issue required balancing society's desire to protect the innocent against its need to punish the guilty. New Haven's leaders accepted the view that it was better to have an innocent man convicted than a guilty one acquitted, a prosecutorial instinct that surfaced elsewhere in their handling of accused criminals.

Cheever's worries (and ours) that New Haven's gloss on the two-witness rule would undermine the rule itself were exaggerated. Colony leaders devised the exception not to defeat the rule but to resolve a conflict between the restrictions that the rule imposed on the judges' power to convict and their commitment to punish known crime. The magistrates applied the gloss just once—in a case of theft. Even in this situation, two witnesses could testify that the accused, Thomas Langden, had butchered a single swine. The court relied on one "witness" apiece to convict Langden of killing two additional swine, not important in determing his guilt, but necessary to decide the appropriate sentence, which depended on the value of the stolen property.[63] Though there was a logical inconsistency in applying to the same case an evidentiary ruling based on the assumption that several incidents could be treated as a single crime and a rule of punishment that considered each incident separately, New Haven's magistrates ignored it. The motive behind their rule of evidence was the wish to assure the punishment of criminals. The rationale of punishment was to penalize the offender as he deserved, according to the magnitude of his offense. In effecting these two moral imperatives, the judges could find no contradiction.

Adherence to the two-witness rule had another, more significant impact on criminal procedure. Two clear witnesses to a crime or their equivalent were often difficult or impossible to obtain, making a suspect's confession the only route to his conviction. When the magistrates strongly suspected that the accused was guilty, the temptation to wring a confession from him must have been great. (On the European continent, where the two-witness rule also applied, the result was a general use of torture.)[64] The Massachusetts magistrates had recognized the difficulty. When they queried the elders about

62. "Trial of Ezekiel Cheever," 50.   63. ATR I, 169–73.
64. John H. Langbein, *Torture and the Law of Proof: Europe and England in the Ancien Régime* (Chicago and London, 1977), 4–5.

the two-witness rule, they also asked how much pressure a magistrate might use to "exact confession from a delinquent in capital
cases." Since Scripture provided no direct answer to this question,
the Puritan ministers relied on their collective (English) conscience
in responding.

> Where a [capital crime] is committed, and one witness or strong presump-
> tions do point out the offender, there the judge may examine him strictly,
> and he is bound to answer directly. But if there be only slight suspicion,
> etc. [sic] then the judge is not to press him to answer, nor is he to be denied
> the benefit of the law, but he may be silent and call for his accusers. Exam-
> ination [under] oath or [by] torture in criminal cases they generally denied
> to be lawfull.[65]

In practice the New Haven magistrates accepted the restrictions on
their power that this policy contained. So far as we can tell, they
respected the injunction against torture, never examined an accused
under oath,[66] and limited their use of "strict examination" to those
few detected capital offenses in which suspicion was indeed great.[67]

"Strict examination" in New Haven consisted of repeated questioning with intervening visits to the town prison, although the
imprisonment of suspected capital offenders was intended as much
to insure their safe custody as to encourage them to confess.[68] Theoretically the magistrates might have kept everyone who was
undergoing a strict examination locked up until a confession was
won. Instead they regularly brought capital cases to trial at the earliest possible court session. Only once did the magistrates delay proceedings in the apparent hope that imprisonment would force a
confession. They kept Thomas Hogg in jail for two or three months
before his trial in the town court, and sent him back to prison for
probably another two months to await the meeting of the Court of
Magistrates to which they referred the bestiality charge laid against
him. The magistrates justified Hogg's imprisonment by explaining
that, in addition to the incriminating evidence of bestiality that God

65. Winthrop, *Journal*, II, 56. Since John Davenport contributed to the elders' decisions and since New Haven's magistrates sought the advice of their Massachusetts counterparts on difficult cases in 1641, 1644, and 1646, I have concluded that New Haven
subscribed to the elders' ruling, as Massachusetts did. On the consultations with Massachusetts magistrates, see Winthrop, *Journal*, I, 73; II, 232, 324.

66. There is no mention of either practice in the Colony Laws and no evidence that
either occurred in any recorded criminal cases, capital or otherwise.

67. Capital cases: CR I, 66–69, 70–72, 295–96, CR II, 29–36, 151, 169–71, CR II
MSS, 89–91. An example of a capital charge without strong suspicion, and therefore no
strict examination, is ATR I, 245–46.

68. CR I, 130: "Whensoever any capital offender shall be apprehended within this
jurisdiction, he shall be sent with all convenient speed to New Haven, there to be kept
in safe custody till he be brought to due tryall."

had provided, "guilt did appear in his carryadge." Other witnesses reported Hogg's inability to keep his private parts private.[69] All these circumstances combined probably explain the magistrates' extraordinary measures in his case.

In allowing strict examination on suspicion of crimes so heinous that Scripture required their punishment by death, the elders implied that extreme measures were unlawful in less serious offenses, where society's need to flush out the culprits was not as great. New Haven's magistrates did employ the tactics of a "strict examination" in one noncapital case, Thomas Langden's hog rustling, and for the same reason that prompted them to accept one witness apiece to portions of his theft—the wish to determine an accurate punishment. Ordinarily in such cases the judges just asked the criminal for the amount of goods stolen, or sold illegally, and accepted his answer. They believed Langden's response when, at the end of his trial, they asked him how much powder he had traded illegally with the Indians. But to find out the true number of hogs that Langden had stolen, the magistrates interrogated him two or three times, and, still unsatisfied with his confession, "agreed to send him to the prison to lye in irons." Despite yet another examination, Langden never managed to convince the magistrates of the truth of any of his versions of the swine stealing. The authorities cannot have had much liking for Langden; he was a notorious character already twice convicted of other crimes, and a persistent liar under examination. But their easier treatment of other obnoxious criminal defendants—and even of Langden himself on the arms-dealing charge—suggests that it was not simply Langden's odious nature that prompted the magistrates' harsh measures. Their bullying of Langden arose from the combination of his character, of admissions he had made that were inconsistent with the available evidence, of their need to know how many swine he had stolen, and, it would seem, of some reluctance to use one witness per swine as long as there was a chance Langden might confess. It was a constellation that formed only once in eighteen years.[70]

Langden might have been better off if he had invoked from the beginning another clause in the elders' edict. In all but the few capital cases accompanied by "strong presumption" of guilt, New Haveners accused of crimes apparently could (since a few did) "seek benefit of the law" by refusing to answer and demanding proof of the charges.[71] The magistrates accepted this tactic willingly enough unless they knew, and believed the suspect knew, that the evidence

---

69. CR I, 295.
70. ATR I, 169–73. Langden's character: ATR I, 52, 55–56, 125–26.
71. ATR I, 152.

against him was conclusive. In the one case that fits this description, they allowed the suspect to remain silent but expressed their dissatisfaction with her unwillingness to cooperate. "By such ways," a magistrate told her, "she will but make her punishment more heavy." She took the risk. Apparently she made no further comments at her trial, nor did the judges ask her to, although they had made it clear that they thought she should.[72]

The magistrates' restraint in using torture and oaths arose from a number of sources. Abhorrence of judicial torture was part of the culture that New Haveners brought with them from England, where the common law forbade its use.[73] Moreover, the same religious concerns that made the judges so wary of allowing a witness to take an oath account for their declining to use it to compel a defendant's testimony. If the magistrates so much as permitted, let alone demanded, the accused's oath, they would be tempting him to sin and contravening their purpose as guardians of a godly society. The entire import of Scripture was to reveal to fallible men that the power they might righteously exercise over each other was limited. The New Haven magistrates' conception of themselves as God's ministers carried within it an acceptance of the moral restrictions God imposed on their power. If they stepped outside the bounds of righteousness in their efforts to uncover crime, they would destroy their justification for seeking it.[74]

72. ATR I, 88–89.

73. Langbein, *Torture*, 73. Langbein argues that the English did not adopt torture as a routine practice primarily for institutional reasons; it would have been unthinkable to allow JPs, those unpaid amateurs, to operate torture chambers of their own, remote from central authority (137–38). But his analysis fails to consider cultural factors. He discounts what he describes as Sir Edward Coke's self-congratulatory tone in explaining that the English had no law for torture (73), and he fails to consider the evidence of Puritans in New England. Because of the two-witness rule, the colonists had every reason that Europeans had to resort to legalized torture. Yet Puritans avoided it. I would suggest that what Coke and New England's settlers had in common was the feeling that judicial torture was an essentially un-English activity. See also Leonard W. Levy, *Origins of the Fifth Amendment: The Right against Self-Incrimination* (Oxford, 1968), 33. Levy believes that the English abhorred torture.

74. To the extent that adherence to the elders' restrictions protected the accused from being compelled to testify against himself, the actions of New Haven's magistrates provided him with a limited privilege against self-incrimination. But the magistrates did not recognize such a right per se, despite claims to it made by Puritans in England confronted with the ex officio oath in Anglican ecclesiastical courts. The right, which may have existed in England to protect godly men from Satan's Anglican minions, did not apply in New England. Now, as God intended, the righteous men were the judges. Good men needed no protection from the power of evil authorities. Neither did the good authorities have any obligation to put weapons into the hands of bad men. A "right" against self-incrimination was unnecessary. The issue, of course, went beyond New Haven, but it is not the only one in which the realities of holding power in New England transformed a policy developed by Puritans in opposition in England. For an extreme view of such changes, see Darrett B. Rutman, *Winthrop's Boston: Portrait of a Puritan Town, 1630–1649* (Chapel Hill 1965). On the issue of self-incrimination in Massachusetts, see Haskins, *Law and Authority*, 200–201.

Within those bounds the magistrates did whatever they could to get accused criminals to confess, whether the crime was capital or not. A magistrate told one examinant, before he could say a word in answer to the charge laid against him, that "[You had] best speak the trueth, for if [you] shall hide or cover it, it will encrease both your sin and punishment and therefore [you are] wished to confess [your] sinne and give glory to God, and to remember what Solomon says, he that hideth his sin shall not prosper."[75] The magistrate who pointed this proverbial finger betrayed no sympathy for the suspect's possible interest in remaining silent. New Haven's judges expected an accused criminal to tell the truth regardless of the immediate personal disadvantages it would cause him.[76] The "truth" might not be a confession—at first the magistrates might accept a statement of innocence as well as an admission of guilt[77]—but if they confronted the accused with the evidence against him and decided he was guilty, they expected him to admit to his crime. As their harsh treatment of Thomas Langden reveals, they could be forceful persuaders in extraordinary circumstances. Even in ordinary cases, the judges attempted to get the defendant to admit his crimes. For example, a magistrate warned one suspect who, despite proof, refused to confess to his "sinfull and lustfull" attempt to ravish a married woman, "it was not his way to deny it before God and a court of justice, for though the court might, God would not cleare him if guiltie. . . . [And] therefore [the judge] desired him not to leave God and himself" by persisting in his denial.[78]

The magistrates urged each suspect to confess, both before and after they could prove his guilt, because for them confession had a twofold significance. It would clarify the case by providing missing

75. ATR I, 497.

76. See Julius Goebel, Jr., and T. Raymond Naughton, *Law Enforcement in Colonial New York* (New York, 1944), 652–59, for a description of the inquisitorial practices used by New York judges after 1664 in summary proceedings that were in many ways identical with the procedures followed by New Haven's judges in all criminal cases. Goebel and Naughton also think the New York judges' attitudes were antithetical to any belief in the accused's privilege against self-incrimination.

77. John Davenport explained the proper way to respond to accusations. "He that will answer *complaints* made against him *with right words,*" the minister wrote,

> must be mindful especially of three things. First for his personall qualification; that he be innocent of the particular charges . . . and . . . from a good conscience bearing witnes of his integrity let him make his answer to men as if he were making it to our Lord Jesus Christ, . . . Secondly, for the matter of the answer, that it be true and satisfying . . . that is, sufficient to take away the strength of all the allegations produced . . . to prove him guilty; . . . [and] Thirdly, for the manner of it; that the rule propounded by the Apostle be observed . . . where it is injoyned, that our speech be *well filled* and *well seasoned* . . . when it expresseth the sanctifying graces of the spirit . . . and . . . godly wisdom and Christian prudence. (*An Apologeticall Reply to a Booke Called An Answer to the Unjust Complaint of W. B. Also an Answer to Mr. J. D.* (Rotterdam, 1636), 1.)

78. CR I, 239; see also CR I, 334.

details, and when two witnesses were lacking it would make conviction possible. Equally important, even when there was sufficient evidence to convict, a suspect's confession marked the start of his voyage
toward repentance, and repentance was a major theme of New Haven's criminal justice system.

According to the Puritan theory of government expounded by John
Davenport, the magistrate's "chief end" was to "promote men's spiritual good, so farre as they are enabled."[79] To advance the spiritual
stock of the guilty, magistrates, declared Davenport, must inspire in
them a desire to repent. For

> when people who have been formerly under the effects of God's displea-
> sure, so turn unto him with unfeigned Repentence, and Reformation of
> their former evil wayes, God will certainly turn unto them in mercy, and
> make all his creatures serviceable for their Good. . . . That is he will alter
> the Effects of his Providences toward them, that whereas formerly they
> had been afflicting, now they shall be comforting, healing, restoring.[80]

Besides the spiritual and material advantages a criminal could hope
to gain from his repentance, the community would benefit from his
reformation. His return to conformity with God's law would add one
more convert to the town's spiritual portfolio. All this gave New
Haven's judges a strong incentive to reclaim town criminals from sin.

The internal process by which a criminal would reach "conviction"
of his own depravity was familiar to the magistrates, since each of
them had gone through a version of it before attaining church membership. The first step toward religious conversion was total self-
effacement before God.[81] John Davenport instructed his followers,
"The Holy Spirit doth prepare men for union with Christ by
powrfull convincing them of sin, . . . and so humbling them to a lost
estate; . . . Because, till men be [so] humbled . . . they will not come
to Christ as they ought. . . . *Humble yourselves* therefore under the
mighty hand of God that he may exalt you in due time."[82] The convert had to develop this humility within himself, and although it could
not be imposed upon him, the church did use certain "means" to
assist the process. Through public sermons, prayer, and private
instruction, the church elders sought to water the seed of grace in
the souls of New Haven inhabitants so that it would emerge from its
dormant state.[83]

79. Davenport, *Discourse*, 17.

80. John Davenport, *God's Call to His People to Turn Unto Him; together with His Promise
to Turn Unto Them* (Cambridge, Mass., 1669), 20.

81. Davenport and Hooke, *Catechisme*, 22–23. On the morphology of Puritan conversion, see Edmund S. Morgan, *Visible Saints: The History of a Puritan Idea* (New York,
1963).

82. Davenport and Hooke, *Catechisme*, 22, and Davenport, *God's Call*, 27.

83. Davenport and Hooke, *Catechisme*, 34–37.

While the criminals who came before New Haven's magistrates might not possess the gift of grace, each one had a "natural conscience" the judges could nurture. To achieve a criminal's "conversion" to a moral outlook, the magistrates adopted the role of the church and ministry. They too used "means" to humiliate the accused. The process began with the examination, which by its very setting conspired to make the examinant humble. The typical New Haven suspect faced a formidable bench. The two or three magistrates and the four deputies he confronted were (along with the church elders) the most exalted men in town. They were "chosen by the Lord from among their Brethren."[84] God singled them out in New Haven, as He did in the rest of New England, by endowing their integrity and piety with wealth, education, and breeding. The group of twenty who served on the New Haven bench from 1639 until 1658 dressed in finer clothing, lived in grander houses, and spoke with greater eloquence than all but a handful of the suspects who appeared before them.[85]

The greatest of these great men was Theophilus Eaton, chief magistrate of the town and governor of the colony continuously until his death in January 1658. Eaton presided over virtually every court meeting and pretrial examination in New Haven for almost nineteen years. Once England's ambassador to Denmark, he came to New Haven with an estate three times greater than anyone else's, and he received a grant of town land to match. Tenant farmers worked his land while he attended to public affairs and invested in trade. Eaton built a mansion for himself in New Haven and furnished it with a splendor unequaled in New England.[86] The townspeople revered him, no less for his apparently inspiring personal traits than for his wealth. By annointing him and his judicial colleagues "Ministers of God," Puritan doctrine graced their material and social prestige with a bit of sanctity.[87] New Haven's judges stood in relation to their community as fathers to their children, deserving of the honor reserved to parents by the fifth commandment. Before *patres patriae* such as Eaton and his associates, an ordinary New Havener had reason to feel humble.

On arriving at Eaton's house for an examination, most suspects had reason to feel uneasy as well. Many did not know what evidence the magistrates had against them, and some were even ignorant of

84. Davenport, *Discourse*, 27.
85. A list of judges and the value of their estates and information from estate inventories will appear as an appendix in my dissertation.
86. George D. Seymour, *Memorials of Theophilus Eaton* (New Haven, 1938), which includes Eaton's will and estate inventory.
87. Davenport, *Discourse*, 17.

the charges.[88] Without friend or counsel, a suspect had to defend himself before the august group assembled to question him, and his interrogators did not extend themselves to make him comfortable. Although how much sting the magistrates put into their examination probably depended on what they knew of the accused and on the evidence against him, they seem generally to have encouraged his feelings of shame or fear. They warned examinants to "speak the truth," or they lectured them. When Mark Meggs at his examination denied the greater part of an accusation of lewd behavior, Eaton reminded him of his "former filthynes" with William Fancy's wife and of his stiff denials at that time, "though the evidence was sufficient for his punishment." The remembrance of all this, Eaton intoned, should have kept Meggs from both his new adulterous behavior and his current denial of it.[89]

Examinants who took the magistrates' warnings to heart and confessed and repented on the spot sometimes reaped material as well as spiritual rewards for their submission. On occasion the magistrates dismissed a sorrowful criminal without sending him to trial at all. Instead of public ignominy, not to mention public punishment, he might get off with a private admonition or a "private correction" by his father or master at home.[90]

While cooperation coupled with spiritual capitulation might work to an offender's advantage, rigorous obstruction of the magistrates' investigations had the opposite effect. Thomas Langden's stubbornness worked against him, and not only because he had to endure extended grilling and probable imprisonment. His grueling examination was unusual, but not so the additional punishment he suffered "for his continued lying with impudency calling God to witness a lye with dreadful asseverations profaning the name of God, ([he] wished the sunn might never shine on him if he was guilty)."[91] From the magistrates' point of view, a suspect who concealed or twisted the facts frustrated God's work and deserved stern treatment. As Davenport explained, "It is in vain for any that continue in their sins to expect any mercy or favour from God. Such ought to expect, that God's wrath incensed against them by their sins and impenitency, may be executed against them by any and all of his creatures, as he is the Lord of hosts."[92] Who better to execute God's wrath than the creatures He chose as magistrates?

88. For examples of cases from which I have drawn such inferences, see CR I, 328, and CR I, 454–55.
89. ATR I, 31, and, in a later case, ATR I, 498.
90. For examples, see CR I, 301, 380, ATR I, 55–56.
91. ATR I, 173. See also CR I, 170–71, 327–28, 469.
92. Davenport, *God's Call*, 55.

At examinations, then, the New Haven magistrates exercised almost unlimited discretion. They decided whether to prosecute and how strictly to examine a suspect, and they could add or subtract charges against the accused. No formal mechanism existed for reviewing their decisions. Though the potential for abuse of the magistrates' power was as unlimited as their discretion itself, before 1658 the court annals record only one person's objections to the magistrates' conduct during pretrial proceedings. Mrs. Brewster, while reproaching the witnesses against her, complained that during an examination the governor had lured Edward Parker into giving evidence against her (as well as into incriminating himself) by looking "wisely upon him, as if by Mrs. Brewster's confession [the governor] had knowne all before, and so drew things out of him." The other magistrates present at Parker's examination cleared the governor of her charge, as did Parker himself.[93]

Mrs. Brewster also protested that the magistrates framed innocent victims. "They goe two and two together," she alleged, "and writt down what scandalous persons say and so hurrey them and compare their writings and if they find any contradictions they are charged for lies."[94] In her recognition of the magistrates' adverse reaction to incongruities in testimony, Mrs. Brewster's claim had a basis in fact.[95] But the magistrates charged people with lying only when they could prove (according to the two-witness rule) a different set of facts. Never under Eaton's leadership was a defendant convicted solely on charges arising out of the investigation of a reported crime. With one exception, everyone punished for lying at an examination was found guilty of having committed the offense he lied about as well.[96] Nor do the magistrates ever appear, in those records of examinations that survive in court annals, to have provoked suspects of whose guilt they were sure into telling lies that would bring further punishment on the accused. In one case Governor Eaton stopped an examinant from ensnaring himself. "To prevent rashness and sinful expressions," Eaton warned him that the magistrates had already collected incontrovertible proof of the charges he was about to deny.[97]

Although the authors of the court records were unlikely to find fault with New Haven's magistrates, the inclusion of Mrs. Brewster's

93. CR I, 249.   94. CR I, 244.
95. See CR I, 285, where the court determined that a couple had stolen a silver spoon in part because their stories about how they acquired it differed.
96. The one exception was James Till. Till was a repeat offender who could not be convicted of violating the Sabbath by working, but his accounts of his Sabbath-day activities were disproved by two witnesses. CR I, 454–55. For other liars, see CR I, 170, 221–25, 327–28, 442–43, 469–70, and ATR I, 125–26. The issue in these cases was not the denial of guilt in itself but the alternative version of facts that the defendant alleged.
97. CR I, 223.

insinuations suggests that town secretaries felt there was nothing to hide in the judges' behavior. Despite their unchecked power over pretrial proceedings, New Haven's magistrates seem to have preserved their judicial integrity in the examination process. But did they preserve their principles at trial? Even historians sympathetic to the Puritans have had difficulty accounting for the seemingly biased behavior of Puritan magistrates toward defendants on trial in New England. New Haven's magistrates are no exception to the rule, of which Mrs. Brewster's case is a good example.

Sworn testimony convicted her, but even before the oaths were administered the magistrates treated her as if she were already convicted. They objected to almost every effort she made to defend herself. After each of Mrs. Brewster's arguments, the court denounced her, either for what she said or for the way she said it. The magistrates once told her that "meeknesse and modesty would better become her," explaining that they "could not allow her answer in point of truth, [the] evidence was strong against her." After another of her outbursts, the magistrates "reprooved [her] for [her] boldness contrary to truth" and warned her that "such rayling languadge was uncomely and sinfull Michell the Archangell durst not carry it soe with the Divell, though he had matter enough against him." Not surprisingly, a frustrated Mrs. Brewster "seemed to charge the court as if she could not be heard."[98]

New Haven's magistrates treated many attempts made by other New Haven suspects to defend themselves in court with as little open-mindedness and as much disdain as they accorded Brewster's. Once, as soon as the accused had spoken on his own behalf, the court informed him that "his answer was thought overbold and uncom[e]ly for a man under such apparent guilt."[99] Such a statement by a supposedly impartial judge makes the Puritans' pious invocations of justice look like so much hypocrisy.

But the magistrates' actions seem unfair only if one assumes that the purpose of a courtroom trial is the impartial assessment of guilt or innocence, and that was not the purpose of most trials in New Haven. The Puritan magistrates established blame long before the accused appeared in court.[100] The man "under such apparent guilt" from the outset of his trial had already defended himself before undecided judges. Thomas Fugill argued his case in private, first with the men (not judges) who originally suspected him, then with the magistrates at an examination after his accusers reported him,

98. CR I, 247–250.   99. CR I, 260.
100. For evidence that Massachusetts magistrates did the same, see Winthrop, *Journal*, II, 276.

and then, again in private, with Governor Eaton. Finally the New Haven town meeting appointed an expert to investigate and aired the whole issue in public—again giving Fugill the chance to defend himself. All of this happened before trial. Granted, Fugill's is an unusual case. He was the town secretary suspected of fraudulent record keeping,[101] and town leaders were unhappy to find in a fellow church member such a betrayal of trust. They gave him every chance to explain himself and recorded all their efforts. In few cases are pretrial activities so well documented. Yet information about similar pretrial confrontations with suspected criminals exists in other cases, including Mrs. Brewster's and Thomas Langden's. These examination records, and confessions in court unprompted by an accuser's public charge or the testimony of witnesses to the crime, suggest that whether or not the records mention a preliminary examination, the magistrates had already confronted most suspects with the evidence before trial.[102] In 1661, in one of the infrequent cases for which the examination is recorded, John Browne asked his examiners for "a reason why he was called to a private house, and not in publick." Although the magistrates replied that they intended only to investigate the case, Browne had good reason to think that his examination was really his trial. By the time it was over, the judges had decided he was guilty, continuing a practice developed years before.[103]

If the magistrates did decide that most suspects were guilty before sending their cases to trial, we should find few New Haven trials that did not result in conviction and should expect a failure to convict only in cases that had not received a prior examination. For the most part we do. Only 14 out of 201 criminal trials of New Haveners in New Haven between June 1639 and January 1658 did not end in convictions on all charges. Of these, 2 occurred in cases for which the records are so sparse we have no way of guessing how they reached the court,[104] and 7 probably came to trial without an examination at all.[105] In only 2 of these 14 cases do we know that trial was preceded by examination. Both were capital cases, the one involving Thomas Hogg, charged with bestiality, and the other involving Eliz-

---

101. We are indebted to Fugill's perfidy. One result of his disgrace was a vast improvement in the detail and accuracy of the New Haven court records. His mistakes insured that his successors avoided his record-keeping techniques.

102. Out of the 137 criminal defendants whose confession or denial is determinable, a number that includes all suspects whose pretrial examinations are known, 92 had probably been confronted with the evidence against them before trial. Of these, 48 had been examined, 36 confessed in court although no proof was presented, and 8 committed their crimes in the courtroom.

103. ATR I, 490.   104. CR I, 29, 39.

105. CR I, 24, 371, 378–79, 470–71; ATR I, 16–17, 178, 182–83, 214–15.

abeth Godman, the accused witch. The gravity of these charges had already caused the magistrates to delay Hogg's trial in hope of a confession and to imprison and strictly examine both suspects. It also accounts for the decision to send to trial cases that the magistrates were not certain they could prove. For these two offenders, trial appears as the final stricture of a "strict examination," a last effort to pressure them into confessing.[106]

Three more cases ending without conviction on all charges may also have proceeded to trial after examination, and like Hogg's and Godman's cases, there are good reasons to view them as exceptional. All three suspects were under strong suspicion of guilt, each had a notorious reputation in the community, and even though the court found one of the charges against each of them unprovable, at the same trials it did convict them, on their own confessions, of related but lesser offenses. In one other case the tactic of trying a doubtful case worked—an accused of similar questionable reputation confessed at trial to an offense far more serious than he would admit to at his examination, and without his confession conviction on the graver charge would have failed.[107]

The magistrates' failure to examine systematically every accused criminal before trial suggests that their practice of allocating blame before trial to criminals they had examined was inadvertent. They did not intend the examination to replace the trial as the scene for determining guilt or innocence; institutional arrangements led them to that result. The men who later judged the crimes they investigated would have been hard pressed to avoid evaluating the evidence during the investigation. If they had not found sufficient evidence of guilt at the examination, they would not (except in rare cases) have sent the accused to trial in the first place. Only a powerful theroetical or doctrinal purpose might have kept them from taking the examination to be conclusive, and none existed.

By the seventeenth century the concept that opposing parties should present conflicting evidence to an impartial judge at trial had been accepted, if not always lived up to, in the settlement of cases

106. This is indicated by the case of Nicholas Bayly's wife. She was suspected of witchcraft, but the magistrates did not examine her strictly, because she was not under "strong presumption of guilt." They also did not try her on the capital charge. The judges mentioned it at the beginning of her trial for lesser crimes. ATR I, 245–46. On Godman and Hogg, see CR II, 29–36, 151–52; CR I, 295–96.

107. For the three nonconviction cases, see CR I, 252–53, 454–55, and CR II, 139. The records do not reveal whether the suspects themselves were questioned before trial, but it appears that the witnesses were. For a case in which taking the accused to trial resulted in his confession, although without it the evidence was insufficient to convict and although he had denied the charge at his examination, see ATR I, 30–31. Unfortunately, for most cases it is impossible to tell whether the magistrates had adequate proof of the charge before trial.

contested by individuals in England. In English criminal cases prosecuted by the crown against individuals, however, the idea that the judge should be uninvolved before trial was barely beginning to emerge. In the England that New Haven's Puritans left behind, a justice of the peace often sat as a judge on a case he himself had prepared (by examining the parties) for court.[108] Puritan theology nowhere explicitly stated that the magistrate must be impartial at public trial. His unbiased opinion was required when he evaluated the evidence, but he could do that when he heard the proof and the accused's rebuttal the first time. By giving both investigatory and adjudicative power to a few specially qualified men who exercised broad discretion over procedure, New Haven law made the practice of deciding guilt before trial a predictable development. New Haven's magistrates did not draw procedural lines sharply, and they probably saw examination and trial as a continuous process in which they might discover the truth at any point. That point, as it happened, was most often reached before public proceedings began. But the variations in criminal procedure that New Haven's magistrates allowed themselves created ambiguities about the purpose and proper conduct of the trial itself.

If New Haven's judges used the trial to determine the accused's guilt or innocence in only a handful of criminal cases, we must consider what purpose most New Haven trials served. Then, as now, a public proceeding was a necessary part of the criminal process. Since Puritan precept required that a public offense and scandal be censured publicly,[109] at trial the magistrates proved to God and men that New Haven was fulfilling its religious mission. The judges used trials to reinforce public opinion against crime and to educate the townspeople in Puritan ideals. At the same time, they satisfied the expectations of the English settlers that government proceedings against individuals would be open to public inspection. The magistrates may have been sure of a person's guilt before trial, but the townspeople were not. Trial convinced the spectators, including, possibly, deputies who had been absent from the examination, that the courts' judgments and sentences were just.[110]

108. See Goebel and Naughton, *Law Enforcement,* 381, 555, and Langbein, *Prosecuting Crime in the Renaissance,* 111 n. 28. Langbein believes that English criminal trials were not regularly adversary until the eighteenth century, although the scantiness of English records makes the development of the adversary mode difficult to trace. Langbein, "Criminal Trial," 263–72. The study of criminal procedure in the American colonies, then, should provide useful information about the development of modern practices.

109. CR I, 222. The same rule applied in the church. See Davenport and Hooke, *Catechisme,* 45.

110. The records contain no indication that anyone in New Haven, other than an occasional criminal, objected to the way that town leaders conducted criminal affairs. There were complaints in other towns that were part of the New Haven Colony against the government based in New Haven. These took the form of protests against the

Trial had another purpose as well, centered not on the community but on the criminal. In deciding whether to send any particular individual to trial, the magistrates could minimize its public functions. Instead they concentrated on the trial's private purposes. Once they established an offender's guilt, the magistrates focused his trial on securing his repentance.

On rare occasions this emphasis is explicit. In one case, for example, the governor examined a group of men in private about their alleged late-night drinking, smoking, and singing of "filthy corrupting songs." He dismissed those men who admitted their "miscarriages and promised amendment," but put the one carouser who "said he saw no evil in" their activities through a trial solely in order to make him repent actions that he confessed to. (He was honest enough to stick to his opinion, although he finally condeded that "if ther was any evill in it he desired to see it.")[111] Even when the purpose of the trial as an instrument of repentance was not made explicit, repentance played a major role. The magistrates hoped for signs of "inward conviction and suitable sorrow"[112] in criminals, and called on them to display them. In one case a magistrate "asked [the defendant] what she said to the charge" and "wished [her] to owne her sinn and show her repentance for it."[113] In another he told the defendant, "it were better for him if he did it to confess it was in a passion and show his sorrow for it."[114]

Criminal trials in New Haven were a continuation of the efforts to reclaim defendants that the magistrates had begun at the examination, and the techniques in both were the same. For the accused a trial was a ritual of humiliation. As at the examination, the circumstances a defendant found himself in at trial were conducive to bringing him to see the evil of his ways. He again faced his formidable judges without counsel, and this time before an audience. While his betters glowered at him from one end of the meetinghouse, his family, friends, and accusers watched him from the other. And as one of the town's few entertainments, trials were probably well-attended affairs.[115]

The more awesome the experience, the more valuable it could be as a means of humbling him. Whether it was a cause or a result of

---

restrictions of the franchise to church members and against colony policies in relations with the Indians and the Dutch. (See, for example, CR II, 47, 62.) Again, there is no suggestion of discontent with the magistrates' handling of judicial matters.

111. ATR I, 55–56. See also ATR I, 191–92, where the magistrates tried an unruly servant in court because private means of correction had not been adequate to bring about his repentance and reform.

112. CR I, 386.   113. ATR I, 88.   114. ATR I, 152.

115. For example, see CR I, 478.

the magistrates' use of the trial as an instrument of repentance, a courtroom appearance was a social disgrace. The magistrates usually avoided raising charges they could not prove (with the exceptions already noted),[116] and because of the high conviction rate, the public could assume that the defendant on trial stood guilty as charged. Townspeople also looked to the magistrates to repair the reputations of people embarrassed by unfounded accusations. On the judges' orders false accusers had to make public acknowledgment in court of their errors,[117] and law-abiding people who claimed damages to their good names through criminal accusations, even if made outside the courtroom, won the slander suits they brought.[118] The defendants called for trial in New Haven were shamed from the moment they stood up before the court.

The magistrates capitalized on the accused's resulting discomfiture. Many criminals willing to confess and repent proved their sincerity to the court's satisfaction, and had the lesson hammered in, by humbling themselves in public. Thomas Meekes came to trial so that he might respond to the charge of fornication as he had at his examination. "He said he could say nothing against w[hat] hath been declared but it is true, and he desires to judge and condemne himself for it in the sight of God and his people."[119] Jeremiah How confessed to the crime as charged and proved his submission by revealing to the court "sundry other things . . . which he saw as evils in his carriage, and professed his sorrow for them, which the court was glad to see and heare."[120] Samuel Hotchkiss also admitted to crimes he had not been charged with, and he managed to repent both his crime and his lack of repentance. "He acknowledgeth his sin," the reporter noted, "and he judgeth in himself that the court cannot passe too heavy a sentence upon him; for he hath sinned against his light and conscience and confesseth he hath formerly been given to this way of theft. It is now the griefe of his hart that he cannot be sufficiently afflicted with it."[121] Repentant criminals like Meekes, How, and Hotchkiss, having satisfied the magistrates and given hope of their reformation, got through their trials quickly. The court pronounced sentence on them and let them go.

When a criminal seemed insufficiently cowed or, worse, completely unrepentant, the magistrates kept him in the arena a little longer and attempted to increase his humiliation. If he had con-

---

116. See ATR I, 253, where the judges did not raise charges they could not prove; see also ATR I, 245.

117. See CR I, 163.

118. See, for example, CR I, 180–81, and ATR I, 209–10, 211. The stigma of public accusation apparently also applied in Massachusetts. See Winthrop, *Journal*, II, 215, 230.

119. CR I, 469.   120. ATR I, 268.   121. CR I, 301.

fessed, they prodded him to recount the details of his crime.[122] Sometimes they would admonish him, as did the magistrate who told two fornicators that theirs was "a sin which . . . shutts [them] out of the kingdome of heaven, without repentance, and a sinn which layes them open to shame and punishment in this court. It is that which the Holy Ghost brands with the name of folly, it is that wherin men show their brutishness, therfore as a whip is for the horse and asse, so a rod is for the fooles backe." The culprits promptly confessed.[123]

Other criminals took more court time before coming around. A suspect who had not confessed would watch while the witnesses proved to the court's satisfaction (and presumably everyone else's) the charges against him. To convince one of Mrs. Brewster's accomplices of her guilt the court marshaled three witnesses, instead of the necessary two, to testify to her face that she had said words reviling the church which she denied. When even that did not suffice, the judges sent out for a fourth witness, who confirmed the testimony of the other three.[124] If the witnesses' performance left the criminal still unmoved, the magistrates asked him to explain his actions, and self-justification earned only a magisterial reproof.[125]

Even though a New Haven suspect faced neither the physical agony of torture nor the spiritual coercion of the oath, he needed an iron determination and a resilient spirit to persist in silence or go on denying the charge once he heard the magistrates' proof against him, either first at his examination or later at his trial. Francis Hall, for example, denied the militia sergeant's charge that he had acted in contempt of authority by refusing an order. But after another witness confirmed the charge, Hall "seemed to fall under it, and said he rather beleived [*sic*] serjant Fowler then himself . . . and submits to the court."[126]

If Hall's self-abnegation in conceding error is atypical, his concession is not. The magistrates needed no more pressure than the coercion applied or inherent in ordinary examinations and trials to bring most New Haveners who were tried to confess to their crimes. Of the 137 tried and the 129 convicted before 1658 whose pleas are known (out of a total of 201 tried and 193 convicted), 118 admitted to their crimes. Between January 1645 and January 1658, at least 102 of the 121 defendants who faced trial (all but 8 of whom were convicted) confessed.[127] And more often than not the magistrates

122. For example, see ATR I, 9–12.
123. CR I, 435; see also CR I, 306, ATR I, 198–99, 529, and CR II, 94, 95, for example.
124. CR I, 253–56.   125. CR I, 316.   126. CR I, 386–87.
127. During New Haven's first years most of the court reporters' entries are terse accounts containing only the criminal's name, his crime, and his sentence. All but 6 of

were able to move the offender from confession to repentance. Before the court passed sentence, 65 of 118 confessing New Haven criminals also repented of their sins and made enough of an impression on the court reporter that he noted their words. Only 8 admitted to the charges while at the same time refusing to recognize their sin, and the remaining 46 either did not make explicit whatever feelings of remorse or resentment they may have had or did not make an impression on the court reporter sufficient to lead him to note their statements.

The magistrates' record of success in bringing offenders to a "conviction" of their own guilt makes the judges' hostility toward the few criminals like Mrs. Brewster who obstinately maintained their own innocence seem less objectionable, if only because it is more understandable. Given the magistrates' foreknowledge of the evidence against a self-righteous criminal, and the concern they felt for the soul of each one, we see that even in those seemingly prejudiced trials the behavior of New Haven's judges was consistent with Puritan ideals of justice and righteousness.

It was not in how they dealt with those defendants whom they convicted but in how they treated those they did not that New Haven's magistrates seem to have violated their own principles. Of the fourteen suspects the magistrates did not convict on any or all charges between 1639 and 1658, only one, John Jenner, so thoroughly convinced them of his innocence that they completely exonerated him.[128] The other thirteen defendants escaped judgment only because they refused to confess and because the evidence mustered against them failed to meet the requirements of the two-witness rule. The court's attitude toward one of these, whose case apparently progressed no further than an unsubstantiated accusation, is unclear.[129] It released

---

the 64 cases for which the suspects' pleas are unrecorded are pre-1645 cases. Therefore, for the entire period, pleas are known in 68 percent of the cases tried. In 86 percent of these, or 59 percent of the total cases tried between 1639 and 1658, the suspect confessed to at least one charge. Between 1645 and 1658, 84 percent of all New Haveners tried, pleas known or not, confessed. Six cases out of the total of 201 in which New Haveners were tried ended in conviction on some charges, and in nonconviction on one, which accounts for the seeming surplus when 193 conviction cases are added to 14 nonconvictions.

128. CR I, 29. At least that is the most likely interpretation of the case report: "John Jenner accused for being drunke with strong waters was acquitted, itt appearing to be of infirmyty and occasioned by the extremyty of the colde." "Itt" refers to his seemingly drunken behavior. I believe this is the only instance in the records where the word *acquitted* is used. Jenner's is a 1639 case; presumably the magistrates dismissed similar cases before trial thereafter.

129. CR I, 24. The report reads, "Thomas Badger being accused upon suspicion of stealing mony from Edward Cox, boatswaine of the Exetor marchant, was referred to further proofe."

only two of the remaining twelve without some show of reluctance. Both were cases of sexual misconduct in which the only evidence was the woman's word. Each accused penitently admitted to part of the charges but denied the most serious allegations, and the court was able to convict him only on the lesser ones. The judges accepted these results without a recorded murmur of discontent.[130]

In the other ten cases, however, they were not so generous. In one the court cleared a militia sergeant of the allegations of partiality made against him, yet blamed him for arousing the suspicions that had led to his appearance in court.[131] Though he was innocent, the court left the stigma of accusation upon him. The nine others suffered a worse disgrace. On top of the shame they incurred by being accused, they remained as stained by suspicion after trial as they had been before it. As the court released these suspects, it made plain its persistent doubts about their innocence. Noting its dissatisfaction with the uncertain state of each case, the court hinted that it would look for further evidence and sometimes warned the unconvicted accused to keep a better check on his behavior in the future.[132]

In four of the ten cases, the magistrates went even further. Although they had been unable to establish guilt and although they stopped short of actual conviction, in their final warning to these four defendants the judges treated them much as if their guilt had been proved. They released with a reprimand a boy accused of committing "filthy wickedness" with other boys convicted of it, because of conflicting testimony. Nevertheless the judges saw fit to add "that if ever any such carriage came forth against him hereafter, the court would call these miscarridges charged upon him to mind again."[133] By implying that a future accusation would substantiate the first one, the magistrates made clear that they actually believed the accused to be guilty. In effect they treated this boy and the three other suspects whom they similarly branded with a "criminal record" more harshly than some admitted criminals. Those confessed culprits the magistrates dismissed after examination got off, not only without punishment, but without even standing for trial. These four, however,

130. ATR I, 182–83, CR II, 139, CR II MSS, 92–93.
131. CR I, 371, 378–79. The court ruled that Thomas Munson had been faithful in performing his duty as militia sergeant. But it added that his actions "had the appearance of negligence but they hoped this [his trial] would be a warning, and so passed it by." By "passing it by," the court indicated that it actually considered punishing Munson for the "crime" of seeming to have acted unfairly. He was vulnerable to this treatment because as a town official he was God's representative and should have forestalled the publication of even unjust complaints against him by dealing with the complainants privately.
132. The nine cases are CR I, 39, 295–96. 454–55, 470–71; ATR I, 16–17, 178–79, 214–15, 252–53, CR II, 29–39, 151.
133. ATR I, 178–79; also ATR I, 214–15, CR I, 39 probably, CR II, 29–36 (see p. 30).

suffered both the humiliation of trial and the possibility of future punishment for crimes that remained unproven.

The magistrates may have had their reasons for clinging to their suspicions of all ten of these defendants. Even at this distance, we can find in half of the cases some evidence of the factors that may have motivated them. Five of the suspects had histories of crimes or criminal accusations at the time of their trials,[134] and events proved the magistrates right at least once. A year after George Wood escaped conviction for stealing two silver spoons, another charge of theft prompted a search of his possessions. The searchers uncovered not only the newly missing item but the spoons as well, and the court convicted Wood of both thefts.[135]

At Wood's first trial the magistrates had deferred ruling on the theft charge, preferring instead to waite "til more light appear." This reservation and their expressions of doubt about the innocence of other unconvictable suspects are unlikely to have been formal attempts to leave unproven charges pending. If they were, the magistrates should have made their continued suspicions clear every time only one witness could testify to a charge, and they did not.[136] They were committed to fulfilling the social covenant regardless of legal formalities; they would have retried any case if a second witness to prove the charge had appeared later. Their refusal to acquit unconvictable suspects resulted from their concern with their town's spiritual well-being, not to mention their own veracity. The magistrates would have found it unethical, and therefore impossible, to pronounce innocent without qualification people whose innocence they still doubted.[137]

134. The five nonconvicted suspects with criminal records were Thomas Hogg (CR I, 295–96), James Till (CR I, 163, 418–19, 454–55), George Wood (ATR I, 252–53), Elizabeth Godman (CR II, 29–36, 151–52), and Jeremiah How (CR I, 422, ATR I, 16–17). The other five nonconvicted yet unacquitted suspects did not have any other criminal charges brought against them prior to or at the time of their trials. At least three of these lived on in New Haven for years without attracting any further recorded accusations. The three are Ellis Mew (ATR I, 182–83, 402, 512), William Westerhouse (CR I, 470–71, ATR I, 49, 53), and John Clark (ATR I, 179, 378, 511). Clark was brought up in New Haven, and his father was one of the town's original settlers (CR I, 9, 17, 92). The remaining two suspects are Henry Boutle, a servant (or tenant farmer) in town at least from 1651 to 1654, whose accusation in court marks his final appearance in town records (ATR I, 214–15, 65, 205, 209), and Thomas Chambers, who appears in the records only the one time, at his trial (CR I, 39).

135. ATR I, 252–53, and CR II, 187–89.

136. Assuming that the magistrates were formally leaving cases pending would also imply that they were deliberately preserving their option to apply New Haven's gloss on the two-witness rule should another witness come in. But there is no other evidence to support such an argument.

137. The magistrates' commitment to strict honesty was such that they objected when a defendant adopted a standard legal ploy, claiming he "either forgott . . . or did not know the order" he violated. Both, pronounced the magistrates, could not be true. CR II, 200.

But if acquittals are too much to expect from New Haven's magistrates, they did overreach the limits of their discretion in threatening to think of four unconvicted defendants as criminals. In these instances the magistrates' determination to get full value out of only one witness was unjustifiable. By decreeing who might be found guilty, the rule also established who must be found not guilty. If it did not require explicitly that the judges treat an unconvicted person exactly as if he had never been accused, it did imply that they should treat him a good deal better than they treated people they could convict. Regardless of how effectively magisterial threats promoted collective virtue, or how consistent they were with the magistrates' duty to ferret out the guilty and return them to the path of righteousness, the magistrates, in issuing them, violated the single rule for protecting the innocent from unjust punishment that Scripture contained.

Nowhere have I seen Puritan magistrates criticized for the way they treated those whom they failed to convict. Yet it was in allowing the enthusiasm that they directed so often against convictable suspects to color their reactions to unconvictable ones that New Haven's judges fell short of their own principles. Since guilt was not in question at most New Haven trials, the magistrates could generally play their role as the town's moral guardians unfettered by the restrictions of the two-witness rule. That may be why in those few cases where their duty to punish and reform sinners conflicted with their obligation to clear those defendants whose guilt was in doubt, they were unable to resist expressing their suspicions. In these cases the freedom from procedural constraints intended by New Haven's leaders to preserve principle instead permitted it to be undermined.

As yet the erosion was slight—four (even ten) cases out of two hundred are negligible—and it went unremarked in the New Haven records. But a student of legal systems who appreciated the virtue of formal legal procedures in preventing the abuse of justice would have foreseen decay and worse. In fact the degree to which New Haven's judges lived up to their ideals during the eighteen years of Theophilus Eaton's magistracy is impressive. So also is the criminal justice system that Eaton and his colleagues created, in spite, Anglo-American jurists might say, of its nonadversary character. What criminal justice in New Haven lacked in formality it made up in an efficiency and a thoroughness modern jurists would envy. Criminal cases came speedily to trial, and few carried over from one court session to another. Each case received a full and thorough investigation, and, once entered into the records, criminal cases came to public conclusions. Despite the burden on the magistrates, who conducted political as well as judicial affairs in town and colony, they did not complain of overwork, although the omission of examinations in some cases may be a sign that they were seeking to reduce the time they devoted to criminal matters.

Most important, perhaps, for the effectiveness of the system was the consistency of purpose that characterized the Puritan criminal process. Efficiency and thoroughness were by-products of the magistrates' efforts to reach their goals, not ends in themselves. The judges rarely lost sight of their search for righteousness. From the moment a magistrate called a suspect for examination to the end of his trial, the defendant's experiences reinforced the Puritan ideals of the community. The system worked well enough that at least half the criminals who confessed to their crimes also repented of them. And all offenders, repentant or not, had yet to suffer punishment, the magistrates' final means of redemption. In devising a criminal procedure, then, New Haven's leaders were in the enviable position of being able to accommodate both moral and practical considerations, and at what was to them a negligible price—the loss of legal formality.

The Rhode Island Civil Code of 1647

G. B. WARDEN

The Yale Law School disposes of its kitchen garbage through a pseudo-Gothic archway bearing the following inscription:

"The law is a living growth, not a changeless code."

Whether comical or typical, the motto expresses an age-old shibboleth of the Anglo-American legal system. To legal scholars who glorify the particular cases, precedents, and gradual accretion of judicial decisions in the so-called common law, codification has been condemned as foreign, arbitrary, despotic, anarchic, flimsy, rigid, papist, atheistic, frivolous, and, perhaps most important, antithetical to the vested interests of the bar and bench. As Lord Mansfield put it, "It would be very hard on the [legal] profession if the law was so certain that every body knew it."[1]

Anglo-American lawyers conveniently forget that, instead of being an eccentric exception, codification has been the rule in all legal systems in all continents from Hammurabi and Moses to Soviet Russia and China. Even in England itself, Anglo-Saxon law was codified in the dooms of Canute and Ethelred. Canon law and Roman civil law dominated the medieval English universities. Codification was a major influence in the creation of the Tudor state. A uniform, rational, and written expression of the law was desirable to Sir Francis Bacon in support of royal authority and to Puritan reformers in support of parliamentary authority, as well as to Levelers in support of popular authority.[2]

---

1. See Jones v. Randall, in Henry Cowper, ed., *Reports of Cases Adjudged in the Court of King's Bench, 14 G. III–18 G. III* (London, 1800), 40.
2. For the context of codification in England, see Barbara Shapiro, "Codification of Laws in Seventeenth-Century England," *Wisconsin Law Review* 2 (1974): 420–65.

Although until this century most attempts at codification have failed in England and America, colonial historians have recognized an orgy of code making that occurred in New England before 1680. (Thomas Dale's *Laws Divine, Moral and Martial* for Virginia in 1615 smacked more of Draconian fiat for a military camp than of a civil code in the usual sense of the term.) Julius Goebel has exhaustively illuminated the influence of manorial law and borough law in New Plymouth's code of 1636. Richard Morris has devastated simplistic notions of the "reception" of the common law in Nathaniel Ward's *Body of Liberties* for Massachusetts in 1641. George Haskins and others have traced the influence of the Bay Colony's *Laws and Liberties* in 1648 on the codes of Connecticut in 1650, the New Haven Colony in 1656, and subsequent elaborations in New Hampshire, New Jersey, New York, and Pennsylvania. Codification, in short, became nearly epidemic in early New England.[3]

The Rhode Island civil code of 1647 has received little attention from historians, perhaps with good reason. Since its beginning, Rhode Island had the reputation of being the eccentric deviation from everything considered normal among its neighbors. Yet the Rhode Islanders agreed with their enemies on the necessity for a civil code, even though the document produced in 1647 differed markedly from the codes enacted across the borders. Nonetheless, the Rhode Island code of 1647 deserves attention in an attempt to understand the complex elements of code making in early New England's legal history.

In order to appreciate the context of the 1647 code, it is necessary to begin with the basic question of whether Rhode Island actually existed at the time. With the possible exception of the rowdies in Sir Ferdinando Gorges's semibaronial province of Maine, no New England colony had more inauspicious beginnings than had Rhode Island. None of the first settlers chose to be there; all were banished there from other colonies. In 1636 Roger Williams established Providence on the mainland for fellow Separatists. In 1638 Anne Hutchinson and William Coddington founded Portsmouth on the northern side of Aquidneck Island for Antinomian outcasts. But in 1639 the Hutchinsonians rebelled against Coddington, who seceded to establish Newport, on the southern side of the island. In 1642 Portsmouth and Newport were reunited under Coddington's leadership. Unlike almost everyone else in New England during the English civil wars.

---

3. The articles by Goebel, Morris, Haskins, and others are in *Essays in the History of Early American Law,* ed. David H. Flaherty (Chapel Hill, 1969). See, generally, Darrett B. Rutman, "The Virginia Company and Its Military Regime," in *The Old Dominion: Essays for Thomas Perkins Abernethy,* ed. Rutman (Charlottesville, 1964), 1–20.

Coddington advocated a royal charter for the island, and Roger Williams of Providence was dispatched to England to procure it. Not being a royalist, Williams instead secured, in 1644, a patent for both of the island towns and Providence from the earl of Warwick's parliamentary committee on plantations. Coddington refused to accept the patent, and it had little influence outside Providence. To make matters worse, William Arnold in Pawtuxet, northeast of Providence, wanted to secede to Massachusetts, and with the Bay's help New Plymouth secured a fraudulent patent from the Warwick committee to the Narragansett lands east of Aquidneck. In 1647 Samuel Gorton from Warwick, southwest of Providence, was seeking parliamentary authority against both Massachusetts and his neighbors.[4]

The assembly that met at Portsmouth in May 1647 to promulgate a civil code was therefore the first to include delegates from the island towns and Providence. The proceedings were to govern Warwick as well, even though it was not directly represented and though Coddington from Newport was conspicuously absent.

It is, I hope, not too farfetched to say that the Rhode Islanders were suffering from an acute identity crisis, which in turn entailed a fundamental crisis of authority, not only among the towns but also in relations with other colonies and with England itself. In the neighboring colonies, civil codes were approved at least ten years after the initial trials of settlement and early feuds over internal authority. If in other colonies the civil codes were a means of consolidating authority, the Rhode Island code by contrast had to bear the burden of creating authority where it had not existed before. Instead of being the creation of popular unity in the state, the Rhode Island code was in effect the means by which the state was to be created.

The parliamentary patent of 1644 offered no help at all as a source of sovereign authority to bind the towns or create a unified state. Indeed, in the search for higher authority, Rhode Island stood alone in getting the 1644 patent. Connecticut and New Haven never bothered to seek any higher authorization from crown or Parliament until almost forced to do so after 1660. New Plymouth passed statutes in the name of the king but never troubled His Majesty by getting a charter. Massachusetts had a royal charter but honored it more in the breach than in the observance; in 1641 the Bay stopped issuing writs in the king's name and in 1644 denied the authority of Parliament beyond the borders of England. A part of Rhode Island's reputation for deviance rested on the fact that, unlike its neighbors, it

4. See Samuel G. Arnold, *History of the State of Rhode Island and Providence Plantations* (New York, 1859–60), I, 47–199, and Sydney V. James, *Colonial Rhode Island: A History* (New York, 1975), 20–60.

sought official English approval for the colony. What may have been normal in other colonies, to the south, ran counter to the political orthodoxy in New England.

If royal or parliamentary authority was a nullity in New England, the other means of establishing sovereignty in Rhode Island and other nearby colonies was an almost ubiquitous reliance on popular civil covenants or compacts as the basis of the civil state. Reliance on such covenants in Rhode Island, however, was problematical since the town covenants were almost mutually exclusive. In 1637 Roger Williams and his neighbors in Providence adopted a covenant based purely on their mutual agreement. In 1638 the Antinomian refugees at Portsmouth mutually agreed to a biblical dictatorship. In 1639, after Coddington had taken his one-man rule to Newport, the Hutchinsonians who were left in Portsmouth adopted a covenant based on loyal obedience to King Charles. When Newport and Portsmouth reunited, in 1642, a new covenant was adopted transforming the jurisdiction into a "democracy . . . in favor of our Prince"—whatever that meant.[5] If Charles Stuart was the "Prince" meant, he might not have enjoyed the compliment of having a democracy established in his name.

The town covenants thus represented a crazy quilt of mutually antithetical political and religious views. With the exception of lip service paid to the crown in the civil covenants of New Plymouth, of Exeter, New Hampshire, and of York, Maine, the popular compacts of New England at the time rested on the bare fact of mutual agreement, and the political consensus, such as it was, in New England towns coincided with a developing consensus centered on the Congregational variant of Reformed religion. Lacking political agreement among the towns, the Rhode Islanders lacked religious agreement as well. The Separatists in Providence, the Antinomians in Portsmouth, and the Biblicists in Newport had little in common with each other, with their Congregationalist neighbors, with a Presbyterian Parliament, or with an Anglican monarchy. If the civil codes of other colonies represented ten years of consolidating authority, the Rhode Island code of 1647 was the culmination of ten years of political and religious feuding.

Eventually the English civil wars would draw away extremists like Thomas Venner and William Aspinwal, who became Fifth Monarchy agitators in England, and eventually George Fox's Quaker faith would provide a religious and political compatibility that was absent

5. For the covenants, see the sources cited in Warden, "Law Reform in England and New England, 1620 to 1660," *William and Mary Quarterly*, 3d ser., 35 (1978): 672–73 n. 9.

in 1647.[6] At the time, however, the Rhode Island code represented
the result not of consensus but of virtual anarchy.

If the conflicting anomalies of authority and governance behind
the code remain obscure, one could say that, as in other New England
colonies at the time, there were fundamental problems of "home
rule" and "who should rule at home."

Having traced the murky sources of authority that form the constitutional context of the 1647 code, a traditional legal historian would
now plunge deeply into the dense text of the document and produce
pages of footnotes comparing and contrasting its clauses with those
in English statutes and those in the codes of New Plymouth, Massachusetts, Connecticut, New Haven, and New Hampshire. But there
are limits to the reader's patience, and such an exegetical exercise
would only allow textual trees to obscure the contextual forest.
Instead, I will concentrate on the three major themes of the code: its
Englishness, its democracy, and its religious freedom.

A traditional question in American legal history concerns the
degree to which the early settlers incorporated the English common
law into their legal systems. Since there are no case reports and only
a few file papers from that era, the answer to the question depends
on the civil codes of the New England colonies. Outside of Rhode
Island, it is now clear, the codifiers depended heavily on the Bible,
on borrowings from Roman civil law as practiced in Scotland and
the Netherlands, and on legal practices developed in English manors
and boroughs rather than on those of the common-law courts at
Westminster. In that context, the Rhode Island civil code of 1647
appears to be the most English of the New England codes. The code
cites the 1644 patent as the basis of legal authority and refers to the
common law of England, and almost every other provision includes
citations of relevant English statutes or digests of the time; there are
few references to the Bible or other sources of law.

Like a cryptographic code, however, the Rhode Island code of
1647 is deceptive in appearance. Since the parliamentary patent of
1644 was unacceptable to the island towns, referring to it as a source
of authority was an example of wishful, rather than realistic, thinking. Also, the parliamentary patent differed from the Massachusetts
charter in that it omitted the clause prohibiting local laws "repugnant" to English statutes or to English law in general. Instead, the
1644 patent required only that local laws be in "conformity" with
English law, and even that provision was limited by the important

6. James, *Colonial Rhode Island*, 38–41, and Carl Bridenbaugh, *Fat Mutton and Liberty of Conscience* (Providence, 1974).

proviso "as far as the nature and constitution of the place will admit."[7]

In short, the 1644 patent did not require the adoption of English law, and that loophole was almost infinitely expandable. Presumably, the intentionally vague language was the work of Roger Williams, who as a protégé of Sir Edward Coke was familiar enough with English law to know what to avoid and that stricter language would have been unacceptable or impractical in the Rhode Island towns. As a Separatist who had objected to the Massachusetts charter as an impious fraud of a corrupt prince usurping the name of Christian, Williams may also have had grave misgivings about accepting any stronger authoritarian language from the members of an unreformed Presbyterian Parliament. It was, however, necessary to maintain at least the appearance of conformity, so "that we may show ourselves . . . unwilling that our popularity should prove (as some conjecture it will,) an Anarchie, and so a common Tyranny . . . ."

Regarding the common-law system based on customs and precedents in case-by-case judicial decisions of the king's courts in Westminster, the Rhode Island code declares:

TOUCHING THE COMMON LAW.

It being the common right among common men, and is profitable eyther to direct or correct all, without exception; and it being true, which that Great Doctor of the Gentiles once said, that the Law is made or brought to light, not for a righteous man, who is a Law unto himselfe, but for the Lawless and disobedient in the Generall . . . upon which, upon the point, may be reduced the common Law of the Realme of England, the end of which is, as is propounded, to preserve every man in his own person, name and estate . . . .

The code then proceeds to specify laws and penalties with references to parliamentary statutes.

It is relatively safe to say that the Rhode Island code's version of common law had little to do with any of the various definitions of the common law current at that time. In fact, the reliance on positive law was the direct opposite of common-law thinking. And, though some ardent adherents argued, together with the Rhode Islanders, for the universality of the common law, none would have gone so far as to declare it "the common right among common men."[8] Like most other Englishmen at the time, the Rhode Islanders probably

7. See John R. Bartlett, ed., *Records of the Colony of Rhode Island and Providence Plantations in New England, 1636–1663* (Providence, 1856–65), I, 143–46 and 158.

8. Equity in its nontechnical sense was universalized by St. Germain and lay reformers as being superior to the particularities of the common law, although later writers tended to romanticize the common law as a cosmic equivalent of divine or natural law. See J. W. Gough, *Fundamental Law in English Constitutional History* (Oxford, 1961).

had little close acquaintance with the arcane technicalities of the common law. In short, while appearing to incorporate the common law, they simply made up a definition of their own.

Like the codes of other New England colonies, the Rhode Island code blithely omitted any reference to the king, Parliament, English statutes, or English law in the oaths required of the colony's officials, commanding them instead to obey only the law of the colony. Still, after giving an almost convincing show of incorporating the English common law, the text of subsequent provisions includes many references to parliamentary statutes, Stamforde's *Abridgment of Statutes,* St. Germain's *Doctor and Student,* and Dalton's *Countrey Justice.* None of the other New England codes contain such references, and, at first glance, it would seem that once again Rhode Island was deviating from its neighbors by placing itself directly in the mainstream of English positive and customary law.

The appearance, especially of the printed text, is deceptive. Although a good number of the statutory citations are embedded in the text in the same orthography and ink, most of the ones included by Bartlett at the end of paragraphs are actually in the margins of the manuscript, in a different ink and in a later style of handwriting.[9] My hunch is that most of the Englishness in the appearance of the text was a later addition rather than a paramount concern of those drafting and approving the text in 1647.

Some pietistic literature in popular Rhode Island histories claims that the code was a uniquely American invention, which clearly it is not. Other early commentators point to the code as the clearest expression of English rights and liberties, which it may be, but perhaps only on the surface. It is now clear that the code's arrangement and many of its substantial provisions were borrowed almost verbatim from Dalton's *Countrey Justice,* a popular digest for rural magistrates. Yet even that reliance does not adequately place the Rhode Island code in the mainstream of English local law. Dalton, for example, devotes morbid attention to the examination, apprehension, and trial of witches, which the Rhode Island code dismisses in one sentence. Though many of the main titles of the Rhode Island code's sections follow Dalton's, the contents of the subsections are drastically rearranged. Whereas Dalton embroiders the margin with

9. The extant manuscript text at the State Archives in Providence appears in a volume of the Rhode Island Colonial Records, 1646–1669, pt. 2, after p. 211, but it is preceded by records of the General Assembly for 1665 and by a note referring to revisions enacted in 1658. The manuscript variations that are most notably different are those given in Bartlett's edition on pp. 164–65, 173, 191–92, 194, and 202. Bartlett's misprint on p. 174 of a statute of William and Mary is actually a statute of Philip and Mary.

several statutory citations and other references, the Rhode Island code, even with later additions, sticks to the bare minimum.[10]

Thus, despite appearances, the Rhode Island code is generally not any more English than are comparable provisions of the Massachusetts and New Plymouth codes. Even though the Rhode Islanders were being just as selective as their neighbors in the matter of adopting English law, further considerations help to explain in part why the Rhode Islanders felt a perhaps greater need to promote the rather shallow appearance of English law.

Perhaps the appearance of conformity to English law was one means of creating unity or a basic consensus among the feuding towns. It may also have been related to the protests by Robert Child in Massachusetts in 1646 against the un-English provisions of the *Body of Liberties*. It would also be useful in thwarting similar criticisms that Samuel Gorton was presenting to Parliament in 1647. The appearance of legal orthodoxy might help to dispel the Rhode Islanders' reputation for anarchy and heterodoxy, perhaps enough to persuade the neighboring colonies to admit Rhode Island into the New England Confederation, for military assistance against the Indians or the Dutch. Apparent conformity might add legitimacy to the colony's status against military and legal threats from the Bay and New Plymouth. And in the midst of the English civil wars, as Massachusetts discovered, a show of Englishness would help to minimize harassment from royalist or parliamentary ships in the area. In terms of content, Rhode Island, like its neighbors, went on its merry "independent" way in church and state.

Considering all the contrary tendencies in the context of the colony's early history and especially considering that the code provisions probably never went into effect anyway, it is difficult to conclude that the document adhered to English law in anything but a superficial way.

The much proclaimed democratic elements in the 1647 code similarly involve peculiar anomalies as well as differences between appearance and content. The preamble to the code states clearly and unequivocally that the government is to be a democracy, without even the proviso "in favour of our prince" that was expressed in the Newport covenant of 1644. In addition, the term is explicitly defined as the free consent of all or of the majority of the free inhabitants.

10. Compare Dalton, *Countrey Justice* (London, 1618), 198–229, with Bartlett, *Records*, 160–67. Chapters from Dalton are cited in Bartlett, pp. 163, 165, and 169, perhaps from the fourth edition (1630), the first to use chapter headings, or from the three subsequent editions published prior to 1647, all but one being in the Treasure Room, Langdell Library, Harvard Law School.

While it stops short of advocating universal equality, the statement is at least far more democratic than many found in other documents of that time in England or New England.

The question again arises whether the expression accurately reflected actual democratic practice. The preliminary orders of the Portsmouth assembly in May 1647 state that the majority of the colony was present, but it is clear that Providence sent only ten delegates. The Newporters also left early and refused to endorse the complete code. No one from Warwick was present. In short, the assembly was more representative than strictly democratic.

The preamble gives the impression that the whole code was considered as a form of civil covenant, since it was to be signed by those present, copied, sent to the towns for additional signatures, and later reratified with amendments. That cumbersome procedure may have taken place, but the only available copy of the code has no signatures. No town copies are extant, and it is doubtful that the towns gathered to approve the document, since by the end of 1647 Providence was in the midst of dissension, Warwick was still separate, and Coddington in Newport was already in opposition. Like the document's Englishness, the code's democratic elements are complex.

It has been aptly pointed out that the governmental structure outlined in the code is not a democracy at all but a federation of towns.[11] Each town was to receive a charter of incorporation from a subsequent assembly, separate from the structure of the alliance between the towns that the code delineates. The document avoided any mention of franchise qualifications for town voting or elections to the assembly. As with the clumsy mechanism for ratification of the code, legislation to be approved by the assembly had to originate in the towns, and any bill in the assembly had to be approved by the towns and then approved again by the assembly before it became law. At any stage, changes or amendments made in the assembly or towns would require the same cycle, perhaps prolonging final approval indefinitely. Other provisions allowed voting by proxy, suggesting that the whole mass of freeman was not likely to appear at future sessions of the assembly.

Nonetheless, it would seem that democracy in some form—either representative in the assembly or direct in the towns—was more than mere show. Certainly, there was a genuine feeling that democracy was necessary, as the preamble stated. In addition, democracy was needed to offset the anomalous situation in Newport. There Coddington had been elected by majority rule, but he seems to have

11. See Samuel H. Brockunier, *The Irrepressible Democrat: Roger Williams* (New York, 1940), 169.

pursuaded his followers that, having once been elected, he should serve a life tenure, in biblical fashion. Scripture did sanction the popular election of judges but contained no provision for annual elections or any other specific term. In Newport, officials were elected for one year "or until another be chosen," a rather wide loophole. In 1634 John Cotton had unsuccessfully tried to get a similar procedure adopted in Massachusetts, so that magistrates would not be turned out of office except for good cause. The long controversy over the standing council of life magistrates in Massachusetts involved similar issues, and in Congregational churches the pastors and elders were, of course, elected for life without any further imposition of accountability.[12]

The Rhode Island code of 1647 contained provisions for annual elections and impeachment. If they reflected a sincere desire for the usual sort of democratic rotation of offices and accountability, it may help to explain why the autocratic Coddington refused to endorse the code. In 1650 he went to England and received from Parliament a patent giving him one-man rule for life over all of Rhode Island, despite the 1644 patent. Meanwhile, in the towns, the Rhode Islanders held annual elections but, like other New England colonists, tended to reelect the same men of substance and probity year after year. In short, actual practice seems to indicate that the Rhode Islanders, for all their reputation as extreme levelers, were no more or less democratic than were their neighbors.

Like other New England codes, the Rhode Island code of 1647 had a "Magna Carta" clause protecting life and liberty and property, except by judgment of peers or by a duly approved law. This, too, differed little from other codes, in its language or its debatable substantive guarantees. Yet the code is remarkable for its federal character, which gave the assembly and the alliance between the towns few of the familiar attributes of centralized authority or legislative power that were commonly granted by other codes. Of course, considering the nature of the towns at the time, it was unlikely that any of them would agree to such an alliance with coercive powers. As with the New England Confederation and later the Continental Congress, the most acceptable and feasible government for Rhode Island was one that governed least and interfered little with the autonomy of the towns. By default or centrifugal fragmentation rather than by harmony, unity, and consensus, the Rhode Island

12. For the situation at Newport, see Arnold, *History,* 132, 137, 159; for Massachusetts, see John Winthrop, *The History of New England,* ed. James Savage (Boston, 1825), I, 132, and Robert E. Wall, *Massachusetts Bay: The Crucial Decade, 1640–1650* (New Haven, 1972), 41–92.

federation represented one variation of its neighbors' political systems.

In older studies Rhode Island has been depicted as the bastion of religious liberty and toleration, while its neighbors have been portrayed as theocracies. More recently, however, we have learned that the simplistic term *theocracy* does not do justice to the complexities in the relations between church and state in New England. Massachusetts and New Haven did make church membership a requirement for voting, later supplemented by a property qualification, but excommunication of a church member did not entail loss of the political franchise. Ministers were forbidden to hold public office or exercise civil power. Massachusetts banished Roger Williams and the Antinomians—not, the Puritans believed, for conscience sake, but only for the improper expression of their beliefs and for civil disturbances. It was an extremely fine hair to split, but the Puritans believed that their handling of dissent kept them free from the taint of being a church state; similar troublemakers went to the stake on the Continent or to the scaffold in England. In New England, they were sent to Rhode Island, a fate worse than death to members of the Bay Colony.

The Rhode Island code prohibits persecution for conscience sake. In contrast to neighboring codes, it completely avoids biblical citations as justification for specific provisions. It omits the sections on the formation of churches that appear in the Massachusetts codes. Once again, the appearance suggests that the Rhode Islanders were creating a totally secular state, free from the theocratic elements that colored the established churches and states of England and Europe.

The context of the Rhode Island towns helps to explain the appearance of a secular state. In Providence, the Separatists who had been considered extremists north of the border moderated their charges against other congregations who refused to denounce the churches of England and Rome. Perhaps the moderation in Providence was going too far; Roger Williams withdrew more and more from worship with his neighbors. On another tangent, Anne Hutchinson in Portsmouth began to deny the authority of any temporal magistracy. In Newport, Coddington preferred his autocratic biblical rule. In Warwick, Samuel Gorton, at the other end of the spectrum, advocated literal adherence to English statutes concerning moral offenses.

Under those circumstances, the appearance of religious neutrality was desirable and nearly inescapable in the Rhode Island code. It did not establish religious freedom, religious rights, or religious toleration by any explicit, positive means. Instead, such toleration was accomplished by the omission of the regulatory provisions contained in other codes and English statutes. By that indirect means alone was it possible to maintain some semblance of accommodation with strict Biblicists in Newport, with Antinomians in Portsmouth, separating Congregationalists in Providence, and with crypto-Anglicans in Warwick. It was the same sort of grudging toleration that Cromwell and the English Independents later allowed in the face of factional friction.

The code's apparent silence on matters of doctrine and polity contrasted with the codes of its neighbors, giving the impression of secular liberalism in Rhode Island. In fact, however, like citizens everywhere at the time, the Rhode Islanders could not dissociate the state from religious sanctions. Most people nowadays looking at the code's criminal provisions would weep in despair at their apparent confusion and illogic. High treason comes under a heading of parricide. Witchcraft is in a section with suicide and assaults. Forgery appears in the same section as trespass. Slander goes along with perjury.

An early commentator, Judge W. R. Staples, confessed that he could make no sense of such an arrangement. Governor S. G. Arnold, in his history, however, thought that the criminal provisions were a model of legal clarity and secular safeguards. Neither man recognized that most of the provisions were borrowed from Dalton. And it is an ironic comment on the state of biblical knowledge in the nineteenth century that neither of them noticed the underlying theme of the criminal provisions. These coincide exactly with the order of the so-called second table of the Ten Commandments—parental honor, stealing, coveting, murder, bearing false witness, and so forth. The appearance is secular, with citations of English statutes, but the Rhode Islanders were incorporating as much biblical substance into their code as their counterparts in Massachusetts, New Plymouth, Connecticut, and New Haven were.

We know now that Roger Williams was far more of a Puritan than a tolerant religious liberal. Like his orthodox neighbors in other colonies, he firmly believed in forbidding ministers and churches to exercise civil power. He differed with them, for obvious reasons, in denying the civil state's power over doctrine and conscience. But, as expressed in the code, Rhode Island agreed with its neighbors about the civil state's need to regulate outward moral conformity and behavior. The code provided some protection from sectarianism but not freedom from religion itself, despite secular appearances.[13]

To someone punished for forgery, it would probably make little

13. See W. R. Staples, *Proceedings of the First General Assembly* (Providence, 1847), 21n; Arnold, *History*, 205–6, and Edmund S. Morgan, *Roger Williams: The Church and the State* (New York, 1967), 118–35.

difference whether the law was based on English precedent or on biblical sources. Puritan beliefs and the local context, however, help to explain why the Rhode Islanders tried to attain clashing goals of apparent secularism and fundamental religion.

I have argued elswehere that important elements of early New England's history need to be considered within the context of the so-called Puritan Revolution during the civil wars, Commonwealth, and Protectorate in England.[14] Other scholars have argued that agrarian practices, "persistent localism," and traditional peasant communitarian values made New England scarcely different from Old England with few distinct departures from customary life.[15] On a level of everyday work, family life, and community relations, such traditionalism would have been understandable; the settlers, after all, could not mentally erase most of their previous experience.

On another level of experience, however, the New Englanders, like other colonists, had to cope with the anomaly of being English but at the same time different within a colonial or provincial setting. Certainly in religion the Congregationalists consciously adopted practices and attitudes directly challenging the traditional state church of England. With varying degrees of self-consciousness, deliberation, and explicitness, the New Englanders were, I believe, attempting to carry out most of the expressed goals of a revolutionary challenge to the status quo in English society, economy, politics, and law as well, no matter how traditionalistic local life, family, and farming may have been.

In popular covenants adopted by a highly diverse array of groups in all the New England colonies, the settlers of various political and religious persuasions tried to change the fundamental bases of legal authority. The civil codes of all the New England colonies were another fundamental expression of that legal revolution. Codification itself marked a sharp departure from the legal and governmental discretion of the royal prerogative. Codification was also a negative reaction against the customary practices of the common-law system.

As the Rhode Island civil code indicates, the legal revolution in early New England involved complicated elements of appearance and substance, of apparent tradition and substantial innovation. The complexities may lead the unwary general or legal historian astray. An exclusive focus on English law, on Puritan beliefs, or on the local context does not provide an adequate understanding of Rhode Island's code and those of neighboring colonies. Simplistic notions

14. See Warden, "Law Reform," 669–70, 687–89.
15. See the works cited ibid., nn. 31, 35.

of consensus or conflict offer little help in understanding the over-lapping anomalies of substance and expression. In that regard, the Rhode Island code provides another dimension to our understanding of fundamental paradoxes of Anglo-American identity, of change and continuity, and of revolutionary goals and search for stable legitimacy within the diverse communities of early New England.

Magistrates, Sinners, and a Precarious Liberty: Trial by Jury in Seventeenth-Century New England*

JOHN M. MURRIN

Maybe the history of liberty in early America has been overstudied. An army of monographs has marched through practically every battleground between a governor and his assembly, until we the spectators finally seem willing to call off hostilities and surrender unconditionally, whatever the contestants chose to do. Distinguished books have examined the origins of the Bill of Rights and the particular rights to religious toleration, freedom of speech and press, and the guarantee against self-incrimination. In the past generation, the constitutional thought and political ideology of the Revolution have received minute and exhaustive attention. So thorough has this analysis been that now only the more painful ambiguities of colonial liberty seem to arouse great interest—the paradoxical growth of freedom and slavery in the same social environment; the ambiguous and, in many respects, deteriorating status of women, blacks, and Indians in colonies whose public values were proclaimed of, by, and for European males; the conspiratorial or "paranoid" dimension of Revolutionary resistance; the uncertain costs and benefits conferred

*Various versions of this paper were presented at Harvard's Charles Warren Center, the Edmund S. Morgan Conference at Yale, the Middle Atlantic Legal History Conference at Princeton, the Philadelphia Center for Early American Studies, the Johns Hopkins University History Department Seminar, and the University of Virginia. The author wishes to thank the participants for their many helpful suggestions. He also expresses his gratitude to various individuals who took the time to provide detailed criticism: Fred Anderson, Barbara Black, Patricia Bonomi, Jon Butler, Thomas Green, David Hall, Douglas Jones, William Jordan, Stanley Katz, David Levin, Donna Merwick, Gary Nash, William Pencak, and Lawrence Stone. The Warren Center and the American Bar Foundation generously funded much of the research for this project.

on the republic by the right to bear arms. Anybody who proposes to write a history of still another liberty, particularly if much of the subject must be approached in traditional institutional terms, risks exposure as the first person to deserve entry to *The Guinness Book of Records* for remorseless pedantry.

Yet much of the boredom that institutional history provokes today arises from the care and excellence with which earlier historians did their job. Nobody likes to embroider around the edges of someone else's masterpiece. But despite all that has been accomplished, one ancient institution has almost completely eluded sustained scholarly attention. Probably because historians have assumed that juries were always there and have not changed or developed significantly over time, the right to a trial by jury has been taken for granted instead of studied. Hugh Rankin finds the jury secure in Virginia by 1642. Zachariah Chafee and George Lee Haskins, no mean authorities on New England law, have reported its thriving condition in seventeenth-century Massachusetts.[1]

Most historians, even those well read in early American history, accept this tradition as valid. Most of them probably also believe that trial by jury was venerated among the settlers chiefly for its role in criminal rather than civil trials. Flatly contradicting this received wisdom is a different view, set forth in a passing remark by Julius Goebel and in introductory essays by Joseph Smith and Neal W. Allen to volumes of colonial court records that only committed specialists are likely to read.[2] All three men have observed that New England courts in the seventeenth century rarely used juries in criminal trials unless the offense was capital. In most New England colonies, on the other hand, ordinary tribunals expanded the function of civil juries far beyond that of contemporary English practice. Evidently the priorities of the settlers differed from our own.

Yet, as we all know, colonists objected strenuously in 1764–65 when George Grenville threatened their right to trial by jury. A quarter of a century later, the Fifth, Sixth, and Seventh amendments to the

---

1. Rankin, *Criminal Trial Proceedings in the General Court of Colonial Virginia* (Williamsburg, 1965), 90 n. 26; Chafee in *Records of the Suffolk County Court, 1671–1680, Publications of the Colonial Society of Massachusetts* XXIX–XXX (1933), at XXIX, xlv–xlvi (hereafter cited as *Suff. Ct. Rec.*, I and II).

2. Goebel, "King's Law and Local Custom in Seventeenth-Century New England" (1931), reprinted in *Essays in the History of Early American Law*, ed. David H. Flaherty (Chapel Hill, 1969), 83–120, at 112–13; *Colonial Justice in Western Massachusetts (1639–1702): The Pynchon Court Record: An Original Judge's Diary of the Administration of Justice in the Springfield Courts in the Massachusetts Bay Colony*, ed. Joseph Smith (Cambridge, Mass., 1961), 144–45 (hereafter cited as *Pynchon Ct. Rec.*); *Province and Court Records of Maine*, ed. Charles Thornton Libby and Neal W. Allen (Portland, 1928–), IV, lxxi–lxxiv (hereafter cited as *Me. Ct. Rec.*).

federal Constitution guaranteed the individual's right to a grand jury for indictment, a petit jury for trial of a federal crime, and a civil jury in any federal lawsuit for more than twenty dollars. Herein lies a story. No apology is necessary for trying to explain how the colonists' attitude toward juries changed from initial ambiguity to reverential acceptance.

The present essay, part of a larger study on trial by jury in colonial America, will concentrate on seventeenth-century New England, the region best served by published court records and scholarly monographs and for which I have also had time to pursue manuscript sources even into the eighteenth century. As every social historian feels obliged to remind us these days, New England was not colonial America, and we cannot with any assurance extrapolate patterns of behavior from this region to other colonies. This caution is in every way commendable. Yet on this specific question, New England represented not a norm or a microcosm of North America but a laboratory in which both the projury and the antijury extremes found elsewhere on the continent achieved elaborate institutional definition in one Puritan society or another. I have now read enough court records for other colonies—most of what exists in print—to make this judgment confidently. Rhode Island nearly equaled Quaker West New Jersey and outpaced Pennsylvania in its fondness for juries. New Haven Colony matched New Netherland and exceeded Virginia in its rejection of juries. In between stood Plymouth, Massachusetts, Maine, and Connecticut, here listed in the order by which they progressed along the spectrum between these two extremes.

Obviously the social dynamic that generated contrasting behavior within New England could differ radically from such forces elsewhere. No other legal system in America could match, for example, New England's ability to mobilize guilt and shame for socially approved purposes. Nevertheless, one major uniformity does emerge. Colonies organized by settlers without strong leadership from a magisterial elite (Rhode Island, West Jersey, North Carolina) warmly embraced juries. Powerful magistrates, and the colonies they dominated (New Haven, Massachusetts, Connecticut, Virginia, early Maryland), embodied a deep suspicion of juries. In New England, a subdued, sometimes almost invisible tension between magistrates and settlers, particularly the more sinful variety, suffuses the first century of the region's history. Even a careful scholar can miss this theme if he or she studies a single colony. The pattern best emerges when we examine the full range of options adopted by the Puritans in all of their colonies. To comprehend this diversity, we must begin the story in England.

I

Colonial America could display such an astonishing variety of behavior because it inherited a thoroughly ambiguous set of traditions from England. The English jury arose as a twelfth-century institution by which private individuals gave government officials (judges, in most cases) the information that they needed to administer the law. Jurors provided facts that royal officials could not easily obtain in any other way, and judges applied the law to those facts. The relationship was always more complex than a simple statement of principle can convey. For example, because popular beliefs justified certain forms of homicide that the law condemned, jurors became adept at altering the facts to create a situation of desperate self-defense where none had really existed.[3] By the Tudor era, however, juries had largely completed their evolution from active knowers of local events to passive receivers of evidence made available to them only in court. In an environment in which bench and jury heard the same information simultaneously through the testimony of sworn witnesses, the jurors lost much of their creative powers over facts. They also became subject to greater discipline from the bench and the objects of a slowly developing legal tradition that would define their activities with greater precision, including their right to acquit in the face of the evidence.[4]

Beginning with the late medieval growth of equity, juries faced other challenges, especially under the Tudors. Until 1640, conciliar government—Star Chamber, the Council of the North, the Council of Wales—dispensed with juries over a broad range of civil and criminal business, sometimes extending even to capital punishment, at least in the borderlands.[5] Below the level of capital crimes, juries encountered a new rival as Tudor, Stuart, and Hanoverian parliaments slowly restricted their powers. One by one, Parliament excluded specific offenses from the benefit of a jury trial, giving jurisdiction instead to one or more justices of the peace "out of sessions"—sitting, that is, outside the regularly scheduled county courts of quarter ses-

3. Catharine H. Kappauf, "The Early Development of the Petty Jury in England, 1194–1221" (Ph.D. diss., University of Illinois, 1973); Thomas A. Green, "Societal Concepts of Criminal Liability for Homicide in Mediaeval England," *Speculum* 47 (1972): 669–94.

4. John H. Langbein, "The Origins of Public Prosecution at Common Law," *American Journal of Legal History* 17 (1973): 313–35; Thomas A. Green, "The Jury and the English Law of Homicide, 1200–1600," *Michigan Law Review* 74 (1975–76): 413–99.

5. For a summary of the literature on this question, see David Thomas Konig, "Criminal Justice in the New World: English Anticipations and the Virginia Experience in the Sixteenth and Seventeenth Centuries" (Paper read before the International Association for the History of Crime and Criminal Justice, 4 September 1980).

sions that routinely used juries. Over time these exceptions grew into a formidable corpus of summary justice so extensive, warned William Blackstone, "as, if a check be not timely given, to threaten the disuse of our admirable and truly English trial by jury, unless only in capital cases." His anxieties were well founded. In the nineteenth century the summary tradition would replace the jury trial as Britain's normal method of handling all but serious crime.[6]

In England throughout the period of American colonial history, juries remained an indispensable component of civil suits at common law, whether at Westminster or with justices on eyre; of felony (capital) trials at local assizes; and of misdemeanor cases at quarter sessions. Assizes still heard some misdemeanors, and sessions sometimes tried felonies in the Elizabethan and early Stuart eras, but as time passed these courts tended to differentiate their criminal functions along the boundary line of capital punishment.[7] Because, especially after the collapse of the prerogative courts in 1641, the growth of summary justice stopped short of trials for life or mutilation, and because Parliament simultaneously indulged its greed for property by vastly expanding the number of capital offenses, the jurisdiction of the assize courts was not threatened by this trend. Instead, summary justice competed directly with the quarter sessions, slowly restricting their criminal business.

Two other trends deserve mention. First, criminal procedure during the early modern era was groping toward a distinction between the prosecutorial and adjudicative functions of the court. This difference could utterly collapse in major political trials in which the bench might insult the defendant and browbeat witnesses and jurors, but in "ordinary" felony or misdemeanor cases, judges increasingly saw themselves as neutral umpires, standing above both prosecution and defense. In trials for life, the bench often warned the accused *not* to plead guilty.[8] Very likely, pleas of guilty remained rather unusual at all levels of the judicial system, as they had been during the Middle Ages as well.[9]

6. Felix Frankfurter and Thomas G. Corcoran, "Petty Federal Offenses and the Constitutional Guaranty of Trial by Jury," *Harvard Law Review* 39 (1925–26): 917–1009, which is primarily a study of the statutory base of summary justice in England and colonial America; William Blackstone, *Commentaries on the Laws of England: A Facsimile of the First Edition of 1765–1769*, ed. Stanley N. Katz et al. (Chicago, 1979), IV, 277–78.

7. J. S. Cockburn, *A History of English Assizes, 1558–1714* (Cambridge, 1972), chap. 6, esp. table 1, pp. 94–96.

8. John H. Langbein, "The Criminal Trial before the Lawyers," *University of Chicago Law Review* 45 (1978–79): 263–316, esp. 278.

9. Ibid., 277–78; Green, "Societal Concepts of Criminal Liability," 671. In Devon, 1598–1639, some 44 percent of the accused at assizes had the charges dismissed or were acquitted, compared with 35 percent brought to trial at quarter sessions. This pattern may suggest a somewhat higher rate of guilty pleas in the lesser court. Cockburn, *English Assizes*, 96.

Second, procedural protections for the accused evolved most rapidly where they mattered the least, in misdemeanor trials at quarter sessions. At this level, defendants began to win the right to postpone trial, ostensibly to prepare a better case, but often more in the hope that the prosecution would not be able to produce its witnesses several months later. The accused also secured the right to obtain a copy of the indictment, engage counsel, and produce sworn witnesses. All of these privileges still seemed much too dangerous to grant to accused felons.[10]

Obviously, then, even when colonists explicitly claimed to be importing or imitating English law, we must be careful about what kind of law they considered most characteristically English. To judge from their behavior, New England magistrates consciously imitated what they evidently regarded as the most progressive and efficient feature of the whole system, the trend toward summary justice. In a culture as addicted to guilt as was Puritan New England, they succeeded overwhelmingly in criminal law, but they had to yield ground over civil disputes that lacked comparable internalized sanctions. Settlers, on the other hand, showed an unmistakable fondness for juries. When given an unimpeded opportunity to develop their preferences, they also moved beyond English limits by expanding the procedural safeguards allowed to accused criminals.

These tensions required time to work themselves out. Perhaps the best way to grasp the social dynamic behind the astonishing variety of New England's jury systems is to pursue the subject in roughly chronological order, beginning with Plymouth.

II

New England's first recorded statute involved juries. ". . . *all* Criminall facts, and also all [matters] of trespasses and debts betweene man & man," declared Plymouth Colony in December 1623, "should [be tried] by the verdict of twelve Honest men to be Impanelled by Authority in forme of a Jury upon their oaths."[11] By then memories of English common law were about fifteen years old, and most of the settlers had doubtless acquired some familiarity with Roman law during their sojourn in the Netherlands. Yet, so far as I know, not a

10. For this pattern, see Lois G. Carr, "County Government in Maryland, 1689–1709" (Ph.D. diss., Harvard University, 1968), I, 196–97, 254–55. For the legal status of defense witnesses, see Sir Matthew Hale, *Historia Placitorum Coronae: The History of the Pleas of the Crown*, ed. Sollom Emlyn, rev. ed. by George Wilson (London, 1778), II, 283–84.

11. *Records of the Colony of New Plymouth in New England*, ed. Nathaniel B. Shurtleff and David Pulsifer (Boston, 1855–61), XI, 3 (emphasis added, brackets in original) (hereafter cited as *Plym. Col. Recs.*).

single Pilgrim had gained experience as a magistrate in England. Only Elder William Brewster even qualified, through his study at Cambridge, as a true gentleman, and he did not hold judicial office in the colony, probably because Puritans regarded the post of ruling elder as incompatible with such a responsibility.[12] Power devolved instead upon such men as William Bradford, a self-educated, orphaned farmer who learned the weaver's trade in Leiden; Edward Winslow, trained as a printer; Thomas Prence, who could barely write; and Isaac Allerton, a tailor who became a merchant and speculator before moving on to New Haven.[13] Except for a brief and unhappy experiment with a renegade Anglican, the colony had no clergy for the first nine years, and nothing like an adequate supply before midcentury. The few who served prior to 1650 either lacked stature or soon departed.[14]

Clearly if Plymouth were going to acquire a magisterial ethos, it would have to build upon someone else's example. Until the settlement of Massachusetts Bay, in the 1630s, nothing of the kind existed near enough to merit imitation. Unfortunately we know practically nothing about the actual administration of justice before the mid-1630s. The sensational trial of the Reverend John Lyford and John Oldham for conspiring to overthrow the colony's government did display Bradford's astute ability to assemble evidence and trap his opponents in open court, but Bradford's account says little about procedure. The accused denied guilt only to confess when confronted with the evidence (Lyford's incriminating letters) and with the refusal of any of their followers to support them. But Bradford never indicates whether a jury was impaneled, or how the court planned to proceed had the two continued to plead innocent. He does reveal his utter disgust at Lyford's hypocritical talent for manipulating Puritan respect for sincere repentance. This trait Lyford had shown upon arrival and continued to display long after his trial until again exposed, this time by his wife. She feared, through her own reading of Scripture, that God might deliver her to the Indians for rape as one way of punishing her husband's sins, including his earlier sexual adventures in England and Ireland. Plymouth was not magisterial, but it did rely upon powerful mechanisms of internalized guilt, even by mere association.[15]

12. John Winthrop, *The History of New England from 1630 to 1649*, ed. James Savage, new ed. (Boston, 1853), I, 97.

13. These men have been traced through the indices of William Bradford, *Of Plymouth Plantation, 1620–1647*, ed. Samuel Eliot Morison (New York, 1959), and George D. Langdon, Jr., *Pilgrim Colony: A History of New Plymouth, 1620–1691* (New Haven, 1966).

14. Ibid., chap. 9.

15. Bradford, *Of Plymouth Plantation*, ed. Morison, 147–63, 165–69.

Only as Plymouth court records start to appear, in 1633, can we try to assess how closely the colony observed its jury mandate of a decade before. A jury decided two civil suits at the "court" of January 1632/33, but probably none participated in the "Acts of the Councell" between courts, which included disposition of a few civil cases.[16] Very likely, juries did attend all "court" meetings (i.e., what would soon be called sessions of the General Court), and by middecade their use had become standard in civil disputes. Criminal trials are harder to evaluate. When the record informs us only that John Holmes "was censured" and fined for drunkenness, or that two couples were "adjudged to sitt in the stocks" for fornication before marriage, we cannot tell whether any or all of the accused pleaded guilty or were condemned summarily. But because at the same court the clerk specifically noted a jury verdict in a civil case "proved by divers testimonies," we can be reasonably certain that no jury participated in the criminal trials.[17] Perhaps inspired by a different example already emerging in Massachusetts Bay, the General Court in 1636 significantly modified its jury guarantee of 1623. A new law permitted freeholders "of good report" to sit with freemen on juries, but the scope of jury activities was narrowed to "All trialls whether Capitall or between man & man," which were to follow "the law of Engl. as neer as may be."[18] As contemporary practice soon demonstrated, nobody believed that this law *prohibited* jury trials for noncapital crimes. In fact, a 1660 statute empowering the magistrates to decide all criminal cases in which the fine did not exceed £10 must have rankled with the public, for it was repealed a year later.[19] Eventually the colony provided distinct oaths for two types of trial jurors: in civil and criminal cases. In Massachusetts and Connecticut the comparable distinction was between civil jurors and jurors of "life and Death."[20]

Although the colony government never attempted to eliminate all noncapital jury trials, summary proceedings did become frequent. Magistrates dispatched some important cases by themselves, including one involving two men accused of homosexual activities that fell short of overt sodomy. For this potentially capital offense, one was banished and the other only whipped.[21] Dismissals and acquittals

---

16. *Plym. Col. Recs.*, I, 5–11. The jury trials are on p. 6.   17. Ibid., 12.
18. Ibid., XI, 12.   19. Ibid., 128.
20. *The Laws of the Pilgrims: A Fascimile Edition of the Book of the General Laws of the Inhabitants of the Jurisdiction of New-Plymouth, 1672 and 1685*, ed. John D. Cushing (Wilmington, 1977), 73; cf. *The Earliest Laws of the New Haven and Connecticut Colonies, 1639–1673*, ed. John D. Cushing (Wilmington, 1977), 128.
21. *Plym. Col. Recs.*, I, 64. For the fine distinctions that courts had to make about degrees of "unnatural vice," see Bradford, *Of Plymouth Plantation*, ed. Morison, 404–13.

happened fairly often under the Plymouth system, but magistrates could also lose patience with a guilty party who stubbornly refused to confess.[22]

Yet in Plymouth, as opposed to Massachusetts and Connecticut, most criminal cases decided without a jury, especially in the early decades, were heard before the General Court, not the Court of Assistants (or magistrates). In Massachusetts, as we shall see, trial before the General Court was explicitly regarded as an alternative to, and hence the equivalent of, a jury trial. Thus by contemporary Massachusetts definition, most such trials in Plymouth should not be regarded as summary. Plymouth *behavior* indicates that many ordinary settlers did not accept this equation. Prior to 1668, every criminal jury trial in the colony occurred before this body, not the Court of Assistants. Between 1668 and absorption by Massachusetts, roughly half still took place there. Faced with the moral equivalent of a traditional jury (by strict Puritan definition), many defendants chose the jury anyway. Apparently they regarded the need for a unanimous verdict among twelve men as a stronger protection than a majority vote in a larger body could provide. Doubtless for the same reason, most civil litigants before the General Court continued to use jury trials. Nevertheless, the frequency of the demand for a criminal jury declined over time despite the steady growth in population. In just over two years, from 1636 to 1638, eight jury trials for misdemeanors occurred. After 1638 the volume fell off sharply. On three occasions (1642–47), 1649–55, 1655–60), the colony went five years, give or take a few months, without a single criminal jury trial.[23]

The Plymouth experience offers an interesting perspective on judicial practice in the rest of New England, especially in the truly orthodox colonies. It suggests what Massachusetts might have become had the deputies won a clean victory over John Winthrop and the magistrates. Perhaps not until the emergence of the college-educated Thomas Hinckley, late in the century, would Plymouth begin to possess a magistracy in a position to claim the kind of authority exercised in the Bay Colony. Plymouth behavior also teaches us to regard with a bit of skepticism the Massachusetts claim that a general court of saints really was an adequate substitute for trial by jury. Too many Plymouth settlers did not think so, even if others accepted the formula. Finally, Plymouth development over time did tend to bring

22. For examples of criminal trials without juries before the General Court, see *Plym. Col. Recs.*, I, 97–98, 105–7, 118–19, 128, 132, 143. For an interesting mix of convictions and acquittals, see the session of 2 January 1637 / 38, ibid., 75. For the pressure to confess, see ibid., II, 86.

23. This paragraph rests on a tabulation of all criminal jury trials found in ibid., I–VII passim.

the colony into closer alignment with its neighbors. In the decade 1630–40, alternative visions of Puritan justice were taking shape around Massachusetts Bay, out in the Connecticut Valley, and off Long Island Sound. All of them embodied severe restrictions on criminal jury trials.

III

The earliest Massachusetts records raise the same difficulties that we have encountered in Plymouth. Entries are usually too brief to tell us what we wish to know about juries. From the start, John Winthrop and his magisterial colleagues probably did respect the right to a jury trial when life was at stake, for they used one in a homicide case of 1630. Juries were also employed for at least some civil cases. In 1631, John Endicott lost a suit for battery by jury verdict, and two years later an absent juror was fined, indicating a broader use of the institution than surviving documents actually show.[24] Because most records of the emerging Court of Assistants either have not survived or are too terse to help much, we have to gain our information from other sources, such as Winthrop's journal or occasional file papers.

As the judicial system acquired form and coherence, court clerks had strong reasons for distinguishing cases decided by juries from those resolved by the bench, if only to compute the jurors' fees, which depended on how many cases they heard. Winthrop's journal is an informal record guided by no such necessity. Perhaps it means nothing, then, that he mentions no jury in describing two potentially capital trials of 1631—that of Henry Lynn, who suffered banishment (an alternative to death) for conspiring against the government, and that of John Dawe, who was whipped for adultery with an Indian, an offense that the magistrates had not yet had time to proclaim capital by some public act.[25] On the other hand, the same General Court of 1634 that created the House of Deputies and demoted Winthrop from the governorship also declared "that noe tryall shall pass vpon any, for life or banishment, but by a jury so summoned or by the Genall Courte."[26] Almost incidentally, the colony's freemen thus revealed their own belief that the General Court, proceeding

24. *Records of the Court of Assistants of the Colony of the Massachusetts Bay, 1630–1692*, ed. John Noble (Boston, 1901–28), II, 9, 15, 35 (hereafter cited as *Ct. Assts. Recs.*).
25. Ibid., 19; Winthrop, *History*, I, 73.
26. *Records of the Governor and Company of the Massachusetts Bay in New England*, ed. Nathaniel B. Shurtleff (Boston, 1853–54), I, 118 (hereafter cited as *Mass. Recs.*). The last five words of this passage were probably added by amendment, according to Shurtleff.

by majority vote, was an adequate equivalent to trial by jury and that in Massachusetts, as opposed to Plymouth, jury trials would take place only in lesser tribunals.[27]

Did this law merely restate accepted practice, or had the magistrates taken to deciding even capital offenses summarily, until called to account in 1634? In all likelihood, we shall never know. But with the beginnings of local "quarter courts" in the mid-1630s (direct ancestors of the "county courts" of the next decade), we start to learn much more. Because this study rests primarily upon these records, a word about them seems necessary. Unless compelling evidence to the contrary exists, I believe what they say. If the record mentions a jury, one was used. If it does not, the proceedings were summary. In Massachusetts, Connecticut, and Maine, such evidence indicates that civil juries flourished from the start, but trial by jury for non-capital crime all but disappeared before 1660.[28] Other sources reveal that the official account is wrong in two cases. Plymouth records mention no jury in Thomas Granger's bestiality trial of 1642, but Bradford's narrative shows that one was indeed used. Winthrop's journal provides a similar corrective to the official Massachusetts entry for the adultery trial of James Brittaine and Mary Latham, who, the official version tersely reports, "being found guilty" were condemned to hang. Winthrop notes that, while James pleaded guilty, Mary confessed only after "the jury cast her."[29]

Fortunately other good reasons exist besides jury fees for assuming that the official records are highly accurate in this regard, especially once court entries had become standardized. Sometimes a court would meet, dispatch its civil business with a jury, and then adjourn criminal matters to a later date, when the court reassembled with no jury present. Absent jurors were often fined after the civil cases but before criminal trials had begun, presumably so that jurors who did

27. For the criminal jurisdiction of the General Court, the best study is Barbara A. Black, "The Judicial Power and the General Court in Early Massachusetts (1634–1686)" (Ph.D. diss., Yale University, 1975), 174–93. For Sarah Roper's challenge to the General Court as the equivalent of a jury, which in her case also amounted to a claim against double jeopardy, see pp. 181–82.

28. See the earliest recorded years in *Plym. Col. Recs.*, I; *Me. Ct. Recs.*, I; *Pynchon Ct. Rec.*; *Records of the Particular Court of Connecticut, 1639–1663, Collections of the Connecticut Historical Society* 22 (1928) (hereafter cited as *Conn. Partic. Ct. Recs.*). The published abstracts for early Essex County do not indicate whether juries were used in civil cases, but the manuscript originals in the Essex County Court House (Salem) show that they were. See *Records and Files of the Quarterly Courts of Essex County, Massachusetts* (Salem, 1912–75), I (hereafter cited as *Essex Ct. Recs.*).

29. Compare *Plym. Ct. Recs.*, II, 44, with Bradford, *Of Plymouth Plantation*, ed. Morison, 320–21; and compare *Ct. Assts. Recs.*, II, 139, with Winthrop, *History*, II, 190–91. After her conviction, Mary Latham accused twelve other men of having slept with her, five of whom were still in the colony. They escaped punishment, apparently for want of a second witness.

attend could then be dismissed. Far too often to be fortuitous, the only criminal jury trial at a court session followed hard upon the civil cases, preceding all other criminal business. Occasionally a request for a jury by someone farther down the criminal docket would force postponement of the trial because the jury had already gone home. These routine procedures strongly suggest that the magistrates did not offer jury trial to the accused. The defendant had to take the initiative, probably *before* appearing in court, if only to be placed in the right slot on the docket.[30]

Assuming, then, that the records mean what they say, I have found only four jury trials for noncapital crimes in Massachusetts before 1660—two in Boston before 1640; a Middlesex case of 1653 involving, not a settler, but an English ship captain; and a paternity trial in Springfield.[31] Connecticut had seventeen criminal jury trials before counties emerged after 1663. All were for "life and death," twelve for witchcraft.[32] Sociologically speaking—and in these days what historian dares be caught talking any other way?—no definable group did nearly as much as accused witches to keep criminal jury trials alive west of Boston before 1660. Maine held one capital jury trial in 1650 and no other criminal jury cases before the Restoration. There the possibility did arise several times, however. A few defendants, presented for various misdemeanors, "traversed" their "present-ments" (the English-language equivalent of a formal Latin indict-ment by grand jury). A "traverse" was a request for jury trial which also permitted the accused to postpone his case to a later court, when, for example, the prosecution might no longer be able to produce its

30. These points can all be illustrated from the Suffolk County records, 1671–86. For criminal sessions without juries present, see *Suff. Ct. Rec.*, I, 119, 125–26. On very rare occasions, a jury might be present at an adjourned session, as in ibid., II, 1168–71. For the fining of absent jurors after the civil cases but before summary criminal proceedings began, see ibid. II, 834, 865, 883, 956, 991 (the last two references containing minor variations on this pattern). Of eleven criminal jury trials in these two volumes, seven either occurred within the civil docket or preceded other, summary criminal trials. Ibid., I, 107–8, 145; II, 626, 866–67, 940 (two cases), 992–93. For the postponement of a trial because no jury was present, see John Clarke's case in Records of County Court, Suffolk, 1680–1692 (Social Law Library, Suffolk County Court House, Boston), I, 194 (hereafter cited as Suff. Ct. Recs., 1680–92). Two exceptions deserve note. William Hawkins, accused of having spirited away a pregnant woman to Barbados in 1671, had his trial postponed as soon as he requested a jury, but another defendant farther down the docket was tried by jury at the same court. *Suff. Ct. Rec.*, I, 82–83. And at least one noncapital defendant in the Court of Assistants was offered a jury trial but declined it. See the 1677 case of William Pope, accused of having abused authority and defamed the women of Boston. *Ct. Assts. Recs.*, I, 104.

31. *Ct. Assts. Recs.*, II, 78, 86; Middlesex County Ct. Records, transcribed by David Pulsifer (County Court House, Cambridge), I, 40–43 (hereafter cited as Midd. Ct. Recs.); *Pynchon Ct. Rec.*, 230–31.

32. *Conn. Partic. Ct. Recs.*, passim. The offense is stated in fifteen cases, but the other two are denoted as trials for "life and death." See pp. 81–82.

witnesses. In Maine before 1660 the traverse became solely a device for evading trial altogether. No one who used it was ever brought to judgment.[33]

To put the matter succinctly, Plymouth Colony resolved twice as many noncapital crimes by jury between 1636 and 1638 as all the rest of orthodox New England combined before 1660. England with its Star Chamber and other conciliar courts, its High Commission and other ecclesiastical tribunals, and its emerging body of summary justice at petty sessions had already created a series of formidable barriers to criminal jury trials. Yet even taken as a whole, these mounting exceptions did not match the challenge that New England was beginning to erect against common-law traditions of criminal justice. Even the region's sharp reduction in the number of capital crimes worked in the same direction, once it became clear that juries should be expected only for those offenses.

But New England's orthodox system departed from England's in more than juries. It was not really an adversary system at all. In the strict technical sense of the term, criminal justice in the orthodox colonies was inquisitorial. Although grand juries emerged around 1635 to accuse people of crimes, the magistrates themselves compiled evidence, prosecuted, questioned witnesses and the accused, judged, and passed sentence. Bound by a strict covenant with the Lord, they knew they had a sacred duty to "discover" and punish sin, and, it was hoped, reclaim the sinner. Throughout orthodox New England, this combination of severe inquiry and genuine compassion for those who repented placed enormous pressure on the accused to plead guilty and created a truly phenomenal rate of conviction, perhaps somewhere in the 90 percent range. So far as I am aware, no English courts could match this performance.[34]

Massachusetts and Connecticut, unlike Plymouth, did possess genuine magisterial talent—never enough to meet all needs but a fully adequate supply to exert a decisive influence. The two John Winthrops, Thomas Dudley, Sir Richard Saltonstall, and Willima Pynchon,

33. For the capital trial, see *Me. Ct. Recs.*, I, 140–43. In another case in 1647, the record claims that Charles Frost was "presented and indicted" for murder, but the full entry suggests that the coroner's jury refused to find a murder and that the grand jury failed to indict. Ibid., I, 109. For use of the traverse, see ibid., I, 118–19, 134–35; II, 13. For a similar case in Old Norfolk County (most of which later became part of New Hampshire), see *Essex Ct. Recs.*, I, 223, 236. In this cae, the accused protected himself after his traverse by appearing at the next court as foreman of the jury that should have tried him!

34. Rates of conviction will be discussed below. For the distinction between inquisitorial and adversary systems, see Leonard W. Levy, *Origins of the Fifth Amendment: The Right against Self-Incrimination* (New York, 1968), chap. 1; and John H. Langbein, *Prosecuting Crime in the Renaissance: England, Germany, France* (Cambridge, Mass., 1974), which makes important distinctions between pretrial and courtroom procedure in this context.

to name only some, had either been magistrates themselves or moved easily in the circles that governed English counties. If anything, the orthodox colonies may also have been rather overburdened with ministerial talent in the first decade. Many New England towns began, in fact, with the migration of a group of people following in the wake of a single magistrate and favorite minister.[35] Within the "Great Migration," those who arrived late in the 1630s, after experiencing the full arsenal of Archbishop William Laud's weapons, seem to have acquired more extreme views than their predecessors had of what God demanded from his followers.[36] Juries had no biblical warranty, after all, and could become a casualty of intense Puritan reform. New England's jury arrangements fit this pattern almost too nicely. Thus Massachusetts restricted juries more than Plymouth had, Connecticut narrowed the Massachusetts model, New Haven abolished the institution entirely, and only the social casualties from these godly activities moved decisively in the other direction when they gathered together as the colony of Rhode Island.

The extremes of projury Rhode Island and antijury New Haven are sufficiently important to require separate consideration. Only after that can we return to the core New England colonies of Massachusetts and Connecticut, both of which were, or eventually became, complex enough to embody the two extremes within the same society.

IV

Rhode Island never achieved much cohesion in the seventeenth century. Even with strong protection from England, it was lucky to escape the eventual fate of New Haven and Plymouth, each absorbed by a larger neighbor. Nearly all of Rhode Island's first settlers had been adjudged heretics by orthodox neighboring colonies, but this heritage of dissent and experience of banishment did not easily generate unity. The range of nonconformity remained too great to permit a firm consensus. Somewhere in his fascinating pilgrimage from Separatist to Baptist to Seeker, Roger Williams founded Providence and discovered that no society could be godly. In practical terms, he demanded a more drastic separation of church and state than existed anywhere else in the Christian world in his day. By contrast, the Antinomian exiles initially created a tight theocracy at Portsmouth under William Coddington, who derived his model of autocratic rule

35. E.g., see Darrett B. Rutman, *Winthrop's Boston: A Portrait of a Puritan Town, 1630–1649* (Chapel Hill, 1965), chap. 2.
36. See the essay by Stephen Foster in this volume.

from the Old Testament's Book of Judges. When the settlers soon wearied of his pretensions and overthrew him, he tramped south to found Newport. From this base he continued to pester the other towns with his Biblicist claims for many years. By then Samuel Gorton, a strange, rather mystical Baptist with a touching confidence in the justice and integrity of English law, had established his own town (eventually named Warwick). In Rhode Island, toleration, the disestablishment of religion, and the decriminalization of the First Table (the first four commandments of the Protestant Bible) triumphed as at least negative points of agreement because these principles met the needs of all but Coddington and his admirers.[37]

Doubtless most justice remained decentralized to the town level, where Coddington happily presided as "Judge" over Portsmouth's early court of "elders," while Warwick under Gorton explored the wonderful merits of juries.[38] Above this level, some records have survived for the quarter court on Aquidneck Island (Portsmouth and Newport), from 1641 to 1646. Here again the clerk's notations are too brief to prove much beyond the presence of jurors, usually designated as either grand or petit. At least seven civil disputes and one criminal trial were decided by juries, but probably others were also. Two other criminal cases were in all likelihood resolved summarily.[39]

Whatever uncertainties remain before 1647, the Rhode Island code of that year resolved them in favor of juries. As G. B. Warden shows elsewhere in this volume, the code is an odd document that stands sharply apart from other New England codes, most of which can be traced to the Massachusetts code of 1648 and the Body of Liberties of 1641. Rhode Island devoted most of its text to criminal justice, which constituted only a small portion of the other documents. Orthodox New England colonies announced their allegiance to divine law so stridently that historians have had to undertake the tedious assignment of demonstrating that they were more English than they let on. Rhode Islanders proudly proclaimed derivation from English law, prompting Warden to show that the code is less English than it seems.

Two features concern us. Orthodox New England codes obtained their capital laws from the Bible, specifically the Ten Command-

37. Sydney V. James, *Colonial Rhode Island: A History* (New York, 1975), esp. chaps. 1–4; Edmund S. Morgan, *Roger Williams: The Church and the State* (New York, 1967).

38. *Records of the Court of Trials of the Town of Warwick, R.I.*, transcribed by Helen Capwell (Providence, 1922). Coddington's precise judicial activities have left disappointingly few traces in the surviving records.

39. This record is in *Documentary History of Rhode Island*, ed. Howard M. Chapin (Providence, 1916–19), II, 132–65. The cases of Job Tyler and Ralph Earle were probably handled summarily. See pp. 142, 158.

ments, which meant including several crimes not capital at common law (adultery, incest, perjury that threatened the life of another, public masturbation in New Haven, and a stubborn and disobedient son in Massachusetts and Connecticut) while excluding most English capital crimes (that is, nearly all of those against property). Rhode Island eliminated capital offenses against the First Table (blasphemy and heresy, but not witchcraft, which was lumped with crimes of violence against others) and followed the order of the Second Table but included only those crimes which were also capital at common law. The rationale seemed to be that no one deserved execution unless condemned by *both* the Bible and English law. Interestingly, even in the orthodox Puritan colonies, the behavior of juries corresponded quite closely to this principle, whatever the law said. Only three people died for adultery, New Haven hanged only one masturbator (without jury, of course), Connecticut hanged just one man for incest, and no ill-mannered son quite made it to the gallows. In Rhode Island, adultery received a specific lesser penalty. Incest, much less public masturbation, was not even mentioned. But certain crimes against property—arson, burglary, and robbery—did become capital. Granting the behavioral patterns of early settlers, who were more likely to commit robbery or burglary than incest or even adultery, Rhode Island seemed, on balance, prepared to execute a higher percentage of its people than were its inquisitorial neighbors.[40]

The second point concerns criminal procedure. Because the Rhode Island code drew heavily on such manuals as Michael Dalton's *Countrey Justice,* much of which described *summary* procedure, the code prescribes jury trials for some offenses but not others. It does begin with a paraphrase of Magna Carta, protecting everyone in his person and property except "by the Lawfull judgment of his Peers, or by some known law," but this safeguard proves little. In Massachusetts and Connecticut it became quite compatible with summary justice. Only when the code describes the duties of court officials does it become quite clear that Rhode Islanders were demanding jury trials for virtually all offenses except drunkenness, which was relegated to trial before a single magistrate. The "President" (the first "Assistant" and thus the presiding or chief justice) of the Court of Trials was required to read the indictment to the prisoner, offer him a jury, summarize impartially the evidence presented, read the jury's verdict, and pronounce sentence.[41] Defendants had the right to coun-

40. For the code, see *Records of the Colony of Rhode Island and Providence Plantations, in New England,* ed. John Russell Bartlett (Providence, 1856–65), I, 147–208 (hereafter cited as *R.I. Col. Recs.*). The adultery and incest cases will be discussed below. For New Haven's public masturbator, see Winthrop, *History,* II, 324.

41. *R.I. Col. Recs.,* I, 204.

sel. Indeed, each town was required to maintain two attorneys for whoever had need of one.[42] In 1650 the colony took the next logical step to complete its system of criminal justice. It created the offices of attorney and solicitor general, thereby separating institutionally the duties of the prosecutor from those of the bench.[43] Presumably to discourage *qui tam* prosecutions (by private persons, usually for assault or crimes against property), the legislature later required that in such cases the *prosecutor* would have to pay the jury's expenses.[44]

Rhode Island, in sum, enacted a highly romanticized version of English criminal justice, binding together some features that were already eroding (firm guarantees of jury trials) with others that were just beginning to emerge (the separation of prosecution from judgment). Why? The colony's utter vulnerability to hostile Puritan neighbors, who openly and cynically coveted its Narragansett lands, encouraged both Williams and Gorton to seek English protection and to advertise the colony's dedication to English law. Gorton, in turn, had barely escaped with his life, after a grim confrontation with Massachusetts justice in 1643–44, when he was tried for blasphemy before the General Court. All but three magistrates favored the death penalty, and only resistance from the deputies led eventually to his sentence of banishment, which in turn permitted him to appeal to England and win the earl of Warwick's protection. Gorton had every reason to think English justice preferable to what he had experienced in Massachusetts.[45] All of Rhode Island's leaders and many ordinary settlers had their own unpleasant memories of magisterial justice in the orthodox colonies. They responded by creating a strongly *anti*magisterial system of their own, one that went well beyond the *un*magisterial features we have seen in early Plymouth.

Nobody discovered the difference more painfully than Roger Williams. No doubt alarmed by the high level of wrangling that characterized public affairs and by what seemed to be an insufficiently rigorous moral code, he responded in a way that threatened the colony's territorial integrity and its tradition of magisterial restraint. After hearing reports from Indians about Richard Chasmore's amorous activities with a heifer, he virtually invited Massachusetts to intervene and punish the abomination. Bay officials did arrest "Long Dick" inside Rhode Island without authorization from any colony court, only to have an impromptu town meeting release him in Providence. Yet Williams did not relent. As president of the Court of Trials, he tried to act much like a Massachusetts magistrate at its next session in March 1656/57, at which Chasmore was acquitted. Wil-

42. Ibid., 200–201.   43. Ibid., 225–26.   44. Ibid., 384.
45. For an excellent account of Gorton's trial, see Robert E. Wall, Jr., *Massachusetts Bay: The Crucial Decade, 1640–1650* (New Haven, 1972), chap. 4.

liams launched ten prosecutions, chiefly against people who had rescued Chasmore. He accused them of "open Defieance . . . agst our Charter," or indicted them as "Comon aposers of all Authority," for "Contempt of the order of the collony," and as "ringleaders in new devisions in the collony." The results were mortifying. Each defendant pleaded not guilty, a jury was impaneled, and then "proclam[ation] was made in open court by o Es [oyez] three times for A prosicutor but none appeared." All ten went free. In Rhode Island, the bench could not prosecute by itself except for contempt, as the vast silence around him ought to have told Williams. Significantly, perhaps, he was not reelected president two months later.[46]

In practice, jury behavior and criminal justice operated even less repressively than the Rhode Island code intended. Strong-willed colonists carried into their jury duties the penchant for disagreement that marked their other activities. In orthodox colonies, juries probably disposed of most cases in ten or fifteen minutes, to judge from the case load they dispatched. But in Rhode Island, a few juries sat for days unable to reach a verdict. One civil jury gave up, announcing "that they cannot Agree to bring in A verdict and will no longer atend upon the case."[47] Even a grand jury could divide so ferociously that the court had to suspend business for two weeks waiting for the indictments![48] Hard work on this scale made the office onerous, no doubt, and fines for absent jurors are frequently noted in the records.

Criminal juries could also divide. One threw up its hands and turned the case back to the court. Another sat four days before declaring itself hung.[49] Much more often, especially before 1660, juries simply acquitted. Only 30 percent of all defendants (32 percent in noncapital cases) were pronounced guilty prior to that year. In the next decade, the rate rose to 52 percent (53 percent in noncapital trials), which may indicate a toughening attitude. However, since thirteen of these trials involved offenses that virtually challenged the government's right to exist (the sort of noncapital case that is not really comparable with anything in the orthodox colonies), the juries had little choice in these cases. If they are subtracted, the conviction rate in the 1660s rose only to 37 percent (or 38 percent in noncapital trials).[50]

Several other points deserve emphasis. First, the danger inherent

---

46. Bradford Fuller Swan, *The Case of Richard Chasmore, Alias Long Dick* (Providence, 1944); *Rhode Island Court Records: Records of the Court of Trials of the Colony of Providence Plantations,* ed. "H.M.C." [Howard M. Chapin?] (Providence, 1920–22), I, 25–27 (hereafter cited as *R.I. Ct. Trials Recs.*).

47. *R.I. Ct. Trials Recs.,* I, 31. Cf. pp. 67–68   48. Ibid., II, 68–69. Cf. p. 80.

49. Ibid., I, 67–68.

50. Based on a tabulation of all criminal jury trials ibid., I–II.

in the code that hangings might become commonplace never materialized before 1670. Only six capital trials occurred. Besides an Indian who confessed to murder (and thus faced no jury before he hanged), juries acquitted two men for murder, Chasmore for bestiality, and another settler for burglary. Only one man, convicted of murder, was hanged.[51] Second, the sheer volume of criminal jury trials is quite remarkable—eighty-four for noncapital offenses, even though the records are complete for only about sixteen years from 1647 to 1670. How many is eighty-four? More than I have found for Massachusetts and Connecticut together for the entire pre-Dominion era, at a time when Rhode Island's population was perhaps a twentieth of theirs. Third, Rhode Islanders did show a greater sense of guilt or sin than most non-New Englanders, even if they lagged well behind their orthodox neighbors in this respect. Pleas of guilty, though not the dominant feature of the criminal-justice system, were fairly common. Many settlers were Puritans, after all. To take but one example, male fornicators frequently confessed, a rarity outside the region and, for that matter, almost unheard of in Massachusetts by the early eighteenth century.

Finally, Rhode Island demonstrates that if neighboring colonies insisted on blending prosecution with judgment, the reason cannot be the lack of adequate precedent or the inability of orthodox magistrates to grasp the implications of their actions. Rhode Island sorted out the issues readily enough and chose its precedents with care. In this respect, Massachusetts, Connecticut, and New Haven did no less. They simply embraced quite a different set of precedents. New Haven in particular deliberately rejected most of the features of criminal justice that Rhode Islanders peculiarly cherished.

V

New Haven Colony abolished juries. A prudent historian, explaining the development of juries, probably should stop there (as others have) and turn to another colony. This temptation deserves to be resisted, if only to discover what a highly principled antijury system looked like in practice. Criminal justice in New Haven manifested important traits that would color Puritan jurisprudence in Massachusetts and Connecticut as well. The colony's records in this respect are so full, so wonderfully detailed in what they tell us about the settlers' behavior and magisterial expectations, that they provide insights into the New England sense of justice difficult to match any-

51. For the capital jury trials, see ibid., I, 6, 26–27, 72, 78, 79–80; II, 97–98 (the one executed). For the Indian, see ibid., I, 71–72.

where else save in Winthrop's journal. Not even Winthrop gives us the verbal exchanges between judges and accused common to New Haven, but extremely rare everyplace else. In the other New England colonies, supporting documents offer us a frequent glimpse of pre-trial activities, but we almost never see what happened in court beyond the barest account of the procedure and the result.

From the moment of its founding in 1638–39, New Haven set exalted magisterial standards for all of New England. Its settlers invested about £36,000 in the Quinnipiac community—a fantastic sum, roughly equal to one-sixth of what the London Company spent on the whole Virginia venture through 1624.[52] It attracted the two most important merchants ever to migrate to early New England: Theophilus Eaton, who had been governor of the East-Land Company and an unofficial emissary from the English court to Christian IV of Denmark; and Eaton's relative by marriage, Edward Hopkins. No other colony in the region could boast a like proportion of wealthy organizers. Of the seventy original proprietors, leadership went from the start to Eaton and his school friend and London pastor John Davenport, who had been silenced by Laud and forced into exile in the Netherlands for several years.[53]

Davenport came rather late to strict Puritan convictions. He wore a surplice and used the Book of Common Prayer until 1632, when John Cotton persuaded him of his error. Driven to a new extreme by Laud's harassment, he arrived in America more grimly committed to a pure church than did any other ministerial contemporary. In New Haven, he insisted on restricting freemanship to church members, and Eaton backed him over the objections of his own brother, the Reverend Samuel Eaton, who soon returned to England. Davenport's own standard of a valid conversion experience probably exceeded that of any other divine in New England. He grilled applicants without mercy in order to ferret out hypocrites and applied the "rule of charity" only after there remained no doubts to be charitable about. In a very real sense, political participation in New Haven proper (as against other towns in the colony that possessed their own ministers) had to be filtered through Davenport. The seven pillars of his church became the colony's first freemen in 1639, and by 1641

52. The investment is calculated by adding all entries under "Estates" in the list of planters printed in *Records of the Colony and Plantation of New Haven, from 1638 to 1649*, ed. Charles J. Hoadly (Hartford, 1857), 91–93 (hereafter cited as *N. H. Col. Recs.*, I). For the London Company, see Theodore K. Rabb, *Enterprise and Empire: Merchant and Gentry Investment in the Expansion of England, 1575–1630* (Cambridge, Mass., 1967), 58–59.

53. Floyd M. Shumway, "New Haven and Its First Settlers," *Journal of the New Haven Colony Historical Society* 21 (1972): 45–67; Bernard Bailyn, *The New England Merchants in the Seventeenth Century* (Cambridge, Mass., 1955), 38.

the town had over sixty male church members, most of them from the self-selected group that had chosen to follow Davenport in the first place.[54]

Eaton, a minister's son, achieved a standard of lay piety that must have daunted contemporaries. He liked to edify his enormous household by reciting entire sermons from memory, doubtless without sufficient warning to allow potential auditors a chance to discover other urgent tasks. He left the deathbed of his adult son rather than miss one of Davenport's Sunday-afternoon sermons, and news of the young man's demise had to be brought to him at the meetinghouse. This gesture awed even Cotton Mather. So severe was Eaton that he supported the excommunication of his own wife, barred her from public worship, and even threatened to banish her when her opinions about baptism strayed too close to those of Roger Williams. It seems almost superfluous to add that he consumed much of his personal estate in supporting the colony. When a man of such terrible godliness denounced juries, mere saints had better listen. They did.[55]

Eaton and his small band of assistants gave New England its purest model of the righteous magistrate. The young Michael Wigglesworth, who grew up in New Haven, may even have shaped his idea of God while watching them administer the law. Far more than did any theological treatise available at Harvard, the New Haven court provided a vibrant model for Christ, the Just Judge of *The Day of Doom* (1662):[56]

> Thus all mens Pleas the Judge with ease
>   doth answer and confute
> Until that all, both great and small,
>   are silenced and mute. . . . (stanza 182)
>
> . . . .
> . . . Their Judge severe doth quite cashier
>   and all their Pleas off take
> That never a man, or dare, or can
>   a further Answer make. (stanza 186)

54. Cotton Mather, *Magnalia Christi Americana,* ed. Kenneth B. Murdock and Elizabeth W. Miller (Cambridge, Mass., 1977–), I, 253–60; Norman Petit, *The Heart Prepared: Grace and Conversion in Puritan Spiritual Life* (New Haven, 1966), 168–76. Compare *N. H. Col. Recs.,* I, 9–10, with Franklin Bowditch Dexter, *Historical Catalogue of the Members of the First Church of Christ in New Haven, Connecticut (Center Church), A.D. 1639–1914* (New Haven, 1914), 1–6.

55. Mather, *Magnalia,* I, 253–60; *N. H. Col. Recs.,* I, 246, 270 (Mrs. Eaton); William Hubbard, *A General History of New England, from the Discovery to MDCLXXX* (Cambridge, Mass., 1815), 320, credits Eaton with the abolition of juries in the colony.

56. *Seventeenth-Century American Poetry,* ed. Harrison T. Meserole (New York, 1968), 102, 103.

New Haven magistrates struggled conscientiously to replace traditional English law with "the judiciall lawes of God, as they were delivered by Moses."[57] Even wills had to meet this standard. Men "may not make wills as they will themselves," pronounced the court, apparently unconscious of the pun, when a testator failed to provide adequately for his children, "but must attend the minde of God in doeing the same."[58] Civil suits scarcely existed at all in the colony's early years but gave way to a system of arbitration and loving conciliation.

Above all, the magistrates handled cases in the way they imagined God would judge them were He to appear visibly in the court. When a disappointed litigant stormed off "irreverently . . . sayeing he would have justice in another place if he had it not here," the court extracted a humble apology for "neglecting the imadge of God of magistrats." John Heardman, accused of drunkenness after downing about a quart of rum, learned from Magistrate Benjamin Fenn that he had broken the law. Heardman retorted,"y^t ye lawes were his [Fenn's] will, or words to y^t purpose, to wch he [Fenn] replied y^t ye lawes were not his will, but he hoped according to ye will of God." Having challenged a judge's divine role, Heardman could not even wriggle away with the humble confession expected of the guilty in New Haven. Fenn stung him with another characteristic of New Haven justice, a little sermon wishing "y^t he were not of a malicious spirit against goodnes & those in authority, & y^t he declared himself to be a sonne of Beliall, not subject to any yoake." If "all men were of his frame," warned Fenn with righteous contempt, "it would be a hell vpon earth & no liveing among them."[59]

Unlike Massachusetts, where magistrates from the start were lenient with penitent offenders, New Haven seemed more interested in retributive justice. Like Christ on the Last Day, the court inquired minutely into the precise degree of guilt and varied its punishments accordingly.[60] Even without the bait of lighter sentences (something that became common only in the late 1650s), offenders quickly learned to demonstrate shame and contrition for their sins. This lesson even reached an escaped Virginia servant, who boasted of having murdered his master while fleeing and who aroused attention by

57. *N. H. Col. Recs.*, I, 130. Cf. the earlier statement (p. 21) "thatt the worde of God shall be the onely rule to be attended vnto in ordering the affayres of gouernment in this plantatiō."

58. *Records of the Colony or Jurisdiction of New Haven, from May, 1653, to the Union. Together with the New Haven Code of 1656*, ed. Charles J. Hoadly (Hartford, 1858), 159–60 (hereafter cited as *N. H. Col. Recs.*, II).

59. Ibid., I, 271–72; II, 271–74.

60. Gail S. Marcus is developing this theme in her Yale dissertation.

his "frequent Curseing & sweareing in a most prophane & blasphemous manner, horrible to be hearde or uttered, & the like not formerly knowne among us, to ye great dishono^r of god, & danger of infection to others." He claimed that "he was sorry y^t he had soe done, but . . . he had beene brought up in such places & company where it was frequently used, & he hoped he should reforme for ye future."[61]

Those whose penitence seemed insincere, insufficient, or merely ritualistic faced acute shame, for as Wigglesworth put it (stanza 57):

> It's vain, moreover, for Men to cover
>   the least iniquity:
> The Judge hath seen, and privy been
>   to all their villany.
> He unto light, and open sight
>   the works of darkness brings:
> He doth unfold both new and old,
>   both known and hidden things.

Robert Meaker discovered the difference between mere admission of guilt and true conviction of sin when he and his wife tried to escape with the bare acknowledgment that "they were sorey" that they had fornicated before marriage. The court had heard too many rumors to leave it at that. Was it true, the magistrates demanded, that he had deliberately gotten her drunk and then "acted his fylthynes" with her while she lay in a complete stupor? The whole seamy (or sodden) incident had to come out—in public.[62] Similarly Benjamin Wright attempted to slip past judicial scrutiny with a vague admission of "ye sinfulnes of his carriage" without confessing to the specific "things charged upon him." Pressed by the court, he turned legalistic, claiming he could not tell whether the charges were true or false because he had been denied a written copy of them. When an official explained that he had offered to read them to him, Wright fell "into a fainting fit" before the court. The governor relentlessly drew the moral that Wright should "consider the providence of God towards him, that as he had beene smiteing at the authority of God, so now God came vpon him as if he would kill him." The routine English privilege in misdemeanors of requesting a copy of the indictment became in New Haven a "smiteing at the authority of God."[63]

Accused persons had few rights or procedural protections in a

61. *Ancient Town Records: New Haven Town Records*, ed. Franklin Bowditch Dexter (New Haven, 1917–62), II, 275–76 (hereafter cited as *N. H. T. Recs.*).

62. Ibid., I, 124–25.

63. *N. H. Col. Recs.*, II, 253–54. Wright would not yield, finally got his copy, but was bound a hefty £50 to good behavior.

society whose major cohesive force was the dynamic emotional interplay between guilt, repentance, conversion, and the punishment of
sin lest the wrath of God harry the land. Wright's fainting spell surely
reveals intense inner turmoil for daring to claim an English protection. Captain How's daughter, accused of profane swearing in her
mother's presence, refused to admit the charge but demanded that
the court prove it. "She was told by such wayes she will but make her
punishment more heavy."[64] Young John Browne, denounced for
drunkenness, objected without effect to being grilled by the deputy
governor in private; "he was told that oath might bee taken in due
time, but the thing now intended was, only examination, to find out
the trueth."[65] His brother Samuel, tried for a like offense five years
later, held out against the pressure, "desired to see his accusers &
did not owne ye Charge." Eyewitnesses obligingly described how he
had staggered along the roadway, collapsed, and gone to sleep with
vomit around his mouth. His arrogant refusal to confess earned him
a triple sentence, everything the court could throw at him.[66] Another
youth, who had joined some friends in vengeful pranks against a
saint whose testimony had placed one of them in the stocks, would
not confess even after a confederate had divulged everything. Like
Wigglesworth's hypocrites, as the clerk reported with disgust in every
word, he "stood stupid & as a sott full of guilt now before ye Court
& at Last being urged to speake the truth he went on in sinfull eva-
sions" until, inevitably, his final, pathetic defenses crumbled.[67]

In England, judicial oaths provided some protection for the
accused. Presumably the terror of God's punishment or at least the
penalty for perjury might compel even disreputable witnesses to tell
the truth. But New Haven magistrates reasoned differently. Few witnesses testified under oath. Horrified at the prospect of affronting
the Lord through a false oath, the magistrates sometimes heard all
testimony first before deciding whom to swear, after which the evidence was repeated. Under this system, only those who would be
believed anyway were sworn. It made sense only under the assumption of broad magisterial discretion. The judges could discern whom
to believe, and they also punished for lying.[68]

The most important protection that an accused person possessed
was the two-witness rule, derived from the Old Testament. Nobody
could be convicted of a crime (or, what really concerned the court, a
public sin) except by open confession or the testimony of two or

64. *N. H. T. Recs.*, I, 88–89.   65. Ibid., 490.   66. Ibid., II, 189.
67. Ibid., 112–13.
68. E.g., see the trial of Mrs. Brewster et al., in *N. H. Col. Recs.*, I, 242–59, esp. 252-
53.

more witnesses. If the defendant had admitted his offense to someone else, either a magistrate or a private person, and then denied
the act in court, testimony of the earlier statement would constitute
not a confession but one of two "witnesses" in the case. Of course,
legal fictions had to be invented to make some heinous sins, such as
rape, punishable at all under this rule. But it could provide real protection to the accused. Very likely when Samuel Browne drank himself sick but refused to admit it, he hoped—vainly—that no more
than one person had seen him in this condition. On the other hand,
this principle encouraged the magistrates to deny guarantees against
double jeopardy. Most acquittals were issued grudgingly for lack of
sufficient evidence. Should another "witness" come to light later on,
the case could be revived and the offender convicted.[69] As much as
any single feature of the New Haven judicial system, this practice
demonstrates the magistrates' governing rationale: the punishment
of sin.

For maybe twenty years New Haven's legal system achieved most
of what its designers had sought, except regenerate offspring for the
founders. It offered swift justice and a conviction rate exceeding 90
percent.[70] Unless we count among major crimes the Guilford masturbator who displayed his art to town youths "above a hundred
times" before attracting the magistrates' attention, it produced a
phenomenally law-abiding society with no homicides, little overt violence, few thefts after the servants of the early years disappear from
the records, and no other crimes more spectacular than bestiality,
perhaps sodomy, and a case of arson by a juvenile.[71] New Haven
justice was far more successful than the English system, even if each
one is measured solely by its internal criteria. Yet magisterial law was
vulnerable to its own peculiar perversions. Two examples illustrate
how institutionalized zeal against sin, the pressure toward believable
confessions, and the two-witness rule could produce grotesque par-
odies of justice.

William Fancy and his wife were poor and no saints. Although
both groped toward minimal decency in a highly demanding society,
he had been fined for drunkenness and she whipped for theft, an

69. See the case of George Wood, who escaped conviction for having stolen two spoons
only to be condemned (banishment under threat of death should he return) a year later,
when one of the spoons was found in his possession. *N. H. T. Recs.,* I, 252–53; *N. H. Col.
Recs.,* II, 187–89. For a fuller discussion of this practice, see Gail S. Marcus's essay in
this volume.

70. For precise statistics, see the Marcus essay.

71. For the masturbator, see Winthrop, *History,* II, 324; for probable sodomy, see *N.
H. T. Recs.,* I, 32, 178–79; for arson, see *N. H. Col. Recs.,* II, 384–87. For stealing livestock, see *N. H. T. Recs.,* I, 148–51, 169–74. Several bestiality cases will be discussed
below.

incident that somehow made her an appealing sexual target for several young men. Perhaps the exposure of an attractive woman's breasts at the whipping post aroused in the viewers a set of emotions rather more elemental than the ones magistrates hoped to stimulate. Whatever the reason, Thomas Robinson frequently tried to seduce or rape her over a harrowing two-year period, once while she was assisting his wife in childbirth. Stephen Metcalfe, while she nursed him to recovery from a nasty wound, forcibly tried to kiss her. Mark Meggs alternately attempted to rape her or to purchase her favors. She always resisted successfully and reported these incidents to her husband. He refused to alert the magistrates because she was a solitary witness and, as a convicted thief, might not be believed. Instead he remonstrated pathetically with his wife's tormentors after each event. He also feared that if he raised an alarm, *he* might be the one to get flogged. Sadly, he was correct. When the messy details finally emerged, both Fancys were severely whipped, she for concealing iniquity and he, equally unfairly, "for his being as it were a pander to his wife." Meggs was also whipped. But Robinson, the worst offender, avoided punishment by fleeing the colony. With no sense of incongruity, the law thus punished the victims more heavily than their assailants.[72]

George Spencer was an ugly, one-eyed servant who had probably been whipped in Boston for receiving stolen goods and punished in New Haven after he botched an escape attempt to Virginia. Having been in court for his misdeeds, he surely knew that convincing repentance was expected of the accused, and he may well have mistaken the court's penalties, finely graded according to the degree of perceived guilt, for leniency to the penitent offender, measured according to the eloquence of the confession. Also, he had witnessed only misdemeanor trials, not capital ones, and he probably knew little of the scriptural hierarchy of sins. As he later explained to the dismay of the saints, he had profited not at all from John Davenport's ministry, had not said a single prayer during his five years in New England, and read the Bible only when ordered to do so by his master. Then one foul day a local sow inconsiderately gave birth to a deformed piglet whose single eye and awkward protrusion from its head like unto "a mans instrumᵗ of genᵉration" oddly reminded the good people of New Haven of George Spencer.

At this point nobody had witnessed a crime (or sin) or even knew whether such an event had occurred. Of course, granting seventeenth-century beliefs about nature and providence, such a "mon-

72. *N. H. Col. Recs.*, I, 233–39 (quotation, p. 239).

ster" had to generate alarm. Nevertheless, had Spencer steadfastly denied all guilt, he would have escaped at least with his life. But recently he had seen a man merely whipped for sexually molesting a six-year old child, an offense that Spencer considered more disgusting than bestiality. Or, incredibly, he may even have buggered the sow. Whatever his reason, he yielded when his neighbors pressed him to confess, only to learn the terrifying truth that admission of a capital offense meant death, whether the offender was contrite or not. Trapped, he recanted, then confessed again under relentless inquisition, and repeated this cycle several times. The court, using the piglet as one "witness" and Spencer's oft recanted confession as another, sentenced him to hang. He died despairing and unrepentant, "a terrible example of divine justice and wrath."[73]

The Spencer case nearly became an appalling precedent. Obliging pigs, through the psychological mechanism of a modern Rorschach test, now and then offered the community a chance to wipe out its most conspicuous deviants. The next abominable piglet resembled a fellow named (what else?) Thomas Hogg, an unfortunate man bent over with his hernia, his genitals sometimes hanging out where his steel truss had worn through his britches. Unmarried, he was once observed chasing away his loneliness by "act[ing] filthjnesse w^{t}h his hands by the fier side." If I read the record correctly, his neighbors thought him guilty because the piglet's misshapen eyes seemed to resemble his scrotum, which apparently had been seen by too many people. But because he firmly and consistently denied all erotic contact with the sow, the court could not hang him without a second witness. Undoubtedly believing that he really was guilty, the magistrates kept him in jail for months, longer than anyone else in the colony's annals, and finally whipped him for general lewdness.[74]

Hogg's persistent denial might have saved someone else's life as well as his own, for in 1653 New Haven produced another monster. The awful beast had a single red eye, what seemed like misplaced teats instead of an ear, and an extra penis on its hairless forehead. By order of the authorities, the entire town filed past, carefully examining the animal to see "if by the visiage or any other markes" somebody's loathsome guilt would be discovered. This time no one was accused.[75]

73. Ibid., 29, 61, 62–73 (quotations from pp. 63, 73). Cf. *Ct. Assts. Recs.,* II, 70, for a possible earlier career of crime in Massachusetts.

74. *N. H. Col. Recs.,* I, 295–96.

75. *N. H. T. Recs.,* I, 158–59. New Haven seems to have been obsessed with the perils of animal sex. When Nicholas Bayley's dog made amorous advances to a sow, a neighbor advised him to kill the dog. Instead Bayley's wife defended it, explaining, "if he had not a bitch, he must haue some thing." A shocked court banished the depraved couple. Ibid., 245–46.

As the colony entered the late 1650s and 1660s, changes appeared, intensified by the political crisis that accompanied the English Restoration and Charles II's grant of a royal charter to Connecticut which absorbed New Haven under Hartford's jurisdiction. Arbitration became less characteristic of civil disputes, and common-law forms, such as "action of ye case" and "action of debt," made at least a nominal appearance. Even before Eaton's death, in 1658, fines rather suddenly replaced whippings as the dominant form of punishment, as the unruly servants of the early years yielded to a new offending element, the offspring of the founders. Sinners had never received much mercy in New Haven, but under Eaton's successors the magistrates slipped rather easily into the pattern that had always characterized Massachusetts justice. Reclamation of the offender replaced retribution, or pure punishment, as the dominant feature of the system. Sinners thus acquired some small power to manipulate even magisterial justice when they happened to be, as often as not, the children of the saints.

By all criteria, absolute and relative, the second generation failed to meet the religious standards set by the first. On one occasion, however, a son did get gruesome revenge against his father. William Potter, "a weake infirme man," had been a saint since 1641. Twenty-one years later, his son caught him buggering the livestock, and when William confessed to a lifelong fondness for that activity, he was hanged. In what must be one of the most awkward moments in colonial court records, he identified for his wife every beast he had loved, no doubt so that they could be slaughtered before his face at the gallows.[76]

More typically, the children offended and their elders responded. Few sinned as blatantly as William Andrewes, Jr., who, after a few incidents of drunken behavior that the court punished leniently, took to sea, where he guaranteed that he would never be able to go home again. He contracted a second, bigamous marriage in Ireland.[77] John Browne reached for similar standards. Already brought to court for drunkenness and for invoking Charles II as a challenge to New Haven's legitimacy, he experimented with something a bit more wicked in 1665. To the amazement and horror of a group of friends, he attempted to summon the devil in the middle of town one night.[78]

Less spectacular omens of creeping irreverence also spread throughout the colony. Jeremiah Johnson provides perhaps the most agreeable example. After helping to free a cow trapped in a swamp,

76. *N. H. Col. Recs.*, II, 180, 440–43; Dexter, *First Church of New Haven*, 6.
77. *N. H. Col. Recs.*, I, 229–30, 334–35, 449; II, 425–27.
78. *N. H. T. Recs.*, II, 129–32; cf. ibid., I, 490–94.

he solemnly cautioned the animal, "goe thy way and sinn no more, least a worss thing come vnto the[e]." The town court found nothing amusing in this quip and sternly related his scoffing attitude to other defects in his character.[79] Sad to relate, the judges were right. Johnson was soon whipped for stealing and proved to be a contentious neighbor, but not even severe punishment could destroy his impish sense of humor. One day he overheard Edmund Dorman praying loudly in a swamp for a wife: "Lord thou knowest my necessity & canst supply it, Lord bend & bow her will & make her sensible of my condition." When a tavern companion later inquired whom Dorman was talking about, Johnson suggested that "it may be his mare that God would make her seruiseable." Like the antics of John and Samuel Browne, this hint of divine complicity in bestiality got Johnson into enough trouble to stimulate his keen interest in the rights of the accused. He challenged witnesses and objected to putting them on oath, insisting that some were motivated only by vengeance.[80] In similar fashion, John Rossiter discovered the value of the English right against self-incrimination when he and his father were accurately charged with circulating seditious papers that challenged the legitimacy of the government. John particularly resented the magisterial practice of interrogating him without a formal "indictmt," a word that had lost all technical meaning under the New Haven system.[81]

Indeed something like a deliberate, calculated profanation of New Haven's most sacred values seems to have emanated from a significant portion of the rising generation. John Browne frequently laughed during Davenport's sermons, and when his father, Francis (a saint, of course), was publicly "acknowledging his evill, that he had not watched over him as he should," John scandalized the congregation by walking "out of the Meeting house smileing."[82] Several young men, after spreading sexual innuendoes about John Thomas's daughter, showed "so little remorse for their evill" that their attitude "was taken notice of wth greife, both by the Court & others y^t were present."[83] Another group of at least eight young fellows waited until the "parents & Masters of most of them were humbling themselves before ye lord in an extraordinary manner" and then used the unsupervised occasion to hold a drunken folic.[84] In fact, whenever someone went out of town, youths liked to invade his house and

79. Ibid., I, 331.
80. Ibid., II, 7–8. Several months later the court tried to cure Johnson's "scoffing & prophanenes" with a device that, so far as I am aware, was unique to New Haven—a good-behavior bond (£10) without time limit. Ibid., 22–23.
81. *N. H. Col. Recs.*, II, 429, 431–38, esp. 436.   82. *N. H. T. Recs.*, I, 434–35.
83. Ibid., 389–90.   84. Ibid., II, 198.

drink far into the night beyond the scrutiny of their elders. Jacob Melyn (whose prominent father, Cornelis, had been banished from Peter Stuyvesant's New Netherland and had moved the family to New Haven) flirted outrageously with Sarah Tuttle during the wedding solemnities of a cripped couple and compounded the impiety by speculating openly about what, or how, the bridal pair "would doe at night."[85] Jacob later used a cunning and intentional misreading of Scripture to seduce his future bride, narrowly avoiding a whipping that could have disgraced him irrevocably among the Dutch with whom the Melyns conducted much of their business.[86]

His brother Isaac went further, inaugurating what seems to have been a planned defilement of John Davenport's household throughout the 1660s. During Sabbath worship, Isaac quietly organized drinking parties to be held outdoors, presumably in secluded areas, on Sunday nights after respectable folk were asleep. On other occasions he spent hours in the chamber of Hester Clark, a young woman living with the Davenports. Nobody could prove it, but presumably the two fornicated cheerfully while the old Puritan snored.[87] Sarah Dowlittell, one of Davenport's servants, surpassed even that achievement when she nearly turned his kitchen into a brothel. Illicit sex under Davenport's nose was becoming one of the few great thrills the community afforded. She seduced both Joseph and Hachaliah Preston. She almost succeeded with a young married man, John Thomas, Jr., for he "lay downe . . . upon her naked body & attempted to penitrate her body" only to prove embarrassingly impotent. Did the grim image of the slumbering Davenport freeze him out of his ardor?[88] The volume, the nature, and the timing of these incidents, all of which became public knowledge, make us wonder whether Davenport had other, more personal and humiliating reasons than the Half-Way Covenant to move to Boston a few months later.

Granting the extensive youthful unrest in the colony, absorption by Connecticut probably did seem a liberation to many, although few could have been as naive as the card-playing John Clarke, who believed that under Hartford's rule "he might liue merrily & sing & daunce &c."[89] Yet beginning in October 1665, New Haven's town court did impanel juries regularly, taking care over the next six years that nearly all jurors were church members and that a few prominent saints served often in this post. Some litigants still preferred to have their cases tried by the bench, and only one accused criminal requested trial by jury. The change of government thus brought New Haven into line with the rest of orthodox New England. It affected

85. Ibid., I, 450–52.   86. Ibid., II, 11–12.   87. Ibid., 65–71.
88. Ibid., 228–29.   89. Ibid., 23–25.

civil litigation dramatically but criminal trials scarcely at all.[90]

In New Haven, to summarize, the colony's judicial institutions departed from England's in important, even spectacular ways. While England was groping toward an adversary system of justice, New Haven's courts were overtly inquisitorial. They differed from the dreaded Spanish example primarily in that they did not use torture, put the accused (or even most witnesses) under oath, or conceal the identity of witnesses from the defendant. But rates of conviction were quite similar.[91] The distinction between prosecutor and bench, still fuzzy in England to be sure, did not exist at all in New Haven, where the magistrates accused, investigated, prosecuted, judged, and punished. No juries stood between defendant and bench, not even for capital offenders. Suspected persons had virtually no procedural rights beyond their ability to manipulate the two-witness rule. Even its protection could prove illusory, as John Thorpe found out when he was punished despite inadequate evidence. The court, in its convoluted decision, found him "apparently suspicious of being guilty" of having fathered Rebecca Potter's bastard.[92] Ominously, all appeals for change came from manifest sinners, not from the saints.

In less extreme ways, the rest of orthodox New England would experience much the same tension between inquisitorial magistrates and uncooperative sinners. Out of this struggle, criminal jury trials would achieve a rebirth rather different from the kind advocated by the ministers. Historians of Massachusetts and Connecticut law would do well to spend less energy digging up obscure English precedents for everything they happen to find. They should pay closer attention to the shining example of magisterial justice in nearby New Haven. It cast a deep shadow.

VI

By 1640 the dominant seventeenth-century pattern of jury usage had already taken hold in Massachusetts, Connecticut, and Maine. To understand it better, we should place it briefly in a broad inter-colonial context. In the Chesapeake colonies, where population scat-

90. Each juror appearing ibid., 152–276 passim, has been checked through the public records. For the criminal trial, see the case of Hodshon (Hudson) and Bristow (1666), at pp. 190–93.

91. The medieval Inquisition did not acquit, but the Spanish Inquisition was more lenient. Yet, as in New Haven, it preferred to release someone under a judgment of "not proven" rather than not guilty. In Toledo from 1575 to 1610, dismissals, suspended cases, and acquittals numbered 179 as against 1,909 convictions. This conviction rate of 91.4 percent was almost identical to New Haven's, which was 93.2 percent. Henry Charles Lea, *A History of the Inquisition of Spain* (New York, 1906–07), III, 105–8, 553; for New Haven's conviction rate, see Gail Marcus's essay in this volume.

92. *N. H. T. Recs.*, II, 183–85.

tered thinly along the river valleys, assembling any jury was troublesome, expensive, and an inconvenience to the settlers themselves. Accordingly, few were used before the Restoration era even in civil cases, and I have yet to find one for a noncapital crime. Compared with local jurisdictions in England, the counties of both the Chesapeake and New England had ludicrously small populations. The median size of English counties grew unevenly from something over 60,000 in 1600 to 160,000 by 1800.[93] As late as 1700 only the *colonies* of Massachusetts and Virginia approached the normal population level of English *counties* a century earlier. The largest Massachusetts counties took most of the seventeenth century to climb past the 10,000 mark. In per capita terms, juries were obviously a heavier burden to maintain in North America than in England.

However true, this argument explains nothing about variations in jury usage *within* New England. After 1640, Suffolk, Essex, and Middlesex counties were probably always more populous than the entire colonies of Plymouth and Rhode Island. By that year, all of these jurisdictions routinely impaneled a jury for each regularly scheduled session of a quarter court. In all of them, use of the jury became standard practice in civil disputes, many for astonishingly trivial sums, a few even after the defendant defaulted.[94] Each of these societies also employed juries for capital offenses. The major variations arose in response to noncapital crimes. Only two such cases went to a jury in Massachusetts between 1640 and 1660, and none in Connecticut or Maine. In these tribunals, as opposed to those in the Chesapeake, juries did sit with each court. But they handled only civil controversies, not ordinary crime.

A quiet struggle over juries did indeed occur in the dozen years or so after 1640, the very period in which the Rhode Island and New Haven systems achieved definition. This contest has left maddeningly few clues behind. The Massachusetts Body of Liberties of 1641, which was largely forced upon the magistrates by the deputies after years of contention, gave either party to a civil suit the right to request a jury and also provided that the "like libertie shall be granted to all persons in Criminall cases."[95] Apparently many of the deputies had reservations about the emerging pattern of summary justice. In the

93. The figure for 1600 is a rough guess based largely on material in E. E. Rich, "The Population of Elizabethan England," *Economic History Review*, 2d ser., 2 (1949–50): 247–65. That for 1800 comes from the British census of 1801.

94. See above, n. 28. For examples of jury trials after default by the defendant, see Midd. Ct. Recs., I, 115, 116. For litigation over trivialities, see Returne Wayte's appeal from the Malden Commissioners' Court (which heard causes worth less than 40s.) to the county court and then the Court of Assistants, where he won on his second jury verdict. Ibid., III, 314; *Ct. Assts. Recs.*, I, 165.

95. *Puritan Political Ideas, 1558–1794*, ed. Edmund S. Morgan (Indianapolis, 1965), 184–85 (Liberty No. 29).

protracted duel over the "negative voice," the deputies never challenged the right of the magistrates to act as judges, but they did attack magisterial discretion and insist that the General Court, sitting together rather than bicamerally for judicial business after 1649, function as the colony's highest court of appeal.[96] The magistrates, on the other hand, shared quite different scruples about juries. In September 1642, the assistants appointed what became a joint committee "to consider (whether in tryall of causes to retaine or dismise [dismiss] iuries)."[97] This tantalizing entry makes sense only when one assumes that most magistrates now hoped to abolish civil juries entirely. New Haven's purer example was becoming contagious.

This issue remained alive into the 1650s. William Pynchon wrote an impassioned letter to Winthrop defending juries, at least in "all controversies about meum and tuum," insisting that the practice was "Consonant to the word of God" and "far above the course of justice in France." Had these been Eaton's arguments for the abolition of all juries?[98] Significantly, Pynchon defended only civil juries. He made no argument for their use in criminal trials.[99] A final clue appeared in May 1652. The magistrates initiated and the deputies approved a measure that shifted at least the initial cost of a jury to anybody who requested its use. He would have to pay 20s. down several days in advance, to be reimbursed only if he won.[100] This law had an immediate practical impact. While it remained in effect, just one civil case went to a jury in the Middlesex, Ipswich, and Salisbury courts. Only Salem showed no change from this measure.[101]

One wonders whether the magistrates had tried to accomplish indirectly what they had been unable to get by overt means for the past decade. If so, they failed. The measure must have been quite unpopular, for it was repealed five months later, and litigation immediately resumed its earlier course.[102] By 1658 the General Court simply took juries for granted when it defined and explained their fact-finding role. The plaintiff's claim must "be proved by sufficyent

96. See Black, "Judicial Power and the General Court," esp. 285–86.

97. *Mass. Recs.*, II, 28.

98. Hubbard (see above, n. 55) credits New Haven's abolition of juries to "some reasons urged by Mr. Eaton (a great reader and traveller) against that way." Could this be the French example that Pynchon had to refute? Although Hubbard does not say so, I also find it hard to believe that Eaton would have taken such a step without finding scriptural justification.

99. Pynchon to Winthrop, 1 March 1646 (probably 1646/47), in *Winthrop Papers* (Boston, 1929–), V, 134–35.

100. *Mass. Recs.*, IV (i), 81; III, 242–43, 262.

101. Based on an examination of the manuscript court records for 1652 in the Essex County Court House (Salem) and the Middlesex County Court House (Cambridge). The *Pynchon Ct. Rec.* has a gap for 1652.

102. *Mass. Recs.*, IV (i), 107.

evidenc, else the case must be found for the defendant," the legislature explained, while in criminal trials "every man is honest & innocent, vnlesse it be proved legally to the contrary." The last half of this statement makes sense if it is assumed to apply to capital crimes, or if we postulate that some people in the colony believed that juries should be used more regularly than they were in ordinary criminal trials.[103]

While Massachusetts magistrates maneuvered to abolish civil juries, their Connecticut counterparts satisfied themselves with weakening the force of the traditional English jury. They experimented with verdicts that needed to be less than unanimous, obviously to increase the likelihood of agreement, and for smaller causes they authorized juries of six men instead of twelve. Despite these precautions, the colony had three hung juries in capital trials during the first generation. Did others produce convictions by majority or two-thirds votes?[104]

Taken together, this evidence suggests several conclusions:

1. Massachusetts magistrates, at least into the 1650s, probably did prefer and did battle for a legal system closer to New Haven's than England's.

2. Ordinary lay saints, as freemen and deputies, fought and won an obscure struggle to preserve juries in civil trials, an issue that Connecticut compromised by removing the unanimous verdict.

3. Some people probably hoped to give juries a criminal role closer to the settlers' English experience, much as Rhode Island was doing at precisely this time. We do not know who these men were or how aggrieved they felt. All of our evidence comes from the House of Deputies, that is, from church members who had become freemen. No surviving documents tells us what the growing population of those who were not church members had to say on this question, although Robert Child may have had this issue, among others, in mind when he drafted his appeal for English law.[105]

4. Except when capital trials were decided by the General Court, instead of a jury, which in turn seems to have been almost a peculi-

---

103. Ibid., 290–91; cf. II, 21, for a 1642 statement on juries.

104. *Conn. Partic. Ct. Recs.,* passim. Although I have found no statutory basis for the phenomenon, Connecticut went through a cycle in 1654 similar to that in Massachusetts in 1652, moving from routine use of civil juries to their abandonment and back to their use. See pp. 122–31. The Connecticut code of 1672 required unanimous verdicts in capital trials. I do not know whether such an understanding had always been in force, but hung juries are far less likely to occur when a verdict need only be by majority vote than when it must be unanimous. See *Earliest laws of the New Haven and Connecticut Colonies,* ed. Cushing, 111.

105. The most recent discussion is in Wall, *Massachusetts Bay,* chaps. 5 and 6 and epilogue.

arity of Massachusetts, all of the other New England colonies dissented from New Haven's decision to try such offenses summarily. Massachusetts, Plymouth, Connecticut, and even Maine routinely used juries for life and death. Nevertheless, the Massachusetts magistrates did find a way around this inconvenience on one occasion. When Benjamin Sawser, a Cromwellian soldier, mumbled in his cups in 1654 that "Jehova is the Devill, and hee [Sawser] knew no God, but his sword, and that should save him," a jury in the Court of Assistants acquitted him of blasphemy "vpon poynt of ignorance." The magistrates rejected the verdict, which under colony law brought the case before the General Court. There Sawser was tried again, a clear example of double jeopardy. After that body convicted him but before it passed sentence, Sawser prudently broke jail and fled the colony.[106]

5. Lesser crimes were handled summarily, almost without exception, save in Plymouth Colony. Developments there from 1640 to 1660 merit brief attention. We have already seen that from 1636 to 1638, just prior to the establishment of New Haven, Plymouth tried eight misdemeanors before juries. Thereafter the pace slackened notably, especially when one remembers that the population was growing rapidly. Eight more cases went to a jury in the 1640s, and four in the 1650s.[107] Even unmagisterial Plymouth was slowly assimilating to the judicial norms that now prevailed in most of New England.

VII

It is much easier to describe than to explain New England's fondness for civil juries and aversion to criminal ones, and the task would be much harder without New Haven's luminous model. No reforming English pamphleteer or contemporary New Englander I have encountered ever provided an explicit rationale for the system that emerged in Massachusetts and Connecticut. Enough does survive, however, to prove that the settlers understood this difference and brought appropriate expectations with them into court. Most revealing are mixed cases, roughly equivalent to modern torts—behavior, that is, straddling the boundary between civil and criminal law. The

106. *Ct. Assts. Recs.*, III, 34–38. The magistrates believed that more than alcohol was wrong with Sawser, probably because he had named his horse Jehova and during one encounter with the governor had mockingly cried, "Jehova where art thou Jehova," to the great amusement of his comrades. See Timothy Jerome Sehr, "Colony and Commonwealth: Massachusetts Bay, 1649–1660" (Ph.D. diss., Indiana University, 1977), 161–62.

107. Compiled from *Plym. Col. Recs.*, II–III passim.

two best examples occurred after 1660, but they reveal assumptions that must have been operative earlier as well.

After a defective boom on a vessel owned by James Stuart and Joseph Ludden killed a man, the two faced a criminal trial before the Boston bench without a jury. Obviously they did not expect to be accused of murder. But when the court ordered them to pay £10 damages to the widow, as in a civil suit, they appealed. They protested that "it had been more Legall for [the aggrieved family] To haue sought theire Remedy if [wronged] Jn the Comon Road of Justice, where: both they & wee might have bin Tryed by o^r Equalls according to the Great & Granted priviledg of Engl[ish]men." With perfect technical accuracy, the other side rejoined that Stuart and Ludden had not been "denyed the liberty of law in being tryed by a Jury (as they unworthily insinuate) they never pleading for it upon theire tryall."[108] For our purposes the issue here is a matter of expectations, not law. At least since the Body of Liberties, Stuart and Ludden, like all criminal defendants, had possessed a *legal* right to demand a jury. But they entered the court believing they faced criminal charges, not a civil suit, and they responded as nearly everybody else did, by submitting to the judgment of the bench. When they found themselves assessed civil damages, they felt cheated because had they foreseen any such result, they would have requested a jury trial.

The second case is an example of skulduggery gone askew, or a moral tale in which the weak and lowly outsmart the corrupt and mighty. Samuel Donnel, Esq., a former York justice, prosecuted his nephew for stealing hay. The real issue seems to have been trespass and title, for Donnel some years before had driven his widowed sister-in-law off a meadow that she and her children had mowed for a decade. He now prosecuted her son for continuing to use it. Integrity on the York (Maine) bench was not terribly high in these years. By pressing a criminal case, Donnel could leave the decision to the justices among whom he had sat until the previous year. Had he brought an action of trespass or ejectment, the issue would have gone to a jury, where a widow's tears and the sad plight of a disinherited orphan lad might have caused trouble. But the nephew thwarted the scheme by demanding a criminal jury trial, where he was acquitted. The jury even assessed charges on Donnel instead of the accused, a fairly good sign of what the jurors believed. Enraged, Donnel appealed, apparently never realizing that, because *he* had made the matter criminal instead of civil, he lacked grounds for appeal and

108. *Suff. Ct. Recs.*, I, 404–8.

was in fact raising the issue of double jeopardy. (Somebody may have pointed this out to him later because the case never did reach the Superior Court, which under the Second Charter could be sensitive to this issue.) His chief argument in his appeal was that "the Law requires noe Jury in Such Case," which was not quite accurate. The law explicitly *permitted* criminal juries, but his statement says a lot about his expectations. He added that the trial jury had been sworn only to handle civil, not criminal cases, which was probably true in Maine even at this late date.[109] What matters here, once again, is Donnel's assumptions. Juries were for civil disputes, not crime.

What, then, are we to make of this pattern that contemporaries understood but never bothered to explain to the world? The best I can offer is a plausible hypothesis that accounts for the data but possesses only indirect literary proof.

In civil cases the primary function of the jury may well have been to express the community's consensus about which disputant owed the other how much. By yielding gracefully, the loser reabsorbed himself into the community and restored harmony with the other party. The jury expressed the will of ordinary church members, rather than of exalted magistrates, and helped to define the community's expectations for everyday behavior. The relationship was not quite one of equals, however, for at least in the early years it tended to align church members against the rest of society. In Salem during the late 1630s, for instance, only 3 suits out of 107 pitted one saint against another.[110] In a society in which most settlers still hoped eventually to gain admission to the church, this statistic does not necessarily betray antagonism. It does indicate who was setting standards for whom.

Crime remained another matter. In New England court records, one reads little about felonies and misdemeanors but a great deal concerning sin, evil, wickedness, filthiness, pollutions, and the like. If (as New England legal historians like to argue) this pattern is supposed to be a mere commonplace of the age or something shared by all Englishmen, we would have to explain why this rhetoric is almost entirely absent from the court records of the early Chesapeake colonies.

The proper response to sin in New England was confession and repentance, not denial of guilt. This behavioral trait set the region apart from the rest of English America. If through misguided sentimentality or a misplaced concern for harmony the community failed

109. *Me. Ct. Recs.*, IV, 293–95 (April 1703).
110. David T. Konig, *Law and Society in Puritan Massachusetts: Essex County, 1629–1692* (Chapel Hill, 1979), 27–28.

to punish known sins, it would break its covenant with God, and He would devastate the land with some appropriate catastrophe. Only educated and experienced saints, the magistrates, could be trusted to make correct decisions in this area, which to contemporaries seemed far more important than the realm of civil law. Even more significant, perhaps, was the defendant's perspective. To ask for a jury signaled lack of contrition, a dangerous attitude to assume before the magistrates, especially if the jury found the person guilty.

Even the magistrates drew the line at capital offenses, but I have never encountered one who explained why. Perhaps the most obvious answer is the best. Puritan justice allowed considerable latitude for reform, often remitting fines long after they had been imposed if the defendant's subsequent behavior seemed to warrant such mercy. (Of course the lower orders, who were usually whipped instead of fined before the 1660s, could claim no such benefit.) The bench could also make amends for some of its mistakes should it later change its mind.[111] But because death is final, the larger community ought to be involved in any judicial decision that terminated life. Had magistrates and ministers possessed no misgivings about this concession to English law, the New Haven system could not have existed. Or at least it would have been denounced as outrageous, much as the Dale regime in Virginia had been earlier. Instead the godly reserved their anathemas for Rhode Island.

Nevertheless, three Connecticut cases strongly suggest that magistrates demanded community sanction before taking a settler's life. In 1672, Thomas Rhood and his daughter Sarah both pleaded guilty to a grand-jury indictment for incest. Legally the court needed nothing more to justify hanging them, but it turned both cases over to a jury, which convicted the pair. The bench hanged Thomas without compunction, but divided over the daughter. The incest began with rape, but over time she accepted the relationship. Recognizing "a great appearance of force layd up upon her spirit by her father['s] overaweing & Tiranicall abuse of his parentall authority," the magistrates whipped her instead.[112] Nearly twenty years later, Mercy Brown confessed to the ax murder of her son but denied malice in the act. The jury convicted her of murder, but the court ruled that she was mentally distracted and ordered her confined for life instead

---

111. See Carol F. Lee, "Discretionary Justice in Early Massachusetts," *Essex Institute Historical Collections* 112 (1976): 120–39.

112. Norbert B. Lacy, "The Records of the Court of Assistants of Connecticut, 1665–1701" (M.A. thesis; Yale University, 1937), I, 35–36, 39, 46 (hereafter cited as "Conn. Ct. Assts. Recs.," I). I have used the copy in the Connecticut State Library, Hartford. In 1682, the court even gave a jury to an Indian after he had confessed to murder, a benefit that not even Rhode Island had allowed in a similar case. Ibid., 112–13.

of hanged. For a defendant to be executed in Connecticut, both court and jury had to concur.[113]

Magistrates saw their role in biblical and inquisitorial terms. Settlers were much more likely to place high value on English protections for the accused. If so, we ought to find a visible tension along the boundary that separated biblical from common-law crimes. Adultery offers such a test. According to the Old Testament, it deserves death. English law did not agree.

The saints struggled with this dilemma for years before taking the plunge, and then they quickly got out of the water. The first known adulterer in Massachusetts was spared in 1631 because the offense had not yet been declared capital.[114] Three more were merely banished in 1637 because the capital law had been proclaimed only in the Court of Assistants, not in the General Court.[115] After the passage of the Body of Liberties in 1641, no such excuse would work. The test came in 1644, and it found some of the magistrates more worried than the jury "because there were not two direct witnesses." A few even questioned the biblical warrant "whether adultery was death by God's law now." With doubts resolved after consultation with the elders, the pair were hanged.[116]

New Haven's magistrates also executed someone for adultery, but we know nothing more than that about the incident.[117] In Connecticut the kind of uncertainty that had troubled the Massachusetts court until 1644 continued to bother John Winthrop, Jr. Even after a jury convicted Hannah Hackleton for this offense *after* she had confessed to it, he could not bring himself to approve the death penalty. More secular in outlook than his father, he evidently could not accept the Bible on this point. Perhaps he used other powerful arguments as well, for he had just obtained a royal charter for the colony and doubtless had strong political reasons for evading this question.[118] His stand must have scandalized the other magistrates because they did not accept his position for nearly a whole year. Hannah remained

---

113. Ibid., 174–75, 193. For an earlier case in which the bench rejected a jury's guilty verdict in a capital trial, see Kateram Harrison's 1669 trial for witchcraft, in which she pleaded not guilty and endured one hung jury before the second convicted her. Ibid., 13–14, 18, 19, 23.

114. *Ct. Assts. Recs.*, II, 19; Winthrop, *History*, I, 73.

115. As did Connecticut after 1665, Massachusetts may have used a jury here even when two of the accused pleaded guilty. See the cryptic entry in *Ct. Assts. Recs.*, II, 70, which also notes that the jury was "of Life & Death." In this case, the ministers persuaded the magistrates that the capital law against adultery had not been adequately promulgated. See Winthrop, *History*, I, 309.

116. Ibid., II, 190–91; *Ct. Assts. Recs.*, II, 139.   117. *N. H. T. Recs.*, I, 32.

118. Robert C. Black III, *The Younger John Winthrop* (New York, 1966), 157–58, notes Winthrop's leniency to adulterers in the 1650s. See chaps. 15–17 for the charter.

in jail all that time and then was released with a whipping.[119] Her escape from the gallows signaled that adultery would no longer be a capital crime in Connecticut, news that made the colony the divorce capital of America in the next several decades.[120]

The real drama over adultery remained in Massachusetts. There, once the magistrates had exacted life, they were willing to do it again, only now the jury had grown reluctant. In 1645 a jury found Henry Dawson and Mrs. Hudson innocent of adultery but "guilty of adulterous behavior" for lying in bed together. Since neither of the suspects confessed and the woman's husband believed her story, the evidence against the couple was inconclusive, as the jury pointed out. Yet, reported Winthrop, this verdict "was much against the minds of many, both of the magistrates and elders, who judged them worthy of death."[121]

Thereafter, Massachusetts juries avoided explicit convictions for adultery. The devices varied. In 1667 Bethjah Bullojne and Elizabeth Hudson were both accused of adultery with Peter Turpin. The jury found each woman "guilty of lieing in bed with Peter Turpin." Unsatisfied with the result, the court sent the jury out again, only to get a special verdict shifting all responsibility to the bench: "If by lawe Bethjah Bullojne lying in bed wth Peter Turpin be adultery wee find her Guilty: If by lawe Bethjah Bullojne lying in bed wth Peter Turpin be not adultery wee find her not guilty." Probably unwilling to accept the responsibility for taking life without explicit community approval, the court sentenced both women to stand on the gallows with ropes about their necks and then receive ten stripes or pay fines of £10. This was the lightest penalty ever inflicted for this offense before 1686. We can only guess whether the court chose to be lenient because it shared the jury's uncertainty or because it lacked a specific verdict of guilty.[122] In 1675 another man and woman were found "not legally Guilty [of adultery] but Guilty of very filthy carriage &c." After their gallows humiliation, they received thirty-nine lashes at the cart's tail, and the man was banished.[123] But when Thomas Davis

119. Hartford County Court Records, 1663–1677 (Connecticut State Library, Hartford), 35–36, 38, 52–53 (hereafter cited as Hart. Co. Ct. Recs., followed by dates in the volume). The government used a public prosecutor in this case.

120. See the adultery trial of John Slead and Abigail Betts, 8 October 1672, for this shift. Conn. Ct. Assts. Recs., I, 37–38. The Connecticut code of 1672, adopted in October, specifically made adultery less than capital. *Earliest Laws of New Haven and Connecticut*, 76–77. Extensive unmined material on divorce can be found in Conn. Ct. Assts. Recs. and in the file papers of the Connecticut Archives, Crimes and Misdemeanors, at the State Library.

121. Winthrop, *History*, II, 305–6.

122. *Ct. Assts. Recs.*, III, 191–93. I have not had the opportunity to examine six unpublished depositions relevant to this case.

123. Ibid., I, 56–57.

and Elizabeth Broune were returned "not Guilty legally" but "Guilty of very suspitious acts leading to Adultery," each got two whippings totaling sixty-nine lashes and the usual ritual on the gallows.[124] If the court's sentence varied somewhat, so did the jury's formulae, as when Philip Darland and Mary Knight were convicted of "vile filthy and abominably libidinous Actions," but still not adultery.[125]

Without something like Winthrop's journal to guide us through these cases, we cannot with certainty explain the variations. Some points do stand out, however:

1. After the executions of 1644, no Massachusetts jury would convict for adultery.

2. The magistrates were not determined to hang everyone accused of this sin. They had the opportunity in the Bullojne and Hudson case and received it again a decade later when another accused couple pleaded not guilty, only to request trial by the bench instead of a jury.[126] In all of these cases the magistrates whipped but did not hang.

3. When the younger Winthrop refused to hang even a convicted adultress, the crime effectively ceased to be capital in Connecticut, whatever the law said, and it was soon changed.[127] The rash of divorce petitions that followed, often using adultery as justification, powerfully suggests that the pressure to execute had always come from above, not below.

4. When the Massachusetts Court of Assistants ordered banishment or double whippings, the judges probably disagreed with the jury's verdict. Believing the defendants deserved to hang, the magistrates did the best they could to placate an angry God. When the issue was death, juries could be soft on sin.

Ironically, when death was not at issue, Winthrop Senior could be soft on sin—and too often was, according to other saints. Dudley, supported by the elders, rejected his argument that in young plantations the magistrate should err toward leniency rather than harshness.[128] The deputies demanded fixed penalties for each particular offense, while Winthrop, eventually backed by nearly all the other magistrates, consistently defended judicial discretion. Denunciations of his "arbitrary" government and its tendency to "tyranny" reverberate through his journal and sound quite modern, or at least eighteenth century, until one recalls a curious fact. He behaved

124. Ibid., 70–71. The jury found Elizabeth "Guilty of Prostituting hir body to him to Committ Adultery." Cf. pp. 73–74 for a similar case.
125. The jury added "whorish" to Mary's verdict. Ibid., 252–53. For another variant, see the Rice-Crocket trial of 1683, at pp. 234, 240.
126. Ibid., 114–15.   127. See above, n. 120.
128. Winthrop, *History*, I, 211–14 and passim.

"arbitrarily" (or, in his version, exercised proper "discretion") mostly by *mitigating* the traditional rigors of the law. Only in the land of the saints could institutionalized compassion attract charges of despotism.

On this issue Winthrop occasionally retreated, but he never surrendered, and he made it abundantly clear why he could not. The magistrates had to understand, not merely whether a particular unlawful act had been committed, but the depth of sin manifested in each crime brought before them. The application of uniform punishment to every theft or lie would make injustice inevitable and provoke divine wrath. Either through pretrial investigation or in the actual courtroom, the judge had to explore the degree of guilt before passing sentence. Even to show compassion, in other words, he had to be an inquisitor.

In all of his discussions of this question, Winthrop cites Scripture, not English judicial precedents. He was trying to tell us something so obvious to contemporaries that no one troubled to make it explicit. His model of magisterial behavior differed only slightly from Eaton's in New Haven. His opponents also have a message for us. Since magistrates were announcing themselves as more lenient than ordinary lay saints who elected juries, why ask for one? And why risk appearing unrepentant, thereby losing the best advantage that the system offered to the accused? The controversy over judicial discretion did not pit magistrates against the "people," but great saints against lesser saints. Only when sinners obtained more leverage in New England would traditional English procedures become viable.[129]

Other signs abound that New England magistrates punished sin, not just crime. Why else would they formally admonish John Woolrige for his fraud and drunkenness committed *before* he came to Massachusetts?[130] Why did William Pynchon whip a man for masturbation and then keep both the offense and the whipping secret?[131] And why, even after some defendants won acquittals, did the bench punish them anyway? Thomas Waters, found not guilty of rape, was then banished nonetheless.[132] Thomas Walter, cleared of felonious theft, still had to purge himself by oath. By swearing to his innocence, did he take the onus for any false acquittal off the community and upon himself?[133]

129. See generally Edmund S. Morgan, *The Puritan Dilemma: The Story of John Winthrop* (Boston, 1958); Winthrop, *History*, II, 67–69, 250–57, 274–82.

130. *Ct. Assts. Recs.*, II, 73.

131. *Pynchon Ct. Rec.*, 224. This offense occurred next to the meetinghouse during sermon time, but if the profanation bothered Pynchon, why did he keep the matter private?

132. *Ct. Assts. Recs.*, I, 158.   133. *Suff. Ct. Recs.*, II, 1066.

For this pattern we do have an explicit statement by a magistrate explaining what the courts were doing, if not why. Gov. Thomas Hinckley of Plymouth, distressed that a jury might free someone whom the judges considered guilty, wrote to the Massachusetts magistrate William Stoughton for advice. He replied:[134]

> The testimony you mention against the prisoner . . . is clear and sufficient to convict him; but in case your jury should not be of that mind, then, if you hold yourselves strictly obliged by the laws of England, no other verdict, but not guilty, can be brought in; but, according to our practice in this jurisdiction, we should punish him with some grievous punishment, according to the demerit of his crime, though not found capital.

In other words, not guilty might mean guilty. When magistrates violated this most elementary of English rights, they did it knowingly and conscientiously.

Likewise New England courts paid only limited heed to the right against self-incrimination. The Massachusetts Body of Liberties permitted torture, not in order to extract a confession, but only to discover the names of confederates from someone already convicted of a heinous crime. Puritans had fought hard in England against the High Commission's oath ex officio, which compelled a person to answer any questions put to him before he knew what he was charged with. New Englanders honored this commitment except on extremely rare occasions, such as the Robert Child affair, when it *may* have been violated.[135]

But forced self-incrimination can occur without oaths. The magistrates agreed after full debate in 1641 that in capital cases in which "one witness or strong presumptions do point out the offender, there the judge may examine him strictly, and he is bound to answer directly, though to the peril of his life. But if there be only light suspicion, etc., then the judge is not to press him to answer, nor is he to be denied the benefit of the law, but he may be silent, and call for his accusers."[136] Article 26 of the Body of Liberties allowed an accused person to have an unpaid attorney (an advantage almost never claimed) but added that this right "shall not exempt the partie himselfe from Answering such Questions in person as the Court shall thinke meete to demand of him."[137]

Nor did rules in court necessarily hold in pretrial proceedings. Thomas Bunam, objecting to his peremptory examination by Connecticut magistrates for a misdemeanor, got an attorney and appealed

134. Thomas Hutchinson, *History of the Colony and Province of Massachusetts-Bay*, ed. Lawrence Shaw Mayo (Cambridge, Mass., 1936), I, 382n.
135. Levy, *Origins of the Fifth Amendment*, 352–54.
136. Winthrop, *History*, II, 56.   137. Morgan, *Puritan Political Ideas*, 184

to the General Assembly for redress. He particularly resented being questioned without first being told his offense. The assembly, to his distress, emphatically applauded this aspect of the magistrates' activity, encouraged them to pass summary sentence whenever such efforts uncovered a breach of the law, denied the right of attorney to anybody else who appealed a misdemeanor conviction, and added a £5 fine to anyone who dared appeal and then lost![138] In Massachusetts, Benjamin Hurd found himself on trial for having advised William Read to plead not guilty to arson. Under the two-witness rule, Hurd explained, "nothing else could hurt him wth severall such like expressions tending to encouradge him in denying his crimes."[139] Reading a prisoner his rights is, of course, a very modern idea. But to make it a criminal offense to point out the law to him travels quite far in the opposite direction at a time when even English judges advised accused felons to plead not guilty.

Magisterial latitude in pretrial hearings knew few limits. Samuel Appleton put a theft suspect under oath before interrogating her in 1683.[140] John Hathorne arranged to sell into Barbadian bondage another accused thief without even bringing him to trial. His motives were at least partially humane, for he feared that the man would freeze to death in jail before the next session of the county court. "Necessity hath noe law," he explained, adding that "I hope y[e] Cuntry well rid of a grand theife."[141] Hathorne could also indulge in the crudest form of leading question, a trait doubtless shared by English justices of the era. "What day of the weeke did you steale the money from Elizabeth Russell?" he asked George Harris in 1684. When that did not work, he tried again: "When was it you tooke the money out of her chest?" "I never took any," replied Harris.[142] Ministers could also practice this tactic, as when Deodat Lawson broke down a suspect in front of witnesses "for the Glory of God and Conviction of Goodm. Boston."[143] Hathorne may have failed to trap Harris, but deferential terror of magistrates probably did compel some individuals to confess to crimes they had never committed. George Spencer and the New Haven sow may be the cruelest example. Samuel French insisted he was another in 1667.[144]

". . . o[r] Coartes at Ipswich was all one [with] the Inquishon howse

---

138. *Public Records of the Colony of Connecticut,* ed. J. H. Trumbull and Charles J. Hoadly (Hartford, 1850–90), I, 394–95.

139. *Suff. Ct. Recs.,* I, 89.   140. *Essex Ct. Recs.,* IX, 142–44.

141. Ibid., 567.

142. Ibid., 398–99. Of course leading questions were undoubtedly a standard practice in English pretrial examinations as well. See Langbein, "Origins of Public Prosecution," as in n. 4, above.

143. *Essex Ct. Recs.,* IX, 569–70.   144. Ibid., III, 398n.

in spayen," complained Thomas Wells, a church member whom some others thought a conjurer; "when a man is onse brought into Coarte ... he knowes not for what: he had as good be hanged."[145] Wells grossly exaggerated, of course, and the magistrates took understandable affront at his Spanish comparison. But he was correct to insist that criminal justice in Massachusetts, as in New Haven, was inquisitorial. Lacking the compulsory weapons of that Spanish tribunal, orthodox New England courts depended heavily upon the accused's sense of guilt, often rewarding with lighter sentences those who convincingly manifested their repentance. One would like to measure the effect, if possible. I suspect, but cannot prove, that brief formulaic phrases in the official records often did describe distinct kinds of courtroom events.

"Jedidiah Strong fined for drunkenness" tells us nothing about how he pleaded or why he was convicted. Other entries reveal more. The meaning seems obvious when the accused "pleaded guilty," "owned the fact," or "confessed." These defendants made no attempt in court to deny guilt, whatever they may have done in pretrial hearings. On the other hand, those "legally convicted" had almost certainly professed innocence only to be condemned under the two-witness rule. More fascinating still are intermediate phrases, especially the variants upon "legally convicted, in part by his own confession." This terminology could reflect conviction for a pretrial statement later denied in court, but that pattern is not likely to have occurred often. In most cases it probably describes a defendant who pleaded innocent, only to disintegrate under withering interrogation from the bench. Several cases in New Haven County, after the merger with Connecticut, support this reading.[146]

The intense impact of internalized guilt often emerges from the records. Thomas Verry confessed that his fornication before marriage "was a great grief and trouble to him and his wife and he asked that the authority would extend their charity to so poor a worm both in respect to estate and guilt."[147] Examples of utter self-abasement can be multiplied almost indefinitely from New England records but scarcely exist in other colonies, most of which rarely bothered, in the seventeenth century, to prosecute fornication before marriage. The psychic toll that shame and fear could exact appeared when Abra-

145. Ibid., IV, 78. Wells appears frequently in these volumes. Interestingly, the three witnesses who heard his remark claimed not to know what the Spanish Inquisition was. The magistrates did, of course, and took offense.

146. New Haven County Court Records, 1666–1698 (Connecticut State Library, Hartford), 52–53, 114, 120 (hereafter cited as N. H. Co. Ct. Recs., 1666–98). Here again New Haven clerks provided details hard to recover elsewhere.

147. *Essex Ct. Recs.*, VIII, 146.

ham Foster learned that Elizabeth Gold had blamed her pregnancy on him. "He did not deny it," reported a witness, "but stood pale and trembling for nearly a quarter of an hour and said he would not answer until he had spoken with Betty."[148]

VIII

Slowly, nonetheless, the system changed. Two new developments emerged in the Restoration era. Settlers began to manifest an inclination to litigiousness disturbing enough to provoke God's wrath. And some people, though not as yet very many, began to demand jury trials for minor crimes. Because the role of juries again became problematic, the time has come to offer a brief word about who sat on them.

Any direct study of jurors would require enormous time and effort. Each jurisdiction held two to four courts per year with separate petit juries and an annual grand jury. Over a fifty-year span, the number of persons involved would be mammoth. Seventeenth-century court records usually do name the jurors, but unfortunately they do not say what town they came from. A more ruthless scholar than I could solve part of this problem by working up from town and church records where they happen to be full enough to be useful. Instead we shall have to make do with a brief statement of legal requirements. In Massachusetts before 1647, jurors had to be freemen— that is, church members. In that year, as one of its concessions during the Robert Child affair, the General Court relaxed this provision, permitting those who were not church members to vote for and hold town office and serve on juries. Interestingly, they could not *elect* jurors. This function remained a privilege of freemen. In short, the church members decided who sat on juries. Connecticut never restricted freemanship to church members or placed any special qualifications upon jurors. But just as most freemen and deputies were church members anyway, so may have been most jurors. New Haven Town (rather than County), once it adopted juries in 1666, did keep the office tightly under the control of eminent church members. Plymouth did not restrict freemanship to church members and permitted nonfreemen to serve on juries, elected presumably by the freemen.[149]

148. Ibid., 381–82.
149. *The Laws and Liberties of Massachusetts reprinted from the Copy of the 1648 Edition in the Henry E. Huntington Library*, ed. Max Farrand (Cambridge, Mass., 1929), 51; David H. Fowler, "Connecticut's Freemen: The First Forty Years," *William and Mary Quarterly*, 3d ser., 15 (1958): 312–33.

Juries and litigants interacted strangely after 1660. Originally the Massachusetts courts had enabled the godly to set standards for the unchurched, but now "to the Scandal of their holy Profession" church brother was "going to Law with Brother, and provoking and abusing one another in publick Courts of Judicature."[150] Church members had probably shed some of their reluctance to sue one another in court, but granting the rapidly declining percentage of saints in the adult male population and the increasing volume of litigation, another trend seems even more likely. Sinners were growing restless. The ideal of village harmony still retained immense appeal and real power, but after 1660 it had become attainable only by the townsmen's relying on the courts to settle disputes that had gotten beyond local control.[151] Paradoxically, some of the devices used by the courts to impose a result did as much to disrupt harmony as to restore it.

New England's odd use of appeals embodied this awkward tendency. Unlike England, which required that appeals be grounded in technical law and be resolved by the bench of a higher court, New England permitted appeals from almost anybody dissatisfied with a verdict in a lower tribunal. Rarely did the higher court unequivocally decide the case on a point of law, although the Massachusetts General Court did tend to specialize in equity suits.[152] Instead the two litigants received a new trial before a different jury and, in Massachusetts and Connecticut, could appeal that verdict to the General Court. If one of them still refused to accept that result, he could even petition for a new trial and start the process all over again at the county level.

Here again, no contemporary gave an explicit rationale for this system. To me, it makes sense only if we assume that the jury was supposed to reflect the community's will and persuade *both* disputants to accept the result. Instead, the moral force of the community as expressed by one jury could be repudiated by the public will embodied in another. From a more disturbing perspective, I think, sinners had learned to turn one jury of saints against another. Between 1674 and 1686, juries in the Massachusetts Court of Assistants upheld county decisions 350 times and overturned them on 204 occasions (37 percent).[153]

150. Williston Walker, *The Creeds and Platforms of Congregationalism* (1893; reprint, Boston, 1960), 430.
151. See Konig, *Law and Society in Puritan Massachusetts,* for a full development of this theme.
152. Black, "Judicial Power and the General Court," stresses the equity jurisdiction of the General Court.
153. Calculated from *Ct. Assts. Recs.,* I. In Plymouth, which lacked counties before 1686, retrials served the same purpose.

Lawsuits thus threatened to become a bizarre lottery that either party could win, especially if he tried often enough. John Godfrey cut a contentious path through Massachusetts court records, appearing on over one hundred occasions. No saint (he was often accused of witchcraft), he won more often than not.[154] Almost as spectacular was the Plymouth career of Capt. John Williams, an embittered man whose marriage broke up over his own admission of impotence and his accusations of his wife's infidelity, which no one else believed. As a young man he attracted attention by abusing an orphaned niece who was quickly removed from his custody, by trying to embezzle the estate of another teenage ward, and by entertaining Quakers and violating the Sabbath. In his mature years, he found ways to turn small incidents into interminable problems. He sued Thomas Wade and Timothy White early in 1683 for carting away what he claimed was some of his timber. He lost then and twice more before he finally got a favorable verdict on his fourth attempt, in July 1684. By now the case had become a staple item for almost every Plymouth court session. Wade and White won a reversal, as did Williams the following year. Their seventh jury trial, in July 1686, led to a special verdict so confusing to the court that it postponed its judgment until October. By then Wade had evidently lost patience. He complicated matters and weakened his defense by using Williams's horses for target practice. Williams appeared to be the winner just as the Dominion of New England closed down the fun. But Wade and White did not forgive and forget. They waited six years until Williams became vulnerable after being convicted of selling liquor to the Indians. This time the court threw out their suit, ending almost a decade of increasingly nasty litigation, all over a load of wood.[155]

Fathergon Dinley died too soon to match these records, but he tried. An exceptionally litigious fellow, he lost the same suit four times to New York's Cornelis Steenwyck, tried again and lost a fifth time in Suffolk (Boston), at the height of the third Anglo-Dutch war, but then won at last on appeal to the Court of Assistants. The Dutch had just retaken New York. We have to wonder whether Dinley called patriotism to the rescue of what was otherwise a hopeless cause.[156]

Appeals and retrials did not exhaust the ingenuity of Massachusetts litigants. In 1672 the General Court, rashly perhaps, took away

154. John Demos, "John Godfrey and His Neighbors: Witchcraft and the Social Web in Colonial Massachusetts," *William and Mary Quarterly*, 3d ser., 33 (1976): 242–65.
155. On the early life and career of Williams, see *Plym. Col. Recs.*, III, 171–72, 185, 189; IV, 50, 93, 106, 107–8, 117, 121, 125–26; VII, 209–10, 213. For some of his other quarrels, see ibid., V 109; VI, 19. For this case, see ibid., VII, 259, 264, 265–66, 276–77, 281, 287–88, 300–301, 303–4, 311.
156. *Suff. Ct. Recs.*, I, 167–73, 246, 292–93; *Ct. Assts. Recs.*, I, 371.

from magistrates the power to reject a jury verdict. (In Connecticut this power continued into the eighteenth century.) This change was part of a complicated compromise between deputies and magistrates. Before 1660, rejection of a verdict in any court sent the case to the General Court for review. In the amended code of that year, the practice was modified so that, when a bench-jury dispute occurred at the county level, the suit went to the Court of Assistants. But the code made no provision for carrying a rejected verdict from the Court of Assistants to the General Court. In other words, magistrates in that tribunal could simply overrule the jury, the "democraticall" component of the judicial process. When the magistrates yielded this power in 1672, they insisted upon some remedy against erroneous juries. To meet this need, the legislature revived an obsolete common-law device, attaint of jury.[157]

Attaint permitted an aggrieved party to take criminal action against jurors who made corrupt decisions. But in Massachusetts it instantly became something quite different, a way to retry the case before a new jury instead of prosecuting the original jurors. It had several advantages, for it obviated even the fairly nominal requirement that one needed new evidence to secure a retrial. It also enabled someone to get a rehearing before the Court of Assistants without first returning to the county level. For some exasperated litigants, in other words, it may have marked a crude bid for improved efficiency. The results were distressing nonetheless. In the March 1681 session of the Court of Assistants, for example, 28 percent of the losers attainted their jury.[158] The public scandal of having the jury in this exalted tribunal denounced year after year as corrupt and vicious, even if only as a legal fiction, finally became too much to bear. Many jurors were church members, after all, and yet attaint gave legal license to the godless to call them something else. The General Court retaliated cleverly and effectively by declaring that anyone who lost a claim of attaint would himself be fined and would also be open to defamation suits from *each* juror.[159]

In these cases the quest for harmony and voluntary conciliation produced only protracted quarrels. Understandably, some men responded with varying degrees of impatience and indignation. Ste-

157. Black, "Judicial Power and the General Court," 329–32. For the law, see *Mass. Recs.*, IV (ii), 508–9.
158. Calculated from *Ct. Assts. Recs.*, I, 179–89.
159. Because one jury normally handled all the cases at a given session, only one litigant had to attaint in any court to raise a public challenge to the jurors' integrity. For the repeal, see *Mass. Recs.*, V, 449–50. For two subsequent efforts to attaint, see *Ct. Assts. Recs.*, I, 282, 287, 293, 294. In the first, Anthony Checkley (the attorney general!) was fined and the fine later suspended. The second case got lost during the transition to the Dominion of New England.

ven Butler could scarcely believe in 1682 that the Suffolk court would dare permit Anthony Checkley (an early lawyer of dubious reputation) to reopen, without new evidence, a case that "hath bin heard & determined by two if not three Generall Courts," but he was wrong. This time around Checkley won, as he did again on appeal to the Court of Assistants.[160] Thomas Walter fared better on a similar occasion. Learning that the assistants were going to rehear John Gifford's complaint against him, he angrily "turned away & went out of Court though Called to Attend." This gesture may have worked, for the magistrates took a formal vote and then threw out Gifford's case.[161] ". . . a Court & jury bee nothing," William Norman sadly observed; "noe," agreed Humphry Hodges, ". . . for what one Court doth another undoeth." For pointing out the obvious, Hodges faced criminal charges.[162]

New England had gone jury mad. This wild expansion of the role of civil juries far exceeded anything imagined for them by any English apologist I have ever read. And yet devotion to juries seemed to rise in direct proportion to the contempt litigants enjoyed displaying for any particular set of twelve men, good and true. Amid all the frenzy, a tiny proportion of the people accused of noncapital crimes also began to demand jury trials.

In Connecticut, no jury trial for ordinary crime had ever occurred before that colony absorbed New Haven, in the mid-1660s. Then, ironically, the first ones appeared in newly created New Haven County, almost certainly because the Eaton-trained magistrates of that jurisdiction did not understand the jury system as it had evolved elsewhere in New England. No doubt they had heard about the famous and quite recent Hannah Hackleton adultery trial, in which the Connecticut court turned the matter over to a jury even though she had already pleaded guilty, only to see her escape death because of the younger Winthrop's reservations.[163] At any rate, the perplexed judges followed that model in November 1666. Otto Janson, a Dutchman who knew even less about juries then did the New Havenites, pleaded guilty to having stolen a horse from one man and some miscellaneous items from another. The bench nonetheless gave both cases to a jury, which dutifully confirmed his guilt. Another sign of magisterial confusion is the way this case is entered in the records. The victims are listed as plaintiffs and Janson as defendant,

160. Ibid., 205–6. Butler was appealing to the Court of Assistants because the inferior court had retried the case and found against him. He also lost the appeal.

161. Ibid., 218

162. *Suff. Ct. Recs.*, I, 190–92. Hodges was fined £10 for his remarks; he appealed but apparently did not pursue the matter to conclusion.

163. For the Hackleton trial, see above, at n. 118.

Table 1

NONCAPITAL ACQUITTALS, MASSACHUSETTS AND CONNECTICUT,
1660–86/7

Court	N Verdicts	N Acquitted	% Acquitted
Boston	23	5	22%
Charlestown	3	0	0
Cambridge	8	2	25
Salem	16	4	25
Ipswich	24	2	8
All Connecticut	7	0	0
Total	81	13	16%

Note: The Boston (Suffolk) totals include one verdict from 1668, mentioned in *Rec. Ct. Assts.*, III, 154–55, which is omitted from the discussion in the text above.

as though the issue were civil litigation. New Haven had much to learn in 1666. But someone soon enlightened the judges, for no one else received a criminal jury in the county court until 1685.[164]

Elsewhere in Connecticut, the Court of Assistants specifically offered a jury to a noncapital defendant in 1671 (he rejected the option), the only such example I have found in the entire colony before the 1690s. Only four actual jury trials for such offenses took place in Hartford in this period, all in the 1680s—three in the Court of Assistants, and one in the Hartford County Court at the very late date of 1687. Connecticut magistrates could hardly have demanded more from juries than they got. In seven trials all seven defendants were convicted.[165] Meanwhile summary justice continued to thrive, even for major noncapital offenses such as attempted rape, adultery after it cased to be capital, and crimes against property.[166]

Change was more dramatic in Massachusetts, particularly in Essex County, where 40 defendants put themselves "on God and the country" between May 1660 and the establishment of the Dominion of New England, a rate of roughly three every two years. Middlesex registered 11 from 1660 to 1686 (the records for 1663–71 recently disappeared and are not included here), and Suffolk produced 22

164. N. H. Co. Ct. Recs., 1666–98, p. 7. See p. 152 for the 1685 case.

165. Conn. Ct. Assts. Recs., I, 95–98 (two cases), 152–53; Hartford Co. Ct. Recs., 1678–97, pp. 128–29. For the man offered a jury, which he refused, see Conn. Ct. Assts. Recs., I, 29–30.

166. For examples of summary trials for serious offenses, see ibid., 37–38 (adultery), 52–53 (bestiality); N. H. Co. Ct. Recs., 1666–98, 10–12, 103 (both rape).

between 1671 and 1686. Because Suffolk convicted 548 other people in the years 1680–86 alone, the percentage requesting juries was very small and most likely would remain tiny even if we knew how many defendants had not pleaded guilty.[167] Of this colonywide total of 73 verdicts, 24, or about one-third, occurred before the Ipswich bench in Essex County, where the local magistrates Daniel Denison and Simon Bradstreet attracted criticism by the 1660s for incompetence, favoritism, and even intoxication on the bench.[168] Criminal defendants grew bolder, it seems, when judges came under attack.

Whatever benefits the accused may have hoped to derive from the bench's embarrassments or from the growing abuse that jurors received from civil litigants, they must have been disappointed. Jurors surely felt baffled by their unstable civil role, but they were chosen by church members in Massachusetts, and there and in Connecticut they still knew sin when they saw it. Their low acquittal rate tells the story. (See table 1.[169])

Farther toward the New England periphery, defendants did better:[170]

Table 2

OTHER NEW ENGLAND ACQUITTALS, 1660–86

Court	N Verdicts	N Acquitted	% Acquitted
Plymouth Colony	29 (45)	10 (18)	34% (40%)
Old Norfolk	8	4	50
York (Maine)	6	3	50
Rhode Island	53 (56)	25 (27)	47 (48)
Total	96 (115)	42 (52)	44 (45)

Note: The Plymouth and Rhode Island totals in parentheses include capital trials. The Rhode Island totals exclude one hung jury, three unknown verdicts, and three trials of March 1659 / 60.

Northern New England had difficulty sustaining the standards of Congregational purity demanded by Massachusetts, and the 50 per-

167. I have calculated convictions through 1686 from Suff. Ct. Recs., 1680–92.
168. *Essex Ct. Recs.*, IV, 76–82, 99, 104–5.
169. Compiled from *Suff. Ct. Recs.*, I–II; Suff. Ct. Recs., 1680–92, I–II; Midd. Ct. Recs., I, III–IV; *Essex Ct. Recs.*, II–IX; Conn. Ct. Assts. Recs., I; Hart. Co. Ct. Recs., 1666–77 and 1678–97; N. H. Co. Ct. Recs., 1666–98.
170. Old Norfolk's records are scattered through *Essex Ct. Recs.* For the other jurisdictions, see *Me. Ct. Recs.*, II–III; *Plym. Col. Recs.*, II–VII; *R. I. Ct. Trials Recs.*, I–II.

cent acquittal rate in Old Norfolk (most of which became part of New Hampshire) and York probably reflects this contrast. Interestingly, these results do not differ to any significant degree from the behavior of juries in Rhode Island unless we subtract the thirteen guilty verdicts that probably challenged that colony's right to exist (see above, at n. 50) and thus raise the acquittal rate to 63 percent. Plymouth stands midway between the true periphery and the orthodox core of New England, acquitting significantly fewer defendants than the northern border or Rhode Island did, but twice as many as the citadels of orthodoxy did. And Plymouth's rate of acquittal was actually declining, from 42 percent in the 1640s and 1650s to 34 percent after 1660. If we assume that the intensity of Puritanism was a major variable in jury behavior, these results match our expectations.

Despite the exceptionally strong performance of Massachusetts juries as moral watchdogs, some evidence indicates magisterial uneasiness at their use. If Suffolk County was at all typical from 1680 to 1686, only 3 percent of the accused went free (not guilty, quash, dismiss) in nonjury trials. Juries did permit an extremely small number of offenders to escape justice. Let us assume, just for argument, that jurors were too charitable every other time that they acquitted someone. If so, all of half a dozen people in Massachusetts and Connecticut from 1660 to 1687 went free to pollute the land.[171] Nevertheless, this possibility upset some magistrates. The Essex bench refused to accept the first acquittal it saw, in which John Upton was accused of helping to steal, among other things, two Bibles.[172] When a Middlesex jury found John Chadwicke "not legally guilty" of fornication, the bench fined him for lying instead.[173] Moses Parker, who had been denounced for trading illegally with the Indians, was convicted by the jury of having accepted "one beaver." The bench probably expected more, for it then fined him summarily for a liquor violation and contempt as well.[174] Sarah Snell impudently denied her "wanton lascivious carriages" and demanded a jury—something that almost never happened for sexual misdemeanors. The jury convicted her, and the court gave her twenty lashes (later commuted to a £10 fine), double the penalty it usually imposed for actual fornica-

171. The only major jurisdictions missing from this calculation are Hampshire County, Mass., New London County, Conn., and Portsmouth, N.H., which I have not yet had time to examine systematically. The Suffolk data are compiled from Suff. Ct. Recs. 1680–92, I–II.

172. *Essex Ct. Recs.*, III, 264–66.

173. Midd. Ct. Recs., III, 2–3. Cf. the witchcraft trial of James Fuller, in which he was fined for lying (boasting of his familiarity with the devil?) after the jury acquitted him. *Ct. Assts. Recs.*, I, 228–29.

174. Midd. Ct. Recs., IV, 28–29.

tion.[175] Her experience suggests that by the 1680s the real danger in juries seemed to be, not so much how *they* might behave, but the lack of guilt or sorrow displayed by the person who requested one.

Ebenezer Austin's trial nicely combined all of these tensions—magisterial misgivings about juries, their actual performance, and the disturbing behavior of defendants. Merely because Austin's wife gave birth four and a half months after the wedding, his grumpy neighbors accused the couple of fornication. He denied the charge, demanded a jury, and introduced a witness (appropriately named "Foull") who testified vaguely that the pair "was mareed at my hous A consederebell time severall weeks before" the date on the town clerk's record. Few jurors had to count on their fingers to calculate that "severall weeks" did not equal four or five months. They found Austin guilty. Awaiting sentence, Austin had second thoughts about his rash actions and obviously feared magisterial reprisals. He addressed a "Humble petition" to the court full of all the proper words of self-abasement without quite admitting, fully and unequivocally, his sin. Theophilus Eaton would have seen through the document, but read quickly, it was convincing. Above all, Austin apologized for his behavior in court: "Indeed if I have offended the Honourd Court in desiring A Jury I am heartely sory for it & begg your favrable construction thereof, for sum freinds thinking [i]t might be for the best, and Nature is precous to use what means may be Lawfully (at hart [hand?]) to preserve it selfe." After a little more groveling, his plea for "Justice mixed with mercy" had its effect. He paid a fine of only £4 for himself and his wife, the minimum then being imposed for fornication before marriage.[176]

Austin had tried to turn his sin into the kind of game that civil litigation was becoming, and he retreated to a stance of expected humility just in time. In the process, he obligingly revealed more specifically and incontrovertibly than anyone else I have encountered that a request for a criminal jury could indeed offend the magistrates.

His effort to brazen out his offense suggests another point. Histories of classic freedoms always seem to provide a few appropriate—and genuine—heroes who endure great suffering for the sake of principle. Among Austin's near contemporaries, one thinks of Roger Williams accepting midwinter exile for freedom of religion, John Hampden battling against taxation by prerogative, or Algernon Sidney dying on the gallows for freedom of thought. But in New England, with the possible exception of Samuel Gorton, those who began to insist on criminal jury trials against regional tradition and

175. *Suff. Ct. Recs.*, II, 940.
176. Midd. Ct. Recs., IV, 225–26. The petition is in Middlesex Files, f. 123.

all odds of success were not an admirable group. They were sinners, not heroes, because where we can check, those who were convicted truly deserved their fate. The list includes Dr. Richard Cordin and Dr. Henry Greenland, who affected deep piety while trying to seduce half the women of Essex County (Greenland later contributed to the progress of mankind by becoming the first settler in Princeton, New Jersey); John Godfrey, a legend of contentiousness in his own day; Capt. John Williams, whom we have met disturbing most of his Scituate neighbors; Richard Martyn, who shamelessly battered his own father; two young men who enjoyed tormenting Thomas Maule, a Salem Quaker; and a highly organized ring of burglars in Essex County. Quakers and Baptists, hounded by the courts for their dissent, did not request jury trials. Quakers apparently got more delight out of denouncing and enraging the magistrates than in seeking acquittal, even when sentiment for toleration ran strong among the deputies and, presumably, the pool of potential jurors as well.[177]

Some moderns might try to make a case for Joseph Gatchell as a martyr, if only because he dared to affirm the blasphemous principle of universal salvation in a Calvinist stronghold. For this crime he got his tongue bored through with a hot iron and—fortunately for him, as it turned out—spent a lot of time in jail. He had already been convicted twice for theft, and while he was still in prison, his friends engineered the most spectacular burglary in seventeenth-century Massachusetts when they stole over £500 from George Corwin's home. Had Gatchell been free, he almost certainly would have joined in this caper, and he may have been one of the few people who knew where the loot was stashed. One of his amusements may have been keeping his brother's wife pregnant. He seems not quite the material of which heroes are made.[178]

Jury trials for noncapital crimes made only limited progress in orthodox seventeenth-century New England colonies, hardly any in Connecticut. Only after the Glorious Revolution and the Second Charter destroyed a regime based ultimately on church membership would this institution win a secure lodging. That is another story for another time and place.

While the saints ruled, sinners paid for their crimes. But their day was coming, and with it another leap forward for American liberty.

177. For Godfrey and Williams, see above, at nn. 154–55. For Greenland and Cordin, *Essex Ct. Recs.*, III, 47–55, 65–66, 88–90, 133–35, 194–97; for Martyn, ibid., IV, 186–87; for Maule's tormentors, ibid., VIII, 346; for the burglary ring, ibid., IX, 271–86. For tolerant sentiments among the deputies, see David D. Hall, *The Faithful Shepherd: A History of the New England Ministry in the Seventeenth Century* (Chapel Hill 1972), 228–30.

178. *Essex Ct. Recs.*, IX, 215, 269, 271–86; *Ct. Assts. Recs.*, I, 253–54. Information on Gatchell's amorous activities comes from Christine Heyrman.

Elites and Electorates: Some Plain Truths for Historians of Colonial America[*]

JOY B. AND ROBERT R. GILSDORF

How does one explain a widely enfranchised, "democratic" electorate that consistently returned "gentlemen" to office? This is one of the most puzzling conundrums of pre-Revolutionary American politics. These days its most fashionable solution involves the notion of deference. Indeed, it is almost impossible to find a study of colonial society or politics that does not use the term. Everybody seems to agree not only that something called deference was operating in colonial politics but also that it functioned in such diverse situations as New England town meetings, the hurly-burly of Pennsylvania politics and gentry-dominated Virginia.[1] Rarely defined precisely, *deference* is usually taken to mean the acceptance or recognition of superiority.[2] Essentially it accounts for legislatures filled with

[*] We wish to express our great appreciation to the staff of the Connecticut State Library for the working facilities that they provided us during our research there in 1977 and 1978, for their comprehensive knowledge of the collections that they maintain so well, and for being such a wonderful group of people with whom to work. Marvin Thompson, an editor of the Trumbull papers, was especially helpful in sharing with us his knowledge and providing us with information. For their reading of and comments on earlier drafts of this paper, we are indebted to Florian Bail, Tom Pocklington, and various reviewers, known and unknown, but especially John Murrin. Monika Porritt, as usual, performed superbly in rendering readable the many drafts of this paper.

1. For instance, see Edward M. Cook, Jr., *The Fathers of the Towns* (Baltimore, 1976), esp. chap. 4; Alan Tully, *William Penn's Legacy: Politics and Social Structure in Provincial Pennsylvania, 1726–1755* (Baltimore, 1977), 79–94; Jack Greene, "Society, Ideology, and Politics: An Analysis of the Political Culture of Mid-Eighteenth-Century Virginia," in *Society, Freedom, and Conscience: The American Revolution in Virginia, Massachusetts, and New York,* ed. Richard M. Jellison (New York, 1976), 14–76.

2. J. G. A. Pocock defined deference in eighteenth-century language as "the voluntary acceptance of a leadership elite by persons not belonging to that elite, but sufficiently free as political actors to render deference not only a voluntary but also a political

"gentlemen" by postulating docile voters. In fact the term is even used as a kind of shorthand to indicate that, in a stratified society, political office went to the upper stratum and that the lower and middle strata—whether pleased or not with this state of affairs—at least were not doing anything to disturb the status quo.[3] Our purpose in this essay is to increase the usefulness of this concept by defining it more precisely than has heretofore been done and to apply this definition to a specific instance, namely, to Connecticut politics in the eighteenth century. Our intent is primarily heuristic rather than descriptive. We must begin with a brief examination of some pitfalls inherent in the current use of the concept of deference.

The deferential interpretation of colonial history originated in an attempt to cope with "the problem of democracy"—the assertion by some historians that there was really no good reason why politics in colonial America could not accurately be described as democratic.[4] As J. R. Pole emphasized in 1962, there was similarly no good reason for not describing Virginia officeholders as an oligarchy. Oligarchies are not found in truly democratic political systems, and consequently Virginia—and any other colony with elite officeholders—simply could not be called a democracy, its broad electorate notwithstanding. Pole suggested rather that colonial politics was deferential in the sense that men of substance commanded the deference of their neighbors and thus naturally were elected to office.[5]

He expanded this thesis later, in his book on representation. Here he was primarily interested in the process by which representation—the theory of which derived from a common political culture—led to revolution on one side of the Atlantic and reform on the other, and eventually to two very different forms of government. In Pole's

---

act." "The Classical Theory of Deference," *American Historical Review* 81 (1976): 517. A more influential definition, and one that underlines the unitary nature of political and social superiority, is that of Bernard Bailyn, who pointed out that the colonists believed "political leadership would devolve upon the natural social leaders of the community, whose identity, it was expected, would be steadily and incontestably visible." *The Origins of American Politics* (New York, 1970), 96. Though these definitions are derived from seventeenth- and eighteenth-century political theory, they are both offered and used as modern analytical explanations of colonial political behavior.

3. See, for instance, James Kirby Martin, *Men in Rebellion: Higher Governmental Leaders and the Coming of the American Revolution* (New Brunswick, 1973), 61.

4. See Robert E. Brown, *Middle-Class Democracy and the Revolution in Massachusetts, 1691–1780* (Ithaca, 1955); and idem with B. Katherine Brown, *Virginia, 1705–1786: Democracy or Aristocracy?* (East Lansing, 1964). John B. Kirby's article "Early American Politics—The Search for Ideology: An Historical Analysis and Critique of the Concept of 'Deference,'" *Journal of Politics* 32 (1970): 808–38, delineates the development of the concept of deference and its relation to earlier schools of interpretation.

5. Pole, "Historians and the Problem of Early American Democracy," *American Historical Review* 67 (1962): 626–46.

interpretation of the American side of the process, the colonists revolted against Britain in order to defend what they conceived of as their legitimate governments. For them the various provincial governments were legitimate because they were representative; the assemblies, in a word, were elective and consequently ruled with the people's active consent. Naturally the legislative branch was the focus of legitimacy since it was the branch to which the colonists gave their explicit consent. Throughout the colonial period its basic legitimacy was underlined for Americans in conflicts with an "alien," that is, appointed, executive branch. Colonial legislatures, skillfully, if sometimes unconsciously, building on the basis of this legitimacy, were thus able to arrogate to themselves the main powers of government. They were not, however—as Pole is at great pains to stress—democratic. What was represented in these legislatures was property, not people. It followed, therefore, that those with the most property had the most right to govern. But because in America property was widespread, the franchise was also extensive, so that it is reasonable to say the colonists acquiesced in the principle of representation by property and thus in the rule of men of property. It was in fact precisely this widespread willingness to defer to their more substantial "betters" which gave colonial legislatures such a strong sense of legitimacy and made them react so sharply to perceived infringements of their rights and liberties on the eve of the Revolution.[6]

This is a fascinating interpretation of colonial history, but it leads Pole into difficulties. In order to be consistent with his stress on property as the central principle of representation, he must insist upon both the independence of the electorate, men with a certain minimum of property, and the dominance of the ruling elite, those who had the most property. But if the voter was truly independent, then how could the elite be dominant? And if the elite was truly dominant, which Pole goes to great lengths to assure us was the case, then in what sense was the electorate independent? Pole ultimately is unable to resolve this paradox and can do no more than make equivocal statements such as the following: "American elections often presented a curious mixture, difficult to understand at its face value, of local turbulence and basic order, of jocular familiarity and implicit deference." He is reduced to describing colonial elections with high turnovers of officeholders as "the equivalent, within republican norms, of peasant revolts, all the safer and more decorous for being

6. Pole, *Political Representation in England and the Origins of the American Republic* (London, 1966), esp. 503–39.

legal and peaceful."[7] It is a strange way to characterize an independent electorate.

In his essay on political culture in Virginia, Jack Greene has made a somewhat more successful attempt to cope with the inconsistencies in the concept of deference by skirting the whole issue of power and equating superiority in socioeconomic terms with inherent individual superiority. Greene takes the tack that the deferential acquiescence of the populace to the rule of the gentry was willing because it was beneficial to all concerned. The freeholders, who "regularly exercised their liberty of choice to select gentrymen to represent them," were simply conforming to the widespread belief that government "should be reserved for and was the responsibility of enlightened and capable men." Thus, "Government by the 'virtuous and enlightened' was not only the ideal but also, to a remarkable degree, the habit of colonial Virginians."[8] In Greene's interpretation the elite ruled not because its members had more property than did other Virginians, although he admits that this was true, but because they were literally superior beings. In this way he is able to evade the whole question of dominant elites and independent electorates by concluding that in deferential politics gentlemen were elected because they really were the most fit to rule.

If historians who consider deference a useful concept in explaining colonial politics have problems with the acceptance or recognition of superiority, those who wish to describe colonial politics as democratic have their own dilemma. The consistent election of wealthy, well-educated, and socially respected men to colonial legislatures does not really square with the image of a democratic polity. Robert and Katherine Brown's well-known study of Virginia shows how difficult it is to come to grips with it. The Browns amass a great deal of evidence intended to prove that the people not only consented to but really controlled the course of politics. But though they do not use the term *deference,* the acceptance of superiority is an important part of their argument. They use it to show that the colony's social stratification, and by implication its political stratification, was minimal. While pointing out that voters "almost invariably preferred a man from the middle or upper social and economic strata," the Browns emphasize that candidates could gain and retain office only by pleasing a sufficient number of voters. "If Virginia had been an aristocratically-controlled society, there would have been no need to cultivate the votes of the lower classes."[9] For the Browns the recognition of superiority or "deference" implicit in the consistent elec-

7. Ibid., 521.   8. Greene, "Society, Ideology, and Politics," 22–25.
9. Brown and Brown, *Virginia, 1705–1786,* 57.

tion of upper-class men was nothing more than the free choice by independent voters of the persons best qualified to represent their interests—a position remarkably close to that of Jack Greene.

It is clear that quite different interpretations of colonial politics have a common weakness when it comes to analyzing the roles of elites and electorates. Whether historians use the term *deference* or not, the acceptance of superiority seems to function in current interpretations of colonial politics as a kind of residual, very nearly tautological explanation. Men who were demonstrably superior, in terms of wealth, status, and the like, were elected to office. Therefore, voters must have chosen them because they were wealthy, of high status, and so forth. Given the apparent absence of coercion, historians have thus only to demonstrate that officeholders in a particular colony or town were superior men in order to be able to label its politics as deferential. Further analysis of the relationship between voters and officeholders need not be undertaken.

At the least this is hardly very informative. At the worst it may well be obscuring the true nature of colonial politics. A deferential interpretation, for instance, glosses over the whole question of choice; yet choice is surely essential to understanding the relationship of the voter to those who governed him. If colonial voters never or rarely had a choice, then how do we know that they were deferring to the individuals they elected? The most we can say is that this was not a democratic system. Such elections offered the voters little more than the opportunity to consent to the existing state of affairs. Without choice, voting could merely have been an acknowledgment of the de facto rule of a particular group. The consent of the ruled confers legitimacy upon any regime and undoubtedly aids the ruler in obtaining compliance, but it is not necessarily the same thing as deference.[10] No-choice elections may indicate not only deferential respect for the voter's superiors but also coercion, an apathetic resignation to the status quo, or satisfaction with the system rather than with those running it. Moreover, how can one make any statements about the independence of the electorate if they had no choice?

In competitive elections in which the voters could choose from among more than one candidate, it is reasonable to assume that they chose the man they considered to be superior. But superior in what way? If all candidates were wealthy, then the only way of showing that wealth was the probable basis for their choice is to demonstrate that the wealthiest candidate won in every election. Whether the voters' choice in this case was deferential, coerced, or secured in some

10. Richard Rose, "Is Choice Enough? Elections and Political Authority," in *Elections without Choice*, ed. Guy Hermet et al. (London, 1978), 197.

other way obviously depends on how the wealthy candidate utilized his advantage.[11] Even then the historian would still have to explain why wealth seemed to be the determining factor in these elections. Finally, if the voter did choose freely from among the candidates, no matter what the basis for his choice—if becoming an officeholder *depended* upon winning votes in a competitive election—then in what way does it make sense to call this deferential politics, unless it was the candidate who was deferring to the voter? In the interests of more clarity and less confusion in dealing with the relationships between elites and electorates, a more precise and hence necessarily abstract definition of deference is needed.

It is important to begin by noting that deference, like influence, authority, and coercion, is subsumed under the general notion of power. It does not refer to a system of government, yet it is not merely descriptive of the manners and mores of social intercourse.[12] It is in fact clearly related to the distribution and exercise of legitimate power within particular societies. To understand it properly, therefore, requires a consideration of the elements shared by all power concepts. In common with most contemporary theorists, we consider power concepts to denote relations between individuals or groups and not cardinal values inhering in particular persons.[13] It is central to the delineation of such concepts that these relations be asymmetrical, such that in specified acts or behaviors person B yields to person A's preferences.[14] Now, if B yields to the preferences of A

11. We use wealth here merely for the sake of simplicity and do not intend to imply that historians believe it was the only basis for deference.

12. Our discussion is explicitly limited to overt political deference, and we exclude a number of usages such as formal "presentation rituals," covert attempts at ingratiation, and those which refer to generalized relationships (e.g., "he deferred to public opinion"). When speaking about collectivities, such as societies, it is meaningful to speak of "deference systems" in the sense used by Edward Shils, "Deference," in *Social Stratification*, ed. J. A. Jackson (Cambridge, 1968), 104–32.

13. While not entirely satisfied with any particular formulation of power, we have drawn mostly on the writings of Robert A. Dahl, esp. *Modern Political Analysis*, 3d ed. (Englewood Cliffs, 1976), chaps. 3 and 4, and "Power," in *The International Encyclopedia of the Social Sciences*, ed. David L. Sills (New York, 1968), XII, 405–15; Harold D. Lasswell and Abraham Kaplan, *Power and Society; A Framework for Political Inquiry* (New Haven, 1950), esp. chaps. 4 and 5. While useful on some dimensions, Shils, "Deference," conceives and applies the term in a broader and less explicitly political way than we do. For a provocative formulation that has also had a good deal of influence on our thinking, see Howard Newby, "The Deferential Dialectic," *Comparative Studies in Society and History* 17 (1975): 139–64. See also Donald D. Searing, "Authority and Power: Social Control in the House of Commons" (Paper presented at the Annual Meeting of the American Political Science Association, Washington, D.C., September 1–4, 1977).

14. Not all theorists accept that limitation, however. See, for example, David A. Baldwin, "Power and Social Exchange," *American Political Science Review* 72 (1978): 1229–1242. That B yields to the preferences of A in one or more instances does not preclude the possibility that A might yield to the preferences of B in other instances. Insofar as

in some matter, and does something he otherwise would not have done—which is to say that A initiated the affair and communicated his wishes to B or that B presumed or already "understood" what it was that A desired—we leap intuitively (and rightly) to the conclusion that A must have had some edge over B, in material possessions, persuasive ability, social position, or whatever.[15] This edge or superiority, to which we shall refer as resources, provides the basis for A's exerting influence, authority, or whatever over B, or his getting B to defer to him. The possession of these resources, however, should be kept distinct from the relation itself. By taking note of a person's resources, we can calculate and refer to his *potential* power; his *actual* power is another matter.[16] Even if all powerful persons by definition have superior resources, it does not follow that all persons with superior resources actually have power in the sense intended here, namely, getting other persons to yield to their preferences. B, in fact, is never without resources of his own in any power relation. Insofar as he chooses to utilize these, he has the potential not only for resistance but for successful resistance. This includes the possibility that he may somehow withdraw from the situation without yielding to A's preferences, the most extreme withdrawal, of course, being a martyr's death. The study of power, therefore, requires the examination of its exercise in actual encounters. In any power relation the proof of the pudding is undoubtedly in the tasting.[17]

The historian, as a student of power, is in the unique position of knowing who prevailed in the particular sequence of encounters he is studying. The pudding has long since been tasted and the verdict rendered. His problem is more subtle. In order to explain why things happened as they did, he must work backward and ferret out the structure, the attitudes, the beliefs, the behaviors that made such an

---

there is a counterbalancing of asymmetric relations among individuals, though, the society becomes a more truly interdependent one, and whether, under such conditions, any given class or grouping could maintain preeminence in the political realm is doubtful. As indicated below, it does not seem that colonial American society was interderdependent in this sense, or at least not extensively so.

15. Developing Carl Friedrich's notion of "anticipated consequences," Dahl, *Modern Political Analysis,* 30–32, distinguishes between "manifest" or "explicit" power (influence) and "implicit" power (influence). In the latter case it is B's perceptions of or assumptions about A's preferences that triggers his behavior; it does not require that A actually communicate those preferences in advance to B.

16. An even more refined distinction could also be maintained, that between "having potential power" (the possession of resources), "having power" (the capability to act), and "exercising power" (actually gaining compliance). For a discussion along these lines, see Felix E. Oppenheim, *Dimensions of Freedom* (New York, 1961).

17. When B's resources match A's, the relation is no longer asymmetric and therefore the interaction between the two parties does not involve power but rather bargaining, negotiation, cooperation, and so forth.

outcome possible. We know in most cases who was elected to office in colonial towns, counties, and legislatures. What we don't know is why. In pursuing this "why," we see that the differences rather than the similarities among the various power concepts become crucial, for it is these which will instruct historians in the kinds of politics with which they are dealing.

There are a number of elements in any encounter which distinguish *deference* from other widely used power terms such as *coercion* and *influence*. The way these elements vary according to the type of power relation is shown in Table 1. For the sake of simplicity, we

Table 1

DISTINCTIONS AMONG COERCION, INFLUENCE, AND DEFERENCE

| | Type of Relation | | |
	Coercion	Influence	Deference
Initial State of Preferences of A and B	Opposed	In disagreement	B's preempted to A's
Final State of Preference of A and B	Opposed	In agreement	B's preempted by A's
B's Calculation of Costs/ Benefits of Compliance/ Noncompliance	Present throughout	Present at outset, but altered by A	Absent throughout in pure case; increasingly present as deference weakens
Interactions between A and B	Conflictual throughout	Conflictual, changing to cooperative	Preemptive throughout
Use of Resources by A	Sanctions, inducements (threats, promises, etc.)	Used to impress B	Used to establish membership in "superior" group
Use of Resources by B	Used against A or surrendered to him	Added to those of A	Expended on A's behalf
Resultant Compliance	Behavioral but not attitudinal modification	Attitudinal and behavioral modification	Attitudes and behavior conform to previous patterns

have differentiated only coercion, influence, and deference.[18] In all three of these relations B yields to the preferences of A. But though the end result is the same in each case, there are a number of variations that add up to substantially different kinds of relations. Coercion starts and ends in conflict, and A's success depends upon his willingness to expend his resources either in punishing or in rewarding B. By matching his resources with those of A, B in turn calculates whether he should resist or comply with A's demands. Whether he resists or chooses not to sacrifice his resources, his attitudes have remained unchanged. He may behave according to A's wishes, but his opposition to these wishes remains unchanged.[19]

In the case of influence, B and A start out in opposition (or at least not in agreement), but A is able to demonstrate to B, by convincing him that he, A, is a sound person arguing a sound case, that his, B's, original position or opinion was not a good one. B is persuaded by A that his interests are best served by going along with his, A's preferences. A thus uses his resources to demonstrate, implicitly or explicitly, the utility or "correctness" of his preferences over those of B, whose calculations of the costs / benefits to himself of yielding to A's preferences are altered by A's persuasions. In the end, A has changed not only B's behavior but also, more important, his attitudes. B is willing to add his resources to A's in order to achieve a newly perceived common interest.[20]

18. Our intention here is that these three terms be used in a modern sense, not necessarily as they were used in the colonial period. It seems to us to make no more sense to use seventeenth- or eighteenth-century terminology as an *analytical* tool in political history than it does for the historian of science to analyze its development using terms like phlogiston, humors, or celestial spheres.

19. *Coercion* or *coercive power,* for want of a better term, denotes positive inducements as well as negative ones or deprivations, and it is not limited here to severe deprivations of inducements. This corresponds to the usage set out by Lasswell and Kaplan, *Power and Society,* 97–98. Some would not include positive inducements under coercion, but would simply call them bribery. See Bernard Gert, "Coercion and Freedom," in *Coercion,* ed. J. Roland Pennock and John W. Chapman (Chicago, 1972), 30–48. We do not go into problems of comparison and measurement of power here.

20. Obviously our definition of *influence* is not at all similar to the technical eighteenth-century term described by Bernard Bailyn (*Origins of American Politics,* 28–29) as the administration's distribution of patronage and electioneering funds and their management of officeholders who held seats in the House of Commons. As we mentioned earlier, we find it unhelpful and confusing to use such terms in their contemporary sense in analytical work. Definitions in *A New English Dictionary on Historical Principles,* ed. Sir James A. Murray (London, 1909), 270, indicate that the mainstream meaning of the word from early times was the informal ascendancy of a person or group over another person or object attained by "insensible or invisible means, without the employment of material force, or the exercise of formal authority." Perhaps the technical sense of the word derived from the fact that in order to determine the outcome of votes in Parliament, one had to influence or persuade one's peers to change their beliefs about some matter. Obviously if one controlled—through what we call coercion—a number of seats, then one's "influence" would have been greatly expanded and the need to persuade proportionately lessened.

Deference involves virtually no expenditure of resources by A, because the relation between B and himself is preemptive, not conflictual. The question of whether B's preferences are in opposition to A's never surfaces, because it is taken for granted by both sides that whatever B's preferences are, A's take precedence. A and B are not in disagreement over A's preferences and B's anticipated response. A must merely make B aware that he possesses those resources which will place him among that class of persons to whom it is right and proper for B to yield. There is no progression or change in the relation of A and B, as there is in the case of influence. B's attitudes and behavior are both what they were in the beginning, or rather his attitudes remain the same and therefore his behavior can be predicted. In fact, if there should be a change in his attitude, if he should question A's preemption of precedence, then it is doubtful that the relation is any longer one of deference. At what point one can say that "deference" stops and influence or coercion begins is hard to tell, but there surely is a point at which B no longer complies as a matter of course with A's dictates or wishes. In the gray zone between "pure" deference and either influence or coercion (or some other type of relation), B might well consider and reject the utility of trying to challenge A. At this point, A prevails as much by default as by preemption. A might well not even be aware of the lessening of B's deference until the latter refuses, passively or actively, to yield to A's preferences in his accustomed manner. Such a refusal might create only a slight ripple in their relation—no more than the uneasy recognition of changed circumstances.

This points up another distinguishing characteristic of deference. As we noted earlier, all power relations are reciprocal as well as asymmetric. This reciprocity derives from the fact that B, as well as A, possesses resources. A's advantage lies in his ability to use his superior resources to "set up" their initial involvement, to put B in the position of *having* to expend his own resources in resisting or complying with A's demands. But even though A can limit B's options to compliance or resistance, he can never initially be sure which of the two B will choose. It is this uncertainty, coupled with his perceptions of his own potential power vis-à-vis B's, that determines A's choice of both the form of power and the limits within which he will attempt to exercise it. From the beginning, A is aware of the reciprocity in his relationship with B. It is perhaps the essence of deference that B is *not* aware of it. In the context in which B has learned or been accustomed to yield to A, he does not question, let alone resist, A's "right" to impose his preferences. He is unaware of or never considers the reciprocal nature of the relationship. Within the limits of deference, A thus does not have to command or persuade and probably seldom has to communicate his desires explicitly to B. By virtue of his acceptance of a system of beliefs and values that indicates who his "betters" are and what his "place" is in certain realms of behavior, B might be said to have been conditioned or "programmed" to yield to A, a demonstrated superior. At the extreme, it could be said that B has been conditioned to conceive of his interests and A's as identical.

Obviously the delineation of the "realms of behavior" within which deferential relations exist can be determined only through empirical investigation. It can never be assumed that because deference characterizes, say, social encounter it will also be found in, say, politics and religion. Surely there are limits or bounds beyond which one person will not defer to the preferences of another—situations in which compliance, if desired, requires the exertion of other forms of power. Continued use of the term *deference* to explain such compliance is utterly misleading.

Since deferential behavior and attitudes tend to be habitual, if not conditioned, and depend to a great extent on A's continued ability to structure the context within which B's responses are made, they operate most strongly and are most precisely calibrated in local contexts. Here the possibilities for reinforcement are greatest, and here the most realistic assessment of a person's resources can be made. As the degree of personal contact is lessened or vanishes altogether, the information that marks out "superiority" necessarily decreases, and deferential behavior must increasingly be based on hearsay and categorical assumptions about the resources likely to be possessed by individuals exhibiting certain characteristics. Cues like dress, speech, lifestyle, and reputation play a greater role as personal contact diminishes. Similarly, the strength of A's control over the context lessens as distance increases.[21]

Consider, for instance, colonial elections. They did not, of course, take place in a void but in a context structured by such formal requirements as the size and type of franchise, the method of balloting, and the time of polling and by such informal requirements as candidate recruitment, setting an agenda of issues (if any), and possibly some form of campaigning. The candidate's (A's) control over

21. See Newby, "Deferential Dialectic," 156–58 and Shils, "Deference," 126–29. One might also say that the local, face-to-face situation, with its greater subtleties and nuances, might have made it more difficult to arrive at a consensus about the local hierarchy, as evidenced by controversies in seating meetinghouses. See Cook, *Fathers of the Times*, 91–93; Michael Zuckerman, *Peaceable Kingdoms: New England Towns in the Eighteenth Century* (New York, 1970), 217–19; Bruce C. Daniels, *The Connecticut Town: Growth and Development, 1635–1790* (Middletown, Conn., 1979), 115–17.

these factors clearly determined the scope of the voter's (B's) options. If he, working alone or with others, controlled all of them, the voter's choices would have been drastically circumscribed, even trivialized. Moreover, within this contextually narrowed sphere of action, the candidate motivated by personal ambition would probably have sought to reduce even further the choices left to the voter by relying on coercion, influence, or deference. Which form he chose would have varied according to the nature of his relationship with different voters. The final election result would have been the outcome of the intersection of all these factors and relationships.

Nevertheless the voter in this as in all power relations retained a degree of choice and thus always had a certain leverage over the candidate, should he choose to employ it. Even in the case of an unopposed candidate, he had the option of refusing to put in an appearance at the polls. If there was more than one candidate, he could, of course, have voted for an opponent. Paradoxically the more trivialized the voter's choice, the greater in certain ways was his leverage over the candidate. If his vote made no substantive difference to the content (or structure) of politics, then beyond the pressure that the candidate could bring to bear on him, he had no particular reason to make an effort to get to the polls. Yet it was obviously crucial to the candidate that a sufficient, even "respectable," number of voters not only arrive at the polls but cast their votes for him. Since he was dealing with many voters, it might have placed a considerable strain on his resources to coerce, cajole, bribe, or otherwise induce each of them to vote as he wished. His best bet would have been to offer to potential voters a general inducement of a relatively trivial and inexpensive nature. It is quite likely that the practice of treating was of this nature. It may in fact have had a double or triple utility for the candidate if deferential relations prevailed between him and many of the potential voters. In this case it would have been another means of signaling to them that he was indeed a man of substance, someone who could afford to treat his fellow citizens to a festive occasion. It would also have insured that the voter came to him rather than he to the voter. In this way his superiority would have been subtly reaffirmed in the eyes of the voter, an affirmation no doubt reinforced by the public commitment tendered to him in the form of a vote that he would have (graciously) accepted with thanks. The relative importance of the occasion for the candidate and the relative triviality of his vote for the voter may thus have been obscured.

The potential difficulties involved in reinforcing deferential responses in such complex situations point up an important attribute of systems of deference. In any such system the position of the elite

is dependent on the stability of the conditioning factors that originally marked out its superiority.[22] The appearance of compelling
issues, the development of competition for office, a significant geographical or social shift in resources, a change in values—any or all
of these destabilizing factors, few of which are subject to elite control, can undermine the deferential responses through which it seeks
to legitimize its power. Of necessity, then, political deference, especially in larger, impersonal contexts must be linked to the broader
social and political structure.

What we have said so far about deference has been couched solely
in terms of encounters between individuals. Most historians are
interested in applying the concept of deference on a systemic basis,
using it to explain or describe, say, the politics of a town or an entire
colony. Can these definitions of power relations between individuals
be used to analyze collective power relations within a system? Will
they help historians understand what went on at the polls in colonial
elections? In particular, are we now in a position to determine whether
relations between a colony's political class—those who ran for and
held office—and its electorate were deferential? Historians, of course,
can never be privy to the voters' states of mind when they cast their
ballots and thus in one sense can never know whether their choices
were fixed through coercion, influence, or deference. It is possible,
however, to make inferences about the relations between voters and
the political class by examining election outcomes in conjunction with
the conditions necessary to predicate deference.

The conditions are quite simple. First of all, there must have been
choice in elections. This is to say nothing more than that there must
have been at least two candidates competing for a single office in any
given election or, if one is looking at a system, that there must have
been competition for office more frequently than not. As we pointed
out earlier, if there was no choice, then it is very difficult to determine whether the voters were deferential or not. The historian simply has no sure way of gauging the voter's state of mind when there
was no electoral alternative.

The second condition that must hold if the historian is to ascertain
the existence of deference is the presence of a widespread, unques-
tioning acceptance of the premise that *only* persons fitting into a particular category were qualified to rule. The often quoted statement
of Samuel Wyllys, a Connecticut magistrate, in 1680, to the effect
that "the making of rulers of the lower sort of people will issue in

---

22. Stability is also a goal of those who seek to establish or maintain a system of deference. "*Stability* is therefore the keynote of deference, for only deference ensures the
long-term maintenance of the power and privileges on which elites can continue to draw."
Newby, "Deferential Dialectic," 146 (emphasis in the original).

contempt, let their opinion be what it will," is a good example of this kind of premise.[23] If Wyllys's opinion was widely shared by his compatriots, then it is *possible* that deference to socioeconomic superiors was present at the polls in Connecticut.[24]

If these two conditions hold, then it follows that the premise in the second condition will be mirrored in election results. Suppose Connecticut voters unquestioningly accepted Wyllys's premise that only men of the better sort were qualified to be rulers. Elected officeholders should then be consistently higher on the socioeconomic scale than their unsuccessful competitors. If this proved to be the case, then historians could infer with a reasonable degree of certainty that the members of the colony's electorate were conditioned to defer to their superiors. Of course, if this relationship was not reinforced by other, nonpolitical relationships, then it was probably a rather fragile one.

Conversely, should it turn out that electoral results do not mirror the premise, whatever it may be, then either the voters were deferring to a different, perhaps not yet determined, category of persons, or they were not deferring at all. In the latter case it is likely that relations of influence obtained—competing candidates used their resources to persuade the voter they were best qualified—or it may be that relations between voters and the political class were symmetrical rather than asymmetrical. At this point it seems most useful to illustrate our reasoning with an analysis of a specific case. We will attempt to do this in the following pages with elections to the upper house of the General Assembly in eighteenth-century Connecticut.

Our first task is to discover whether there was competition in elections for the upper house. Fortunately we can do this rather easily

23. Quoted in Richard L. Bushman, *From Puritan to Yankee: Character and the Social Order in Connecticut, 1690–1765* (Cambridge, Mass., 1967), 12.

24. Wyllys was clearly referring here to what we would call socioeconomic superiority. Nevertheless, in New England, one is always tempted to look for indications of deference to sanctity as symbolized by church membership. One instinctively feels that sainthood must have carried some weight politically even in the eighteenth century. In the study of the Connecticut political class described below, we concentrated on socioeconomic factors for several reasons. First, these seem to be of the most concern to historians studying colonial politics. Second, the colonists themselves never made church membership a condition for holding high public office. Although magistrates were expected to be men of virtue and "nursing fathers" to the church, the Puritan tradition of a sharp separation between civil and ecclesiastical jurisdictions apparently carried over into their conception of the proper qualifications for office holding. Finally, we were able in our study to confirm this to some extent by correlating church involvement (ranging from no membership through being a deacon) with political success. The correlation turned out to be zero. All this should not be taken to mean that religion played no role in eighteenth-century Connecticut politics. We feel, to the contrary, that it was one of the most dynamic factors in the colony's political development.

by examining the colony's constitutional framework. Under the charter of 1662, the basic constitutional document, freemen chose not only the town representatives or deputies who constituted the lower house, but also the twelve assistants, governor, and deputy governor who together functioned as an executive council and as the upper house.[25] Twice a year every town's freemen gathered to elect two deputies for the forthcoming session (held in October and May) of the General Assembly. At the fall meetings in September, they also nominated by written ballot candidates for the upper house, including the governor and deputy governor. Since there were no qualifications other than freemanship for any office, any freeman in the colony could theoretically nominate any other freeman for these positions. When the votes from all the towns were tallied at the October session of the assembly, the twenty men who received the highest number became candidates for the spring general election and were voted upon at the April freemen's meetings. Balloting for the governor and deputy governor was at this time separate from that for assistants, and in order to stand for these two positions it was not necessary for a man to have been one of the top twenty nominated in the fall.[26] Frequently there were "scattered votes" for others besides the obvious front-runners, and on at least one occasion, in 1740, a "write-in" candidate gave the incumbent, Gov. Joseph Talcott, a run for his money.[27] For some years there was ambiguity about how many votes it actually took to elect a governor or deputy governor—whether an absolute majority or merely a plurality—but eventually it was settled that it required an absolute majority. Short of that, the election was decided by the assembly.[28] For the assistants, the candidates in April had to have been formally nominated in October, and the voter was allowed to cast up to twelve votes for candidates on the list. The twelve with the highest votes were the ones chosen assistants for the coming year. Members of the upper house were thus directly nomi-

25. For the charter, see *The Public Records of the Colony of Connecticut, 1636–1776*, ed. J. H. Trumbull and Charles Hoadley (Hartford: 1850–1890), II, 3–11 (hereafter cited as *PR*). Subsequent legislative enactments altered the details of elections. For a good description of nomination and election procedures, see Bruce Stark, "The Upper House in Early Connecticut History," in *A Lyme Miscellany, 1776–1976*, ed. George J. Willauer, Jr. (Middletown, Conn., 1977), 142–47.

26. A ruling to this effect was made in January 1708 when the General Assembly wished to clear the way for the election of Rev. Gurdon Saltonstall as successor to Fitz-John Winthrop. *PR*, V, 39.

27. See Bruce Stark, "The Election of 1740 in Connecticut," *Connecticut History* 22 (1981): 7–13. We do not entirely agree with his interpretation, however.

28. The question first came up in connection with the election of Roger Wolcott as deputy governor in 1748. See Bushman, *From Puritan to Yankee*, 239–40. Governors frequently obtained fewer nomination votes in the fall than did the most popular assistants.

nated and elected by the freemen in annual, colonywide elections.

It is obvious not only that was there competition for places in the upper house but that it was mandated by the colony's constitution. Unless they were willing to tamper with the charter, the colony's only guarantee of virtual autonomy within the empire, no elite could avoid competition at the polls. Clearly, under these circumstances, the voter always had a choice, and the first condition was thus fulfilled.

Unfortunately, determining whether the second condition held is more difficult. Certainly the dominant political culture of Connecticut during the eighteenth century gave the common man little, if any, encouragement to play an active role in politics, let alone to aspire to a public office of any prominence. Without doubt all colonists were agreed throughout the colonial period on the need for good rulers and the necessity for freemen to cast their ballots wisely and disinterestedly.[29] No one, then or now, would argue for the choice of bad rulers, but an emphasis on personal qualities rather than on policy positions as proper criteria for leadership potential, combined with a stress on the "independence" of the freeman, could only have played into the hands of those who favored the status quo.[30] As many have since pointed out, the appeal for nonpartisanship or "independence" both undercuts efforts of the disadvantaged to concert their efforts in their own interests and gives the game by default to those possessing superior material and other social resources.[31]

Whether there was an equation in the general political culture of Connecticut between the attributes of the good ruler and the trappings of wealth, education, breeding, and social status, or whether the position of the well-born was enhanced by default, is a difficult question. Richard Bushman states quite bluntly that there was such an equation, that it was religiously based, and that it was strongly entrenched. He argues that subordination to such rulers was internalized, though he feels it waned considerably between the turn of

29. In the oath prescribed in 1704 for persons being admitted to freeman status, individuals had to swear that "whensoever you shall give your vote or suffrage touching any matter which concerns this Colonie, being called thereunto you will give it as in your conscience you shall judge may conduce to the best good of the same, without respect of persons or favour of any man." *PR*, IV, 483.

30. The "independence" of the freeman was repeatedly stressed in the newspapers. See, for example, Roger Wolcott, "A Letter to the Freemen of Connecticut," *Connecticut Gazette*, 28 March 1761; *New London Gazette*, 20 February 1767; *Connecticut Courant*, 5 March 1770 and 2 April 1770; *Norwich Packet*, 4 November 1773. Alexander King, a deputy from Suffield, noted in his diary on 20 September 1774: "so much undue practice to influence the minds of the Freemen in the Election of Deputies I never knew in this Town before." As a cryptoloyalist, he perhaps had particular cause to complain. Connecticut Historical Society, Diary No. 3, 1774.

31. The best discussion of the effects of nonpartisanship in local elections in the United States is Willis D. Hawley, *Nonpartisanship and the Case for Party Politics* (New York, 1973).

the century and the Revolution.[32] Timothy Breen, on the other hand, argues that by 1700 such a cultural presumption was temporally and intellectually far from any of its religious roots. It was, according to his interpretation, more a matter of a secularly based ideology, espoused by those of "court" persuasion who were eager to secure their own power in government. Naturally these men found it expedient to restrict eligibility for high office to a small and select group— an elite of wealth and status identical with themselves. Those opposed to their persuasion, the "country" interest, did not argue that the good ruler had to have certain social characteristics; they emphasized instead the need for all rulers to be fully accountable to the people. However, they too felt that certain charactristics were beneficial if possessed by the aspiring ruler, notably education and economic means sufficient to protect a man from the temptations of corruption.[33]

Without attempting to answer the question which of these two persuasions the colonists embraced or how deep its hold was, we will posit, as a point of departure, that the dominant political culture of Connecticut at the start of the eighteenth century did hold that for the public good, only men at the upper reaches of society were qualified to rule. We begin, therefore, with the assumption that other things being equal, the ordinary freeman would have cast his vote without question for any man superior to him in socioeconomic status who was either explicitly or implicitly a candidate for office. All that the superior would have had to do was to indicate that he was available in order to garner the freeman's vote. In most cases this probably would have involved little or no expenditure of resources on the candidate's part, and availability would probably have been conveyed implicitly more often than explicitly. The freeman, in a word, deferred to the candidate, his superior.

While this cultural presumption engendered a situation that can be characterized as a power relation, in that all A's (socioeconomic superiors) would have tended to prevail over all B's (ordinary freemen), it would necessarily have been a rather diffuse and ultimately quite fragile relationship. In most cases it probably was not strongly reinforced by the social or economic relationships actually pertaining between the freeman and the well-educated, well-off, well-con-

<hr>

32. Bushman, *From Puritan to Yankee*, chap. 1. Just about everyone else seems to accept this as a given. See, for example, Stephen Foster, *Their Solitary Way: The Puritan Social Ethic in the First Century of Settlement in New England* (New Haven, 1971), and Donald M. Scott, *From Office to Profession: The New England Ministry, 1750–1850* (Philadelphia, 1978).

33. T. H. Breen, *The Character of the Good Ruler: A Study of Puritan Political Ideas in New England, 1630–1730* (New Haven, 1970), esp. chaps. 6 and 7. Breen, it should be noted, devotes the bulk of his discussion to Massachusetts.

nected candidate. The freeman, after all, was in no case a tenant of the candidate and must rarely, if ever, have been his employee. Nor can one assume that the social distance between the two was very great. If the candidate had a college education, the freeman was no doubt literate. In Connecticut both were likely to be descended from "ancient," if not equally distinguished, families. Moreover, the freeman was quite likely to have held at least a minor town office. Much as people like Samuel Wyllys would have liked it, Connecticut did not have a gentry such as Virginia's.[34] In Connecticut any nexus of deference between voter and candidate would therefore have been dictated primarily by cultural beliefs or assumptions. The situation was further complicated by the fact that elections for the upper house were direct and colonywide. It is easy to see that deference in this larger context would be even more fragile than in a local setting. In most cases there would have been no possibility of a direct relationship between the candidate and the voter in which the former could reinforce his dominant position with social or economic sanctions. The nexus would be both primarily cultural and indirect.

Of course, any serious candidate for assistant had to become known to and supported by voters throughout the colony. If deference was to operate, then the candidate, who was sometimes but one among fifty or more, somehow had to indicate that he was a member of that class for which the freeman habitually voted. Whatever his antecedents and achievements, this would not have been an easy task. And if the candidate had a problem in getting his name before the electorate, the freemen would have had their own information problem. Even assuming, as we are, that they were conditioned to act deferentially when casting their ballots, they still would have had to know who their "betters" were and who among the competing candidates were the "best." In local contexts this would not have been too difficult; but when it came to candidates from the other side of the colony, they would have required guidance. An easy solution for the freemen would have been to nominate or vote for those they knew best, men from their own and neighboring towns. As the few surviving local tabulations of nomination votes show, such localism or regionalism was probably quite prevalent.[35] But consistent voting on

34. See Jackson Turner Main, "The Distribution of Property in Colonial Connecticut," in *The Human Dimensions of a Nation Making: Essays on Colonial and Revolutionary America*, ed. James Kirby Martin (Madison, Wisc., 1976), 54–104; and idem, *Connecticut Society in the Era of the American Revolution* (Hartford, 1977).

35. The main collection of town tabulations of nomination lists, with votes for seven towns in 1737 and six in 1745, is at the Connecticut Historical Society, in Connecticut Secretary of State, Statistics. See also in the same collection the county breakdown of votes for the 1770 nominations.

this basis would have produced no more than a host of relatively equally supported candidates, none of them standing much above the rest. Since this is obviously not what occurred, we must consider how the transmission of information between individual candidates and widespread voters affected the members of an electorate culturally conditioned to defer to their betters.

The one situation that would have enabled both candidates and voters to overcome their common information problem is that of the incumbent assistant standing (as he always did) for reelection. The man who was already an assistant would automatically fall into the category of those who were qualified to rule, simply because otherwise he would not have been elected in the first place. If the best-qualified rulers were to be found among the better sort, then it followed that anyone who was already a ruler could be assumed to possess the requisite socioeconomic background. Thus, apart from direct personal knowledge, the one reliable cue the voter had as to the worthiness of a candidate was his incumbency, and this, in turn, probably triggered a conditioned, deferential vote for him. (Of course, any blemish in his performance in office would have provided a different and conflicting cue.) Since incumbent assistants were by definition fit for office and presumably available and certainly visible to the electorate, cultural presumption would have been enough to keep them in office.

Given this situation, the extraordinary stability of patterns of office holding in Connecticut is not particularly surprising.[36] Writing in 1795, Zephaniah Swift, himself a member of the political class, could see such continuance in office as a "noble sentiment" that seemed to be "interwoven in the character of the people."[37] Whatever the sentiment toward incumbent rulers, though, one cannot leap to the conclusion that the same, presumably deferential, sentiment also

36. For figures on tenure in office of the assistants, see Stark and Harold E. Selesky, "Patterns of Officeholding in the Connecticut General Assembly: 1725–1774," also in Willauer, *A Lyme Miscellany*, 166–98. Perhaps more to the point, out of 524 individual contests involving incumbent assistants standing for reelection between 1730 and 1774, only 22 (4.2 percent) resulted in their defeat. Still, during the four decades preceding the Revolution, the number of assistant careers terminated by defeat (17, since some of the above were reelected at a later date) was higher than the number terminated by death (11).

37. Zephaniah Swift, *System of the Laws of the State of Connecticut* (Windham, 1795), I, 93. But, as he points out, the practice of reading off the names in the April freemen's meetings in order of seniority of first election as an assistant probably had the tendency to work against nonincumbents. "In such cases we find that there is a wonderful mechanism in voting. The freemen in general will not have any personal attachment to the persons nominated, and they will generally vote for those who are first called. There may be some places where local feelings may operate, but this will rarely be sufficient to counteract the general indifference." I, 84.

operated between voters and nonincumbent candidates. It cannot, in other words, be assumed merely because they commanded deference once in office, that the assistants had gotten there in the first place because of deference to their social prominence. Regardless of their resources, persons making a bid for the office of assistant confronted greater electoral difficulties than did those who had already won it. No matter how wealthy or socially prominent a man was, these resources would have been of no avail unless voters throughout the colony knew about them. In the absence of appropriate mass media—which were lacking in Connecticut until the 1750s and which were even then not very informative—the most feasible means of doing this would have been through a network (or networks) of intermediaries, men in every part of the colony who were linked not just to a class of betters but to specific candidates and who were prepared to pass along information about their qualifications to the freemen. Ideally, of course, such networks would have consisted of men who were themselves deferred to by the freemen.

There were a number of possible networks that the "well-qualified" candidate, or for that matter any other candidate, might have used. First and most obvious would have been a network of friends, relatives, and business associates. Since such intermediaries would quite likely have been of equivalent social position, a network of this type should have been very efficacious with a deferential electorate. As we shall see, however, when we examine electoral outcomes, connections of this kind do not seem to have been particularly useful to candidates in Connecticut. A second network might have been the colony's ministers. Commentators as varied as Samuel Peters and Lyman Beecher have pointed out that the minister was in an ideal position to influence the freemen.[38] But even if such networks existed, it is difficult to imagine that they would have been of great help to individual candidates. Whatever was done by way of recommending a candidate would have had to be done indirectly. Few, if any, ministers would have been willing to make explicit recommendations in their public utterances. Even the Reverend John Owen, an ardent champion of the New Lights, was apparently only prepared to pray "that ye Freemen might (when giving in yr Votes for Rulers) be constrained to vote for such as knew Christ That we might no more have

---

38. Generally on the potential role of the clergy in elections, see Scott, *From Office to Profession*; J. William T. Youngs, Jr., *God's Messengers: Religious Leadership in Colonial New England, 1700–1750* (Baltimore, 1976); David M. Roth, *Connecticut: A Bicentennial History* (New York, 1979), 60–61. For Peters's comments on the influence of ministers, see *The Works of Samuel Peters of Hebron, Connecticut: New England Historian, Satirist, Folklorist, Anti-Patriot, and Anglican Clergyman (1735–1826)*, ed. Kenneth W. Cameron (Hartford, 1967), 64, 70.

such to rule over us, as were Enemys to the Work & Grace of God."[39] While such indirection might have sufficed to cue in the voter on occasion, it probably was not normally an effective means of getting one's name and qualifications before the freemen. If the minister endorsed a candidate privately, then he would have been doing no more than any other friend or relative.

Organized parties would have been a logical, and in retrospect the most efficient, network for getting to the voters and garnering support colonywide. But organized and competing parties, especially if the lines were drawn on the basis of clear-cut issues, would have undermined the whole foundation of a deferential system since the voters would have been compelled to evaluate not merely the candidates' personal qualifications for office but also their stands on these issues.[40] Throwing in one's lot with a partisan group would therefore have meant endangering and quite possibly forgoing deferential responses from the electorate that were based on one's superior status. The dominant political culture of the colony never legitimated parties, in any event, but their backfire potential is no doubt part of the reason that they came relatively late to Connecticut and never made much headway there until the end of the century. Nevertheless, by the 1739–40 round of elections the advantages of at least circulating a list of candidates had become apparent to some. The resulting defeat of three assistants and the sharp challenges to the reelection of both Gov. Joseph Talcott and Dep. Gov. Jonathan Law were such shocks that they provoked the upper house into passing a bill providing for severe penalties for the circulation of such lists. The lower house did not concur, and this was the last that was heard of it.[41] As the century wore on, however, the advantages of a "partisan" network of men committed to particular views increased to the point that, by the middle of the 1760s, the New Lights were holding fairly regular nomination-strategy meetings before elections as well as circulating lists of candidates and inserting general appeals in the newspapers.[42] By 1763, William Samuel Johnson commented with a

39. Connecticut State Library, Archives. Ecclesiastical, 1st ser., VIII, 281.
40. But competition and the nature of this competition are crucial. See, for example, Ronald P. Formisano, "Deferential-Participant Politics: The Early Republic's Political Culture, 1789–1840," *American Political Science Review* 68 (1974): 473–87.
41. Connecticut State Library. Archives. Civil Officers, 1st ser., II, 399.
42. For discussion, see Bushman, *From Puritan to Yankee*, pt. 5; Oscar Zeichner, *Connecticut's Years of Controversy, 1750–1776* (Chapel Hill, 1949; reprinted 1970); Christopher Collier, *Roger Sherman's Connecticut: Yankee Politics and the American Revolution* (Middletown, Conn., 1971), esp. chaps. 2 and 3. For a good summary of the 1759 events surrounding the religious controversy over the Dana affair in Wallingford and Thomas Clap's leadership of Yale College, see Louis Leonard Tucker, *Puritan Protagonist: President Thomas Clap of Yale College* (Chapel Hill, 1962), chap. 9.

trace of envy that the New Lights "have acquired such an influence as to be nearly the ruling part of the government owing to their superior attention to civil affairs and close union among themselves in politics."[43]

As electoral networks, however, protoparties such as the New Lights had at best only moderate success. Trends over the years in total votes for candidates of known ideological-religious persuasion do show a definite clustering of the votes of like-minded candidates from just before the Stamp Act crisis on into the 1770s. But the strong regional cast to party alignments during the pre-Revolutionary years indicates their failure to become truly colonywide organizations. Interestingly enough, regional patterns of voting disappeared after 1800 when the clash between the Republicans and the Federalists developed.[44] Moreover, a calculation of the percentage of the votes in both nomination and general elections that went to incumbents shows that there was virtually no change at all from the 1730s to the 1770s.[45] Nor were parties successful in gaining control of the recruitment of candidates, as steadily increasing numbers of contestants for the upper house show.[46] Thus, because of organizational weaknesses and the general opposition to parties, partisan networks may not have proved to be consistently effective for aspirants to the upper house.

By far the most plausible and, as we shall see, most efficacious network of intermediaries would have been the town deputies. If a candidate could make a name for himself in the General Assembly through committee service, debate, and the like, the deputies and assistants might be sufficiently impressed to put his name before the freemen in their respective towns. Another equally attractive possibility for the candidate lay in the hands of the assembly, for it conferred various public positions that brought a candidate before his

43. A letter sent to J. Beach, printed in *Samuel Johnson: His Career and Writings*, ed. Herbert and Carol Schneider (New York, 1929), III, 266.

44. See Edmund B. Thomas, Jr., "Politics in the Land of Steady Habits: Connecticut's First Political Party System, 1789–1820" (Ph.D. diss., Clark University, 1972), 218, 269.

45. Calculating the percentage of votes for incumbents (including those for governor and for deputy governor in the fall nominations) for both nomination and general elections between 1731 and 1774 gives an idea of how things might have changed both over time and between the two types of elections. The average in nine nomination elections was 67 percent, and for seven general elections, 81 percent. (If an incumbent had died before the nomination election, the first-ranking nonincumbent was substituted and considered an incumbent.) The trends in percentages do not vary consistently over time. As one can see, though, voters felt freer to nominate nonincumbents than to vote for them in the April elections.

46. Colonywide, the average number of candidates with at least 100 votes in the fall nomination elections was under 40 in the 1730s, 43 in the 1750s, 50 in the 1760s (to a maximum of 62 in 1769), and 58 in the early 1770s.

countrymen as the incumbent of a post of public trust, albeit a lesser one than that of assistant. The voter would thus have been provided with an unmistakable cue as to the candidate's fitness for office. Judicial posts in particular would have given the additional advantage to both the candidate and the voter of possible direct contact. A freeman in Connecticut might often come in contact with the courts through service as a grand juror, involvement in litigation, the settlement of an estate, or petitioning the county court for various kinds of permits or assistance. (Lawyers practicing before the courts no doubt also benefited from exposure of this type.)

There are two important implications here for relations between nonincumbent candidates and voters. First, unless the deputies themselves were deferred to by the freemen in their respective towns, they would have functioned only as transmitters of information and opinions and not as a network of primary power relations, reinforcing the cultural presumption of a link between social position and proper qualifications for office.[47] Second, we must bear in mind that gaining a reputation among one's peers, the deputies, would have revolved primarily around matters of competence and performance in various offices of responsibility. It is hard to imagine the deputies conferring such responsibilities on men merely because they were of some appropriate station in life. It is even harder to imagine the deputies going back to their towns to praise the worthiness of some candidate or other on that basis alone. They would have been conveying knowledge, or at least impressions, of capabilities for office. In the process the basis of the original cultural presumption would have been subtly but definitively altered; the equation in the voters' minds would now have been not between high status and fitness for high office but between political experience or demonstrated competence and fitness for high office.

To sum up our discussion of the second condition: the voter, per-

47. Although many would assume that the deputies were deferred to by the people, this is something that cannot be taken for granted. William Samuel Johnson seemed to be assuming that this was the case when he wrote to Eliphalet Dyer in 1770, regarding Dyer's chances of being elected deputy governor. "But we must be Contented with what the People please to do who so generally follow the lead of the Assembly, upon these occasions that I fear there is little hopes of seeing any alteration in yr favour next May." Printed in *The Susquehannah Company Papers*, ed. Julian P. Boyd, IV (Wilkes-Barre, 1930), 34. On the other hand, when the issues were ones that people really cared about, then the deputies do not seem to have been able to carry the day if their opinions differed from those of the people. See the report on the Litchfield Sons of Liberty meeting in February 1766, during which Col. Ebenezer Marsh, a longtime deputy, opposed the sending of representatives to a county meeting. Notwithstanding the fact that Marsh and one S.S. (probably Stephen Stone) "employ'd all their Power to render it abortive" and "also opposed by their Votes, almost every Motion that was made to forward it," the gathering of forty to fifty people did send representatives. *Connecticut Courant*, 10 February 1766.

haps initially culturally conditioned to defer to high status persons, but often lacking information about who these persons were, naturally would have first responded to the "infallible" cue of incumbency. In its absence, the deferential voters would have had to resort to their own knowledge of local and regional notables, probably using more often than not the cue of incumbency, albeit at a lower level. When it came to other candidates, though, they would necessarily have depended on information conveyed to them through a number of possible sources—friends of the candidates, deputies, perhaps ministers, and on occasion "partisan" spokesmen, as varied as the Sons of Liberty or itinerant preachers.[48] Depending upon the source, this information would have been conveyed to them in quite different terms. If it came primarily through the deputies or through partisan spokesmen, then the voters would necessarily be casting their ballots on grounds other than that of socioeconomic status. It would, therefore, have been very risky for a nonincumbent candidate to rely on the kind of culturally based deference postulated at the beginning of this section in order to achieve office. Moreover, the increasing complexity of the colony's affairs and the impact of changes in its society and economy would have rendered such deference ever more tenuous. Clearly, as the eighteenth century progressed, a man who wanted to be elected to the upper house would have had to muster resources other than those pertaining to his socioeconomic characteristics and, insofar as he was able, to utilize them in influential or persuasive ways rather than to attempt to secure deferential responses. This in turn would have meant that the road to political success was progressively opened to men with few resources beyond their own talents for achievement. The potential field of candidates would thus have been greatly expanded.

In fact, the number of candidates for the upper house did increase substantially in the decades preceding the Revolution. Certainly the opportunities for distinguishing oneself in terms of government services—whether judicial, military, or legislative—expanded with the growth of the colony. Outside of government service, opportunities in the professions, in business, and in land speculation were equally expansive. Even the establishment of Yale College broadened the chances to acquire status through education. No matter to what cues the voters were responding or by what criteria they were judging nonincumbent candidates, they unquestionably had to choose from among an increasing number who were equally well qualified. A can-

48. For the potential effect of itinerant preachers, see Harry Stout, "Religion, Communications, and the Ideological Origins of the American Revolution," *William and Mary Quarterly*, 3d ser., 34 (1977): 519–51.

didate must have found it increasingly attractive, if not always effective, to differentiate himself from his no less well-qualified competitors by staking out positions on issues of interest to his potential constituents.

At this point it behooves us to ask whether the voters can any longer be said to have been deferring to their superiors. Clearly there are difficulties in maintaining that our postulated second condition, namely, voter identification of high status with fitness for office, held in Connecticut throughout the century. Nevertheless, before concluding that the colony's electorate was not deferential, let us examine the outcomes of elections to see whether they confirm the hypothesis sketched out above.

In a comparison of 213 politicians from three levels of the legislative elite (deputies, unsuccessful candidates for the upper house, and assistants) between 1735 and 1773, we found that the factors most highly correlated with political success were *not* those traditionally associated with the colonial elite—namely, family connections, family wealth, and father's position.[49] Nor did a man's own wealth and status play the role commonly imagined. This is not to say that these men were ordinary. Like politicians in nearly every other time and place, the men in our sample were a cut above average in wealth, education, occupational status, and family background. But they were also exceptional in that those who sought and succeeded in attaining high office were ambitious, entered politics at an early age, and pursued political careers more assiduously than did those who were content to remain deputies. It was, moreover, precisely these factors that contributed most to their eventual success. In elevating men to the

49. The 213 individuals examined here are an aggregation of men chosen from each stratum during three periods, 1735–38, 1753–56, and 1770–73. In each period all members of the upper house, including the governor and deputy governor, and all nonincumbent official nominees (top 20) were selected. The candidates consist of those on candidate lists for each period. In the periods 1753–56 and 1770–73 there were candidate lists for each year, and all listed candidates were selected. For the period 1735–38 only one colonywide list was found, that for 1737, plus seven town lists for 1737. Candidates were selected if they met certain criteria, i.e., if they were listed on a town list and the colony list, on more than one town list, or, if only on the colony list, if they had 70 votes or more. (We discovered a colony list for 1739, unfortunately only after we had completed our research.) Deputies were chosen in each period by taking a random sample of towns in each county and then a random sample of the deputies from these towns. Individuals are classified according to the highest level attained during their political career, which in effect means that a few of the assistants studied actually reached that position after 1773. Candidates, however, never attained that position; included among them are 13 top-20 nominees who never became assistants. Wherever possible, particularly for political careers and genealogical aspects, data were coded on the situation pertaining up to the time of a man's first election as an assistant, or, if he was never an assistant, to the end of his political career. It was not possible to date things so specifically, of course, for social or economic data.

upper house, voters apparently cast their ballots more on the basis of a man's political accomplishments than on his social or economic position, whether it was something he achieved in his own right or derived from his family.

The most salient factors examined are listed in Table 2, which for lack of space compresses a wealth of detail into a few key figures: the percentage of those at each level of the legislative elite with high values on the variable in question and the overall correlation (Tau-B) between the given variable and political success, that is, election as an assistant.[50] Let us look first at the "ascribed" factors, the resources a person derived from the circumstances of his birth and the kind of town in which he resided.

The deferential thesis leans especially heavily on the influence of family in the attainment of high office, sometimes implying a sort of family-perpetuated oligarchy. But as the findings displayed in Table 2 show, the fact of the matter is quite different from such a supposition. No one of the three family-background factors investigated (Father's social status, father's wealth, and family connections with past and present legislators) was especially highly related to political success.[51] Because of the emphasis in the literature on the importance of family connections and our own speculations on the useful-

50. Table 2 abstracts only the percentage "high" on the indicated variables. Because the group studied is not, strictly speaking, a random sample, we shall not report levels of statistical significance for relationships.

51. The social-status variable used for both the individuals themselves and their fathers is a composite one, based on the conjunction of occupation, education (college or not), and scale of operations. Basically, the high-status category comprises lawyers, ministers, larger merchants and traders, and larger manufacturers. Variables on wealth (both father's and own) used in the study are not absolute inventoried wealth, but are based on deviations from means of the inventoried wealth of samples of the general population. The samples used were drawn from probate records for twenty-year periods in the eighteenth century for Connecticut by Bruce C. Daniels, "Probate Inventories as a Source for Economic History in 18th Century Connecticut," *Connecticut Historical Society Bulletin* 37 (1972): 1–9. In order to minimize distortions due to inflation, we converted all of Daniels's inventories and our own for the first half of the century to lawful money, using contemporary, year-by-year conversion tables. We next calculated the means and standard deviations for Daniels's data in each period. Using these, we then in effect calculated standard scores (i.e., the number of standard deviations from the mean) for each individual in our sample who had an inventory that included real wealth. The variables were trichotomized (lowest to 1.0, 1.1 to 3.5, 3.6 and over) and adjusted for age by excluding all persons sixty or older who were not wealthy, i.e., in the highest category. The resulting variables are thus really a measure of how far the individual departed from the norm of inventoried wealth at roughly the time of his death compared with the rest of our sample.

Wealth, especially a man's own wealth, ought to be treated with great caution here. Apart from the difficulties inherent in using inventories to measure an individual's relative economic position, it may be that one enhanced one's wealth by being politically successful. If this was so, then a large estate might be caused by political success rather than the reverse. Obviously the wealth of his father is the more relevant indicator here of the role that wealth played in a man's career.

Table 2

BACKGROUND FACTORS OF THREE LEVELS OF THE
LEGISLATIVE ELITE IN EIGHTEENTH-CENTURY
CONNECTICUT AND THEIR RELATIVE IMPORTANCE

Factors	Percentage			Tau-B[a]	N[b]
	Assistants	Candidates	Deputies		
Ascribed Factors					
High-Status Father[c]	43.4	42.0	11.8	.25	(198)
High Asst. Links[d]	31.5	30.4	8.8	.29	(213)
High Father's Wealth[e]	50.0	48.5	37.6	.12	(84)
"Central" Town[f]	40.7	39.2	8.8	.34	(213)
Achieved Factors					
High Pers. Status[c]	72.2	61.0	16.4	.41	(204)
High Pers. Wealth[e]	72.2	58.1	56.7	.12	(109)
Entry Age 34 or Under[g]	50.0	32.5	16.3	.35	(211)
High Prior Positions[h]	81.5	55.7	20.0	.50	(213)
High Committee Service[i]	78.8	64.9	17.5	.48	(206)
N[j]	(54)	(79)	(80)		

[a] Correlation between position on the full scale and political success or highest position attained. Tau-B can vary between −1.0 and 1.0, and the higher the value the stronger the relationship between the factor and political success. Values of Tau-B of .50 or better are usually considered to be quite respectable; those under .20 of relatively little import.

[b] N's vary because of missing data for some cases. Total N is 213.

[c] Composite measure based on primary occupation, scale of operation where relevant, and college education, trichotomized.

[d] Score of family relationships with persons who served as assistant (or higher), weighted by number of years such persons served and closeness of family relationship. Here the scores are trichotomized: high score, low score, and none.

[e] Inventoried wealth, excluding those for whom specific determinations could not be made and those over age 59 unless they were wealthy.

[f] Composite measure based on population density, commercialization (taxes per acre), and whether the town was an administrative center.

[g] Age of first civil position (usually that of town deputy) at colony level, trichotomized for calculation of Tau-B.

[h] Composite score based on office holding before election as assistant or to end of political career for all nonassistants. For details of the offices used and weights given to them in computing "scores" for office holding, see n. 64. A "high" score in the table is 9 or more points. Tau-B was calculated with a four-interval ordinal scale as set out in n. 64.

[i] Service on general or policy committees as a deputy, calculated as the rate per 100 regular sessions in the house prior to election as assistant or until end of political career if never an assistant. For purposes of analysis the score was dichotomized. A "high" score is a rate of service equivalent to over 11.5 committees served on for every 100 regular sessions (excluding nondeputies). For further details, see n. 63.

[j] N's reported are the totals for each level, according to highest position attained. Some assistants actually won office after 1773, the cutoff for the group studied; and some, of course, had become assistant prior to 1735, the earliest date at which persons actually serving were included. Candidates never attained the office of assistant, either after 1773 or at any time in their careers. Included among the candidates are 13 persons who made it to the top-20 listing but were never elected assistant. The N's vary, of course, in the actual computations, because of missing data for some cases.

ness of family networks for voter support, we went into this aspect in great detail and constructed a variety of measures. Suffice it to say here that we found these measures to be interrelated and that compared with others, those who became assistants had both more and geographically wider family ties with previous and contemporary legislators.[52] Interestingly enough, more ministers (ordained in Connecticut) also figured among their kin.[53] A fourth of the assistants, slightly over a fifth of the unsuccessful candidates, but only 8 percent of the deputies examined were the sons of governors or assistants. Nevertheless, strictly paternal political ties proved to be less efficacious (Tau = .15) than the ties with assistants that a man accrued from the two preceding generations of his family plus what he gained through marriage, which, as Table 2 shows, had a correlation of .29.[54] Although this was apparently the most telling aspect of a man's familial background in the eyes of the voters, and a possible indication that this type of family network aided an aspiring assistant, it was less important than where he lived.

Most of the men in our sample pursued their political careers from the towns in which they had been born.[55] A few—for example, Roger Sherman, Oliver Wolcott, and Elisha Sheldon—did move to a town that offered them more scope for their economic or political ambitions. These three, at least, seem to have made good choices, since each of them was elected to the upper house. But for most of the individuals studied it has to be said that their town was a given factor in their background, not ascribed in quite the same sense as family— they could, after all, change their town—but tending toward that. Edward Cook has shown that New England towns of some size and economic importance were more likely than were less significant towns

52. We traced both maternal and paternal family relationships for three generations, excluding great-uncles and cousins but including uncles by marriage, as well as immediate spousal relatives. We awarded relatives with legislative service as deputy or above points for years of legislative service, weighted according to the closeness of the relationship. An individual's total genealogical score was the sum of the scores of all his relatives. A year of legislative service by a father or brother was worth 5 points, the maximum possible. Thus a score of 50, however obtained, would be equivalent to ten years of service by a father or brother. We researched family relationships in the Connecticut State Library and, wherever possible, checked them against vital statistics, church records, and probate material.

53. The average numbers of ministers ordained in Connecticut with which the individual was related are as follows: assistants, 1.72; candidates, 1.48; and deputies, 0.68.

54. The genealogical measure concerned specifically with kinship connections with present or former members of the upper house was determined in the manner outlined in n. 52. The resulting "assistant score" was trichotomized: high, low, and no relations with members of the upper house.

55. Precisely two-thirds of the group had lived all their lives in the town in which they resided at the time; another 26 percent had lived there twenty or more years. Years of residence did not vary according to highest position attained.

to have disproportionately high numbers of men holding important positions in the government of the colony.[56] This was certainly the case in Connecticut. Ranking the towns in terms of size, economic function, and the degree to which they were administrative centers of the government, we developed a scale of town "centrality" which is roughly equivalent to Cook's.[57] As can be seen in Table 2, coming from a larger, more thriving town, usually a commercial and / or administrative center, helped a man's political advancement more than did his father's standing or family political connections. About four out of ten assistants and unsuccessful candidates came from the highest-ranking towns, whereas fewer than one in ten of the deputies did. Since the men who came from higher-ranking towns had only marginally better family backgrounds than those who did not, it might be argued that visibility was a key element in the moderately strong relationship (Tau = .34) between town "centrality" and political success.[58]

The advantages an individual derived from his family or town were obviously of some importance to his eventual success in politics, but the significance of both of these ascribed factors fades compared with the effect that his own status had. Wealth as such does not seem to have made much difference, regardless of whose it was. But the men who were lawyers or merchants, who engaged in farming or manufacturing on an appreciable scale, and / or who had a college education, were the ones most likely to make it to the upper house. According to the composite social-status measure used, over seven out of ten assistants and six out of ten candidates were ranked as high in status, whereas this was true for only a sixth of the deputies. Since the scales used for fathers and for sons are identical, comparisons in status can be made.[59] They show that across the board, but especially among the assistants and the candidates, the sons were a

56. Cook, *Fathers of the Times,* chaps. 6 and 7.
57. The index of centrality of town was constructed by ranking towns on each of three aspects—commercialization (taxes per acre), population density, and whether it was an administrative center (and what kind)—then summing up these for an overall ranking. This, in turn, was collapsed to a simpler, if cruder, three-interval scale. Too late for our own work, we discovered that Bruce Daniels (*Connecticut Town,* Chap. 6) had also done this for Connecticut towns.
58. The more important the town, the higher one's own social status (Tau = .39) and that of one's father (Tau = .29). Those coming from the more important towns also tended to be more closely connected to assistants through their family (Tau = .31). Clearly, these advantages were cumulative for those who lived in the more major centers. But it is obvious, too, that there was no one-to-one correspondence between the importance of a man's town and his social standing. As Daniels notes, in *Connecticut Town,* chap. 6, personal status and family background were more closely associated with political success the less important the town.
59. For details of the scale, see no. 52.

good deal more likely to be higher in status. More important, the effect of their own status on their success in politics was much greater than that of their fathers (.41 versus .25). Personal or achieved status was not merely a reflection of a man's having come from the "better sort" of family, for it is only moderately related to father's status (Tau = .38), father's wealth (Tau = .33), or family political connections (Tau = .30).[60] There was by no means an exclusive connection between the right background and personal success, though then, as now, having the right background obviously helped.

Most necessary of all for the aspirant to the upper house, though, was the prior achievement of political stature and a reputation of demonstrated competence in governmental affairs. We did not look systematically into the town offices held by members of the sample, but an examination of extant lists of selectmen in a number of towns shows that high proportions (from 60 to 90 percent) of their deputies to the assembly had served as selectmen, most of them before having been chosen as deputy.[61] If there was an apprenticeship system of political advancement in Connecticut—and we think there was—then it started in the towns and moved upward through the lower house. Certainly service in the lower house was virtually a sine qua non for election as an assistant. It was not, however, mere longevity of service that turned the trick; nor was the lower house simply a comfortable station for those en route to the top.[62] The men who were most likely to be elected as assistants were those who dis-

60. The composite measure of social status includes education, but for those interested specifically in that, we might note a few things about it. Not quite a third (32.4 percent) of the group had a college education, most often from Yale College. Naturally, education and political success were related; over half (52 percent) of the assistants had a college education, about 40 percent of the candidates, and only 11 percent of the deputies. The overall relationship between education (college or not) and political success is not as strong (Tau = .34) as that of social status. The fact that a man had a college education was by no means a simple reflection of the status of his family; the relationship between having a college education and coming from a high-status family is only moderate (Tau = .26).

61. The towns and percentages of their deputies who served as selectmen (or, in some cases, moderator or town clerk) are as follows: New Haven, 61 percent (95 percent were selectmen first). See History of the City of New Haven to the Present Time, ed. Edward E. Atwater (New York, 1887). Litchfield, 86 percent (95 percent first). See Payne Kenyon Kilbourne, Sketches and Chronicles of the Town of Litchfield, Connecticut (Hartford, 1859). Suffield, 71 percent (50 percent first). See Robert Hayden Alcorn, The Biography of a Town: Suffield, Connecticut, 1670–1970 (Hartford, 1970). Tolland, 60 percent (67 percent first). See Loren P. Waldo, The Early History of Tolland (Hartford, 1861). Derby, 82 percent (88 percent first). See Samuel Orcutt and Ambrose Beardsley, The History of the Old Town of Derby, Connecticut, 1642–1880 (Springfield, Mass., 1880). Stamford, 76 percent (70 percent first). See E. B. Huntington, History of Stamford, Connecticut: From Its Settlement in 1641, to the Present Time (Stamford, 1868). Stonington, 73 percent (63 percent first). See Richard A. Wheeler, History of the Town of Stonington, County of New London, Connecticut: From its First Settlement in 1649 to 1900 (New London, 1900).

62. Of the 213 men, 206 (96.7 percent) had served as deputies. The mean numbers of regular sessions served as a deputy (prior to first election as assistant or to end of career) were as follows: assistants, 17.4; candidates, 24.4; and deputies, 17.3.

tinguished themselves sufficiently to win appointments to important legislative committees and / or judicial and military posts. As can be seen from Table 2, either of these "routes" offered a much higher chance of eventual success than did any other factor examined.

Both lay fully in the hands of the incumbent legislators, which meant in effect the members of the lower house. It was naturally the lower house that decided which of its members to nominate for the joint ad hoc committees that constituted the legislature's most important governing tool.[63] Similarly, the deputies filled all judicial posts up to and including that of justice of the quorum through nomination by county caucus.[64] The role of the upper house, apart from nominating its own members to joint committees and the higher judicial posts, was mostly to confirm, though occasionally also to veto or to add to the names proposed by the lower house. The lower house, in turn, played a similar role vis-à-vis the nominations of the upper house. The crucial political breakthrough, therefore, for the nonincumbent candidate had to be made in the lower house.

It is possible, of course, that the voters were responding independently to the men who won these appointments. It seems more likely, though, given the sparse information available to them, that they were responding to the cues provided either directly, by incumbency in these posts, or indirectly, through the reports of the deputies. If

---

63. Membership on three types of committees was determined by going through the volumes of the *Public Records,* since house journals are not available for the whole period: local, having to do with strictly local matters; housekeeping, having to do with the keeping of records, tabulation of votes, etc.; and general committees, having to do with general or policy matters. Because the total number of committees a man was on is obviously a function of the time served in the lower house, the totals for all the above were normalized on a per (regular) session basis. The mean indexes of committees served on per session (x 100) are as follows:

	Local	Housekeeping	General	All Committees
Assistants	27.1	28.4	35.0	90.5
Candidates	39.7	37.0	30.7	107.4
Deputies	18.6	11.7	7.3	37.5

Membership on general committees was the most discriminating variable, and consequently is the one used in the analysis.

64. The measure of prior position holding covers a range of positions that were weighted according to our estimation of relative importance. Judicial positions were scored from 8 for Superior Court to 4 for JP; militia positions, from 7 for general to 1 for ensign; speaker of the lower house, 8; clerk of the lower house, 5; colony secretary, colony treasurer, 8; court clerks according to level of court, 5 for Superior Court clerk and 3 for county- or probate-court clerk; naval officer and county sheriff, 4; county surveyor and king's attorney, 3. Most of these positions, except for those of colony secretary and treasurer, naval officer, perhaps, Superior Court and county-court judges, and court clerks, were under the control of the lower house. Scores were assigned only once for each type of position, according to the highest level attained before the first election as an assistant, or, if he was never an assistant, up to the end of the man's political career. Total scores were collapsed into four categories: high, 13–28 points; medium-high, 9–12; medium-low, 5–8; and low, 0–4. No one with a score below 4, which would mean being the equivalent of a JP, got to be an assistant.

this was true, then the assembly, particularly the lower house, acted as a kind of screening mechanism for prospective candidates for assistant, no doubt removing from serious consideration all those whose views were not in conformity with the broad goals of society as perceived by its members.[65] Thus it is not improbable that a lengthy, somewhat circuitous, but nonetheless responsive nominating procedure existed as the backbone of Connecticut politics, in which the lower house served as a sort of permanent nominating convention whose popularly elected delegates annually selected and assessed potential candidates for higher office.[66]

Both aspects of political experience were relatively distinct in that there was only a slight tendency for men scoring high on the one dimension to score high on the other (Tau = .23). As the correlations show (see Table 2), the effects of both on political success were practically the same. Yet their effects, if equivalent in magnitude, may have been different in nature.[67] High-level appointments, especially in the case of county or probate judgeships, enhanced a man's political visibility in a direct way and demonstrated that he was sufficiently capable and responsible to have been vested with a great public trust. Active service on general committes of the lower house brought far less public recognition, since there was no public journal of assembly proceedings. Those who were most active in the lower house were no doubt placed on committees because they were initially thought to be competent by their colleagues and subsequently so proved themselves. But the word of their superior performance could have gotten back to the voters only through the expressed judgments of the deputies.[68]

65. The most notorious instance was the purging of the ranks of the judiciary during the Great Awakening. Some of this also occurred after the Stamp Act crisis of 1765–66. We have done some preliminary analysis of ideological-religious leanings and how they are related to political success and the like. Taking a strong position rather than the content of that position seems to be most highly correlated with political success. While our data on this aspect cannot be assumed to pertain to a man's position before attaining office, they do seem to suggest that moderates or "low-profile" types were *not* the ones who made it to the top.

66. It is barely conceivable that some small group or clique dictated these selections. But such a group would have had to be in control in all counties, the basis for judicial and field-grade militia appointments, control the house itself, and be on good terms with the upper house. The existence of such a group also implies that it had sufficient power to elevate itself, if it wished, to the upper house; and if it did that, it would be coterminous with the assistants we are studying.

67. Both aspects of political experience tend to compensate for one another as well as to have a greater effect jointly than either does alone. Each has its strongest effect on ultimate political success among those lower on the other aspect. Combined into a joint measure of prior political experience, the correlation between this variable and political success is .60.

68. The importance of these two routes to higher office is suggested not only by the tenacity with which the lower house maintained its privileges in this area but also by

Both position holding and committee service were related in some measure to the individual's own social status—the social-background variable most closely related to political experience—the correlations being .26 and .44, respectively. Neither of these is sufficiently strong to suggest that the link between political experience and later political success can be attributed solely to high social position. But the higher correlation between general-committee service and one's own social status suggests that men of lower status may have found it necessary to progress through posts that conferred greater visibility. Perhaps, too, the deputies were quick to recognize the ability of men whose social position was frequently an achievement in its own right.[69]

Political advancement in Connecticut does not appear to have been determined solely by birth or good fortune. Ambition and sheer ability—two factors often discounted in historical analyses of this type, for lack of direct evidence—need to be considered here too. Perhaps Connecticut was different from most other American colonies in offering a greater role for ability in achieving high office. Whatever the reason, men started relatively early in politics in Connecticut, and those who made it to the top started at a considerably earlier age than did those who tried and failed; these, in turn, started at an earlier age than did those who never tried. For our sample the mean entry or starting age in provincial politics (usually as town deputy) was 38.2 years, exactly 4.5 years younger than the mean age at which Cook found men starting town office.[70] For assistants, however, it was 33.9 years; for candidates, 37.2 years; and for deputies, 42.0 years. This pattern parallels that found by Cook, which he interprets as having been primarily the result of social advantages that conferred a head start on those of better family or with a college education. According to him, the voters in a self-fulfilling hypothesis read into their social attainments equivalent political abilities.[71] Multivariate analysis of our data, however, demonstrates that an early

demands made during the imperial crisis that monopolization of public office cease and proceedings of the assembly be made public. See the instructions given by the freemen to Windham's deputies in 1766, *New London Gazette*, 31 October 1766. They must have reached a considerable number of people, since they were also reprinted in the *Connecticut Courant*, 10 November 1766, and the *Connecticut Gazette*, 15 November 1766. What was of main concern was not corruption but the fact that some seemed to be getting more than their fair share of important positions. Viewed in the context of other instructions given to the deputies pertaining to debtor-creditor relations, the complaint suggests that its inspiration came from economic and political entrepreneurs who were frusted by the lack of openings in the system. See Martin, *Men in Rebellion*, for a strong argument along these lines.

69. See Robert Zemsky, *Merchants, Farmers, and River Gods* (Boston, 1971), esp. 285–300, for a study of committee service and its relationship to social background. There are definite parallels between his findings and ours.

70. Cook, *Fathers of the Towns*, 111.   71. Ibid., 112–18.

starting age in provincial politics in Connecticut was not primarily associated with a prominent social background.[72] Even when the combined effects of several background factors (the person's own social status, that of his father, and the ranking of his town) are taken into account, the mean starting ages remain quite unchanged—33.9 for assistants, 38.9 for candidates, and 41.2 for deputies.[73] Those who started out earlier in provincial politics seem therefore to have been more highly motivated and / or more able, because once we have ruled out anything more than a very slight relationship between starting age and social background, there remains in our view no other plausible interpretation. In the correlations listed in Table 2, earliness of entry age ranks among the more important factors in political success, equal in strength (Tau = .35) to the centrality of a man's town and stronger than any of the family-related factors.

Those who embarked on their political careers relatively early served longer as deputies and also achieved better records in the number of level of offices held (Tau = .34) and the number of general committees served on per session (Tau = .34). While it was a longer route to the top, an apprenticeship system thus held out definite possibilities for those who lacked social resources.[74] The correlations between political experience and political success in our sample are usually always higher among those ranking low on family and personal social resources.[75] This can be seen from the findings presented in Table 3, which shows the level of ultimate political success according to personal social status and prior political experience on

72. The correlation of earliness of starting age in provincial politics with social eminence is quite low: own social status, .21; father's status, .15; father's wealth, .09; connections with assistants, .09. The correlation is no greater (.05) with importance of town.

73. Analysis of variance and Multiple Classification Analysis (MCA), with starting age as the "dependent" variable and political success and varying combinations of background variables as the "independent" variables, show that eventual political success consistently "explains" variation in the starting age more than do any of the social-background variables or the importance of a man's town. Moreover, the combined effect of the three social-background variables plus the town variable is quite minimal; their combined, multiple correlation (R) is only .32. Introducing them into the analysis along with legislative success has very little effect on the original relationship with success. The procedures used in these analyses are discussed in Norman H. Nie et al., *Statistical Package for the Social Sciences*, 2d ed. (New York, 1975).

74. As the negative correlations between earliness of starting age and rapidity of ascent—from start to nomination and to becoming an assistant—show (−.30 and −.28, respectively), the early starters took longer to get there.

75. Since the patterns for both of the two political-experience variables, taken separately, are quite alike, we shall for the sake of simplicity note a few for the combined political-experience measure. (See n. 67.) Controlling for his own social status, the correlations between the combined political-experience variable and political success are as follows: high status, .31; medium status, .70; and low status, .55. Using other background variables as controls (e.g., father's status, assistant connections, importance of town), we find similar patterns of compensating or offsetting resources and routes.

Table 3

HIGHEST LEVEL ATTAINED BY PRIOR POLITICAL
EXPERIENCE AND PERSONAL SOCIAL STATUS
(Percentage at Level Indicated)

	High Position Holding[a]		Low Position Holding	
	Committee Service[b]		Committee Service	
	High	Low	High	Low
High Personal Status[c]				
Assistant	51.1	46.7	30.4	0.0
Candidate	44.4	40.0	52.2	50.0
Deputy	4.4	13.3	17.4	50.0
N	(45)	(15)	(23)	(8)
Medium Personal Status				
Assistant	58.3	18.2	7.1	0.0
Candidate	25.0	45.5	71.4	0.0
Deputy	16.7	36.4	21.4	100.0
N	(12)	(11)	(14)	(23)
Low Personal Status				
Assistant	50.0	16.7	25.0	0.0
Candidate	50.0	41.7	25.0	15.4
Deputy	0.0	41.7	50.0	84.6
N	(4)	(12)	(4)	(26)

[a] A score of 9 or more on the composite scale of prior office holding. For details on the construction of the scale, see n. 64.

[b] Service on general or policy committees of the lower house. High service is equivalent to a rate of service on more than 11.5 committees per 100 regular sessions served in the house (excluding nondeputies). For further details, see n. 63.

[c] Composite measure of personal social status. For details of the construction of the scale, see n. 51.

both dimensions. Without a higher level of prior experience either in terms of committee work or position holding, the chances of getting to the top, whatever one's social status, were nil. Of those who scored high on both aspects of political experience and had high status, over half became assistants and only 4 percent never even tried (as far as we know) to get nominated. High social status might have helped those who ranked high on one of the two dimensions of political experience, but it made no difference at all for those who were high on both. Throughout, as we can see, political experience made a difference, but it was especially important for those whose status was below the top category.[76]

The results of this analysis demonstrate convincingly that simple deference interpretations of elite-voter relations do not apply to election to the upper house in eighteenth-century Connecticut. If it were true that voters consistently deferred to men from prominent families, then family indicators should have been the ones most highly associated with political success. Undeniably there were certain advantages in having such a background, but advancement within the political class was much more a function of factors other than family background. Starting out at an earlier age, coming from the right town, and having achieved high status in one's own right counted for more. The role played by ascribed factors, as opposed to achieved factors, is suggested in the overall pattern of percentage figures in Table 2. Ascribed factors seem to have provided only an initial advantage, marking off candidates from deputies but not assistants from candidates. Perhaps they functioned here to lend greater visibility to certain deputies, but only within a geographically restricted context. On the other hand, a high ranking on achieved factors separates not only the candidates from the deputies but the assistants from the candidates. Again, political-experience variables at each career stage are the most discriminating of the achieved factors. Obviously we can only surmise what was in the voters' minds when they chose their rulers, but what seemed to matter most of all to them was a man's political experience.

This essay emerged from our dissatisfaction with prevailing formulations and usages of the concept of deference by historians of

76. If we cross-tabulate personal social status and political success and control for combined political experience, we find that much of the original impact of status is reduced. The original relationship between personal social status and political success is .41. But for those with high combined political experience it is −.01; among those higher on one but not on both dimensions, .26; and among those low on both, .12.

There was at least one other route to the top, one in which family connections, and presumably deference, did play a larger role. This is indicated by the sequence in which persons held deputy, as opposed to judicial, positions. About 15 percent of the men studied were JPs before becoming a deputy, and it was among these men that family political connections figured most prominently. Whereas only 19 percent of those who were deputies first had high assistant connections, 41 percent of those who were JPs first had such connections; and 34 percent of the latter, but only 15 percent of the former, were sons of governors or assistants. (The groups did not differ in regard to family wealth or social status, however.) Those who were JPs first were also more likely to make it to the top (41 percent as opposed to 25 percent) and to get there faster. Most of them were late starters too. See John M. Murrin, "Review Essay," *History and Theory* 11 (1972): 226–75, for some interesting findings and interpretations on the situation in Massachusetts. But, while there are parallels between Connecticut and Massachusetts on this score, it must be remembered that only 15 percent of the group of men we studied fell into the favored category of becoming a JP first and that only 24 percent of the assistants studied could have attained the position by that route.

colonial politics. It seemed to us that scholars writing about who controlled pre-Revolutionary politics (and why) were stretching the concept of deference to cover virtually all political relations while
simultaneously denying that deference had anything to do with
power—largely on the ground that it involves "softer" modes of
interaction. This anomaly, we felt, was obscuring rather than clari-
fying certain aspects of colonial politics. But though our intentions
are in part critical in this essay, the reader ought by now to be aware
that they are primarily heuristic. We claim neither originality nor
comprehensiveness for our theoretical formulation of the concepts
of coercion, influence, and deference. We hope, though, that our
attempted formulation will provide a useful starting point for further discussion and for testing through the analysis of specific areas
of pre-Revolutionary political history. Concepts are meant to be tools,
to help organize thoughts and marshal empirical evidence, and it is
incumbent on historians no less than on other students of society to
use them in that way. Regrettably, the more fashionable the concept
of deference has become, the more uncritical and a priori has its use
become. It is admittedly rarely easy to analyze historically far-removed
periods in theoretical, conceptual terms. No doubt this discomfits
most historians who naturally want concepts that are practicable. But
let us not confuse the analytical aims and requirements of concept
usage with the hopes and frustrations of the historian in unearthing
and piecing together the data necessary to apply concepts rigorously.
If all we can do is make suggestive inferences from these fragments
and arrive at tentative conclusions about the kind of power relations
that pertained then between elites and electorates, so be it. As someone once said, anything worth doing well is worth doing half well.

The use of the concept of deference—or, for that matter, coercion
and influence—must be undertaken with full recognition of the
environmental factors that impinge upon the development of power
relations. It is clear that such factors had a significant effect in Connecticut. In fact, it is quite possible that Connecticut was founded
with a clear-cut and systematic intention of establishing and foster-
ing deferential relations that because of a quirk of fate—the pro-
curement of the charter from Charles II—was derailed by institutional
and economic realities beyond the control of a would-be elite. The
combination of an agrarian economy based on small freeholds, a
strong religious culture that insisted upon the unmediated independence of each person's relationship to God, and an unalterable constitutional mandate for annual, colonywide nominations and elections
combined to work strongly against the establishment of a deferential
electorate. Even in the case of incumbent assistants, it may not be

useful to describe their relationship to the electorate as deferential. If anything, it was more of a deference to their occupancy of high office than to their social or economic eminence. Ordinarily no one today attempts to explain the high rates of reelection of congressmen by supposing that modern voters defer to incumbents.

Contrast this situation with developments in Virginia, where chaotic beginnings eventually resulted in an economy characterized by much greater disparities and much more frequent dependencies, by a diverse religious culture, and by institutions much more fully subject to the control of a favored few. One would anticipate that power relations would develop in quite a different way from that in Connecticut. Naturally this can be verified only through the empirical *analysis* of whatever evidence is available.

It is certainly not our intention to generalize our findings in Connecticut to include the other colonies—not even Rhode Island, which was most similar to it. It is even less our intention to create convenient new certainties for colonial historians to apply uncritically to politics. Our discussion of these power relations and their illustration by the analysis of a small portion of the totality of politics in colonial America will do no more and no less, we hope, than make historians aware of the dangers in too simplistic an approach to such matters.

THREE

*Culture, Society,
&
the Revolution*

The Culture of Agriculture:
The Symbolic World of the
Tidewater Planter, 1760-1790 *

T. H. BREEN

Sometime late in the 1760s, Richard Henry Lee composed an essay entitled "That State of the Constitution of Virginea [*sic*]." Considering Lee's reputation as an outspoken defender of American liberties, one might assume that the document dealt primarily with British corruption and parliamentary oppression. In point of fact, however, Lee focused his attention upon other topics. After briefly describing the colony's political structure, he turned to "our staple" and explained how Virginians cultivated tobacco. Lee analyzed each step in the long agricultural routine—sowing, transplanting, weeding, topping, cutting, curing, and packing—for, in his opinion, it was important that people unfamiliar with this culture know exactly "how much labour is required on a Virginean estate & how poor the produce."[1]

Lee's preoccupation with the production of tobacco would not have surprised his neighbors on Virginia's Northern Neck, men like Landon Carter and George Washington. After all, it is modern historians who insist upon treating these people as lawyers, as lawmakers, as political theorists, as almost anything in fact except as planters.[2] This perspective has distorted our understanding of the world of the

* The author wrote this essay while a member of the Institute for Advanced Study, Princeton, New Jersey. He thanks not only the staff of the Institute and the editors of this volume but also Jacob Lassner, Stephen Foster, Clifford Geertz, Richard Beeman, Emory Evans, Josef Barton, Richard Bushman, Chester Pach, and Michael Zuckerman for encouragement and suggestions.

1. Lee Family Papers, Mssl. L51, f. 378, Virginia Historical Society. The essay was not published. See Pauline Maier's sketch of Lee's political ideas in *The Old Revolutionaries: Political Lives in the Age of Samuel Adams* (New York, 1980), 164-200.

2. For example, the fullest account of the careers of these Virginians remains Charles S. Sydnor's *Gentleman Freeholders: Political Practices in Washington's Virginia* (Chapel Hill,

eighteenth-century Virginians. Tobacco touched nearly every aspect
of their existence. It was a source of colonial prosperity, a medium
for commercial transactions and payment of taxes, and a theme of
decorative art, and the majority of the planters' waking hours were
spent, as they would have said, in "making" a crop.[3] Almost every
surviving letter book from this period contains a description of
tobacco production, and even Thomas Jefferson, who never distinguished himself as a planter, instructed a European correspondent
in the mysteries of cultivating the Virginia staple.[4]

However much the Virginians themselves wrote about tobacco,
historians seldom show much interest either in its production or in
its relation to the culture of the great Northern Neck families: the
Carters, Corbins, Fitzhughs, Lees, and Taylors, to cite just a few of
the more prominent names.[5] The reasons for this oversight are clear.

1952). Like other historians who have written about the great planters—-Douglas S.
Freeman, Louis Morton, Aubrey C. Land represent notable exceptions—Sydnor concentrated on politics and paid virtually no attention to the role of tobacco in shaping
gentry culture. The crop did not even appear in Sydnor's index.

3. For an example of tobacco employed as a theme of decorative art, see the tobacco
finials on a mideighteenth-century Chesapeake walnut high chest (G59.17.5) in the Winterthur Museum, Winterthur, Delaware.

4. To G. K. van Hogendorp, with papers, "On Tobacco Culture," 4 May 1784, in *The
Papers of Thomas Jefferson*, ed. Julian P. Boyd (Princeton, 1950–), VII, 209–12.

5. The generalizations advanced in this essay about the culture of agriculture are
based on extensive research in the letters and diaries of the great planters of Tidewater
Virginia, particularly those of gentry families living on the colony's Northern Neck. This
group included members of the Baylor, Beverley, Burwell, Byrd, Carter, Corbin, Fitzhugh, Lee, Taylor, and Washington families. These planters marketed their crops primarily through the consignment system, that is, they shipped their tobacco each year to
a British agent who then sold it for the highest price that he could obtain. This representative also purchased goods, usually manufactured items, for the Virginians and kept
an account of the planter's balance. See Arthur Pierce Middleton, *Tobacco Coast: A Maritime History of Chesapeake Bay in the Colonial Era* (Newport News, 1953), chap. 4; Jacob
M. Price, *Capital and Credit in British Overseas Trade: The View from the Chesapeake, 1700–
1776* (Cambridge, Mass., 1980).

Two questions immediately arise concerning an analysis based on the experiences of
such a small elite group. What about the small planters? The slaves? One would like to
know how Virginia's less prosperous planters perceived the culture of tobacco. For the
most part, they do not seem to have recorded their thoughts on this subject; at least,
very few documents of any sort written by these people have survived. There is no
reason, however, to believe that their relation to the Virginia staple differed significantly
from that of the great planters. See, for example, Aubrey C. Land, "Economic Behavior
in a Planting Society: The Eighteenth-Century Chesapeake," *Journal of Southern History*
33 (1967): 469–85. On this point, it is interesting to note that Philip Fithian, Robert
Carter's tutor at Nomini Hall, claimed that "the People of fortune . . . are the *pattern of
all behaviour here.*" Fithian to Rev. Enoch Green, 1 December 1773, in *Journal and Letters
of Philip Vickers Fithian*, ed. Hunter D. Farish (Williamsburg, 1945), 35 (emphasis added).

Slaves performed most agricultural jobs on the large Tidewater plantations, and the
pattern of their lives was inescapably influenced by the cultivation of tobacco. My intent
is not to reduce the blacks' role in agricultural production; rather, it is to explore the
work culture of the large planters, the men who made the decisions on what seed to use,
what fields to cultivate, when to begin each chore, and who, unlike staple planters in

First, since many planters became revolutionaries, researchers have naturally emphasized the Virginians' grievances against the British imperial system and their thoughts about a new form of government.

But the members of this particular ruling group were unusual in a second way. Unlike other landed elites that Western historians have studied, this one actually directed the production of a staple crop. In other words, Virginia planters did not retire to metropolitan centers, divorcing themselves from the annual agricultural routine. And third, twentieth-century scholars find it difficult to comprehend the productive aspects of agrarian culture. In their analyses of preindustrial societies, they seize upon the familiar—the nuclear family or urban conflict, for example—while ignoring the daily activities of the great majority of the population. As a result of this bias, we possess substantial studies of colonial cities, urban artisans, and mob violence, but almost nothing perceptive about the work culture of the early American farmers.[6]

Modernization theory has exacerbated these interpretative difficulties. Colonial American historians—sometimes quite unconsciously—anticipate the birth of a new industrial society and therefore depict farmers and planters as persons whose lives must inevitably be transformed by social forces beyond their control. Early American cultivators become a homogeneous group. No distinction is made between different kinds of agriculture; no attention is paid to different relations between crop and cultivator. Thus, all too often, the farmers of pre-Revolutionary America appear either as simple rural folk about to be overwhelmed by an expanding market economy or,

---

other parts of the New World, actually resided on the plantation. Even though the Carters and Corbins did not toil in the fields, their lives were as intimately bound up with what grew there as were the lives of their slaves. See Gerald W. Mullin, *Flight and Rebellion: Slave Resistance in Eighteenth-Century Virginia* (New York, 1972), chap. 1.

6. Obvious exceptions to this generalization are Lewis Cecil Gray, *History of Agriculture in the Southern United States to 1860* (New York, 1941), and Ulrich B. Philips, *Life and Labor in the Old South* (Boston, 1941), chap. 8. See also James A. Henretta, "Families and Farms: *Mentalité* in Pre-Industrial America," *William and Mary Quarterly*, 3d ser., 35 (1978): 3–32, and, for a provocative discussion of the relation between planter culture and agricultural production at a slightly later point in American History, Eugene D. Genovese, *The Political Economy of Slavery: Studies in the Economy and Society of the Slave South* (New York, 1967), esp. chaps. 1 and 6.

To appreciate the dimensions of this interpretative problem, one has only to compare what little we know about colonial farm life with the rich insights into early nineteenth-century factory culture that we have gained from scholars such as E. P. Thompson, Merritt Roe Smith, and Anthony F. C. Wallace. E. P. Thompson, "Time, Work-Discipline, and Industrial Capitalism," *Past and Present*, no. 38 (1967): 56–97; Merritt Roe Smith, *Harpers Ferry Armory and the New Technology: The Challenge of Change* (Ithaca, 1977); and A. F. C. Wallace, *Rockdale: The Growth of an American Village in the Early Industrial Revolution* (New York, 1978).

less frequently, as agricultural innovators busily hustling their neighbors down the road toward modernity.[7]

To avoid such interpretive problems, one must understand the agrarian population on its own terms, as people bound by rules developed within a specific cultural and physical environment. As anthropologists have discovered, forms of cultivation influence the character of a people's culture. Analysis of agricultural activities in narrow economic terms, as simply a matter of counting bushels and bales, of calculating rates of growth, obscures the relation between crop and cultivator. Plants assume special significance for the grower, and over several generations the products of the fields become associated with a particular set of regional values, a pattern of land tenure, a system of labor, even a festive calendar. This connection is especially obvious in areas relying upon a particular staple such as sugar, cotton, or coffee.[8] Whether the cultivation of certain plants generates values or merely reinforces values already present in the society is not clear. Probably both processes are at work, and the dominant crop both shapes and gives meaning to the local culture. "The culture of agriculture" is a convenient label for this complex interplay between values and behavior, between production and culture.

In the study of Caribbean agriculture, the relation between crop and cultivator occupies a central place. Indeed, these island societies established staple economies at approximately the same time and under roughly similar conditions as did the Tidewater planters, and the Caribbean experience provides insights into the development of Virginia's culture of agriculture. In the case of Cuba, for example, scholars speak of a "sugar mentality," a specific pattern of behavior and turn of mind connected with the production of sugar. In plantation societies dependent upon sugar cane, the crop affects the cultivators' attitudes about proper land use and work habits, about time and space, about the very character of most human activities. Because this crop has had such a long history in the Islands, it is not surprising that one anthropologist concluded, "Sugar . . . rules the Antilles."[9] In neighboring areas in which coffee was the chief staple, one finds a similar cultural configuration. As one investigator of a subregion

7. I have discussed these interpretive problems at greater length in "Back to Sweat and Toil: Suggestions for the Study of Agricultural Work in Early America," *Pennsylvania History* 49 (1982): 241–58.

8. See Clifford Geertz, *Agricultural Involution: The Process of Ecological Change in Indonesia* (Berkeley, 1963); Carville V. Earle, "A Staple Interpretation of Slavery and Free Labor," *Geographical Review* 68 (1978): 51–65.

9. Sidney Mintz's foreword to Ramiro Guerra y Sánchez, *Sugar and Society in the Caribbean: An Economic History of Cuban Agriculture* (New Haven, 1964), xliv.

of Puerto Rico discovered, "coffee culture is not merely a business [it is also] . . . an environmental pattern and a social structure."[10]

Colonial Virginians concentrated on tobacco. Nevertheless, the relation of their culture to the dominant crop was not unlike that found in the Sugar Islands. On the eve of the American Revolution, the cultivation of tobacco gave both *shape* and *meaning* to planter culture. Indeed, in view of the centrality of a single staple in the colonists' lives, one can write confidently of a "tobacco mentality," a distinct culture that leaders of the Northern Neck like Carter, Lee, and Washington took for granted. The relation between plant and planter was complex, far more so than might at first appear. Certainly, the distinction between "shape" and "meaning" is crucial to a full understanding of the region's culture of agriculture.

On one level, the crop shaped general patterns of behavior. The plant possessed a special, even unique, set of physical characteristics that in turn influenced the planters' decisions about where to locate plantations and how to allocate time throughout the year. In other words, tobacco affected perceptions of time and space; and without doubt, the Virginia work routine—very different from that associated with sugar and coffee—contributed powerfully to the development of a tobacco mentality.

On a second level, however, tobacco gave meaning to routine planter activities. It was emblematic not only of a larger social order, its past, its future, its prospects in comparison with those of other societies, but also of the individual producers. The personal link between planter and tobacco is fundamental to the argument of this essay. The staple provided the Lees and Carters of eighteenth-century Virginia with a means to establish a public identity, a way to locate themselves within an intricate web of human relationships. The crop served as an index of one's worth and standing in a community of competitive, highly independent growers; quite literally, the quality of a man's tobacco was the measure of the man. Both aspects of the tobacco mentality—as shaper of everyday experience and as source of individual and corporate meaning—help to explain the intensity of the planters' commitment to the staple and to the customs that it spawned.

The planters of Lee's generation not only grew tobacco but also participated in a revolution—an unlikely course of action for a group of wealthy landowners. The two occurrences may have been more closely connected than historians have realized. In the period immediately preceding the Declaration of Independence, the great plant-

10. Cited in Julian H. Steward et al., *The People of Puerto Rico: A Study in Social Anthropology* (Urbana, Ill., 1969), 171, also 93–94, 161–68.

ers of the Northern Neck were forced either to abandon the
cultivation of tobacco or at the very least to contemplate doing so.
Their symbolic world, intimately bound up with a single staple, deeply
rooted in Virginia's history, seemed threatened. In fact, at precisely
the same time that Parliament redefined the character of the British
empire, the great planters of this region experienced a crisis of self-
perception. It is not surprising that, in a situation in which the familiar fabric of everyday life was filled increasingly with problems, these
particular Virginians were unusually receptive to bold, even radical,
political ideas.[11]

Tobacco as Shaper of Culture: Space and Time

Colonial Virginians acknowledged the profound impact that
tobacco had had upon the development of their society. They were
less certain, however, whether the results had been beneficial. A case
in point was the planters' settlement pattern, a use of space that clearly
set them apart from other colonial Americans. The earliest Virginians had carved out riverfront estates often located miles from the
nearest neighbor. As time passed, colonists spread west and north
along the waterways in search of fresh lands on which to establish
their sons and daughters. Each generation faced the same problem;
each behaved much as its predecessor had done. Crown officials
complained that dispersed living discouraged urban development
and invited military disaster, and while Virginians recognized the
desirability of prosperous commercial centers—New England towns

11. In recent years, scholars have depicted the leaders of Revolutionary Virginia,
especially Thomas Jefferson, as intellectuals almost totally divorced from the productive
aspects of their society. Not surprisingly, the planters appear in this growing literature
on the ideology of the American Revolution as Enlightenment figures, as rural geniuses
who drew notions about politics directly from English or Scottish publications rather
than from everyday life on the large Tidewater plantations.

In 1966 Gordon Wood analyzed the separation of political rhetoric from social reality
with particular reference to Virginia and suggested that the planters' shrill, often hys-
terical pronouncements about the loss of virtue were related in some way to "strains
within Virginia society." "Rhetoric and Reality in the American Revolution," *William and
Mary Quarterly*, 3d ser., 23 (1966): 27–30. In a series of provocative articles, Rhys Isaac
tried to define the precise character of these strains. He concluded that the pre-Revolutionary gentry felt that its hegemony was threatened by the vociferous opposition of
the colony's Protestant dissenters and that thus the great planters' political beliefs and
behavior in this period must be interpreted in part as a response to an unprecedented
cultural challenge. See esp. Isaac, "Evangelical Revolt: The Nature of the Baptists' Challenge to the Traditional Order in Virginia, 1765 to 1775," ibid., 30 (1974): 345–68.
Neither Wood nor Isaac attempted to connect tobacco cultivation to the development of
distinct subculture or, more to the point, to the planters' receptivity to certain English
political ideas during a time of agricultural change. See Bernard Bailyn, *The Ideological
Origins of the American Revolution* (Cambridge, Mass., 1967); Joseph Ernst, " 'Ideology'
and an Economic Interpretation of the Revolution," in *The American Revolution*, ed. Alfred
F. Young (De Kalb, Ill., 1976), 161–85.

without Puritans—they refused to abandon their isolated plantations.[12]

By the middle of the eighteenth century, dispersed settlement was
accepted as an inevitable product of a particular type of agriculture.
Tobacco may not in fact have caused dispersion—the planters might
have maintained the fertility of their original tracts—but contemporary Virginians nevertheless blamed their staple for creating a dispersed population. In 1775, for example, the anonymous author of
American Husbandry informed his readers of what every Virginian
knew from firsthand experience: "A very considerable tract of land
is necessary for a tobacco plantation." The writer estimated that
planters required at least fifty acres for each laborer, for if they possessed less land, "they will find themselves distressed for want of
room."[13]

The cultural implications of Virginia's dispersed settlement pattern were obvious. Social relations among the colony's great planters
were less frequent, less spontaneous than were those enjoyed by
wealthy towndwellers in other parts of America. The majority of the
planter's life was spent on his plantation in the company of family,
servants, and slaves. Some Virginians found this "solitary and unso-
ciable" existence difficult to endure.[14] Like William Fitzhugh, Virginia's most successful seventeenth-century planter, they relied on
libraries to compensate for the absence of "Society that is good and
ingenious."[15] But books must sometimes have seemed poor substitutes for regular contact with outsiders. In 1756 Edmund Pendleton,
a young planter and promising lawyer, protested that he had failed
to hear an important piece of news because he was isolated in "a
forest."[16]

12. See John C. Rainbolt, "The Absence of Towns in Seventeeth-Century Virginia,"
Journal of Social History 35 (1969): 343–60; Kevin P. Kelly, " 'In dispers'd Country Plan-
tations': Settlement Patterns in Seventeenth-Century Surry County, Virginia," in *The
Chesapeake in the Seventeenth-Century: Essays on Anglo-American Society and Politics*, ed. Thad
W. Tate and David L. Ammerman (New York, 1980), 183–205.

13. *American Husbandry*, ed. Harry J. Carman (New York, 1939), 165. This anonymous book was originally published in 1775. Avery O. Craven, *Soil Exhaustion as a Factor
in the Agricultural History of Virginia and Maryland, 1606–1860*, University of Illinois Studies in the Social Sciences, vol. 13, no. 1 (Urbana, Ill., 1926); and Carville V. Earle, *The
Evolution of a Tidewater Settlement System: All Hallow's Parish, Maryland, 1650–1783* (Chicago, 1975).

14. "A Letter from Mr. John Clayton Rector of Crofton at Wakefield in Yorkshire, to
the Royal Society, May 12, 1688," in *Tracts and Other Papers Relating Principally to the
Origin, Settlement, and Progress of the Colonies in North America . . .* , ed. Peter Force, III
(Washington, D.C., 1844), no. 12, p. 21.

15. Richard Beale Davis, ed., *William Fitzhugh and His Chesapeake World, 1676–1701:
The Fitzhugh Letters and Other Documents* (Chapel Hill, 1963), 15.

16. Cited in David John Mays, *Edmund Pendleton, 1721–1803: A Biography* (Cambridge, Mass., 1952), I, 102.

Other tobacco planters viewed their situation more positively. While admitting that their lives were slow-moving, even a bit dull, they bragged that physical isolation generated personal independence. The cultivation of tobacco transformed them into "Patriarchs," men who depended upon no one but "Providence."[17] Landon Carter, for example, described Sabine Hall in 1759 as an "excellent little Fortress . . . built upon a Rock . . . of *Independence.*"[18]

However cranky Carter may have appeared to contemporaries, his celebration of untrammeled individualism was not unusual in this colony. Visitors reported that an independent turn of mind was a central characteristic of planter society. "The public or political character of the Virginians," declared Andrew Burnaby in 1760, "corresponds with their private one: they are haughty and jealous of their liberties, impatient of restraint, and can scarcely bear the thought of being controuled by any superior power."[19] Tobacco alone was not responsible for the planters' passionate resistance to external authority—whether political or ecclesiastical. Nevertheless, the spatial context within which they developed ideas about church and state served to heighten aggressive self-reliance.

The cultivation of tobacco also shaped the planters' sense of time, their perception of appropriate behavior at particular points throughout the year. A comparison with other staples helps make the point. Each crop, be it coffee, sugar, or tobacco, possesses a distinct character and thus places different demands on the people who grow it. Some staples, for example, require a great expenditure of labor over a relatively short period of time, perhaps a month or two of drudgery around the harvest; in sugar-producing regions especially, this exhausting season can be followed by months of unemployment or underemployment. Other staples are associated with more balanced work rhythms. The tasks necessary to transform their seeds into a marketable commodity are spread out over the entire year, and there is no extraordinary crisis period, such as when the

17. William Byrd II to Charles, earl of Orrery, 5 July 1726, in "Virginia Council Journals, 1726–1753," *Virginia Magazine of History and Biography* 32 (1924): 27.

18. Cited in Jack P. Greene, ed., *The Diary of Colonel Landon Carter of Sabine Hall, 1752–1778,* Virginia Historical Society Documents, vol. 4 (Charlottesville, 1965), I, 19. Peyton Randolph expressed a similar view. Writing to protest the actions of several British merchants, Randolph bragged, "I shall never be affected with any Reply that can be made, having an excellent little Fortress to protect me, one built on a Rock not liable to be shaken with Fears, that of *Independency.* . . . ." *A Letter to a Gentleman in London, from Virginia* (Williamsburg, 1759), 27.

19. Rev. Andrew Burnaby, *Travels through the Middle Settlements in North America, in the Years 1759 and 1760; With Observations upon the State of the Colonies,* in *A General Collection of the Best and Most Interesting Voyages and Travels in All Parts of the World. . . ,* ed. John Pinkerton, vol. 13 (London, 1812), 715.

cane is cut, which alone determines whether the enterprise will be a success.

Work schedules, of course, influence the timing of other, seemingly unrelated activities. In many countries, the personality of the major crop determines when festivals are held—in other words, when the cultivators have the leisure to organize such events. In the coffee-growing sections of early twentieth-century Puerto Rico "traditional ceremonies . . . marked a sharp transition from work to non-work."[20] In the cultivation of other staples, such a clear break between labor and leisure might have made little sense.

As grown in eighteenth-century Virginia, tobacco placed major demands upon the planter throughout the year. There was no "dead season" when laborers turned their attentions to other pursuits. From the moment they put out the seed to the time that they loaded hogsheads on British ships, the workers were fully occupied in making a crop. Tobacco was not like wheat, a plant that farmers sowed and simply waited for to mature.[21] The Virginia staple could never be taken for granted. It dictated a series of jobs, any one of which, if improperly performed, could jeopardize the entire venture. Each step in the process required personal skill, judgment, and luck. No wonder a French traveler explained that "the culture of tobacco is difficult, troublesome, and uncertain."[22]

Colonial planters followed a fairly well-established routine. As one observer noted, "This process varies more or less in the different plantations, but the variations are not by any means considerable."[23] This generally shared production schedule, repeated annually throughout a planter's lifetime, on plantations scattered throughout Virginia, was a powerful element in the development and persistence of a tobacco mentality. Moreover, unless one understands exactly what was at stake at every point—the dangers, the requirements, and the critical, often subtle decisions made by planters throughout the year—one cannot fully comprehend the relation of culture to agriculture.

The production cycle for Northern Neck tobacco began in late

20. Steward et al., *People of Puerto Rico*, 200.

21. See Harold B. Gill, Jr., "Wheat Culture in Colonial Virginia," *Agricultural History* 52 (1978): 386; Douglas S. Freeman, *George Washington: A Biography* (New York, 1948–54), III, 195–96; Rhys Isaac, *The Transformation of Virginia 1740–1790* (Chapel Hill, 1982), 22–30.

22. Duc de La Rochefoucauld Liancourt, *Travels through the United States of North America* (London, 1799), II, 84.

23. Ibid., 85. An excellent discussion of this annual process can be found in David O. Percy, *The Production of Tobacco along the Colonial Potomac*, National Colonial Farm Researdh Report, no. 1 (Accokeek, Md., 1979). For a modern account of tobacco production throughout the world, see B. C. Akehurst, *Tobacco* (London, 1968).

December or early January. The commonly accepted date for planting seed in specially enriched beds was about twelve days after
Christmas. The precise timing depended upon a number of variables, but according to one prosperous gentleman, "The best time
for sowing the seed is as early after Christmas as the weather will
permit."[24] The small seedbeds, usually not larger than a quarter of
an acre, were carefully manured. Some were even fertilized with wood
ash. In either case, once the seed had been placed in the ground, the
planter covered the entire bed with branches in order to protect the
tobacco from possible frost damage. Knowledgeable producers prepared several different "plant-beds," frequently separated by considerable distances. This practice insured that the accidental
destruction of one bed by cold, disease, or pests would not deprive
the planter of an opportunity to make a good crop. But there were
always risks. Prudent Virginians understood that the odds against a
single plant's surviving to maturity were exceedingly high, and during this initial stage, "an experienced planter commonly takes care
to have ten times as many plants as he can make use of."[25]

The second phase of tobacco cultivation, transplanting seedlings
from the beds to the main fields, occupied the full attention of the
plantation labor force for several months. The work usually com-
menced in late April, but as in all stages of tobacco production, the
exact timing depended in large part upon the planter's judgment.
He alone decided whether the tiny plants were sufficiently developed to survive the operation. According to common wisdom, the
tobacco leaves were supposed to be "as large as a dollar." Virginians
looked for additional signs—the thickness of the young leaves, the
general appearance of the plants—subtle indicators that one learned
to recognize through long experience.[26]

However skilled the planter may have been, transplanting was an
anxious time for everyone. Chance played a central role in this procedure. Success required frequent rains, for soaking moisture loosened the soil and allowed the planter to pull up the seedlings without
harming their roots. The work was difficult and unpleasant. Because
no one could predict when the rains would fall, one had to take
advantage of major storms, termed "seasons" by colonial Virginians.

24. A man identified as Judge Parker is quoted in William Tatham, *An Historical and
Practical Essay on the Culture and Commerce of Tobacco,* ed. G. Melvin Herndon (Coral
Gables, 1969), 118–19. Tatham's book was published in London in 1800. See also Curtis
Carroll Davis, ed., " 'A National Property': Richard Claiborne's Tobacco Treatise for
Poland," *William and Mary Quarterly,* 3d ser., 21 (1964): 99–110.
25. J. F. D. Smyth, *A Tour in the United States of America* (London, 1784), II, 129. See
also Lee Family Papers, Mssl. L51, f. 378.
26. Jefferson, "On Tobacco Culture," *Papers,* VII, 210.

"When a good shower . . . happens at this period of the year," wrote one well-informed grower, "the planter hurries to the plant bed, disregarding the teeming element, which is doomed to wet his skin."[27] Laborers rushed frantically from the beds to the fields where small tobacco hills had already been laid out. A seedling was dropped on "every hill . . . by the negro-children; the most skilful slaves then . . . planting them."[28] Under perfect conditions, transplanting could be finished by late May, but in fact the job spilled over into June. William Tatham, an eighteenth-century Virginian who published a detailed description of tobacco cultivation, explained that the fields were seldom fully planted until "the *long season in May;* which (to make use of an Irishism) very frequently happens in June."[29]

As the tobacco ripened over the summer, the planter and his slaves performed a number of tedious chores. The crop could not be ignored, not even for a week. Producers waged constant battle against weeds, and over the course of the growing season, each tobacco hill was hoed as many as three times. Since major planters like Landon Carter cultivated more than a hundred thousand plants, weeding obviously took a considerable amount of time. After eight to twelve leaves appeared on each plant—how many depended upon "the fertility of the earth"—the planter ordered his workers to begin topping.[30] This operation, literally the removal of the top of the plant, prevented the tobacco from flowering. The goal was to channel the plant's energies into the leaves. No sooner had the topping been completed than the tobacco started putting out suckers, secondary shoots that had to be removed before they deprived the leaves of important nutrients. Throughout this period each plant received regular, individual attention; each task was done by hand.

The next step, cutting the tobacco, generated considerable tension on the plantations of the Northern Neck. It was well known that the operation took place sometime in September. The difficulty came in determining the exact day on which to start. As every planter understood, even a slight error in judgment could ruin the entire crop. An early frost, for example, was capable of destroying every plant that stood unprotected in the fields, and as the September days passed, the danger of frost increased. On the other hand, it was folly to cut tobacco that was not fully ripe. Immature leaves seldom cured properly. The decision to cut, therefore, tested the planter's competence.

27. Tatham, *Historical and Practical Essay,* 15.
28. Smyth, *Tour,* II, 130.
29. Tatham, *Historical and Practical Essay,* 14. See also Lee Family Papers, Mssl. L51, f. 378.
30. Jefferson, "On Tobacco Culture," *Papers,* VII, 210. See also Smyth, *Tour,* II, 131–37.

And yet, notwithstanding the critical importance of this moment in the production cycle, Virginians offered no universal description of ripe tobacco. Each planter had to rely on his own judgment. He simply sensed when the tobacco was ready for cutting; it had the "right" appearance. According to Tatham, "The tobacco, when ripe, changes its colour, and looks greyish; the leaf feels thick, and if pressed between the finger and thumb will easily crack." He then added, "experience alone can enable a person to judge when tobacco is fully ripe."[31] Richard Henry Lee, a man who possessed the necessary experience, advised growers to look for "spots appearing on the leaf."[32] Other planters adopted different guidelines, a mixture of local custom and informed intuition, none of which guaranteed success.

Colonial Virginians did not refer to the September cutting as a harvest. Such a term would have suggested finality, the completion of the annual agricultural cycle. But for the tobacco planter, cutting led immediately to another arduous task, curing, and if he failed at this stage, it did not much matter how skillfully the transplanting or cutting had been performed. One English visitor who closely studied the cultivation of tobacco claimed that proper curing represented the planter's most difficult challenge, "and, for want of knowledge and care, there are every year many hogs-heads spoiled, and worth nothing." He insisted, in fact, that "the curing of tobacco is an art." Another man termed it "an art most difficult of attainment."[33]

Again, the crucial factor was personal judgment. The cut tobacco was hung in special curing barns and dried until it seemed ready for packing. The trick was to produce a leaf neither too dry nor too moist. Excess moisture would almost certainly cause the tobacco to rot while being shipped. But leaves that were allowed to dry too long became brittle and sometimes turned to dust before reaching Great Britain.

Wise planters naturally tried to terminate the curing process at the moment that the tobacco became dry yet pliable, a time that Virginians called simply "case." This point, Tatham explained, "can only be judged of safely by long experience." The problem was that the condition of the tobacco could change from hour to hour, moving in and out of "case" depending upon the humidity. Wet days supposedly gave the cured tobacco leaves greater flexibility and thus

31. Tatham, *Historical and Practical Essay,* 124–25.
32. Lee Family Papers, Mssl. L51, f. 378.
33. Richard Parkinson, *A Tour in America, in 1798, 1799, and 1800* (London, 1805), II, 418, 423; N. F. Cabell, "Some Fragments of an Intended Report on the Post Revolutionary History of Agriculture in Virginia," *William and Mary Quarterly,* 1st ser., 26 (1918): 155.

made them easier to handle. "This condition," observed Taham, "can only be distinguished by diligent attention, and frequent handling; for it often changes this quality with the change of the weather in a very short space of time."[34] If the colony experienced a particularly rainy fall, however, the planter was sometimes forced to light fires in the curing barns. The heat assisted the drying process but could create other difficulties. As Jefferson reported, "great care is necessary as it [the tobacco] is very inflammable, and if it takes fire, the whole, with the house, consumes as quickly as straw would."[35]

Successful curing did not mean that the tobacco was ready for market. Several complex operations still remained. When the leaves reached "case," workers quickly "stripped" them from the stalks on which they had hung in the barn. Those planters who obtained the highest returns for their tobacco also "stemmed" the leaves. This was a monotonous job. Slaves, both men and women, removed "the largest stem or fibres from the web of the leaf," leaving a handsome product that could be packed easily. The speed with which stemming was accomplished depended upon the slaves' "expertness." One had to learn the necessary skills, and "those unaccustomed to it find it difficult to stem a single plant."[36] Regardless of the workers' training, these operations required considerable amounts of time, and during the autumn months it was not unusual for the slaves to labor long into the night over the individual leaves.

Only when these tasks had been completed could the planter order "prizing" to begin. Layer after layer of leaves was placed in hogsheads manufactured by plantation coopers. Men then pressed or "prized" the leaves until there was space for additional layers. This process was repeated until the hogshead weighed at least a thousand pounds. Sometimes the pressure on the tobacco cracked the staves, and the hogshead burst. No wonder that Tatham concluded that prizing "requires the combination of judgment and experience."[37] These jobs—stripping, stemming, and prizing—continued throughout the fall. A prosperous Virginia planter, Richard Corbin, advised a plantation manager that with careful planning of the work routine, "the Tobacco will be all prised before Christmas, weigh well, and at least one hhd [hogshead] in Ten gained by finishing the Tobo thus early."[38] But Corbin counseled perfection. Often the hogsheads were

34. Tatham, *Historical and Practical Essay*, 37.
35. Jefferson, "On Tobacco Culture," *Papers*, VII, 211.
36. Tatham, *Historical and Practical Essay*, 40–41.   37. Ibid., 43.
38. "Instructions given by Richard Corbin, Esq., to his agent [James Semple] for the management of his plantations; Virginia, 1759" in *Plantation and Frontier Documents, 1649–1863: Illustrative of Industrial History in the Colonial and Ante-Bellum South*, ed. Ulrich B. Phillips (Cleveland, 1909), I, 112.

not ready for shipment to the public warehouses and inspection until well after the New Year.

Not until the following spring, a full fifteen months after the sowing of the tobacco seed, did the planter send loaded hogsheads to the European market. By that time, of course, another crop was in the ground, and he faced a new round of agricultural decisions. The schedule contained few slack periods, no time during which the grower could be completely free of anxieties about the state of his crop. Richard Corbin explained the tobacco cycle to an inexperienced employee. Sounding suspiciously like a New England Puritan, Corbin observed that "To employ the Fall & Winter well is the foundation of a successful Crop in the Summer: You will therefore Animate the overseers to great diligence that their work may be in proper forwardness and not have that to do in the Spring that ought to be done in the Winter: there is Business sufficient for every Season of the year."[39] And when Richard Parkinson, an Englishman, first arrived in Virginia, planters told him that it required a "year's work to go through the process" of cultivating tobacco, to which Parkinson later exclaimed, "so it is"! He ticked off a full calendar, each month corresponding to some specific task.[40] This demanding routine barely left time to clear fresh land for future plantings or to cut wood for fences and fuel.

This onerous production schedule affected eighteenth-century planter culture in several significant ways. First, the staple became the arbiter of time, of work and play. The tobacco calendar discouraged communal activities. It contained no clear culmination, no point at which the producer could relax and enjoy the fruits of his labor.[41] Even cutting tobacco could not be termed a genuine harvest. It never generated autumn festivals, for curing followed hard upon cutting. One task was as important as the other. Recreational activities—cockfights and horse races, for example—had to be scheduled around the cultivation of tobacco, fit somehow into the established work routine. It is not surprising that after George Washington dropped the cultivation of tobacco for that of wheat, he discovered that he had more time for fox hunting, his favorite pastime. As one of his biographers explains, wheat altered the pace of Washington's life, for in this type of agriculture, "The ground was plowed; the grain was planted; after that, nothing need to be done or could be done, except keep livestock away, until harvest."[42]

39. Ibid., 111.

40. Parkinson, *Tour in America*, II, 415–16. See also Freeman, *Washington*, III, 194–96.

41. For an analysis of a different agricultural work routine, see Steward et al., *People of Puerto Rico*, 199–200.

42. Freeman, *Washington*, III, 196.

Second, the staple promoted social cohesion. This claim appears paradoxical, for how could a crop that restricted communal activities, that heightened the planter's autonomy, generate a sense of common identity and purpose? The answer lies in a shared work process. The production of tobacco provided highly individualistic planters with a body of common rules and assumptions that helped bind them together. As one labored in the fields, whatever the time of year, one knew that people on other plantations were engaged in the same agricultural routine. A planter did not actually have to see other men at work to know what they were doing.

This shared framework of labor experience made distant, often unrelated planters appear less alien than they would have had they been urban artisans or cultivators of other crops. The tobacco production schedule became a kind of secular litany, and at the drop of a hat, planters recited the steps necessary to transform seeds into marketable leaves. The fabric of rules tied an individual not only to his neighbors but also to his predecessors. Since time out of mind— or so it must have seemed—Virginians had followed the same calendar, and thus the very process of cultivating tobacco placed a man within a tradition as old as the colony itself. Predictably, one visitor discovered that "the planters never go out of the beaten road, but do just as their fathers did."[43] Social cohesion was a product of common agricultural assumptions, shared symbols, and collective judgments. Indeed, it was out of these strands of tradition, rules, and judgment that the staple planters of tidewater Virginia created a distinct culture.

Tobacco as Source of Meaning

Because tobacco very powerfully shaped the patterns of everyday work experience, the plant acquired considerable symbolic importance. Indeed, its emblematic qualities were central to the development of a tobacco mentality. On one level, the dominant staple reflected the entire social order. It was synonymous with Virginia, and when one mentioned tobacco in the Anglo-Saxon world of the eighteenth century, one inevitably evoked images of wealthy planters, slave laborers, and great houses. On a second level, the crop came to represent the individuals who cultivated it. In itself tobacco was culturally neutral, but in the absence of an adequate circulating currency, it provided Virginians with a means to forge a public identity, a mechanism for placing people into a generally accepted hier-

43. *American Husbandry,* ed. Carman, 160. For an interesting discussion of the culture of agriculture in the contemporary United States, see Mark Kramer, *Three Farms: Making Milk, Meat and Money from the American Soil* (Boston, 1980), 3–107.

archy. In both cases, the *colonial* and the *individual,* tobacco was the measure of the people who produced it.

By the middle of the eighteenth century, Virginia society and the cultivation of tobacco were generally regarded as being synonymous. To be sure, the colonists grew other crops, such as corn, but these plants never shared tobacco's prominence. According to one Frenchman who visited Virginia in 1765, "the produce of the Soil is hemp, Indian Corn, flax, silk, Cotton and great quantity of wild grapes, but tobacco is *the* staple Commodity of virginia [*sic*]."[44] The evidence in support of this observation was overwhelming. The leaf appeared to be ubiquitous. One encountered it growing on the small farms scattered along the colony's back roads, on the vast fields of the great riverfront plantations, on the wharves near the public warehouses. It dominated conversation in Williamsburg and Fredericksburg. No wonder an English traveler labeled tobacco "the grand staple of Virginia."[45] Robert Beverley, a Tidewater planter who avoided extravagant language, called tobacco simply "our staple."[46]

Beverly took it for granted that Virginians—at least all those he cared to know—relied on this crop. It defined their lives. In fact, being a Virginian before the American Revolution meant putting out hills of tobacco every spring. This connection between tobacco and society struck some outsiders as excessive, but they never questioned the plant's importance. "The Virginians," observed Andrew Burnaby in 1760, "are content if they can but live from day to day; they confine themselves almost entirely to the cultivation of tobacco; and if they have but enough of this to pay their merchants in London, and to provide for their pleasures, they are satisfied, and desire nothing more."[47]

The colonists, of course, saw nothing unusual about the relation between this plant and their society. They assumed that tobacco had always had a special symbolic significance in Virginia. Indeed, the staple's long history made it plausible, even self-evident, that the fortunes of the plant were inseparably bound up with the progress of the colony itself. The culture and its staple were one, and time only increased the intensity of the identification. Tatham provided an example of this turn of mind. While he was conducting research in seventeenth-century documents related to the regulation of the tobacco trade, he was suddenly overwhelmed by an awareness of the

44. "Journal of a French Traveller in the Colonies, 1765," pt. 1, *American Historical Review* 26 (1920–21): 743 (emphasis added).

45. Symth, *Tour,* I, 32–33.

46. Robert Beverley to John Bland, 1764, Beverley Letter Book, 1761–1793, Library of Congress, Washington, D.C.

47. Burnaby, *Travels,* 717.

centrality of tobacco in the colony's development. "We learn from these laws," he declared, "how much the subject of this staple was interwoven in the spirit of the times; and how nearly the history of the tobacco plant is allied to the chronology of an extensive and flourishing country, whose measures contribute greatly . . . to give a tone to the affairs of the American union."[48] Tatham may have exaggerated, but for Virginians who believed that tobacco possessed important emblematic qualities, it was not easy to imagine the colony without the staple.

The close identification with the crop also operated on a personal level. In colonial Virginia, tobacco provided a medium—a cultural ether—within which the planter negotiated a public reputation, a sense of self-worth as an agricultural producer. In part, the deep ties between the Virginia planter and the staple resulted from the peculiar characteristics of tobacco. As we have seen, its cultivation required personal attention; at every stage the planter made crucial judgments about the crop's development. His attention throughout the year was focused not on whole fields or on specific plants but on individual leaves. According to Fernando Ortiz, a modern Cuban anthropologist, "This is why tobacco-raising is such a meticulous affair, in contrast to [sugar] cane, which demands little attention. The tobacco-grower has to tend his tobacco . . . leaf by leaf. . . . The ideal of the tobacco man . . . is distinction, for his product to be in a class by itself, the best."[49] The Virginia planters naturally insisted on being present at every step of the process, and however boring life on the isolated plantations may have seemed, they seldom were in a position to become absentee owners. Growing tobacco was a personal challenge.

Of course, the planters recognized that their presence did not in itself guarantee success. Many aspects of tobacco cultivation were beyond their control. Regardless of his skills, the planter still had to reckon with luck, with chance factors like pests and weather that undermined the best-laid plans. Such "accidents," as Virginians sometimes called them, were an inescapable part of farming. In 1768 Henry Fitzhugh, a wealthy planter of northen Virginia, encountered

48. Tatham, *Historical and Practical Essay,* 184. The persistence of a distinctive culture also struck the marquis de Chastellux. During a visit to Virginia, Chastellux noted, "The Virginians differ essentially from the inhabitants to the north and eastward . . . not only in the nature of their climate, that of their soil, and the objects of cultivation peculiar to it, but in that indelible character which is imprinted on every nation at the moment of its origins, and which by perpetuating itself from generation to generation justifies the following great principles, that *everything which is, partakes of that which had been.*" *Travels in North America, 1780–1782* (Dublin, 1787), II, 174–75.

49. Fernando Ortiz Fernandez, *Cuban Counterpoint: Tobacco and Sugar* (New York, 1947), 24.

a series of misfortunes in making a crop. In words that other Virginians might have written just as well, he described his reverses. "We have had so cold & dry a Summer," Fitzhugh recounted, "that nothing coud grow, & abt the middle of Augt we had a very violent Rain which drowned a great deal of tobo on low grounds, & caused that on the high land to spot very much." An early frost, "destroyed a great deal of tobo in the Backwoods."[50] In such a situation the planter felt helpless. Landon Carter knew this sensation. In 1771 he predicted that he would bring in a fine crop. But then came a "terrible dry spell," and the soil on his plantation baked "into a mere solid Mass." Carter responded to these adverse conditions as best he could, but his efforts were in vain. *Fortuna* had won. "Had I not been honestly sensible that no care had been wanting nor diligence neglected," Carter confided to his diary, "I should be uneasy more than I am; but as I have nothing of this sort to accuse myself with, I must and do submit."[51]

In fact, however, Carter and his contemporaries were unwilling to submit. Fatalism was foreign to their outlook. Instead, they believed in the existence of an agricultural *virtù,* a set of personal attributes that ultimately determined the quality of a man's crop. This sense of power—and, of course, responsibility—is the reason why colonial planters came to regard their tobacco as an extension of self. To be sure, "accidents" might ruin a crop or two, but over the long haul there was no explanation other than incompetence why an individual could not produce good tobacco. William Nelson responded almost arrogantly to an English merchant who suggested in 1770 that the soil of Virginia was too exhausted to make a fine export leaf. "You make me smile," Nelson lectured, "when you talk of the Lands being too much worn & impoversh'd to bring good Tobo. . . . I know that a skillful Planter can make it fine from any Land, it being his Part & Interest to improve any that he finds worn or wearing out."[52]

Landon Carter shared Nelson's assumptions. When a young man in his neighborhood—an overseer, no less—announced that *only* the "accident of the rains" could account for Carter's handsome tobacco crop, Carter exploded. It was management that made the difference. He expressed gratitude for "the assistance of heaven" but nevertheless insisted that his superior skills as a planter brought suc-

50. Henry Fitzhugh to Steuart and Campbell, 28 June and 20 October 1768, Henry Fitzhugh Papers, Manuscript Division, William R. Perkins Library, Duke University, Durham, N.C. Permission to quote from this collection was granted by the Perkins Library, Duke University.

51. Entry of 16 August 1771, in Greene, ed., *Diary of Landon Carter,* II, 614.

52. William Nelson to Samuel Athawes, 26 July 1770, Nelson Letter Book, Colonial Williamsburg, Inc., Research Center, microfilm.

cess. "This I assert," Carter fumed, "if our July had not been so drye and hot . . . *My management* would have appeared more conspicuous than that of others; for I dare bet anything that none of the Tobacco tended as they have done can be [as] thick as mine."[53]

The highest praise one could bestow on a Virginia planter was to call him "crop master," a public recognition of agricultural excellence. Many aspired to this rank, but success proved elusive. One contemporary observed that growing tobacco was "an art, that every planter thinks he is proficient in, but which few rightly understand." Tatham defined the qualities that were expected of a man who held this title. A master cultivated his own "estate." An absentee could never acquire the requisite knowledge; the demands of the work schedule were too heavy. According to Tatham, the crop master "understands the whole process of the culture, and gives instructions concerning the various operations, though perhaps he does not attend personally to their execution." A crop master demonstrated an ability to make quick, accurate judgments about each stage of production. Possession of these characteristics transformed the ordinary planter into a "lord of the soil."[54]

Tatham knew what he was writing about. Eighteenth-century planters worked hard at being—or at least appearing to be—proficient managers. Richard Corbin, for example, instructed an assistant, "Let me be acquainted with every incident that happens & Let me have timely notice of everything that is wanted, that it may be provided."[55] If nothing else, the person who received these orders could assume that his employer was a legitimate crop master.

Virginians quickly learned which planters possessed superior judgment, and at critical points in the production process, they turned to crop masters for advice. Cutting the tobacco was such a time. Writers like Tatham provided inexperienced planters with general descriptions of ripe leaves and changes in color and thickness, but books somehow never conveyed adequate information. In frustration, Tatham declared that ripening is "easier to understand than to express." "It is a point," he concluded, "on which I would not trust my own experience without consulting some able crop-master in the neighbourhood."[56]

It was certainly wiser to call on a local expert than to trust one's luck. Carter preached this lesson to anyone who bothered to listen.

---

53. Entry of 8 September 1770, in Greene, ed., *Diary of Landon Carter,* I, 482 (emphasis added).
54. Tatham, *Historical and Practical Essay,* 100; *American Museum,* June 1789, p. 537.
55. "Instructions," in *Plantation and Frontier,* ed. Phillips, I, 111.
56. Tatham, *Historical and Practical Essay,* 23–24.

In 1770 John Purcell, "master of the Patrol in this neck," chased a runaway slave into a curing barn belonging to one of Carter's neighbors and discovered, among other things, that the planter's tobacco was "dung" rotten. Carter immediately ascribed the condition of the crop to poor personal judgment. The plants had been "cut down not half ripe and of course too thin to stand the sweat of the house. Thus is 9/10 of the tobacco spoilt every year."[57] The planter stood twice condemned. He not only was an incompetent producer but also had failed to consult a crop master.

Even the names given to the various kinds of tobacco testified to the close personal relation between the planter and his crop. People unfamiliar with the cultivation of this staple assumed that colonial Virginians grew only two varieties, Oronoko and sweet scented. While this information may have been technically correct, Virginians recognized finer distinctions. "Question a planter on the subject," one man explained, "and he will tell you that he cultivates such or such a kind: as, for example 'Colonel Carter's sort, John Cole's sort,' or some other leading crop master."[58] Sometimes visitors reported finding different "species . . . with names peculiar to the situation, settlement, and neighborhoods, wherein they are produced," but on closer inspection one usually discovered that an excellent local tobacco was identified with a specific planter.[59] This practice was certainly prevalent along the lower York River. The planters in this area claimed that they produced the best leaf in the entire Chesapeake region. But according to Andrew Burnaby, the very best York crops came from the fields of Col. Edward Digges. Indeed, Digges enjoyed a reputation for consistent quality that French wine makers would have envied.[60] Digges's tobacco "is in such high estimation that . . . [he] puts upon every hogshead in which it is packed, the initials of his name; and it is from thence called the E.D. tobacco, and sells for a proportionally higher price."[61]

The centrality of tobacco in the lives of these men spawned a curious system of social ranking, one strikingly different from that normally associated with modern industrial societies. The planter's self-esteem depended—in part, at least—upon the quality of his tobacco. This measure, of course, was highly subjective. It left him extraor-

57. Entry of 11 September 1770, in Greene, ed., *Diary of Landon Carter,* I, 487.

58. Tatham, *Historical and Practical Essay,* 4–5.   59. Smyth, *Tour,* II, 130.

60. The comparison between these two crops is instructive. Both involved highly personalized agricultural processes, and even after the product left the vineyard or plantation, it bore the name of a specific individual. His honor was at stake wherever people drank wine or inspected tobacco leaves. See Leo A. Loubère, *The Red and the White: A History of Wine in France and Italy in the Nineteenth Century* (Albany, N.Y., 1978).

61. Burnaby, *Travels,* 706–7; "Journal of a French Traveller," 743.

dinarily vulnerable to the opinion of other men. However excellent a person regarded his own crop as being, a sharp-eyed critic could always find flaws in it. Virginians worried about these negative judgments and, as we shall see, took them quite personally. Indeed, the planters seem to have cultivated tobacco as much to gain the respect of merchants and neighbors—in other words, of people with whom they maintained regular face-to-face contacts—as to please the anonymous chewers, smokers, and snuffers who ultimately purchased the staple in Europe.

Even Virginians whose crops were not so renowned as those of Edward Digges took pride in making outstanding tobacco. In fact, the planter's self-respect was so tightly bound up with the quality of his tobacco that it was sometimes difficult to discern whether a man's reputation or his tobacco was being shipped to market. Henry Fitzhugh staked his honor on twelve hogsheads of sweet-scented tobacco. "It was made on the plantation [where I] live," he informed a British merchant, "& therefore as I saw to the whole man[age]ment of it my self [I] can with authority reco[m]mend it to be exceeding good."[62] Philip Ludwell Lee, Richard Henry's brother, modestly called the crop produced at Stratford in 1771 "as fine as ever was made."[63] William Nelson wrote a sharp note in 1766 to a merchant who seemed unappreciative of having received some of "*my* Hanovers stem'd Tobo."[64] The emphasis was on the planter's skill and judgment, on his personal involvement with production. In 1772 Robert Beverley predicted that his plantation would not produce a large crop, but he consoled himself with the thought "that the Quality is remarkably fine." Certainly, there was nothing about the appearance or taste of these leaves that embarrassed Beverley in front of his censorious neighbor and future father-in-law, Landon Carter.[65]

If Virginia planters had been less intimately involved in production, they might not have been so sensitive to what other men said about their tobacco. But this was not the case. Within this particular agrarian culture, planters calculated not only their own standing but also that of their competitors by the appearance of fully cured tobacco leaves. "I know in this neighbourhood," Carter declared, "people are very fond of speaking meanly of their neighbour's Crops and I am certain mine has been so characterised." Fortunately for Carter, as he rode about the Northern Neck gratuitously inspecting other men's

62. Henry Fitzhugh to James Buchanan, n.d., Henry Fitzhugh Papers.

63. Philip Ludwell Lee to William Lee, 25 July 1771. Lee Family Papers, Mssl. L51, f. 252.

64. William Nelson to James Gildart, 26 July 1766, Nelson Letter Book (emphasis added).

65. Robert Beverley to [?], 27 December 1762, Beverley Letter Book.

tobacco, he did not "see any so good [as mine]," and he even ven-
tured "a wager with the best of them both as to quantity and quality."[66] Robert Beverley also kept an eye on his neighbors and in 1774
was able to recommend one of them to a British correspondent
because "He is thought to make very good Tobacco."[67] Richard Mason
was not such a man. According to George Mason, the colony's famed
constitutional theorist, "Dick's" failure as a planter called into question his moral character. After all, he "handled his Tobacco in so
careless & slovenly a Manner that more than half of it was rotten, &
even the best of it . . . will run some Risque at the Warehouse."[68]

Not surprisingly, the price they received for their tobacco obsessed
colonial planters. The sources of this preoccupation were cultural as
well as economic. To be sure, men like Carter and Lee strove to
maintain a favorable balance with the British merchant houses. They
hated debt. Nevertheless, they were also concerned with the judgment of other planters. Price provided a reasonably unambiguous
measure of the worth of a man's tobacco, its quality; and in this sense
a high return validated a person's claim as crop master. Historians
who described these Virginians solely as agricultural capitalists eager
to maximize income miss a crucial aspect of the tobacco mentality.
These planters competed in the market not only for pounds and
pence but also for honor and reputation.[69]

66. Greene, ed., *Diary of Landon Carter,* I, 474.
67. Robert Beverley to Samuel Athawes, 1774, Beverley Letter Book.
68. Robert A. Rutland, ed., *The Papers of George Mason, 1725–1792* (Chapel Hill, 1970),
I, 57.
69. It is important not to be misunderstood on this point. I am not arguing that the
planters were indifferent to profits or that they were incapable of responding to economic incentives. Obviously, they grew tobacco to make money, and, judging from some
correspondence from this period, they were quite upset when they failed to obtain a
price that they had anticipated. In 1766, for example, William Beverley explained to an
English merchant, John Bland, "You must be sensible, it is my Duty to Act in such a
Manner as may be most conducive to my Interest, as far as is consistent with Integrity &
Honour, if therefore I find any Commodity of mine in lower esteem with one Man than
another, I shall certainly be Justifiable in making Choice of that person who entertains
the best opinion of it." 27 March 1766, Beverley Letter Book. Beverley sounds like a
hard-nosed businessman, the kind of clever entrepreneur who agricultural economists
tell us inhabits rural America.
I believe, however, that such considerations governed the planters' behavior only in
part. Their thinking was not unlike that of the Balinese peasants that Clifford Geertz
observed placing bets on fighting cocks. "This [symbolic analysis]," Geertz declared, "I
must stress immediately, is *not* to say that the money does not matter, or that the Balinese
is no more concerned about losing five hundred ringgits than fifteen. Such a conclusion
would be absurd. It is because money *does,* in this hardly unmaterialistic society, matter
and matter very much that the more of it one risks, the more of a lot of other things,
such as one's pride, one's poise, one's dispassion, one's masculinity, one also risks, again
only momentarily but again very publicly as well." *The Interpretation of Cultures: Selected
Essay* (New York, 1973), 433–34. And it was precisely because tobacco mattered in Virginia society so very much that it became in the eye of the major producers a measure
of self, a source of meaningful society identity, as well as a means to maintain a high
standard of living.

Rumors of price spread rapidly. Whenever Virginians congregated, they traded information about the local market, and while each planter conducted his business in private, everyone seemed to know exactly how much money he had received. These gatherings filled Virginians with considerable anxiety. They wanted to discover how well other producers had done, to establish an index by which they could measure their own performance. On the other hand, to learn that one had settled for a lower price than that offered to competing planters in the area was galling. It amounted to a public loss of face. Robert ("King") Carter, the wealthiest Virginian of his generation, could not bear the thought of losing out to his neighbors. "In discourse with Colonel Byrd, Mr. Armistead, and a great many others," Carter lectured an English merchant, "I understand you had sold their tobacco . . . at good rates. I cannot allow myself to come behind any of these gentlemen in the planter's trade."[70] Carter assumed not only that the news of his sales circulated widely but also that low returns compromised his standing within the community of planters.

Isaac Giberne understood such matters. Although this Anglican parson was not a typical Northern Neck planter, he was very much involved in the local tobacco culture. In 1773 he wrote to William Lee, a former neighbor who was then trying to establish himself as a London tobacco merchant. "In yours of 25th Jany. last," Giberne observed, "you say you can only promise me *Neighbour's Fare* for my Tobaccos last year." That agreement Giberne enthusiastically accepted, but he warned, "Pray remember my good Friend, that as Colo. Frans. Lee is literally and almost my next door neighbour, that my sales do not fall short of his; otherwise your promise fails, as I shall be content in *the Equity* of *his* price, let it be what it will."[71] At stake was Giberne's honor, and, as William Lee must have learned as a boy in Virginia, planters kept no secrets about tobacco prices.

Criticism of a man's tobacco, however tactfully phrased, set off a frenzy of self-examination. Whenever planters received a low price, for example, they assumed that somehow they must be at fault. Their reaction was almost reflective. The problem, they reasoned, must have been in production, in the management of the labor force—in other words, in themselves—and they usually accepted responsibility

70. Louis B. Wright, ed., *Letters of Robert Carter, 1720–1727: The Commercial Interests of a Virginia Gentleman* (San Marino, Calif., 1940), 93–94.

71. Worthington Chauncey Ford, ed., *Letters of William Lee* (Brooklyn, 1891), I, 74. In another part of the same letter (8 July 1773), Giberne declared, "I must say I expected something more than my proceeds for the Tobaccos . . . which went in Walker. Mr. Russell far exceeded those sales. Nor can I understand the difference you mention of the north side of Rappahannock Tobacco. My overseers at Home and at the Glebe, are reckon'd neat Planters, and it is *generally* allow'd our Tobaccos are more valuable than the Potomack; and yet we get no better prices, or scarcely so good" (I, 73).

for the poor showing of their tobacco in the British market. In 1766 the London firm of Steuart and Campbell notified Henry Fitzhugh that some sixty hogsheads of his "own Crop sold much lower" than had the "rent" tobacco made by Fitzhugh's tenants. This was extremely embarrassing. The questionable hogsheads displayed his personal seal, "HF," and he had expected they would "all have sold . . . at a very highprice." The problem was in the curing. "You say," Fitzhugh declared, "the tobo was very good, & neatly handled but many hhds very much effected with Smoke." This malodorous quality could not have been avoided, the planter argued, since without fires in the unusually moist curing barns, the entire crop would have rotted. Fitzhugh promised to do better next time.[72] Robert Beverley received so many complaints about his early crops that he began to doubt whether he would ever become a master grower. Each year he tried to improve the quality of his leaves, until in 1765 he wrote to England in frustration, "I don't think it necessary for a Man to serve his whole life an apprenticeship."[73]

In a sense, the planters were too caught up in an endless cycle of production, too blinded by the tobacco mentality, to become fully successful capitalists. They were trapped by the assumptions of a staple culture. There seems no other plausible explanation for their extraordinary naiveté about international market procedures.[74] One

72. Henry Fitzhugh to Steuart and Campbell, 18 February 1766, Henry Fitzhugh Papers.

73. Robert Beverley to Edward and Samuel Athawes, 21 September 1765, Beverley Letter Book.

74. Economic historians discovered—with evident surprise—that eighteenth-century planters actually knew very little about the subtleties of the English tobacco market. Aubrey C. Land wrote, for example, "Small producers or great, all were bound to the tobacco market, whose workings few understood well and almost none perfectly. Many honest planters regarded the marketing mechanism with suspicion and professed to see tobacco production as a kind of bondage to a shadowy, somewhat sinister group of merchants across the water." Land, "Economic Behavior in a Planting Society," 474. In support of this generalization, Land cites Samuel M. Rosenblatt's fine essay on the London consignment firm of John Norton and Sons. As Rosenblatt explains, tobacco merchants regularly received a "drawback," or return, on certain customs duties paid on tobacco reexported from England. Some of this money should have been credited to the planters against whom all duties and fees were charged, but most Virginians possessed only the vaguest comprehension of these procedures. In this case, what they did not know *did* hurt them, for the drawbacks generated fairly large sums. "The situation as it related to ready cash, discount, and interest, was very involved," Rosenblatt declares. "While there can be little question of the merchants' awareness of the profit that came to them when they had ready money . . . the great body of planters were not so alert. Some of those who knew of this advantage did not realize its magnitude." Even such successful planter-merchants in Virginia as Nathaniel Littleton Savage and William Nelson seemed uncertain how the system operated, and, as Rosenblatt concludes, "If William Nelson, a leading mercantile and political figure in the colony, was so poorly informed about the complexities of English customs procedures, it stands to reason that other less business-oriented Virginians were even more uninformed." Rosenblatt, "The Significance of Credit in the Tobacco Consignment Trade: A Study of John Norton &

experienced Virginia merchant complained that the planters held "wild & chimerical notions" about price-setting mechanisms.[75] Indeed, men who exercised the closest scrutiny over cutting and curing seem to have been mystified about what happened to their tobacco once it left America. They speculated about factors of supply and demand, but about commercial practices that ate into their profits, they remained ignorant. In 1774, for example, Fitzhugh confessed to an English merchant with whom he had dealt for more than a decade, "I really do not understand your manner of keeping my Interest Act [Account]."[76]

Two Virginians, Landon Carter and George Washington, left particularly vivid insights into the tobacco culture, especially into the producer's pursuit of honor and reputation through his crops. Like Washington, Carter kept a diary. The master of Sabine Hall, a large plantation located on the Rappahannock River, took considerable pride in his ability to grow quality tobacco. In late September 1770—after most of his plants had been cut and carried to the curing barns—he congratulated himself. "By being carefull and early in topping, worming and suckering," Carter wrote, ". . . I have produced I believe as to goodness as fine tobacco as ever was seen[,] And as to quantity very large."[77]

Contemporaries learned to play upon Carter's vanity. One clever associate who came to Sabine Hall looking for scarce planking took care to accompany his request with the observation that Carter's tobacco was "by far the thickest he had ever seen."[78] Such comments obviously pleased Carter, and he recorded every fulsome word in his diary. He could hardly contain his satisfaction when "some Gentlemen" who sat on the county court with him expressed admiration for Carter's fine crop. "One of them," Carter noted, "ignorantly was

---

Sons, 1768–1775," *William and Mary Quarterly*, 3d ser., 19 (1962): 390–94. Since so many of the colony's great planters had been educated in England, one cannot convincingly argue that they lacked an opportunity to learn more about the drawbacks.

75. Francis Jerdone to Alexander Speirs and Hugh Brown, 11 June 1759, Francis Jerdone Papers, College of William and Mary Library, Williamsburg, Va. William Nelson expressed amazement at the high prices that Scottish traders gave for Virginia tobacco. He could not understand how they carried on their business and suspected that they knew something about the mysteries of commerce that even the English merchants did not comprehend. He explained to Edward and Samuel Athawes, two experienced London merchants, "Depend upon [it], my Friend, they [the Scots] have some secrets in the Tobo. Trade, that you & I are unacquainted with, or they could not give such prices here & carry all before them as they do." 12 August 1767, Nelson Letter Book. See also entry of 20 May 1774, in Greene, ed., *Diary of London Carter*, II, 813.

76. Henry Fitzhugh to Steuart and Campbell, 29 September 1766; Fitzhugh to Campbell, 5 December 1774, Henry Fitzhugh Papers.

77. Entry of 23 September 1770, in Greene, ed., *Diary of Landon Carter*, I, 501.

78. Entry of 8 September 1770, ibid., 482.

going to seperate [*sic*] the leaf immagining it had been double."[79]
Incidents like these reaffirmed Carter's reputation as an outstanding
manager, a skillful judge of production; and while he savored even
the slightest praise from neighbors, he showed almost no interest in
how his hogsheads were marketed in England. He wanted direct,
immediate confirmation of high standing in the agrarian community.

A bizarre exchange with a British merchant in 1774 revealed the
extent to which Carter's self-esteem was bound up with his tobacco.
The merchant accused Carter of exporting a low-grade leaf, and to
support this claim, he returned a sample of the planter's latest crop.
The offending leaves "rolled up in blue paper" mortified Carter. He
examined the leaves and reported they "smelt very fine." Still, he
was uneasy. Carter turned to members of his family. "Even my
daughter," the planter observed, ". . . praised it." But her testimony
failed to reassure the master of Sabine Hall. The more he stared at
the contents of the blue package, the more anxious he became. "I do
suppose by a thousand ways I should have been ashamed of bad
tobacco and had thought it must be changed; but I see it is according
to my home method of managements and it is very fine." To be sure,
the tobacco was "a trifle dusty," but Carter did not think its low quality warranted humiliation. Finally, unable to contain his shame and
doubt any longer, Carter bit into the sample. "I took some of it to
chew. It is very fine," he repeated, "and [I] shall tie up the rest; for
I love a good quid."[80] Few planters would have gone to such lengths
to defend their product, but most surely would have understood
why Carter was so upset.

Robert Wormeley Carter certainly understood. Landon's son
played upon his father's pride, and in so doing revealed much about
the workings of the tobacco mentality. Landon desperately craved
Robert Wormeley's respect. Next to his son, neither merchants nor
neighbors mattered, but for complex reasons, the two men constantly quarreled.[81] Sometimes tensions between them became
unbearable and exploded in a torrent of mutual abuse and criticism.
Landon upbraided Robert Wormeley—by the 1770s a middle-aged
planter—for sloth, gambling, but most of all for filial ingratitude. In
his turn, Robert Wormeley accused his father of producing medio-
cre tobacco. The charge deeply wounded the senior Carter. Within
this particular agricultural society such behavior represented the
height of disrespect, for both men fully understood the symbolic role
that tobacco played in their culture.

79. Entry of 6 September 1770, ibid., 480.
80. Entry of 21 May 1774, ibid., II, 831–14.   81. Ibid., I, 48–61.

In July 1770 Robert Wormeley visited Sabine Hall and immediately began to point out imperfections in the way Landon cultivated his crop. Why, the father asked, did the tobacco plants now ripening in the fields not meet his son's expectations: "I was told by the most insolent as well as most imprudent person amongst men (my son) That was because I would follow *my own way.*" Landon embraced martyrdom. The "scoundrel [was] determined to abuse his father," and the plantation tour continued. Landon had broken the soil improperly; his judgment on other aspects of production was suspect. The senior Carter held his tongue, but in his diary he vented his emotion. "He has not seen my estate this whole year," Landon cried, "but in Passing by, and yet he will find fault because sworn to do it with his father. If I ask him why richer lands in my neighborhood don't exceed me in cropping [in quantity], Then I am answered to make better tobacco."[82] On other occasions, Robert Wormeley was less censorious, but he knew how to defend himself against his father's barbs.[83] He could not directly insult the patriarch of Sabine Hall. By calling Landon's tobacco management into question, however, he accomplished the same end.

Like Landon Carter, George Washington assumed that a man's reputation was only as good as the tobacco he grew. After the conclusion of the French and Indian War in Virginia (by late 1758 the war with France no longer threatened the colony's frontier), Washington returned to Mount Vernon determined to become a successful planter. At this point, in 1759, it did not occur to him to cultivate another staple. Virginians grew tobacco, and he saw no reason to doubt that he could make a quality leaf. In 1762 he offered an overseer a monetary incentive to bring in a better crop than normal because of the "well known intention of the said George Washington to have his tobacco made and managed in the best and neatest manner which in some manner lessens the quantity."[84] To whom Washington's intentions were well known was not spelled out in this agreement, but he probably realized that his Northern Neck neighbors—the Lees, Fitzhughs, and Carters—kept a sharp watch over his progress as a planter.

The results humiliated Washington. He was a proud man, and no matter how diligently he worked the stubborn fields of Mount Vernon, he could not produce the kind of quality leaves that one saw on the plantations of the James, Rappahannock, and York rivers. In his own eyes, the crucial measure was price. However hard he tried, he

82. Entry of 6 July 1770, ibid., 436–37 (emphasis added).
83. For example, see ibid., I, 482; II, 615.
84. Cited in Freeman, *Washington,* III, 81.

still received lower returns than did his friends and neighbors. In bitter frustration, Washington wrote to an English merchant complaining, "I am at a loss to conceive the Reason why Mr. Wormeleys, and indeed some other Gentlemen's Tobaccos should sell at 12d last year and mine . . . only fetch 11½." Washington knew that the results of his sales were no secret. These much publicly discussed prices provided an index to his skills as a producer, and it was with the conventions of Virginia culture in mind that he protested, "Certain I am no Person in Virginia takes more pains to make their Tobo. fine than I do and tis hard then I should not be well rewarded for it."[85]

Hard indeed. Frustration turned to depression. In 1762 Washington wrote painfully of his own failure as a planter. "I confess," he scribbled, "it [tobacco cultivation] to be an Art beyond my skill, to succeed in making good Tobo. as I have used my utmost endeavours for that purpose this two or 3 years past; and am once again urged to express my surprise at finding that I do not partake of the best prices that are going."[86] At this point in his life, Washington was a captive of the tobacco mentality. He could have turned aggressively to other crops in the early 1760s, but to have done so would have made him less a Virginian. It would have cut him off from the only source of public esteem other than soldiering that he had ever known.

Frustration eventually gave way to anger. Throughout his long military and political career, Washington's self-control impressed contemporaries. He sometimes seemed incapable of showing passion of any sort. But in September 1765 his pitiful tobacco sparked a remarkable outburst. He reminded an English correspondent, Robert Cary, that the price he had obtained for his tobacco was "worse than many of my Acquaintances upon this River, Potomack." The comments that he imagined men were whispering behind his back were too much for Washington to bear. "Can it be otherwise . . . a little mortifying than to find, that we, who raise none but Sweet-scented Tobacco, and endeavour I may venture to add, to be careful in the management of it . . . ," he asked rhetorically, "should meet with such unprofitable returns? Surely I may answer No!"[87] These were words for Patrick Henry, not for the reserved Washington. He decided that if he could not excel at the planter's trade, not become a tobacco crop master, then he would shift his attention to a different plant. It is essential to recognize how the decision was made. He began with the traditional culture. For a decade he persisted. Wash-

---

85. George Washington to Robert Cary and Company, 3 April 1761, in *The Writings of George Washington*, ed. John C. Fitzpatrick (Washington, D.C., 1931–44), II, 357.
86. Ibid., 378 (28 May 1762).   87. Ibid., 427–28 (20 September 1765).

ington was not drawn into the wheat market, because he carefully calculated that grain would bring increased profits. Rather, he was forced out of the tobacco market.

Virginians, then, were planters. However much political theory they had read, however familiar they were with the writings of John Locke or Francis Hutcheson, however much time they spent impressing one another in Williamsburg, they remained products of a regional agrarian culture. Tobacco shaped their society and defined their place within it. From the perspective of a cultural anthropologist, the plant possessed immense symbolic significance for the planters and their families. By the middle of the eighteenth century, this staple had been tightly woven into the fabric of the colonists' everyday life; it gave meaning to their experience. One would predict, therefore, that any alteration in the traditional relation between planter and tobacco would have far-reaching, even revolutionary, implications for the entire society.[88]

Crisis of Self-Perception: Tobacco and Wheat

Sometime in the 1760s—an exact date is impossible to establish— Northern Neck planters began to discuss tobacco in a way they had not done before. Their comments betrayed doubts about the future of their staple and, by extension, about a world of symbols associated with tobacco. "I am afraid," Robert Beverley declared in 1764, "we shall not gain much Advantage by the Cultivation of Tobacco."[89] He exaggerated, but a growing number of Virginians shared this anxiety. Arthur Lee, a colonist who had gained a broader perspective on the planters' problems from his experiences in England and Scotland, counseled his brother Richard Henry: "Tobacco, your present staple, seems to be [a] very precarious commodity."[90]

A major source of the Virginians' uneasiness was the low price that they received for their tobacco. To be sure, they aspired to produce a quality leaf, but suddenly none of the planters seemed to be doing very well. Persons who prided themselves on having mastered the cultivation of this crop found themselves slipping ever deeper into debt. The agricultural skills they had acquired, the ability to judge

88. On this point, see Marc Engal and Joseph A. Ernst, "An Economic Interpretation of the American Revolution," *William and Mary Quarterly*, 3d ser., 29 (1972): 3–32. They observe, on p. 9, "The forward part played by the Northern Neck of Virginia in pushing that colony toward Independence demands an investigation of colonial society far beyond treatises on whig ideologies, just as the presentation of America as a nation of prosperous middle-class farmers overlooks a diversity of sharply differing regional economies."

89. Robert Beverley to William Hunter, 5 March 1764, Beverley Letter Book.

90. Arthur Lee to [Richard Henry Lee], 1763, *Lee Family Papers, 1742–1795*, ed. Paul P. Hoffman, 8 reels (Charlottesville, 1966), reel 1.

the precise moment when to cut or transplant—these attributes were incapable of restoring the expansive prosperity that William Byrd II and Robert ("King") Carter had enjoyed. "For my part," George Braxton grumbled in 1756, "I get such small prizes [prices?] for my Tobacco that I would make a Tryal of any commodity rather than wear my Negroes out in making and cultivating a worthless weed."[91]

For some planters of the Northern Neck, the state of the colony's agriculture created genuine despair. Their culture seemed to have been turned on its head by forces thoroughly beyond their control. Instead of reinforcing personal independence, tobacco generated staggering debt and, worse, a debilitating sense of obligation to distant merchants. To be sure, earlier Virginians had experienced debt, but before the 1760s few men saw the situation as hopeless.[92]

For planters like Carter, Washington, and Lee, the very condition of being financially bound to a British firm compromised individual freedom. They felt trapped, desperate. In 1766 an anonymous Virginian declared with cool matter-of-factness, "That this colony is in a declining State, or, I may rather say on the Brink of Destruction, I fear is too evident to the most superficial Observer, to need any arguments to prove."[93] The writer referred not to a specific act of Parliament but to a pervasive crisis of confidence that swept the commonwealth. Beverley expressed the same thought more poignantly. In 1764 he foresaw little "Possibility of this wretched Country [Virginia] (as it certainly is in its Present situation) once more moveing upon its own Leggs—But I dredd very much from the Apearances of this Day that it will be condemned forever to a state of Vasalage & Dependence."[94]

While Virginians had difficulty pinpointing the exact source of their society's ills, they suspected that it was somehow related to the cultivation of tobacco. Indeed, planters came up with several theories, none of which called into question their reputation as crop masters. Landon Carter, for example, argued that changes in the colony's climate made it almost impossible for men like himself to produce outstanding tobacco. An unusually cold growing season in 1764 brought to mind a prediction he had heard as a youth, "that Virginia would in time cease to be a tobacco Colony." Six years later he still blamed a general cooling trend for the depressed state of the col-

91. Cited in Frederick Horner, *History of the Blair, Banister, and Braxton Families* (Philadelphia, 1898), 141. See also *Plantation and Frontier*, ed. Phillips, I, 83.

92. See [Daniel Dulany], *Considerations on the Propriety of Imposing Taxes in the British Colonies for the Purpose of Raising a Revnue*, in *Pamphlets of the American Revolution, 1750–1776*, ed. Bernard Bailyn (Cambridge, Mass., 1965), I, 652–58.

93. *Virginia Gazette* [William Rind], 11 December 1766.

94. Robert Beverley to John Bland, 1764, Beverley Letter Book.

ony's economy. "I cannot help observing," he jotted in his diary, "as I have before done that this climate is so changing [that] unless it return to his [its?] former state Virginia will be no Tobacco Colony soon." Carter worried about the implications of his analysis. What if he was correct? "What then," he asked plaintively, "can we tend?"[95]

The rational solution, of course, was for the planters like Carter to drop tobacco. A few Virginians apparently discussed such bold action. "We also hear," announced the *Georgia Gazette* in 1765, "that the inhabitants of that colony [Virginia] intend to give over the culture of tobacco, as it greatly impoverishes their land, and to introduce a species of agriculture that will be a more general utility, and better adapted to the good of their soil."[96] George Mason could easily have supported this plan. In fact, he advocated a complete break with Virginia's traditional staple, and in a letter published in 1769, he challenged "the principal Gentlemen . . . [to] set the Example, that will be quickly followed by the Bulk of the People." It was obvious to Mason at least what had to be done. "If we were to desist purchasing Slaves, and making Tobacco," he calculated, "we shou'd have a Number of Spare Hands to employ in Manufactures, and other Improvements; every private Family wou'd soon be able to make whatever they wanted, for their own Use."[97] All one had to do was accept the necessity of change.

Few planters of the Northern Neck welcomed such advice. To be sure, they were deeply troubled by the state of the tobacco economy; they were not fools. Still, they found it difficult to desert a known, albeit frustrating, staple for an unfamiliar substitute. Such changes came slowly; they were upsetting. Tatham understood the continuing hold the tobacco mentality had upon these men, and while he wished the innovators well, he knew they faced deep-seated resistance. "I have hopes," he explained, "that the obstinancy of habitual practice, and the trodden paths of our ancestors, will prove no obstacle to those experiments, and comparisons, which may be helpful to agricultural knowledge, especially in Virginia . . . if men would but trust themselves a little way beyond the *leading-strings of their forefathers.*"[98]

Early efforts to effect agricultural change were halting, tentative, and unenthusiastic. In the years following the French and Indian War (1758–1759), a few Virginia planters attempted to liberate themselves from tobacco. These trials, however, were conducted with

95. Greene, ed., *Diary of Landon Carter,* I, 280, 433; II, 635.
96. Cited in Louis Morton, *Robert Carter of Nomini Hall: A Virginia Tobacco Planter of the Eighteenth Century* (Charlottesville, 1941), 143.
97. The letter of "Atticus," 11 May 1769, *George Mason Papers,* ed. Rutland, I, 108.
98. Tatham, *Historical and Practical Essay,* 112 (emphasis added).

a notable lack of zeal, and when Andrew Burnaby traveled through the colony in 1760, he found most planters cultivating tobacco in exactly the same ways that their fathers had done. "Some few," Burnaby admitted, ". . . have been rather more enterprising, and have endeavoured to improve their estates by raising indigo, and other schemes: but whether it has been owing to the climate, to their inexperience in these matters, or their want of perserverance, I am unable to determine but their success has not answered their expectations."[99] If the visitor had bothered to ask John Baylor, a well-known Tidewater planter, Burnaby might have gained greater insight into the failure of indigo. Baylor tried the new crop and hated it. Indigo was unfamiliar and culturally alien, and as soon as the tobacco market revived even slightly, Baylor announced excitedly that he had returned to "my favourite employment Tobo."[100]

Hemp fared little better. When Col. Adam Gordon toured Virginia in the early 1760s, he was persuaded that the planters would soon give up tobacco. "From the high Duty on that Commodity," the English officer reported, "its value is fallen, and many people are going upon Hemp, which it is hoped may succeed, if the Bounty is continued."[101] It is not certain to whom Gordon had spoken. Perhaps the men who had time to chat with strangers in Williamsburg overestimated the planters' willingness to produce hemp. Francis Fauquier, Virginia's royal governor, knew better. In 1763 he informed the Commissioners for Trade and Plantations that "the Inhabitants seemed contented with their Staple Tobacco, and cannot *as yet* be brought to cultivate those articles for which the Society for the Encouragement of Arts and Manufactures in London offer so large Premiums."[102] Virginians working on isolated plantations clung to the cultivation of tobacco, hoping, as farmers often do, that chance factors would dramatically raise the price they received for their crops. One good year and no one would have to fiddle with hemp or indigo.[103]

But for the tobacco planters of the Northern Neck, the good times

99. Burnaby, *Travels,* 717.

100. Frances Norton Mason, ed., *John Norton and Sons Merchants of London and Virginia* . . . (Richmond, Va., 1937), 10 (16 September 1760).

101. Col. Adam Gordon, "Journal of an Officer who Travelled in America . . . 1764 and 1765," in *Travels in the American Colonies,* ed. Newton D. Mereness (New York, 1916), 404.

102. Francis Fauquier, "Answers to the Queries Sent to Me by the Right Honourable the Lords Commissioners for Trade and Plantation Affairs," 30 January 1763, Colonial Office Papers, class 5, no. 1330, Public Record Office, London, microfilm, Colonial Williamsburg, Inc., Research Center.

103. Thomas Jefferson, *Notes on the State of Virginia* (New York, 1964), 159; Robert Beverley to John Bland, 1764, Beverley Letter Book.

never returned. Prices continued to disappoint everyone, and as the years passed, more and more planters could no longer avoid being overwhelmed by debt.[104] These conditions forced some of Virginia's leading families to liquidate their entire holdings. The *Virginia Gazette* regularly carried advertisements of personal lotteries, sad testimonials to an individual's inability to satisfy creditors.[105] Almost everyone knew a bankrupt planter, and while tobacco alone seldom accounted for a person's financial woes, the old staple proved unable to save anyone from ruin.[106]

When confronted with insolvency—and sometimes only then—various Northern Neck planters began sowing wheat where once they had grown tobacco.[107] By 1774 a Fredericksburg merchant, Charles Yates, stated confidently that the planters were determined "to drop planting & turn their Lands to Farming as wheat yields more profit."[108] Yates stretched the truth. No doubt, the conversion from one crop to another was neither as sudden nor as great as he reported. Indeed, the planters in this particular region had grown wheat for

104. Robert Beverley to Landon Carter, 16 January 1766, Landon Carter Papers, Mssl, C2462a, Virginia Historical Society, Richmond, Va. A dramatic account of a planter's growing indebtedness is contained in John Syme's correspondence (Jones Exors. vs. John Syme, U.S. Circuit Court, Virginia District, Ended Cases [1797], microfilm, Colonial Williamsburg, Inc., Research Center). See also Emory G. Evans, "Planter Indebtedness and the coming of the Revolution in Virginia," *William and Mary Quarterly*, 3d ser., 19 (1962): 511–33, and idem, "Private Indebtedness and the Revolution in Virginia, 1776 to 1796," ibid., 28 (1971): 349–79; Mays, *Edmund Pendleton*, I, 144–46.

105. For example, Landon Carter noted, in his diary, "I was surprised this day to hear that in the Philadelphia *Gazette* the whole R[alph] W[ormeley] estate on Shenandoah, Slaves and all, were to be sold. I say I was surprised because there had been a prodigious boast of great Profits made there, and not long ago I heard A Gentleman declare his [estate] was then clear of debt." Entry of 6 May 1774, in Greene, ed., *Diary of Landon Carter*, II, 805; for a particularly large number of personal lottery advertisements, see *Virginia Gazette*, 3 October 1767.

106. Bernard Moore to James Hunter, 22 April 1767, Hunter-Spotswood Family Documents, transcript, Colonial Williamsburg, Inc., Research Center; Richard Henry Lee to Arthur Lee, 5 April 1770, in *The Letters of Richard Henry Lee*, ed. James Curtis Ballagh (New York, 1970), I, 43; John M. Hemphill, ed., "John Wayles Rates His Neighbours," *Virginia Magazine of History and Biography* 66 (1958): 303–6; *Writings of Washington*, ed. Fitzpatrick, II, 457–60, 473–76.

107. About this difficult transition, the historian Richard B. Sheridan writes, "Tidewater planters, who were burdened with debts that were often passed down from father to son, were compelled to change their agricultural system and to discover new staples that were adapted to worn-out soils. The transition which had been underway since midcentury was painful, even though some planters found a partial solution by growing wheat, settling new plantations in the backcountry, or engaging in manufacturing enterprises." "The British Credit Crisis of 1772 and the American Colonies," *Journal of Economic History* 20 (1960): 184; Paul G. E. Clemens, "The Operation of an Eighteenth-Century Chesapeake Tobacco Plantation," *Agricultural History* 44 (1975): 517–31; Edward C. Papenfuse, Jr., "Planter Behavior and Economic Opportunity in a Staple Economy," *Agricultural History* 46 (1972): 297–312. See also Phillips, *Life and Labor*, 50–51, 98–99; Geertz, *Agricultural Involution;* and Loubère, *The Red and the White*.

108. Cited in Gill, "Wheat Culture in Colonial Virginia," 382.

many generations. The problem, as far as they were concerned, was emphasis rather than change. However many acres were actually involved, a shift called into question the planters' self-perception. It was an indication, along with disquieting political and social trends, that a familiar tobacco mentality was in jeopardy. A symbolic world of tobacco and kings seemed to be crumbling around them, and in this unsettling atmosphere men may have been unusually receptive to new ideas about agriculture and government, religion and slavery, all expressions of a traditional culture.

At the very time when established values were being called into question, wheat increasingly became the focus of planter attention.[109] Robert Beverley expressed amazement in 1769 at "the great Quantities of our most valuable Lands being so generally employed into the cultivation of Wheat."[110] One after another, planters of the Northern Neck committed themselves more fully to cereal production. In 1767 George Washington stopped planting tobacco altogether and within a short time had discovered a lucrative local market

109. The colony's overall level of tobacco production did not drop in the years immediately preceding the Revolution. Much of the tobacco came, however, from newly developed lands west of the Tidewater. As Roger Atkinson, a resident merchant, explained in 1769, "20 years ago when the Quantity [of tobacco] was trifling compared with what it is now, for I remember when we took only 500 Hogsheads at these Warehouses, whereas now in a good year the Quantity is 10,000.... Now the Quantity here owing to the backlands' settlements is amazing[ly] encreased." *Virginia Magazine of History and Biography* 15 (1970): 346.
No specific data on the amount of acreage in the Northern Neck devoted to wheat and tobacco are available. We do know, however, that by the 1770s wheat had clearly become Virginia's second staple and that the colonists exported more wheat than did the farmers of Maryland and Pennsylvania combined. The problem of gathering more precise statistics is compounded (1) because much wheat produced in Virginia was consumed there and consequently does not appear on the export records and (2) because much exported wheat went to scattered New World markets (including a growing coastal and overland trade with other American colonies) and was therefore less well recorded than was the tobacco that was shipped almost entirely to British ports. Moreover, the shift from tobacco to wheat took place at different times and at different paces throughout the Chesapeake region. Maryland's eastern shore clearly led the way. David C. Klingaman estimates that by the 1760s the grain exports were the "dynamic element" in the Virginia economy, and the evidence points to an accelerating transition from tobacco to cereals in the Tidewater area. As Carville Earle and Ronald Hoffman explain, this change in agricultural production had a significant impact on urbanization in the Chesapeake colonies. See Gill, "Wheat Culture in Colonial Virginia," 382–83; Paul G. E. Clemens, "Chesapeake Tobacco Plantation," 517–31; Carville Earle and Ronald Hoffman, "Staple Crops and Urban Development in the Eighteenth-Century South," *Perspectives in American History* 10 (1976): 7–76; and David C. Klingaman, *Colonial Virginia's Coastwise and Grain Trade* (New York, 1975), 98–125; Paul G. E. Clemens, *The Atlantic Economy and Colonial Maryland's Eastern Shore: From Tobacco to Grain* (Ithaca, 1980), 111–223.

110. Robert Beverley to Samuel Athawes, 6 September 1769, Beverley Letter Book. While he was traveling through Virginia in April 1773, Josiah Quincy, Jr., observed, "The Culture of corn and wheat is supplanting very fast that of tobacco in this province." "Journal of Josiah Quincy, Junior, 1773," *Proceedings of the Massachusetts Historical Society* 49 (1915–16): 467. W. A. Low, "The Farmer in Post-Revolutionary Virginia, 1783–1789," *Agricultural History* 25 (1951): 122–27.

for his wheat.[111] His neighbor Robert Carter began switching to grain in the early 1760s, but for many years—perhaps out of force of habit—he continued to make a few hogsheads of tobacco. But even that token enterprise ceased in 1774. Carter informed William Taylor, his agent in Westmoreland and Richmond counties, that tobacco "for several years last passed, yeald no profit to me, but on the contrary, other funds have been applied to support them [tobacco plantations], and to preserve [*sic*] in growing tobacco at those places I apprehend would be a mark of folly and not discretion."[112] Even Edmund Pendleton, a brilliant lawyer of conservative temperament, gave up tobacco at this time. The cultivation of grain presented Pendleton with unanticipated difficulties, and in 1778 he managed to harvest only "Crops of weavel eaten wheat." Fleetingly, he contemplated returning to Virginia's traditional staple, but by that time, as he recognized, it was "perhaps too late."[113]

Some Virginians gradually came to perceive wheat in positive terms, as being emblematic of individual liberty. For them, cereal production provided a possibility of severing ties with English tobacco merchants, of escaping from the burden of debt, of reestablishing independence not only for the planters but also for the entire society. In 1772 a Virginian, Roger Atkinson, excitedly informed an English merchant, "Sir it is with great Pleasure I acq't you that we have now got another staple of late years, as it were created, viz: Wheat, w'ch will I believe in a little time be equal if not superior to Tob'o—is more certain & of w'ch we shall in a few years make more in Virg'ia than all the Province of Pennsylvania put together."[114] William Allason wrote in less breathless prose, but he well understood the implications of wheat culture for Tidewater society. He was pleased to hear of an unexpectedly large grain harvest in 1774, "and this is the more fortunate as most [planters] had gone more on it [wheat] than heretofore, their dependence on Tobacco being much lessened."[115] Wheat could create a personal sense of liberation. It seems to have done so for Henry Fitzhugh. "I shall not," he declared

111. Freeman, *Washington*, III, 179.

112. Cited in Morton, *Robert Carter*, 262. See esp. 118–48.

113. Cited in Mays, *Edmund Pendleton*, I, 117. Some great planters of eastern Virginia migrated west into the Piedmont region and the Shenandoah Valley during this period and there continued to cultivate tobacco. See Robert D. Mitchell, "Agricultural Change and the American Revolution: A Virginia Case Study," *Agricultural History* 47 (1973): 130–32; Joseph Clarke Robert, *The Tobacco Kingdom: Plantation, Market, and Factory in Virginia and North Carolina, 1800–1860* (Durham, N.C., 1938), 3–53.

114. Atkinson to Lyonel and Samuel Lyde, 25 August 1772, *Virginia Magazine of History and Biography* 15 (1908): 352.

115. "The Letters of William Allason, Merchant of Falmouth, Virginia," ed. D. R. Anderson, *Richmond College Historical Papers*, vol. 2 (Richmond, Va., 1917), 154.

to a British merchant house to whom he was heavily indebted, "I hope have occasion to draw on you for much for [credit] as I have now got into a way of making large Crops of Wheat at my Back quarters."[116]

An extraordinary period of cultural redefinition had begun. Even the language of agriculture changed. Virginians who cultivated wheat no longer called themselves *planters;* grain transformed them into *farmers.* New crops generated new symbols. N. F. Cabell, a man who in the early nineteenth century wrote a short "History of Agriculture in Virginia," described with considerable perspicacity how the movement from tobacco to wheat affected individual Virginians. "Many planters," Cabell declared, "first lessened their crops of tobacco and then abandoned it altogether. Planters thus became farmers, and as such entered on a general course of improvement, but suffered much during the period of transition."[117]

About the character of planters' suffering, little is known. No doubt, some individuals found adjusting to the demands of the new crop difficult. In 1769 Richard Corbin, a leading figure in the royal government of Virginia, complained that "the old beaten Path[,] Industry in the Planter's Way, will not suit the present Modern improvement in Husbandry."[118] Corbin was a man who had formerly derived great satisfaction from producing high-grade tobacco. But as time passed this personal identification with "our staple" lost significance. In fact, it would have made little sense to speak of the "tobacco mentality" after the Revolution. Beverley had been correct about its being the end of an era. When an English traveler visited Mount Vernon following the War, he described its owner in a way that reflected the profound shift that had taken place in the agriculture of Virginia. "General Washington," he explained, "who formerly had been a planter, but lately a farmer, had no land left that would bring a crop of tobacco."[119]

On another level, Tidewater Virginia was no longer synonymous with tobacco. It may have been a "tobacco" colony, but it certainly was not a "tobacco" state. The very process of shifting from one crop to another took on symbolic meaning. The colonial crop had been tobacco, a staple now associated with royal government, ruinous debt, slave labor, soil erosion, lack of independence—in other words, with a host of negative qualities.[120] But wheat helped to free the common-

116. Fitzhugh to Steuart and Campbell, 20 October 1768, Henry Fitzhugh Papers.
117. Cabell, "Some Fragments of an Intended Report," 115. See also Gill, "Wheat Culture in Colonial Virginia," 382.
118. Richard Corbin to Hannah Philippa (Ludwell) Lee, 10 June 1769, Lee Family Papers, Mssl. L51, f. 527.
119. Parkinson, *Tour in America,* II, 423–24.
120. See Earle, "Slavery and Free Labor," 56–59.

wealth from these burdens. Grain rejuvenated the land and, presumably, the human spirit as well. "Wheat and other corn . . . ," wrote
the author of *American Husbandry* in 1775, "are raised principally on
old tobacco plantations that are worn out without assistance of much
manure. This is a point which deserves attention: exhaust the lands
. . . as much as you will with tobacco, you will leave it in order for
grain."[121] Other Virginians stressed the appropriateness of wheat
for the new society. In his "Report to President Washington on Agricultural Conditions in Northern Virginia" (1791), Dr. David Stuart
commented that "people are generally exchanging tobacco for wheat;
I flatter myself the face of our Country will soon assume an appearance that will not only do honor to our climate but ourselves." From
Stuart's perspective, "the old Tobacco grounds" were merely
reminders of the "slovenly" agricultural practices that Virginians had
once accepted without second thought, and in the post-Revolutionary period the "old" fields evoked no fondness for a lost culture.[122]

Like Stuart, Jefferson welcomed the transition from tobacco to
wheat. He understood the relation between culture and agriculture
more fully than did his contemporaries, and even before the conclusion of the American Revolution, he decided that the citizens of an
independent republic should be discouraged from growing tobacco.
His views on this subject were not drawn from the works of European philosophers; they were the product of experiences he had had
while growing up on a Virginia plantation. In 1758, Jefferson
recalled, the planters had exported the largest number of hogsheads
in the colony's history. Soon after this, however, they began to cut
back on tobacco cultivation, a trend Jefferson applauded. He hated
the staple for what he thought it had done to the land and its people.
"It is a culture productive of infinite wrechedness," he declared with
uncharacteristic passion. "Those employed in it are in a continual
state of exertion beyond the power of nature to support. Little food
of any kind is raised by them; so that the men and animals on these
farms are badly fed, and the earth is rapidly impoverished." By contrast, wheat liberated men from these crushing burdens. It freed
them from the mind-dulling tasks that Jefferson feared would destroy
intellectual curiosity and undermine political vigilance. "Besides
clothing the earth with herbage, and preserving its fertility," he

121. *American Husbandry,* 187.
122. Gertrude R. B. Richards, ed., "Dr. David Stuart's Report to President Washington on Agricultural Conditions in Northern Virginia," *Virginia Magazine of History and
Biography* 61 (1953): 286, 287. In 1799 the duc de La Rochefoucauld Liancourt reported
from western Virginia that "here, and on James-River, and in fact throughout Virginia,
tobacco is yearly replaced by wheat, which becomes gradually almost the general object
of culture; and the present fall in the price of wheat does not seem to render the planters less attached to this *change in their system of cultivation.*" *Travels through the United States,*
II, 84 (emphasis added).

insisted, "it [wheat] feeds the laborers plentifully, requires from them only a moderate toil, except in the season of harvest, raises great numbers of animals for food and service, and diffuses plenty and happiness among the whole."[123] The message was clear. A cultural revolution was taking place in the fields of Virginia, one that would insure the survival of a new nation.

The change from tobacco to wheat did not cause the planters of the Northern Neck to support the Revolution. To make such a claim would be to indulge in a crude form of agricultural determinism. Rather, it would seem that important alterations in the planters' traditional work culture, their sense of time and space, and their self-perception coincided with Parliament's decision to tax Americans without their consent. Under any circumstances, Virginians like Richard Henry Lee and George Washington would have resisted the Stamp Act and the commercial regulations that followed.

It is equally plain that even in the absence of political and social tension, the transition from one crop to another would have generated considerable anxiety. No one who lives by the soil surrenders "the old beaten Path" with enthusiasm. But it so happened that at the same time when Virginia tobacco planters had begun to contemplate a redefinition of the culture of agriculture, they were also forced to restructure their political culture.[124]

123. *Notes on the State of Virginia,* 159.

124. Changes in agriculture did not "cause" Tidewater planters to adopt the political ideology that Bernard Bailyn describes in his *Ideological Origins of the American Revolution.* The inadequacy of this type of crude correlation has been demonstrated by Emory Evans and Thad W. Tate in their analyses of the relation between the planters' English debts and support for independence. Thad W. Tate, "The Coming of the Revolution in Virginia: Britain's Challenge to Virginia's Ruling Class, 1763–1776," *William and Mary Quarterly,* 3d ser., 19 (1962): 323–43; Evans, "Planter Indebtedness," 511–33.

My point is that profound changes in patterns of agricultural production—changes involving a restructuring of the elements of everyday experience—heightened the planters' receptivity to certain new political ideas. As Gordon Wood has stated, "Out of the multitude of inherited and transmitted ideas available in the eighteenth century, Americans selected and emphasized those which seemed to make meaningful what was happening to them." Wood, "Rhetoric and Reality," 24. I have shown why men in one section of Virginia—one that produced many of the nation's Revolutionary leaders—might have felt compelled at this particular time to select one group of ideas over another.

The Problem of Allegiance in Revolutionary Poughkeepsie

JONATHAN CLARK[1]

It was, as John Shy has reminded us, a civil war.[2] And that fact continues to pose challenges to our understanding of the nature of the American Revolution. Studies of mob violence and the treatment of Loyalists suggest that American revolutionaries did not differ so greatly from their French successors as we had once supposed. They may not have practiced the excesses of intolerance, but they did not lack its spirit. They may not have made heads roll to enforce conformity, but they substituted effective alternatives, ranging from destruction of property and simple assault to dressing the disaffected in coats of tar adorned with feathers. They also managed partially to purify their society by forcing thousands of Loyalists to leave it.[3] Granting all that, the American Revolution still seems positively polite. It saw no guillotine, no terror, no Robespierre of the wilderness embarking on a campaign to make Americans embody the national will by disembodying those found wanting. Even the most fiery rebels never contemplated undertaking a bloody crusade against the enemy at home. Instead, known Loyalists were rapidly reintegrated into American society, and in some areas that process began long before the war ended. All of which raises a question: Why did

1. Portions of this paper were presented (under a different title) at the conference honoring Edmund S. Morgan. The author wishes to thank the participants at the conference, especially John R. Howe, Jr., for their comments and suggestions. Additionally, Thad W. Tate gave to a later draft the valuable benefit of his gentle but firm editorial pencil.

2. John Shy, "The Loyalist Problem in the Lower Hudson Valley: The British Perspective," in *The Loyalist Americans: A Focus on Greater New York,* ed. Robert East and Jacob Judd (Tarrytown, 1975), 3.

3. See esp. Gordon S. Wood, "A Note on Mobs in the American Revolution," *William and Mary Quarterly,* 3d ser., 23 (1966): 635–42. Robert R. Palmer, *The Age of the Democratic Revolution* (Princeton, 1959–64), I, 188–90.

so many Patriots and Loyalists, despite the animosities and acts of violence of the pre- and early-war years seem so willing, so soon, to live and let live?

What follows is an attempt to answer that question for Poughkeepsie, New York, a town deeply divided over the question of independence. Poughkeepsie was characterized by ethnic diversity (even some slaves spoke both English and Dutch)[4] and by a religious tolerance that bordered on indifference (during the war years no regular services were held at either the Reformed or the Episcopalian church).[5] It was a growing town, containing in 1775 about five hundred people in the village proper and another thousand or so in the surrounding countryside. As a river town, situated on the Hudson about halfway between New York City and Albany, it had its share of merchants and storekeepers. As the county seat for Dutchess, it could boast (or bemoan) more lawyers than most towns its size. Yet despite these distinctive qualities, Poughkeepsie shared three fundamental attributes with most of the rest of America: it was overwhelmingly rural, parochial, and Protestant. Rural enough that a village physician received a large portion of his pay either in farm products or by having his patients perform farm labor for him,[6] and sufficiently parochial for voters at the annual town meetings to show great concern about keeping sheep behind fences but to give little notice to the impending conflict with England.[7] At the very least, the Poughkeepsie experience made up a small part of the American experience, and thus the problem of allegiance in Poughkeepsie may offer one small step toward a fuller understanding of the American Revolution.

I

When the movement for independence is brought down to the local level—where many names remain, but very few faces, and where little of what men may have read or written survives—it takes on a different aura. The evidence does not lend itself to judgments about "central themes" or "underlying causes" or even why men chose the side they did. To look to home is to look at the Revolution from the inside out, and from that perspective grand commitments, whether

4. [Poughkeepsie] *New York Journal*, 16 October 1780.
5. Helen Wilkinson Reynolds, *The Records of Christ Church, 1755–1910* (Poughkeepsie, 1911), 50.
6. Robert Noxon, [Account] Book, 1784, Ledger B, passim. Dutchess County Historical Society, Poughkeepsie.
7. Town Records: Town of Poughkeepsie, 1742–1754, Adriance Memorial Library, Poughkeepsie.

to independence or to continued union with England, serve only as contexts in which committed men directed their energies toward trying to ensure that their side prevailed.

In Poughkeepsie, as in so many rural communities, most men would have had a nodding acquaintance, if nothing more, with one another and an awareness of those men to whom deference was due. They would very likely have had a sense of which way locally prominent and, if not prominent, vocal men leaned on imperial issues. Men who had neighbors and family and taverns to visit, as well as town meetings to attend, would most certainly have realized by 1775 that they, too, might soon have to make a choice of allegiance. These, of course, are assumptions, but without them we cannot even try to recapture (in many instances through numbers) what the participants would have articulated differently but have known more intimately and experienced more vividly.

This is expecially true of the prominent men in town who had by 1775 made up their minds to follow either the dictates of the king or the resolves of the Continental Congress. Their dilemma was not one of choosing sides but of persuading others to join their cause and, once they had gotten them on the right side, of keeping them there. It was not a problem they could ignore, because neither side could depend on readily available forces from outside the country capable of compelling allegiance.

Before the summer of 1776, Poughkeepsie Patriots might be proclaimed rebels, but George III lacked the wherewithal to punish them. Likewise, the Continental and Provincial congresses might pass whatever illegal resolutions they wished, but their enforcement was left, of necessity, in the hands of local officials. Nor did the situation change drastically during the year and a half after New York tardily joined the other states in declaring its independence, on 9 July 1776. Poughkeepsie lay but seventy-odd miles upstream from the British army headquarters in New York City directly in the path of the inevitable attempt by British forces to divide the states in two. In late 1777, Patriots in Poughkeepsie were told they had lost more by the fall of Fort Constitution (across the Hudson from West Point) than Americans had ever gained by the surrender of Burgoyne's army.[8] A few months later William Emmot advised Capt. Stephen Hendrickson "to turn [to the king], that he might still have a pardon, that at that time only the leading men would be hung."[9] Certainly until 1778, no one in Poughkeepsie could confidently predict whether a

8. Hugh Hastings, ed., *The Public Papers of George Clinton, First Governor of New York, 1777–1795, 1801–1804* (New York, 1899–1914), II, 539, 543–46.
9. Ibid., 543–44.

triumphant Howe or a victorious Washington would finally ride through town. Under such circumstances, Patriot leaders in particular would have been fools not to keep a close count of men they could depend on, of men who would acquiesce in, if not actively support, the resolves of Congress and of those likely to join the ranks of the disaffected.

And fools they were not. When Gilbert Livingston, the son of the county clerk, received word in 1776 that the Convention of Representatives planned to begin work on a new constitution, he warned his fellow delegates that they had first better make sure they had a state to govern before concerning themselves with the proper mode to govern it by.[10] Other men in Poughkeepsie probably shared Livingston's position. They knew well how precarious their situation was in a town divided, and how fragile their hold—even over men who preferred to remain unobtrusive and uncommitted. They had managed to push their community toward independence by 1776; they had managed to keep it there during the next two, trying years; and the very process by which they had succeeded in doing so helped dictate the way they treated the enemy at home.

Until the summer of 1775 Poughkeepsie remained, at least to outward appearances, a hotbed of Loyalism. The man most responsible for that appearance was Bartholomew Crannel, the town's leading lawyer and the acting surrogate for Duchess County. Crannel had moved up to Poughkeepsie from New York City in the early 1740s. He subsequently married into the Van Kleeck family, helped found the Anglican Christ Church, and later married off his three daughters to local young men of good family and promise.[11] Crannel had long since become a pillar of the community when, as he later told British authorities, he discovered, in the summer of 1774, that the rebels in town had "Independence in Contemplation."[12]

During that August the precinct supervisor had called a special town meeting of "the Freeholders and Inhabitants" in order to decide whether the town would establish a local committee to correspond with the Committee of Fifty-one in New York City and have a voice in selecting delegates to the First Continental Congress.[13] Bartholomew Crannel had, by his own later account, used his considerable

10. Gilbert Livingston and Christopher Tappen to the New York Convention, Aug. 9, 1776, in Peter Force, ed., *American Archives*, 5th ser., I, 1541–42.

11. Edmund Platt, *The Eagle's History of Poughkeepsie from the Earliest Settlements, 1683–1905* (Poughkeepsie, 1905), 24–38.

12. Helen Wilkinson Reynolds, "Loyalist Transcripts" (Transcriptions of manuscript records in the New York Public Library, Adriance Memorial Library, Poughkeepsie).

13. Force, ed., *American Archives*, 4th ser., II, 701–2.

clout to put a stop to that move: the motion was soundly defeated.[14] Worse—from the perspective of precocious Patriots—the meeting directed the supervisor to forward three resolutions to the Committee of Fifty-one. One affirmed that the people in Poughkeepsie continued "unshaken in their allegiance" to King George III and adamantly opposed "American Independence." A second asserted their belief in the principle of no taxation without representation and their hope that the New York Assembly would prepare one more "humble Petition and Remonstrance" saying so. The final resolution attested to their willingness to bear their fair share of the "national expense."[15] In his first contest with the rebels for the votes of the people, Crannel had won hands down. And he repeated his victory in the spring of 1775 when another town meeting decided, by a vote of 110 to 77, to have nothing to do with the Second Continental Congress.[16] In so far as votes on issues meant anything, Poughkeepsie had all the makings of a Loyalist stronghold.

Matters were not quite that simple, though. Backward as one majority may have been in imperial matters, another majority of the same voters had, since 1772, elected known radicals to influential town offices. In that year, John Frear, a future colonel of the militia, was elected one of the two assessors.[17] In the following year, Lewis Dubois captured the other assessor's post and held it until he joined Montgomery in the ill-fated invasion of Canada. In 1773 as well, John Bailey, who would soon command his own regiment of the militia, was chosen constable.[18] Finally, in the spring of 1775, for the fourth year in a row, men in Poughkeepsie once again elected perhaps the most conspicuous radical in town, Zephaniah Platt, to serve as their town supervisor.[19] In other words, there probably existed a swing group of voters who respected rebel leaders but wanted no part in fomenting a rebellion. Loyalists could command a majority on imperial issues, not because the majority favored the cause of empire, but because it wished to steer clear of trouble. And until news of Lexington and Concord indicated that conflict might be inevitable, the easiest way to avoid trouble was to vote down any measure that might lead to it.

In 1774 and 1775, men with Loyalist predilections were favored both by inertia and by the established provincial government (such as it was). Radicals had no recourse except to largely self-selected committees if they wanted to reverse, or at least neutralize, decisions made by public majorities. And so they resorted to committees.

14. Ibid.; Reynolds, "Loyalist Transcripts."
15. Force, ed., *American Archives*, 4th ser., II, 701–2.   16. Ibid., 304–5.
17. Town Records, 1770–1775.   18. Ibid.   19. Ibid.

Zephaniah Platt and Gilbert Livingston were among the members of the committee that made certain that Dutchess County (and with it, Poughkeepsie) had an indirect voice in the First Continental Congress in 1774, and sent delegates to the subsequent Provincial Convention and Congresses in 1775.[20] They had twice learned the dangers of going public: not by accident would no elections (except for town offices) be held in Poughkeepsie between the spring of 1775 and the summer of 1777 (under the auspices of the first state constitution).[21]

Before July 1775, Patriots lacked the means to pressure the uncommitted to acquiesce in measures they might think necessary. Without that support they could not realistically expect to control the Tory-minded. Well after news of Lexington and Concord reached town, the Loyalist sheriff, Philip Livingston (not a Poughkeepsie resident), had no trouble rounding up a large posse to help him teach the rebels a lesson. The posse marched out to John Bailey's house, where Bailey and a few friends—including the town supervisor, Zephaniah Platt—stood guard under a patriotic flag. The sheriff ordered the flagpole cut down as a public nuisance. That accomplished, he drew his sword and threatened to arrest the town supervisor on the charge of treason. Platt picked up a club and offered to beat the sheriff's brains out should he try it.[22]

In this instance, push did not come to shove. The sheriff backed down and marched his posse back to the village of Poughkeepsie. But the lesson could not have been lost on Platt and his friends that they would have to remain on the defensive and that whatever actions they might choose to take would have to be merely symbolic or conducted through self-appointed committees. But that situation abruptly changed when the First Provincial Congress began to reform the militia and composed the New York Association, a pledge of allegiance to whatever resolutions the Continental and Provincial congresses might make.[23]

During July and August of 1775, local committeemen canvassed

20. Force, ed., *American Archives*, 4th ser., II, 324, 356–57.

21. The elections in 1777 were held under the aegis of New York State's first constitution. Dutchess Delegates made very clear why elections needed to be avoided when they presented their credentials to the Provincial Convention. Force, ed., *American Archives*, 4th ser., II, 356–57. For a contrasting view, see Staughton Lynd, *Antifederalism in Duchess County, New York* (Chicago, 1965), 57–58. Lynd has mistakenly argued that delegates to the Provincial Congress replaced the delegates to the Provincial Convention. They did not. Those two bodies were quite distinct and charged with different responsibilities.

22. J. Wilson Poucher, "Dutchess County Men of the Revolution Period: Zephaniah Platt," *Year Book of the Dutchess County Historical Society* 29 (1944): 54 (hereafter cited as *Year Book*).

23. Force, ed., *American Archives*, 4th ser., II, 597.

Poughkeepsie for signatures to the Association. It was their first opportunity to put the uncommitted and disaffected on the defensive. It gave them the edge they needed to prod the town to move into the mainstream of Revolutionary America. Obtaining a man's signature was no guarantee of his allegiance to Congress, but anyone who refused to sign was automatically isolated and identified as a suspect. Local committeemen intelligently used their new weapon more as a carrot than as a stick. When Dirck Brinkerhoff (from the neighboring Rombout Precinct) forwarded the lists of the county Association lists to Congress, he felt obliged to apologize for the many erasures among the rolls of the non-signers. "[O]n account," he wrote, "of persuing lenient measures," several men who had initially refused to sign had afterwards apparently decided that being a rebel against their king would prove less dangerous than being deemed an enemy to their country.[24] In Poughkeepsie, at least 196 men finally signed, while another 79 resisted all blandishments and adamantly refused to do so.[25] Predictably, perhaps, April's rebel minority of 77 against 110 had become a better than two-to-one majority by August.

II

The Patriots now enjoyed a majority at least on paper. It was undependable perhaps, fickle most assuredly, which meant that once the shooting started, rebel leaders would have to decide how far they were willing to go and what policies they were prepared to pursue in order to keep Poughkeepsie in the patriotic front. While they would undoubtedly have preferred to demand political conformity, they lacked the power to enforce it. They thus would have to determine somewhere along the line what varieties of disaffection or noncommitment would constitute a clear danger to the patriotic cause. This problem was especially acute in Poughkeepsie, where different men seemed intent on choosing every option of allegiance available— except, that is, neutrality.

The Association lists of 1775, when combined with the tax lists of the same year, offer the most complete accounting of Poughkeepsie's free male population before the federal census of 1790. Of the 329 men who definitely resided in Poughkeepsie in 1775, the careers of 239 (a bit less than three-fourths of the total) can be followed

24. Ibid., 600.
25. The Association lists for Dutchess County appear ibid., 597–607, but a much more accurate list can be found in *Calendar of Historical Manuscripts Relating to the War of the Revolution* (Albany, 1868), I, 77–79. A few signers did not reside in town, committeemen often signed twice, and either some men managed to evade the committeemen or else one list has not survived.

closely enough to determine their allegiances with some precision.[26] The 90 whose allegiances remain unknown do appear in various records, but the records often offer only inconclusive evidence. Robert Kidney, for instance, signed the Association, paid taxes, and served in the county militia.[27] Hendrick Bush, too, did all of the above. Robert Kidney sold some barrel hoops to the local Commission on Conspiracies.[28] That same commission had Hendrick Bush "fetched down" because of Loyalist activities, and he later forfeited his property for the same reason.[29] While it is unlikely that the Commission would have purchased supplies from a known Loyalist, the allegiance of Kidney must, in light of Bush's record, remain undetermined.

Stretching the evidence, we could perhaps count men like Robert Kidney as neutral. But we could not do so with the remaining 239: 101 committed themselves to the cause of independence, and another 61 stayed loyal to the king.[30] The 69 left over hardly constituted a body of pristine fence sitters. While they did not steadfastly adhere to either cause and while many of them were not resolute or constant in their allegiance, they invariably, despite their fears or their preference for farming above fighting, spoke or acted in ways sufficiently telling to allow us to count them as either Occasional Patriots or Occasional Loyalists.

Those latter categories of allegiances are not simply artificial slots in which to put men who switched sides. No one in Poughkeepsie could be called a poor man's Benedict Arnold, unless the Association of 1775 is considered as the standard of allegiance. In that case, switching sides becomes rampant, because twenty-one men who signed the Association ended as outright Loyalists, while four who would have nothing to do with the Association in 1775 actually volunteered for service in the Continental line.[31] But those signatures

26. For selected information about each these men, see the Appendix.
27. Platt, *Eagle's History*, 300; Dutchess County Tax Lists to 1778, Adriance Memorial Library, Poughkeepsie; James A. Roberts, *New York in the Revolution as Colony and State*, 2d ed. (Albany, 1898), 244; *Minutes of the Committee and the First Commission for Detecting and Defeating Conspiracies in the State of New York*, Collections of the New-York Historical Society 58 (1925): 346 (hereafter cited as *Commission for Conspiracies*).
28. Platt, *Eagle's History*, 300; Tax Lists; Roberts, *New York in the Revolution*, 243; Hastings, ed., *Papers of Clinton*, IV, 18–19.
29. Roberts, *New York in the Revolution*, supplement, 253; Platt, *Eagle's History*, 301.
30. See the Appendix.
31. The twenty-one who joined the Loyalist cause very likely signed the Association under pressure. The four who refused to sign yet later emerged as Patriots deserve special note. Two, Samuel Hall and Elias Thompson, paid no taxes in 1775 and joined the Continental line. The third, Nathaniel Babcock, was illiterate. The fourth, Felix (sometimes called Phoenix) Lewis, was elected an ensign (later promoted to lieutenant) in the militia, but by 1783 he found himself in debtors' prison. See the Appendix; Berthold Fernow, ed., *Documents Relating to the Colonial History of the State of New York*, vol.

were gathered a full year before New York declared its independence, and the evidence available from the summer of 1776 onward suggests not that men of less than firm allegiance found it easy to recross Rubicons but that they oscillated between a strong commitment to a political cause and an equally compelling desire to maintain their place in the community. Their allegiances, in sum, were occasional only.

Simeon Leroy, Jr., provides one variant of the Occasional Patriot. Not only did he sign the Association and volunteer for the militia in 1775, but the men in his company thought highly enough of Leroy to elect him their second lieutenant.[32] In 1777, though, he left a hint of disaffection when he added his name to a petition requesting a reprieve for William Jaycocks, a teenage Tory condemned to hang. (Gov. George Clinton denied the request, suspecting with some reason that the petitioners had offered to act as parole officers mainly to facilitate Jaycocks's escape to the British.)[33] That hint turned to a strong suspicion in 1783 when Leroy himself was indicted for "adhering" to the enemy.[34] Perhaps he persuaded the court of his innocence, for he still lived in Poughkeepsie when the first census was taken, in 1790.[35] Even so, his dedication to the Patriot cause remained occasional at best.

Another such man was John Child. Though on the surface he was a firmer Whig than was Leroy, many of his acquaintances thought him a borderline case. In 1775 Child signed the Association—as a local committeeman he had little choice.[36] Unfortunately, that was when Peter DeWitt complained from Albany that the "Committee-Men in *Dutchess County* are false and treacherous: nothing can be concerted but it transpires to the Tories."[37] Whether Child had a hand in that transpiring remains unknown, but when someone nominated him for the post of assistant commissioner for conspiracies, the Council of Safety squelched the nomination, writing that men "who desert from the enemy, and surrender themselves" had no business in such sensitive positions.[38] Such an appointment would have exempted Child from militia duty, but even without it he managed the trick in 1779—and caused a near riot.[39] Perhaps Richard

---

15, State Archives, vol. 1 (Albany, 1897), 227, 229; 281; *The New York Packet and the American Advertiser* [Fishkill], 17 April 1783.

32. Fernow, ed., *Documents*, 280.   33. Hastings, ed., *Papers of Clinton*, IV, 738.

34. *New York Packet*, 17 April 1783.

35. *Heads of Families at the First Census of the United States, Taken in the Year 1790—New York* (Baltimore, 1976), 90–91.

36. Force, ed., *American Archives*, 4th ser., III, 1692.   37. Ibid., 458.

38. Pierre Van Cortlandt to the Assistant Commissioners, 28 August 1777, *Commission for Conspiracies*, II, 444.

39. Ibid., II, 350–51.

Everitt, himself a suspected Loyalist, best captured the reality of John Child when he candidly told a part-time spy that Child played at being a Patriot "only to earn a sustenance."[40]

As the likes of Leroy and Child and the twenty-seven other Occasional Patriots only sporadically supported the cause of independence, so another forty men leaned toward Loyalism. Among the Occasional Loyalists was Everitt, who had a penchant for accusing others of taking the king's side—at least until 1780, when he himself was indicted for Loyalism.[41] He may have beaten that rap, or he may have picked up a newly found self-importance during his long sojourn behind enemy lines, but in either case he had his occupation listed as "Gentleman" in a 1783 voting list, apparently the only one in town.[42] Peter Leroy, Sr., provides a slightly different version of the Occasional Loyalist. In 1775, at the age of fifty-three, he had refused to have anything to do with the New York Association.[43] Two of his sons made their allegiance more noticeable when they went off to fight for the British and after the war settled in the colder, but more hospitable, climate of Canada.[44] Leroy's own loyalties undoubtedly also lay with the king, but there is an indication that his brother-in-law John Frear, an active patriot and militia colonel, persuaded him not to act on them and to keep his political views to himself.[45] Men like Everitt and Leroy, though their hearts belonged to the king, lacked the intensity of allegiance that characterized outright Loyalists.

That proved most assuredly to be the case with William Emmot, a prototype of the Occasional Loyalist. Twenty-seven years old in 1775, a saddler by trade and an active member of the Anglican Christ Church, Emmot was one of those men who had the uncanny capacity, when offered a choice between two alternatives, to get away with choosing both of them.[46] Like Peter Leroy, he refused to sign the Association in 1775, but by 1777 he had decided—apparently in good conscience—that he could take an oath of allegiance to the state of New York.[47] So patriots in Poughkeepsie left him to his own devices—that is, until Governor Clinton granted him a pass to go to Long Island, behind enemy lines. Once word of the pass leaked out, local

40. Ibid., 327.   41. *Commission for Conspiracies*, 326–27.

42. *New York Historical and Genealogical Register* 2 (1871): 150.

43. For further information on Leroy and other men of known allegiance, see the Appendix, which provides in table format some of the relevant data on which this essay is based.

44. "Papers of the Leroy Family," *Year Book* 12 (1927): 41. Leroy was among several heads of families on whom a special tax was levied for the rash actions of their sons in joining the British. Hastings, ed., *Papers of Clinton*, VI, 586.

45. "Papers of the Leroy Family," 39–41.   46. Reynolds, *Christ Church*, 57–58.

47. Hastings, ed., *Papers of Clinton*, II, 544.

residents bombarded Clinton with requests that he rescind it. Peter Tappen (who was both the brother-in-law of Clinton and the son-in-law of Bartholomew Crannel) told the governor that the Tory-minded Emmot also happened to be a "sligh Designing fallow, and Every bodey here knows him to be such." (It was Emmot, after all, who suggested that Captain Hendrickson should convert to the king's side.)[48] Clinton revoked the pass, and William Emmot had to stay home. But his craft, if that is the word for it, continued to stand him in good stead. The 1783 poll list gave his occupation as "Esquire,"[49] three years later he was serving as clerk of elections, and in 1798 he received his appointment as a county justice of the peace.[50] No other Occasional Loyalist did half so well.

On the other hand, there appears little reason to question the patriotism of Capt. Bernardus Swartwout simply because he was cashiered for calling out the classes of militia as he saw fit rather than the way Col. John Frear ordered.[51] Nor were Hendrick Bush, Ezekial Pinkney, or John Miller any less Loyalist simply because they were members of the militia.[52] Whig leaders in Dutchess County had early on instituted a policy of drafting known Tories in the hope (not always realized) that they would either pay for substitutes or leave the county.[53]

It is true that participants did not designate four categories of allegiance into which they could divide their contemporaries. But surviving evidence makes it clear that they perceived the problem of allegiance as being far more complex than one of good Whigs against bad Tories. As early as 1775, one Dutchess County committeeman found, besides the firm Whigs and the "black roll of Tories" for whom he had no use, a third group that he designated "middle Whigs."[54] From 1776 to 1778, the varying reactions of local leaders toward the discontented make clear their awareness of even more variations of allegiance, even if that awareness can now be recaptured only by numbers.

Local authorities of necessity—New York being New York—had to assume the task of keeping Poughkeepsie in the Revolutionary mainstream. Thus the way they perceived their strength in numbers (based on an experienced past and an uncertain future in 1776) would

48. Ibid., 543–46.   49. *Genealogical Register*, 150.
50. Platt, *Eagle's History*, 61.
51. Hastings, ed., *Papers of Clinton*, IV, 280–83; 299–300.
52. See the Appendix.
53. Egbert Benson to the Representatives of Dutchess County, 15 July 1776. *Journals of the Provincial Congress, Provincial Convention, Committee of Safety and Council of Safety of the State of New York* (Albany, 1842), II, 309.
54. Force, ed., *American Archives*, 4th ser., III, 606.

influence the treatment they might accord to those men on whom they could not depend with confidence. Had, for example, men like Platt and Livingston thought of their neighbors as either Patriots (138) or Loyalists (101), they would have confronted a potentially active minority of dissidents too large to control without the imposition of harsh measures. Had they gone one step further and imagined a buffer group of 69 neutrals (a combination of "occasionals"), between 109 Patriots and 61 Loyalists, they might have concluded that some form of permanent house arrest would suffice to keep the disaffected at bay.

But such possibilities ignore the realities of political life in Revolutionary Poughkeepsie. In the first place, prominent men of clear convictions would probably not be content simply to comfort themselves with their own righteousness. Most would also want to convert others to their cause, and in those circumstances any men who thought neutrality a virtue would find themselves less a buffer than one of the buffeted. In the second place, any ardent Patriot who harbored visions of undertaking a "scorched-earth" policy against local Loyalists would have quickly and completely alienated the rest of the community.

Patriot leaders lacked a range of options in dealing with the disaffected for the most basic of reasons: the Revolution in Poughkeepsie was, above all else, a family affair. Since the 1740s the town had become, if nothing more, a place to move to, and families with names like Frear, Westervelt, and Dubois had purchased large chunks of land in town at about the time of Crannel's arrival.[55] They were later joined by men like Zephaniah Platt, who left Long Island for good after purchasing his fine farm along Wappingers Creek in 1761.[56] The town continued to grow throughout the last half of the eighteenth century, and community ties were cemented by that most natural of means—intermarriage.[57]

By 1775, people in Poughkeepsie had no trouble in identifying the enemy at home, for the enemy was, if not a neighbor or an acquaintance, more than likely a relative or an in-law. A large proportion of Poughkeepsie residents would have known of someone, related to them by blood or through marriage, who chose an allegiance other than their own. Even within immediate families, allegiances could run the gamut (except that most wives appear to have stood by their

55. As late as 1756, William Smith thought Poughkeepsie "scarce" deserved the name of a village. Platt, *Eagle's History*, 25–27.

56. J. Wilson Poucher, "Dutchess County Men of the Revolutionary Period: Zephaniah Platt," *Year Book* 29 (1944): 53.

57. Many of these relationships can be traced by consulting various local genealogies on file at Adriance Memorial Library, Poughkeepsie.

husbands). For example, Joel Dubois, an Occasional Patriot, was one of those men who could never keep his signals straight. In 1770, at the age of twenty-eight, he had been elected a constable. In that same year the court of general sessions found him guilty of assault and battery and of keeping a disorderly house.[58] In 1775 he signed the Association and later joined the land-bounty militia, even as, in the spring of 1777, he stored three guns in his house for the use of his brother Benjamin and some friends who William Denny, a spy, thought were to "go off to the enemy." Benjamin Dubois, five years younger than Joel, emerged as an Occasional Loyalist. He had in fact planned to leave home and cross enemy lines. But he was less interested in fighting for the British than he was in verifying the rumor that he and his friends "could continue on Long Island at peace without being obliged to fight."[59]

Two other brothers joined the Whig cause. Jeremiah, Jr. (who, along with his older brother, had in 1770 been found guilty of assault and battery), and the youngest brother, Matthew, had signed the Association and joined the militia.[60] While on duty defending the Hudson, both surely could have used the weapons Joel had stored for Benjamin, for both were listed among the poor soldiers unable to buy guns.[61] Joel got his just deserts, but not until 1788, when he was advertised as an insolvent debtor.[62] And what of the father of this disparate brood? Jeremiah Dubois, Sr., was a full-fledged Loyalist. His refusal to sign the Association served only as a prelude to his being packed off to Worcester as a dangerous suspect, where he remained until 1779.[63]

Jeremiah Dubois's brother Elias had lost his life fighting for the English during the French and Indian War. Ironically, Elias's son Lewis spent most of the Revolutionary War fighting against the English as commander of the Fifth Regiment of the New York line. What Lewis Dubois thought of his uncle Jeremiah or of his wayward cousins remains unknown, but in any case he helped extend the interfamilial ties among Poughkeepsie's side takers when he married Alida Van Kleeck. He thus gained as in-laws the members of the prolific family that by the 1770s served as a kind of string, if in-laws of in-laws are counted, that bound together a good part of Pough-

58. Court of Common Pleas, Dutchess County, 1770, microfilm ed., Adriance Memorial Library, Poughkeepsie.

59. *Commission for Conspiracies*, 244, 282–83.

60. Court of Common Pleas, 1770; see also the Appendix; Hastings, ed., *Papers of Clinton*, IV, 283.

61. Hastings, ed., *Papers of Clinton*, IV, 283.

62. [Poughkeepsie] *Country Journal*, 22 April 1788.

63. Hastings, ed., *Papers of Clinton*, V, 74.

keepsie's population into one large family.[64] Through the Van
Kleecks, Lewis Dubois was connected to Henry Van Der Burgh. This
old and valiant Tory had been ordered deported to New Hampshire, apparently went and returned, and then found himself apprehended when he mistook the Patriot Stephen Hendrickson for his
Loyalist friend Abraham Ferdon; sent off to the fleet prison, he
escaped and proceeded to hide out in the woods until old age (he
was just past sixty) finally forced him to come in from the cold.[65]
Van Der Burgh in turn connected Dubois to two of *his* nephews, the
Occasional Loyalist Richard Everitt and the Occasional Patriot
Thomas Poole. Everitt, in his turn, connected Dubois to John Frear,
since Everitt's sister married one of Frear's nephews. All of this
reconnected Dubois back to the Van Kleecks, because John Frear
married Maria Van Kleeck, one of whose cousins married Cornelia
Livingston (daughter of James). A cousin of Cornelia had married
Bartholomew Crannel, who in turn was the father-in-law of the Patriot
Peter Tappen, as well as the Loyalist rector of Christ Church, John
Beardsley, and the Patriot Henry Livingston's son Gilbert.[66] The
connections spread out into the families of Westervelt, Swartwout,
Lassing, Van Den Bogart, Low, Winans, and Palmatier.[67] When, in
1783, the Loyalist Francis Peter Leroy wrote from Canada and ended
his letter with a request that his Occasional Loyalist father "give my
Compliments to Uncle John Frear [the Patriot militia colonel] and
his family,"[68] that simple postscript epitomized the rule in Poughkeepsie, not the exception.

Simply being related—however distantly—to other people in town
has never served as a guarantee for keeping the peace. In fact, if
ever a ripe opportunity came along for people in Poughkeepsie to
settle old scores with one another or to carry on long-standing feuds
with a new vengeance, it did so with the outbreak of the Revolution.
But few men in town seemed ready or willing to take advantage of
the breakdown of constituted authority. Nor did leading Patriots or
prominent Loyalists appear to have any proclivity for goading others
to divide the town through physical violence.

After independence was declared, Loyalists lost the offensive by
default; but their potential strength kept Patriots cautious. On 15
July 1776, Egbert Benson (who would spend the later years of the

64. Platt, *Eagle's History*, 19–25.

65. J. Wilson Poucher, "Dutchess County Men of the Revolutionary Era: James Van
Der Burgh," *Year Book* 15 (1930): 37.

66. Platt, *Eagle's History*, 30.

67. These can be traced through local genealogies on file at Adriance Memorial Library,
Poughkeepsie.

68. "Papers of the Leroy Family," 41.

Revolution in Poughkeepsie) warned the Convention of Representatives to forbear ordering a general call-up of the county militia. While precinct committees drafted Loyalists and "disarmed a great number of people," problems remained. The bolder young men who could have helped leash the Tories had gone off—with their guns—to join Washington's army. To issue a general call-up would have been to lose control of the militia, especially since the government of the convention—such as it was—had too shaky a foundation to persuade the people of Dutchess County "to yield a willing obedience."[69]

Before 1776, neither the Patriots nor the Loyalists would be confident of enough support to dare alienate the uncommitted by attempting to force them into line. Benson nicely summed up the dilemma of the Patriot leaders when he averred, "we always thought, we should be happy if we were capable of combating our internal foes"—to say nothing of combating the British.[70]

While the Patriots in town could count on a nearly two-to-one majority (109 to 61) during the war, those figures do not accurately represent Loyalist strength, for not all Loyalists—or Patriots, for that matter—were equal. In Poughkeepsie, as in other rural towns, rank or wealth alone did not necessarily follow status unless it was accompanied by a length of residency that conferred a sense of permanence. Even in a growing town, old money received preference over new. In Poughkeepsie's case, when men who resided in town in 1775 and who had also paid taxes ten years earlier are isolated from the known population as a whole, they are seen to have formed a breed apart. Whether Patriot or Loyalist, these longtime residents were a cut above their neighbors in relative wealth. The average of their tax assessments in 1775 was more than half again as high as that for all men of known allegiances.[71] These men also controlled town affairs to the extent that they kept the more important town offices exclusively to themselves until 1777.[72] From the ranks of these longtime residents came both the upper echelon of Patriot leaders and the Loyalist elite. Men who had lived in town at least since 1765 enjoyed more wealth and probably greater stature than did their neighbors. They quite likely wielded an undue influence over political decisions, whether in open election or in committee. And they were divided

---

69. *Journals of the Provincial Congress*, II, 309–10.   70. Ibid., 309.
71. The figures are as follows, ten-year residents compared with the 1775 average:
   Patriots—£6.4 vs. £3.4
   Occasional Patriots—£9.3 vs. £3.6
   Occasional Loyalists—£4.0 vs. £3.0
   Loyalists—£4.2 vs. £2.6
72. Poughkeepsie Town Records, 1765–1777.

much more evenly in their loyalties than were the rest of the townsmen.

In 1775 just above half of the Loyalists (31 of 61) and Occasional Loyalists (21 of 40) had lived in Poughkeepsie for at least ten years. By contrast, barely 40 percent of the Patriots (43 of 109) and a mere 20 percent of the Occasional Patriots (6 of 29) had paid taxes in 1765. In fact, if the four categories are combined into two, the Tory-minded men held a majority of 3 (52 to 49) over those who leaned toward independence.[73] Local Patriots, of course, could not have kept an accurate tally of the actual allegiances in 1775, nor could they have predicted precisely who would end up on which side. However, they could not have failed to recognize (though they would not have stated that recognition in numbers) that the leading men in town were more deeply and more evenly divided than was the population at large. Patriot leaders had to tread softly, for they did not know how big a stick they carried.

Even had they known, common sense would have opposed using it if they wished to maintain what may have been their most decisive advantage: the reality that the majority of men with substantial means were well disposed to the cause of independence. Eighteenth-century tax lists obviously provide a very imperfect measure of wealth. They reflect only the real and personal property a man owned locally.[74] There is always the possibility that a man of seemingly modest means assessed at, say, £2—also just happened to own half of New Jersey and in actuality was far and away the richest man around. Yet despite the unknowns, tax lists still offer the best available indicator of relative wealth during a given year. And in Poughkeepsie, no matter which way it is cut, Patriots as a group were, on the average, relatively wealthier than Loyalists.

Poughkeepsie was neither an impoverished town nor a community where the few rich could lord it over the large numbers of poor. Of the 329 residents whose names appear on the Association lists, fully 256 were assessed taxes in 1775.[75] If those who paid no taxes are counted as having a zero assessment, the average assessment for the Patriots is approximately £3.4 compared with £2.6 for the Tories.[76] Even if we exclude the £38 assessed to Henry Livingston, the county clerk and the highest taxpayer in town, we find that the Patriots' assessment still averaged nearly half a pound higher than that of the Loyalists. And if we limit the pool to those men who were actually assessed taxes, we find that the Whigs continued to receive higher

73. See the Appendix.   74. Tax Lists, 1775.
75. These figures represent a comparison of Association lists and tax lists.
76. See the Appendix.

assessments than did the Tories by an average of £4.4 to £3.5.[77]

The averages alone are enough to make Poughkeepsie an exception to the traditional notion that in New York Tories tended to be richer than Whigs. But breaking down the assessments into categories of wealth yields even more valuable information. Assuming that the men who were assessed only £1 or who paid no taxes at all made up, for want of a better phrase, Poughkeepsie's lower economic class, we can say they were attracted to the Patriot and Loyalist sides in most equal proportion (55 of 109 Patriots, 31 of 61 Loyalists).[78] It would be very difficult to argue that, in Poughkeepsie, political loyalty was in any way a product of a man's position on the lower rungs of the economic ladder.

But differences do begin to emerge on the next-higher rungs. A disproportionate number of the Loyalists were assessed between £2 and £4. Men in this group constituted slightly more than one-third of the total number of Loyalists, but less than one-fourth of the total number of Patriots. The most striking disparity, though, occurs in the £5-to-£9 bracket. Out of that group came 19 Patriots but only 5 Loyalists, and of those, 4 were assessed at the £5 minimum. In fact, the solid citizens assessed £5 and over contributed 28 men to the Patriot cause but only 9 to the Loyalist. The known Patriots outnumbered the known Loyalists by a margin of less than two to one in Poughkeepsie. But the well-heeled Patriots outnumbered the well-heeled Tories by a ratio of better than three to one. These figures suggest that the higher a man's estate was assessed the less likely he was to become an outright Loyalist, perhaps because of the vested interest that such a man probably had in his home and community.[79]

The relative wealth of the 40 Occasional Loyalists adds force to that possibility. They constituted the most economically moderate category in almost every way. That category held little attraction for men who owned no taxable wealth. Only 4 of them paid no taxes in 1775. Including those 4, the Occasional Loyalists' average assess-

77. A total of 45 Loyalists and 84 Patriots were assessed taxes.

78. For the Patriots, 25 men were not assessed at all and 30 were assessed at £1. On the Loyalist side, 16 were not assessed and 15 were assessed at £1. The traditional interpretation that Loyalists were wealthier than Patriots may well need revising far beyond the bounds of Poughkeepsie. Most studies of Loyalists have been precisely that—and not examinations of comparative wealth. Even the comparative studies completed to date, though they shed light on some aspects of the problem, are flawed when relative wealth is at issue. A sample of Loyalists and Patriots, chosen primarily because evidence about them survives, is just not a representative sample. See, for example, N. E. H. Hull, Peter C. Hoffer, and Steven L. Allen, "Choosing Sides: A Quantitative Study of the Personality Determinants of Loyalist and Revolutionary Political Affiliation in New York," *Journal of American History* 65 (1978): 344–66.

79. This would seem particularly the case because 22 of their number had resided in Poughkeepsie since 1765 at the latest.

ment was £3.0. Like the Loyalists, they had a disproportionate number of assessments in the £2-to-£4 range (14); but, unlike the Loyalists, they also had a surprisingly large number in the £5-to-£10 range. While only 7 of 61 Loyalists fell into that bracket, 10 of 40 Occasional Loyalists did.[80] Their allegiance may have been to the empire, but something more important to them than political loyalty kept them from taking the final step to unequivocal Loyalism.

Meanwhile, the Occasional Patriots composed the party of extremes. Their numbers were disproportionately high at both the richest and poorest ends of the scale, and disproportionately low in the middle range. Of the 29 Occasional Patriots, fully 19 were either assessed at £1 or not at all in 1775, and three of them became insolvent debtors at one time or another in the 1780s.[81] But even including those 19, the average assessment was £3.6, skewed upward by the £35 assessment of Leonard Van Kleeck and helped along by assessment of between £10 and £20 of the three other Occasional Patriots.[82]

Combined, the Patriot and Occasional Patriot categories accounted for 13 of the 15 large (£11 and above) taxpayers in town (the other two, Bartholomew Crannel and Richard Snedeker, were Loyalists). Local leaders could thus depend on the well-off and the well-to-do to acquiesce in, if not support, whatever measures might have to be taken to push Poughkeepsie into the revolutionary movement and to keep it there. They had little to fear from those with little economic stake in society, since such men were divided among themselves.

In fact, it is difficult to find a "factor" that can help explain why men chose the side they did. The two physicians not serving in the Continental line were Patriots, but the lawyers, merchants, clergy, artisans, and farmers were divided. The hatmaker was a Patriot, the barber an Occasional Loyalist.[83] Some families, Henry Livingston's, for instance, united on one side or the other.[84] Others, like that of Jeremiah Dubois, Sr., had members joining every conceivable side. Ethnicity might have made more of a difference, had intermarriage not broken down ethnic barriers. As it was, men with Dutch, English, Scottish, and French surnames could be found on all sides. Actual membership in the Reformed Church is difficult to trace, but those who attended it were Patriots more often than not, as was its pastor.

80. See the Appendix.
81. They were Joel Dubois, Abraham Frear, Jr., and Austin Creed.
82. See the Appendix.
83. William Terry was the hatter; James Douglass, the barber.
84. That included James Livingston, who had served as county sheriff in the 1760s.

It is also true that, compared with the total known population, a higher proportion of Christ Church's communicants became Loyalists, or belong in one of the "Occasional" categories.[85] Yet not only did some Anglicans become Patriots, but, Zephaniah Platt excepted, Poughkeepsie's Revolutionary leaders were Anglicans as well.[86] The available evidence suggests that Loyalism held a disproportionate attraction for men who had reached or passed their forty-fifth birthday by 1775.[87] Even more significantly, an unusually large number of men ranging in age from the late twenties to the midforties firmly supported the movement for independence.[88]

In the long run, an excess of intolerance, ending in terror, would seem to depend largely upon having a definable group on which to wreak vengeance. If that is true, rabid patriots in Poughkeepsie would have been hard put to hate the enemy at home, where they had only a few old Tories to attack. Even had they tried that, the earnest men of middling age and middling wealth who had recently come to power would quickly have put a stop to it. These men conducted Revolutionary affairs differently.

III

The demography—so to speak—of allegiance in Poughkeepsie limited the options available to local leaders in dealing with the enemy in their midst. The issue was complicated by the varieties of Loyalism that different men exhibited, ranging from Peter Leroy's benign hope that England would prevail to Richard Snedeker's active proselytizing for the king and a few young men's dashing off to join Loyalist regiments. Finally, the resolution of the Loyalist problem rested in the hands of men who, having made themselves noticeably large fish in a small pond, were as intent on saving their town as on saving their country. The destruction of their community, as they knew it, was not a price they would pay for victory.

The men most responsible for prodding Poughkeepsie to move toward independence had much in common with each other. All had lived in Poughkeepsie since at least the early 1760s. All had played an active role in town affairs: Zephaniah Platt and Gilbert Livingston had served as town supervisors, John Frear and Lewis Dubois as assessors, and John Bailey as constable. All were involved in local

---

85. See the Appendix.

86. Platt's religious affiliation remains unknown. For others, see the Appendix.

87. See the Appendix for the ages available. Of the 23 Loyalists whose birthdates are known, 13 were over forty years of age and 9 were above fifty years in 1775.

88. The Patriot group contained 39 (62 birthdates known) men between twenty-six and forty-five years of age in 1775, but only 7 over fifty.

committees in 1774 and 1775. They had reached the age of political awareness during the years, beginning in 1756, when England's imperial presence had begun to make itself visible—and felt. In 1775, Zephaniah Platt was forty years of age; Gilbert Livingston, thirty-two; Lewis Dubois, thirty-one; John Frear, forty-five; John Bailey, forty-three.[89] As they were not especially young or old, so they were not particularly rich or poor: Platt's tax assessment the highest, at £18, Livingston's the lowest, at £6. Dubois was assessed at £13, Frear and Bailey each at £11.[90] Solid citizens, permanent residents, and—by Poughkeepsie standards—precocious revolutionaries, they were far more inclined toward sober stubbornness than righteous intolerance.

During the war years only Dubois—having gone national as a line officer—stayed away from town for extended periods of time. The other four were periodically in and out of town, Frear and Bailey as commanders of militia units, Livingston and Platt as delegates to Provincial Congresses and the Convention of Representatives. Platt, in addition, served on the twelve-man Council of Safety, which until 1778 functioned, in effect, as New York's government for months at a time, and on the original Committee for Conspiracies as well.[91]

When that Committee first met in mid-October 1776, its members gave signs that they might be ready to act like classical radicals. Without hesitation, they ordered the deportation of one hundred suspected Loyalists to Exeter, New Hampshire. Eight of those banished, including Richard Snedeker, Henry Van Der Burgh, John Low, and Johannes Medler, called Poughkeepsie their home.[92] Over the next year more than a dozen other residents spent time in Worcester, Massachusetts, in New Windsor, or in the fleet prison that floated off Kingston. The committee and its successor, the Commission for Conspiracies, working with the cooperation of precinct committees and the military, seemed more than ready to send out of sight any man who got out of line.

During the crucial months between the fall of 1776 and the end of 1777, Platt was invariably in a position to influence any decision affecting a Poughkeepsie resident. On the Committee for Conspiracies, he would have known best the Poughkeepsie residents whom he helped ship to New England, if other members knew them at all. On the Council of Safety, his acquaintance with local men and affairs probably made his the deciding voice in the council's refusal to appoint John Child an assistant commissioner for conspiracies. When,

89. See the Appendix.   90. Tax Lists, 1775.
91. *Journal of the Provincial Congress,* I, 917; *Commission for Conspiracies,* I, 3–6.
92. Commission for Conspiracies, I, 3–6.

in May of 1777, the Convention of Representatives took upon itself the task of filling the appointive offices provided for in the recently proclaimed constitution, Gilbert Livingston undoubtedly had a hand in having Platt named a judge and himself appointed the surrogate for Dutchess County. (Livingston was an obvious choice to replace his law partner and father-in-law, the Loyalist Bartholomew Crannel, as was the selection of Livingston's father, Henry, to succeed himself as county clerk.)[93]

While Platt served as the Poughkeepsie connection in state affairs, Gilbert Livingston, John Frear, and John Bailey, Jr., longtime committeemen all, appeared to retain an informal grip on the town. Not by accident did Livingston chair the committee—on which Frear and Bailey served—that set and enforced price controls on basic commodities when runaway inflation hit in 1779.[94]

Associated with these men were a group of relative newcomers who formed a second tier of local leaders. The eldest, Samuel Dodge, had moved to town in 1770, at the age of forty.[95] Peter Tappen and Andrew Billings were younger and did not arrive in Poughkeepsie until the early 1770s. Curiously enough, whoever controlled appointments to local commissions largely passed over natives in favor of these more recent immigrants. Homebred young men received commissions in the militia, but little else.[96] Meanwhile, Dodge served on the Commissions for Sequestration and for administering poor relief, while both Billings and Tappen were appointed to the Commission for Conspiracies.[97] If these men were not handpicked (Dodge would seem an unlikely successor to Platt as town supervisor unless his candidacy had been agreed to), then family ties may have had great influence (Tappen, an in-law of Governor Clinton, married a sister of Gilbert Livingston's wife, while Billings married a Livingston).

Until 1778, when the duly constituted government of the state began gradually to exert its power over county affairs, these eight men assumed the responsibility of maintaining civil order without law and of administering justice—if that is the word for it—without courts. Their methods were extralegal, informal, and hardly subtle. But the evidence that survives makes clear that their actions (or lack of action, in some instances) served as a means to achieve a rigor-

93. *Journal of the Provincial Congress*, I, 916–17.
94. [Poughkeepsie] *New York Journal*, 9 August 1779.
95. At least, he did not appear on the Tax List until 1770.
96. [Poughkeepsie] *New York Journal*, 25 January 1779.
97. J. Wilson Poucher, "Dutchess County Men of the Revolutionary Era: Dr. Peter Tappen," *Year Book* 19 (1934): 38, and his similarly entitled article on Maj. Andrew Billings, ibid., 30–35.

ously consistent end. They were not out to punish the guilty or even to reform the wayward so much as to enforce a patriotic consensus. Having in 1775 forced men to choose sides, they began in 1776 to reduce the alternatives: those who wished to continue to live in Poughkeepsie now had to choose between acting like Patriots and silent acquiescence. No other option was acceptable. Over the longer run, the policy was successful. Yet it also proved insidious, not because Patriots forced Loyalists out, but because they kept welcoming dissidents back—on the condition, of course, that they would dissent no more.

Perhaps the most unjustly treated victims of patriotic justice were men who belonged, or very likely would have belonged, in one of the "occasional" categories. One poor man, who not inaccurately referred to continental currency as "Linsey-woolsey money," found himself rudely hauled before the Commission for Conspiracies and forced to pledge once more his allegiance to the state.[98] Josiah Bartley ended up in the forced-labor camp at New Windsor, the only evidence against him having been a statement by Zephaniah Platt that Bartley lived with "an equivocal character—that all the Connections are equivocal" and that, in an election (probably that of 1775) on the question of forming a committee, he "was of that party which voted against a Committee."[99]

An equally effective method of enforcing consensus consisted of selective lapses in the maintenance of order. Peter Mesier, for instance, though not a Poughkeepsie resident, exhibited the traits of an Occasional Loyalist. One of the "poor" (in fact, a well-off storekeeper) who left New York City after the British occupied it,[100] Mesier opened a shop just outside the town limits. In May of 1777, he decided to sell tea at the price the market would bear, only to discover that several local women suddenly found him unbearable. After a few minor confrontations, the women took matters into their own hands. They broke into his store, drank his liquor, vandalized the premises, and apparently climaxed their day with a rock-throwing contest in which Mesier and his servants were the targets. They forgot only to take the tea. Mesier, a law-abiding man, preferred to press charges against the women in the only court available—the Commission for Conspiracies. The commissioner took his deposition, then simply let the matter drop.[101]

John Davis was another Occasional Loyalist whom justice blindly bypassed. After the Reverend John Beardsley's forced departure for New York City, the vestry of Christ Church voted to install Davis in its glebe house. Once he had moved in, Davis found himself a near

---

98. *Commission for Conspiracies,* I, 220.   99. Ibid., 23.
100. Ibid., 111.   101. Ibid., 301–3.

neighbor to Samuel Curry, a blacksmith—and stalwart Patriot—who had appropriated for himself some of the land belonging to the church. In the summer of 1778, Curry decided that he needed more than the twenty-five acres that he lived on but had no title to. As Davis put it, Curry "began to be troublesome." He knocked down Davis's fences, then turned his livestock loose in Davis's cornfield. He cut and kept Davis's hay, and then used the rails from the fences he had torn down to build a fence of his own to keep Davis out.

Davis went to court. But for some reason (that Platt was the only judge in town might be relevant) his case was not heard for nine years. Davis finally won by default in 1787, long after both he and Curry had changed addresses.[102] Even men like Davis, who placed community above cause, learned the cost of dissidence, no matter how muted.

By contrast, men who had once demonstrated their patriotism to the satisfaction of local leaders, but who later wavered, were forgiven their lapses as soon as they consented to rejoin the consensus. A mere two months before Burgoyne led his army south from Canada, several men in Capt. Isaac Hageman's militia company apparently decided to try the British side for a while, and they talked Hageman into joining them. But someone informed the authorities, and Hageman, along with seven of his men, was hustled off to jail. Less than three weeks later the Commission for Conspiracies received a petition on Hageman's behalf. The thirty petitioners—John Frear and Peter Tappen among them—argued that Hageman "had been deluded," and asked the commission to set him free. The commissioners, conceiving it "their duty . . . to pardon all such convinced of their error who are willing to return again to their duty," not only released Hageman (he contritely took the oath of allegiance) but gave him back the command of his company. He did not deviate again.[103]

Known Loyalists, of course, provided the most visible candidates for the program dedicated to realizing consensus. Most of the Poughkeepsie men sent to prison prior to the summer of 1777 were allowed to return to town even before the Battle of Saratoga. On their arrival, they were to appear before the Commission for Conspiracies. If they took the oath of allegiance, they were released on their own recognizance. The commissioners were prepared to place on parole even well-known and well-hated Tories who refused to take the oath; but they did not do so, because they feared that "pernicious consequences" (namely, bodily harm) would result.[104] They readily issued passes to go behind enemy lines to those Loyalists whom they thought beyond redemption. Such a pass had been given to

102. Reynolds, *Christ Church*, 62–63.
103. *Commission for Conspiracies*, I, 271–73, 294–95, 309.   104. Ibid., 445.

Richard Snedeker after his return from New Hampshire (his initial crime consisted of "Treasonable Practices"). George Clinton, a brigadier general at the time, had him arrested again because he had not made it to Manhattan—only to Haverstraw, where he was "spreading his Banefull Influence."[105] In the rare instances in which local authorities forced Loyalists like Henry Van Der Burgh, Bartholomew Crannel, and John Beardsley to sail for New York, they did so mainly to protect their lives.[106]

Backsliders were simply exposed to the same treatment again. Richard Snedeker, twice imprisoned, twice released, was left alone after June 1777, when he took the oath of allegiance.[107] Before the end of 1777, Johannes Medler, too, had been twice jailed and twice let go; John Miller, once jailed, once let go, along with Arie Medler, John Van Der Burgh, John Low, Alexander Haire, Isaac Lassing, and others.[108] Patriot leaders made only two demands, even of backsliders: they must take the oath of allegiance and thereafter keep their political sentiments to themselves.

By and large the policy succeeded. When Christ Church resumed services, in 1785, the congregation could publicly demonstrate its commitment to consensus. At least on Sundays, William Terry, a Patriot hatter, could kneel alongside James Douglass, a barber and Occasional Loyalist. The Patriot tavern owner Stephen Hendrickson could keep an eye on his competitor from down the street, Thomas Poole, an Occasional Patriot. The Loyalist Richard Snedeker could sit across the aisle from Col. Lewis Dubois or Gilbert Livingston or John Frear or John Bailey. Occasional Loyalists like John Davis and William Emmot could pray that the Loyalist Samuel Pinckney might prosper (he needed their prayers, because his property had been confiscated).[109] And so it went. The community—the extended family of sorts—that had prayed together had, after a fashion, stayed together.

Loyalists had paid a high price for having supported the king. At least twenty-seven men who lived in Poughkeepsie in 1775 later forfeited their property for their allegiance.[110] Another score or so spent

105. Hastings, ed., *Papers of Clinton*, I, 849.
106. *Commission for Conspiracies*, I, 441, 445–48.
107. Ibid., I, 4, 182, 208, 317; II, 426, 441.
108. For Johannes Medler, see ibid., I, 4, 102–5, 158, 243–45, 291; II, 337, 350; for Miller, see ibid., I, 4, 188; II, 320–22, 328; for the remaining men, see ibid., I, 4, 104–6, 114–15, 182, 208, 271–73, 260.
109. See the Appendix; Platt, *Eagle's History*, 301; Roberts, *New York in the Revolution*, Supplement, 256.
110. Platt, *Eagle's History*, 301, lists 46 men who forfeited their property. Some of those moved to Poughkeepsie only after 1775, and for others I can find no corroborating evidence.

a small part of the war in prison. More than a dozen left for Canada.[111] And if jail terms were relatively short, and if in some cases property that had been seized was repurchased by an in-law or relatives who at least kept it in the family, some scars were bound to remain. Former Loyalists could not, for example, have made themselves immune to the outbreak of fury (it quickly subsided) that followed the peace of 1783, even though that outcry was directed in general against Tories who had left town during the war, and specifically against a "B.C." (Bartholomew Crannel), who received public notification that he would "get his head broke" if he returned to practice law in Poughkeepsie.[112]

Ties to family, to farms, and to the community—ties that were enhanced by the quest for consensus undertaken by Patriot leaders—proved to a surprising extent stronger than political causes. The ties alone were strong enough that 54 of the 109 Patriots—including all of the leaders—still lived in town when the 1790 census was taken. The policy of pressing consensus may well have helped ensure that 18 of 29 Occasional Patriots and 22 of 40 Occasional Loyalists were also counted in the census. And that policy undoubtedly accounted in part for the continued residence of 15 former Loyalists—including 4 who had forfeited their property—and those numbers would probably have been higher, had not death due to old age decimated their ranks.[113]

The consensus achieved by the Patriots—manifested, if nowhere else, in the willingness of former enemies and halfhearted friends to stay on—also exacted its price. While former Loyalists and "occasionals" from both sides were reintegrated into the social fabric of Poughkeepsie, all of them, with the single exception of the Occasional Loyalist William Emmot, were excluded from an active voice in the political affairs of post-Revolutionary Poughkeepsie. Property owners, no matter what their former allegiances, were allowed to vote. But outside of Emmot, only the Patriots of '76 held even the most lowly of town offices. Leonard Van Kleeck, an Occasional Patriot who had in 1775 paid more taxes than anyone else in town except Henry Livingston, never again held office after his final stint as town supervisor in 1767. Richard Snedeker, once a prominent lawyer, had also served as supervisor, but his third term, which ended in the spring of 1772, marked the last time he held any town office. When, in 1788, delegates met in Poughkeesie to debate the merits of the

111. See Esther Clarke Wright, *The Saint John River* (Toronto, 1949), 86.
112. [Fishkill] *New York Packet*, 8, 15, and 29 May and 3 July 1783.
113. By 1790, 13 of the 23 Loyalists of known age would have passed their fifty-fifth birthday.

new federal constitution. Snedeker had been reduced to playing the role of a "carney." For a shilling apiece, the curious could come to his house and stare at the strange sight of two camels, only recently imported from Arabia.[114]

The cost of consensus was thus not restricted to individual instances of deprivation. At least in practice, it extended to the point of denying even political legitimacy to men whose political loyalties had not been shared by the weight of the community. In 1775, local Patriots had lacked the power to quell dissent. Moreover, the use of force would have entailed the risk of alienating the uncommitted. In 1776, they probably realized that they enjoyed a majority in members, wealth and, prestige, but not a sufficiently large majority to allow purification through either violence or banishment without destroying the community as they knew it. Their subsequent policy of enforcing consensus through lenient measures was undoubtedly an unthinking decision.

But surely a natural one. Independence would be meaningless without a community in which to enjoy it. And since the only requirement really imposed on former "occasionals" and Loyalists was that they became permanently apolitical, reasonable men on both sides could be counted on to make the best of a good thing. The Patriots got their consensus, but at the cost of helping create an atmosphere in which quiet acquiescence was deemed a virtue, and vocal opposition a danger to the nation.

APPENDIX: ALLEGIANCES IN POUGHKEEPSIE

The following lists consist of (1) data on men whose allegiances have been determined and (2) the names of men whose allegiances could not be determined. While another investigator might, in a very few instances, decide to assign to an individual an allegiance slightly different from the one I assigned, the general conclusions regarding allegiance would, I am confident, still stand.[115]

Key to list of allegiances:

P = Patriot	O / C = Occasional Loyalist
O / P = Occasional Patriot	S = Signed the Association list

114. [Poughkeepsie] *Country Journal*, 18 June 1788.
115. The evidence for religion, occupation, age, and allegiance comes from Reynolds, *Christ Church; Records of the First Reformed Church; Year Book;* Poucher and Reynolds, *Old Gravestones;* Reynolds, *Notices of Marriages and Deaths;* Platt, *Eagle's History;* Force, ed., *American Archives;* Fernow, ed., *Documents; Calendar of Historical Documents; Commission for Conspiracies;* Hastings, ed., *Papers of Clinton;* [Fishkill] *New York Packet;* [Poughkeepsie] *New York Journal;* and [Poughkeepsie] *Country Journal*.

R = Refused to sign   R = Reformed
E = Episcopalian

The numbers under "Amount of 1775 Tax Assessment in £" refer to the total assessment in pounds, not to the amount of tax actually paid.

Name	Allegiance	Association List	Age in 1775	Occupation	Religion	Appeared on 1765 Tax List	Amount of 1775 Tax Assessment in £	Appeared in 1790 Census
David Ackerman	P	–				+	5	
Gulian Ackerman	P	S		Farmer		+	8	+
Ephraim Adams	P	S			R		1	
George Ame	O/P	R					0	+
Nathaniel Ashford	P	S		Laborer			0	
Nathaniel Babcock	P	R					1	
Ebenezer Badger	O/P	R	29	Shoemaker	E?		1	+
John Bailey, Jr.	P	S	43	Farmer (Esq.)	E	+	13	+
George Balding	O/P	R		Farmer			2	
Isaac Baldwin	O/P	R			E		16	+
Isaac Baldwin, Jr.	O/P	R		Farmer	E		2	+
Henry Barns	O/P	R					1	+
John Barns	P	–					1	+
William Barns	O/L	R			E	+	5	+
Josiah Bartley	L	S				+	1	
Simon Bartley	P	S				+	1	
Thomas Bayeaux	P	S		Farmer	E		1	+
John Beardsley	L	–		Clergyman	E		5	
Andrew Billings	P	S	32		E?		2	+
Cornelius Brewer	P	–					2	+
James Brooks	P	–					1	
Underhill Budd	P	–					1	+
Matthew Burnett	L	S					1	
Thomas Burnett	L	S				+	3	
William Burnett	L	S					0	
Zachariah Burwell	P	S					0	
Christian Bush	L	S					1	
Hendrick Bush	L	S				+	0	
Martin Bush	L	S					2	
Gideon Buyce	L	S					0	
Caleb Carmen	O/P	S		Farmer	E	+	4	
Joseph Chatterton	P	S					1	
John Child	O/P	S			E		2	
Robert Churchill	O/L	R				+	9	+
John Coapman	O/L	R	38	Wheelwright	E	+	1	+

Name	Allegiance	Association List	Age in 1775	Occupation	Religion	Appeared on 1765 Tax List	Amount of 1775 Tax Assessment in £	Appeared in 1790 Census
John Concklin	P	S				+	9	
Matthew Concklin	P	S		Farmer			1	+
Samuel Cooke	P	S	37	Surgeon		+	3	
Ezekial Cooper	P	S		River Trader/ Joyner			3	+
Bartholomew Crannel	L	R	55+	Lawyer (Esq.)	E	+	19	
Austin Creed	O/P	R					0	+
Samuel Curry	P	S	31	Blacksmith	R		1	+
Lodowick Cypher	L	S					1	
John Davis	O/L	S	34		E		4	
Richard Davis	O/P	S	41	Merchant/ Mariner	E	+	12	+
John DeGraff	L	R	55	Mariner		+	4	
Henry Dodge	P	S	18	Surveyor	Bap		0	+
Samuel Dodge	P	S	45				5	
James Douglass	O/L	R		Barber	E		1	
Benjamin Dubois	O/L	–	28		E		0	+
Henry Dubois	P	–	22				0	
Jeremiah Dubois	L	R	54			+	2	
Jeremiah Dubois, Jr.	P	S	30			+	1	
Joel Dubois	O/P	S	33			+	1	+
John Dubois	O/P	S	28				3	+
Lewis Dubois	P	S	31			+	11	+
Matthew Dubois	P	S	28				3	
Nathaniel Dubois	P	S	32	Farmer/ Miner			0	+
Peter Dubois	L	R	51			+	1	
Peter Dubois, Jr.	L	R					0	+
Henry Ellis	P	S		Gunsmith		+	1	+
Henry Ellis, Jr.	P	S	25				2	
Eli Emmons	L	R			E	+	1	
John Emmons	L	R		Brickmaker	E		1	
William Emmot	O/L	R	27	Saddlemaker (Esq.)	E		3	+
Richard Everitt	O/L	S	26	Gentleman	E		2	+
Abraham Ferdon	O/L	S			E	+	1	+
Jacobus Ferdon	L	R			E	+	3	+
John Ferdon	L	R	55			+	2	+
John Ferdon, Jr.	L	R	50		E	+	5	
Zachariah Ferdon	L	R			E	+	5	
William Foreman	P	S		Physician		+	3	+
Abraham Fort	P	S	25	Tavern Owner/ Farmer	R		2	+

Name	Allegiance	Association List	Age in 1775	Occupation	Religion	Appeared on 1765 Tax List	Amount of 1775 Tax Assessment in £	Appeared in 1790 Census
Johannes Fort	P	S	45	Farmer		+	11	+
Abraham Frear	L	R	45	Farmer		+	2	+
Abraham Frear, Jr.	O/P	R	23	Farmer	R		0	+
Elias Frear	P	S	27				0	+
Jacobus Frear	P	S	40	Farmer	R	+	5	+
John Frear	P	S	45	Esquire	E	+	11	+
Simeon Frear	O/L	R	54	Farmer		+	5	+
Simeon Frear, Jr.	O/L	R	31				2	+
Thomas Frear	L	R					1	+
Hendrick Hagerman	O/P	S	33		E		0	+
Alexander Haire	L	S		Merchant			0	
Stephen Hendrickson	P	S	25	Tavern Owner/ Stable Owner	E		0	+
Zachariah Hill	L	–			R		1	
Carel Hoefman	P	S	48	Farmer	R	+	3	+
Henry Hoff	P	S					0	
Robert Hoffman	P	S	39	Farmer	R	+	22	+
Thomas Holmes	P	S					0	
Lemuel Howel	P	S					0	
Samuel Hull	P	R					0	
John Hunt	O/L	R					1	+
Benjamin Jaycocks	O/L	S					1	+
Francis Jaycocks	O/L	S				+	2	+
William Jaycocks	L	S				+	10	
William Jaycocks, Jr.	L	–	20				0	
John Johnson	P	S					1	+
James Kelly	O/L	R		Cooper			1	
Jonas Kelsey	P	S	31	Cobbler	E		3	+
Francis Kip	P	S	30				1	+
Hendrick Kip	P	S		Farmer			0	+
Peter Lansing	L	–		Cooper			1	+
Isaac J. Lassing	L	R	30				2	
Johannes P. Lassing	L	–	35	Farmer		+	4	
Johannes W. Lassing	L	–				+	1	
Lawrence Lassing, Jr.	L	S	25				0	
Peter Ab. Lassing	P	S					2	
Peter An. Lassing	P	S		Farmer		+	4	+
Peter J. Lassing	L	–				+	0	+
Simeon W. Lassing	P	S	40	Farmer		+	3	
Jonathan Lawrence	L	R					2½	
Thomas Lawrence	L	R					2½	
Andries Lawson	O/L	–					0	+
Francis P. Leroy	L	–		Laborer		+	0	

Name	Allegiance	Association List	Age in 1775	Occupation	Religion	Appeared on 1765 Tax List	Amount of 1775 Tax Assessment in £	Appeared in 1790 Census
Peter Leroy	O/L	R	53		R	+	6	+
Simeon Leroy, Jr.	O/L	S	29	Farmer	E		2	
Simeon J. Leroy	L	S	26				0	
Simeon P. Leroy	O/L	–	25				2	
James Letson	O/P	S		Farmer			0	+
Alanson Lewis	O/P	–					1	
Felix Lewis	P	R		Farmer			1	+
Gilbert Livingston	P	S	32	Lawyer	E	+	6	+
Henry Livingston	P	S	60	Lawyer	E	+	38	+
Henry Livingston, Jr.	P	S	27		R		7	+
James Livingston	P	S	47		E	+	15	
John Lovot	P	S					0	
Jacob Low	P	S	28	Farmer	R		3	
John Low	L	R	53		R	+	2	
Peter Low	P	S	51	Farmer		+	7	+
William Low	O/L	R				+	2	+
James Luckey	P	S		Farmer		+	3	+
Wines Manney	P	–	45	Mason		+	5	+
John Maxfield	P	S			R		0	
Arie Medler	O/L	R			E	+	2	+
Johannes Medler	L	S			E	+	4	+
Hendrick Miller	O/L	R					1	
Johannes Miller	L	R				+	3	
Jonathan Morey	L	R					0	
Joshua Moss	P	S		School-master		+	6	
John Mott	L	S	33	House Car-penter			1	
Cornelius Noble	P	S					0	
Robert North	P	S		Boat Captain	E		3	+
Bartholomew Noxon	L	R	72			+	2	
Robert Noxon	O/P	S	25				0	+
Simon Noxon	L	R	53	Miller?			2	
James Odell	O/L	–		Blacksmith			0	
Hendrick Ostrum	O/L	–	37			+	1	
Jacobus Ostrum	O/L	–		Farmer			1	
Francis Palmatier	L	R	29				0	
Jacob Palmatier	L	R	41	Farmer		+	10	+
John Palmatier	O/L	R	53	Cordwainer	R	+	2	+
Peter Palmatier	L	–	33	Boatman		+	2	
Evert Pells	O/L	R	54			+	8	
Francis Pells	O/L	R	30	Farmer			2	+
Hendrick Pells	P	S		Farmer		+	2	
Hendrick Pells, Jr.	P	S		Farmer			0	+

Name	Allegiance	Association List	Age in 1775	Occupation	Religion	Appeared on 1765 Tax List	Amount of 1775 Tax Assessment in £	Appeared in 1790 Census
Michael Pells	O/L	R	60+			+	10	
Ezekiel Pinkney	L	R		Carpenter	E	+	2	+
Samuel Pinkney	L	R			E	+	4	+
Thomas Pinkney	O/L	R		Farmer		+	3	
Zephaniah Platt	P	S	40	Farmer, Esq.		+	18	+
Wilhelmus Ploegh	P	S				+	0	
Thomas Poole	O/P	S		Tavern Owner/ Tailor	E	+	5	+
Eli Read	O/P	R/S		Silversmith	E		1	
John Read	P	S	31	Carpenter	E		1	
John C. Ringland	P	S					5	
Thomas Rowse	P	S					0	
John Michael Rutsen	L	R			E		2	
Myndert Rynders	L	R			R	+	1	
George Sands	O/L	S					7	
John Schenck, Jr.	P	S		Merchant			13	
Paul Schenck	P	S	34	Merchant			5	+
Jacob Schryver	P	S					0	
Joseph Scott	O/L	–		Farmer			3	+
George Shannon	P	S					1	
Samuel Smith	O/L	S	44	Boatman	E	+	3	+
Richard Snedeker	L	S	40	Lawyer	E	+	25	+
Abraham Swartwout	P	S	32			+	1	+
Bernardus Swartwout	P	S	44	Farmer	R	+	3	+
Bernardus J. Swartwout	P	S	32	Farmer			1	
Johannis Swartwout	P	S	61	Miller/ Brewer		+	7	+
Johannis Swartwout, Jr.	P	S	29	Farmer by '84			0	
John Tappen	P	S		Laborer			0	
Peter Tappen	P	S	27	Physician	E		4	+
Teunis Tappen	P	S	47			+	1	+
William Terry	P	S		Hatter	E	+	1	+
Elias Thompson	P	R					0	
Elias Van Benschoten	P	S	57	Farmer	R	+	8	
Elias Van Benschoten, Jr.	P	S	26	Farmer	R-E		1	+
Jacob Van Benschoten	P	S		Farmer		+	6	
Marcus Van Bommel	P	–	48			+	1	+
Jacob Van Den Bogart	P	S	26				1	+
Myndert Van Den Bogart	P	S	54	Farmer		+	4	
Myndert M. Van Den Bogart	O/P	–	30				1	
Peter Van Den Bogart	O/P	–	18				0	

Name	Allegiance	Association List	Age in 1775	Occupation	Religion	Appeared on 1765 Tax List	Amount of 1775 Tax Assessment in £	Appeared in 1790 Census
Henry Van Der Burgh	L	R	58	Lawyer?	E	+	6	
Henry S. Van Der Burgh	L	R					0	+
John Van Der Burgh	L	R	47		E	+	5	
Peter Van Der Burgh	O/L	R	25		R		0	
Richard Van Der Burgh	L	R				+	0	
Abraham Van Keuren	O/P	S	38			+	1	+
Matthew Van Keuren	P	S	69	Ferry/Tavern Operator		+	5	+
Matthew Van Keuren, Jr.	P	S	40				1	+
Baltus Van Kleeck	O/L	R	51		E	+	7	+
Hugh Van Kleeck	P	–	31			+	2('74)	+
Jacob Van Kleeck	P	S	51	Farmer		+	0	
John L. Van Kleeck	P	S	21				2	+
John T. Van Kleeck	P	S	34	Esquire	E	+	6	
Lawrence Van Kleeck	O/P	S	26				1	+
Lawrence J. Van Kleeck	O/P	S	23				1	
Leonard Van Kleeck	O/P	S	51			+	35	
Myndert Van Kleeck	O/P	S			E		12	+
Peter Van Kleeck	O/L	S	60			+	10	
Peter B. Van Kleeck	P	S	30				2	+
Peter B. Van Kleeck	O/L	R	25			+	1	
Simeon P. Van Kleeck	L	–	26	Yeoman			0	
Richard F. Van Steenbergh	L	R					1	+
Stephen Van Voorhees	P	S		Clergyman			1	
Garrett Van Wagenen	P	S	32				1	
Cornelius Viele	O/L	S	57	Farmer		+	6	+
Richard Waddel	P	S					1	
Richard Warner	P	S	54		E		1	
Michael Wellding	O/L	R				+	1	
Albertus Westervelt	L	S	21				2	
Benjamin Westervelt	P	S	48			+	5	
Casparus B. Westervelt	P	S	23				2	
Casparus C. Westervelt	P	S	18				0	+
Cornelius Westervelt	P	S	49			+	8	
Henry Willsie	P	S				+	3	+
John Willsie	O/P	S	28	Farmer			0	+
William Willsie	O/P	S	20				1	+
John H. Wilson	O/P	–					1	
James Winans, Jr.	P	S	32	Mariner	E		4	+
Azariah Winchester	P	S					0	
James Wood	L	R		Cooper			1	
William Yates	L	S					0	+
Gail Yelverton	O/L	R		Storekeeper		+	1	

ALLEGIANCE UNKNOWN: NAMES APPEARING
ON ASSOCIATION LIST

Abraham Bartley
Henry Bayeaux
Sylvanus Beckwith
John Boerum
John Briener
James Brisban
George Brooks
Caleb Carmen, Jr.
Alexander Chaucer
Nathanial Concklin
James Elderkin
Samual Ferdon
Jacob Ferris
Nathan Frear
Sylvanus Greatraknis
Alexander Griggs
Thomas Jacocks
Johathan Johnston
William Kelly
John Kidney
Myndert Kidney
Robert Kidney
Benomi Kip
Matthew Kip
William Lassing
William Lawson
Barent Lewis, Jr.
Melancton Lewis
William Lossing
Samuel Lucky
Peter Muller
John Pinckney

Abraham Pitt
Isaac Poole
Aaron Read
Jacob Rhodes
William Roach
John Robinson
Isaac Romeyne
John Romeyne
John Saunders
John Seabury
John Seabury, Jr.
Edward Simmon
Gorus Storm
Mindert Swartwout
John Townsend
Peter F. Valleau
Francis Van Den Bogart
John Van Den Bogart
Henry Van Der Burgh, Jr.
Jacob Van Der Burgh
Steven Van Der Burgh
Henry Van Vlercome
Frederick Van Vliet
Garrett Van Vliet
Peter Van Vliet
Nehemiah Veal
John Waterman
Andrew Watts
Andrew Week
Càsparus R. Westervelt
Michael Yerry

ALLEGIANCES UNKNOWN: NAMES OF RESIDENTS
NOT ON ASSOCIATION LIST

Thomas Buyce
David Cypher
Thomas Dearing
Peter Deyo, Jr.
Clear Everitt
Daniel Fisher
Isaac Fitchett
William Hare
Richard Johnson
Garret Lansing
Francis Laroy
Murray Lester
Leonard Lewis
Jury Michael

John Noll
Matthew Moss
Benjamin Nollerton
John Paiton
Jacob Palmatier
John Record
John Roemer
Casparus Romeyn
Joseph Simson
Samual Strickland
Marcus Van Bommel, Jr.
John S. Van Kleeck
Moses Van Kleeck
James Wellding

Why Men Fought in the American Revolution

ROBERT MIDDLEKAUFF

In the Battle of Eutaw Springs, South Carolina, the last major action of the Revolutionary War before Cornwallis surrendered at Yorktown, over 500 Americans were killed and wounded. Nathanael Greene had led some 2,200 men into the Springs; his casualties thus equaled almost one-fourth of his army. More men would die in battles in the next two years, and others would suffer terrible wounds. Although the statistics are notoriously unreliable, they show that the Revolution killed a higher percentage of those who served on the American side than any war in our history, always excepting the Civil War.[1]

Why did these men—those who survived and those who died—fight? Why did they hold their ground, endure the strain of battle, with men dying about them and danger to themselves so obvious? Undoubtedly the reasons varied from battle to battle, but undoubtedly there was some experience common to all these battles—and fairly uniform reasons for the actions of the men who fought despite their deepest impulses, which must have been to run from the field in order to escape the danger.

Some men did run, throwing down their muskets and packs in order to speed their flight. American units broke in large actions and small, at Brooklyn, Kip's Bay, White Plains, Brandywine, Germantown, Camden, and Hobkirk's Hill, to cite the most important instances. Yet many men did not break and run even in the disasters to American arms. They held their ground until they were killed, and they fought tenaciously while pulling back.

In most actions the Continentals, the regulars, fought more bravely

---

1. *The Toll of Independence: Engagements and Battle Casualties of the American Revolution,* ed. Howard H. Peckham (Chicago, 1974), p. 90 for Eutaw Springs, pp. 132–33 for the comparison of the Revolution and the Civil War.

than the militia. We need to know why these men fought and why the American regulars performed better than the militia. The answers surely will help us to understand the Revolution, especially if we can discover whether what made men fight reflected what they believed—and felt—about the Revolution.

Several explanations of the willingness to fight and die, if necessary, may be dismissed at once. One is that soldiers on both sides fought out of fear of their officers, fearing them more than they did battle. Frederick the Great had described this condition as ideal, but it did not exist in ideal or practice in either the American or the British army. The British soldier usually possessed a more professional spirit than the American, an attitude compounded of confidence in his skill and pride in belonging to an old established institution. British regiments carried proud names—the Royal Welsh Fusiliers, the Black Watch, the King's Own—and their officers usually behaved extraordinarily bravely in battle and expected their men to follow their examples. British officers disciplined their men more harshly than American officers did and generally trained them more effectively in the movements of battle. But neither they nor American officers instilled the fear that Frederick found so desirable. Spirit, bravery, and a reliance on the bayonet were all expected of professional soldiers, but professionals acted out of pride—not fear of their officers.

Still, coercion and force were never absent from the life of either army. There were, however, limits on their use and their effectiveness. The fear of flogging might prevent a soldier from deserting from camp, but it could not guarantee that he would remain steady under fire. Fear of ridicule may have aided in keeping some troops in place, however. Eighteenth-century infantry went into combat in fairly close lines, and officers could keep an eye on many of their men. If the formation was tight enough, officers might strike laggards and even order "skulkers," Washington's term for those who turned tail, shot down.[2] Just before the move to Dorchester Heights in March 1776, the word went out that any American who ran from the action would be "fired down upon the spot."[3] The troops themselves approved of this threat, according to one of the chaplains.

Washington repeated the threat just before the Battle of Brooklyn, later that year, though he seems not to have posted men behind the lines to carry it out. Daniel Morgan urged Nathanael Greene to

---

2. *The Writings of George Washington*, ed. John C. Fitzpatrick (Washington, D.C., 1931–44), V, 480.

3. Jeanette D. Black and William G. Roelker, *A Rhode Island Chaplain in the Revolution: Letters of Ebenezer David to Nicholas Brown, 1775–1778* (Providence, R.I., 1949), 13.

place sharpshooters behind the militia, and Greene may have done so at Guilford Court House. No one thought that an entire army could be held in place against its will, and these threats to shoot soldiers who retired without orders were never widely issued.[4]

A tactic that surely would have appealed to many soldiers would have been to send them into battle drunk. Undoubtedly some—on both sides—did enter combat with their senses deadened by rum. Both armies commonly issued an additional ration of rum on the eve of some extraordinary action—a long, difficult march, for example, and a battle were two of the usual reasons. A common order on such occasions ran: "The troops should have an extraordinary allowance of rum," usually a gill, four ounces of unknown alcoholic content, which if taken down at the propitious moment might dull fears and summon courage. At Camden no supply of rum existed; Gates or his staff substituted molasses to no good effect, according to Otho Williams. The British fought brilliantly at Guilford Court House unaided by anything stronger than their own large spirits. In most actions soldiers went into battle with very little more than themselves and their comrades to lean upon.[5]

Belief in the Holy Spirit surely sustained some in the American army, perhaps more than in the enemy's. There are a good many references to the divine or to Providence in the letters and diaries of ordinary soldiers. Often, however, these expressions are in the form of thanks to the Lord for permitting these soldiers to survive. There is little that suggests soldiers believed that faith rendered them invulnerable to the enemy's bullets. Many did consider the glorious cause to be sacred; their war, as the ministers who sent them off to kill never tired of reminding them, was just and providential.[6]

Others clearly saw more immediate advantages in the fight: the plunder of the enemy's dead. At Monmouth Court House, where Clinton withdrew after dark leaving the field strewn with British corpses, the plundering carried American soldiers into the houses of civilians who had fled to save themselves. The soldiers' actions were so blatant and so unrestrained that Washington ordered their packs searched. And at Eutaw Springs, the Americans virtually gave up victory to the opportunity of ransacking British tents. Some died in

4. *Writings of Washington*, V, 479–80; Christopher Ward, *The War of the Revolution* (New York, 1952), II, 786.

5. Otho Williams, "A Narrative of the Campaign of 1780," in William Johnson, *Sketches of the Life and Correspondence of Nathanael Greene* (Charleston, S.C., 1822), I, 494; "A British Orderly Book, 1780–1781," ed. A. R. Newsome, *North Carolina Historical Review* 9 (1932): 289.

6. For typical references to Providence, see Herbert T. Wade and Robert A. Lively, *This Glorious Cause: The Adventures of Two Company Officers in Washington's Army* (Princeton, 1958).

their greed, shot down by an enemy given time to regroup while his camp was torn apart by men looking for something to carry off. But even these men probably fought for something besides plunder. When it beckoned, they collapsed, but it had not drawn them to the field; nor had it kept them there in a savage struggle.[7]

Inspired leadership helped soldiers face death, but they sometimes fought bravely even when their leaders let them down. Yet officers' courage and the example of officers throwing off wounds to remain in the fight undoubtedly helped their men stick. Charles Stedman remarked on Captain Maitland, who at Guilford Court House was hit, dropped behind for a few minutes to get his wound dressed, then returned to the battle.[8] Cornwallis obviously filled Sergeant Lamb with pride, struggling forward to press into the struggle after his horse was killed.[9] Washington's presence meant much at Princeton, though his exposure to enemy fire may also have made his troops uneasy. His quiet exhortation as he passed among the men who were about to assault Trenton—"Soldiers, keep by your officers"—remained in the mind of a Connecticut soldier until he died fifty years later.[10] There was only one Washington, one Cornwallis, and their influence on men in battle, few of whom could have seen them, was of course slight. Junior and noncommissioned officers carried the burden of tactical direction; they had to show their troops what must be done and somehow to persuade, cajole, or force them to do it. The praise that ordinary soldiers lavished on sergeants and junior officers suggests that these leaders played important parts in their troops' willingness to fight. Still, important as it was, their part does not really explain why men fought.

In suggesting this conclusion about military leadership, I do not wish to be understood as agreeing with Tolstoy's scornful verdict on generals—that despite all their plans and orders they do not affect the results of battles at all. Tolstoy did not reserve all his scorn for generals—historians are also derided in *War and Peace,* for finding a rational order in battles where only chaos existed. "The activity of a commander in chief does not at all resemble the activity we imagine to ourselves when we sit at ease in our studies examining some campaign on the map, with a certain number of troops on this and that

7. Orderly Book, 12 June–13 July 1778, Benjamin Fishbourne et al., Huntington Library MS BR96.

8. Charles Stedman, *The History of the Origin, Progress, and Termination of the American War* (Dublin, 1794), II, 38.

9. Roger Lamb, *An Original and Authentic Journal of Occurrences during the Late American War* (Dublin, 1809), 362.

10. William S. Powell, "A Connecticut Soldier under Washington: Elisha Bostwick's Memoirs of the First Years of the Revolution," *William and Mary Quarterly* (hereafter *WMQ*), 3d ser., 6 (1949): 102.

side in a certain known locality, and begin our plans from some given moment. A commander in chief is never dealing with the beginning of any event—the position from which we always contemplate it. The commander in chief is always in the midst of a series of shifting events and so he never can at any moment consider the whole import of an event that is occurring."[11]

The full import of battle will escape historians as surely as participants. But we have to begin somewhere in trying to explain why men fought rather than ran from Revolutionary battlefields. The battlefield may indeed be the place to begin, since we have dismissed leadership, fear of officers, religious belief, the power of drink, and other possible explanations of why men fought and died.

The eighteenth-century battlefield was, compared with that of the twentieth, an intimate theater, especially intimate in the engagements of the Revolution, which were usually small even by the standards of the day. The killing range of the musket—eighty to one hundred yards—enforced intimacy, as did the reliance on the bayonet and the general ineffectiveness of artillery. Soldiers had to come to close quarters to kill; this fact reduced the mystery of battle, though perhaps not its terrors. But at least the battlefield lost some of its impersonality. In fact, in contrast to twentieth-century combat, in which the enemy usually remains unseen and the source of incoming fire unknown, eighteenth-century battles involved a foe who could be seen and sometimes even touched. Seeing one's enemy may have aroused a singular intensity of feeling uncommon in modern battles. The assault with the bayonet—the most desired objective of infantry tactics—seems indeed to have evoked an emotional climax. Before it occurred, tension and anxiety built up as the troops marched from their column into a line of attack. The purpose of their movements was well understood by themselves and their enemies, who must have watched with feelings of dread and fascination. When the order came sending them forward, rage, even madness, replaced the attacker's anxiety, while terror and desperation sometimes filled those receiving the charge.[12] Surely it is revealing that the Americans who ran from battle did so most often at the moment when they understood that their enemy had started forward with the bayonet. This happened to several units at Brandywine and to the militia at Camden and at Guilford Court House. The loneliness, the sense of isolation reported by modern soldiers, was probably missing at such moments. All was clear—especially that glittering line of advancing steel.

11. *War and Peace*, bk. 11, chap. 2.
12. See Samuel Webb to Silas Deane, 11 July, 1775, in *Proceedings of the Massachusetts Historical Society*, 1875–76, p. 83.

Whether this awful clarity was harder to bear than was losing sight of the enemy is problematical. American troops ran at Germantown after grappling with the British and then finding the field of battle covered by fog. At that time groping blindly, they and their enemy struggled over ground resembling a scene of modern combat. The enemy was hidden at a critical moment, and American fears were generated by not knowing what was happening—or about to happen. They could not see the enemy, and they could not see one another, an especially important fact. For, as S. L. A. Marshall, the twentieth-century military historian, has suggested in his book *Men against Fire,* what sustains men in the extraordinary circumstances of battle may be their relationships with their comrades.[13]

These men found that sustaining such relationships was possible in the intimacy of the American battlefield—and not just because the limited arena robbed battle of some of its mystery. More important, it permitted the troops to give one another moral or psychological support. The enemy could be seen, but so could one's comrades; they could be seen and communicated with.

Eighteenth-century infantry tactics called for men to move and fire from tight formations that permitted them to talk and to give one another information—and reassurance and comfort. If properly done, marching and firing found infantrymen compressed into files in which their shoulders touched. In battle, physical contact with one's comrades on either side must have helped men control their fears. Firing the musket from three compact lines, the English practice, also involved physical contact. The men of the front rank crouched on their right knees; the men of the center rank placed their left feet inside the right feet of the front; the rear rank did the same thing behind the center. This stance was called—in a revealing term—"locking." The very density of this formation sometimes aroused criticism from officers, who complained that it led to inaccurate fire. The front rank, conscious of the closeness of the center, might fire too low; the rear rank tended to "throw" its shots into the air, as firing too high was called; only the center rank took careful aim, according to the critics. Whatever the truth of these charges about accuracy of fire, men in these dense formations compiled a fine record of holding their ground. And it is worth noting that the inaccuracy of men in the rear rank bespoke their concern for their fellows in front of them.[14]

13. *Men against Fire* (New York, 1947), esp. chap. 10.
14. Eighteenth-century tactics are discussed with discernment by R. R. Palmer, in Edward M. Earle, *Makers of Modern Strategy* (Princeton, 1941); William B. Willcox, *Portrait of a General: Sir Henry Clinton in the War of Independence* (New York, 1964); Franklin

British and American soldiers in the Revolution often spoke of fighting with "spirit" and "behaving well" under fire. Sometimes these phrases referred to daring exploits under great danger, but more often they seem to have meant holding together, giving one another support, reforming the lines when they broke or fell into disorder— disorder such as overtook the Americans at Greenspring, Virginia, early in July 1781 when Cornwallis lured Anthony Wayne into crossing the James with a heavily outnumbered force. Wayne saw his mistake and decided to make the best of it, not by a hasty retreat from the ambush, but by attacking. The odds against the Americans were formidable, but as an ordinary soldier who was there saw it, the inspired conduct of the infantry saved them—"our troops behaved well, fighting with great spirit and bravery. The infantry were oft broke; but just as oft rallied and formed at a word."[15]

These troops had been spread out when the British surprised them, but they formed as quickly as possible. Here was a test of men's spirits, a test they passed in part because of their disciplined formation. In contrast at Camden, where the militia collapsed as soon as the battle began, an open alignment may have contributed to their fear. Gates placed the Virginians on the far left, apparently expecting them to cover more ground than their numbers allowed. At any rate they went into the battle in a single line with at least five feet between each man and the next, a distance that intensified a feeling of isolation in the heat and noise of the firing. And to make such feelings worse, these men were especially exposed, stretched out at one end of the line with no supporters behind them.[16]

Troops in tight lines consciously reassured one another in several ways. British troops usually talked and cheered—"huzzaing" whether standing their ground, running forward, or firing. The Americans may have done less talking and cheering, though there is evidence that they learned to imitate the enemy. Giving a cheer at the end of a successful engagement was standard practice. The British cheered at Lexington and then marched off to be shot down on the road running from Concord. The Americans shouted their joy at Harlem Heights, an understandable action and one that for most of 1776

and Mary Wickwire, *Cornwallis: The American Adventure* (Boston, 1970). For "locking" and other aspects of firing and marching, see Humphrey Bland, *An Abstract of Military Discipline* (Boston, 1747); Edward Harvey, *The Manual Exercise as Ordered by His Majesty in 1764* (Boston, 1774); Timothy Pickering, *An Easy Plan of Discipline for a Militia* (Salem, Mass., 1775).

15. *The Diary of Josia Atkins* (New York, 1975), 38.

16. The *Virginia Gazette*, 6 September 1780, contains an account of the extended disposition on the left. Ward, *War of the Revolution*, II, 722–30, provides a fine study of the battle, as does Wickwire, *Cornwallis*, 149–65.

they rarely had the opportunity to perform.[17]

The most deplorable failures to stand and fight usually occurred among the American militia. Yet there were militia companies that performed with great success, remaining whole units under the most deadly volleys. The New England companies at Bunker Hill held out under a fire that veteran British officers compared to the worst they had experienced in Europe. Lord Rawdon remarked on how unusual it was for defenders to stick to their posts even after the assaulting troops had entered the ditch around a redoubt.[18] The New Englanders did it. They also held steady at Princeton—"They were the first who regularly formed" and stood up under the balls "which whistled their thousand different notes around our heads," according to Charles Willson Peale, whose Philadelphia militia also proved their steadiness.[19]

What was different about these companies? Why did they fight when others around them ran? The answer may lie in the relationships among their men. Men in the New England companies, in the Philadelphia militia, and in the other units that held together were neighbors. They knew one another; they had something to prove to one another; they had their "honor" to protect. Their active service in the Revolution may have been short, but they had been together in one way or another for a fairly long time—for several years, in most cases. Their companies, after all, had been formed from towns and villages. Some clearly had known one another all their lives.[20]

Elsewhere, especially in the thinly settled southern colonies, companies were usually composed of men—farmers, farmers' sons, farm laborers, artisans, and new immigrants—who did not know one another. They were, to use a term much used in a later war, companies of "stragglers" without common attachments, with almost no knowledge of their fellows. For them, even bunched tightly in line, the battlefield was an empty, lonely place. Absence of personal bonds and their own parochialism, coupled to inadequate training and imperfect discipline, often led to disintegration under fire.[21]

17. Tench Tilghman to his father, 19 September 1776, in *Memoir of Lieut. Col. Tench Tilghman* (Albany, 1876), 139.

18. Francis Rawdon to the earl of Huntington, 20 June 1775, Hastings Papers, Huntington Library.

19. Charles Willson Peale Diary, 3 January 1777, Huntington Library.

20. For a fine study of a Massachusetts town and its militia, see Robert A. Gross, *The Minutemen and Thier World* (New York, 1976); for a general view of the colonial militia, John Shy, "A New Look at the Colonial Militia," *WMQ*, 3d ser., 20 (1963): 175–85, is outstanding.

21. The conclusions in this paragraph were suggested by Edward C. Papenfuse and Gregory A. Stiverson, "General Smallwood's Recruits: The Peacetime Career of the Revolutionary War Private," *WMQ*, 3d ser., 30 (1973): 117–32. The Nathanael Greene Papers in the Huntington Library contain materials that tend to confirm these impressions.

According to conventional wisdom, the nearer the American militia were to home, the better they fought, fighting for their homes and no one else's. Proximity to home, however, may have been a distraction that weakened resolve; for the irony of going into battle and perhaps to their deaths when home and safety lay close down the road could not have escaped many. Almost every senior American general commented on the propensity of the militia to desert—and if they were not deserting they seemed perpetually in transit between home and camp, usually without authorization.

Paradoxically, of all the Americans who fought, the militiamen best exemplified in themselves and in their behavior the ideals and purposes of the Revolution. They had enjoyed independence, or at least personal liberty, long before it was proclaimed in the Declaration. They instinctively felt their equality with others and in many places insisted upon demonstrating it by choosing their own officers. Their sense of their liberty permitted, even compelled, them to serve only for short enlistments, to leave camp when they liked, to scorn the orders of others—and especially those orders to fight when they preferred to flee. Their integration into their society drove them to resist military discipline; and their ethos of personal freedom stimulated hatred of the machine that served as the model for the army. They were not pieces of a machine, and they would serve it only reluctantly and skeptically. At their best—at Cowpens, for example—they fought well; at their worst, at Camden, they fought not at all. There they were, as Greene said, "ungovernable."[22] What was lacking in the militia was a set of professional standards, requirements, and rules which might regulate their conduct in battle. What was lacking was professional pride. Coming and going to camp as they liked, shooting their guns for the pleasure of the sound, the militia annoyed the Continentals, who soon learned that most of them could not be trusted.

The British regulars were at the opposite pole. They had been pulled out of society, carefully segregated from it, tightly disciplined, and highly trained. Their values were the values of the army, for the most part, no more and no less. The officers, to be sure, were in certain respects very different from the men. They embodied the style and standards of gentlemen who believed in service to their king and who fought for honor and glory.

With these ideals and a mission of service to the king defining their calling, British officers held themselves as aloof as possible from the

22. Greene to Gov. Reed, 18 March 1781, Nathanael Greene Papers, Huntington Library. On 3 February 1781, Greene wrote Gov. Nash that 20,000 militia would not provide 500 effective troops, the way they "come and go."

peculiar horrors of war. Not that they did not fight; they sought combat and danger, but by the conventions that shaped their understanding of battle, they insulated themselves as much as possible from the ghastly business of killing and dying. Thus the results of battle might be long lists of dead and wounded, but the results were also "honourable and glorious," as Charles Stedman described Guilford Court House, or reflected "dishonour upon British arms," as he described Cowpens. Actions and gunfire were "smart" and "brisk" and sometimes "hot," and occasionally a "difficult piece of work." They might also be described lightly—Harlem Heights was "this silly business" to Lord Rawdon. To their men, British officers spoke a clean, no-nonsense language. Howe's terse "look to your bayonets" summed up a tough professional's expectations.[23]

For all the distance between British officers and men, they gave remarkable support to one another in battle. They usually deployed carefully, keeping up their spirits with drum and fife. They talked and shouted and cheered, and coming on with their bayonets at the ready "huzzaing," or coming on "firing and huzzaing," they must have sustained a sense of shared experience. Their ranks might be thinned by an American volley, but on they came, exhorting one another to "push on! push on!" as at Bunker Hill and the battles that followed.[24] Although terrible losses naturally dispirited them, they almost always maintained the integrity of their regiments as fighting units, and when they were defeated, or nearly so as at Guilford Court House, they recovered their pride and fought well thereafter. And there was no hint at Yorktown that the ranks wanted to surrender, even though they had suffered dreadfully.

The Continentals, the American regulars, lacked the polish of their British counterparts, but, at least from Monmouth on, they showed a steadiness under fire almost as impressive as their enemy's. And they demonstrated a brave endurance: defeated, they retired, pulled themselves together, and came back to try again.

These qualities—patience and endurance—endeared them to many. For example, John Laurens, on Washington's staff in 1778, wanted desperately to command them. In what amounted to a plea for command, Laurens wrote, "I would cherish those dear, ragged Continentals, whose patience will be the admiration of future ages, and glory in bleeding with them."[25] This statement was all the more extraordinary coming from Laurens, a South Carolinian aristocrat.

23. Stedman, *Origin*, II, 382, 360; Rawdon to the earl of Huntington, 3 August 1775, 23 September 1776.
24. Rawdon to the earl of Huntington, 20 June 1775.
25. To his father, 9 March 1778, in *The Army Correspondence of Colonel John Laurens* (New York, 1897), 136.

The soldiers he admired were anything but aristocratic. As the war dragged on, they came more and more from the poor and the propertyless. Most probably entered the army as substitutes for men who had rather pay than serve, or as the recipients of bounties and the promise of land. In time some, perhaps many, assimilated the ideals of the Revolution. As Baron Steuben observed in training them, they differed from European troops in at least one regard: they wanted to know why they were told to do certain things. Unlike European soldiers who did what they were told, the Continentals asked why.[26]

Continental officers aped the style of their British counterparts. They aspired to gentility and often, failing to achieve it, betrayed their anxiety by an excessive concern for their honor. Not surprisingly, like their British peers, they also used the vocabularies of gentlemen in describing battle.

Their troops, innocent of such polish, spoke with words from their immediate experience of physical combat. They found few euphemisms for the horrors of battle. Thus Pvt. David How, September 1776, in New York noted in his diary: "Isaac Fowls had his head shot off with a cannon ball this morning." And Sgt. Thomas McCarty reported an engagement between a British foraging party and American infantry near New Brunswick in February 1777: "We attacked the body, and bullets flew like hail. We stayed about 15 minutes and then retreated with loss." After the battle inspection of the field revealed that the British had killed the American wounded— "The men that was wounded in the thigh or leg, they dashed out their brains with their muskets and run them through with their bayonets, made them like sieves. This was barbarity to the utmost." The pain of seeing his comrades mutilated by shot and shell at White Plains remained with Elisha Bostwick, a Connecticut soldier, all his life: A cannon ball "cut down Lt. Youngs Platoon which was next to that of mine[;] the ball first took off the head of Smith, a Stout heavy man and dashed it open, then took Taylor across the Bowels, it then Struck Sergeant Garret of our Company on the hip [and] took off the point of the hip bone[.] Smith and Taylor were left on the spot. Sergeant Garret was carried but died the Same day now to think, oh! what a sight that was to see within a distance of six rods those men with their legs and arms and guns and packs all in a heap[.]"[27]

The Continentals occupied the psychological and moral ground

26. *Rebels and Redcoats,* ed. George F. Sheer and Hugh F. Rankin (New York, 1957), 354.
27. *Diary of David How* (Morrisania, N.Y., 1885), 28; "The Revolutionary War Journal of Sergeant Thomas McCarty," ed. Jared C. Lobdell, *Proceedings of the New Jersey Historical Society* 80 (1964): 45; Powell, "Bostwick's Memoirs," 101.

somewhere between the militia and the British professionals. From 1777 on, their enlistments were for three years or the duration of the war. This long service allowed them to learn more of their craft and to become seasoned. That does not mean that on the battlefield they lost their fear. Experience in combat almost never leaves one indifferent to danger, unless after prolonged and extreme fatigue one comes to consider oneself already dead. Seasoned troops simply learn to deal with their fear more effectively than raw troops do, in part because they have come to realize that everyone feels it and that they can rely on their fellows.

By the winter of 1779–80, the Continentals were beginning to believe that they had no one save themselves to lean on. Their soldierly qualifications so widely admired in America—their "habit of subordination,"[28] their patience under fatigue, and their ability to stand sufferings and privations of every kind may in fact have led to a bitter resignation that saw them through a good deal of fighting. At Morristown during this winter, they felt abandoned in their cold and hunger. They knew that food and clothing existed in America, to keep them healthy and comfortable, and yet little of either came to the army. Understandably their dissatisfaction increased as they realized that once again suffering had been left to them. Dissatisfaction in these months slowly turned into a feeling of martyrdom. They felt themselves to be martyrs to the "glorious cause." They would fulfill the ideals of the Revolution and see things through to independence because the civilian population would not.[29]

Thus the Continentals in the last four years of the active war, though less articulate and less independent than the militia, assimilated one part of the "cause" more fully. They had advanced further in making American purposes in the Revolution their own. They had in their sense of isolation and neglect probably come to be more nationalistic than the militia—though surely no more American.

Although these sources of the Continentals' feeling seem curious, they served to reinforce the tough professional ethic these men also came to absorb. Set apart from the militia by the length of their service, by their officers' esteem for them, and by their own contempt for part-time soldiers, the Continentals slowly developed resilience and pride. Their country might ignore them in camp, might allow their bellies to shrivel and their backs to freeze, might allow them to wear rags, but in battle they would not be ignored. And in battle

28. Laurens to his father, 14 January 1779, in *Army Correspondence*, 108.
29. S. Sidney Bradford, "Hunger Menaces the Revolution, December 1779–January 1780," *Maryland Historical Magazine* 61 (1966): 5–23; *Correspondence and Journals of Samuel Blachley Webb*, ed. W. C. Ford (New York, 1893), II, 231–32.

they would support one another in the knowledge that their own moral and professional resources remained sure.

The meaning of these complex attitudes is not what it seems to be. At first sight the performance of militia and Continentals seems to suggest that the great principles of the Revolution made little difference on the battlefield. Or if principles did make a difference, say especially to the militia saturated with natural rights and a deep and persistent distrust of standing armies, they served not to strengthen the will to combat but to disable it. And the Continentals, recruited increasingly from the poor and dispossessed, apparently fought better as they came to resemble their professional and apolitical enemy, the British infantry.

These conclusions are in part askew. To be sure, there is truth—and paradox—in the fact that some Americans' commitments to Revolutionary principles made them unreliable on the battlefield. Still, their devotion to their principles helped bring them there. George Washington, their commander-in-chief, never tired of reminding them that their cause arrayed free men against mercenaries. They were fighting for the "blessings of liberty," he told them in 1776, and should they not acquit themselves like men, slavery would replace their freedom.[30] The challenge to behave like men was not an empty one. Courage, honor, gallantry in the service of liberty, all those words calculated to bring a blush of embarrassment to jaded twentieth-century men, defined manhood for the eighteenth century. In battle those words gained an extraordinary resonance as they were embodied in the actions of brave men. Indeed it is likely that many Americans who developed a narrow professional spirit found battle broadly educative, forcing them to consider the purposes of their professional skill.

On one level those purposes had to be understood as having a remarkable importance if men were to fight—and die. For battle forced American soldiers into a situation that nothing in their usual experience had prepared them for. They were to kill other men in the expectation that even if they did they might be killed themselves. However defined, especially by a Revolution in the name of life, liberty, and the pursuit of happiness, this situation was unnatural.

On another level, one which, perhaps, made the strain of battle endurable, the situation of American soldiers, though unusual, was not really foreign to them. For what battle presented in stark form was one of the classic problems free men face: choosing between the rival claims of public responsibility and private wishes, or in

---

30. *Writings of Washington,* V, 479.

eighteenth-century terms choosing between virtue—devotion to the public trust—and personal liberty. In battle, virtue demanded that men give up their liberties and perhaps even their lives for others. Each time they fought, they had in effect to weigh the claims of society and liberty. Should they fight or run? They knew that the choice might mean life or death. For those American soldiers who were servants, apprentices, or poor men substituting for men with money to hire them, the choice might not have seemed to involve a moral decision. After all, they had never enjoyed much personal liberty. But not even in that contrivance of eighteenth-century authoritarianism in which they now found themselves, the professional army, could they avoid a moral decision. Compressed into dense formations, they were reminded by their nearness to their comrades that they too had an opportunity to uphold virtue. By standing firm, they served their fellows and honor; by running, they served only themselves.

Thus battle tested the inner qualities of men, tried their souls, as Thomas Paine said. Many men died in the test to which battle put their spirits. Some soldiers called this trial cruel; others called it glorious. Perhaps this difference in perception suggests how difficult it was in the Revolution to be both a soldier and an American. Nor has it ever been easy since.

The Origins of "The Paranoid Style in American Politics": Public Jealousy from the Age of Walpole to the Age of Jackson

JAMES H. HUTSON

The "Paranoid Style in American Politics" is one of those concepts that has become a staple in American historical writing. In describing and analyzing the widely shared convictions, which have recurred at frequent intervals in American history, that persecutory conspiracies were afoot and had fixed the country's citizens in their sights, Richard Hofstadter, in his celebrated 1964 essay, presented a thesis that many scholars have subsequently employed.[1] In 1969, for example, David Brion Davis published *The Slave Power Conspiracy and the Paranoid Style,* in which he showed how the decades before the Civil War were suffused with paranoid fears of conspiracies, which contributed to the outbreak of that conflict.[2] In 1970 James M. Banner, Jr., borrowed Hofstadter's "useful notion of a 'paranoid style' " to describe the mentality of New England Federalism.[3] More recently, we see Hofstadter's hand in Robert Kelley's ambitious attempt in 1976 to write a history of American political culture: Kelley sees a "characteristic paranoia" in the two political coalitions that he describes as contesting each other in the 1790s as Federalists and Republicans and continuing their antagonism today as Republicans and Democrats.[4]

1. "The Paranoid Style in American Politics," in Richard Hofstadter, *The Paranoid Style in American Politics and Other Essays* (New York, 1965), 3–40.
2. David B. Davis, *The Slave Power Conspiracy and the Paranoid Style* (Baton Rouge, 1969).
3. James M. Banner, Jr., *To the Hartford Convention: The Federalists and the Origins of Party Politics in Massachusetts, 1789–1815* (New York, 1970), 32n.
4. Robert Kelley, "Ideology and Political Culture from Jefferson to Nixon," *American Historical Review* 82 (1977): 559–60.

Hofstadter confined his investigation of the paranoid style to the national period of our history—to the period after the adoption of the federal Constitution. Recently, historians have found considerable evidence of it before and during the American Revolution. So many assertions have been made, for example, that Revolutionary leaders were afflicted with paranoia[5] that in 1976 an essayist concluded that "it is not uncommon for whig publicists and leaders to be viewed as paranoid."[6] Neither is it uncommon for their ideas to be considered in the same way: their thinking, one scholar declares, displayed a "paranoid outlook"; another is struck by the extent to which it was suffused with a "paranoiac mistrust" of power; a third observes that "the insurgent whig ideology had a frenzied even paranoid cast to it"; a fourth hears it sounding a "paranoiac note." Some blame the ages itself for what appears to be the pervasive political pathology: "the era of the American Revolution was a period of political paranoia," a recent scholar writes. Others look elsewhere— even to colonial child-rearing practices—for clues to the origin of the phenomenon.[7]

Can Hofstadter, who ignored the Revolutionary period, be regarded as the source of the widespread attribution of paranoid characteristics to the persons and ideas of the Revolutionaries? I think not. Rather, it appears that the writings of Bernard Bailyn—contrary, it would seem, to this intentions—have inspired the ascriptions of paranoia.

In a series of recent books, Bailyn has presented an ideological interpretation of the American Revolution.[8] Americans of the Revolutionary generation, he contends, had absorbed—had been saturated with—an ideology propounded by a group of British opponents of Sir Robert Walpole. The opposition writers developed a theory of politics which stressed the vulnerability of liberty to the aggressions of the holders of power, who were depicted as operating through

5. I am aware that, clinically, paranoia is a rare species of the paranoid disorder. It is used here, and throughout the essay, not in its exact medical sense, but as a rhetorical device to avoid excessive repetition of the word *paranoid*.

6. Rhys Isaac, "Dramatizing the Ideology of Revolution: Popular Mobilization in Virginia, 1774 to 1776," *William and Mary Quarterly*, 3d ser., 33 (1976): 360.

7. Robert Shalhope, "Toward a Republican Synthesis: The Emergence of an Understanding of Republicanism in American Historiography," *William and Mary Quarterly*, 3d ser., 29 (1972): 72; Gordon S. Wood, *The Creation of the American Republic, 1776–1787* (Chapel Hill, 1969), 17; James K. Martin, *Men in Rebellion: Higher Government Leaders and the Coming of the American Revolution* (New Brunswick, N.J., 1973), 34; J. G. A. Pocock, *The Machiavellian Moment* (Princeton, 1975), 507–8. Lance Banning, "Republican Ideology and the Triumph of the Constitution, 1789 to 1793," *William and Mary Quarterly*, 3d ser., 29 (1974): 171; Philip Greven, *The Protestant Temperament* . . . (New York, 1977), 348–59.

8. Bernard Bailyn, *The Ideological Origins of the American Revolution* (Cambridge, Mass., 1967); idem, *The Origin of American Politics* (Cambridge, Mass., 1968); idem, *The Ordeal of Thomas Hutchinson* (Cambridge, Mass., 1974).

conspiracy and corruption. When the British ministry began to administer America with unaccustomed vigor at the end of the Seven Years' War, its actions were refracted, in the colonies, through the prism of opposition ideology, which caused them to be perceived as steps in a conspiracy to enslave America; such an intolerable design was resisted with arms.

Bailyn explicitly states that it was the Americans' conviction that they were victims of a "constant, unremitted uniform" conspiracy to enslave them, conducted by a corrupt British ministry, which "propelled them into Revolution."[9] Historians have known for decades— as opponents of the Revolution declared at the time—that this notion was chimerical.[10] Was it also pathological? Was it a collective delusion of persecution, a massive paranoid conclusion? No, Bailyn would answer—nothing would do greater violence to the historical record than to reduce the Revolution to a mass psychosis. The American Revolutionaries, he insists, were "profoundly reasonable people," men of "businesslike sanity."[11] Although their feverish fears of a conspiracy of power against liberty might have seemed neurotic to complacent British contemporaries, they were, he explains, realistic responses to the sociopolitical environment of the New World.

In straining for language to convey the intensity of American feelings, Bailyn at times employs the vocabulary of psychopathology, thus appearing to contradict his assertions of colonial rationality. "These extravagant, seemingly paranoiac fears," he writes, at one point, regarding the incessant American charges of conspiracy.[12] Looking over Thomas Hutchinson's shoulder, he finds American Revolutionary ideologues "morbid, pathological, paranoiac."[13] And at the conclusion of his life of Hutchinson, he writes that the governor "could find only persistent irrationality in their [the Americans'] arguments and he wrote off their agitations as politically pathological. And in a limited logical sense he was right."[14] Is it any wonder, then, that commentators on Bailyn's work write of Whig rhetoric having a "paranoiac obsession with a diabolical Crown conspiracy?"[15] Or ask "Is Bailyn saying it was all paranoia and not principle?"[16]

To say that Bailyn rather than Hofstadter is the inspiration of those scholars who are finding paranoid characteristics everywhere in the

9. Bailyn, *Ideological Origins*, ix, 95; idem, *Origins of American Politics*, 11; idem, *Thomas Hutchinson*, 206.

10. *Ideological Origins*, 149.   11. Ibid., 18–19.   12. Ibid., 158.

13. *Thomas Hutchinson*, 2; see also 15.   14. Ibid., 380.

15. Gordon Wood, "Rhetoric and Reality in the American Revolution," *William and Mary Quarterly*, 3d ser., 23 (1966): 25.

16. Alfred Young, "The 'Bailyn' Thesis and the Problem of 'Popular' Ideology" (Remarks made at the Organization of American Historians Meeting, April 1974).

American Revolution does not sufficiently emphasize how little influence Hofstadter has had on them. Between them and his "Paranoid Style" a barrier exists, a barrier created not by mutual ignorance—Hofstadter knew and cited Bailyn's work,[17] and scholars of the Revolution know Hofstadter's writings—but rather by the special position the Revolution occupies in our national life. Americans, as Edmund S. Morgan has observed, have always considered the Revolution a "good thing."[18] Hofstadter considered the paranoid style a bad thing; "the term 'paranoid style' is pejorative," he asserted.[19] One of Hofstadter's purposes in writing "The Paranoid Style in American Politics" was to mount a scholarly polemic against the political right wing of his own time, against the "Goldwater movement," which he accused of sharing with Sen. Joseph McCarthy the view that the United States was in the grasp of a vast, heinous conspiracy—"a conspiracy on a scale so immense as to dwarf any previous such venture in the history of man."[20] The right wing, Hofstadter contended, was the victim and practitioner of the paranoid style. To discredit it, he traced its antecedents back through American history, emphasizing the ludicrous and repellent aspects of selected waves of conspiratorial thinking. The Revolution, even though produced, as Bailyn would have it, by a conspiratorial conviction diffused through the population, could not serve Hofstadter's purposes, for it was "good," and to locate the ancestry of the right-wing mentality of the 1960s in its beneficent fermentation would sanctify the benighted rather than discredit them. Hence, in pursuit of the paranoid style Hofstadter pulled up short of the Revolution, stopping at 1798, at the obscure and morally "safe" Bavarian Illuminati episode.

Value judgments also seem to have inhibited scholars of the Revolution from "linking up" with Hofstadter. To connect the "good" Revolution, caused by conspiratorial convictions though it might have been, with the "bad" paranoid style, would be, for Revolutionary historians, akin to imitating the ancient tyrant Mezentius's binding of the living with the dead. Such a coupling would pollute the Revolution, and because the Revolution created the American nation, it could conceivably impugn the legitimacy of the national experience. To a remarkable degree, historians have been guardians of the Revolution's goodness and sanity. Therefore, they have had little incli-

17. Hofstadter, "Paranoid Style," 12n.
18. Edmund S. Morgan, "Conflict and Consensus in the American Revolution," in *Essays on the American Revolution,* ed. Stephen G. Kurtz and James H. Hutson (Chapel Hill, 1973), 289.
19. "Paranoid Style," 5.   20. Ibid., 7–8.

nation to make it the first link on Hofstadter's paranoid chain.

So the Revolution is a chasm, separating its historians from Hofstadter. A curious, disjointed kind of history results. On the one hand, we have scholars who are concluding that the Revolution was produced, more or less, by a paranoid mentality. On the other, we have Hofstadter finding in the Bavarian Illuminati episode, scarcely twenty years after 1776, the prototype of the paranoid style. Yet there is apparently no connection between the conspiratorial thinking of the 1770s and the 1790s. Are we to assume, to put it another way, that so powerful a causative agent as the American Revolution, insofar as it was a product of a conspiratorial conviction, had no influence whatever on a similar ideational development a score of years later? It is the thesis of this essay that there was a continuity between the conspiratorial thinking of the 1770s and the 1790s—a continuity that extended into the age of Jackson and beyond. The continuity was created by an attitude that was elevated from relative inconspicuousness by the pre-Revolutionary agitation into a key component of the mentality of independent, republican America. That attitude was jealousy.

Today the word *jealousy* has acquired a meaning it did not have in the eighteenth century. We now use it as a synonym for the word *envy*. A modern dictionary gives its primary definition as "resentment against a rival, a person enjoying success or advantage etc. or against another's success or advantage itself."[21] The eighteenth century carefully distinguished between jealousy and envy, however;[22] for it, the principal meanings of jealousy were those which are subordinate in today's dictionaries: vigilance and suspicion.

In equating vigilance with jealousy, the eighteenth century frequently associated it with the eye. The "jealous eye" became, in fact, a cliché in colonial America,[23] occasionally improved by the classically minded who spoke of "Argus-eyed jealousy."[24] Leaders urged

21. *The Random House Dictionary of the English Language—The Unabridged Edition* (1971), s.v. "jealousy."

22. For a particularly good example of the distinction, see John Adams, *Discourses on Davila* (reprint; New York, 1973), 27.

23. See, for example, Daniel Dulany, *Considerations on the Propriety of Imposing Taxes in the British Colonies* (Annapolis, 1765), in Bailyn, ed., *Pamphlets of the American Revolution* (Cambridge, Mass., 1965), 626; [Samuel Adams], "Vindex," *Boston Gazette,* 12 December 1768; Richard Henry Lee to Francis L. Lee, 21 May 1775 and 11 May 1776, in Paul H. Smith, ed., *Letters of Delegates to Congress, 1774–1789,* I (Washington, D.C., 1977), 367; *Collections of the New-York Historical Society* 5 (1872): 25; Samuel Adams to James Warren, 7 January 1776, in Smith, ed., *Letters of Delegates,* III, 51; Carter Braxton, *An Address to the Convention of . . . Virginia,* Peter Force, ed., *American Archives,* 4th ser., VI, 749; Wood, *Creation of the American Republic,* 442.

24. Russell Kirk, *John Randolph of Roanoke* (Chicago, 1964), 105–6.

"watchful jealousy," "Jealousy and Attention," upon their fellow citizens and in the next breath exhorted them to be "watchful and jealous of their liberties," to cultivate "a spirit of vigilance and public jealousy."[25] But watchfulness was not the marrow of the meaning of jealousy. Not for nothing are people watchful and vigilant. These postures are produced by suspicion. And suspicion was, in fact, the core meaning of jealousy in the eighteenth century. Every entry under the word *jealousy* in Dr. Johnson's *Dictionary* begins with suspicion. In everyday usage it might be said, as it was of Arthur Lee, that he was "jealous and suspicious." Or it might be said, as it was of the Society of the Cincinnati, that it would attract "the well-merited suspicions and jealousy of every man of any thought on the continent." Or state legislatures might be complimented as "suspicious and jealous guardians of the rights of the citizens."[26] Jealousy-suspicion meant more than distrust, however. It conveyed the sense of fear, of apprehension—to use a modern word, of anxiety. Thus, in speaking of a friend who feared the sea, Benjamin Rush boasted, "I am not in the least jealous of that element."[27] In a draft speech in the spring of 1775, John Dickinson wrote of "Fears and Jealousies" produced by British colonial policies. A year later an anonymous Connecticut pamphleteer related how British plots "unavoidably create jealousies and fears in every patriotick breast." "Fears, our extreme jealousies," complained Alexander Hamilton in 1788, would not give sound government a chance.[28] In 1774 John Adams entreated General Gage to stop fortifying Boston so "that the Jealousies and Apprehensions of the People may be quieted." In 1777 Thomas Burke predicted that Congress would become an "object of very jealous apprehension"; and in the *Federalist* No. 67 Hamilton complained about oppo-

25. John Adams, *A Dissertation on the Canon and Feudal Law*, in Robert J. Taylor, ed., *The Papers of John Adams*, I (Boston, 1977), 121; Noah Webster, *An Examination of the Leading Principles of the Federal Constitution* in Paul L. Ford, ed., *Pamphlets on the Constitution of the United States* (New York, 1968), 60–61; James Lovell to Samuel Adams, 8 July 1782, Edmund C. Burnett, ed., *Letters of Members of the Continental Congress*, VI (Washington, D.C., 1933), 379; "Argus," *Independent Chronicle* (Boston), 26 April 1782, quoted in Jackson T. Main, *The Anti-Federalists* (Chapel Hill, 1961), 82n.; Plain Truth, *Pennsylvania Packet*, 21 December 1778.

26. Silas Deane, "Narrative, Read before Congress," 21 December 1778, *Collections of the New-York Historical Society* 21 (1888): 154; [Aedanus Burke], *Considerations on the Society or Order of Cincinnati* (Hartford, 1783), 17; Publius (Hamilton), *Federalist*, no. 26, in B. F. Wright, ed., *The Federalist* (Cambridge, Mass., 1961), 217.

27. Rush to Charles Nisbet, 15 May 1784, in L. H. Butterfield, ed., *Letters of Benjamin Rush*, I (Princeton, 1951), 334.

28. John Dickinson, Proposed Resolution, [23–25 May 1775], Smith, ed., *Letters of Delegates*, I, 384; *To the Inhabitants of the United Colonies*, 24 June 1776, in Force, ed., *American Archives*, 4th ser., VI, 1059; Hamilton, Speech at New York Ratifying Convention, 21 June 1788, Harold C. Syrett, ed., *The Papers of Alexander Hamilton*, V (New York, 1962), 51.

nents of the Constitution trying to "enlist all their jealousies and apprehensions" against it.[29] Since fear and apprehension could turn into hatred of the object that provoked them, the eighteenth century sometimes used *jealousy* as a synonym for *animosity*. "There was an hereditary hatred of New England in England," wrote John Adams as Novanglus, and it "was likewise thought there was a similar jealousy and animosity in other colonies against New England."[30] Jealousy, wrote John Taylor of Caroline, could be used "to convey an idea . . . of distrust, hatred, and implacability."[31] When used in this sense, jealousy was usually denounced as "evil," "bad," "malevolent."[32]

Was jealousy an affect, a habit, a characteristic, or an affliction? Just what was it? It was, most observers agreed, a passion.[33] The eighteenth century has been called the age of passion,[34] because of its obsessive concern with the passions as motives of action. Passions were endlessly scrutinized and dissected, especially by writers seeking to explain their operations in the political process. But jealousy, though a venerable concept used by political writers as early as the time of the English Commonwealth,[35] was treated as a foundling, abandoned without systematic analysis. Francis Hutcheson, the leading moral philosopher of the age, could, for example, write two treatises on the passions and scarcely mention it.[36] The reluctance of writers to anlayze jealousy may have been prompted somewhat by its acidulous, unchristian flavor—suspicion and apprehension mocked the charity and love enjoined in the Gospels—yet the moral reputation of the passions did not, in other instances, frighten off investigators. Avarice—material self-aggrandizement—was considered "bad," yet a host of eighteenth-century British writers from Mandeville to Adam Smith explored it and proposed ways of putting it to

29. Adams to Gage, [ante 10 October 1774], Taylor, ed., *Papers of John Adams*, II (Cambridge, Mass., 1977), 158; Burke, Abstract of Debates in Congress, 12–19 February 1777, in Burnett, ed., *Letters of Members of the Continental Congress*, II, 261–62; Wright, ed., *Federalist*, 436.

30. Taylor, ed., *Papers of John Adams*, II, 300.

31. John Taylor, *An Inquiry into the Principles and Policy of the Government of the United States*, ed. Roy F. Nichols (New Haven, 1950), 116.

32. Ibid., 116, 381, 460; Taylor, ed., *Papers of John Adams*, I, 197.

33. See, for example, Taylor, ed., *Papers of John Adams*, I 79, 197; John Taylor, *Inquiry*, 381; "S.C.," *Pennsylvania Gazette*, 9 July 1783; Rufus King to James Madison, 20 January 1788, in Charles R. King, ed., *The Life and Correspondence of Rufus King*, (reprint, New York, 1971), I, 314.

34. Gerald Stourzh, *Alexander Hamilton and the Idea of Republican Government* (Stanford, 1970), 76.

35. By Marchmont Needham, for example. See John Adams, *A Defence of the Constitutions of the . . . United States of America* (New York, 1971), III, 328, 416, 454.

36. Francis Hutcheson, *An Essay on the Nature and Conduct of the Passions and Affections* (London, 1728), 190; idem, *A System of Moral Philosophy* (London, 1755), 164, 165.

public use. Americans like Alexander Hamilton in no way lagged behind them in these inquiries. The reason that jealousy was slighted in the scholarship of the passions—in Britain, at least—was apparently this: although the term was in broad popular use, it signified an ambiguous, potentially destructive passion, which could not easily be reconciled to the political ideals of eighteenth-century Britain. Therefore, most analysts kept it at arm's length. Only in the writings of the Walpolian opposition is much attention paid to it.

Given the opposition's emphasis on the "aggressiveness" of power, on its "endlessly propulsive tendency to expand itself beyond legitimate boundaries,"[37] one would expect a countervailing emphasis in its writings on jealousy—on fear of power and on vigilance in detecting its advances. Commendations of jealousy, it is true, can be found among Walpole's opponents, as well as in the writings of their ideological sires, the country-party politicians of a generation earlier. "Distrust of the executive," wrote one country spokesman, was the chief "principle on which the whole of our Constitution is grounded."[38] In 1706 the country Whig James Stanhope professed to be delighted at "enacting mistrust between the people and those who may govern hereafter," because "the onely charm, the onely sure preservative which a free people can have against the encroachments of tyrants is an eternal mistrust and jealousy."[39] Stalwarts of the Walpolian opposition, Trenchard and Gordon, wrote in the same vein: "Political Jealousy . . . in the People," they claimed, "is a necessary and laudable Passion," because "Power would extinguish Liberty; and consequently Liberty has too much Cause to be exceeding jealous."[40]

But jealousy was invoked sparingly, not profusely, by Walpole's foes; scores of pages of an opposition canon like *Cato's Letters* can be turned without meeting it. For every favorable reference to jealousy, there is, moreover, a squirming at its malevolent tendencies. Stanhope regarded it as the Victorians did sex: as something indecent, if necessary. The "argument" for jealousy, he wrote, was "unfitt to be used in the house [of Commons], or at a conference," even though it should somehow be "incalcated" in the body politic.[41] For Cato, it was the bane of the "virtuous and modest" public servant: "public

37. Bailyn, *Ideological Origins*, 56.
38. Quoted in Jack P. Greene, "Political Mimesis: A Consideration of the Historical and Cultural Roots of Legislative Behavior in the British Colonies in the Eighteenth Century," *American Historical Review* 75 (1969): 343.
39. Quoted in Geoffrey S. Holmes, *British Politics in the Age of Anne* (London, 1967), 123.
40. [John Trenchard and Thomas Gordon], *Cato's Letters* (1755; reprint, New York, 1971), I, 260–61; also 6–7, 191.
41. Quoted in Holmes, *British Politics*, 123.

Jealousy," he wrote in Letter 19, "will misrepresent his whole Conduct, render his best Designs abortive, his best Actions useless."[42] To what, asks Cato in another place, can the excesses of tyrants be ascribed? "Tiberius, Caligula, Claudius, and Nero took Rome chiefly for the Scene of their Cruelty, and destroyed many great and good Men, some out of Wantonness, and more out of Jealousy."[43] The ambivalence of the opposition toward Jealousy is captured by an anonymous pamphleteer, who, in the beginning of his work, praised "jealousy of their liberties" as being "characteristic of true Englishmen," but who a few pages later declared, "Jealousy is a difficult antagonist to encounter and overcome. It is a monster that makes the food it feeds on."[44]

The opposition's sensitivity to the demonic potential of jealousy—Cato cites the regressive sequence "Jealousy, Mistrust, Fear, and Hatred"[45]—made it wary of it as a political instrument. Jealousy appeared to promote conflict in an age whose political ideal was consensus, so much so that political opposition and its vehicle, the political party, had not yet obtained legitimacy, being regarded in some circles as quasi-seditious. Like their contemporaries, therefore, the men in the opposition to Walpole placed a premium on harmony between ruler and ruled. "What a fatal and crying Crime it would be," wrote Cato in Letter 25, "to break the Confidence between the Prince and his People. . . . There is no Mischief which this mutual Mistrust and Aversion may not bring forth. They must therefore be the blackest Traytors, who are the first Authors of so terrible an Evil" as sowing suspicion between the prince and people.[46] Such a conviction would appear to preclude promoting jealousy, yet the opposition did not repudiate it. One of its pillars, Bolingbroke, tried to develop a rationale for using it which would resolve the contradiction between jealousy and confidence by conceiving of them as existing in a kind of creative tension in which leaders were expected to efface suspicion and create confidence by governing well. According to Bolingbroke,

> Men may be jealous, on account of their liberties, and I think they ought to be so, even when they have no immediate distrust that the persons, who govern, design to invade them. An opportunity of invading them open'd, is reason sufficient for awakening the jealousy: and if the persons, who have this jealousy, apply to those, who govern, to help to cure it, by remov-

---

42. *Cato's Letters*, I, 128.   43. Ibid., III, 80; IV, 115.
44. [Anonymous], *A Speech Intended to Have Been Delivered in the House of Commons, in Support of the Petition from the General Congress at Philadelphia* (London, 1775). This pamphlet may have been written by Arthur Lee, whose political thinking was shaped in the circle of Wilkes, Burgh, and other "second generation" opposition thinkers in Britain.
45. *Cato's Letters*, I, 186.   46. Ibid., 194.

ing the opportunity, the latter may take this, if they please, as a mark of confidence, not distrust; at least, it will be in their power, and surely it will be for their interest, to show that they deserved confidence, in this case, not distrust.[47]

The majority of opposition thinkers were more reluctant than Bolingbroke to exploit jealousy, and it therefore remained, in their view, a potent, but suspect, quality, whose value in public life was in constant danger of being compromised by its corrosive tendencies.

The status of jealousy in eighteenth-century America before the Stamp Act was both similar to, and different from, its place in opposition thinking. The term retained its meaning of vigilance-suspicion as it crossed the Atlantic. Colonists frequently used it in that sense. In 1713, in a sermon at Hartford, Connecticut, the Reverend John Bulkley asserted that "we are a People, very tender of our Civil Interests and jealous lest by any means they are invaded or taken from us."[48] That such a declaration should have issued from a Congregational pulpit was appropriate, because a "tense mutual watchfulness," a "collective watchfulness," is said to have been characteristic of Puritanism.[49] (That this aspect of Puritanism persisted is demonstrated by Samuel Adams, a protagonist of primitive Puritan values, who, as the Revolutionary struggles developed, conceived of himself as being in, and recommended to others, the role of " 'watchman on the wall,' alerting his city to new threats to its freedom.")[50] In 1733 a New York newspaper writer complained of attacks on Whigs "who from a just zeal and jealousy for their liberty endeavor to defeat schemes of power destructive of liberty."[51] Twenty years later another New York newspaper complimented the provincial legislature for being "widely jealous of the Liberties of their constituents."[52]

But jealousy was not the central idiom in the political vocabulary of early eighteenth-century America. Nor could it compete with consensus as the prime political value. In America, as in England, consensus was the political ideal, elusive as it often proved to be. "We have always been careful," the Massachusetts House of Representatives informed Governor Burnet early in the eighteenth century, to act "in the most decent and respectful manner [lest] something should

47. Henry Saint-John, 1st viscount Bolingbroke, *A Dissertation upon Parties* (London, 1754), xi.

48. Quoted in Perry Miller, *The New England Mind: From Colony to Province* (Cambridge, Mass., 1953), 377–78.

49. Michael Walzer, *The Revolution of the Saints* (London, 1965), 221, 223, 301.

50. Pauline Maier, "Coming to Terms with Samuel Adams," *American Historical Review* 81 (1976): 36.

51. Quoted in Bailyn, *Origins of American Politics,* 126.

52. William Livingston, William Smith, Jr., and John Morin Scott, *The Independent Reflector,* ed. Milton Klein (Cambridge, Mass., 1963), 12 April 1753, p. 193.

drop that might be offensive, and interrupt that Harmony and good Understanding between Your Excellency and the House, which is so conducive to Your Ease, so necessary to the publick Good, and so very much desired and valued by Us,"[53] a sentiment repeated as late as 30 June 1768, when the Massachusetts house informed Lord Hillsborough that any attempt to impress the king "with a jealousy of his faithful subjects . . . is a crime of the most malignant nature; as it tends to disturb and destroy that mutual confidence between the Prince and the subject, which is the only true basis of public happiness and security."[54] Americans, moreover, shared with their British brethren the belief that jealousy could easily become a social cancer. Men like Jonathan Edwards and John Adams acknowledged its pernicious tendencies by using it to describe the ugly passions aroused by their towns' chronic animosities over the disposition of their common lands.[55] By the middle of the eighteenth century, however, some Americans had begun to conceive of jealousy in new, positive ways that foreshadowed its enthusiastic acceptance in the independent United States. Especially in New York and Pennsylvania, two of the more heterogeneous of the American colonies, jealousy was coming to be regarded as a constructive force. Writing of the conflict between various religious-ethnic groups for control of a proposed college in New York, a newspaper essayist in 1753 remarked, "For as we are split into so great a Variety of Opinions and Professions: had each Individual his Share in the Government of the Academy, the Jealousy of all Parties combating each other, would inevitably produce a perfect Freedom of each particular Party."[56]

That jealousy would be a force to be reckoned with in America in the future was predicted by the New Yorker William Livingston in 1753: "should the Supreme Head of a free State attempt to lay impositions upon them [the Americans], without their Consent . . . would it not be deemed such an Advancement of the Royal Prerogative, as is utterly inconsistent with the nature of such a Constitution? An Attempt of this Kind, would raise an honest Jealousy in the Breast of every Lover of Liberty."[57] The Sugar and Stamp acts made Livingston a prophet by exciting jealousy in the form of vigilance

53. Richard Bushman, "Corruption and Power in Provincial America," in *The Development of a Revolutionary Mentality* (Washington, 1972), 67.

54. Harry Alonso Cushing, ed., *Writings of Samuel Adams* (reprint, New York, 1968), I, 222.

55. Richard L. Bushman, "Massachusetts Farmers and the Revolution," in *Society, Freedom, and Conscience*, ed. Richard M. Jellison (New York, 1976), 109; Taylor, ed., *Papers of John Adams*, I, 54.

56. Klein, ed., *Independent Reflector*, no. 20, 12 April 1753, p. 195.

57. Ibid., 17 May 1753, pp. 232–33.

throughout the colonies. That there was a good deal of reluctance to employ jealousy against king and mother country was evident from the efforts of American leaders to justify it, to prove that it was not un-British. "No people have been more wisely jealous of their liberties and priveleges than the British," wrote Oxenbridge Thacher in 1764. The British nation, another writer assured his audience, had always been "enthusiastically jealous of its rights."[58] Thus, it was made to appear that for Americans to indulge their jealousy was to affirm their Britishness. "Like their British Ancestors," wrote Samuel Adams in 1765, "they are jealous of their liberties." "We have," wrote John Adams in the same year, "the jealous Watchful Spirit of true Britons, over all Attempts" to violate our rights.[59]

The speedy repeal of the Stamp Act caused many Americans to hope that an aberration had been rectified and that good will between the metropolis and the colonies would be permanently restored. Others, however, were uneasy about what the Stamp Act portended. Writing in a Boston newspaper in 1769, "Alfred" remarked that "tho' it was soon repeal'd, it yet created such a jealousy between the mother country and the colonies, as it is to be fear'd will never wholly subside."[60] In this usage, of course, the word *jealousy* meant apprehension, fear—not watchfulness. Subsequent parliamentary activity justified the pessimists, for in 1767 another tax, the Townshend duties, was imposed on the unrepresented Americans. As a result, "the Minds of the People were filled with Anxiety, and they were justly alarmed with Apprehensions of the total Extinction of their Liberties."[61] Fear spread, and in 1768 John Dickinson, in the most influential political writings published in America before *Common Sense,* tried to spread it even more.

At the beginning of the eleventh number of his *Letters from a Farmer in Pennsylvania,* Dickinson made the arresting declaration that "a perpetual jealousy respecting liberty is absolutely requisite in all free states." "Of all the states that have existed," he continued, "there never was any in which jealousy could be more proper than in the colonies."[62] By *jealousy* Dickinson did not mean watchfulness; the time when alertness alone could protect American liberties had passed, he believed. Like Owen Glendower, he was summoning the stronger

---

58. Oxenbridge Thacher, *The Sentiments of a British American,* in Bailyn, ed., *Pamphlets of the American Revolution* 490; Peter Thacher, "Oration Delivered at Watertown, March 5, 1776," in, *Principles and Acts of the Revolution in America,* ed. Hezekiah Niles (reprint, New York, 1971), 23–24.

59. Samuel Adams to John Smith, 19 December 1765, in Cushing, ed., *Writings of Samuel Adams,* I, 47; Taylor, ed., *Papers of John Adams,* I, 136.

60. Cushing, ed., *Writings of Samuel Adams,* I, 386.

61. Taylor, ed., *Papers of John Adams,* I, 315.

62. [John Dickinson], *Letters from a Farmer in Pennsylvania* (Dublin, 1768), 96.

spirits, invoking the affective side of jealousy—fear, apprehension. Specifically, he recommended that "a spirit of apprehension may be always kept among us."[63] In other words, Dickinson was attempting to mobilize American anxiety and to commit it to the battle with the British Parliament. And such an attempt was likely to succeed, for there was, scholars now tell us, an abundance of anxiety in eighteenth-century America.

The discovery of anxiety in colonial America is a recent phenomenon. The conventional view of colonial life has been that Americans, having made a successful adjustment to the conditions of the New World, were by the middle of the eighteenth century brimming with confidence and optimism. While recent writers do not deny the sanguine strain in the eighteenth-century temperament, they emphasize the anxiety that was weighing upon it.[64] The sources of anxiety are represented as having been social and political. Socially, anxiety is said to have been caused by the development of a prosperous, materialistic milieu in eighteenth-century America. The acquisitive, aggressively individualistic conduct engendered by this society conflicted with the exacting Christian values inherited from the seventeenth century and produced, it is claimed, widespread guilt and anxiety. Perry Miller's description of New England in 1730—"the complex, jostling reality of this anxious society"—seems to have been among the first signals to scholars of the existence of socially induced anxiety in eighteenth-century America.[65] Both Richard Bushman and Alan Heimert believe that in New England some of this anxiety was assuaged by the Great Awakening of the 1740s.[66] Yet its persistence is a major theme in the writings of Gordon Wood and Jack Greene. Both Wood and Greene find "increasing anxiety" in Virginia on the eve of the Revolution, produced by a "social crisis" among the gentry caused by the sapping of moral standards by deviant behavior. Both apply their conclusion about Virginia to the colonies at large, where they detect "chronic anxiety passed along from one generation to another and never far below the surface of colonial life, over the failure of later generations to measure up to the standards" of their forefathers.[67]

63. Ibid., 97.

64. "Anxiety and despair, as much as confidence and optimism, have characterized our history from the beginning. The anxiety quotient has always been abnormally high in American history. Indeed this higher level of anxiety and larger admixture of despair may well distinguish Americans from all other people in history." Page Smith, "Anxiety and Despair in American History," *William and Mary Quarterly,* 3d ser., 26 (1969): 417.

65. Miller, *New England Mind,* 482–85.

66. Richard Bushman, *From Puritan to Yankee: Character and the Social Order in Connecticut, 1690–1765* (Cambridge, 1967), 147 ff.; Alan Heimert, *Religion and the American Mind* (Cambridge, Mass., 1966), 138.

67. Gordon Wood, "Rhetoric and Reality," 27–30; idem, *Creation of the American Republic,* 108; Jack P. Greene, "Society, Ideology, and Politics: An Analysis of the Political Culture

Politically, anxiety was induced by the memories and experience of arbitrary government. By the middle of the eighteenth century, a smaller proportion of the colonists than at any previous time were refugees from the political, religious, and economic oppression of European autocracies. Yet most Americans were sons or grandsons of such refugees, and the terrors of their experiences were vivid in the popular consciousness. "The people of this country in general, and of this province [Massachusetts] in special," wrote John Adams in 1775, "have an hereditary apprehension of and aversion to lordships temporal and spiritual. Their ancestors fled to this wilderness to avoid them—they suffer'd sufficiently under them in England. And there are few of the present generation who have not been warned of the danger of them by their fathers or grandfathers."[68] Martin Van Buren recorded similar apprehensions among the people of the middle colonies: "nothing could therefore be more natural than that they and their immediate descendants, made familiar with the wrongs and outrages practiced on their fathers by absolute tyrants, should have been jealous of their liberties," should have regarded all authority with "suspicious watchfulness."[69] The political presumptions of Revolutionary Americans had been forged in their ancestors' struggles with arbitrary power. Greene has recently argued that the anti-Stuart, "seventeenth-century opposition tradition, with its overriding fear of prerogative power . . . continued to occupy a prominent place in [American] politics at least until the middle of the eighteenth century and did not entirely lose its force until after the Declaration of Independence."[70] Opposition ideology, which stressed rampaging executive power, also had its roots in the struggles with the Stuarts and was credible to Americans because of the survival in the colonial executive of archaic seventeenth-century powers, the danger of whose capricious use was a "source of perpetual anxiety."[71]

Finally, any inventory of eighteenth-century American anxiety must include that aroused by religious developments, specifically by the pervasive dread that the Church of England would be established in the colonies. The "fear of an ecclesiastical conspiracy against American liberties, latent among nonconformists throughout all of colonial history," became so intense in the 1760s that the decade can be

---

of Mid-Eighteenth-Century Virginia," in *Society, Freedom, and Conscience,* ed. Jellison, 65–75; idem, "Search for Identity: An Interpretation of the Meaning of Selected Patterns of Social Response in Eighteenth-Century America," *Journal of Social History* 3 (1970): 204.

68. Taylor, ed., *Papers of John Adams,* II, 265.

69. Martin Van Buren, *Inquiry into the Origin and Course of Political Parties in the United States* (New York, 1867), 18.

70. Greene, "Political Mimesis," 343.   71. Ibid., 351.

said, in Bailyn's words, to have "climaxed years of growing anxiety that plans were being made secretly to establish an American episcopate."[72] "The Great Fear, 1766–1770" is the way Carl Bridenbaugh described American anxiety over this threat in the years in which it reached a crescendo.[73] His words do not seem too strong.

By the 1760s, America was awash in anxiety, apprehension, fear—the terms can be used interchangeably;[74] as John Adams put it in 1782, "before the war . . . the American mind was possessed with all that fear, which is essentially the characteristic of monopolized colonies."[75] Adams's remark contained a hint of disapproval, which reflected how Americans felt about their anxieties. Although they were not prepared to apologize for them—they felt that they were justified by present and past events—they nevertheless regarded them as somehow discordant or untoward. By declaring that jealousy was a vital element in the conflict with Britain, Dickinson meant to redeem anxiety, to convert it from a liability to an asset, a process that was being repeated in many areas of American life, where Revolutionary pressure was transforming into desiderata various attitudes and practices that had previously been considered deviant.[76]

The Whig leadership harkened to Dickinson's invocation of jealousy. Citing the commendation of "perpetual jealousy" by the "dispassionate and rational Pennsylvania Farmer," Samuel Adams declared that "the true patriot therefore will enquire into the causes of the fears and jealousies of his countrymen and if he finds that they are not groundless, he will be far from endeavouring to allay or stifle them. On the contrary . . . he will by all proper means in his power foment and cherish them." "The spirit of apprehension," Adams asserted, in a dictum that combined both meanings of jealousy, "should be kept up among [the people] in its utmost vigilance."[77] Saluting the "patriotic Farmer," Adams's colleague James Lovell declared that "watchful, hawk-eyed jealousy" must be encouraged.[78] "The public mind," Alexander Hamilton recalled some years later, began to be "influenced by an extreme spirit of jealousy . . . to

72. Bailyn, *Ideological Origins*, 96–97.

73. Carl Bridenbaugh, *Mitre and Sceptre: Transatlantic Faiths, Ideas, Personalities, and Politics, 1689–1775* (New York, 1962), 260–87.

74. It should be pointed out that some psychologists distinguish between these affects. See John C. Nemiah, "Anxiety: Signal, Symptom, and Syndrome," in Silvano Areti, *American Handbook of Psychiatry*, 2d ed. (New York, 1974), III, 97–98.

75. John Adams, "Letter from a Distinguished American," *Parker's General Advertiser* (London), 17 October 1782.

76. Bernard Bailyn, "Political Experience and Enlightenment Ideas in Eighteenth-Century America," *American Historical Review* 67 (1962): 350–51.

77. Cushing, ed., *Writings of Samuel Adams*, II, 149–50, 288, 293.

78. "Oration, Delivered at Boston, April 2, 1771," in Niles, ed., *Principles and Acts of the Revolution*, 4.

nourish this spirit, was the great object of all our public and private institutions."[79]

Where so much jealousy-anxiety already existed, it could easily be nourished. As 1776 approached, it became luxuriant. "The fears and jealousies of the people," wrote Samuel Adams in 1771, had "become general."[80] "Jealousy and suspicion, concluded Charles Carroll of Maryland in 1773, had become the very basis of American politics."[81] "Jealousy . . . is plentifully produced in our House of Representatives," because it is "so natural to their Habits," observed Elbridge Gerry in February 1775.[82] The hearts of Americans "now burn with jealousy and rage," exclaimed Joseph Warren a month later.[83] Americans, declared the Olive Branch Petition of 8 July 1775, were filled "with the most painful fears and jealousies"; "procure us relief from our afflicting fears and jealousies," they besought the king.[84] By the summer of 1775, fear and jealousy of Britain had become so intense that prospects of an accommodation faded away. In the next year the colonies declared their independence.

How did jealousy, so pervasive in America by 1776, become the link between the paranoid conditions detected by scholars of the Revolution and, subsequently, by Hofstadter? What was there about eighteenth-century jealousy that caused twentieth-century scholars to describe its operations as paranoid? Suspicion and apprehension, synonymous with jealousy, have been identified by experts on paranoid disorders as being among the principal characteristics of the paranoid condition.[85] Therefore, the profusion of jealousy in Revolutionary America created what, at the very least, can be called a paranoid tone in its politics; the persistence of jealousy into the nineteenth century perpetuated that tone.

But jealousy did more than give a distinctive tone to Revolutionary politics; it sent its roots below the surface of that politics to become one of the principal components of the Revolutionary mentality. One need not follow Bailyn in reducing that mentality to an expression of Walpolian opposition ideology to recognize that he identifies and

79. Speech at New York ratifying convention, 24 June 1788, in *The Debates in the Several State Conventions, on the Adoption of the Constitution,* ed. Jonathan Elliot (Philadelphia, 1896), II, 301.

80. Cushing, ed., *Writings of Samuel Adams,* II, 148–49.

81. Wood, *Creation of the American Republic,* 16.

82. George A. Billias, *Elbridge Gerry: Founding Father and Republican Statesman* (New York, 1976), 63.

83. "Oration, Delivered at Boston, March 6, 1775," in Niles, ed., *Principles and Acts of the Revolution,* 20.

84. Boyd, ed., *Papers of Thomas Jefferson,* I, 220, 222.

85. David W. Swanson, Philip J. Bohnert, and Jackson A. Smith, *The Paranoid* (Boston, 1970), 14–15.

stresses many of its key elements and, in so doing, makes comprehensible why the mentality is susceptible to attributions of paranoia by twentieth-century historians. The fear of power, which Bailyn finds pervading the Revolutionary mind, was articulated in a way that invites the ascription of paranoia, for the principal symptom of the paranoid condition is persecutory delusions, and Revolutionary Americans conceived of power as a constant assailant of liberty, as nothing less than a persecutor of it—liberty, said John Adams, was "hunted and persecuted in all countries by cruel power."[86] Bailyn also isolates a belief in conspiracy as a key element of the Revolutionary mentality; he demonstrates that, between 1763 and 1776, Americans of every political persuasion were convinced that their adversaries were participants in a malign conspiracy.[87] The political process itself was conceived to be conspiratorial, with the result that political opponents were routinely reviled with interchangeable epithets like *conspiracy, junto,* or *faction* (often the terms were joined into "junto conspiracy" or "conspiratorial faction"),[88] thus creating an atmosphere in which political opposition and political parties were rejected as illegitimate and evil. In the popular mind and in the psychological literature, the presence of a conspiratorial mentality is considered to be an indicator of the paranoid condition—Hofstadter claimed that belief in conspiracy was "the central image of the paranoid style"[89]—so on this account, too, the ascription of paranoid comes easily to twentieth-century historians of the Revolutionary period.

Fueling the twentieth-century impression that Revolutionary thinking was paranoid is the tendency of the Revolutionary generation to combine their conceptions of power and conspiracy and to conceive of power—the essence of politics—as being both persecuting and conspiratorial: Madison, for example, warned against the "silent encroachment of those in power"; Richard Henry Lee cautioned against "the silent powerful and ever active conspiracy of those who govern."[90]

To power conceived as conspiratorial, the Revolutionaries fused jealousy, a synthesis that produced a compound which can be described as ideology, for the word *ideology* comprehends within its meaning not only abstract precepts but also suspicions, fears, and passions of the sort that jealousy represented. The fusion of jealousy with power seems, in fact, to have been irresistible to the Revolution-

86. Bailyn, *Ideological Origins,* 59.   87. Ibid., 144–59.
88. Ibid., 122, 151 n.   89. Hofstadter, "Paranoid Style," 29.
90. Elliot, ed., *Debates in the Several State Conventions,* III, 87; Lee to George Mason, 1 October 1787, in *The Papers of George Mason,* ed. Robert Rutland (Chapel Hill, 1970), III, 997.

ary mind. The bonding of the two became a kind of cliché, expressed by Congressman Thomas Burke of North Carolina on 11 March 1777 in the following characteristic manner: "the delusive intoxication which power naturally imposes on the human mind . . . inevitably leads to an abuse and corruption of power, and is in my humble opinion the proper object of political vigilance and jealousy."[91] So well did Revolutionary Americans understand the relationship between power and jealousy that writers like Alexander Hamilton could condense the concepts into a phrase like "jealousy of power" (which he capitalized for emphasis) and be sure that he would not be misunderstood.[92] In fact, the term *jealousy* was frequently used singly to convey the whole range of meaning of the ideological amalgam into which it, power, and conspiracy were fused.

Jealousy was thus used as a shorthand for a larger ideological construct, containing a mix of elements, two of which—power and conspiracy—were conspicuous in the thinking of the enemies of Walpole. The persistence of the word *jealousy* in the American political-intellectual vocabulary thus becomes a sign of the survival and the continuity of Walpolian opposition ideology in the United States. Bailyn insists on the continuity of that tradition, exemplified by the fear of power, down to the present day.[93] Pocock, Murrin, and Banning find aspects of opposition ideology, which they call by an older name, country ideology, thriving in Jeffersonian America and operating for an indeterminate time thereafter.[94] In tracing jealousy from independence to the Jacksonian period, as the remainder of this paper will do, I will be approaching, from a fresh direction, the problem of the continuity of opposition-country ideology in the United States. But the principal purpose of following jealousy, as it devolved into the Jacksonian period, is to demonstrate that it was the continuous source of those contemporary interpretations of political activities which twentieth-century historians describe as paranoid. As long as jealousy, and the cluster of ideas and emotions for which it stood, retained its grip on the American mind, so long would efforts by politicians to augment the power of the state—or indeed to take practically any action—be interpreted by sizable numbers of Americans as evidence that a conspiracy of power to persecute them

91. Thomas Burke to Richard Caswell, 11 March 1777, North Carolina State Archives, Raleigh, N.C.

92. "The Continentalist," 12 July 1781, in Syrett, ed., *Papers of Hamilton,* I, 652.

93. Bailyn, "The Central Themes of the American Revolution," in Kurtz and Hutson, eds., *Essays on the American Revolution,* 27.

94. Pocock, *Machiavellian Moment;* John Murrin, "The Great Inversion: or, Court versus Country" (Folger Library Conference, 21–22 May 1976); Lance G. Banning, "The Quarrel with Federalism: A Study in the Origins and Character of Republican Thought" (Ph.D. diss., Washington University, 1972).

was underway. In other words, so long as jealousy flourished, so long would a point of view that the twentieth century calls paranoid also flourish.

After independence was declared, Americans turned on each other the jealousy produced by the conflict with Britain. The evidence on this point is overwhelming. "The time is now past when the least danger is to be apprehended to our liberties from the power of Britain," wrote Benjamin Rush in 1778. "Tyranny can now enter our country only in the shape of a whig. All our jealousy should be of ourselves." "The jealousy of the people in this country," Noah Webster observed, is "directed against themselves." "A certain jealousy of government," explained a Massachusetts writer in the 1780s, was "first imbibed in the beginning of our controversy with Britain, fed by our publications against the British government, and now by length of time became in a manner habitual." "The prejudices which the revolution had engendered against the arbitrary government of Great Britain," wrote William Plummer of New Hampshire, "made the people jealous of giving to their own officers so much power as was necessary. . . ." "The people in this country," declared another New Englander, "cannot forget their apprehensions from a British standing army . . . and they turn their fears and jealousies against themselves." "The principles which had taught us to be jealous of the power of an hereditary monarch," asserted Hamilton in the *Federalist*, were "extended to the representative of the people."[95]

So strong was jealousy in the newly independent United States that it is no exaggeration to say that for a few years it dominated the American mind. In 1777 a British spy reported Silas Deane as saying that "Jealousy is the ruling feature in the American Character," "that its greatest degree was now excited in America."[96] The evidence indicates that Deane was correct. Americans from north to south remarked on the prevalence of jealousy, on the "universal jealousy . . . which the leaders of the revolution had found it necessary to foster and cultivate."[97] In Massachusetts James Warren observed how it was "no difficult Matter to engage the prejudices of the people in a Country where Jealousy is excited on the slightest surmise," while in North Carolina James Iredell marveled at "how easy it is to excite

95. Butterfield, ed., *Letters of Rush,* I, 221; Wood, *Creation of the American Republic,* 378, 325; Main, *Anti-Federalists,* 16n; Webster, *Examination,* in Ford, ed., *Pamphlets on the Constitution,* 51; *Federalist,* no. 26, in Wright, ed., *Federalist,* 215.

96. Paul Wentworth to William Eden, 22 December 1777, B. F. Stevens, *Facsimiles of Manuscripts in European Archives Relating to America 1773–1783,* II (London, 1889), no. 234.

97. Noah Webster, *History of the United States* (New Haven, 1832), 252.

jealousy."[98] Jealousy was perceived as being characteristic of the new state governments. "I cannot help remarking the singular jealousy of the constitution of Pennsylvania," declared one politician.[99] "Jealousies are very apparent in all our State Constitutions," wrote Thomas Jefferson, who was perhaps thinking specifically of Virginia, where delegates to the state constitutional convention in 1776 were being instructed by their constituents to "endeavour to fix a publick jealousy in the Constitution, as an essential principle of its support."[100] The Articles of Confederation, submitted to the states in 1777, were also seen as incorporating jealousy—not enough for Thomas Burke of North Carolina, who thought that the government created by the Articles would be "an object of very jealous apprehension, unchecked and unlimited as it is," too much for Alexander Hamilton, who retrospectively complained, in 1788, that in "forming our confederation, this passion alone seemed to actuate us."[101] Reflecting Hamilton's attitude, another Federalist remarked in the same year that "when the confederation was made . . . we were then jealous of the power of our rulers, and had an idea of the British government when we entertained that jealousy."[102]

Jealousy dominated the American mind because most Americans approved it. It was extolled as a "virtue." "Jealousy, especially at such a time is a political virtue: nay I will say it is a moral virtue," wrote Samuel Adams on 27 January 1772; a decade later his conviction that "Jealousy is a necessary political virtue, especially in times like these," had not abated.[103] "Virtuous jealousy" became, in fact, a kind of watch cry for Americans, recommended by men as various as William Tudor of Massachusetts and William Hornsby of South Carolina.[104] So valuable did jealousy appear to Samuel Adams and Arthur Lee that they were loath to set its limits. "It is a spirit," wrote Lee,

98. James Warren to John Adams, 1 January 1779, in *Warren-Adams Letters,* II, 84; [Iredell], *Answers to Mr. Mason's Objections to the New Constitution,* in Ford, ed., *Pamphlets on the Constitution,* 364.

99. Webster, *Examination,* in Ford, ed., *Pamphlets on the Constitution,* 34n.

100. Thomas Jefferson, "Autobiography," in *The Life and Selected Writings of Thomas Jefferson,* ed. Adrienne Koch and William Peden (New York, 1944), 83–84; Buckingham County Instructions, 15 May 1776, in Force, ed., *American Archives,* 4th ser., VI, 459.

101. Thomas Burke, Abstract of Debates, 12–19 February 1777, in Burnett, ed., *Letters of the Members of the Continental Congress,* II, 261–62; Syrett, ed., *Papers of Hamilton,* V, 68.

102. Wood, *Creation of the American Republic,* 539.

103. "Candidus," 27 January 1772, in Cushing, ed., *Writings of Samuel Adams,* II, 323; Samuel Adams to Arthur Lee, 21 November 1782, in R. H. Lee, ed., *Life of Arthur Lee, LL.D.* (reprint, New York, 1969), II, 230.

104. William Tudor, "Oration, Delivered at Boston, March 5, 1779," in Niles, ed., *Principles and Acts of the Revolution,* 37; Jackson T. Main, *Political Parties before the Constitution* (Chapel Hill, 1973), 404–5.

that "we ought to respect, even in its excesses."[105] Fearing that America was "too unsuspecting long to continue free," Adams insisted that he himself be constantly scrutinized. Upon learning that he had been reelected a Massachusetts delegate to Congress, Adams fretted: "What do frequent Elections avail, without the Spirit of Jealousy and Strict Inquiry which alone can render such Elections any Security to the People?"[106] The political opponents of the Adamses and the Lees esteemed jealousy as much as they did. In defending Silas Deane against the accusations of Arthur Lee, Matthew Clarkson on 21 December 1778 invoked "public jealousy" as an antidote to Lee's machinations, while a fortnight later William Duer declared that "jealousy of those in power is very necessary, nay, inseparable to freedom" and urged his countrymen to instruct their representatives in Congress to employ it, so that "treachery and deceit in the servants of the public should be exposed to public view."[107] Jealousy, in short, was approved on all parts of the political spectrum.

The highest compliment paid to jealousy was its "republicaniza-tion." The decision for independence was also a decision for repub-licanism, which Americans regarded as both a form of government and a way of life, whose attainment was the highest ambition of many. With apparently no dissent, jealousy was considered to be a genuine republican quality. David Ramsay noted "the extreme jealousy of . . . new republics."[108] Silas Deane "insisted that Jealousy was prevalent in Republicks." Samuel Adams saluted the "Republican Jealousy" of Deane's enemy, Arthur Lee. Tench Coxe extolled "Republican Jeal-ousy, the guardian angel of these States." In the *Federalist* both Mad-ison and Hamilton paid their respects to the "maxims of republican jealousy," while the leading Anti-Federalist pamphleteer, the Fed-eral Farmer, applauded "true republican jealousy and vigilance, the strongest guard against the abuses of power."[109] Jealousy was already in high repute among Americans who credited it with having played a vital role in discovering the enormity of British intentions in the

105. [Arthur Lee], *An Appeal to the Justice and Interests of the People of Great Britain in the Present Disputes with America* (London, 1774), 62.

106. Samuel Adams to John Adams, 8 December 1777, and to Samuel Cooper, 25 December 1778, in Cushing, ed., *Writings of Samuel Adams*, III, 416; IV, 106.

107. Clarkson, "Plain Truth to Common Sense," 21 December 1778; Duer, "To the Free and Independent Inhabitants of the State of New York," 11 January 1779, *Collec-tions of the New-York Historical Society* 5 (1888): 121, 339.

108. David Ramsay, *History of the United States . . .* (Philadelphia, 1816–17), III, xi.

109. Paul Wentworth to William Eden, 22 December 1777, Stevens, *Facsimiles*, II, no. 234; Samuel Adams to Benjamin Austin, 9 March 1779, in Cushing, ed., *Writings of Samuel Adams*, IV, 135; [Tench Coxe], *An Examination of the Constitution of the United States of America . . .* , in Ford, ed., *Pamphlets on the Constitution*, 151; *Federalist*, nos. 29, 38, 64, 70, in Wright, ed., *Federalist*, 228, 276, 424, 457. Walter H. Bennett, ed., *Letters from the Federal Farmer to the Republican* (University, Ala., 1978), 40; see also Hamilton to Wash-ington, 25 March 1783, in Syrett, ed., *Papers of Hamilton*, III, 306.

years leading up to 1776. Putting the imprimatur of republicanism upon it consummated its legitimization in America and decisively differentiated it from its status in Britain, where it remained an equivocal element and gradually lost its political significance as the heirs of the Walpolian opposition declined in importance in the course of the eighteenth century.[110]

A reaction against the reign of jealousy occurred around 1781. That the fear of power was being carried to excessive lengths even Richard Henry Lee, whose credo was a "Spirit of Liberty is a jealous spirit," was willing to concede. Writing to a Virginia recruiting officer whose efforts were being impeded by popular distrust of the army, Lee on 29 January 1782 sarcastically remarked, "the times are productive of wonders, or else it would surprise that any jealous genius should be found to deny you the powers necessary for preservation of the constitution for fear that the constitution should be injured."[111] But it was not men of Lee's political stripe who were most exercised by the excesses of jealousy. The sharpest critics were a group of middle-state and southern nationalists, who while in control of the Continental Congress, between 1780 and 1783, sponsored various programs to strengthen the central government. One of their favorite measures was a 5 percent impost, proposed on 31 January 1781, which was intended to stave off a national bankruptcy by giving Congress an assured revenue. But since the impost was an augmentation of the central government's power, it excited widespread jealousy. James Varnum of Rhode Island reported to Governor Greene on 2 April 1781: "an extreme, tho perhaps well-meant Jealousy, in many Members of Congress, especially those of long Standing, seems to frustrate every Attempt to introduce a more efficacious System. Prudent Caution against the Abuse of Power, is very requisite for supporting the Principles of republican Government; but when Caution is carried too far, the Event may, and probably will prove alarming."[112] Less circumspect, Alexander Hamilton, as the "Continentalist," railed on 12 July 1781 at the "extreme jealousy of power" which "is the attendant on all popular revolutions . . . It is to

110. Country-opposition politicians, professing an updated version of the old ideology, experienced a resurgence in Britain in the 1760s and 1770s, only to suffer a final dissipation of their strength and a transformation of their creed in the years thereafter. See John Brewer, *Party Ideology and Popular Politics at the Accession of George III* (Cambridge, 1976), 249, 253–56, 264, 268. For the use of jealousy by one of the intellectual leaders of the opposition resurgence, see James Burgh, *Political Disquisitions* (reprint, New York, 1971), I, 370; III, 311.

111. Richard Henry Lee to Charles Lee, 11 May 1776, and to William Davies, 29 January 1782, in James Ballagh, ed., *Letters of Richard Henry Lee* (reprint, New York, 1970), I, 189; II, 267.

112. James Varnum to William Greene, 2 April 1781, in Burnett, ed., *Letters of the Members of the Continental Congress*, VI, 41.

this source we are to trace many of the fatal mistakes, which have so
deeply endangered the common cause; particularly that defect which
will be the object of these remarks, A WANT OF POWER IN CON-
GRESS."[113] A vivid specimen of the jealousy that so annoyed Hamilton, of the paralyzing fear of power in such notoriously feeble hands
as those of the Continental Congress, is furnished by the Rhode Island
delegates Jonathan Arnold and David Howell, who explained on 15
October 1782 that they opposed the impost because it was a "perpetual grant."

> After Congress shall have obtained a Perpetual permanent revenue at their
> disposal, will it not be a Temptation to that August body, after the Exam-
> ple of Holland . . . to vote themselves Perpetual. . . . Would it not be in the
> power of Congress, having the perpetual Revenue at their disposal, and
> having the Command of your Armies and navys to block up your Harbors,
> and bring war into your State? . . . But, we hear some minion of Power
> reply, you are excessively Jealous, you are affrighted at nothing. We answer
> a degree of Jealousy is necessary, where it is extinguished Liberty expires.
> Did not similar Jealousies bring about the present glorious revolution? Did
> America resist the power of Britain to avoid only three pence on a pound
> of tea, or was it . . . not rather Oppression and violence Apprehended and
> which existed in our well grounded fears and reasonable Jealousy that
> brought on the present war?[114]

Other jealous Americans described the consequences of the adoption of the impost in even starker terms. It was, claimed a group of
Rhode Islanders, intended "to serve the purposes of aristocracy" by
"perpetually enslaving the common people." A South Carolina
newspaper writer agreed: the impost was a "charter of slavery."[115]

Perhaps the most systematic arraignment of jealousy written during the Confederation period was produced by one "S.C." in the
Pennsylvania Gazette of 9 July 1783. Provoked by the opposition to
the congressional impost of 1783, "S.C." assailed jealousy as the
handmaiden of hypocrisy: "To be jealous of power is now, with some,
the cant phrase of the day and . . . is a passion which may be possessed by the bravest or basest mind, for the best or the worst of
purposes . . . he who wants to avoid a duty, which the circumstances
of his country call for, will affect to be jealous of power, as a pretence
for his delinquincy. It is therefore in itself no virtue, and in its best
stages is but a vice refined." Continued "S.C.":

113. Syrett, ed., *Papers of Hamilton*, II, 650.
114. Arnold and Howell to William Greene, 15 October 1782, in Burnett, ed., *Letters
of the Members of the Continental Congress*, VI, 504.
115. Joseph L. Davis, *Sectionalism in American Politics, 1774–1787* (Madison, Wis., 1977),
37; Main, *Anti-Federalists*, 94.

But if we must deify a vice, and give it a place in the pantheon of America, pray let us, for our honor's sake, put it in the most obscure corner of the building, and never let its sneaky visage be seen until the amiable goddess confidence gives some symptoms of sickness.

There is some consistency in being jealous of power in the hands of those who assume it by birth, or without our consent, and over whom we have no controul, nor the power of removal, as was the case with the crown of England over America. But to be jealous of those whom we chuse, the instant we have chosen them, shews either the folly of our choice, or the absurdity of our politics; and that in the transition from monarchy to a republic, we have unfortunately bastardized our ideas, by placing jealousy where we ought to place confidence.

Let us, concluded "S.C.", put some controls on this "little, mean, sneaking, and sneaky temper of jealousy, this poison of human happiness, and which in a thousand instances for one to the contrary, is only the stalking horse of party and private design."

The conflict over the impost was one of the sharpest in a series of struggles, culminating in the adoption of the federal Constitution of 1787, over the strengthening of the central government. The controversy has been described in a number of ways; as much as anything else, though, it was a dispute between various segments of American society over the degree of jealousy necessary to sustain republican government in the United States. The proponents of stronger government—the nationalists of 1780–83, the Federalists of 1787—approved jealousy but argued that it must be under some restraint, that it must be used with moderation. One of their number summarized their position by declaring, in 1783, that although government must be scrutinized with a " 'watchful and distinguished eye' . . . this was 'far different from that excess of jealousy, which from a mistaken fear of abuse, withholds the necessary power.' " "Manly jealousy," a spokesman for the group asserted, was appropriate; "unmanly Jealousies" and "mean suspicion" were not.[116]

At the Constitutional Convention of 1787 and at the state ratifying conventions, the Federalists forthrightly asserted their position on jealousy. "A certain degree of it is highly necessary to the preservation of liberty," asserted Randolph of Virginia. It was "useful," said Jay; "prudent," agreed Madison; "lawful," said Ellsworth; "undoubtedly to be commended," declared Iredell.[117] Specific functions were

116. Davis, *Sectionalism in American Politics*, 148, 150; Credentials of Virginia delegates to Constitutional Convention, 16 October 1786, in Max Farrand, ed., *The Records of the Federal Convention of 1787*, 4th printing (New Haven, 1934), III, 560.

117. Elliot, ed., *Debates in the Several State Conventions*, III, 70; *Federalist*, nos. 41, 64, in Wright, ed., *Federalist*, 298, 424; The Landholder [Oliver Ellsworth], no. 10, in Ford, ed., *Essays on the Constitution*, 191; Marcus [James Iredell], *Answers to Mr. Mason's Objections . . .* , in Ford, ed., *Pamphlets on the Constitution*, 363. Madison later pronounced jealousy "natural." Farrand, ed., *Records of the Federal Convention*, III, 542.

envisioned for it. Hamilton saw it as a weapon of the state legislatures, which "will always be not only vigilant but suspicious and jealous guardians of the rights of the citizens against the encroachments
from the federal government." It would, he observed on another
occasion, protect the citizens against the army, which had "better be
in those hands of which the people are most likely to be jealous than
in those of which they are least likely to be jealous." And in advocating a single rather than a plural executive, he contended that "it is
far more safe there should be a single object for the jealousy and
watchfulness of the people."[118] Madison, who feared the "legislative
power" in the new government, asserted that "it is against the enterprising ambition of this department that the people ought to indulge
all their jealousy and exhaust all their precautions."[119] Might the
Constitution permit the president to become a monarch? "Let the
jealousy of the people once take alarm," wrote Hanson of Maryland,
and "at the expiration of his term he is dismissed, as inevitably as
light succeeds the darkness."[120]

Although Federalists praised "the honest patriot who guards with
jealous eye the liberties of his country, and apprehends danger under
every form,"[121] they charged that opponents of the Constitution were
discrediting jealousy by overindulging it. Again and again, they complained that the Anti-Federalists were so besotted with jealousy that
their judgments were impaired. Anti-Federalist jealousy was
denounced as "causeless," "overscrupulous," "groundless," "extreme,"
"stale and careless," "green eyed hell-born."[122] Many did not doubt
that it was pathological: it was "distempered," "a delirium of the
imagination," a "strange madness."[123]

Far from being intimidated by their opponents, the Anti-Federalists defiantly defended jealousy and proclaimed their intention of
employing it to its fullest extent. Repeatedly, they insisted that they
"had a right to be jealous of our rulers," that it was "just," "absolutely
necessary," and their "duty to indulge a jealousy of the human character," and that "jealous care and watchful anxiety" were mandatory.
"Fear, or jealousy, or watchfulness over those we have entrusted with

118. *Federalist*, nos. 25, 26, 70, in Wright, ed., *Federalist*, 209–10, 217, 457.
119. *Federalist*, no. 48, ibid., 344.
120. Aristides [Alexander Contee Hanson], *Remarks on the Proposed Plan of a Federal
Government*, in Ford, ed., *Pamphlets on the Constitution*, 233.
121. [Hugh Williamson], *Remarks on the New Plan of Government*, in Ford, ed., *Essays
on the Constitution*, 402.
122. Elliot, ed., *Debates*, II, 130, 147; *Federalist*, no. 1, in Wright, ed., *Federalist*, 91;
Ford, ed., *Pamphlets on the Constitution*, 47; Merrill Jensen, ed., *The Documentary History of
the Ratification of the Constitution* (Madison, Wis., 1976), II, 179, 649.
123. *Federalist*, no. 59, in Wright, ed., *Federalist*, 395; Landholder [Oliver Ellsworth],
nos. 10 and 2, in Ford, ed., *Essays on the Constitution*, 191, 144.

power," they claimed, were "so far from being the main spring of despotism" that they were "indispensably necessary for the preservation of liberty." "Those who would wish to excite and keep awake your jealousy and distrust are your truest friends," was the Anti-Federalist credo.[124] They believed that jealousy should never relax, that it should at all times be mobilized to the fullest extent.

The Anti-Federalists were, indisputably, more jealous than the Federalists. Why? One explanation is that, being older than the Federalists (as students of the Constitution assure us they were),[125] they were active in politics earlier than were their adversaries. They would have been more deeply involved, therefore, in the preindependence struggle with Britain and may have gained a deeper commitment to jealousy, with which American politicians armed themselves during that contest. The Anti-Federalists were, in fact, fond of stressing their Revolutionary credentials. They were the "Old Patriots of 75," "men of 1776."[126] In a revealing pamphlet, *Letters from the Federal Farmer,* Richard Henry Lee related Anti-Federalism to the preindependence period by citing Dickinson's *Letters from a Farmer in Pennsylvania.* Lee's purpose was to dissuade his fellow Anti-Federalists from being too trustful. The confidence of the Federalists in their ability to establish a government that was both powerful and free was, Lee warned, "very repugnant to that perpetual jealousy respecting liberty, so absolutely necessary in all free states spoken of by Mr. Dickinson. However, if our countrymen are so soon changed, and the language of 1774, is become odious to them, it will be vain to use the language of freedom."[127] For Lee, the language of 1774 was that of jealousy. Having served the country so well in the period leading up to the war with Britain, it was, he believed, the appropriate posture for 1787. Anti-Federalists agreed with him.

The jealousy of the Anti-Federalists produced the same interpretation of the Federalists' actions that prewar jealousy produced of the British ministry's policies; in both cases a conspiracy to enslave was detected. The Federalists, wrote a New York Anti-Federalist,

124. Elliot, ed., *Debates,* II, 28, 60, 399; Ford, ed., *Essays on the Constitution,* 58, 110, 379; Jensen, ed., *Documentary History,* II, 396. "A True Friend," Philadelphia *Independent Gazetteer,* 22 December 1787; "An Honest American," ibid., 19 January 1788; Centinel, XV, ibid., 22 February 1788.

125. Stanley Elkins and Eric McKitrick, *The Founding Fathers: Young Men of the Revolution* (Washington, D.C., 1962), 23–25.

126. Morton Borden, ed., *The Antifederalist Papers* (East Lansing, 1965), 2; Wood, *Creation of the American Republic,* 538.

127. Ford, ed., *Pamphlets on the Constitution,* 318. Gordon S. Wood has disputed the attribution of the Federal Farmer pamphlets to Lee. See *William and Mary Quarterly,* 3d ser., 31 (1974): 299–308. For a recent discussion of the problem, which concludes with a suspension of judgment on authorship, see Bennett, ed., *Letters from the Federal Farmer,* xiii–xx.

had turned the Constitutional "Convention into a Conspiracy," "as deep and wicked a conspiracy," declared another New York Anti-Federalist, "as ever was invented in the darkest ages against the liberties of a free people." To a Philadelphian, the Federalists were "a set of the basest conspirators that ever disgraced a free country" and their handiwork, the Constitution, was a document that "proceeded from a wicked combination and conspiracy against the liberties of their country." As Gordon Wood put it, "the fear of a plot ran through the anti-Federalist mind."[128] The purpose of the plot, they believed, was to enslave America, to bring to fruition an "insidious and long meditated design of enslaving their fellow citizens." From Patrick Henry, who "strongly and pathetically expatiated," in the Virginia ratifying convention, "on the probability of the President's enslaving America," to the western Pennsylvanians who were convinced that the Constitution would "rivet the fetters of slavery" upon them and to the Massachusetts Anti-Federalists who believed that their opponents were "a set of men who will seek every opportunity to enslave us," the continent rang with charges that a conspiracy was afoot to transform Americans "from respectable, independent citizens, to abject, dependent . . . slaves." The Anti-Federalists, said Benjamin Rush in an effort to turn truth to ridicule, were "men capable of believing that . . . the President of the United States will blacken their faces, seize their plantations, press their wagons, and afterwards sell them for slaves at public vendue."[129]

A recent historian has labeled Anti-Federalist fears "paranoia."[130] Although Hofstadter did not examine the Anti-Federalists, their fears were a precise example of what he calls the paranoid style: the conviction of large numbers of Americans—Jackson T. Main suggests the Anti-Federalists may have been a majority[131]—that they were the target of a malign conspiracy. Jealousy produced the Anti-Federalist conviction, just as it produced the prewar belief in a British ministerial conspiracy, which scholars have called paranoid. The jealousy that flourished in America between the Stamp Act and the Constitutional Convention was, therefore, both the creator of the paranoid style and the link between its manifestations. What happened was that efforts to augment the power of government—by taxation and

128. Staughton Lynd, "Abraham Yates's History of the Movement for the United States Constitution," *William and Mary Quarterly*, 3d ser., 20 (1963): 223; Catherine D. Bowen, *Miracle at Philadelphia* (Boston, 1966), 106; Jensen, ed., *Documentary History*, II, 643; Ford, ed., *Pamphlets on the Constitution*, 74; Wood, *Creation of the American Republic*, 487.

129. Jensen, ed., *Documentary History*, II, 290, 652, 237; Elliot, ed., *Debates*, III, 59–60, 148; II, 167.

130. Joseph Davis, *Sectionalism in American Politics, 1774–1787* (Madison, Wis., 1977), 153.

131. Main, *Anti-Federalists*, 249.

customs reform after 1764, by changing the structure of government in 1787—aroused the jealousy of citizens who opposed the reforms and caused them to interpret them in a way that twentieth-century historians call paranoid.

As jealousy in America did not disappear with the adoption of the Declaration of Independence, so it did not disappear with the adoption of the Constitution. It continued to flourish in the 1790s and became one of the features that distinguished the political parties of that decade. Those parties, an older view held, were formed in the struggle over the Constitution, Federalists remaining Federalists, Anti-Federalists becoming Jeffersonian Republicans. We now know that this thesis was wrong when applied to the Federalists, many of whom, like Madison, became leaders of the Republicans. On the other hand, there seems to have been considerable continuity between the Anti-Federalists and the Jeffersonian Republicans (among the leaders, at least),[132] with the result that so thoroughly did they infuse the Republican party with the intense jealousy which they had displayed in the conflict over the Constitution that it might be called—although the phrase was never used at the time—the party of jealousy.

Republican leaders shared the attitudes of their followers. Jefferson himself feared power—he thought it made men "wolves"—and as early as 15 March 1789 declared that "jealousy . . . is a precious reliance."[133] His most memorable encomium on jealousy appeared in the Kentucky Resolutions of 1798, which became a kind of party creed: "it would be a dangerous delusion were a confidence in men of our choice to silence our fear for the safety of our rights . . . confidence is everywhere the parent of despotism—free government is founded in jealousy, and not in confidence; it is jealousy, and not confidence, which prescribes limited Constitutions, to bind down those whom we are obliged to trust with power."[134] Jefferson's lieutenants esteemed jealousy as much as he did. John Randolph of Roanoke was fond of exclaiming that "this is a government of suspicion, not confidence." And, in what some scholars regard as the best summary of Jeffersonian principles, Randolph in 1813 asked, "What are they? Love of peace, hatred of offensive war, jealousy of the State Governments toward the General Government: a dread of standing armies; a loathing of public debt, taxes, and excises; tenderness for the liberty of the citizens; jealousy, Argus-eyed jealousy,

132. On this point, see Norman K. Risjord, "The Virginia Federalists," in *Essays on the Early Republic, 1789–1815,* ed. Leonard W. Levy and Carl Siracusa (Hinsdale, Ill., 1974), 81.

133. Jefferson to Edward Carrington, 16 January 1787, and to Madison, 15 March 1789, in Boyd, ed., *Papers of Jefferson,* XI, 49; XIV, 660.

134. Paul L. Ford, ed., *The Works of Thomas Jefferson,* VIII (New York, 1904), 474.

of the patronage of the President."[135] A year later John Taylor of Caroline, "the philosopher of Jeffersonian Democracy," published *An Inquiry into the Principles and Policy of the Government of the United States,* which was the most systematic (as far as any of Taylor's convoluted writings can be called systematic) analysis of jealousy in government yet published in America. His volume was an attack upon John Adams's *Defence of the Constitutions of the United States of America* and upon the "evil principle, jealousy," which Taylor claimed that Adams made the key to his system. Claiming that Adams mistook the function of jealousy in politics, Taylor proposed to demonstrate its proper use. Fearing what he variously called the "monied interest" and the "aristocracy of paper and patronage," he argued that Americans should be more apprehensive of it than of their traditional bugaboo, the standing army: "all are jealous of soldiers, and therefore they will not be watched; few are jealous of stockjobbers, and therefore they will be watched." Taylor was full of directions for using jealousy: "jealousy by a government of a nation is always criminal, because a nation cannot usurp its own rights; but jealousy by a nation of a government, is always laudable, because a government may usurp the rights of the nation." Finally, in writing of the "jealousies of nations," Taylor presented a theory reminiscent of Bolingbroke's on the creative tension between jealousy and confidence. "The jealousies of nations and factions are however different passions," wrote Taylor. "The first is inspired by a love of liberty; the other by ambition and Avarice. The first is extinguished by the virtues of justice and moderation and returns love and respect . . . the first is demonstrated in the existing relation, between the united nations of these states, and their governments."[136]

A superficial reading of the Federalists' literature of the 1790s would suggest that they repudiated jealousy as being the cant of opponents seeking to impair their ability to govern. Their attitudes ranged from the measured condemnation of "illiberal prejudices and jealousy" in Washington's "Farewell Address" to the irritation of Hamilton, who in 1797 complained of public service because "the opportunity of doing good, from jealousy of power and the spirit of faction, is too small in any station to warrant a long continuance of private sacrifices," to the disgust of other Federalists, for whom jealousy was "a mania, a dementia quod hoc . . . [a] hydrophobia, baffling our attempts to describe its nature or its remedies."[137] Yet most

135. Kirk, *John Randolph of Roanoke,* 71, 105–6.
136. Taylor, *Inquiry,* 52, 68, 381, 416, 460.
137. Felix Gilbert, *To the Farewell Address* (Princeton, 1961), 137; Hamilton to William Hamilton, 2 May 1797, in Syrett, ed., *Papers of Hamilton,* XXI, 78; Seth Ames, ed., *Works of Fisher Ames* (reprint, New York, 1969), II, 113.

Federalists adhered to the position of the supporters of the Constitution (which they usually had been) that although excessive jealousy
was inimical to the state, jealousy in moderation was legitimate. Fisher
Ames, for example, in a 1796 speech to the House of Representatives on the Jay Treaty condemned unrestrained jealousy: "while these
prepossessions remain, all argument is useless . . . the ears may be
open, but the mind will remain locked up, and every pass to the
understanding guarded. Unless, therefore, this jealous and repul-
sive fear for the rights of the house can be allayed, I will not ask a
hearing." Ames, however, in the same speech praised the "jealous
affection which a body of men is always found to bear towards its
own prerogatives and power . . . this very spirit is a guardian instinct
that watches over the life of this assembly . . . without its existence
with all the strength we see it possess, the privileges of the representatives of the people, and, mediately, the liberty of the people would
not be guarded, as they are, with a vigilance that never sleeps, and
an unrelaxing constancy and courage."[138]

Ames himself furnishes good evidence of the strength of jealousy
in the early United States. While his party was in power and its programs were being opposed by the Republicans, Ames railed at their
jealousy. But when the election of 1800 transferred power to the
Republicans and put Ames in opposition, he displayed a jealousy
that matched the most feverish productions of his adversaries. He
was convinced that if the "jacobins," as he always called the Republicans, prevailed, they would institute a tyranny "more vindictive,
unfeeling, and rapacious, than that of Tiberius, Nero, or Caligula,
or any single despot that ever existed." By 1805, confronted with
what seemed to be an irreversible Republican ascendancy, Ames's
fears pitched him into panic: "our days are made heavy with the
pressure of anxiety, and our nights restless with visions of horror.
We listen to the clank of chains, and overhear the whispers of assas-
sins. We mark the barbarous dissonance of mingled rage and triumph
in the yell of an infatuated mob: we see the dismal glare of their
burnings and scent the loathsome steam of human victims offered
in sacrifice."[139]

Further evidence of the strength of jealousy among Federalists is
provided by the Reverend Jedidiah Morse of Charlestown, Massachusetts. It was Morse who first brought the Bavarian Illuminati to
the nation's attention, alleging in a sermon of 9 May 1798 that they
were a brotherhood of international conspirators, dedicated to over-
throwing the government and religion of the United States. Yet in
the sermon "exposing" the Illuminati, Morse warned about excessive

138. Ibid., 40–41.   139. Ibid., III, 354.

jealousy: "while on the one hand, we would avoid passive obedience and non-resistance, let us not vibrate into the other extreme, and believe it a duty to be jealous and suspicious of every thing which is done by our rulers."[140] That Morse did not regard the Illuminati exposé as an example of excessive jealousy demonstrates how wide a scope the Federalists were willing to allow it.

Jealousy, then, was pervasive among Republicans as well as Federalists. It showed itself as soon as steps were taken to implement the new Constitution. Predictions were made in the Constitutional Convention that the "new Government will be regarded with that Jealousy inseparable from new Establishments,"[141] and these predictions were accurate. Every move to put the government into effect aroused the fears of those who soon became identified as Republicans. Before the new government "had done anything there was nothing oppressive or tyrannical which it was not accused of meditating," wrote Fisher Ames; "when it began its operations, there was nothing . . . right or beneficial that it did, but from an insidious design to delude and betray the people."[142] The jealousies and suspicions of the Republicans were, as the decade progressed, reciprocated by the Federalists and were articulated by each side as the conviction that the other was conspiring to ruin the republic. Republicans accused the Federalists of "liberticide," of conducting "a carefully controlled conspiracy to destroy republican government," or engaging in "a vast plot to establish a pro-British, tyrannical plutocracy wearing the gaudy cloak of monarchy";[143] Federalists believed that Republicans were conspiring with France to subject the country to a Jacobinical reign of terror. The result was, in the words of two recent historians, that "the political debates of the 1790s were in fact characterized by . . . bitterness, vituperation, mistrust, even paranoia."[144]

It is ironic—and may reflect a Jeffersonian bias in historians—that they ascribe to Federalists, who were on record as being more discriminating in using jealousy than Republicans, a greater affinity for paranoid interpretations. By 1795, writes James Banner, "Americans of all political stripes" were using conspiracy theories to explain the political developments of the day, but "Massachusetts Federalists were more susceptible to seeing plots and secret plans in the most

140. Jedidiah Morse, *A Sermon Delivered at the New North Church in Boston . . . May 9, 1798* (Boston, 1798), 27–28.

141. Joseph R. Strayer, ed., *The Delegate from New York* (Princeton, 1939), 54.

142. Ames, ed., *Works of Ames*, II, 372.

143. Banning, "Republican Ideology and the Triumph of the Constitution," 183–84; Marshall Smelser, "The Jacobin Phrenzy: The Menace of Monarchy, Plutocracy, and Anglophilia, 1789–1798," *Review of Politics* 21 (1959): 241.

144. Levy and Siracusa, eds., *Essays on the Early Republic*, 144.

innocent acts" than were their Jeffersonian counterparts. According to Banner, the Federalists saw malign conspiracies everywhere: "Plots were laid within the cabinet, in midnight caucuses of 'Jacobin' malcontents, in Napoleon's carriage somewhere in Europe. There were conspiracies of 'internal foes' and of 'external enemies.' There were small conspiracies to seize elections and larger 'secret and systematic' foreign intrigues 'by wicked and artful men, in foreign countries' to 'undermine the foundations of [Christian] Religion and to overthrow its Altars.' " Federalists, Banner concludes, were victims of "paranoia."[145] Marshall Smelser makes the point a bit stronger: "Federalists began to show symptoms of what can be called 'social paranoia' . . . Suspicions regarding even their nearest and dearest came quickly to mind . . . Something like the true paranoiac's hallucinations seized them and tormented them—conspiracy at home, intrigues abroad, sedition among the farmers and town workers, treason in high places."[146] Out of this seedbed arose the fear of the Bavarian Illuminati of 1798, the prototype of Hofstadter's paranoid style. Banner dismisses the Illuminati episode as "farcical."[147] The description seems just, for the historian of the event treats it with amused contempt, regarding it as the invention of the Reverend Morse, which interested a small circle of Federalist intellectuals, but which left the people at large unmoved and unconcerned.[148] Compared with the powerful waves of conspiratorial fears generated by the jealousy of both parties in the 1790s, the Bavarian Illuminati incident was an ephemeral whitecap.

Thomas Jefferson's election in 1800 set in motion in the United States an intellectual detoxification of power. By reducing the scope of the government that he inherited from the Federalists and by not ravening the country's liberties like a wolf, Jefferson belied both his own and his party's predictions about the poisonous seductiveness of power; at the same time, his conduct in office discredited the nightmarish fears that Federalists like Ames were passing along to the public about an orgy of democratic tyranny. Jefferson proved and Madison confirmed that the possession of power need not make a man a monster or a despot. By the end of the War of 1812, it even occurred to some Republicans that power might be beneficent, and the "party after 1815 adopted with embellishments of its own the old

145. James M. Banner, Jr., *To the Hartford Convention: The Federalists and the Origins of Party Politics in Massachusetts, 1789–1815* (New York, 1970), 32, 43–44.

146. Marshall Smelser, "The Jacobin Phrenzy: Federalism and the Menace of Liberty, Equality, and Fraternity," *Review of Politics* 13 (1951): 457–58.

147. Banner, *To the Hartford Convention*, 43.

148. Vernon Stauffer, *New England and the Bavarian Illuminati* (reprint, New York, 1967), 301–20.

Hamilton system that included a national bank, a protective tariff, and a federally sponsored system of internal improvements."[149] Many Republicans, however, were uneasy about this flirtation with power, and they kept their guard and their jealousy up. One such man was Jefferson's former private secretary, William Burwell, upon whose death John Quincy Adams remarked in 1821, "Jealousy of States rights and jealousy of the Executive were the two pillars of Burwell's political faith, because they are the prevailing popular doctrines in Virginia . . . Virginia teems with his breed more than any other state in the Union. . . ."[150]

The march of time, however, was making Burwell's kind of jealousy more difficult to sustain. John Randolph of Roanoke continued to preach it, but, as Robert Dawidoff has recently shown, his advocacy of jealousy and the other tenets of country ideology served only to certify him as an anachronistic eccentric.[151] As each year passed without an egregious abuse of power, the assumption on which jealousy was founded—that such an event was inevitable—became less credible. The success of republican government was, in short, becoming the enemy of republican jealousy. Americans were not bashful about broadcasting their success. By the time of Monroe's first inaugural address, Jefferson's simple statement, in his first inaugural, that the nation was "in full tide of successful experiment" had been amplified into "nor ever was success so complete." "Our government," Monroe continued, "has approached to perfection . . . we have no essential improvement to make."[152] Two decades later, Andrew Jackson in his "Farewell Address" asserted with characteristic braggadocio, "Our constitution is no longer a doubtful experiment; and, at the end of nearly half a century, we find that it has preserved unimpaired the liberties of the people, secured the rights of property, and that our country has improved and is flourishing beyond any former example in the history of nations."[153]

Jackson believed that the success of the American experiment made the traditional objects of jealousy inappropriate. Take those minions of power who were the scourge of the average European: "the officers of the police, the collectors of taxes, the customs men." To his astonishment, Tocqueville discovered that in Jacksonian America they

---

149. Norman K. Risjord, *The Old Republicans: Southern Conservatism in the Age of Jefferson* (New York, 1965), 161.

150. Ibid., 227.

151. Robert Dawidoff, *The Education of John Randolph* (New York, 1979), 294–95.

152. Quoted in Henry S. Commager, "America and the Enlightenment," *The Development of a Revolutionary Mentality* (Washington, D.C., 1972), 29.

153. Harold C. Syrett, *Andrew Jackson: His Contributions to the American Tradition* (Indianapolis, 1953), 260.

were not feared but "honoured," because they were considered agents of the people.[154] Jackson saw no reason to worry about the abuse of power by a people's government: "It is true that cases may be imagined disclosing such a settled purpose of usurpation and oppression on the part of Government as would justify an appeal to arms. These, however, are extreme cases, which we have no reason to apprehend in a Government where power is in the hands of a patriotic people."[155] Nor should a people's army be apprehended. "In many countries it is considered unsafe to put arms into the hands of the people. . . . That fear can have no place here when it is recollected that the people are the sovereign power."[156] In his approach to jealousy, Jackson was, therefore, so far from attempting to reaffirm the attitudes of the Old Republic (as one scholarly interpretation holds)[157] that he was trying to release his fellow citizens from fears inherited from it. In 1840, in fact, Henry Clay specifically accused Jackson of repudiating the old Jeffersonian attitudes of "vigilance, jealousy, and distrust."[158]

Jackson and the national political success of which he boasted seem to have succeeded in assuaging some part of the public's jealousy. By 1840 the profuse jealousy of Jeffersonian times was incomprehensible to many Americans. Addressing the Ohio legislature in 1840, Thomas Corwin, the governor-elect, attempted to account for the remarkably weak executive established by the state's 1802 constitution. The "fearful jealousy of executive power" written into the constitution, Corwin explained, "can probably only be rationally accounted for by reference to the times which gave it birth," times in which, he explained, the Jeffersonian-Federalist conflict was at white heat.[159] In 1848 John C. Calhoun pronounced what he assumed was an epitaph for public jealousy. "There is no solicitude about liberty now," Calhoun lamented. "It was not so in the early days of the republic. Then it was the first object of our solicitude. The maxim then was, that 'Power is always stealing from the many to the few.' 'The price of liberty is perpetual vigilance.' . . . It is not so now." And why was it not so? Because "we have ceased to remember the tenure by which liberty alone can be preserved. We have had so many years of prosperity—passed through so many difficulties and dangers

154. George W. Pierson, *Tocqueville in America* (Garden City, N.Y., 1959), 250.
155. Syrett, *Andrew Jackson*, 266.
156. Seventh Annual Message, 7 December 1835, in James D. Richardson, ed., *A Compilation of the Messages and Papers of the Presidents*, III (New York, 1897), 1390.
157. Marvin Meyers, *The Jacksonian Persuasion* (Stanford, 1957), chap. 1.
158. Speech, Hanover Co., Va., 27 June 1840, in Calvin Colton, ed., *Works of Henry Clay*, VI (New York, 1897), 206–7.
159. Isaac Strohm, ed., *Speeches of Thomas Corwin* (Dayton, Ohio, 1859), 283–84.

without loss of liberty—that we begin to think that we hold it by right divine from heaven itself."[160] Success, in Calhoun's opinion, had subverted jealousy.

But jealousy was a hardier specimen than Calhoun, who himself was striving desperately to keep it alive, imagined it to be. Jackson and his allies had not, in fact, repudiated it. The president commended his supporters for "the jealous maintenance of their rights," and his admirers were always ready to flatter themselves with such stock phrases as a "people jealous of its liberties."[161] Regarding jealousy as a valuable asset, Jackson sought to redirect it from the federal executive to those whom he considered more dangerous than a government that time and experience had proven innocuous. "Jealous anxiety"—a phrase (and a tautology) that Jackson used in his second inaugural address, in 1833, and in his "Farewell Address," in 1837[162]—should be principally focused on men trying to arouse sectional tensions (Calhoun and his confederates) and on "corporations with exclusive privileges" (the Second Bank of the United States). Jackson, in other words, was suggesting that the object of jealousy cease to be exclusively public, that it be shifted from the government itself to quasi-public or private entities.

By the 1830s a similar shift had occurred in the concept of conspiracy. No longer could it casually be affixed to political organizations, for parties had now ceased to be regarded as illegitimate and seditious.[163] Gone was the eighteenth-century view that "ever 'the best party is a kind of conspiracy' " against the nation,[164] parties were now accepted and extolled. They were, as Clay and Calhoun stated in identical words, "honest and patriotic."[165] "Parties may meet," declared a Philadelphia newspaper in 1832, "struggle, triumph, and fall, and the country and its freedom remain unimpaired. They all, or at least the great mass of each, cherish but one object, the welfare of their country; and whatever party succeeds, its members will be found too honest as well as too numerous to be corrupted, or rendered subservient to designs on the republic. The constant change of parties, like the ebbing and flowing of the sea, will keep the gov-

160. Speech against the acquisition of Mexico, 4 January 1848, in Richard K. Cralle, ed., *The Works of John C. Calhoun* (reprint, New York, 1968), IV, 417–18.
161. Seventh Annual Message, 7 December 1835, in Richardson, ed., *Compilation*, III, 1386; *Niles' Weekly Register*, 28 December 1833.
162. Richardson, ed., *Compilation*, III, 1223; Syrett, *Andrew Jackson*, 261–62.
163. Richard Hofstadter, *The Idea of a Party System: The Rise of Legitimate Opposition in the United States, 1780–1840* (Berkeley, 1970), chap. 6.
164. Quoted in Isaac Krammick, *Bolingbroke and His Circle: The Politics of Nostalgia in the Age of Walpole* (Cambridge, Mass., 1968), 153.
165. Clay, Speech, Lexington, Ky., 16 May 1829, in Colton, ed., *Works of Clay*, V, 372; Calhoun, Speech on force bill, 9 April 1834, in Cralle, ed., *Works of Calhoun*, II, 391.

ernment pure and safe."[166] Since parties were now conceived to be aggregations of honest citizens promoting the public welfare, castigating a political opponent as a conspirator became more uncommon.[167] In the future the stigma of conspiracy would more often be applied to private enemies than to public ones.

The refocusing of jealousy and conspiracy was not an exercise in which every group in Jacksonian America indulged. Jealousy was incompatible with Whiggism, which emphasized the use of governmental power in society, and few Whigs were therefore disposed to hunt out new objects on which to focus it (indeed, most Whigs believed that if jealousy had a role in their times, it was as a check on Jackson himself, whom they regarded as an aspiring despot). Many of Jackson's supporters were content to see jealousy abate, now that the achievement of a stable political system seemed to make it unnecessary. But there were sectors of the population in Jacksonian America in whom jealousy remained alive and who did redirect it onto nongovernmental entities (although not necessarily onto those which Jackson recommended).

The groups to which they applied it—the Masonic order, the Catholic church, the forces of slavery—had been around for a long time and had not been perceived, until now, as aggressively subversive. In colonial America there had, it is true, been undercurrents of suspicion of Freemasonry, but until the 1820s and 1830s not many people had become exercised about it. Similarly, until the 1830s slavery had never been perceived as a serious threat to large numbers of white Americans, and, in fact, whatever harm it portended had apparently been averted in 1820 by the Missouri Compromise. There had been, to be sure, virulent hatred and fear of Catholicism in colonial America, but the animosity toward this church seems to have been somewhat muted by the Revolution, and until the 1830s decreasing numbers appear to have tormented themselves about the machinations of the pope. In the 1830s, however, segments of the American population began to believe that all of these entities were conducting diabolical conspiracies against them. What suddenly made them appear so malignant? The answer seems to be that jealousy, disengaged from its familiar governmental and political objects, was played upon them by a portion of the population, which began to

166. *Niles' Weekly Register*, 20 October 1832.
167. The habit died hard, however. In 1834 the Jacksonian Robert Rantoul assailed the American System as "the conspiracy of avarice against liberty," while in the same year the Whig Tristram Burges attacked Jackson's removal of the deposits from the Second Bank of the U.S. as a "Catalinarian Conspiracy." Luther Hamilton, ed., *Memoirs, Speeches, and Writings of Robert Rantoul, Jr.* (Boston, 1854), 144; Arthur M. Schlesinger, Jr., *The Age of Jackson* (Boston, 1945), 108.

see their actions as persecutory conspiracies, an interpretation of conduct which strikes twentieth-century observers as paranoid. Thus, jealousy continued to be the source of what Hofstadter called the paranoid style, which he described as enjoying a heyday in the 1830s. Consider, for example, the Slave Power Conspiracy and observe how it was undergirded with jealousy.

Garrison, one of the inventors of the Slave Power Conspiracy, commended "holy jealousy" to his followers.[168] In extolling jealousy, Wendell Phillips yielded to none of the Jeffersonian stalwarts whom he despised: "there is no republican road to safety but in constant distrust," he declared.[169] Phillips and his Abolitionist colleagues subscribed to the opposition ideology's conception of power, which was engrafted into the concept of jealousy, that it was constantly and insatiably aggressive. "Power is ever stealing from the many to the few," he wrote, in the exact phrase used by Calhoun. "The hand intrusted with power becomes, either from human depravity or espirit de corps, the necessary enemy of the people."[170] That this notion was not confined to the Abolitionist elite is demonstrated by one Nathaniel P. Rogers, an obscure friend of Garrison, who regarded every "president or chairman as an embryo Caligula or Nero."[171] In the jealous abolitionist mind, the Slave Power could not be static: it must be, as all power was, dynamic, relentlessly encroaching. It must, said Phillips, send "out its poisonous branches over all our fair land." It must, agreed Garrison, be "like a cancer . . . eating out the vitals of the republic. We are under the absolute dominion of the Slave Power—a Power, which, like the grave, is never satisfied—and, like the horse-leech, is every crying, Give! Give!"[172] The result of the Slave Power Conspiracy (such an inimical force naturally received the epithet "conspiracy") would be the visitation of the most frightful persecution on every place, on every person, in the United States. The Slave Power must be opposed, declared Phillips, "that it may not result in Northern Slavery." It must be stopped, concluded Garrison, lest it lead "to the enslavement of others—of a community— of a people—of myself."[173]

168. Garrison to Orson S. Murray, 11 August 1837, in *The Letters of William Lloyd Garrison*, ed. Louis Ruchames, II (Cambridge, Mass., 1971), 278.

169. "Public Opinion," 28 January 1852, in *Speeches, Lectures, and Letters* (reprint, New York, 1968), 54.

170. Ibid., 52.

171. Garrison to Henry C. Wright, 1 October 1844, in *The Letters of William Lloyd Garrison*, ed. Walter M. Merrill, III (Cambridge, Mass., 1973), 267.

172. Oscar Sherwin, *Prophet of Liberty: The Life and Times of Wendell Phillips* (New York, 1958), 126; Garrison, "Free Speech and Free Inquiry," *Selections from the Writings and Speeches of William Lloyd Garrison* (New York, 1968), I, 260.

173. Sherwin, *Prophet of Liberty*, 126; Garrison to Peleg Sprague, 5 September 1835, Merrill, ed., *Letters of Garrison*, I, 508.

It is well known that the Abolitionists themselves were implicated in a malign conspiracy by those whom they accused of being principals in the Slave Power Conspiracy: the southern extremists, the "fire eaters," whose intellectual mentor was Calhoun. In the 1830s these southerners believed that they had discovered an "abolition conspiracy," which, in due course, they depicted as evolving into a Black Republican conspiracy, acting in the tradition of the "Jacobins, Illuminati, and Freemasons."[174] Infusing the conspiratorial conception was jealousy, for which Calhoun vigorously proselytized in the 1830s. His speeches were laced with adjurations to his followers to watch "with the greatest jealousy," "with ceaseless vigilance," because the "angry waves of power, impelled by avarice and ambition . . . driven furiously over a wide and broken expanse, would be resistless."[175] Instructed by jealousy, Calhoun's adherents and intellectual heirs interpreted the actions of their northern opponents as steps in a persecuting conspiracy. By extolling a "wise jealousy of executive usurpation," the framers of the constitution of the Confederate States of America kept the tribal faith.[176]

Jealousy was, then, the common denominator of the various paranoid styles in the 1830s. But it was no longer common to most Americans. It had loosened its grip on the political center, which regarded it as inappropriate in a political system that had achieved success. Those whom it continued to influence and who, as a result, discovered the congeries of conspiracies for which the 1830s were remarkable tended—like the Abolitionists and southern extremists—to be on the margins of the American body politic. The migration of jealousy to the periphery of American politics in the 1830s is strikingly similar to the fate of the country-opposition ideology in England a century earlier. Having achieved stability under Walpole, Britain became intellectually complacent and the country-opposition ideologues were forced to the margins, left and right, of politics. Their creed (of which the power-jealousy nexus was a principal component) became one of the mainstays of American thought until the 1830s, when the achievement of political stability once again forced it to the margins of public life. And with jealousy on the margins, what twentieth-century commentators call the paranoid interpretation of political events also receded to the margins of American politics, and it has, except for occasional incursions into the political mainstream, remained there.

174. Davis, *Slave Power Conspiracy and the Paranoid Style,* 38, 40 ff.
175. Cralle, ed., *Works of Calhoun,* III, 641; II, 386; VI, 135, 142, 190.
176. Jabez L. M. Curry, *The Civil History of the Government of the Confederate States of America* (Richmond, Va., 1901), 74.

Looking back on jealousy from the 1830s shows it to have had a long history. It was in use during the English civil wars. The Walpolian opposition helped to transmit it to America, where it attained a status that it never enjoyed in the mother country. In America it encapsulated fears deeply imbedded in the political culture and fused with an ideological conception of power which reflected those fears. Considered a passion by eighteenth-century Americans, it resembled an ideological distillate, a concentration of attitude and idea, of affect and affirmation. Recommended and used as a weapon in the struggle with the British king and ministry between 1763 and 1776, it emerged at the Declaration of Independence with authentic revolutionary credentials; by being wrapped in the mantle of republicanism, it was virtually canonized. All Americans regarded it as a positive force in the new nation, many approving even its excesses. It thrived into the Age of Jackson, when it changed its focus from public to private groups. For at least the century in which it was most potent, from 1730 to 1830, it caused Americans to interpret events as diverse as British ministerial policies, the movement for the Constitution, Federalist and Republican political activities, and the conduct of the forces of slavery in a manner that modern scholars call paranoid. It was the source of, and supplied the continuity to, the various manifestations of the paranoid style.

Ascribing paranoid manifestations to jealousy raises numerous questions about Hofstadter's conception of the paranoid style as it operated through the middle of the nineteenth century. Hofstadter conceived of the paranoid style in terms of a mental-illness model, as being produced by the interaction of precipitate and predisposition. He postulated a standing predisposition to paranoia among a segment of a country's citizens: "a mentality disposed to see the world in the paranoid's way may always be present in some considerable minority of the population."[177] The precipitate that stimulated this predisposition into action was, in his view, social conflict that involved an "ultimate scheme of values" and brought "fundamental fears and hatreds, rather than negotiable interests" into play.[178] It has been the thesis of this essay that the jealousy which produced what scholars have called paranoid manifestations in eighteenth- and nineteenth-century America was shared by almost all Americans, not by a minority. Furthermore, it has been claimed that what kindled jealousy into paranoid-style episodes was not social or, as Hofstadter states in another place, ethnic and religious conflicts,[179] but efforts of adversaries to augment political power, sometimes by increments

177. "Paranoid Style," 39.   178. Ibid.   179. Ibid.

that Americans themselves admitted were intrinsically trifling, such
as a three-pence duty on tea. The disposition to paranoid type thinking was, in other words, far more pervasive than Hofstadter imagined and the precipitating factors were far less cosmic.

The liberal use of a term like *paranoid style* in an historical essay
creates the danger that readers will infer that the author is implying
that the totality of the politics in the period he is examining were
pathological. I mean nothing of the sort (nor did Hofstadter). It cannot be denied that Americans in the colonial and early national
periods seem to have been addicted to a belief that those holding
power, or trying to get more of it, intended, often with the aid of
conspiring confederates, to abuse it, to use it to persecute their
opponents. But the fear of power was what Freud would have called
an objective anxiety,[180] a realistic apprehension grounded in hard
facts. For most Americans had experienced the abuse of power. The
Stuarts had harried many of their ancestors out of England. After
1688, colonial governors often wielded regressive powers irrespon-
sibly. The War of the Revolution itself was just such a wanton abuse
of power as the political ideology of the time predicted. The trauma
caused by the Revolution was deep. "It is scarcely possible at this
distant day," recalled Martin Van Buren in retirement, "to appreciate the terror of irresponsible and arbitrary power which had been
impressed upon the minds of men who had themselves suffered from
its excesses or had witnessed the cruelties it had inflicted on others."[181] In this climate of fear it was easy to imagine another egregious abuse of power, inflicted by an American Lord North.
Therefore, the fears of Anti-Federalists, Republicans, and Federalists of a persecutory conspiracy of power holders are altogether
credible. As time passed, however, as the memory of the War of the
Revolution became less vivid, as nothing remotely resembling it was
repeated, and as the American political process achieved success and
stability, the earlier jealousies became untenable. Sensing this,
Americans either relinquished them or transferred them to non-
public entities like Freemasonry and the so-called Slave Power. Since
it was difficult to demonstrate that these organizations had committed past despotic excesses against white Americans, fears of them
were less realistic than those previously entertained. It is at this
point—and at this point only—that it becomes possible to speak of
those fears veering off toward pathology. Up to 1830, *paranoid*, with
its connotation of pathology, is not a suitable term to apply to the

180. Sigmund Freud, *A General Introduction to Psychoanalysis,* 20th ed. (New York, 1969),
401–2.
181. Van Buren, *Origin and Course of Political Parties,* 40.

beliefs in persecuting power which surfaced so frequently in American politics: it gives a false impression and has impeded analysis of the continuity of those beliefs. *Jealousy,* a neutral term that suggests the same idea as paranoid, would be an improvement in accuracy and felicity. We might then speak of a jealous strain in American politics between 1730 and 1830 rather than of a paranoid style or complexion.

In 1876, Wendell Phillips delivered a centennial lecture at the Old South Church in Boston in which he tried to make some sense of the agitations that seemed to be forever bestirring that city. "What does Boston mean?" asked Phillips. "Since 1630 the long fibre running through the history which owns that name means jealousy of power."[182] That same long fiber, though no longer entwining the political center, ran through the nation at large, up to the moment at which Phillips was speaking. Even today, it can be detected in the United States.

182. Wendell Phillips, *Speeches, Lectures, and Letters,* ed. Theodore C. Pease, 2d ser. (1891; reprint, New York, 1969), 236.

Doctoral Students of Edmund S. Morgan

Brown University

1951

MALCOLM FREIBERG

Prelude to Purgatory: Thomas Hutchinson in Provincial Massachusetts Politics, 1760–1770

1952

IRVING H. BARTLETT

The Romantic Theology of Horace Bushnell

JOHN BLANCHARD MACINNES

Rhode Island Bills of Public Credit, 1710–1755

ROBERT J. TAYLOR

Western Massachusetts in the Revolution

1954

DAVID S. LOVEJOY

The Licentious Republic: Rhode Island, 1760–1776

1955

PHILIP S. CAMPBELL

Cotton Mather

JOHN E. SELBY

A Concept of Liberty

MACK E. THOMPSON
Moses Brown, Man of Public Responsibility

1957

LUCILLE B. GRIFFITH
The Virginia House of Burgesses, 1750–1774

1960

THADDEUS W. TATE, JR.
*The Theory of the Social Contract in
the American Revolution, 1776–1787*

Yale University

1960

HECTOR G. L. KINLOCH
Anglican Clergy in Connecticut, 1701–1785

1961

GEORGE D. LANGDON, JR.
New Plymouth: A History of the Old Colony

ROBERT L. MIDDLEKAUFF
*Ancients and Axioms: A History of Secondary Education
in Eighteenth-Century New England*

1962

PHILIP H. JORDAN, JR.
*Connecticut Politics during the Revolution
and Confederation, 1776–1789*

1963

JEANNE H. GOULD BLOOM
*Sir Edmund Andros: A Study in
Seventeenth Century Colonial Administration*

JOHN R. HOWE, JR.
*The Search for Stability: An Essay in
the Social Thought of John Adams*

JESSE L. LEMISCH
*Jack Tar vs. John Bull: The Role of
New York's Seamen in Precipitating the Revolution*

1964

DAVID D. HALL
*The Faithful Shepherd: The Puritan Ministry
in Old and New England, 1570–1660*

JAMES H. HUTSON
*John Adams and the Diplomacy of
the American Revolution*

PATRICIA S. WATLINGTON
The Partisan Spirit: Kentucky Politics, 1779–1792

1965

ALETHA J. B. GILSDORF
*The Puritan Apocalypse: New England Eschatology
in the Seventeenth Century*

ROBERT E. WALL, JR.
*The Membership of the Massachusetts
General Court, 1634–1686*

1966

STEPHEN FOSTER
*The Puritan Social Ethic: Class and Calling in
the First Hundred Years of Settlement in New England*

JOHN M. MURRIN
*Anglicizing an American Colony:
The Transformation of Provincial Massachusetts*

MYRA L. RICH
The Experimental Years: Virginia, 1781–1789

DAVID J. RUSSO
*The Southern Republicans and
American Political Nationalism, 1815–1825*

GERARD B. WARDEN
Boston Politics, 1692–1765

1967

ROBERT G. POPE
*The Half-Way Covenant: Church Membership
in the Holy Commonwealths, 1648–1690*

ALVIN R. RIGGS
Arthur Lee and the Radical Whigs, 1768–1776

ROBERT M. ZEMSKY
The Massachusetts Assembly, 1730–1755

1968

TIMOTHY H. BREEN
*The Character of the Good Ruler: A Study of
Puritan Political Ideas in New England,
1630–1730*

1969

JOSEPH J. M. ELLIS III
*The Puritan Mind in Transition: The American
Samuel Johnson (1696–1772)*

1971

WILLIAM C. DENNIS II
*A Federalist Persuasion: The American Ideal
of the Connecticut Federalists*

KENNETH W. KELLER
*Diversity and Democracy: Ethnic Politics in
Southeastern Pennsylvania, 1788–1799*

1972

JONATHAN C. CLARK
The Hopes and Fears of a Yesteryear: 1787

ARNOLD A. SHERMAN
*Commerce, Colonies and Competition: Special
Interest Groups and English Commercial and
Colonial Policy, 1660–1673*

1973

JAMES W. DAVIDSON
Eschatology in New England: 1700–1763

MICHAEL D. SCHAFFER
*The Good Citizen of the American
Republic, 1789–1800*

1974

DAVID W. ROBSON
*Higher Education in the Emerging
American Republic, 1750–1800*

1975

BARBARA A. BLACK
*The Judicial Power and the General Court
in Early Massachusetts (1634–1686)*

DAVID E. STANNARD
*The Puritan Way of Death: A Study in
Religion, Culture, and Social Change*

STEPHEN E. WIBERLEY, JR.
*Four Cities: Public Poor Relief in
Urban America, 1700–1775*

1977

CHRISTINE L. HEYRMAN
*A Model of Christian Charity: The Rich and
the Poor in New England, 1630–1730*

BRUCE MANN
*Parishes, Law and Community in
Connecticut, 1700–1760*

1978

WILLIAM K. BREITENBACH
*New Divinity Theology and the Idea
of Moral Accountability*

JAMES ESSIG
*Break Every Yoke: American Evangelicals
against Slavery, 1770–1808*

MATTHEW SECCOMBE
*From Revolution to Republic: The Later
Political Career of Samuel Adams, 1774–1803*

1979

RACHEL KLEIN
*The Rise of the Planters in the South Carolina
Backcountry, 1767–1808*

1980

CAROL F. KARLSEN
*The Devil in the Shape of a Woman:
The Witch in Seventeenth-Century New England*

1983

BARBARA C. SMITH
*The Politics of Price Control:
Massachusetts, 1776–1779*

Dissertations Still in Progress with Tentative Titles

SARAH BLANK, Ministers, Merchants, and Mechanics: Church and Society in Eighteenth-Century Boston

PETER DIMOCK, The Years of Many Generations: Local New England Historians, Community, and the Historical Imagination in the Nineteenth Century

GAIL SUSSMAN MARCUS, "All Due Means to Prevent Sin": The Criminal Justice System as a Means of Social Control in Colonial New Haven, 1638–1665

MARY MACMANUS RAMSBOTTOM, Visible Symbols and Sensory Piety: New England Religious Experience, 1680–1740

HAROLD E. SELESKY, A Colonial Society at War: Connecticut, 1636–1785

ROBERT TRENT, Sacred Cod, Profane Fishermen: Marblehead in the Seventeenth Century

ANN WITHINGTON, Article Eight of the Association of 1774

ROSEMARIE ZAGARRI, Conceptions of Space in Late Eighteenth-Century Virginia

Index

Burroughs, George, 54
Burton, Henry, 26
Burwell, William, 364
Bush, Hendrick, 292, 295
Bushman, Richard, 222–23, 344
Butler, Steven, 200–201
Byrd, William, 269, 276

Cabell, N. F., 282
Cadiz, English loss at, 5
Calhoun, John C., 365–66, 368–69
Calvinists, Calvinism:
    Laudians vs., 4
    see also Puritans, Puritanism
Cambridge Platform, 7, 28–30
Cambridge Synod, 28, 29
Camden, Battle of, 318, 320, 322,
    324, 326
Camp, Edward, 114
Canada:
    Loyalists in, 294, 309
    Montgomery's invasion of, 289
canon law, 138
capital offenders, 103
    banishment of, 161
    in England, 156
    evidentiary rules for, 119–20
    jury trials for, 153, 155–56, 159,
        161–62, 170, 183, 189–90
    mental distraction as mitigating
        factor in, 189–90
    nonjury trials of, 161–62
    strict examination of, 118–19
Carroll, Charles, 347
Carrier, Martha, 45
"cartail act" of 1661, 34
Carter, Landon, 247, 254, 257, 264–
    66, 267–68, 271–73, 276–77
Carter, Robert ("King"), 269, 276
Carter, Robert Wormeley, 272–73,
    281
Carter family, 248, 251, 273
Cary, Robert, 274
Catholics, 58, 367
Cato, 339–40
Cato's Letters, 339–40
Chadwicke, John, 204

Chafee, Zachariah, 153
Charles I, king of England, 14, 141
Charles II, king of England, 37, 87,
    179, 243
Chasmore, Richard, 168–70
Chauncey, Charles, 5
Checkley, Anthony, 201
Cheever, Ezekiel, 116–17
Child, John, 293–94, 304
Child, Robert, 145, 185, 194, 197
Christmas celebrations, Sewall's
    opposition to, 79, 84
circumstantial evidence, 114–16
    supernatural forces and, 115–16
civil codes, 138, 139, 142, 149, 157
    see also Rhode Island Civil Code
        of 1647
Civil War, U.S., 318, 332
Clark, Hester, 181
Clark, Susan, 107
Clarke, John, 181
Clarkson, Matthew, 352
Clay, Henry, 366
clergy:
    colonial elections and, 226–27,
        230
    "consociations" of, 10–11
    growing power of, 28–29
    ordination of, 28
    in Plymouth Colony, 158
Clinton, George, 293, 294–95, 305,
    308
Clinton, Henry, 320
Coddington, William, 139–40, 146–
    47, 148, 165–66
coercion vs. deference, 211, 214–16,
    218, 219, 243
Cogswell, Adam, 62–63
Coke, Sir Edward, 143
Coldom, Clement, 44, 47
Cole, John, 266
Collins, Samuel, 70
Colony Court of Magistrates (New
    Haven), 105, 108
Commission for Conspiracies, 304,
    306
Commission on Conspiracies, 292

ALVERNO COLLEGE LIBRARY
Saints and revolutionaries
974.02S157

2 5050 00275452 7

156652

974.02
S157

REMOVED FROM THE
ALVERNO COLLEGE LIBRARY

Alverno College
Library Media Center
Milwaukee, Wisconsin

DEMCO